Introduction to
PHILOSOPHY
Deducing Answers

Jeffrey
Watson
Arizona State University

Kendall Hunt
publishing company

Contents

Unit 6–Ethics and Free Will   459

Final Unit   553

Appendix   573

How to Use This Textbook

✳✳

A textbook is a **resource** for you to use to help you learn.

There are many resources you get in a class to help you learn: lectures, recorded materials, discussions with your classmates, feedback from your instructor. Since every student learns differently, every student will rely on a different combination of resources in order to learn the same subject matter.

Studying philosophy takes more than reading a textbook. Studying philosophy is more than knowing which philosopher thought what. To really study philosophy, you have to spend time thinking about these ideas on your own, trying to come up with your own objections and arguments. However, a textbook is an important tool to sharpen your philosophical thinking by enountering the arguments of others who came before you.

This textbook is divided into six main units, plus a short introductory section and a short final section. In the appendix of the book are resources for writing in philosophy and for making arguments.

Each main unit in this textbook contains the following materials to help you:

* An **overview** which helps you understand the topics covered in the unit. Reading this first will help you understand the questions which the unit is about.

* A set of **notes** which help explain the main ideas in the source texts. Reading this will help you interpret the source texts and study for quizzes and exams. These notes are written for an introductory level class.

* Copies of the **source texts** which the discussion in the unit is based around. Reading these will help you see where the arguments discussed in this class come from! These texts are very difficult,

because they were written over the course of 2,500 years of history, in several languages, for a variety of audiences. Most were not written for introductory students. However, trying to read them, even if you don't understand all of what you read, helps you encounter the origins of these ideas. You may find you understand more when you re-read the texts after listening to lectures.

* A list of **study questions** which you can ask yourself at the end of the Unit. Would you know how to answer these questions if someone asked you? Practicing answering them is a good way to study.

Enjoy studying philosophy!

Overview: Introductory Unit

✻✻✻

In this Unit, we'll discuss what Philosophy is and discuss the four important tools we'll need in the rest of the course: giving *reasons*, constructing *arguments*, *evaluating* arguments, and writing clear *definitions*.

✤ 0.1 What Is Philosophy? ✤

✳ ✳

The word "Philosophy" itself comes from a compound of two Greek words: philos- (love) and -sophia (wisdom), meaning "the love of wisdom".

However, this doesn't tell us much about what philosophers actually do. Perhaps it makes it sound like philosophy has to do with collecting wise sayings, which is something a philosopher might choose to do, but not really what philosophy is about. So, instead, I prefer to define philosophy in this way:

> **φιλοσοφιά**
> Philosophia, the love of wisdom.

Philosophy is thinking clearly and carefully about interesting and difficult questions.

First, philosophy involves *thinking*. This means that philosophy isn't just a matter of reading what others have written. We do read what others have written, since that's a source of interesting things to think about. And we do write down our thoughts, since that's a way of communicating them. But the core of philosophy is simply sitting down—or walking, or hiking, or whatever you prefer—and thinking about things.

Clear and Careful

We want our thoughts to be *clear*. That is, philosophical thinking isn't quite like imagining or free-associating thoughts or letting one's mind wander from topic to topic. We want our thoughts to be something that we can explain to others and feel confident that they'll have understood exactly what we meant. That means we want to avoid relying on ambiguous terms, poetic but muddled language, or confused concepts. Instead we want to strive toward clearer *definitions* of the concepts we are thinking about, to know clearly what it would take for the propositions we consider to be true, and ultimately to understand the true natures of the subjects we are thinking about.

We also want our thinking to be *careful*. That is, we want to avoid logical *fallacies* and to structure our thoughts into *arguments*. Philosophical thinking is highly disciplined thinking. We want to make explicit everything we are assuming, even things that seem so obvious that everyone takes them for granted. We want to be sure that the

© Rob Wilson/Shutterstock.com

premises in our arguments, if they turned out true, would *guarantee* that the conclusions of our arguments also had to be true. We want to think critically and discipline our thoughts through *logic*.

Imagine if a philosophy class was just everyone stating their own opinions on a topic without giving any *justification* for them: "I think this is true!" "Well, I think you're wrong!". At first, simply having the dialogue would be good, since it would let us hear many

> *Philosophy is thinking clearly and carefully about interesting and difficult questions.*

points of view. But part of that wouldn't be helpful, because we'd never hear *why* anyone believed what they did. So instead we want to know what *justifies* someone's opinion, not just what their opinion is. When we read source texts, we'll want to know what arguments each philosopher offered for his or her views, not just bullet points about what their views were.

Interesting Questions

Of course, philosophers don't just think, but they need to think about *something*. While most fields of study at a University are highly specialized and focused in on one aspect of reality—for example, sociologists study societies, and biologists study living organisms—philosophy is the most *general* of the disciplines. Philosophers may want to think about a specific aspect of reality (as a social theorist, or a philosopher of biology might do). But they might also want to simply think about the structure of reality as a whole (as a metaphysician does) or about the nature of our knowledge (as an epistemologist does).

Epistemology: What do we know? How do we know?

Philosophy

Metaphysics What's the structure of reality as a whole?

Ethics What ought to be done and ought not be done?

What limits the questions philosophers think about are two criteria: first, philosophical questions must be *interesting*, and secondly, they must be *difficult*.

What do I mean by "interesting"? After all, it seems like all it takes for something to be interesting is for somebody to *find* it interesting. Take any two people, and what each of them finds "interesting" is going to differ pretty greatly: one person might be interested in other cultures, another in earthworms, and another in classic cars. Further, it seems like our interests can change, and this is partly under our control: We can choose to *take an interest* in something and in the process of learning about it develop more interest than we had at first. Perhaps, it's best to say this: *Nearly every possible subject has some degree of interestingness, and some of us discover what's interesting about one subject, yet never discover what's interesting about another subject, even though others do the reverse.*

I've chosen a small handful of philosophical questions in this book because many people have found them interesting across distant times, places, and cultures. There are, of course, many other questions which many people have found interesting that aren't in this book, and you might find other questions more interesting; it might take a planet full of books to encompass everything that people have found interesting. However, you might try to take an interest in these questions, to at least see why others found them interesting, and perhaps to see if you can find what is interesting about them. Here are some examples:

1. What makes something *true*?
2. What can I *know* about anything?
3. What is the nature of this experience I'm having?
4. What makes someone a person or *self*?
5. Why is there anything at all?
6. What is our moral responsibility, if anything?

Many of these questions are about what's called *Metaphysics*: that is, they're questions about the structure of reality as a whole and the nature of things within it. However, before doing that we'll first have to answer some questions about *Epistemology*: questions about what knowledge is, what we can know, and how we know it. Finally, at the end of the book we'll touch on questions related to *Ethics*: questions about what one ought to do or ought not to do.

Difficult Questions

What these philosophical questions have in common, unlike some other interesting questions, is that they are *difficult*. What do I mean by "difficult"? Here I have a special definition in mind, different than the ordinary definition of "difficult". (Fair warning: This often happens in philosophy, where a word is defined in a specialized sense rather than the everyday ordinary sense). Think of there are being four types of questions, only one of which philosophy is concerned with:

1. *Easy Questions* are questions where we can specify what process of observations would be needed to find the answer, in principle, even if we can't actually go through that process.
2. *Difficult Questions* are questions where we can't specify what process of observations would be needed to find the answer, although they have an answer we could understand.
3. *Nonsense Questions* are questions where we can't specify what process of observations would be needed to find the answer, because they have no answer we can understand, because the question itself is mistaken and nonsensical.
4. *Mysterious Questions* are questions where we can't specify what process of observations would be needed to find the answer, because they have no answer we can understand, even though we can understand the questions.

An example of an Easy Question might be "who killed John F. Kennedy?" or "how many stars are there in the universe?" or "what is a cure for the common cold?". In the everyday sense, these are not "easy" questions, of course! They'd take a lot of work to answer. However, in principle, we can specify the process by which one would go about finding an answer. For instance, if someone had a videotape of the shooter of JFK firing, and we could see that the bullet which killed him came from the firing of that gun, then that would tell us who killed John F. Kennedy.

> **"Easy" question:** possible to specify observations which would answer the question.

If we had the ability to travel very quickly through all of space and count all of the stars, that would tell us how many stars there were. In principle, enough study on microorganisms, chemistry, and human physiology might tell someone, someday, a cure for the common cold.

An example of a Difficult Question, by contrast, is something like "how certain do you have to be in order to know something?" or "why am I having a conscious experience right now?" or "what makes an action morally wrong?". What makes these questions difficult is not just that they'd take a lot of hard work and careful thinking to answer. What makes them difficult is that it's not even clear at first how to find an answer. Telescopes and microscopes and old film reels won't help us answer these questions. Searching the internet won't help.

When we try to tackle difficult questions in this book, what we will do is figure out all of the possible views someone could hold, weigh the reasons for and against each view, and then select the answer which has better reasons on its side. Some of those reasons will involve observations, but others may not.

Just because a question is Difficult to answer doesn't make it unanswerable. There can be better and worse answers to philosophical questions, answers which are more supported by reasons and less supported by reasons. Likewise, just because a question is Difficult doesn't mean there's no correct or incorrect answer. Philosophical claims must be either true or false like any other sort of claims. But it does mean that on most philosophical issues, you'll have to use your own judgment to decide what the best answer is. In this textbook, I'll help rule out some possible answers as clearly incorrect, but I won't be able to tell you between the remaining possibilities which you should think is correct.

At a few points we'll discuss whether some questions that seemed like good, difficult philosophical questions might be either nonsense questions or mysterious questions. Nonsense questions are questions like "how many cats does a duck?" or "when infinitely eats Tuesday, will Congress yesterday?" Most nonsense questions are silly and easy to spot. But some aren't so easy to spot. For example, "if time stopped, what would happen next?" or "if you weren't yourself, who would you be?". These at first might look like perplexing philosophical questions! But part of doing philosophy is recognizing

> **Method for Studying Subject S**
> 1. Determine all of the possible views about S.
> 2. Weigh the reasons for and against each view about S.
> 3. Pick the better answer based on the balance of reasons.

that they're nonsensical. If time truly "stopped", there would be no "next". You couldn't not be yourself. Someone who asks these questions doesn't clearly understand the question they're asking; when doing philosophy provides that clarity, the questions disappear.

Finally, we may encounter some mysterious questions. Mysterious questions are questions which can't be answered, even though they must have answers. Unlike nonsense questions, the questions can be clearly understood, and given certain assumptions, it would follow that there is some fact of the matter about the correct answer. But unlike difficult questions, we could never possibly understand the answers to them, because any answer which we could understand would raise the same question all over again: We simply can't go on thinking about the question any further. Since deciding that an answer to a question is "mysterious" in this way is tantamount to giving up knowing the answer to it, in general we want to try very hard to get answers before deciding a question is mysterious.

Key Points:

* Philosophy involves clearly defining our terms, justifying our views, and giving logical structure to our arguments.

* Philosophical questions include questions about
  * Metaphysics: the structure of reality as a whole the natures of things in it
  * Epistemology: the theory of knowledge
  * Ethics: what ought to be or ought not to be

* Philosophical questions are "difficult" in the sense that we can't easily say what sort of observations one could make to answer them, but they still have answers we could hope to understand.

❊ 0.2 Why Study Philosophy? ❊

✳ ✳

© Berkomaster/Shutterstock.com

Q1. What's the point of taking a Philosophy class?

Q2. Why these texts?

Q3. Why read philosophy?

Q4. Should everyone study Philosophy?

Q5. Is Philosophy practical?

Q6. What good has philosophy done over the last 2,500 years?

Q1. What's the point of taking a Philosophy class?

Upon announcing that you've enrolled in a philosophy course, you are likely to have some well-meaning relative ask you:

"You mean, psychology?"

And when you explain that you don't mean psychology, but philosophy—then they'll likely say something like,

"What's the point of studying *that*?"

Studying philosophy seems like a horrible waste of time to many people. At least with another class, you'll walk away with some possibly practical information about how the world works. But in philosophy, none of the information you get is practical. No one is ever going to ask you to explain David Hume in 2 minutes during a job interview. You will not pull out your pocket copy of Plato's *Republic* when figuring out how to jump-start your car battery. Who cares what strange things this or that philosopher said?

However, this is the result of a misunderstanding of what philosophy is about. People tend to think philosophy is about what this or that philosopher said. Studying what someone else said does not seem like a very interesting or worthwhile thing to study.

But philosophy is not about learning *information* about what someone else said. Instead, philosophy is about gaining *skills* in thinking through difficult problems and evaluating arguments. What famous philosophers said is interesting because their arguments are novel and interesting, not because they were famous. Their arguments are something we can evaluate today. But we also study not-so-famous philosophers who happened to make interesting arguments.

The point of taking a philosophy class is two-fold. First, taking a philosophy class will let you explore topics that no other field at the University allows you to study so freely: We'll consider the nature of the self, the existence of God, the nature of morality, whether or not there is free will, and how we can know anything at all. These are not topics other classes will allow you to think so freely about, and for many people they are meaningful questions that impact how they choose to live life, so they are worth taking some time to consider. Second, a philosophy class will train you to think and communicate your ideas to others in a more clear, structured, and orderly way. Gaining practice using logic to defend your views in a philosophy class can make you a more confident communicator and help you explain your views to others, even when you're discussing something "practical".

Q2. Why these texts?

Another question someone might ask is, "Why are so many of the texts selected in this book written by Westerners?"

People of all ages, times, and places have thought philosophically about philosophical questions in a number of ways. Thus, it is not really honest to speak of philosophy beginning in a particular place or time or cultural setting or to think of it as limited to one geographic region. It is not necessary to use the Greek word "philosophy" in order to be doing serious philosophy, of course.

However, the goal of this textbook is not to provide a survey of *all* philosophy through all of history. That would take a much larger book! Instead, the goal is to give you a few peeks at *one* larger conversation.

It is easier to do philosophy within one "philosophical tradition" that shares a common history and vocabulary than many at once, all using different terminology and having different assumptions and motivations. Even though they may disagree with one another, those working within the tradition are already familiar with many of the same texts, references, problems, methods, and concepts employed by others in the tradition, so that there is more potential for fruitful debate. Everyone understands the references that others make and the terminology that they are using.

You should consider reading a book about another philosophical tradition after you read this book. This text will give you an idea of the questions and approach in just one, but there are others.

Q3. Why read philosophy?

We might ask: if philosophy is just *thinking*, why take a course on philosophy that involves reading texts? Why not just sit down and do it on our own?

Thinking on your own is great, of course—and part of philosophy. But consider how thinking about these questions is often more efficient when we know what other people have thought about them. It can improve our own reasoning skills to read works by better reasoners. It can help us avoid errors or traps that others before us discovered, make distinctions that others saw but we might not have noticed, and use a common language when talking to other people in the present day.

Q4. Should everyone study Philosophy?

No. I don't think it's true that everyone should study philosophy. For one thing, not everyone really wants to study philosophy. Some people find it a bit too abstract to get a grasp on. Some people feel more comfortable in life avoiding difficult and deep questions. And some students have a very clear, step-by-step plan for exactly what they're going to do for the rest of their lives, and taking philosophy might get in the way of those plans.

That said, I think a lot of students do find philosophical questions intensely interesting, enjoy abstract thinking, are willing to be a bit uncomfortable having their own beliefs challenged by others, and prefer the open-endedness of the philosophy degree. I've seen many students make themselves unhappy by trying to study something that they aren't interested in, because friends or relatives think it is "practical". And I've seen many students who studied philosophy go on to be successful in law school or the "real world" to believe that studying philosophy isn't also practical.

Q5. Is Philosophy practical?

Why do people who are interested in philosophy decide to not major in it? The main reason is a general perception that the humanities are "impractical".

It's true that, unlike nursing or engineering, a B.A. in History or Philosophy doesn't give you a straight and narrow career path right out of college. That said, lack of forced direction can be a very good thing! Few people do know what they want to do with the rest of their lives at age 18–22 and most people change their minds several times in their 20s and pursue many different fields. The world changes quickly now—and much of the "practical" training someone got 10 years ago is out of date today. That's reality.

What's the best preparation for this brave new world that changes quickly, where you have the freedom to change career paths or fields throughout your life? The most general sort of study possible. Philosophy is the most general sort of training for life you can get.

The analytical and reasoning skills that you pick up in philosophy courses serve you well in life, whatever you end up doing. People respect those who can think independently and confidently offer solutions to difficult problems that no one has encountered before. They look to people like that to manage and to lead.

Will the topics you cover in, say, epistemology class come in handy when your employer looks to you to make a tough decision? Probably not. But will the skills you gained in epistemology class, come in handy when making decisions? Yes, definitely.

Q6. What good has philosophy done over the last 2,500 years?

People question whether philosophy has made any progress, or whether it is simply repeating back and forth the same arguments for centuries. However, you might think of it this way: philosophy spent the last 2,500 years having children.

Philosophy has many children—it is sometimes called the "Mother of the Sciences". Most disciplines on your campus had their origins in philosophy, if you trace them far enough.
For instance:

* **Computer Science.** Modern computing is the direct result of developments in logic produced by Bertrand Russell and Alfred North Whitehead in their *Principia Mathematica*, as well as others like Gottlob Frege who came before them. Their works were meant to answer questions once posed by Plato about how we can know the most basic truths of Arithmetic, but the end result was the philosopher Alan Turing's invention of computing.

* **Sociology** was founded by the philosopher Auguste Comte, the "father of sociology", and one of the most influential sociologists was the philosopher Emile Durkheim.

* **Physics** has improved and grown incredibly since its origins in the Pre-Socratic philosophers of ancient Greece. But at each turn, physics has advanced in part because of philosophical advances. For instance, the philosophical turn away from received tradition and toward the empirical methods of Francis Bacon moved physics forward. Isaac Newton was also a philosopher. Einstein's theories of relativity harken back to philosophical debates about the relativity or absoluteness of space and time that long preceded Einstein. Contemporary Quantum Mechanics raises a host of new philosophical questions.

* **Chemistry** as the study of what the basic elements are and how these atoms combine to form matter at the level we know it also finds its origins in the thought of the classical Greek atomists.

* **Biology** finds one of its earliest expositions by Aristotle, and the work of Aristotle and his students remained the basis of biology through most of the Middle Ages. The great revolution in biology that came about through Charles Darwin's theory of evolution, involved rejecting Aristotle's purpose-based view of nature and a return to Greek thought prior to Aristotle.

* **Economics** in its modern form has its origins in the philosopher Adam Smith's *Wealth of Nations*. Karl Marx's critique of Smith's capitalism, on the other hand, had its origins in the works of the philosopher Georg Hegel.

* **Political Science** is an outgrowth of the political theory that originated in philosophers like Aristotle and Machiavelli. Modern political theory continues to be considered as part of philosophy.

* **Linguistics** in its modern form is closely tied to the philosophy of language and attempts by logicians and philosophers of language to analyze the structure of language and determine its semantics. Noam Chomsky's work challenged the view of John Locke that humans were a "blank slate".

* **Anthropology** was foreseen as a distinct field by the philosopher Immanuel Kant, and developed out of the idea in Enlightenment philosophy that something universal could be known about "humankind".

What other new disciplines will philosophy produce down the road? What do you think?

Further, even in those disciplines that originated independently of philosophy in Western History—law, medicine, business, and religion—philosophy is an important field of study today. For example, many students eager to go to Law school seek a Bachelor's degree in philosophy as preparation for their field: this is probably a good preparation as evidenced by the high Law School Admission Tests (LSAT) scores the philosophy majors on average receive! Philosophy majors also tend to have some of the highest average scores on the GRE (Graduate School), GMAT (Business), and MCAT (Medicine). Medical students are expected to be able to think philosophically about difficult ethical decisions. Operating a business requires an ability to make rational decisions and avoid logical fallacies. And many religious traditions have a long history of interaction with philosophy and philosophical reasoning.

So, if you're thinking of majoring in philosophy, but then a well-meaning relative asks you: *What can you do with a philosophy degree?* You can let them know that you're studying the most basic and general field there is, so that you're ready to do anything.

❉ 0.3 Reasons and Causes ❉

© chrupka/Shutterstock.com

People have different opinions on philosophical topics. Sometimes people say "everyone is entitled to their own opinion". Legally and socially, that's true. You can't be punished in court for having the wrong opinion. Perhaps, we're most likely to get along best with one another when we generally don't try to make each other feel ashamed, embarrassed, stupid, taboo, or outcast simply for disagreeing with us.

However, it's misleading to say that someone is *entitled* to his or her opinion. If you want to communicate your opinion to others, then it's not enough to say that you hold your opinion *because* you hold it, because it's your *right* to hold it.

"Listen to me! I believe something . . . *because I'm entitled to!*"

Sure, you have the right to your opinion. Other people also have the right to ignore you.

If you want anyone to listen to you and take you seriously, you're going to have to give them *reasons* for your beliefs. You'll have to explain why you believe what you do, and not just assert that you believe it because you do. Presenting reasons allows other people to weigh and consider what you have to say for themselves.

Now, the word "reason" can be ambiguous—it can have multiple senses or meanings. What we mean by a "reason" for a belief in philosophy is *justification*: something which gives you the right to be certain about that belief, or at least increases your confidence that the belief is true. For example, I believe that most cats eat meat and do not eat vegetables. My justification for this belief consists of many reasons: that I've seen my cat eat meat but snub vegetables repeatedly, that I've seen other cats do the same, that other people have told me their cats do the same, and that I've never heard of a cat eating only vegetables. These are all things that make it more likely that "most cats eat meat, not vegetables" is true. "Reason" in this sense has to do with my process of reasoning that backs up what I believe.

However, the word "reason" in English also sometimes means *cause* or *explanation*. Various factors cause or motivate us to hold the beliefs we do. But often the causes of our beliefs are not the same as what justifies our beliefs. For instance, one cause of my belief that most cats eat meat is probably watching a lot of cartoons growing up—in these cartoons, cats went after fish and foul but not cabbage or carrots. However, that I saw cats in cartoons eating meat is not such a good reason to believe that cats truthfully eat meat; after all, I also watched cartoons growing up in which tiny blue people lived in mushroom houses, and in which intergalactic fighting robots transformed into motor vehicles; yet, neither is true. Another cause of my belief that cats eat meat is probably a process of social indoctrination through constant repetition of the message "cats eat meat" in advertisements, jokes, and stories about cats. But this isn't a justification for my belief either. Advertisements and jokes and stories are also used to repeat and spread messages that are false—consider how many jokes simply play off of existing stereotypes. The mere repetition of a message is not enough reason to think it is true.

Sometimes, when you separate out the mere causes of your belief from the actual justifications for your belief, you find a number of beliefs that aren't as certain as you thought!

Test yourself for a moment: What do you actually know about, say, feudal life in Medieval Europe? What do you actually know about American Indian Civilization prior to the landing of Europeans? What do you actually know about Islamic law? What do you actually know about the Spanish Inquisition or the American Civil War?

When you think about *how* you know this, can you find a *justification* for what you believe? Or is what you find just a set of *causes* that aren't *reasons*: a repeated series of cultural images from movies, television, things your friends posted on the internet, and stories people tell? Are your beliefs justified by evidence, or did you simply pick them up from people around you?

When someone asks in philosophy for the *reasons* you hold a belief, they're not asking for what initially caused that belief, but for what justifies it. This is particularly important when we consider topics like the existence of free will, the nature of morality, or the existence of God. Everyone will have *different causes* behind their beliefs on these topics: perhaps they were raised with a certain set of beliefs, perhaps their current peers or friends hold these beliefs, perhaps they felt persuaded by something they heard or read, perhaps they have a certain psychological motivation to believe or not believe something, or perhaps they gain socially by believing or not believing something. However, the ultimate reasons that justify their beliefs will tend to be very similar.

Keeping in mind the distinction between the justifying reasons for a belief and the causes of a belief during this course will help you in several ways:

* When you read the source texts by major philosophers, ask yourself *why* they believed the positions they held. However, don't focus on asking *why* in terms of their psychology, their point in history, their social influences, or their hidden motives. Instead, focus on asking *why* in terms of the reasoning and argumentation they used to justify their positions—arguments which remain equally relevant today.

* When you're asked for the reasons behind your view, don't think in terms of what originally caused you to hold those views, but rather in terms of what reasons you have to think that your views are likely to be true. You may not think your views are absolutely certain, but in holding them you naturally think they are more likely to be true than the alternatives – so explain why you think that is so.

* When you're asked to give an argument for your views, you'll need to avoid many of the tools that are normally used in persuasive writing: rhetorical style, powerful language, personal stories, and appeals to emotion, popularity, or authority. Those things might *cause* someone else to change their mind and agree with you, but they won't *justify* the other person in agreeing with you. Instead, focus on things which the person you are writing to already believes, and show how your view follows from what they already believe.

* When you try to find objections to someone else's argument, look for reasons to think that their premises (their assumptions) are probably false. Try to object to the premises that lead to their conclusion rather than simply objecting to their conclusion.

Offer reasons rather than causes, and other people might even come to share your opinion!

Key Points:

* A "reason for a belief" sometimes means the cause which produced the belief, but in philosophy it has to do with the justification for that belief.

* Justification for a belief has to do with the evidence or argumentation someone has to support that a belief is true, not simply their sense of certainty about the belief.

* Giving reasons for your beliefs can help others understand your views.

❈ 0.4 Constructing Valid Arguments ❈

✳ ✳

© Gwoeii/Shutterstock.com

Extracting Arguments

Most of the time, arguments in philosophy are written out in essay form as a series of paragraphs accompanied by many examples and illustrations. However, sometimes it is helpful to pull out the essential pieces of the argument from the examples and illustrations. We call this *extracting* an argument from the text. There is a formal style for extracting an argument, or for presenting one's own argument. The formal way of doing it helps make it easier to see whether the argument is *valid* or *invalid*.

The Form of an Argument

When you extract an argument, you write it down as a numbered series of **premises** followed by a **conclusion**, with intermediate **steps** along the way showing your reasoning. For example:

1. Either John or Mary or Todd will win the election (Premise).
2. Todd will not win the election (Premise).
3. If Mary wins the election, then John will retire (Premise).
4. Either John or Mary will win the election (from 1, 2).
C. Either John will win the election, or John will retire (from 3, 4).

Premises are those things where both the person making the argument and the person to whom the argument is made agree upon, or are at least willing to assume for the sake of the argument. The conclusion is what the person making the argument thinks of the person to whom the argument should believe, given a belief in the premises. Intermediate steps help show how someone gets from the Premises to the Conclusion.

> **Structure of an Argument**
> **Premises:** *shared assumptions*
> **Steps:** *how the conclusion is reached from the premises*
> **Conclusion:** *what one is supposed to believe given the premises*

A person who accepts the premises of a valid argument should accept the conclusion; a person who wishes to reject the conclusion of a valid argument has to reject one or more of the premises.

You can label the premises with numbers like 1, 2, or P1, P2. The conclusion can be labeled "C", or it can simply be the next number in the chain.

More Examples

P1. Tom wants to go to Law school.

P2. If Tom wants to go to Law school, he'll need to do well on the LSAT.

P3. If anyone wants to do well on the LSAT, they should study philosophy.

P4. Tom needs to do well on the LSAT (P1, P2).

  C. Tom should study philosophy (P3, P4).

  1. Everyone who is a philosophy major understands logic.

  2. Kendra is a philosophy major.

  C. Kendra understands logic (1, 2).

Validity

The most important concept in our study of logic will be the concept of validity. In philosophy, we define a valid argument this way:

    (Valid) An argument is valid if and only if there is no logical possibility of true premises with a false conclusion.

In other words, there's no way that the conclusion can be false when the premises are true.

The three arguments given above as examples were valid. It's not possible that Kendra doesn't understand logic, if Kendra is a philosophy major and all philosophy majors understand logic. It isn't possible for it to be false that Tom should study philosophy, if it's true that (i) he wants to go to Law school, (ii) if he wants to go to Law school he has to do well on the LSAT, and (iii) if anyone wants to do well on the LSAT they should study philosophy.

> An Argument is **Valid** if the conclusion can't be false in any possible scenario where the premises are true.

Validity doesn't necessarily mean the conclusion is true. It is possible that Kendra doesn't understand logic, because it's possible that not all philosophy majors understand logic. It's possible that Tom shouldn't study philosophy, because it's possible that there are people who want to do well on the LSAT but who have no interest in philosophy and who would be better off studying something else. In a valid argument, the conclusion can be false *only if* the premises are false.

Validity does not require knowing whether the premises are true or false. The reason why validity is such a useful tool is that it tells us whether a conclusion follows from certain premises without requiring us to know whether or not those premises are true or false. The definition of "validity" asks whether it is *impossible* for the premises to be true with the conclusion false, and not whether we happen to know the premises are true or the conclusion is false.

> Logic is less concerned with what **is actually true**, than with what **could or couldn't be true** given a set of assumptions.

For instance, this argument is valid:

1. If there are unicorns, then there are unicorn dance parties.
2. There are unicorns.
C. There are unicorn dance parties.

Premise 1 and premise 2 are false, and the conclusion is false. However, *were it the case* that premise 1 and premise 2 were true, then the conclusion would have to be true. It is irrelevant to validity that the premises are false.

On the other hand, this argument is invalid:

1. The Mississippi River is in the United States.
2. The Gulf of Mexico is south of the United States.
C. The Mississippi River flows south into the Gulf of Mexico.

Even though all of the premises are true, and the conclusion is also true, it's still *possible* for the premises to have been true with the conclusion false. Can you think of a way that might have been the case, perhaps in a world slightly different from our own?

© Rainer Lesniewski/Shutterstock.com

Some Bad but Valid Arguments

Most students wrongly assume a "valid" argument is just a "good" argument. But that's not true. The word "valid" used in logic is used in a very particular, carefully defined way. In everyday English, a "valid" point is just a "good point". But in logic an argument can be valid even though it's a bad argument.

Notice that an argument can be valid even if the conclusion doesn't follow from the premises:

1. The moon is made of tacos.
2. Tacos are a type of food.
C. $5 + 0 = 4 + 1$

Why is this a valid argument? Because **it is not possible for the conclusion to be false,** whether the premises are true or not, so it is not possible for the premises to be true with the conclusion false. Since it's impossible for 5+0 not to be equal to 4+1, the conclusion can't be false, no matter what the truth of the premises are. Of course, even though it's valid, it's a stupid argument! The conclusion has nothing to do with the premises.

Consider another bad, but valid argument:

1. Jeff lives in Mesa.
2. Jeff does not live in Mesa.
C. Aliens rule the world through a secret society based in underground tunnels in Detroit.

Why is this a valid argument? Because **it is not possible for the premises to be true**, regardless of the conclusion, it is not possible for the premises to be true with the conclusion false. The premises contradict each other: There's no possibility of Jeff living in Mesa and not living in Mesa (at the same time), since that's a contradiction. Since there's no possibility of true premises, there's no possibility of true premises with a false conclusion. By definition, it's valid. Of course, it's also a silly argument! We might have written *anything* in for the conclusion.

A valid argument can also have unnecessary premises. For example:

1. Jeff lives in Mesa.
2. Mesa is in Arizona.
3. Jeff does not like milk.
C. Jeff lives in Arizona.

Here, only premise 1 and 2 are needed to make the argument valid. It's impossible for Jeff to live in Mesa, which is in Arizona, and yet not live in Arizona. Premise 3 is completely irrelevant to whether Jeff lives in Arizona or not. But adding it doesn't make the argument invalid, just longer than it needs to be.

Good Invalid Arguments

Conversely not all good arguments are valid. Here is an example of an invalid argument, even though it's not such a bad argument.

1. The mail carrier arrived at 3 p.m. every day last week.
2. The mail carrier arrived at 3 p.m. yesterday.
3. The mail carrier arrived at 3 p.m. today.
C. The mail carrier will arrive at 3 p.m. tomorrow.

© Steven Good/Shutterstock.com

Why is this argument invalid? Because even though it isn't unreasonable to think that the mail carrier will keep a tight schedule, it's still not logically guaranteed that the mail carrier will arrive at 3 p.m. tomorrow simply because he's done so in the past. Maybe he or she will get a flat tire.

Just because an argument isn't valid doesn't mean it isn't persuasive. Consider the argument below. Many people seem to find it persuasive; though, logically speaking, the argument is invalid:

1. There is no practical application for most philosophical debates.
2. If something has no practical applications, it is not useful.
C. Studying philosophy is useless.

This argument is invalid, because it is possible that studying philosophy is useful, even if most philosophical debates are not useful. It is possible for the conclusion to be false even if one grants that the premises are true.

For example, suppose that the process of studying "useless" debates in philosophy sharpens one's ability to think critically in an abstract and unbiased way, in a manner in which studying "useful" debates would not. If thinking critically is useful, then studying philosophy could be useful, even if philosophy weren't about anything useful. Or, it might be that philosophical debates are important not because they have particular practical applications, but because they shape one's overall perspective toward life itself. In that case, studying philosophy might be useful for life itself even if it had no particular practical applications to, say, how to design a better motor or engine.

Consider this argument:

1. Lemonade is made from water.
2. Water evaporates in the heat.
C. Lemonade evaporates in the heat.

This is a good, commonsensical argument, with true premises and a true conclusion. But it's invalid. Why? Because it's *logically* possible for the premises to be true and the conclusion false. This is logically possible, even though it is not a possibility in our world given our laws of nature. There's no contradiction in saying "lemonade is made from water, which evaporates in the heat, but lemonade doesn't evaporate in the heat". To understand why, substitute "lemonade" with 'concrete'. Concrete is made from water, but concrete doesn't evaporate in the heat. Logic isn't supposed to assume anything about the world we live in or take anything for granted.

Learning from Invalid Arguments

We can learn from invalid arguments by figuring out which premises are needed to make them valid.

1. The mail carrier arrived at 3 p.m. yesterday.
2. The mail carrier arrived at 3 p.m. today.
3. *The mail carrier will arrive tomorrow at whatever time he or she arrived today.*
C. The mail carrier will arrive at 3 p.m. tomorrow.

1. There is no practical application for most philosophical debates.
2. If something has no practical applications, it is useless.
3. *If something is useless, then studying it is useless.*
C. Studying philosophical debates is useless.

Finally:

1. Lemonade is made from water.
2. Water evaporates in the heat.
3. ***Everything which is made from water will evaporate in the same circumstances as water does.***
C. Lemonade evaporates in the heat.

Now these arguments are valid. We made them valid by adding a premise. By making the invalid arguments into valid arguments, we revealed the hidden assumptions that the invalid arguments were making. We can now question those assumptions.

How to Use Validity

First, you can use this as a tool to **present your own arguments**. Before arguing for a position you hold, you can ensure that your premises **entail** your conclusion: that is, there is no way your conclusion could be false if your premises were true.

You can also use it as a tool in **interpreting what you read**, or to presenting an argument you've read, heard, or can imagine someone making. For example, we will read an essay by Descartes. Descartes doesn't set out his argument in a formal way. But by setting out his argument in a formal way which is valid, you can see what assumptions Descartes is making.

You can use the format to show that someone's argument isn't valid. You can also use it to show that in order to make someone's argument valid, you have to add an absurd premise. Or you can use it to assist someone who is making an argument by showing them what assumptions they need to make clear.

Some Argument Forms Guaranteed to Be Valid

Certain forms of argument are guaranteed to be valid, regardless of the content of those arguments. You can employ these when you are constructing an argument, to help guarantee that the argument is valid.

MODUS TOLLENS	MODUS PONENS
Form:	Form:
1. IF A THEN B 2. Not B C. Not A	1. IF A THEN B 2. A C. B
Example:	Example:
1. If it's snowing, then it's cold. 2. It's not cold. C. It's not snowing.	1. If it's snowing, then it's cold. 2. It's snowing. C. It's cold.

DISJUNCTIVE SYLLOGISM	CATEGORICAL SYLLOGISM
Form:	Form:
1. EITHER A OR B 2. Not A C. B	1. EVERY P IS Q 2. A IS P C. A IS Q
Example:	Example:
1. Either I'm dreaming, or the world is seriously messed up. 2. I'm not dreaming. C. The world is seriously messed up.	1. Every parent has children. 2. George Bush is a parent. C. George Bush has children.

REDUCTIO	ARGUMENT BY IDENTITY/ANALOGY
Form:	Form:
1. ASSUME A 2. IF A THEN B 3. B 4. NOT B C. NOT A	1. A is (like) B. 2. B is C. C. A is C.
Example:	Examples:
	Identity
1. Children have no free will (Assumption). 2. If someone has no free will, they will go along with whatever you tell them to do. 3. Children will go along with whatever you tell them to do (by 1 & 2). 4. Children do not go along with whatever you tell them to do (real observation). CONTRADICTION C. Children do have free will.	1. Barack Obama is the President. 2. The President deserves respect regardless of your political views. C. Barack Obama deserves respect regardless of your political views. *Analogy* 1. Politics is like war in all of the relevant ways. 2. War destroys innocence. C. Politics destroys innocence.

Key Points:

* An argument is valid if and only if there is no logically possible world where the premises are true and the conclusion is false.

* Valid arguments might be bad arguments; invalid arguments might be good arguments.

* Some forms of argument are always valid, no matter what the premises say.

❀ 0.5 Extracting, Explaining, and Evaluating an Argument ❀

© exopixel/Shutterstock.com

EEE-ing an argument is a three-step method for studying philosophy:

Extracting a valid argument with premises leading to a conclusion

Explaining the premises of the argument and the conclusion

Evaluating the premises of the argument and the conclusion

You'll notice your instructor using this method sometimes in lectures. You'll want to use this method both when you're trying to *interpret* what philosophers have written and also when you're trying to formulate arguments of your own.

I. Extracting an Argument

You'll notice that most philosophers use formal arguments sparingly, and instead write in lengthy prose. So, how do you go about presenting someone's argument as a formal argument, if they haven't given you a formal argument to work with?

How do you get started?

EXTRACTING an argument from a bit of philosophical prose is a three-step process:

STEP 1. Find and simplify the Conclusion.
STEP 2. Find and simplify the Premises
STEP 3. Add Premises to Make the Argument Valid

27

STEP 1. Find and simplify the Conclusion

Extracting an argument means writing it out as a **valid argument** with a series of premises and a conclusion, where the truth of the premises would guarantee the truth of the conclusion. You don't have to stick to the original wording or sentence structure when presenting an argument. You can rephrase the terms to make sure the terms in each premise line up with the terms in the conclusion.

> **Extracting** an argument means finding and simplifying, the conclusion, finding and simplifying the premises, and adding premises to make it valid.

What is the point? What does the author want to persuade you is true? Notice that this has nothing to do with the *order* the sentences appear in.

For example, suppose someone makes this argument:

> *We shouldn't vote for the school bonds because that would mean higher taxes for no real benefit. Education has enough money being wastefully thrown at it and it never gets better, and it won't get better until we deprive it of money.*

Here the conclusion is very clear:

C. We shouldn't vote for the school bonds.

Sometimes it can be harder to extract a conclusion, particularly when reading older philosophical texts. For instance, take this paragraph by Francis Bacon, from his *Novum Organum*, published in 1620:

The first step is to figure out what the section you're reading is trying to get you to conclude.

> *Those who have handled sciences have been either men of experiment or men of dogmas. The men of experiment are like the ant, they only collect and use; the reasoners resemble spiders, who make cobwebs out of their own substance. But the bee takes a middle course: it gathers its material from the flowers of the garden and of the field, but transforms and digests it by a power of its own. Not unlike this is the true business of philosophy; for it neither relies solely or chiefly on the powers of the mind, nor does it take the matter which it gathers from natural history and mechanical experiments and lay it up in the memory whole, as it finds it, but lays it up in the understanding altered and digested. Therefore from a closer and purer league between these two faculties, the experimental and the rational (such as has never yet been made), much may be hoped.*

© Everett Historical/Shutterstock.com

How do we find the conclusion of Bacon's argument? First, look at the first and last sentence of the paragraph. Those are places where a conclusion tends to go. Second, look for words which indicate a conclusion, like "therefore", "thus", "as a result", "so"—whereas words like "because" or "since" tend to indicate a premise. Looking at the last sentence of the paragraph, we see the word therefore. That's a word which tends to indicate a conclusion. So Bacon's conclusion is something like:

> *Therefore from a closer and purer league between these two faculties, the experimental and the rational (such as has never yet been made), much may be hoped.*

But that's a bit wordy! So, let's try to summarize what Bacon is saying in fewer words. Bacon is saying that:

C. If the experimental and the rational faculties work together, then more knowledge will result than if they work separately.

STEP 2. Find and simplify the Premises

Next, we need find the premises for our argument. What reasons are given for the conclusion?

Let's start with the argument that we shouldn't vote for the school bonds. An initial stab at this argument might look like this, listing the reasons as premises and what the person wants to convince us of as a conclusion.

1. It would mean higher taxes for no real benefit.
2. Education has enough money being wastefully thrown at it.
3. Education never gets better.
4. Education won't get better until we deprive it of money.
C. We shouldn't vote for the school bonds.

However, we need to simplify the argument a bit, to get to the core of it. First, we need to use consistent terms: "It" in the first premise should be replaced with "School bonds".

Second, we should distinguish between *premises* of our argument, and *support for* the premises. Premises 2–4 are actually not arguments for the conclusion. Instead, they're arguments for the truth of premise 1; namely, that school bonds would bring no real benefit.

Third, we need to make sure we're using words precisely. The phrase "no real benefit" is misleading—are there "unreal benefits"?—so instead we might want to say "no *significant* benefit".

Fourth, we want to break up premises into small, independent claims. Premise 1 really contains two independent claims: first, that school bonds would raise taxes, and second that they'd bring no real benefit.

The core of the argument is this:

1. School bonds would mean higher taxes.
2. School bonds would bring no significant benefit.
C. We shouldn't vote for the school bonds.

What reasons does Francis Bacon give in the excerpt from *Novum Organum* above for the conclusion that "if the experimental and the rational faculties work together, then more knowledge will result than if they work separately"?

We'll need to ignore the aspects of Francis Bacon's writing that are more literary and metaphorical and simplify or reinterpret the passage to get to his core reasoning. Not everything in the paragraph has to appear as a premise, after all. In fact, looking at the paragraph above, it seems like Bacon repeats the same argument twice, first by analogy to ants and spiders, and then more directly speaking of philosophers.

Take this: *the men of experiment are like the ant, they only collect and use.*

Knowing the conclusion we're aiming for, we might simplify this to:

1. If the experimental faculty works alone, then it only collects raw data.

What about this? *The reasoners resemble spiders, who make cobwebs out of their own substance.*

Again, knowing the conclusion we're aiming for, we can simplify this to:

2. If the rational faculty works alone, then it has no data to understand and digest.

And what about this? *But the bee takes a middle course: it gathers its material from the flowers of the garden and of the field, but transforms and digests it by a power of its own.*

What Bacon is saying could be put this way:

3. If the experimental and rational faculties work together, then the raw data will be understood and digested.

Notice that we didn't add everything as a premise. Not every premise in the argument is necessary to make it valid. For instance, we don't need to further add this as a premise:

4* Ants are like experimenters and spiders are like reasoners.

or this:

4** The business of philosophy is to rely neither solely on the powers of the mind nor the powers of the senses.

Because 4* is just part of the metaphor that illustrates the argument, and 4** is another way of stating the conclusion. We want to eliminate any premises that aren't necessary for the conclusion to be true—otherwise the argument will get very long!

The result we get is

1. If the experimental faculty works alone, then it only collects raw data.
2. If the rational faculty works alone, then it has no data to understand and digest.
3. If the experimental and rational faculties work together, then the raw data will be understood and digested.
C. If the experimental and the rational faculties work together, then more knowledge will result than if they work separately.

STEP 3. Add Premises to Make the Argument Valid

Part of philosophy is always being on the look-out for leaps in reasoning that reveal hidden assumptions. Many times it's the things we all take for granted and assume that get us in trouble. That's why validity is so important when formulating arguments: we want arguments where the premises would guarantee the conclusion, were the premises true.

> Making an invalid argument valid can usually be accomplished by adding premises to bridge the gap between the premises and the conclusion.

Sometimes authors make assumptions that they don't bother to mention or disclose. These can be commonsensical, but they can also sometimes be open to a challenge. So, by figuring out what premises we need to add to make an argument valid, we can reveal these hidden assumptions.

Look at the arguments we created at the end of the last step. Are they valid?

1. *School bonds would mean higher taxes.*
2. *School bonds would bring no significant benefit.*
C. *We shouldn't vote for the school bonds.*

The argument is *not* valid. "We shouldn't vote" appears in the conclusion, but it isn't clear how the premises entail it. Nothing in either premise mentions what we "should" do, nor do the premises mention voting. We need a third premise to link up the premises with the conclusion:

1. School bonds would mean higher taxes.
2. School bonds would bring no significant benefit.
3. **If something leads to higher taxes for no substantial benefit, then we shouldn't do it.**
C. We shouldn't vote for the school bonds.

We're close! But we've said "would mean" in premise 1, but "leads to" in premise 3. We said "for no substantial benefit" in premise 3, but "bring no substantial benefit" in premise 2. And we said "do it" in premise 3, but "vote for" in the conclusion. We need to be consistent! Here's our final version:

FINAL EXTRACTED ARGUMENT

1. School bonds lead to high taxes.
2. School bonds bring no significant benefit.
3. If something leads to higher taxes and brings no significant benefit, then we shouldn't vote for it.
C. We shouldn't vote for school bonds.

Now the argument is clearly valid. If premise 3 is true, and premises 1 and 2 are true, then the conclusion has to be true.

Now let's look at the argument from Francis Bacon's *Novum Organum*.

1. *If the experimental faculty works alone, then it only collects raw data.*
2. *If the rational faculty works alone, then it has no data to understand and digest.*
3. *If the experimental and rational faculties work together, then the raw data will be understood and digested.*
C. *If the experimental and the rational faculties work together, then more knowledge will result than if they work separately.*

This argument *makes sense* and, maybe even, *seems persuasive*. But that's not what "valid" means. Validity requires that there is no way that the conclusion could be false if the premises were true. Yet in this argument we're taking something for granted.

We're assuming that *only collecting raw data* or *having no data to understand and digest* are situations that will produce *less knowledge* than raw data being understood and digested.

That seems plausible! But imagine for a moment a scenario in which this is false. Imagine that we all had very twisted reasoning which took raw data and spit out paranoid nonsense and lead us to believe many falsehoods: suppose everytime someone told us the weather was sunny outside, we'd use our "reasoning" to conclude from this data that trolls were about to invade. That would seem like a case where just having raw data would be much better and produce more knowledge than allowing this "reasoning" to understand and digest the data.

The point of this silly scenario isn't that it undermines the argument, of course. It's just that we need to add a premise. We need to be explicit that we are assuming:

> Extracting an argument
> often reveals **hidden
> assumptions.**

4. *If the experimental faculty only collects raw data or the reasoning faculty has no data to understand and digest, then less knowledge will result than if the raw data is understood and digested.*

So, let's add in this premise, to produce our new, valid argument:

FINAL EXTRACTED ARGUMENT

1. If the experimental faculty works alone, then it only collects raw data.
2. If the rational faculty works alone, then it has no data to understand and digest.
3. If the experimental and rational faculties work together, then the raw data will be understood and digested.
4. If the experimental faculty only collects raw data or the reasoning faculty has no data to understand and digest, then less knowledge will result than if the raw data is understood and digested.
C. If the experimental and the rational faculties work together, then more knowledge will result than if they work separately.

II. Explaining an Argument

Explaining an argument requires explaining **each premise** of the argument. To do this, you need to both (i) **define** the terms in each premise precisely, and (ii) give **reasons to believe** the truth of the premise. Let's tackle this argument:

1. School bonds lead to high taxes.
2. School bonds bring no substantial benefit.
3. If something leads to higher taxes and brings no significant benefit, then we shouldn't vote for it.
C. We shouldn't vote for school bonds.

Premise 1, (i) Definitions

School bonds lead to high taxes.

Here some of the terms are pretty straightforward. We'll assume "school bonds" refers to some particular set of bonds at issue in an election, and that "higher taxes" means that property tax rates will go up. "Lead to" is talking about causation.

Premise 1, (ii) Reasoning

We'll assume the reasons behind this premise are also uncontroversial. Even proponents of the bonds will agree that they have to be paid for by property taxes, and that means higher taxes than if the bonds weren't passed.

Premise 2, (i) Definitions.

School bonds bring no substantial benefit

We're familiar with "school bonds", and we'll assume "bring" also involves causation. The word "benefit" is hard to define, but the idea seems to be that a benefit involves someone's being made better off than they would have been otherwise. But what about "no *significant* benefit". We don't want to define this in a circular way, so we can't say "no benefit worth paying higher taxes for", since this would beg the question. We don't want to imply that there's no benefit at all to the school bonds, since surely someone will get some benefit out of it. So we'll have to acknowledge that the term "significant" is **vague**. It means something like "enough to be worth noticing", but it's hard to nail this down.

> Explaining an argument means helping your reader understand why author of the argument thinks the premise are likely true.

Premise 2, (ii) Reasoning

Here's where we can turn to the original argument. The reasons given were *education has enough money being wastefully thrown at it, education never gets better, and education won't get better until we deprive it of money*. Certainly all three of these, if they are true, give reasons to be skeptical about the benefits of the bonds. If money is being "wastefully thrown at" education, then more money is likely to have the same effect. If education never gets better, then there's no point in trying to make it better. And if education won't get better until we deprive the system of money, passing the school bonds won't help.

Premise 3, (i) Definitions

If something leads to higher taxes and brings no significant benefit, then we shouldn't vote for it.

Here the only phrase in need of definition is "we shouldn't vote for it". We'll assume "we" is the audience of the argument who can vote on the bonds, and we'll assume voting is pretty straightforward. The word "should" is a difficult word, though. It seems like it isn't so much a matter where one *morally* shouldn't vote for the bonds—as though casting a "Yes" vote were immoral or evil. Instead, the issue seems to be that we *prudentially* shouldn't vote for the bonds—that means, we shouldn't as a matter of our mutual self-interest.

Premise 3, (ii) Reasoning

Here the premise seems to be built on a slightly deeper principle. It's not just that we should only vote for higher taxes if they are justified by some benefit. Instead, the principle being assumed here seems to be that we shouldn't *bring about* anything which will lead to *a harm* without *more significant benefits*. That is, we shouldn't make ourselves worse off in one way (taxes) unless it's compensated for by some benefit (a better education system). This seems like a fairly intuitive principle.

Of course, it's possible to explain an argument in a less structured way—in a short paragraph, for example. The point of explaining an argument is two-fold. First, you help the person reading your extracted argument understand the reasons *why* someone would believe the premises. Second, you make clear what would be needed in order to *object* to one of the premises, which is part of a critical evaluation.

Now that we've explained the premises, there's not much needed to explain the conclusion: the outcome of this argument is that one shouldn't vote for the school bonds.

III. Evaluating an Argument

Now begins the fun part. Evaluating an argument requires *you* to enter the picture and say what *you* think about the argument. You want to say whether or not you think it is sound:

(Sound) An argument is sound if and only if it is valid and all of the premises are true.

Since we made sure the argument was valid in Step 1, we're now going to **evaluate each premise** to make sure, we think, each premise is true.

> Validity
> + All premises True
> Soundness

Sometimes it's easy to say that a premise is false or that a premise is true. But often it's not easy to say. Some premises are more controversial or harder to judge. You're free to have your own opinion in this class when you evaluate the premises, so long as you give some explanation for opinion. For example:

Premise 1: School bonds lead to higher taxes.

This premise seems uncontroversial, since even proponents of the bonds agree with it.

Premise 3: If something leads to higher taxes and brings no significant benefit, then we shouldn't vote for it.

This is supposed to be an application of a general principle that one shouldn't lead to a situation where there's a greater harm with insufficient benefits to justify it. I think I would accept the principle.

Premise 2: School bonds bring no substantial benefit

Unlike the other two premises, this premise seems very controversial! Proponents of the bonds would certainly disagree. The reasons given involved not wanting to throw money at education that goes as waste. You might form your own opinion on this issue. But I wonder if it's really true that education never gets better—it seems like peoples' education has improved substantially over the last 100 years, even if it's too slow for us to notice. And I wonder if it's true that Education won't get better unless it's deprived of money: it seems like this is a recipe for things to only get worse. And I don't know

> Evaluating an argument can mean **objecting** to it, or **defending** it, or simply pointing out its **strengths** and **weaknesses**.

whether or not the education system is likely to waste most of the money from the school bonds. So, I think premise 2 is doubtfully true.

So—there you have it! An explanation of how to present, explain, and evaluate an argument. Let's look at one last example to see how this works.

Last Example

Original argument: *People think of the mind as if it were a computer, but it's not. It's not just that the mind doesn't literally have a "hard drive or "ram". Now, our gloriously spontaneous, random, and sometimes senselessly irrational mind can't be predicted based on inputs and programming the way a computer can be predicted. It's chaotic. Maybe someone will produce a computer more perfect than our minds someday, more rational, more pure; but will they ever produce something capable of the pure absurdity of falling in love?*

1. Extract

1. Computers can be predicted based on inputs and programming.

2. Minds can't be predicted based on inputs and programming.

3. Something which can be predicted based on inputs and programming isn't like something which can't be predicted based on inputs and programming.

C. The mind isn't like a computer.

2. Explain

Premise 1—Define.

Can be predicted means that an idea observer could know based on the thing's past that an event in the future would occur to it.

   Programming means the software on which the computer runs.

   Inputs mean what an outside agent or force enters into the computer, such as typing on a keyboard, clicking with a mouse, and so on.

Premise 1—Reasons.

Even though modern computers may not always be predictable by us, they operate by a series of steps where each step leads inevitably to the next, so that an ideal reasoner could know the future simply by knowing its past. Even the "random number" generators in computers simply involve going through a sophisticated algorithm which could, in principle, be traced back to its sources.

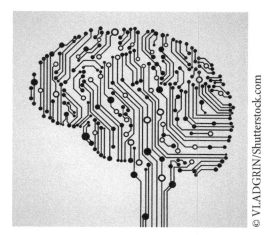

© VLADGRIN/Shutterstock.com

Premise 2—Define

Mind means a conscious, cognitive, reasoning faculty like the one which you and I have.

Premise 2—Reasons

Perhaps, people seem very difficult to predict even in principle. We experience ourselves acting in what seems like spontaneous ways that no one on the outside could ever know.

Premise 3—Define

Like—two things are alike if they have all of the same properties.

Premise 3—Reasons

A can't be like B if A has property X and B does not.

3. Evaluate

Premise 1: The way in which computers currently operate does still seem to be entirely predictable *in principle* by an ideal mathematical mind (perhaps, no human mind). If it weren't so, computers couldn't be programmed!

Premise 2: Here we have to be careful, though, to be consistent. Just like computers can't be predicted by most of us, it seems clear that minds—the thoughts and decisions that people make – can't be predicted by most of us. But why not think that an ideal mind, given a complete scan of our brains and knowledge of the exact workings of our psychology, wouldn't be able to predict what we'd do next? Just because I don't see how *other people* could predict my "spontaneous" actions, why think that my actions are somehow indeterminate even by an ideal mind?

Premise 3: This seems like a trivial truth: how can something be like something else and yet not like it? But surely the person who says "minds are like computers" doesn't mean *alike in every way possible* or *having all of the same properties*. Otherwise, nothing would like anything else but itself! The word "like" is **ambiguous**. Minds aren't like computers in terms of not being made of silicon, but they might be like computers in other ways. What person means is that the mind and computers are alike *in some interesting ways* or in some *relevant* ways. Perhaps, both minds and computers are comparable in terms of information storing capacity, for instance. So the premise as stated here is far too strong.

Key Points:

* Extracting an argument involves producing a numbered list of premises, followed by a conclusion, where the premises, if true, would guarantee the truth of the conclusion.

* Explaining an argument means precisely defining any important terms in the argument and offering reasons why the person making the argument would think the premise is true.

* Evaluating an argument means considering whether you think the premises of the argument can be objected to or not, and either presenting objections to them or defending them against objections.

❀ 0.6 A Guide to Writing Definitions in Philosophy ❀

✳ ✳

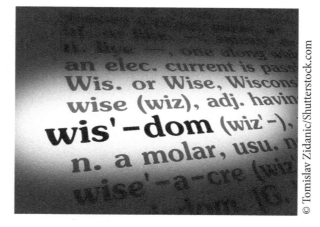

© Tomislav Zidanic/Shutterstock.com

The purpose of a dictionary definition is to provide the reader with a sense of what a word means and to guide the reader in how to use it. A dictionary definition helps someone learn unfamiliar parts of a language.

Philosophers are interested in understanding the **concepts** behind our words, and not just how to use the words themselves. When we attempt to "define" words in philosophy, what we're really trying to do is understand how one concept is related to other concepts. This is sometimes called "conceptual analysis". Our goal is to break down a concept into pieces in order to have a more precise understanding of our concepts.

The process of writing definitions in philosophy involves trying to resolve ambiguity and further define sub-terms in one's own definition, while aiming to provide necessary and sufficient conditions, and while avoiding circularity.

Resolving Ambiguity

The first step in developing an initial definition is to distinguish the many different senses or meanings of a word. If a word has multiple meanings, then you'll need a different definition for each meaning. For example, there are at least two meanings to the word "bank": (i) the sense in "the left bank of the river" and (ii) the sense in "Bank of America". There are at least three meanings of the word "know": (i) the

37

sense in "I know Terry", (ii) the sense in "I know how to speak Mandarin", and (iii) the sense in "I know that Phoenix is north of Tucson". You'll want to distinguish each sense of the word being used, to be clear about what you mean.

For instance, does every use of the word "free" mean the same thing? What about every use of the words "will" or "determined"? Clarifying these terms is necessary to understand what we're talking about when we debate whether free will is compatible with determinism.

Defining the Terms in the Definition

After coming up with an initial definition, the next step is to define all of the unclear or disputable sub-terms within the definition. It's fine for a dictionary to say that love is a "passionate affection", but what counts as "passionate" and what is "affection"? A dictionary can define "authority" as "the right to control", but what's a "right" and what is "control"? This process has to stop somewhere. We could try to define "water", but there's not much dispute about what water is. But don't stop until you get to clearer terms than you started with.

For example, suppose someone were to define a "free choice" as "not being forced to make a decision". Then it will be necessary to define *forced* and *make a decision*.

Noncircularity

A basic principle of writing good definitions in philosophy is avoiding circularity! Don't use the concepts you're trying to define within the definition! This can happen in obvious ways: for instance, defining "love" as "the state of loving" will be unhelpfully circular. But it also can happen in more subtle ways. For example, suppose we tried to define "money" as "what a rich person has". This definition will ultimately be circular, because in order to define "rich" we'll likely have to talk about money.

To consider another example, suppose we had defined "free choice" as "not being forced to make a decision". We couldn't then, in our definition of *forced*, define "forced" as "the opposite of free", and we couldn't define "make a decision" as "to bring about a choice", since both would appeal to the terms we were trying to define in the first place.

Necessary Condition

A good definition in philosophy provides necessary conditions for the thing it defines. A definition needs to be broad enough to include all *possible* cases of the term. If every possible instance of T is X, then X is a necessary condition of T. For example, "is a mammal" is a necessary condition of being a dog, because nothing could be a dog if it were not a mammal. However, "barks a lot" is not a necessary

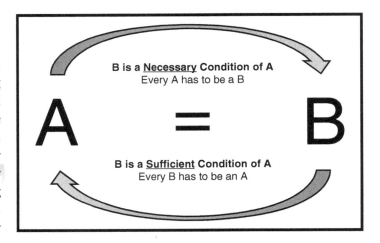

B is a **Necessary** Condition of A
Every A has to be a B

A = B

B is a **Sufficient** Condition of A
Every B has to be an A

condition of being a dog, because Siberian huskies don't bark a lot, yet they are dogs. "Something you learn from someone else" isn't a good definition of knowledge, because it isn't a necessary condition. A person could discover new knowledge on his or her own. On the other hand "being believed" is a necessary condition of being known. Everything that is known has to be believed.

Many people have argued that *having the ability to do otherwise* is a necessary condition of free will. That is, every instance in which someone acts "freely" is necessarily a case in which they had the ability to act differently than they did. However, this might not be all there to acting freely. Perhaps, free will requires more than merely having the ability to act differently: perhaps, it requires a kind of control.

Sufficient Condition

A good definition in philosophy also provides sufficient conditions. A definition needs to be narrow enough not to include anything that isn't a case of the term. For instance, "is a Chihuahua" is a sufficient condition for being a dog, because necessarily every Chihuahua is a dog. However, "creature with four legs" is not a good definition of "dog", because cats also have four legs, and cats aren't dogs. Just because something has four legs isn't enough to guarantee that it is a dog. Similarly, "true belief" isn't a sufficient condition of knowledge. For example, I might believe that it's true that I'm going to win the lottery because I believe I'm a very lucky person. Suppose it turns out that I've won the lottery. Surely I didn't *know* that I was going to win the lottery. On the other hand, "blue" is one sufficient condition for "having color". While not everything that has color is blue, everything that is blue has color.

Some people think that *being morally responsible* for something is a sufficient condition for having free will. That is, they think that it isn't possible to be morally responsible for something unless you did it freely.

Objecting to a Definition

So, now that you know how to write definitions in philosophy, how would you object to a definition that someone else offers?

One way to object to a definition is to present a **counterexample**. A counterexample is an instance that demonstrates a definition hasn't yet given complete necessary and sufficient conditions for a concept. Here's how to present a counterexample:

"Adam says that the definition of 'pain' is 'an experience which the subject dislikes.' However, masochists like pain. So, pain isn't necessarily an experience which the subject dislikes."

Definitions must hold true in any possible way the world could have been, not just the way the world happens to be at the time. It so happens that all species on earth that have kidneys also have hearts. Someone might think that part of the definition of being a "species with a kidney" is "being a species with a heart." However, it's *possible* that some species with kidneys, perhaps on some distant planet, might not have any hearts. The possibility of a species with a kidney but no heart still counts as a counterexample to the definition.

A Final Note

It's very hard to come up with definitions for our concepts. Most definitions will ultimately have counterexamples. But a better definition is one where the counterexamples are harder to find and less obvious. There are few things for which we actually could give necessary and sufficient conditions without counterexamples. But the *process* of trying to do so helps us understand better the limits of our concepts.

Finally, note that most definitions will ultimately include some *vague* concepts. This is because many of our concepts simply are vague and have vague boundary-lines. At what point does fast turn to slow, or poor turn to rich? At what point does a chair become a sofa, or a sofa become a bed? How old does something have to be to qualify as *ancient*? So long as one is aware of the vagueness of the terms used in a definition, it is probably best to be tolerant of it, as something that can't be eliminated from most of our ordinary concepts.

Overview: Unit 1
Truth and Logic

✳ ✳

In this unit, we'll do an overview of what philosophy is all about. What's the history of philosophy? What's the goal of philosophy? What methods do philosophers use? What does the Standard View assume about the world?

By the end of this unit, you should be able to:

* Recognize major figures and events in the history of philosophy, like Socrates.

* Recognize Locke's views on the purpose of philosophy.

* Categorize an argument as deductive, inductive, or abductive.

* Recognize distinctions between different senses of "necessary" and "possible" and consider alternative possibilities to ordinary scenarios.

* Evaluate an argument as valid or invalid, and recognize invalid inferences.

* Evaluate the premises of an argument as stronger or weaker.

* Distinguish sentences from propositions; ambiguity from vagueness; the sense of a word from its referent.

✳ Relate the truth of a proposition to facts about the world, and facts to opinions about the facts.

❀ 1.1 Notes on Unit 1 Source Texts ❀

❋ ❋

Before we delve into considering specific philosophical questions, it is important to get a bit of background. First, we should get a bit of historical background about the history of philosophy, so that it's possible to understand the context of the texts in this class. Second, we should get a handle on the basics of logic and argumentation, and some of the vocabulary that philosophers use.

A. Notes on a Brief History of Western Thought

B. Notes on a Guide to Philosophical Argument

C. Notes on Plato's "Apology"

D. Notes on Plato's "Allegory of the Cave"

E. Notes on Locke's "Enthusiasm"

A. Notes on a Brief History of Western Thought

"Western" thought is, broadly speaking, the ongoing philosophical conversation that traces its orgins to Europe, the Middle East, and North Africa. It is distinguished from the distinct schools of thought that developed relatively independently in East Asia, India, Sub-Saharan Africa, and the Americas. These geographical boundaries are increasingly artificial, of course. In a globalized world, one can study Eastern philosophy in London and Western philosophy in Mumbai.

The "Brief History of Western Thought" gives a narrative that walks briskly through the three major eras of Western thought that brought us into the present day:

1. The Ancient era
2. The Medieval era
3. The Enlightenment era

Giving an exhaustive history of philosophy in a few pages would be impossible! Instead, the goal is to provide a bit of context to the readings in this course in terms of the major social, religious, and political events happening in the world at the time.

The Philosophers in this textbook are *not* mere "products of their time". Thinking of something one reads as a mere "product of its time" is a way of dismissing it as though it were now irrelevant. It's true that some things written in the past are irrelevant today. In this class we won't read Aristotle's works on biology, or Descartes's works on Astronomy, because contemporary science now understands biology and astronomy much better than they did. But assuming that *everything* written in the past is irrelevant today simply reflects an irrational prejudice toward the present, an unjustified assumption that people at other times were simply less intelligent and more simple-minded than people are today. Philosophical problems about knowledge, consciousness, personal identity, God, ethics, and free-will are discussed by contemporary thinkers in our own day just as they were by philosophers in the past. When you read philosophy, you should read it as presenting an argument intended for you to consider and respond to, rather than distancing yourself from it by speculating about the author's psychological or social situation or his or her hidden motives.

That said, understanding the changes in the way information spread through history, who was responsible in each era for spreading information, and the political and religious changes that lead information to be transferred or lost from each generation to the next, helps explain why philosophy had the structure it did.

When information is hard to transfer, for instance, philosophy becomes associated with a handful of dominant "great names" with an interesting biography, while other thinkers tend to be lost to history. On the other hand, now that information is transferred cheaply and quickly and with little effort, philosophy has become more of a collaborative enterprise, pushed onward through debates in journals on specialized topics, rather than one or two Great Treatises on Everything.

When writing philosophy requires being independently wealthy or keeping the favor of wealthy patrons, philosophy tends to express a different set of values than it does when, say, writing philosophy requires taking a vow of poverty and living in a religious commune. Now that it is feasible for more people to spend the time it takes to write philosophy, a much wider and more diverse collection of values can be expressed, debated, and considered.

The most noticeable change from the past to the present has been the inclusion of women. Women contributed to philosophy throughout history, especially during the Enlightenment period, when figures such as Elizabeth of Bohemia, Catherine Cockburn, and Mary Wollstonecraft influenced thought at the time. However, Western society has tended to obscure the contributions of women, discounting their works or minimizing the importance of what they had to say. This tendency began to change in the middle of the twentieth century, as figures such as Ruth Barcan Marcus, Elizabeth Anscombe, Philippa Foot, and Hannah Arendt became widely read and influential thinkers. Furthermore, feminist philosophers brought attention to approaches in philosophy that seemed to reflect the concerns of a socially "normal" male perspective rather than truths of pure reasoning.

The twenty-first century promises to be the first in which Western thought advances equally through the contributions of women and men. Roughly one-sixth of all professional philosophers today are women, and the American Philosophical Association has made a priority of encouraging interested women to pursue philosophy. When people think of what a "philosopher" looks like in the future, their image will no longer be of a man with a white beard.

B. Notes on a Guide to Philosophical Argument

One thing that is common to philosophy in all places and times is that it is conducted in a language. The second piece of background in this unit involves the philosophy of language, and the Standard View of how our language relates to the world. Understanding how language relates to the world is essential for understanding and using logic.

Recall that we defined a valid argument as one in which *there is no possible world in which the premises are true with the conclusion false.* The "Guide to Philosophical Argument" is meant to help define each of these terms that are used in the definition of a valid or invalid argument. By the end of reading the Guide, you should know the standard definitions for all of these terms:

1. Representation
2. Reality
3. World
4. Fact
5. Concept
6. True and False
7. Proposition
8. Sense
9. Reference
10. Object
11. Property
12. Opinion
13. Ambiguous, Vague, and Relative
14. Actual World and Possible World
15. Possibility and Necessity
16. Logical, Natural, Epistemic, and Moral Necessity
17. Premise and Conclusion
18. Valid and Sound
19. Inductive, Deductive, and Abductive
20. Fallacy

One reason studying these terms is so important is because these words are not used the same way in philosophy that they are in everyday language. For example, in everyday language an "opinion" is a personal feeling about something or reaction to it. However, in philosophy an opinion is a belief about a proposition. In everyday language a "proposition" might be a situation where one person proposes an agreement to another person, like a proposition of marriage. In philosophy, on the other hand, a proposition is a representation of a fact, which can be either true or false. In everyday language, a "fact" is something that we know. In philosophy, on the other hand, a fact is a state of the world, whether anyone knows it or not. In everyday language, the "world" means either something like our earth or something like our universe. In philosophy, the "world" is reality as a whole, insofar as it can be represented. You can see how not knowing what these words mean would quickly make philosophy confusing!

Central to the Standard View is the concept of a *representation*. Something is a representation if and only if it can be correct or incorrect with respect to some other reality that it represents. For example, a portrait of George Washington represents George Washington: The real Washington is not the portrait, but the person the portrait is about. If the portrait represents Washington as having bright white teeth, but Washington didn't really have bright white teeth, then the portrait is incorrect.

Similarly, a map of Arizona represents Arizona: The real Arizona is not the map, but the territory the map represents. If the map represents Arizona as having a beach, the map is incorrect. The map is incorrect with respect to what it represents, not with respect to itself. Our language also seems like a kind of representation: The sentence "Neil Armstrong landed on the moon" is not a man on the moon, but it represents reality as containing a man landing on the moon in the past. If Neil Armstrong didn't land on the moon, then the sentence is incorrect. The same can be said of our thought, or of our perceptions. When I open my eyes and see my computer, the image in my head is not my computer, but rather it is something which represents reality as containing a computer. If there is no computer, then I'm hallucinating, and my representation is incorrect.

Before taking a philosophy class, many students who grew up in Western society became accustomed to thinking of their beliefs as divided into "objective beliefs" about things that are measurable and quantifiable, and "subjective beliefs" about qualitative or controversial things. Because most of the measurable and quantifiable issues in philosophy have been "outsourced" to the sciences, contemporary philosophy seems to many people to be something subjective, which no one can answer.

Philosophers do not usually think in these terms, however. Instead, *objectivity* in philosophy has to do with the world *out there* independently of how we consciously experience it, and *subjectivity* in philosophy has to do with the conscious experiences within our own minds. *Every* belief we have is subjective, in this sense, because every belief takes place in our minds. However, on the Standard View, every belief we have is *about* an objective world which does not depend on our minds. When I believe something, my belief isn't about my belief, but about how the world would be even if I didn't believe it. Beliefs are subjective states about an objective world. The subjective *represents* the objective.

The upshot of this approach is that questions in philosophy are about how the world is objectively also. Philosophical questions can have answers. Sometimes we can come to reasonable and justified conclusions about what those answers are, and other times the best we can manage is a tentative "best guess" at the answer—but in this regard, philosophy is no different than any other field of study. Like philosophy, answering a question in the sciences is never *just* a matter of conducting an experiment or collecting data, since someone must interpret these results critically and use them to argue for a conclusion. Like the sciences, answering a question in philosophy is not just a matter of considering my own subjective experiences, but requires comparing and confirming my conclusions with others who are studying the same thing.

C. Notes on Plato's Apology

One of the most famous ancient Greek philosophers was Socrates, who lived in Athens. During most of the life of Socrates, Athens was ruled by an "elected" oligarchy known as the Thirty. Practically speaking, The Thirty were a puppet government run by the neighboring city-state of Sparta, and they had become regarded by a group of Athenians as tyrants. Socrates was ordered by The Thirty to join a group to fetch a former general and political opponent of the regime, and Socrates committed an act of civil disobedience by refusing to follow this order, making him some powerful enemies.

Eventually the Thirty were deposed, and Athens returned to its traditional democracy. However, some still regarded Socrates as a traitor, and did not forget their grudge against him. Further, Socrates had made a habit of questioning and embarrassing prominent members of the city, attempting to show that they didn't really know anything at all, making him more enemies. Eventually, the enemies of Socrates were able to find someone willing to charge Socrates in court, a young man named Meletus. A jury of

501 members was chosen for the trial. Athenian juries operated by majority vote, rather than requiring unanimity.[1]

Socrates defended himself at his trial from the charges. Ultimately, however, he was convicted and sentenced to death. Socrates accepted the outcome of the trial and died drinking poison given to him by his executioners. Socrates never wrote a book. However, his student Plato sought to make Socrates's story and philosophy known and wrote a number of dialogues in which Socrates was the main character. The *Apology* is Plato's account of what was said at Socrates's trial.

D. Notes Plato's The Allegory of the Cave

A later work written by Plato was *The Republic*. One section of the Republic gives an argument about what the meaning of philosophy is, that is, what a philosopher is supposed to be up to. The argument is made using an allegorical story, to make it vivid and easier to remember and understand, involving a man in a cave in which he found only shadows, who leaves the cave to find the source of light outside of the cave, the sun.

Recall that we defined a representation as something that can be correct or incorrect with respect to some other reality which it represents. But now, consider the following argument:

1. Something is a representation if and only if it can be correct or incorrect with respect to some other reality which it represents.
2. States of the world can be correct or incorrect.
C. States of the world are representations of some other reality.

The first premise is simply a version of the definition of a representation. But think for a moment about the second premise. It says that there are ways in which events in our world can be just or unjust, moral or immoral, right or wrong, good or bad . . . all of which are just other ways of saying "correct" or "incorrect". When people are treated fairly, something is correct. When people are treated unfairly, something is incorrect. For many people, this seems like common sense.

However, the conclusion goes against common sense! The conclusion says that the real world is itself a representation of some other, "higher", reality. Just like our concepts or sentences or pictures are representations of the world at our level of reality, Plato's argument says that our reality represents a reality at an even higher level.

For Plato, things in at our level of reality were mere reflections or shadows of a higher reality. Our circles are not perfectly round and our squares do not have perfect right angles, but we call them "circles" and "squares" *because* they represent the form of the perfect Circle and the form of the perfect Square, which exist in a higher reality. Similarly, in the higher reality, one finds the perfect Human, the perfect State, perfect Justice, and the ultimate form of the Good itself. Things in our world aim to match up to this ideal, although they don't always do so.

Plato's higher reality is sometimes called the realm of the *forms*. For Plato, the task of the philosopher was to leave behind sensory experiences in this world, and through the intellect to seek out this

---

[1] See Nails, Debra, "Socrates", The Stanford Encyclopedia of Philosophy (Spring 2014 Edition), Edward N. Zalta (ed.).

higher world of forms. The task was to abandon the copies, and seek out the originals—to leave the shadows, and to seek the ultimate source of light.

A philosopher who managed to do this—to understand this higher realm of forms—shouldn't expect to be greeted warmly upon returning to a society of people who still mistook shadows for reality. Instead, the philosopher should expect to be a bit of an outcast, or even a source of amusement. And as the philosopher challenged those who claimed to have knowledge, but only knew our world of mere appearances, the philosopher should expect to suffer the same fate as Socrates.

E. Notes on Locke's Essay on Enthusiasm

John Locke had a very different view of philosophy than Plato. For Locke, philosophy was very much about this world that we live in and experience through the senses. Rather than seeking to know a higher world, philosophy sought to know and truly understand our world—philosophy was the love of truth. Of course, we couldn't always be certain about what the truth was. Philosophy did not give us knowledge with absolute certainty and could not rule out every possibility that we were wrong. Instead, philosophy was simply following a principle that related our *beliefs* about reality to our *evidence*. A philosopher was someone who was more sure when there was more evidence, and less sure when there was less evidence.

Someone who loved the truth for truth's sake would follow this principle:

degree of confidence in your belief that p = degree of probability on your evidence that p is true

Your beliefs should be stronger and more certain when you have more evidence, and weaker and more tentative when you have less evidence. For example, suppose your evidence shows that 20% of homes in your neighborhood built when yours was have lead paint, and you have no evidence that your house is an exception. How confident should you be that your home does not have lead paint? According to Locke, you should be 80% sure. Being more certain or less certain than that is a sign that you're moved by emotions or feelings rather than reason. How sure should you be that you'll win a coin toss? 50% sure. How sure should you be that you are going to die and pay taxes? Basically certain.

Locke thinks that most people don't actually love the truth for truth's sake. Even though they'd claim to always follow this principle if you asked them, the truth is that they form some beliefs based on a desire for something to be true or false, not based on their evidence. Locke believed that the people he called *enthusiasts* were guilty of this. As Locke portrays them, the enthusiasts believed that they received direct revelations from God whenever an idea stood out strongly and vividly in their minds, and that through this they could obtain special knowledge about other people, the future, or new religious doctrines. Locke said that this amounted to circular reasoning: it was a revelation from God because they believed it, and they believed it because it was a revelation from God.

Locke's principle that one's degree of belief should match one's degree of evidence seems to apply in most cases. However, can you think of any exceptions to Locke's principle? For example, suppose you had a serious disease and a doctor told you that you have a 2% chance of survival. Suppose the only way anyone ever survives the disease is through staying optimistic and believing that a very difficult, painful, long and arduous treatment for the disease will work . . . though nearly all of the optimists also die, none of the pessimists survive. How confident should you be that you are going to survive?

Locke's principle leads us on to questions about knowledge, and whether we can know anything at all. We'll deal more with those issues in Unit 2!

❈ 1.2 A Brief History of Western Thought ❈

✳ ✳

Since Philosophy is simply thinking philosophically about philosophical questions, philosophy is something that anyone can do. And it's something which, naturally, humans have done for a very long time, all over the world.

This textbook focuses on source texts that have played a significant role in the history of "Western" thought. This isn't because we're assuming that "Western" thought is superior, or that interesting and difficult questions haven't been raised in other parts of the world. Rather, this is because your instructor and the majority of your classmates are likely to be part of a Western culture already, broadly speaking, and so this approach to philosophy is likely to seem more familiar to them, and so it will make for an easier introduction.

What is "Western" Thought?

By "Western" thought, we mean the philosophical tradition that originated in a community of thinkers interacting across Europe, North Africa, and Western Asia (the "Middle East").

Thinkers in these areas share a common heritage in Ancient Greek thought and have been part of an ongoing conversation for at least 2,300 years.

The tradition is diverse, and includes ancient works in Greek, Latin, Syriac, Hebrew, Arabic, and Farsi, as well as modern works in scores of languages. These thinkers came from several different religious and non-religious backgrounds.

"Western" thought is often contrasted with the "Eastern" thought of Chinese philosophical schools, such as Taoism and Confucianism, and of the many schools of philosophy in India. It is also typically distinguished from philosophical traditions in Sub-Saharan Africa and the Americas.

However, the label is misleading. Schools of thought all over the world have been interacting frequently for several centuries now, and this interaction is only increasing in pace with globalization. To give one clear example, Buddhism is generally considered to be part of "Eastern" religious thought. However, the Buddhist teaching that the self is impermanent and always changing has been highly influential on the debates about personal identity we discuss in Unit 4.

If you're a student who comes from one of these backgrounds, you're likely to find your instructor interested to hear and learn from comparisons or contrasts that you can draw between your background knowledge and what you're studying in this class.

The Era of Ancient Greek Philosophy

Philosophy neither began nor ended with ancient Greek thought. However, the "Western" philosophical tradition usually traces itself back to thought in Greek city states like Miletus, Elea, and Athens. So, for context, it will help to know a few major figures.[1]

Thales of Miletus

One of the earliest Greek philosophers, perhaps the first to bear that name, was Thales of Miletus (624–546 BCE). Thales sought to investigate the natural world independently, rather than relying on the stories handed down from prior generations. He theorized that despite all of the differences we observe, everything was composed of one substance: one single type of stuff. He thought this substance was water.

Although the idea that everything is water might seem silly to us now, the idea that everything is composed of the same substance is not: We know that when you break down chemical structures, the same sub-atomic particles (protons, neutrons, electrons, and quarks) compose both a mound of earth and a balloon full of air. So, in a way, Thales was ahead of his time.

One of the earliest complaints about Greek philosophy was, apparently, that it was useless and impractical. So, as the story goes, Thales set out to prove to his fellow Milesians that philosophy was useful. He purchased most of the Olive presses in the city in advance of the harvest, apparently anticipating a major harvest. When harvest time came, and the harvest was in fact abundant, he rented out the olive presses at a premium, and used the monopoly to make a lot of money. Thales apparently claimed not that he was seeking wealth, but that he was showing that philosophers could use their philosophy to become rich if they wanted to, and the only reason they weren't rich was that they didn't care much about material goods. Philosophy made wealth possible, and also removed the desire to pursue it.

Pre-Socratics

A number of other philosophers taught in this early era in the seventh to fifth centuries in the various Greek city states, including Miletus, Ephesus, and Elea; although few of their direct writings have survived, reports of their views were passed down by the philosophers who followed them. Some of the most famous philosophers of this period include

* **Pythagoras** of Samos, known for his view that the structure of mathematics was the structure of the world, and for his views about the migration of the soul after death.
* **Heraclitus**, known for his view that everything was in a state of constant change and flux, which is summed up in his quote that "one never steps in the same river twice."
* **Zeno of Elea**, known for his many paradoxes, such as one showing that simply running a race from one point to another appears to require completing an infinite series of actions, assuming that space and time are infinitely divisible.
* **Democritus**, known for his *atomism*, the view that the world was made up of basic particles, and that the combinations of these small-scale particles produced the large-scale properties we observe.

---

[1] The author acknowledges as a helpful source Patricia Curd, "Presocratic Philosophy", The Stanford Encyclopedia of Philosophy (Winter 2012 Edition), Edward N. Zalta (ed.).

Of course, by calling these philosophers "*Pre*-Socratics", we're implicitly defining them in terms of who they came *before*: a far more influential figure named Socrates.

Socrates, Plato, and Aristotle[2]

Socrates (469–399 BCE) was a philosopher who lived in the city state of Athens. Socrates never wrote any books, so most of what we know about him comes from his student, Plato, who wrote a number of *dialogues* featuring Socrates as the central character. These dialogues feature Socrates engaged in questioning prominent people of the time, and through questioning attempting, to reveal their ignorance. No one in Athens was too high up the social ladder to escape the questions of Socrates. Rather than teaching a set of claims about the world, Socrates used the technique of questions and answers in an attempt to get those he spoke with to arrive at a state of utter puzzlement.

In one of these dialogues, the *Phaedo*, Socrates asserts that philosophy is a *preparation for death*. He didn't mean that Philosophy is about being especially morose or morbid all of the time. Rather, because Socrates believed the mind separated from the body at death, he saw philosophers as preparing for death by separating their reasoning minds from physical passions.

Πλάτων
Plátōn

Σωκράτης
Socrates

Ἀριστοτέλης
Aristotélēs

© mishabender/Shutterstock.com

One way to get insight into Socrates's thought is consider what he called the "virtuous life", the model of the life which is good for a human to live. For Socrates, the key to virtue was looking after the health of one's individual soul. Compare this to a philosopher who lived in China a short time before Socrates (551–479 BCE). For Confucius, the virtuous life involved qualities such as being deferential to one's parents, doing what was appropriate in all significant relationships, and being respectful of the customs of one's society. For Socrates, the focus was inward and individual, whereas for Confucius the focus was outward and relational.[3]

Socrates was put on trial and sentenced to death in Athens, after having made a number of enemies. We'll read more about Socrates's trial in Unit 1. Socrates's student Plato then went on to found the *Academy* in Athens, when remained open for centuries after his death and took in many students.

> *The picture of intellectual reasoning as completely separated from emotion has been very influential in Western thought. But is it right? Does good reasoning really require being unemotional? Or can some emotions sometimes help us reason more properly?*

---

[2] The author acknowledges as a helpful source for this section lectures given by Prof. Michael J. White at Arizona State University, as well as the *Stanford Encyclopedia of Philosophy,* plato.stanford.edu.

[3] Students may refer to Solomon, Robert (2007). "The Little Philosophy Book".

Plato (429–347 BCE)wrote many philosophical dialogues on a wide range of topics, from explorations of the nature of knowledge, to the nature of justice, to the proper organization of society, to the nature of reality itself. Two of the ideas that Plato introduced, which we'll study more when we get to Unit 1, are the idea now called *a priori* knowledge, and the idea of a reality at a higher level than our own, filled by what he called the *forms*.

As the Academic School of philosophy in Athens grew, a competing school of philosophy also arose, founded by none other than Plato's most famous student, Aristotle.

Aristotle (384–322 BCE) founded the Peripatetic school of philosophy in Athens at a public meeting place known as the lyceum. Unlike his teacher Plato's back-and-forth conversational dialogues, Aristotle's writings were methodical and highly organized, containing lists of definitions for terms and arguments for each view. Aristotle seemed less interested than Plato in finding the forms in a higher level of reality, and more interested in finding them at the level of reality at which we live.

© Viacheslav Lopatin/Shutterstock.com

Aristotle developed argumentation into a formal system of logic, known as syllogistic logic, which allows one to determine whether or not an argument is valid simply by looking at the *structure* of the argument, independent of the *content* of the argument. We'll look more at argumentation in Unit 1. Besides founding the science of zoology and developing early accounts of physics, linguistics, and political science, Aristotle also wrote extensively on the topic of Metaphysics, a small portion of which we'll read in Unit 3. Further, he lectured extensively on topics in Ethics, and it's widely believed that Aristotle's son Nicomachus compiled these lectures into the work called *Nicomachean Ethics*, which we'll read in Unit 6.

Aristotle had many famous students. His student Theophrastus, for instance, is sometimes called the "father of *botany*" for his observations of the structure and variety of plants.[4] His student Aristoxenus wrote on musical theory.[5]

However, Aristotle's most famous student was not a philosopher at all. Instead, he was a bloodthirsty Military Leader who within 10 years had conquered an empire of nearly 2 million square miles and subdued over a quarter of the world's population.

The Macedonian Empire and Hellenization

Aristotle's famed student's name was **Alexander the Great**. The son of the King of Macedonia, Alexander conquered territory spreading from Greece to Egypt to Persia, before dying at the young age of 32.[6]

Alexander spread with him Greek culture and philosophy to all of the territories he conquered, including, of course, the philosophy of his tutor Aristotle. The city of Alexandria, in Egypt, eventually became one of the intellectual centers of this empire.

---

[4] "Theophrastus" (1998). In Routledge Encyclopedia of Philosophy, 337.

[5] "Aristoxenus". (2015). In Encyclopædia Britannica.

[6] "Alexander the Great" (2015). In Encyclopædia Britannica.

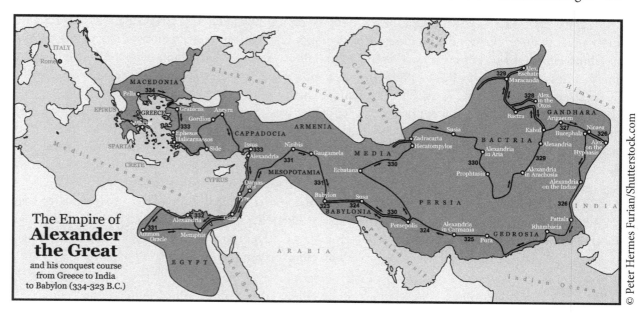

The Empire of **Alexander the Great** and his conquest course from Greece to India to Babylon (334-323 B.C.)

© Peter Hermes Furian/Shutterstock.com

After his death, Alexander left his empire to his generals, who immediately began fighting for control of the territory and eventually divided it among themselves. These smaller dynasties which followed sought cultural domination over the territories they conquered, seeking to supplant local customs with Greek culture, language, and thought. In some ways this was destructive to local culture, and it was at times resisted and fought by the conquered people. But one positive effect was producing across a wide territory a common system of communication and a new kind of intellectual community, where thinkers from different nations were able to share ideas with one another.

Among the schools of thought that arose during this period:

* **Stoicism**, founded by figures such as Zeno of Citium and Chrysippus, and carried on later by Roman thinkers, taught that the world was *deterministic*: everything which happened, *had* to happen. As a result, ethics had to do not with promoting a better world, but with obtaining inner freedom from one's judgments on the world, so that one was emotionally unmoved no matter how things in the world occurred. The Stoics also developed a distinct system of logic from Aristotle.[7]

* **Epicureanism**, founded (naturally) by Epicurus, developed on the earlier atomism and materialism of Democritus. It also promoted the idea that the good life involved maximizing long-term pleasures and seeking complete tranquility, the absence of pain.[8]

* **Skepticism**, whose most well-known thinker was Sextus Empiricus, questioned whether we could have any knowledge at all. Doubting everything, the most radical of the skeptics sought to abstain from either affirming or denying any proposition, endeavoring to suspend all beliefs. Although this might have seemed extreme, it did raise an important question for Epistemology: How is knowledge possible?[9]

---

[7] Baltzly, Dirk, "Stoicism", The Stanford Encyclopedia of Philosophy (Spring 2014 Edition), Edward N. Zalta (ed.).

[8] Konstan, David, "Epicurus", The Stanford Encyclopedia of Philosophy (Summer 2014 Edition), Edward N. Zalta (ed.).

[9] Vogt, Katja, "Ancient Skepticism", The Stanford Encyclopedia of Philosophy (Winter 2014 Edition), Edward N. Zalta (ed.)

The drastic differences between these schools of philosophy in ancient Greece parallel the dramatic differences that can be found in competing philosophical schools in other regions of the world, such as in Chinese philosophy. For instance, **Confucian** philosophy emphasized an approach to life that involved maintaining the law and social order—the ideal of the perfect "gentleman". Aristotle had a similar conception of the good life, as one that aligned with being an upstanding benefactor of the *polis*, or city. By contrast, the **Daoist** school of philosophy, following Lao Tzu, emphasized harmony with nature even at the expense of social propriety. What mattered was following the way or pattern of nature, rather than resisting it through trying to control nature by the will. Hence, the Daoists told stories about outcasts, thieves, and hobos who violated the pretentions of high society. A similar opposition to social pretentiousness can be found in later Greek thinkers who were inspired by the story of Socrates.

Only a couple of centuries later, many of the territories originally conquered by Alexander were swept up into a new empire. This new empire brought with it a new system of law and government, a high level of military and civil organization, and technological advancements. However, instead of creating a distinct intellectual culture, it adopted Greek intellectual culture and philosophy as its own.

The Roman Empire

The Roman Empire was a powerful force that lasted for centuries and covered an expansive geographic territory, spreading across Europe, North Africa, and Western Asia. As a result of the Roman Empire, areas on the outskirts of civilization in Western Europe were now linked culturally and

© Peter Hermes Furian/Shutterstock.com

intellectually to the larger philosophical conversation that had been ongoing in Greece, Egypt, and Mesopotamia.

The early centuries of the Roman empire saw further developments of the various Greek schools, including the Stoic, Epicurean, Peripatetic, and Academic schools. Some of the philosophers who wrote during this era whose names are still recognized today include Lucretius, an Epicurean an author of the poem *On the Natures of Things*, the statesman and orator Cicero, and the Stoics Epictetus (a slave) and Marcus Aurelius (an emperor). This period, lasting from the first century CE until roughly the fourth century CE, is generally seen as the final stage of the era in Ancient Greek philosophy.

A major shift in culture, religion, and thought was soon to arrive on the scene.

The Era of Medieval Philosophy

Constantine to Theodosius[10]

The transition from the era of Ancient Greek philosophy to the Medieval era has its roots in two actions taken by the emperor Constantine I, who reigned from 306 to 337 CE.

The first was Constantine's decision to move the capital of the Roman Empire from the city of Rome to a new city farther east, which he named Constantinople (after himself) and is today known as Istanbul. Although the empire had already been administratively divided at times between West and East, moving the capital to the East marked a shift in the center of power.

The second was Constantine's decision to embrace rather than resist the gradual conversion of the Roman Empire to Christianity. Both Christianity and Judaism had been persecuted on and off by various

Roman emperors from the first century onward, but Christianity had grown in popularity. Constantine's mother Helen had converted to Christianity, and by the end of his life Constantine himself had converted.

Christian and Jewish thought were concerned about entirely different subjects than traditional Greek and Roman thought. Rooted in **Hebrew philosophy**, they were primarily concerned with the notion of *God*, a transcendent being who was beyond and outside of the world, and the reason the world existed, and the relationship between God and a particular

---

[10] Information in this section is taken from Dr. Donald L. Wasson, "Constantinople" (2015) and "Constantine I" (2015) In *Ancient History Encyclopedia*, accessed via http://www.ancient.eu/.

community or nation of people chosen by God. Unlike pantheistic religions, in which God was identified with the world as a whole, the God of Hebrew philosophy was independent of the world. Unlike the Greek or Roman gods, which were supposed to be powerful and immortal beings that existed *within* the world, which could be represented by pictures, statutes, or actors in a drama, the God of Hebrew philosophy was not part of the world, and thus incapable of being represented by anything in it. Yet, at the same time this transcendent being was also believed in Hebrew philosophy to be personal rather than impersonal—God had a name and spoke to particular individuals throughout history.

The next 70 years of Roman history were tumultuous, with some Emperors and other officials providing support for the new religion, and other Emperors and officials seeking to reverse it and restore traditional Roman paganism as a state religion. Since philosophy was associated with paganism, it was viewed by many Christians as the enemy: for instance, the philosopher Hypatia was murdered by a mob of Christians. Eventually, during the reign of Theodosius, Christianity became the state religion of the Roman Empire. The Academy of Athens, founded by Plato, was soon closed permanently by the emperor Justinian.

Although not everyone is compelled to join a State religion, members of a State religion tend to receive many privileges in their society. Hence it is common to participate in a State religion out of a desire for personal gain, or to maintain social status. Thus, the intellectual elite during these years moved out of the classic philosophical schools of Plato and Aristotle and instead applied philosophical thinking to questions about Christianity.

The result was that Greek philosophy entered into religious debates about doctrinal boundaries and the definition of heresy. Instead of rejecting philosophy as pagan, Christians began to incorporate its methods and terminology.

For example, there were a series of debates over whether Jesus was divine. This orthodox view was popular among many common folk, but seemed clearly contradictory to many philosophical thinkers of the time—among other unacceptable things, it seemed to imply that God was finite, that God experienced suffering, and that God had died. The Egyptian thinker Arius held instead that Jesus was not identical with God, since God was necessarily infinite and unchanging. Other thinkers at the time—such as Basil of Caesarea and Gregory of Nazianzus, both of whom had studied philosophy in Athens, argued for the orthodox view, which ultimately prevailed at the council of Nicea.[11]

Over the next two centuries, three things happened that are important to understand in order to make sense of Medieval philosophy:

* The Spread of Monasticism

* The Arrival of Islam

* The Collapse of the Western Roman Empire

---

[11] See "St. Gregory of Nazianzus", "St. Basil the Great", and "Arius" In *Encyclopædia Britannica*, www.britannica.com.

The First Event: The Spread of Monasticism

Buddhism and Hinduism both have monastic communities—separate groups of individuals who leave the pattern of ordinary life in order to pursue what they believe to be a purer and more spiritual form of life. Monasticism is associated with a strict, austere, exclusive way of living. Starting with Anthony the Great in the third century, Christianity also had developed a form of monasticism, with monks living sometimes as hermits, sometimes in small groups, and sometimes in large monasteries.

Over time, monasticism spread across the empire. The primary consequence of monasticism for the history of Western Philosophy was that monasteries soon became centers of intellectual study and debate. Monks gathered, preserved, and commented upon texts—including some of the philosophical works of ancient Greece, like writings by Plato and Aristotle. Keep in mind that in an era before printing or storage in an electronic "cloud", texts had to be painstakingly copied by hand every few generations as the older copies of the text wore out. Whatever wasn't copied within a few generations was lost forever! Thus the preservation of "pagan" Greek philosophy was largely in the hands of the monks: Whatever they chose to copy, we have today.

The Monasteries remained the center of intellectual culture in the Eastern Roman (Byzantine) empire throughout the Middle Ages. Byzantine philosophers both inside and outside of the Monasteries tended to be heavily influenced by Aristotle, but also by mystical readings of Plato, in addition to Christian scriptural texts. They were concerned about questions in ontology, especially concerning the nature of the Trinity and concepts needed to explain the trinity, such as substance, essence, being, and personhood. They also were concerned with questions about the nature and immortality of the soul, which unlike most philosophers they distinguished from the intellect or mind, and the concept of human free-will played an important part in their account of the cosmos. Byzantine thought went on to heavily influence Russian philosophy in the nineteenth and twentieth century, and it continues today as a distinctive and influential strain within Western philosophy.[12]

The Second Event: The Arrival of Islam

The second major event was the rise of a prophet in Mecca, Arabia. Beginning in the seventh century CE, Muhammad rejected the practices and beliefs of Arabian paganism. Instead, Muhammad proclaimed the oneness (*tawhid*) of God (*Allah*). Muhammad preached around the Arabian Peninsula and most of the people in it converted to Islam. He became the spiritual and political leader of this new Muslim community. The Qur'an presented, in the view of these Muslims, a direct revelation from God.[13]

Following Muhammad's death, a dispute arose between his followers over who he intended his successor to be. Some of them sided with Muhammad's father-in law, Abu Bakr, while others sided with his son-in-law, Ali. This division would later develop into the split between Sunni and Shia Muslims. Yet in spite of this division, the community maintained its unity the first four caliphs, a time known as the age of the Rightly Guided Caliphate. During this time the lands of the Muslim community grew and spread quickly, and began launching a military conquest of the lands that had previously belonged to the Persian Empire and the Roman Empire. The State which resulted became known as the Caliphate.

---

[12] Ierodiakonou, Katerina and Bydén, Börje, "Byzantine Philosophy", The Stanford Encyclopedia of Philosophy (Spring 2014 Edition), Edward N. Zalta (ed.).

[13] Voll, John. Encyclopedia of Politics and Religion, ed. Robert Wuthnow. 2 vols. (Washington, D.C.: Congressional Quarterly, Inc., 1998), 383–393.

Within 30 years the Caliphate had conquered most of Western Asia and also Egypt; within 60 years, it had conquered the rest of North Africa and also Spain. Soon it reached the frontier of China. How'd it happen so quickly?

Part of the story is that the Roman Empire, short on funds, occupied with invasions and wars by various barbarian tribes in central Europe, was simply unable to defend these territories on the edge of its empire. However, another part of the story is that the Roman citizens of these territories, while themselves predominantly Christian or Jewish, considered the Caliphate preferable to remaining part of the Roman Empire.

توحيد

Tawhid – the oneness of God

Consider that once a religious group accepts the authority of the State to intervene in religious debates, the State can begin using or even creating religious disagreements to serve its objectives. Thus, from the fifth to the seventh century, it is hard to question that the Roman Empire used heresy as a political tool for conducting foreign and domestic policy. During this period, churches located outside of the Empire, such as those in Ethiopia, India, and Armenia, as well as churches located in the subjugated and poorer parts of the empire, such as North Africa and the Middle East, were all found guilty of the heresy of *Monophysitism* and cut off from the official church. People living in North Africa and Western Asia had been reduced to a position of second-class citizenship in the Empire.

Thus, in comparison to the Roman Empire, the early Caliphate offered greater religious freedoms for these indigenous Christians, as well as greater religious freedom for Jews, and greater local control. Although the leadership and elites in the Caliphate consisted only of Muslims, the majority of the population was not required to convert to Islam.

After the Caliphate had been established for a few generations, the intellectual heritage of the Greeks was thus transferred to a new group of Islamic thinkers and Islamic scholarship.[14] These thinkers began commenting on the works of philosophers, debating philosophical questions about fatalism and free will, and attempting to interpret these philosophical questions within an Islamic framework.

Although there were many schools of thought which arose in the Islamic world between the ninth and twelfth centuries, the most influential historically on Western thought were the Peripatetics, who took the works of Aristotle as a basis. These included:[15]

* **Al-Farabi**, who developed Aristotle's logic, expanded on Plato's Social theory in the Republic, and also wrote on topics in Metaphysics, Aesthetics, and Psychology.

* **Ibn Sina**, also known as Avicenna, who wrote on metaphysics, medicine, the philosophy of religion, and many other topics, and sought to reconcile Greek philosophical thought and Islamic thought.

---

[14] D'Ancona, Cristina, "Greek Sources in Arabic and Islamic Philosophy", The Stanford Encyclopedia of Philosophy (Winter 2013 Edition), Edward N. Zalta (ed.).

[15] Bertolacci, Amos, "Arabic and Islamic Metaphysics", The Stanford Encyclopedia of Philosophy (Summer 2015 Edition), Edward N. Zalta (ed.).

© Zufar/Shutterstock.com

* **Al-Ghazali**, who wrote on topics in epistemology and metaphysics, and argued against Ibn Sina, holding that Platonic and Aristotelian views in philosophy were contrary to Islam, and arguing in favor of a kind of mystical knowledge.

* **Ibn Rushd**, also known as Averroes, who argued against Al-Ghazali and in favor of Ibn Sina, and who produced an extensive attempt to reconcile Islamic and Aristotelian thought, though at time producing work in tension with common Islamic beliefs.

Finally, **Moses ben Maimon** (also known as Maimonides or Rambam), a Jewish philosopher of that era, who built on the work of Al-Farabi, and wrote on many topics, including epistemology and the philosophy of religion, with the goal of reconciling Aristotelian and Jewish thought. Maimonides established a distinctive tradition of Jewish philosophy, which remains a very active branch of the Western philosophical tradition.[16]

The classical age of Islamic philosophy, and with it the Peripatetic school, ended as the political center shifted to Europe with the crusades. However, Islamic thought went on to develop several other distinct schools of philosophical thought, many of them centered in Iran, which at times supported and at times conflicted with standard belief. Islamic philosophy continues to be active today.

The Third Event: The Fall of the Western Empire

Returning back in time several centuries, recall that Constantine had moved the capital to Constantinople and away from Rome. A variety of Germanic tribes—Vandals, Goths, Visigoths, Franks, and others—had grown in population and began attacking the Western half of the empire, making speedy gains. It was only a generation after the capital was moved, in 410, that the Visigoths reached Rome and sacked the city.

Soon after, the Western half of the Roman Empire crumbled. Although it continued to exist in name throughout most of its former territory, with officers in each region still even holding official Roman titles, in practice most of the territory of the Western Roman Empire was occupied by the various "barbarian" armies. Rome had fallen.

It is difficult to imagine the psychological effect for people who lived in these territories. In place of one interconnected empire under one emperor with one history and one legal system, there were suddenly a variety of local warlords, each making claims on different bits of territory, with very little in the

---

[16] Seeskin, Kenneth, "Maimonides", The Stanford Encyclopedia of Philosophy (Spring 2014 Edition), Edward N. Zalta (ed.).

© Mazolino/Shutterstock.com

way of protection from bandits and no predictable or established rules. There is a reason this era has been called the "dark ages".

Consider that in the present-day culture of Europe and the Americas, it's common to assume that the world is always getting better. We generally look to the future. Change is good, because change means *progress*. When a product is advertised, it's a good thing if it's "New". Technology is gradually leading us to a better tomorrow in which there is less disease, less poverty, less injustice, and fewer mild inconveniences. Our world is gradually becoming more united and less violent. Even if things aren't perfect for us, better days are always ahead for the next generation, because we're always learning more than people knew before us. Or, at least, this is a common way for people to think.

But suppose you lived in the era after the collapse of the Roman Empire. The golden age would be behind you, not ahead of you! Every year the roads would fall into greater disrepair and the amount of trade with the rest of the world would shrink. The future held only disease, poverty, injustice, disunity, and violence. Change would be bad, because change meant falling even further away from the memory of civilization. Being "new" would be bad; what you wanted, if you could find it, was something old, something that linked you to the glory days of Rome. Every generation, your society would know less than the society that came before you. Soon, no one would read Greek anymore, or know how to read at all. Your only source of knowledge you could hope to maintain was memory—that is, the tradition handed down from the Roman era.

What the new barbarian leaders lacked was *legitimacy* in the eyes of the local population. They couldn't claim to be part of a centuries-old empire, continuing the legacy of a great culture. They were just groups of illiterate warriors claiming authority through the power to kill their enemies.

However, there was one Roman institution which survived the barbarian invasions and the collapse of the Roman state. This institution had maintained its tradition and the intellectual link with the past.

It was the one institution that the average person respected. It was also the only thing left that united everyone throughout all of the former Western Roman Empire; the only thing that could legitimately be called "Roman": the Roman Catholic Church.

Feudalism

To put it somewhat simplistically, the Roman Catholic Church eventually decided to compromise with the descendants of the warlords who had conquered the Western Roman Empire. The warlords, many of whom previously followed a form of Arianism, converted to orthodox Christianity and submitted to the Pope. In exchange, the Pope obtained the authority to crown the warlords as Kings and other local authorities, an act which made them legitimate in the eyes of the average person. Their various military ranks—terms such as *Duke, Count, Earl,* and *Baron*—were now transformed into the titles of a new Aristocracy. This Aristocracy found its culmination in the crowning of Charlemagne as King of the Franks, reuniting Western Europe for the first time since Rome had fallen. Although governments in the feudal system were not very powerful compared to, say, modern governments, they had enough power to establish enough stability and law that trade and commerce could continue, which was an improvement.

Intellectually, the monasteries now became essential to the preservation and spread of knowledge. Since the only source of information about science or philosophy was what one could pull out of tradition, the authority of past writers held exceptionally great weight. Philosophers of the era typically worked with very limited excerpts of what philosophers like Aristotle or Plato had said, although they built on what they read and attempted to find parallels in Christian thought. Because they held this knowledge, Monasteries added prestige to the communities they were located in, and this meant they gained financial support from the new feudal governments. Because the Church was the source of legitimacy for feudal governments, Monasteries became a means through which the Church could exercise political power.

Crusades

After several centuries, around the eleventh century, Europe was beginning to climb out of the dark ages. The Papacy provided a kind of new unity to Western Europe, in a position that was both spiritual and political. Warfare between European feudal states was declining as a movement in the Catholic Church pushed for "God's Peace" and developed rules for just warfare. This peace and unity rested on the mutual submission of the feudal kings and lords of Europe to the Pope.

However, in the year 1054, the Catholic Church was split into two in the most dramatic division of its history. A subtle theological dispute arose between Pope Leo IX, representing the churches in Western Europe, and Patriarch Michael of Constantinople, representing the churches in the Eastern Roman

(Byzantine) Empire, over a single word which the Western Churches had added to the creed produced by the council of Nicea. The debate developed into one about the larger issue of the authority of the Pope, and as a result each Church excommunicated the members of the other. The *schism* (division) between the Eastern Orthodox and Roman Catholic churches remains today.

The Catholic Church now was a small shell of the glory it had claimed during the Roman Empire. In its mind, it had lost the majority of its territory and followers in North Africa and the Middle East to the spread of Islam, and now had lost half of what remained, in Eastern Europe and Asia Minor, to the schism.

In 1095, Pope Urban II called for a new war. The official purposes of this war, according to Urban II, was to re-take the former lands of the Roman empire in Spain, North Africa, and Western Asia from the Caliphate, to reunite the schimatic Christians in these lands into the Catholic church, and to make holy sites were available for pilgrimages. Exaggerated descriptions of the cruelty and barbarism of Muslims were used to raise an army to liberate the Middle East.

The Crusades were a dark period in history, lasting 200 years and consuming millions of lives. Whatever their original motives, the crusaders became known for their cruelty, indiscriminate killing of innocents, and love of plunder. The crusaders ended the classical era in Islamic philosophy, set back the progress of civilization, and left an unforgettable memory in the peoples they attacked, both Muslims and the indigenous Christians. The crusaders massacred the inhabitants of Jerusalem, both Muslim and Jewish, and they sacked Constantinople, leading to the decline of the Byzantine Empire. All of the various "crusader kingdoms" were eventually defeated. The credibility of the church hierarchy in claiming to represent Christianity was left tarnished by its open participation in bloodshed.

However, one thing the Crusaders brought back with them was knowledge that had been lost to Western Europeans for centuries. In addition to the texts of works by Ibn Sina and Ibn Rushd, they brought copies of works from the Ancient Greek era that was thought to be lost for ages. For the first time since the fifth century, over 600 years, new knowledge from the past had reached the monasteries of Europe.

Scholasticism[17]

©Andrei Nekrassov/Shutterstock.com

Reading these new texts, translated into Latin in the first time, inspired a fresh school of philosophers in Europe, who wrote from the eleventh through the sixteenth centuries, known as the *scholastics*. Much as Ibn Rushd (Averroes) had sought to make Aristotelian philosophy consistent with Islam, the scholastic philosophers sought to make Aristotle's philosophy consistent with Christianity.

The most notable philosopher of this period was **St. Thomas Aquinas** (1225–1274), who wrote on questions concerning metaphysics, ontology, political organization, ethics, and the nature of God. For generations afterward, his works became the standard for scholastic philosophers.

---

[17] Information in this section is taken from Spade, Paul Vincent, "Medieval Philosophy", The Stanford Encyclopedia of Philosophy (Spring 2013 Edition), Edward N. Zalta (ed.).

The Scholastic era in Europe also saw the rise of a new institution, the *University*. The descendent of "Cathedral schools" founded by a bishop for the purpose of training young clergy, the Universities grew to train young people in far more general variety of fields besides theology, including medicine, law, and the liberal arts—including philosophy.

Medieval philosophers, such as William of Ockham, John Duns Scotus, St. Bonaventure, John Buridan, and Fransisco Suarez, were especially concerned with topics in metaphysics concerning the logical structure of reality and the essential natures of things. They were also concerned with the compatibility of various theological claims about God with reason, such as the compatibility of God's being all-powerful, all-good, and all-knowing with the existence of evil, or the compatibility of God's knowledge of the future with human free-will.

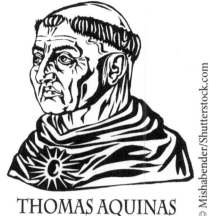

The scholastic incorporation of Aristotle into Christian thought remained the dominant paradigm in European philosophy until the sixteenth century, the standard for science and education across the continent.

THOMAS AQUINAS

© Mishabender/Shutterstock.com

Reformation and Renaissance

Three major events happened in the fifteenth century. The first, in 1492, was the well-known discovery by Christopher Columbus of a new continent that no one in the Western philosophical tradition had known about, and which, notably, did not appear to have been mentioned in any of the religious texts which thinkers at the time took to be authoritative.

© Everett Historical/Shutterstock.com

The second, in 1436, was the first European development the printing press, by Johannes Gutenberg. The printing press freed knowledge from the limitations of what monks and university students could write in a short period of time, and opened it up to widespread dissemination.

The third, in 1453, was the fall of Constantinople to the Ottoman Turks, and with it the fall of the Eastern Roman Empire. The eastern empire had lasted for an entire millennium longer than the western empire, and had been a place of rich philosophical and intellectual work. However, its territory had slowly and gradually gotten smaller and smaller every generation, until in the end the "Roman Empire" was smaller than most US States.

When the empire fell, many of its intellectuals chose to flee to Western Europe, bringing with them knowledge of the Greek language and more copies of Greek texts that had been lost to Western Europeans during the Dark Ages, and remained lost for over 1,000 years. One of the texts which Western Europeans had not seen in Greek for over a millennium was the core religious text of Christianity, the Bible. Although it had been read and studied in Latin, it hadn't been read or studied in Greek. The Greek Biblical text that arrived from Byzantium, sometimes called the *Textus Receptus*, became the source used by Erasmus of Rotterdam to retranslate the Bible from Greek into a new Latin edition, which was then distributed widely by printing press. The result was a flurry of new translations of the Bible: at first into

Latin, but soon after into the common languages like German or English, all printed and distributed widely for anyone who could afford a copy to read.

This change in the availability of information led to a significant change in European religion. A group of reformers, such as Martin Luther and John Calvin, proclaimed that the Bible was contrary to many of the things that the Church had been passing down as tradition. When paired with a number of scandals that the Papacy had experienced in prior generations, this started to erode popular confidence in the trustworthiness of tradition in some places, and in turn with Catholic Church. The result was the rise of Protestantism, as congregations or whole countries broke away from the Catholic Church, a situation that also led to greater political independence.

The Protestant reformers undermined the epistemological assumptions on which scholasticism was based: no longer was a tradition going back to the glory days of Rome or Greece—reason enough to believe that something was true. Tradition could be wrong.

Sixteenth-century scholastic scientists had extracted from Aristotle and a bit of deduction a number of claims about the world. They had built their entire understanding of the world on these claims, and took them for granted. For example, they believed that:

© Nicku/Shutterstock.com

Galileo Galilei.

* Everything in the natural world had a purpose behind it which propelled it forward: acorns were moved by an inner purpose to grow into oak trees.

* Humanity was at the center of God's plan for the universe; therefore, humanity was at the physical center of the universe.

* Motion required a mind; therefore, the stars either had minds or were moved around by angelic beings with minds.

* Elements such as Water, Earth, Fire, and Water all reacted differently and seemed to follow different laws; therefore, they were distinct substances.

When Astronomers and Scientists began making discoveries that undermined these assumptions, like Copernicus's discovery that the earth revolved around the sun, what were the Scholastic scientists to do? They tried to use Church authority to suppress those who challenged Aristotle, as was seen at the famous trial of Galileo. But Church authority was no longer universal after the reformation, and the printing press made it impossible to suppress ideas. The impact of encountering a new and unheard of civilization in the Americas had overturned all confidence in looking to the past—the only way ahead was forward.

A new thinker, Francis Bacon, called for a brand of scientific investigation of the world that focused not on attempting to deduce a logical model of physics or biology but instead on studying the world through sharing the results of observable, repeatable experiments—something made possible across great distances and numbers of people through the printing press. Bacon envisioned philosophy cooperating with science, rather than standing against it:

"Those who have handled sciences have been either men of experiment or men of dogmas. The men of experiment are like the ant, they only collect and use; the reasoners resemble spiders, who make cobwebs out of their own substance. But the bee takes a middle course: It gathers its material from the flowers of the garden and of the field, but transforms and digests it by a power of its own. Not unlike this is the true business of philosophy; for it neither relies solely or chiefly on the powers of

the mind, nor does it take the matter which it gathers from natural history and mechanical experiments and lays it up in the memory whole, as it finds it, but lays it up in the understanding altered and digested. Therefore from a closer and purer league between these two faculties, the experimental and the rational (such as has never yet been made), much may be hoped.[18]

© Shaiith/Shutterstock.com

The period of intellectual, scientific, and artistic flourishing that followed is sometimes called the *Renaissance*, or "rebirth". It marked a dramatic shift in perspective. Instead of a view of history on which the future was progressively getting worse and moving further from the golden age of the Roman empire, this new mindset was one in which the future was progressively getting better and advancing to new heights. This new mindset marks the beginning of the "Early Modern" era in philosophy, also known as the Enlightenment.

The Enlightenment Era in Philosophy

Descartes to Kant[19]

Descartes

© Georgios Kollidas/Shutterstock.com

Rene Descartes (1596–1650) was a mathematician and scientist who began a new era in philosophy. You may be familiar with Descartes's name from your algebra classes, if you've ever used a *Cartesian* coordinate plane to draw out an equation, something Descartes invented. Among Descartes's early scientific works were some books on optics and a book purporting to show that the earth was not the center of the universe, but rather that the earth revolved around the sun. However, after seeing Galileo put on trial for making this very claim, Descartes decided not to publish the book. Descartes wanted very badly not to be at the center of controversy.

Instead, Descartes sought to find a way to reconcile the new and budding empirical sciences—that focused on what we do and don't observe—with rationally oriented philosophy, which focused on what we can and can't conceive. In particular, Descartes wanted to show that philosophy, science, and religion were consistent with each other.

Descartes did this by delving into *Epistemology*, the theory of knowledge. He proposed that the foundation of knowledge was neither what we can observe, nor what the church taught, nor the logic of Aristotle, but *I myself* and my consciousness, since this is the one thing I know for certain. He argued that our scientific knowledge of the empirical world depended on our knowledge of the goodness and

---

[18] From Bacon, *Novum Organum*, XCV, Translated by Spedding, Ellis, and Heath, published 1863, Taggard and Thompson.

[19] Much of this information is taken from the Stanford Encyclopedia of Philosophy, plato.stanford.edu.

trustworthiness of God, which depended on our knowledge of rational truths about the essential natures of things, which ultimately depended on our knowledge of ourselves. In this way, he believed he had shown we could have scientific knowledge, but we had to acknowledge that this depended on a philosophical foundation. We will do a closer study of Descartes in Unit 2.

Rationalists and Empiricists

© ChameleonsEye/Shutterstock.com

Following in the path of Descartes were a number of so-called *rationalists*, who agreed with him and emphasized the priority of *what we know simply through reasoning about what we can and can't conceive*, or *a priori* knowledge, over what we know through sensory experience. Among the most famous rationalists were the Jewish philosopher Baruch Spinoza (1632–1677), who created lenses for a living, and the German Philosopher Gottfried Leibniz (1646–1716), who worked as a diplomat. Aside from inventing Calculus, Leibniz is best known in philosophy for developing the notion of a "possible world", or another way the world could have been without contradiction. This notion of a possible world will appear frequently in this textbook, especially when we discuss The Philosophy of Mind in Unit 3. Most controversially, Leibniz and Spinoza both defended the claim that our world was the best of all possible worlds. The argument that our world is not the best of all possible worlds will become the source of the "Problem of Evil", a major topic in Unit 5.

© Georgios Kollidas/Shutterstock.com

In opposition to the rationalists were a group of philosophers known as the *empiricists*, who believed that our knowledge was limited to what we could obtain through sensory experience and were skeptical about claims that were supposed to be known purely through reasoning. Among the most famous empiricists were John Locke (1632–1704), David Hume (1711–1776), and George Berkeley (1685–1753). We'll study Locke and Hume's views of the extent of our knowledge in Unit 2, since Locke will call into the doubt any claim that we have knowledge innately, Hume will call into doubt the assumption that we know anything as basic as cause and effect relationships, and Berkeley will question whether we should think there is an external, material world outside of our minds at all. We'll also look at their differing accounts of personal identity in Unit 4.

Kant

Immanuel Kant (1724–1804), one of the most influential philosophers in history, was born, raised, lived, and died in Königsberg (Kaliningrad), in the German-speaking country of East Prussia. After completing college at the University of Königsberg and working for a few years teaching children, Kant at the age of 31 began teaching as a lecturer at the University of Königsberg without any salary. He was entirely dependent on payments by the students who showed up to his lectures for a living, and hence he worked as a librarian for additional money. During this time, Kant wrote a number of books that were not considered particularly significant in his own time or in ours, and maintained a very active social life. Finally, after 15 years of teaching, Kant was offered a permanent position at the University.[20]

Then, in 1781, at the age of 57, Kant wrote something entirely new that changed the history of philosophy. In the Critique of Pure Reason, a work of which we will read a tiny portion in Unit 2, Kant developed a synthesis of rationalism and empiricism. (A synthesis involves combining two seemingly contrary views to form a new, original view.) Kant agreed with the empiricists that experience was the source of all knowledge. However, Kant pointed out that we know not only what we actually experience, but we also know the limits of what we could ever possibly experience. So, Kant also agreed with the rationalists that we could obtain knowledge by reflecting on what we could and couldn't conceive. However, this wasn't knowledge of the necessary structure of the world

Immanuel Kant.

© Nicku/Shutterstock.com

(metaphysics) but rather knowledge of the necessary structure of our own minds. All knowledge depended on experience, but we could have a priori knowledge by considering the boundary line of possible experience—and this would give us knowledge of Metaphysics.

Following this idea, in 1785, Kant wrote the Groundwork for the Metaphysics of Morals, which we'll study in Unit 6. Kant sought to move Ethics away from discussions of feelings and sentiments and into the realm of pure logic. Grounding Ethics in logic, he thought, would avoid the skepticism that many people have about our ability to know truths in Ethics. Other major works by Kant include the Critique of Practical Reason (1788), the Critique of Judgment (1790), Religion within the Boundaries of Mere Reason (1793), and two works on the Metaphysics of Morals in 1797.

Yet, while Kant provided a foundation for our knowledge of Ethics and some questions in Metaphysics, there were other philosophical questions which in the *Critique of Pure Reason* he declared outside of the bounds of anything we could ever know—they were neither knowable by experience, nor *a priori*, because they were outside of the limits of any possible experience. These questions included the existence of God, the essential nature of the self, and the existence of free will—questions which previous philosophers had considered highly important. (It also included questions about the infinite divisibility and infinite extent of space and time). Yet if we can't now whether or not God exists, what our own essential nature is, whether or not we have free will, and what reality in itself was—and these are the very topics which drive people to study philosophy to begin with—what use is philosophy anymore?

Philosophy After Kant

Analytic and Continental

After Kant, philosophy in the West divided into two major schools. Although there is no clear way to draw a line between the two, there is diversity of thought and disagreement within each school, and there is interaction between the two schools, it is generally agreed that they represent two different methods of doing philosophy.

The first approach, known as the *analytic* school of philosophy, focuses on studying our conceptual structure—the limits of conceivable experience—since this was one thing Kant granted we could have certainty about. Although we might not be able to know sweeping conclusions about the nature the cosmos by this method, we can use philosophical tools like clear definitions to get clear about what exactly we're trying to ask when we ask more focused and narrow philosophical questions. So, we might not be able to prove that there is or isn't free will, but we will be able to see how "free will" might be defined and, once it is clearly defined, whether any scientific evidence we have we weighs on one side or the other of it, or whether the evidence is relevant at all to the concept we call "free will".

Analytic philosophers disagree about how much our study of concepts should be influenced by ordinary language, "common sense" intuitions, and the views of the majority of people, or whether we should be lest trusting of our ordinary concepts and prefer instead the specialized concepts developed by logicians and metaphysicians, or the concepts developed by scientists. Neither extreme can be right, of course. We can't simply accept all "common sense" at face value, since "common sense" is often wrong or even self-contradictory. But we also can't doubt all common sense, since our reasons for doubting common sense will themselves appeal to common sense about what we should doubt.

The second approach, known as the *continental* school of philosophy, focused instead on studying what it is like to have the lived conscious experience that we have, since this was also something Kant granted we could have knowledge about. Rather than seeing our conceptual structure as something fixed and shared, continental philosophers are more likely to be critical of our concepts, as something which reflect historical or social forces, our individual psychological tendencies, or even our own actively taking a role in shaping how we think. So, whether or not there is such a "real" thing as "free will", there is certainly an experience we have which we call "freedom", and we can describe what it is like to have that experience, which is very real to us. Maybe part of that experience is the freedom to determine what freedom will mean. Or, perhaps part of that experience is having our freedom limited by the presence of others.

Although the divide between analytic and continental philosophers is not as strong today as it was 100 years ago, it is still typical for Western philosophers to identify as belonging to one or the other approach. Both sides have in common that there are influenced by reflecting on the limitations which Kant placed on human reason, and so they both tend to be more tentative and restrained in their conclusions than philosophers who wrote in other centuries.

Philosophy Today

Many people mistakenly think that philosophy is simply the study of the history of philosophy, and not an active, living discipline. However, while philosophy has taken many different turns through history, it remains an active field of inquiry today. There are today people who investigate questions about all of the major philosophical fields, including:

* Logic, the study of reasoning
* Ethics, the study of what ought to be and ought not to be
* Epistemology, the study of what we know and how we know it
* Metaphysics, the study of the necessary structure of reality as a whole

Despite Kant's influential conclusions, much like was true in past eras, there are many respected philosophers today who continue to think and write about topics like free-will, the existence of God, the nature of the self, whether we can know there is an external world, and whether time and space are infinitely divisible or not. However, unlike in past eras, the philosophical community today is no longer limited in its ability to transfer information. Because of this, philosophy no longer has to be defined in terms of merely commenting on a handful of "Great Men" who rose above the rest to have their Grand Treatises on Everything published widely enough to be remembered after their deaths.

Instead, philosophy today works more like the sciences: Philosophers are men and women who promote arguments for particular claims, usually very specific and narrow, by publishing articles in journals that have to be peer reviewed by other philosophers and meet standards of scholarship and argumentation. Other philosophers then respond to these arguments by publishing their own articles with objections or defenses of the argument. Through this process, all arguments receive a hearing, and the weaker arguments are shot down, while the stronger arguments rise to the forefront. Over time, while philosophy may not reach any hard and fast conclusions, this process of producing philosophy piece-by-piece allows for an exploration of the whole of logical space and a picture of the strengths and weaknesses of every possible position someone could hold, as well as the ways in which each position depends on other positions. There can be no "Great Philosophers" anymore (and those who try to be come off as a bit pretentious!), but this is a good thing, because philosophy as a whole progresses faster when more hands are working on it.

Libraries and the internet have made it possible to find older articles that have been neglected or authors whose work was notable but went unappreciated at the time it was written—for example, we now have free or inexpensive access philosophical texts written by women during the Enlightenment period, texts which proposed arguments that influenced thinkers at the time, but which were nearly lost as the prejudices of later generations failed to reproduce their work. Likewise, they've made it possible for ideas to spread very quickly: A new idea may catch on in the course of 5 years rather than taking several decades. Of course, they've also made it harder for potential students to focus: Instead of a small canon of a few Great Philosophers, students are now faced with more writing on philosophy than anyone could possibly read in a lifetime. But this also means that every student of philosophy is already in a position to begin contributing to philosophy, simply by responding to the arguments they read.

There is a widespread narrative that philosophy is dead and we can do without it, because philosophy makes no progress and never comes up with any answers. This is not true. Philosophy has made progress. Sometimes the progress simply involves narrowing down the number of consistent options someone can choose. We understand many things within philosophy, like the relationship between logic and causation, or the nature of language and reference, or what makes consciousness so difficult to explain, better than philosophers a few generations ago did. Of course, the answers are not simple answers, and it takes patience to appreciate the progress. The answers never put an end to questioning; they only raise more questions.

The world has changed substantially since Plato and Aristotle first wrote. Philosophy has played a role in that change. However, looking toward the future, there are good reasons to think that we'll need philosophy more than before, not less. After the development of computing, itself a product of philosophical advances in logic, technology took a massive leap forward past the boundaries of what we might normally have thought possible.

We now live in a world in which information is available almost instantly, but the information we get is often contentious and contradictory. What do we know?

We now live in a world in which we are beginning to understand the brain and its relationship to perception and thought. Can we expect someday to have an explanation of consciousness?

We now live in a world in which medicine does not just allow us to heal diseases, but to enhance and improve our bodies, or even remove unpleasant thoughts or memories. What consequences does this have for personal identity?

We now live in a world in which science explains much of what was mysterious to previous generations. What is the role of religious belief in such a world?

We now live in a world in which we understand enough of human psychology that we can manipulate how people feel and think to suit our purposes. Does this threaten our free will?

We now live in a globalizing world in which we can no longer pretend that everyone shares the same cultural values that we do. How do we resolve conflicts over morality?

Technology has increased, rather than decreased, the number of interesting and difficult questions that students of philosophy have to think about and try to address. Even today, philosophy is something we can't do without.

Try to argue that we *can* do without it, and you're already doing philosophy!

Key points:

* The History of Western Philosophy is usually divided into four periods: Ancient, Medieval, Enlightenment, and Contemporary.

* New movements in philosophy tend to accompany changes in the availability of philosophical writing.

* The Enlightenment era in philosophy was especially concerned with questions about what we can and can't know.

* Thinking carefully and precisely is not made less important by new technological discoveries; quite possibly, it is made more important.

❄ 1.3 A Guide to Philosophical Argument ❄

✳✳✳

Reading philosophy is hard, so having this background will help you think like many of the authors we're reading think. As you read this guide, you'll notice practice questions at the end of each section to help you understand what you read.

Sections:

0. Introduction
1. Reality and Representation
2. Sense and Reference
3. Facts and Opinions
4. Sentences, Propositions, and Facts
5. Possibility and Necessity
6. Premises and Conclusions
7. Validity and Soundness
8. Strengths and Weaknesses
9. Types of Deductive Argument
10. Inductive and Abductive Arguments
11. Avoiding Fallacies

0. Introduction

Philosophers like to *argue*. But the way the term "argument" is used in philosophy isn't exactly how most of us use the word "argument". By "argument", most of us mean a dispute or a fight between two people—we might get into an argument over whose turn it is to wash the dishes or whether or not the most recent *Star Trek* was a good movie. In philosophy, an "argument" is something which doesn't always involve a dispute between two people (though sometimes it does). A philosophical argument is just a way of presenting thoughts in a structured way. You can use an argument to reason through alternatives, to discover a new conclusion, or to explain why you believe something.

This is a guide to the *standard* or "classical" account of how arguments work. What I'm presenting here has only developed a little bit over the years from the way the Greek philosopher Aristotle (384–322 BCE) thought of argumentation. You can find many of these ideas in his *On Interpretation*.

Even though I've called this the "Standard View", if you ever go into more advanced areas of philosophy, you'll find that almost everything in this guide is itself the subject of dispute and argument! Nearly every claim in this guide has been challenged somewhere by good arguments. In fact, some of the things we'll read in this introductory class will challenge the standard view. So, if something in this guide doesn't quite sound right to you, know that you're not the only one to think so, but you have to at least understand what the rules of the game are first before you can challenge them.

So, here are the rules to arguing in philosophy.

1. Reality and Representation

There is a difference between *reality*, and our *representations* of reality. Imagine a professional photographer who takes your portrait while you're in his or her studio. The finished printed photo that you hang on the wall is a *representation* of you, but it isn't you. Or, imagine that you write in a diary what happened to you in the course of a day. What you wrote in the diary is a representation of your day, but it isn't your day *really*. You can misrepresent how your day went by lying in your diary—or a photograph can misrepresent your face, because it's been altered in Photoshop. A misrepresentation in some way fails to match up with reality. There are many kinds of representation.

Perceiving is one kind of representation. Suppose you're looking at a field, and there is a sheep in the distance. What do you see? In one sense, you see the sheep, even if you don't see it very clearly and you can't make out much of it in detail. In another sense, what you "see" is just an image in your mind: the blurry white spot that your mind interprets as a sheep. The sheep is reality. The image in your mind is a representation of the real sheep. The sheep wouldn't cease to exist if you stopped looking at the field.

Hearing a sound is another type of perception, and another kind of representation. Have you ever listened to a recording of your own voice that sounded strange and unfamiliar? The way you hear your voice when you speak represents your voice in one way. The recording represents your voice in another way. Your voice doesn't change, but the representation does.

Conceiving is a different kind of representation. Think for a moment about a distant relative of yours who you haven't seen in a while. Your thought about that person is a representation of that person. The real person might be very different from your thoughts about them. But your thoughts are still a representation of them.

Conception is different from perception. Your perception of something is how it immediately *appears* to you through your senses. Your conception of something is how you think about it even when it isn't around. For example, my current perception is of my computer monitor and not my philosophy class. But I still have a concept of my philosophy class.

Describing is another kind of representation. When we talk to one another, sometimes we represent to each other in language the way reality is. When someone asks for directions to 6th Street, and you say "6th street is north of here", you represent the world as being a place where the place called "6th street" is the direction called "north" of the location called "here" which you're standing in. However, in some ways, language can be a *representation* of a *representation*. Language represents our concepts, and our concepts represent the world. The term "6th street" represents our concept of *6th street*, which in turn represents a real street in a real city. The term "north" represents our concept of *north*, which in turn represents a real direction on the globe relative to earth's axis at the North Pole.

All representations have in common that they can be either accurate or inaccurate of what they represent. An inaccurate description of something is said to be *false*, and an accurate description of the world is said to be *true*. For instance, the sentence "Mt. Rushmore is made of jelly" is false, because the sentence misrepresents Mt. Rushmore. An inaccurate conception of something might be called *confused* or *mistaken*. For example, if I think of Mt. Rushmore as being made of jelly, then I have a confused and mistaken conception of Mt. Rushmore. An inaccurate perception might be called an *illusion*. Suppose that I am in South Dakota, at the base of Mt. Rushmore, and I look up and see the faces of the four presidents as being made of jelly. My perception would be illusory!

By "*reality*", then, we mean that which is not merely represented, but that which makes representations accurate or inaccurate. Because we define perception, conception, and description in terms of how they represent reality, reality must be to some extent independent of how we perceive of it, conceive of it, or describe it. Even if we thought of reality differently, or we ceased to be around perceiving reality at all, reality would still be there.

By "the *world*", we mean *reality insofar as it is representable.* Here is the idea. We can represent some things as concepts which we could never see, like a polygon with 10 billion sides. We can also represent some things in perception that we don't have concepts for. Imagine someone wearing polka dots. You'll perceive all of the polka dots individually, but you won't have a distinct concept for each one. We can conceive of something or perceive something that can't currently be described in our language—forcing us to invent a new word, or perhaps to give up trying to describe it entirely. There are some ideas better communicated with pictures, and some better with words. So, none of our many kinds of representation are *exhaustive*; that is, no single kind of representation can represent *all* of reality. We can't assume, then, that everything which is real is capable of being represented by some means or other. We can't rule out that there is a part of reality which simply isn't capable of being represented by any of our thoughts, or perceptions, or any expressions in our language. Of course, if this is so, then we can't say anything about it, because, obviously, if we could talk about it, then we'd be representing it in our language . . . and then it wouldn't be unrepresentable any more! A reality beyond any possible representation, if there were such a reality which isn't part of the world, would be called *transcendent*. So, we'll define the world as the *representable* part of reality, the part we can actually describe and conceive.

Each of us in what we see, what we think, and how we talk, is trying to represent the world. Again, by "the world", we don't mean the planet earth. Instead, we mean *all* that is the case—the collection of all of the *facts*. Everything from the fact that doctors recommend Acetaminophen for pain relief, to the fact that I dislike tomatoes, to the fact that Christopher Columbus sailed in 1492, to the fact that 2+2=4, is a part of the world. The world includes all of space and time, not just the present moment. Genghis Khan and Marco Polo are part of the world, even though they are no longer present. There are facts about the future, even though they have not yet occurred, such as the fact that the sun will rise tomorrow. These facts are also part of the world.

So, here's the picture we're working toward (and will expand on later):

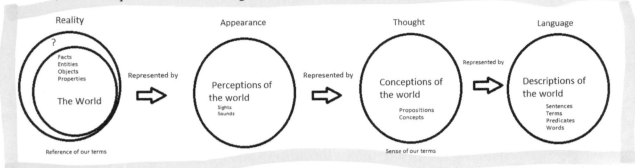

The world is the representable part of reality. The world consists of facts, whose elements are entities and properties. Perception is a representation of the world in sight, hearing, and touch. A concept is a representation of the world, formed as a result of what we've perceived. These concepts are structured together into propositions, which represent facts. A description in language is a representation of our concept of the world, which consists of sentences, that are themselves made of predicates (verbs and adjectives) and nouns (direct objects, indirect objects, etc.). Sentences represent propositions, which represent facts.

Practice Question: Which of the following are representations of the world?
(a) the sight of Niagara falls, (b) a non-fiction book, (c) a conversation about movies, (d) a cough, (e) a bicycle, (f) a road map, (g) a disturbing thought, (h) a landscape painting, (i) a house, (j) my hearing birds chirping, (k) childhood memories, (l) a landscaping company.

2. Sense and Reference

We can't read each others' minds, but we can understand each others' sentences. Because our language is the one thing that we all have equal access to, many philosophers take language as their starting point.

Of course, we don't all speak the same language. Some people say "bread", while others call it "*Brot*" or "*pan*" or "*chleb*" or "*khubz*". While English "bread" isn't the same word as Polish "*chleb*", bread is the same thing as *chleb*, and in some sense the idea behind "bread" is the same as the idea behind "*chleb*".

The common idea behind the words "bread" and "*chleb*" is the *concept* of bread. Different words can express the same concept. For example, the word "sick" and the word "ill" both express the same concept: the concept of being sick is the same as the concept of being ill.

Sometimes the same word can be used to express different concepts. The concept expressed by "sick" in "my dog is sick" is the concept of having a biological illness. On the other hand, "sick" in "he is a sick, dirty old man" expresses a very different concept! In contrast to

Note: when I put a word in quote marks "", I'm talking about the word itself, or *mentioning* the word, not actually *using* the word. For example, "cats" is made out of four letters, but cats are made out of flesh and blood, not letters. Hounds come from all over the world, but the word "hound" comes from German. Jeff is one person, but "Jeff" is the name of many different people.

both of these, "sick" in "that slapshot was so sick!" spoken in a hockey game, expresses a concept of being admirable or amazing.

What do our words or concepts *mean*?

People sometimes think of the meaning of a word as the mental pictures they personally associate with the word. For example, the meaning of the word "bear" to me will be a mental picture of a stuffed black bear in a museum. But that can't be right. Other people have different mental pictures than I do. Perhaps someone else associates the word "bear" with a polar bear in the zoo, and another person associates it the fear and terror they felt when running into a grizzly bear in the woods, and another person associates it with an adorable Koala bear they once held. In spite of these drastic differences in the images and feelings we associate with words, we manage to communicate with one another effectively. We all manage to mean the *same thing* by "bear" even though we don't have the same associations or images.

So, the meaning of a word or concept can't be an image in our heads. The meaning of a word or concept is shared by a society as a whole, and some people might understand the meaning of a word better than others. This shared meaning has to do with the criteria involved in deciding whether or not something is a bear. Consider all of the possible creatures out there which would rightly be called a "bear". That is the *sense* of the word "bear".

The *sense* of a word or phrase like "world's tallest bear" is its shared meaning, the conditions under which a thing could be truthfully called the "world's tallest bear". This is different from the *referent* of a word or phrase. What a word *refers* to is the object, entity, or property in the world that it stands for. The sense of a word determines what it refers to, but sense isn't the same as reference. For example, take the word "mammal". The sense of the word "mammal" is the concept we have in mind when we think about mammals—the concept of a creature that has mammary glands and generally speaking gives live birth. Is there anything in the world which this concept applies to? Yes! Lions, for example. And Tigers. And Bears. Take the collection of all of the things which this concept applies to, and you get the *reference* of the term "mammal". The sense of "world's tallest bear" is such that it refers to *whatever* bear happens to be the tallest at the time. You understand the sense of this phrase even if you don't know what the referent of "world's tallest bear" is, for which you'd need to consult the Guinness Book of World Records.

Think for a moment about submarines. Consider that before submarines were invented, someone still had the idea of a submarine, and even used the word "submarine" to talk about this futuristic vessel. The word "submarine" wouldn't have referred to anything at the time, but it would still have a sense. You can have a perfectly good concept that nonetheless doesn't refer to anything.

Or, take the word "unicorn". The word "unicorn" doesn't refer to anything—there are no unicorns. However, the word "unicorn" does have a *sense* and it expresses a perfectly good concept: the concept of a horse-like creature with a horn on its head. The word is meaningful. We can understand the sense of "unicorn" by thinking about what we mean by "unicorn", but we can't know whether it refers to anything unless we take a look at the world around us. Similarly, a phrase like "the current King of America" might have a sense, but doesn't refer to anyone. The sense of an expression might stay the same, but what it refers to might change. Right now, "President of the United States" refers to Barack Obama. But in four years, it will refer to someone else.

Suppose we take a more difficult term, like "love". What does "love" mean? One way to answer the question would be to give a number of examples of love. That might help a little, because we'd know some of the things that "love" referred to. However, it wouldn't really explain *why* the word love refers to those examples and not others. To understand that, we need to know the sense of love: what is the *concept* expressed by the word "love"? Perhaps there are many different concepts expressed by the word. If a cynical person said, "love doesn't exist", they would mean that the word "love" doesn't refer to anything. But they'd still acknowledge that there was a concept of "love"—it's just that the concept had no actual instances.

Practice Question: for each of the following terms and phrases, what concept(s) are its sense(s), and what object(s) does it refer to? Are there any terms or phrases that have a sense, but don't refer to anything? (A few of these don't have clear answers.)

(a) passion, (b) the tallest man in the world, (c) Martians, (d) the oldest US Supreme Court Justice, (e) beautiful, (f) peanut butter, (g) the first US President from Arizona, (h) the big city, (i) pine, (j) Valhalla, (k) liberty, (l) Congo, (m) war, (n) dream, (o) dinner.

3. Facts and Opinions

Facts are parts of the world.

It is a fact that heat is molecular kinetic energy, and it is a fact that the capital of Arizona is Phoenix. It is a fact that Christopher Columbus sailed across the Atlantic in 1492. There are also much more mundane facts. It is a fact that I brushed my teeth this morning. It is a fact that I like borscht. There are some facts which none of us knows. There is a fact about whether the number of Zebras on earth at this moment is even or odd. Either it's a fact that the number is even, or it's a fact that the number is odd. None of us knows or has the means to find out that fact (if we started counting, a Zebra might die or give birth in the process, changing the number). Likewise, there is a fact of the matter about whether increasing the national budget deficit will harm or help the economy. It's hotly debated what the fact is: Some people think the fact is that it will harm the economy, and some people think the fact is that it will help the economy. There can be facts about things that no one knows.

The way we're using the word "fact" here is different from the way many people learn it in elementary or secondary schools. Schools sometimes teach that "facts" are those things which we know, and "opinions" are those things where no one really knows—no opinion is correct. On this view, it's a fact that water boils at 212° F, but a matter of opinion whether OJ Simpson was guilty of killing his wife, or why Stonehenge was built, because we don't really know.

The trouble with the way high schools often teach the fact/opinion distinction is that it's not clear what criteria determine whether something is a fact or merely an opinion. What determines whether *we* know something to be true or not? Is it a fact that Lee Harvey Oswald killed John F. Kennedy, or is it just an opinion? Is it a fact that parents should vaccinate their children, or is it just an opinion? Is it a fact that a particular famous athlete uses performance enhancing drugs, or just an opinion? In practice, people end up appealing to some *authority* to tell us what we know and what we don't know, what the established facts are and what is open for opinion. The authorities have the facts, and what everyone else believes is "just an opinion" and not worth debating about. The authority might simply represent popularity. If most people believe it, then it is a "fact", and if it is controversial, then it is an "opinion".

Instead, on the way we're using the words "fact" and "opinion" in this guide, and the way most of the philosophers we'll study use them, *there is a fact of the matter about every well-formed question*. We might not always *know* what the fact of the matter is, but there is still some fact of the matter. Who killed JFK? Either it is a fact that Oswald killed JFK, or it is a fact that someone else killed JFK. Either it is a fact that a given famous athlete uses performance enhancing drugs, or else it is a fact that he doesn't—we might not know, but he does. What does Barack Obama dream about at night? None of us know. But there is some *fact* about what he dreams about.

On this way of using "fact" and "opinion", *opinions are beliefs about what the facts are.* In one person's opinion, the fact is that human actions are the cause of global warming. In another person's opinion, the fact is that natural forces outside of human control are the cause of global warming. Which person's opinion is right? It depends on what the facts are. An opinion, or a belief, is a representation of the facts. Some beliefs accurately represent the facts, and some beliefs inaccurately represent the facts. The beliefs that reflect the way the world really is are true, and the beliefs that don't reflect the way the world really is are false.

Should parents vaccinate their children? Either it is a fact that they should, or it is a fact that they shouldn't. People can have different beliefs about what the facts are. They can have legitimate debates about what the facts are, and appeal to different evidence to support their opinions. However, there is some fact of the matter as to whose beliefs correctly represent the world, and whose doesn't. One person is right, and the other is wrong—one person's beliefs are true, and the other person's beliefs are false. For two people to disagree about something, but not believe there is a fact of the matter about it, would be pointless.

There is a difference between whether a belief is true or false, and whether someone should hold that belief given the evidence. The evidence might point you clearly in one direction—and you should base your beliefs on the evidence. Nonetheless, the evidence might actually point you in the wrong direction, and the belief you form is false! For example, suppose you buy a lottery ticket for $1, and someone offers to buy it from you for $2. All of the evidence you have says that you should not believe that your ticket will win the lottery—it's extremely unlikely. You should believe your ticket is a loser, and sell it for $2. Nonetheless, suppose that your ticket wins the lottery! If you believed that your ticket was a loser, your belief was false, and your opinion that your ticket would lose was incorrect! Yet, even though it was an incorrect belief, it was also the right belief to hold, given the evidence you had.

Practice Questions: explain why, on the standard view given here, (a) sometimes the right belief to hold on the evidence is false, (b) every opinion is either true or false, (c) it is both a fact that the earth revolves around the sun, and an opinion, (d) people can disagree about the facts, but there is still a fact of the matter, (e) everyone has their own opinions, but not everyone is right, (f) either it is a fact that an asteroid killed the dinosaurs, or it is not a fact that an asteroid killed the dinosaurs, even if people debate what killed the dinosaurs.

A Very Easy Quiz:

Which of the following are claims about facts, and which are opinions?

i. Cabbage is expensive.
ii. My belief that cilantro is tasty.
iii. Cilantro is tasty.
iv. Your belief that World War II happened.
v. Everyone's belief that the earth revolves around the sun.
vi. It is the case that civilization is progressing.
vii. Tomorrow it will rain.
viii. Driving 75 mph is driving fast.

ix. $7 + 5 = 12$.
x.   Jeff's belief that $7 + 5 = 12$.
xi.   Jeff believes that $7 + 5 = 12$.
xii. Jeff's belief that Jeff believes that $7 + 5 = 12$.

[Answer: i, iii, vi, v, vi, vii, and ix are claims about what the facts are]

4. Sentences, Propositions, and Facts

Many declarative sentences offer a description of how the world is in a particular language. Sometimes, two different sentences describe the world in the same way. They express the same idea—both of them mean the same thing. When this is the case, we say that the *two sentences express the same proposition*. For example, "Joe built that chair" and "That chair was built by Joe" are two different sentences, but they express the same proposition. The English sentence "I am a man", the Spanish sentence "*Soy un hombre*", and the Russian sentence "*Ya chelovek*" all express the same proposition. We can say that two sentences are *synonymous* when they both express the same proposition. In other words, however the world is, either both sentences will be true at the same time, or both sentences will be false at the same time.

Propositions are representations of the world that are in some sense language-independent. Perhaps, there are propositions that can't be expressed in any language. What makes a proposition true or false is whether the proposition *corresponds to a fact*. If a proposition corresponds to a fact, then it is true; if not, then it is false. For example, the fact that the earth is roughly spherical is part of the world. The proposition that the earth is roughly spherical is true, since it corresponds to a fact. The proposition that the earth is flat is false, since it doesn't correspond to a fact. It is a fact that the earth is not flat. So, the proposition that the earth is flat is false. The sentence "the earth is flat" is false; and the sentence "the earth is not flat" is true. Why? Because the first sentence expresses a true proposition, and the second sentence expresses a false proposition. We might say that the sense of a sentence is a proposition, but that the sentence refers to a fact.

Sometimes it is hard to tell what proposition a sentence expresses. Consider the sentence, "The governor's speech was incredible!" This one sentence could be interpreted in at least four different ways, each corresponding to a different proposition:

* *What the governor said was very good.* For example, perhaps she said that the state should pursue the cause of justice, even if it is unpopular.

* *What the governor said was impossible to believe.* For example, perhaps she said that the state was ruled by subterranean reptile-people.

* *The way the governor spoke was very good.* For example, perhaps she spoke persuasively and forcefully with great emotional pull.

* *The way the governor spoke made it difficult to believe.* For example, perhaps she was shifty-eyed and stared at her notes.

Which proposition should we understand the sentence "the governor's speech was incredible" as expressing? It depends what we mean by "speech" (the way the governor spoke, or what the governor said) and what we mean by "incredible" (very good, or dubious). So, is the sentence true or false? Well, that depends on whether the proposition it expresses is true or false, which depends upon the facts: what actually happened when the governor spoke?

When a word has multiple senses, or a sentence could be interpreted as expressing multiple propositions, we say that the word or the sentence is **ambiguous**. The sentence "I went to the bank" is ambiguous between the two senses of "bank", one a financial institution, and the other edge of a river.

Some sentences don't express propositions. For example, take the sentences "Go away and leave me alone!" or "Please pass the salt!" These sentences don't express propositions, because they don't say anything about the way the world is. Instead, they issue comments or requests. Similarly, sentences like "Oh wow!" and "Boy howdy, Charlie!" express an attitude or a feeling, but don't express a proposition.

Some sentences are true or false **relative** to the context they are spoken in and what the relevant comparisons are. For example, consider the sentence "A 6-foot man is tall". If this sentence is spoken in our society, then perhaps it is true. If this sentence is spoken in a society where most people are shorter than 5 feet tall, then it is certainly true. If this sentence is spoken in the NBA, where many players are much taller than 6 feet, then the sentence is certainly false. Or, consider the scribbles of a talented 3-year-old in magic markers. Perhaps "these are beautiful!" is true when the relevant comparison is other 3-year-olds, but false relative to the standards of most professional artists. Is turning 30 getting old? It depends on whether you're talking to college students, or college professors.

Finally, some sentences are **vague**. Consider the sentence, "It's not too far to the supermarket". How far is "not too far"? It's hard to draw a line. Is 2 miles not too far? What about 2.01 miles? Or consider the sentence, "I'm hungry now". Was there a precise moment when I got hungry? Not really: I went from not-hungry, to sort-of not hungry, to sort-of hungry, to hungry, with lots of gradient in between. Vagueness happens when a concept lacks precise cut-off points. Don't confuse being vague with being ambiguous or being relative.

Once we've resolved ambiguity in a sentence, and acknowledged issues of relativity and vagueness, and considered *what the world would have to be like in order for the sentence to be true or false*, we are dealing with a proposition. We can now ask, "does this proposition correspond to a fact?" How would we determine that?

Sentences are made up of two basic parts, *subjects* and *predicates*. For example, in "the hill is grassy", "the hill" is the subject of the sentence, and "is grassy" is the predicate of the sentence. In the sentence "Smoking endangers children", "smoking" is the subject, and "endangers children" is the predicate.

On the Standard View, facts have a structure that parallels the structure of sentences. The fact that the hill is grassy is made up of two parts, the *object* which is the hill, and the *property* of being grassy. The fact that people smoking endangers children is made up of two parts also: first, *a set of objects*, events of someone smoking, and then a property, endangering children. The basic difference between an object and a property is that a property can possibly apply to multiple things, whereas an object is a particular thing. So, to see whether our sentence "people smoking endangers children" is true, we'll need to first look to the world to see what sorts of things endanger children, and then look to the world to see if events where someone is smoking are among those things.

Objects like hills or the event of someone smoking are called *concrete* objects, meaning that they exist in space and time. Anything which does not exist in space and time is called an *abstract* object. For example, it is a fact that prime numbers larger than 2 are not divisible by 2. So the property of not being divisible by 2 applies to a set of objects, the set of prime numbers larger than 2. But prime numbers don't take up space, aren't located anywhere in particular, and don't change over time. So prime numbers are abstract objects. On the other hand, horses are concrete objects—they exist in space and time—and unicorns, if they were to exist, would be concrete objects, because the concept of a unicorn is the concept of something that exists in space and time.

Practice Question: explain what it means for (a) two sentences to be synonymous, (b) a sentence to be ambiguous, (c) a sentence to be true, (d) a proposition to be false, (e) a sentence not to express a proposition, (f) a sentence to be relatively true, (g) a sentence to be vague, (h) something to be abstract or concrete, (i) a sentence to correspond to the facts.

5. Possibility and Necessity

What makes a proposition true or false is the way that the world is—what the facts are. Consider the proposition that Napoleon won the battle of Waterloo. This proposition is false—as a matter of fact, Napoleon famously lost the battle of Waterloo. However, there is a sense in which this proposition *could have been true*. It could have turned out that Napoleon won the battle of Waterloo, if the world had been different. Hitler didn't conquer all of Europe, but he *might* have done so. The South didn't win the Civil War, but there's a way the world could have been where the South did win the Civil War. We say that something is *possible* in the broadest sense of "possible" if there is a way the world could have been that would make it true. Sarah Palin wasn't elected Vice-President, but it's possible that she could have been. Put together what the facts would have to be in order for a proposition to be true. Instead of the actual world, where we live, you might call this a *possible* world.

The *actual* world is the world that you and I live in. But, as the philosopher Gottfried Leibniz first proposed, there are many other possible ways the world could be or could have been other than how it actually is, or *possible worlds*.

Some of these are not too far removed from the actual world. You might have taken this class in a different semester, for example. You might have sat down to read this text a minute or two later, or earlier, than you did. Or I might have written one more or one less word in the last sentence than I did. But other worlds are farther removed from the actual world. There is a possible world in which you have three arms. There is a possible world in which this textbook was written in ancient Hittite. There is a possible world in which the earth is ruled by apes and humans do not exist. There's a possible world in which nothing exists in the universe except for a giant penguin. There is a possible world in which there is no gravity.

The broadest sense of "possible" is sometimes called *logical possibility*. A logical possibility is a scenario (a possible world) which contains *no contradictions*. Even though it's highly *improbable*, and would involve violations of all sorts of laws of nature, it is logically possible for money to grow on trees and for pigs to fly. Why? Because there's nothing contradictory about money growing on trees or pigs flying. On the other hand, it isn't logically possible for something to be both red and green all over, or for 2 + 2 = 5, or for triangles to have five sides, or for bachelors to be married. All of those scenarios involve a contradiction. If something is red, then it isn't green all over—contradicting its being green all over. So, it's logically *impossible* for something to be red and green all over.

When a proposition is a *logical necessity* (or a "necessary truth"), that means that every possible way the world could be is one in which the proposition is true. For example, the proposition "all cats are cats" is logically necessary. Why? Because there couldn't be a cat that isn't a cat—that's a contradiction. When it is *impossible* for a proposition to be false, then it is necessary for it to be true.

There are more narrow senses of possibility and necessity, besides logical necessity and possibility. Here are three more to consider:

* *Natural possibility*. Something might be logically possible, but contradict with one of the laws of nature—for instance, the law of gravity. So, while it is logically possible for me to fly by flapping my arms rapidly (something I might have attempted as a child), this would violate the law of

gravity, making it naturally impossible. It isn't logically necessary that hydrogen and oxygen combine to form water, but it is a natural necessity.

* *Epistemic possibility* (or "probability"). Something might be, given the evidence I have, highly unlikely to be true. I'll then say that it is impossible, in the epistemic sense. For example, it is impossible that pigs can fly and that money grows on trees. Why? Because I know, having seen many pigs and trees, that these things are highly improbable. It is a nomic possibility, and a logical possibility, that the United States will rejoin the British Monarchy. However, knowing the culture of the United States, this is epistemically impossible—it is improbable that it would ever happen. Epistemic possibility comes in degrees. Some things are more probable or less probable.

* *Moral possibility* (or "permissibility"). Often people say that you *need* to do this or that, or that it is *necessary* for you to do this or that—for example, it is necessary for you to cite your sources and not plagiarize the work of others. This doesn't mean that it is a logically necessity that you cite your sources, but rather than it is a *moral* necessity. Failing to do so, by trying to pass off the work of others as your own, would contradict a moral principle of honesty.

Throughout this class, it will be important to keep these senses of possibility and necessity straight. Generally speaking, what we're interested in arguments is the notion of *logical* possibility. We'll say something is "possible" because it isn't logically contradictory, even though it is "impossible" given what we know about the world.

Logical possibility matters so much because it doesn't assume anything further about the world we live in without making it explicit, not even that the laws of physics remain constant. This makes it the foundation of arguments.

Practice Question: Label each of the following as possible/necessary/impossible, logically, morally, epistemically, and nomically. (That means four answers for each): (a) that Tucson is the capital of Arizona, (b) that a square has four right angles, (c) that a mile is closer than a yard, (d) that the lottery is a scam, (e) that aliens will wipe out all life on earth, (f) that mud is made of dirt and water, (g) that I can't walk from Phoenix to Beijing in one hour.

6. Premises and Conclusions

With these tools in our tool belt, we're ready to turn to our original topic: arguments!

In philosophy, an argument is a set of premises followed by a conclusion. Both the premises and the conclusion must be sentences that express propositions. The premises are the sentences that you either already believe to be true or assume for the sake of the argument. The conclusion is the point that the argument is working to lead you to believe.

Here are a few examples of arguments. One way of formalizing an argument is to list out the premises in order, followed by the conclusion. Notice how we label premises like "(P1)" or "(P2)" and conclusions like "(C)".

Argument: My brother says it's snowing outside, and he always lies, so it's not snowing outside.
    (P1) My brother says it is snowing outside.
    (P2) My brother always lies.
    (C) It is not snowing outside.

Argument: Everyone's left work today, and if everyone's left work then it must be a holiday, so today must be a holiday.
(P1) Everyone has left work today.
(P2) If everyone has left work today, then it must be a holiday.
(C) It must be a holiday.

Argument: Either taxes are going up, or we're never getting out of this deficit. We are going to get out of the deficit, so taxes are going up.
(P1) Either taxes are going up, or we're not getting out of this deficit.
(P2) We are getting out of this deficit.
(C) Taxes are going up.

Making an argument is proposing that someone who believes the premises should believe the conclusion also. You want the premises of the argument to be something that the person you are arguing with accepts are likely to be true. You also want to make sure you include all of the premises needed to reach the conclusion, without leaving anything hidden or assumed.

Practice Question: Write out the following argument, as a series of three premises leading to a conclusion: *Someone spilled milk all over the floor, and it wasn't me, but the only two people who could have spilled milk over the floor are me and Carla. So, obviously, Carla spilled milk all over the floor.*

7. Validity and Soundness

Two ways in which we evaluate arguments are in terms of whether they are *valid* and whether they are *sound*. These are technical terms. Don't trust your intuitions as to whether an argument is valid or not—check it in terms of these definitions.

An argument is valid when, and only when, *there is no logical possibility of the premises being true and the conclusion being false*. Think about that definition carefully. It doesn't say that the premises have to be true, and it doesn't say that the conclusion has to be true. It doesn't say that the premises have to lead to the conclusion, or that the conclusion has to follow from the premises. What it says it that it must be logically impossible for the conclusion to be false *if* the premises are in fact true. The following argument is valid:

(P1) All dogs are mammals.
(P2) Old yeller is a dog.
(C) Old yeller is a mammal.

Because, even though old yeller doesn't exist, there's no possible scenario where old yeller is a dog, and all dogs are mammals, yet old yeller isn't a mammal. That would be a contradiction—old yeller would both be a mammal and not be a mammal—and so a logical impossibility. On the other hand, the following argument is invalid:

(P1) Jeff smiles a lot.
(P2) Many contented people smile a lot.
(C) Jeff is a contented person.

The conclusion of this argument is, in fact, true—Jeff is a contented person. The premises are also both true. However, it's not a valid argument. Why not? Because there is a logically possible world in which Jeff smiles a lot, but he's not one of the contented people who smile a lot—perhaps he smiles for another reason—and so Jeff is not a contented person. This isn't the way things really are, but its one way things could have been. So, the argument is invalid. Here's a similar example:

(P1) Barack Obama is eligible for the presidency.
(P2) Barack Obama got the majority of electoral votes in the presidential election.
(C) Barack Obama is the President.

Again, all the premises and the conclusion are true. However, the premises don't guarantee the truth of the conclusion, so the argument isn't valid. It *could* have been that there was a military coup.

Why is validity important? Because it teaches us *not to assume anything without explicitly putting it into our argument as a premise.* By making our assumptions explicit, we help someone who disagrees with us know where exactly they disagree. Suppose we wanted to make the previous invalid arguments into valid ones. Here's what we could do to the Smiling argument:

(P1) Jeff smiles a lot.
(P2) Only contented people smile a lot.
(C) Jeff is a contented person.

or to the Presidential argument:

(P1) Barack Obama is eligible for the presidency.
(P2) Barack Obama hasn't been removed from office.
(P3) Barack Obama got the majority of electoral votes in the presidential election.
(P4) Anyone who is eligible for the presidency and receives the majority of electoral votes in the presidential election and hasn't been removed from office is the President.
(C) Barack Obama is the President.

These arguments are valid. Now, if someone wanted to disagree with our conclusions, they'd have a list of premises that they'd have to deny in order to disagree with us. You can't disagree with the conclusion of a valid argument without denying at least one of the premises.

An argument that is valid *and* has all true premises is called *sound*. I believe that the revised Presidential argument is sound—all of the premises are true, and the argument is valid. Someone who believes that (P1) is false would deny that the argument is sound, and so could deny the conclusion. On the other hand, I don't believe that the revised Smiling argument is sound. I don't believe (P2)—I think that some people smile a lot who aren't contented. The more probable the premises are, the more likely the argument is sound.

So, there are two ways you can challenge an argument: you can challenge that it is valid, or you can challenge that it is sound by denying one of the premises.

Practice Question: Write the definition of a valid argument out. Then, look at the following argument. Explain why it is invalid, according to the definition you wrote. Then, re-write it to make it valid. As re-written, do you think it is sound? Why or why not?

(P1) When immigration increases, then unemployment increases.
(P2) Unemployment has increased since 2008.
(C) Increased immigration has caused the increased unemployment since 2008.

8. Strengths and Weaknesses

When considering particular arguments, we may evaluate them in terms of their validity and soundness. However, most of the time we'll be evaluating broad philosophical *views*. A view often involves a series of conclusions that an author comes to after a series of arguments. How do we evaluate philosophical views, provided that the arguments are valid? Not every view supported by valid arguments is a *plausible* view supported by *good* arguments.

It's not easy or obvious how to evaluate philosophical views. However, here are a few criteria that we often have in mind when we evaluate views. These are strengths:

1. *Probability of the premises*. Given the evidence we have, how probable is it that the premises in the arguments are true? That is, how likely is it that the arguments are sound? You can come up with a valid argument with very unlikely premises, like this one:

> (P1) All kittens are made entirely of water.
> (P2) All water is made entirely of happiness.
> (C) All kittens are made entirely of happiness.

Unfortunately, it's almost certain that (P1) and (P2) are false, and so it's likely that the argument isn't sound. Someone whose view depends on arguments with plausible or likely premises is better than someone whose view depends on highly unlikely assumptions.

2. *Explanatory power*. How much does a view explain? How many unanswered questions would it answer? Suppose Bob loses coordination when he drinks alcohol. One theory says that Bob has an "alcohol allergy", which causes him to lose coordination when he has too much alcohol. Another theory says that alcohol causes everyone to lose coordination in this way—it's not just an allergy specific to Bob. One theory explains more cases than another.

3. *Verifiability*. Does the view make predictions about our observations that are testable? If they aren't, are the claims justified by rational reflection? If they aren't, is there another reason to believe them? Some claims aren't testable, like the claim that all points on the diameter of a perfect circle are the same distance from the center of the circle. There are no observable perfect circles. However, we have other justifications for believing this claim about perfect circles: it helps us predict what distances we'll observe with the more ordinary, imperfect circles we encounter every day. On the other hand, suppose a theory says that the sun experiences painful angst when solar flares occur. How would we test this view?

4. *Parsimony*. A theory is more parsimonious when it is only as complicated as needed to explain things. A "complicated" theory involves more objects and properties, or more assumptions about the world, than a simpler theory. Suppose someone proposes that the moon is made of cheese, but that the cheese turns to rock any time that a person tastes, touches, looks at, or tests its composition. This is a coherent theory that's consistent with our evidence, but why should we believe it? It seems much more complicated than believing that the moon is made out of rock, and not out of cheese. The principle of parsimony is sometimes called Occam's razor. Don't confuse this with the claim that "the simplest explanation is always the best one." Children come up with plenty of simple explanations, but they are rarely true ones. Simplistic explanations usually fail to explain everything that needs explaining. But if two or more explanations are competing, and both explain everything we want to explain, then we prefer the simpler one.

5. *Reflective Equilibrium*. Some philosophical questions go beyond anything that can be evaluated by the earlier standards. For these questions, the best we can go off of is an attempt to reflect on the question

without biases or other assumptions, take in all of the information and competing views that we can, find the balance between all sides, and make our best guess about the answer from what we've taken in. Sometimes there are processes of reasoning that are hard to formalize or put into words, a kind of "intuition", or "reflective equilibrium". There's no guarantee that they're correct, since the world is often unlike our intuitions say, but they can help us get a sense of how plausible or implausible a new idea is at first. Conversations with others, particularly those who don't come from the same background, can help us see where our assumptions or intuitions will be viewed by others as eccentric.

6. *Modesty.* Finally, a view shouldn't require overturning everything else that we believe about the world *unless* it offers us a lot of gains in the other categories. Some of the views we'll discuss in class require turning everything we thought we knew on its head. Modesty isn't a strength of these views. However, these authors believed that their radical views were compensated for by gains in the other areas, so it was worth the cost.

These are some of the strengths of arguments. Weaknesses usually involve the lack of one of the strengths above.

Practice Question: For each of the six criteria given above, come up with an example of a view that is weaker than a competing view because it fails to meet the criteria given.

9. Types of Deductive Argument

The kinds of arguments we've been talking about so far, which are evaluated in terms of being valid or invalid, are typically called **deductive** arguments. A valid deductive argument is one in which the truth of the premises guarantees the truth of the conclusion. There are a variety of forms that a valid deductive argument can take. Here are five of the most common forms that you're likely to see in our class.

a. Modus Ponens

In this form of argument, traditionally called "*modus ponens*", one premise has the form of an "if… then…" sentence, like "If you are hungry, then you should go to the Thai buffet on Dobson Road." A second premise then contains the proposition expressed by the "if" half of the "if… then…" sentence. The conclusion contains the proposition expressed by the "then" half of the "if… then…" sentence. For example:

> (P1) If you are hungry, then you should go to the Thai buffet on Dobson Road.
> (P2) You are hungry.
> (C) You should go to the Thai buffet on Dobson Road.

b. Disjunctive Syllogism

In this form of argument, one premise has the form of an "either… or…." sentence, like "Either you will meet deadlines, or you will face my wrath". Another premise has the form of the *negation* of the proposition expressed by one half of the "either… or…" sentence—by "negation", I mean that it says the proposition is *not* true, or that it is false. The conclusion then contains the proposition in the other half of the "either . . . or . . . " sentence. For instance:

> (P1) Either you met deadlines, or you faced the client's wrath.
> (P2) You did not face the client's wrath.
> (C) You met deadlines.

Both modus ponens and disjunctive syllogism are guaranteed to be valid. There's no way that both premises could be true, yet the conclusion false.

C. Reductio

A Reductio argument starts out by assuming something, then proving that the assumption is false, because a contradiction can be deduced from the assumption. If you take on a certain view, and that view leads to something contradictory or absurd, then the view must be false. Reductio arguments are sometimes confusing at first, because an author seems to be arguing against what he or she was arguing for just a moment earlier. Remember that the assumption in a Reductio is only *temporary*, for the purposes of the argument.

For example, suppose that someone wants to argue that the just thing to do is not necessarily what the law says to do. A Reductio argument starts out like this: *assume that the just thing to do is necessarily what the law says to do. In other words, everything which is against the law is unjust, and everything which is unjust is against the law.* The arguer doesn't actually believe this, but he or she assumes it to see where it will lead. *Consider that the law can say anything. So, there could be a law that says that one should not follow the law. Not following the law would be unjust, but not following the law not to follow the law would also be unjust.* This is a contradiction. Since the assumption leads to a contradiction, the original assumption must be false.

Here's another example. Suppose that Harry says that *one should only believe a claim is true if it can be proven scientifically.* Terry wishes to prove Harry wrong. So, Terry assumes that Harry is right. *Assume that one should only believe a claim is true if it can be proven scientifically.* Terry's Reductio goes as follows. *Consider the principle that one should only believe a claim is true if it can be proven scientifically. Assume that one should believe that this principle is true. If this is so, then the principle can be proven scientifically. However, it can't be proven scientifically.* There is no experimental test which scientists can perform to tell us whether or not we should believe the claim that "one should only believe a claim is true if it can be proven scientifically". *So, according to the principle, one should not believe that the principle is true.* This is a Reductio that proves that the original view is false.

d. Arguments by Identity and Analogy

The last type of deductive argument we'll look at in this guide are arguments from the identity or similarity of two things. Let's start with an argument by identity. "Jeff" and "Dr. Watson" are two terms for the same person. Jeff = Dr. Watson. So, if something is true of Jeff, then it must be true of Dr. Watson, and vice versa. We can use this in a deductive argument:

(P1) Jeff lives in Arizona.
(P2) Jeff = Dr. Watson
(C) Dr. Watson lives in Arizona.

This should be a pretty obvious form of argument. However, it can always be applied to cases where there are two *distinct* things, but where they are "roughly identical" or *similar in all relevant respects*. For example, suppose that I have two mugs made of the same material filled with exactly 2 cups of water each, filled from the same tap at the same time. The mugs of water aren't exactly identical—they are two distinct mugs. However, if I know that the water in one of the mugs will boil at 212 degrees Fahrenheit, then I know that the water in the other mug will boil at the same temperature. The two mugs are identical in every *relevant* way, when it comes to water boiling. Similarly, suppose that an editor is deciding whether a children's book should be published. The editor knows that a book with the same style and subject matter and quality was published recently and was very successful. If these are the only things that are relevant to the success of the book (and they may not be), the editor could conclude that the children's book should be published, because it will also be very successful:

(P1) Toby the Train was successful.
(P2) Ernie the Engine is just like Toby the Train in all the relevant ways.
(C) Ernie the Engine will be successful.

Sometimes two cases are clearly very different, but they are relevant in *some* respect which is important to the issue at hand. One case is an *analogy* for the other. By assuming the two cases are relevantly similar, one can form an *argument by analogy*. For example, everyone knows that one country invading a foreign country, as a geopolitical event, is very different from one person invading another person's house, a local event. Country invasions and home invasions are very different. However, consider someone who makes this argument by analogy:

(P1) Even if your neighbor is an abusive father, you still shouldn't necessarily break into his house, wave a gun around, and light his living room on fire, because that likely won't help the children.

(P2) Invading another country in order to free it from a cruel dictatorship is relevantly like breaking into your abusive neighbor's house, waving a gun around, and lighting his living room on fire in order to save his children.

(C) Even if another country is a cruel dictatorship, you still shouldn't necessarily invade it, because that likely won't help the people in the country.

The person who makes this argument is asserting that the two cases are *morally* similar even if they aren't similar in scale. Is this argument sound? *It depends on whether or not the two cases really are relevantly similar.* Can you think of a morally relevant difference between invading a country for these reasons and invading a neighbor's house? Perhaps the existence of police forces and child protective services in the neighbor case makes it relevantly different, since there's no equivalent authority in international affairs?

Practice Question: Label the following four arguments, in terms of whether they are (a) Reductio, (b) modus ponens, (c) disjunctive syllogism, (d) argument by analogy.

Argument 1. (P1) Alcohol should be legal for adults to purchase.
(P2) Marijuana is similar to Alcohol in the relevant ways.
(C) Marijuana should be legal for adults to purchase.

Argument 2. (P1) You benefit from government.
(P2) If you benefit from government, then you should pay for it.
(C) You should pay for government.

Argument 3. (P1) Either Hannah gets a raise, or she quits.
(P2) Hannah's not getting a raise.
(C) Hannah quits.

Argument 4. (P1) *Assumption*. There is a largest number.
(P2) For any number, you can add 1 and get a larger number.
(C1) You can add 1 to the largest number and get a larger number.
(C2) There is a number larger than the largest number.
(!) *Contradiction*
(C) There is no largest number.

10. Inductive and Abductive Arguments

The arguments we've been discussing in this guide have primarily been *deductive* arguments, which are evaluated in terms of whether they are valid or invalid. In deductive arguments, the premises are supposed to guarantee the truth of the conclusion—there is no way for the premises to be true and the conclusion false.

However, there are two weaker types of argument than deductive arguments. These arguments are useful for establishing that a conclusion is *probable* or *plausible* given the premises, even though it isn't a deductive proof that makes the conclusion *certain* given the premises.

Inductive arguments start with a series of particular truths about individual instances, and draw a general conclusion about a large group of instances. For example:

(P1) Jon works here, and he likes pizza.
(P2) Ted works here, and he likes pizza.
(P3) Anna works here, and she likes pizza.
(P4) I asked 300 other people who work here, and all of them like pizza.
(C) Everybody who works here likes pizza!

Inductive arguments are invalid. Just because many people who work here like pizza, that doesn't mean that everybody who works here likes pizza. There might be one person who hates pizza.

However, an inductive argument with a large enough sample size can make a conclusion highly probable. How do we know that the sun will rise tomorrow morning? Well, it rose yesterday, and the day before, and the day before . . . going back as far as we know. That seems like a good reason to think that it will *almost* certainly rise tomorrow morning. However, it doesn't guarantee that the sun will rise tomorrow morning. Some drastic solar event we couldn't foresee might happen and obliterate the solar system overnight.

If you put salt into boiling water over and over and over again, and every time the salt dissolves in the water, then an inductive argument can establish that if you do it again, the salt will probably dissolve again:

(P1) Salt dissolved in boiling water on try 1.
(P2) Salt dissolved in boiling water on try 2 . . . .
(P50000) Salt dissolved in boiling water on try 1000.
(C) Salt will dissolve in boiling water on try 1001.

Abductive arguments are even weaker than inductive arguments. While inductive arguments make a conclusion *probable* given the premises, abductive arguments merely establish that a conclusion is a *plausible* working hypothesis, not that it is true or even likely true. Sometimes these arguments are called cases of *inference to the best explanation*. In this sort of argument, one tries to find a reason that would explain why some mysterious phenomenon is the case. If we're not sure why an effect happens, we might go through a series of possible causes of the effect.

Suppose that you're sleeping in your bedroom at night, and you hear a knock on the door. The knock is frantic. You know that, if your neighbor were in trouble, your neighbor would knock frantically at your door. So, you think "maybe it's my neighbor at the door". Then, you consider that your Uncle Eddie also has a frantic way of knocking, and a tendency to visit you in the wee hours of the night to share tales of sorrow and woe. So, you think instead, "maybe it's Uncle Eddie at the door". You aren't *certain* that it's Eddie or that it's your neighbor at the door. Perhaps neither of these is even particularly likely, because it could be a whole host of people knocking frantically at your door. However, given the very limited evidence you have, you might pick one of these as the best explanation for the knocking, and go with it for the time being until a better explanation comes along or the evidence changes:

(P1) If my neighbor's house is on fire, then I would hear a frantic knocking.
(P2) I hear a frantic knocking.
(C) My neighbor's house is on fire.

This isn't a valid argument. Why is it invalid? Because it is possible for both premises to be true, and yet the conclusion to be false. Imagine a world where you hear a frantic knocking, but it's caused by your Uncle Eddie, not your neighbor. Your neighbor *would* knock frantically on your door if his or her house was on fire, but it's not—your neighbor is sleeping safely in bed. (P1) and (P2) are true, and (C) is false, so it's invalid. However, it's still a *useful* argument for explaining why the hypothesis that your neighbor's house is on fire is at least *plausible*, given that it's one of the better possible explanations for why you're being woken up by a frantic knocking in the middle of the night.

Practice Question: To practice distinguishing deductive, abductive, and inductive arguments, write out one of each from some set of premises (your choice—make them up) to the following conclusions: (a) composing music takes talent, (b) people are worse drivers in the summer, (c) every object has parts, (d) dogs are mammals.

11. Avoiding Fallacies

The final thing that you'll want to be sure to avoid when arguing is logical *fallacies*. Fallacies in reasoning are either cases where an argument is invalid, but sometimes people treat it as though it were valid, or else cases where an argument is valid, but flawed in a more subtle way. Read through this list of a few common fallacies to see if you can explain why each argument is flawed.

(A) An ***ad hominem*** argument is an argument against the character of one's opponent, instead of against their reasons.

P1. Bertrand Russell opposed the war.
P2. Bertrand Russell has had many extramarital affairs.
P3. Someone who has many extramarital affairs is wrong.
C. Bertrand Russell was wrong about the war.

(B) More subtle is the fallacy is ***begging the question***. When the premises of your argument and the conclusion of your argument would be judged true or false for the exact same reasons, your argument is valid but not persuasive. The reverse of your argument would be equally good. For example:

P1. Nature is a grand accident.
P2. If Nature is a grand accident, then a Designer doesn't exist.
C. A Designer doesn't exist.

or

P1. A Designer exists.
P2. If a Designer exists, then nature is not a grand accident.
C. Nature is not a grand accident.

The trouble is that the belief that nature is not a grand accident is the very same belief as the belief that a Designer (like God) exists, only put in slightly different words. Someone who thinks one is true will think the other is true, and vice versa. So, even though the argument is valid, it simply "begs the question".

(C) Inferring *causation from correlation* involves concluding that one thing is the effect of another simply because the two things are statistically related. For instance:

P1. The probability that one will be seriously ill while in the hospital is very high.
P2. The probability that one will be seriously ill while at home is very low.
C. Going to the hospital causes people to become seriously ill.

Of course, this ignores that being seriously ill is what brings someone to the hospital in the first place!

(D) A *false dilemma* involves a situation where you assume that one of the two options must be true, without ruling out the possibility of a third option or a middle ground.

P1. It's not true that the government should run everything in society.
C. The government should not run anything in society.

or

P1. It's not true that the government should run *nothing* in society.
C. The government should run everything in society.

(E) The fallacy of *equivocation* happens when an argument employs a term that has two meanings, but a different meaning is used in each premise.

P1. Being in a dreamless sleep = being *unconscious*$_1$
P2. The mountains are *unconscious*$_2$
C. The mountains are in a dreamless sleep.

(F) An *appeal to force* involves threatening someone to come to the conclusion rather than persuading them through reasons.

P1. If you don't agree with me, then I will hurt you.
P2. You don't want me to hurt you.
C. You should agree with me.

(G) The *genetic fallacy* assumes that an object has a property because its point of origin had that property.

P1. Listerine was originally designed to treat dandruff.
P2. Dandruff treatments are for your head, not your mouth.
C. Listerine is for your head, not your mouth.

(H) Making a *hasty generalization* involves concluding that something is true generally or universally simply because it is true in some cases. For example:

P1. I know College students who abuse alcohol.
P2. Everyone else I know knows College students who abuse alcohol.
C. All College students abuse alcohol.

(I). A fallacy of *irrelevance,* also called a "*Red Herring*", is a case where the premises of an argument are entirely independent of the conclusion. For example:

P1. Last year, ASU Students spent over $2 million dollars on Music and Entertainment.
P2. Music and Entertainment are luxuries, not necessities.
C. We should raise tuition for ASU Students.

The argument above isn't valid, but notice that an argument could be *valid* and yet still involve the fallacy of irrelevance. For example, suppose we add a self-contradictory premise to the argument. Then, there would be no possible way that the premises could be true with the conclusion false, because there would be no possible way that the premises could be true. Yet even though the argument would be valid, it would still be a fallacy:

P1. Last year, ASU Students spent over $2 million dollars on Music and Entertainment.
P2. Music and Entertainment are luxuries, not necessities.
P3. Triangles have four sides (self-contradictory premise).
C. We should raise tuition for ASU Students.

Irrelevance is what makes the difference between appealing to an *authority* and appealing to an *expert.* The following argument appeals to someone's relevant expertise:

P1. Barack Obama is the President.
P2. The President generally knows the truth about international events.
P3. The President believes that there is a famine in Country X.
C. There is probably a famine in Country X.

On the other hand, the following argument appeals only to an irrelevant position of authority.

P1. Barack Obama is the President.
P2. The President believes that Colgate is the best brand of toothpaste.
C. Colgate is the best brand of toothpaste.

(M) A *misleading comparison* or "false analogy" is an argument by analogy where the analogy is not tight enough to support the conclusion. Something might be like another in some ways, without being like it in all of the relevant ways.

P1. A car is like a human body, and the oil of a car is like the blood.
P2. Cars need oil changes regularly.
C. Humans need blood transfusions regularly.

(N) Assuming that *newer is better* is a common mistake, since we have no reason to assume that the future will always be an improvement over the past.

P1. In the past, people celebrated a variety of holidays and festivals.
P2. Now, people sit at home alone and watch streaming online videos.
C. Watching streaming online video is better than holding holidays and festivals.

(O) Assuming that *older is better* is the reverse of the newer is better fallacy. We have no reason to assume that the past was better than the present.

P1. The traditional method of wine-making required that everyone involved in making the wine must be a blood relative of the others.
P2. Nowadays, wine-makers use contracted laborers who are not relatives.
C. We should return to requiring people involved in wine-making to be blood relatives of each other.

(P) *Popular appeal* makes the mistake of assuming that, because a belief is popular (or unpopular), it must be true. This is also called the "bandwagon" fallacy.

P1. The mainstream media does not report that there are war crimes.
P2. Only the alternative media reports that there are war crimes.
C. There are no war crimes.
or

P1. The mainstream media does not report that chemtrails are real.
P2. Only the alternative media reports that chemtrails are real.
C. Chemtrails are real.

(Q) The fallacy of *tu Quoque*, Latin for "you too!" involves arguing that because your opponent does something irrational, you are entitled to do something irrational also.

P1. Even people who oppose discrimination still discriminate in subtle ways or have hidden prejudices that they haven't fully considered.
C. I am justified in supporting discrimination.

(R) Engaging in *Rationalizing* involves deciding what you want to believe first, and then coming up with reasons to support it, instead of forming your belief on the basis of reasons.

P1. I believe that immigration should be stopped.
P2. If immigration is a drain on the economy, then it should be stopped.
C. I believe that immigration is a drain on the economy.

(S). A *Slippery Slope* is an argument that, because a certain concept is vague and has no clear boundaries, if we accept any borderline cases, then we must accept the most extreme cases on the spectrum.

P1. Assume that compensating organ donors is not unjust.
P2. There is no clear borderline between compensating an organ donor and paying a corporation to harvest organs from living clones of ourselves kept in living stasis to be accessed whenever we are injured in order to enable the wealthy to live forever.
P3. Enabling the wealthy to live forever by buying body parts from the rest of us would be unjust.
C. Compensating organ donors is unjust.

(T) *Tribalism* means assuming that your own 'tribe' (nation, family, group, company, community, and region) is more likely to be correct than anyone else's tribe.

P1. America is awesome.
P2. Americans believe that free-market economics is best.
C. Free-market economics is best.

(U) Engaging in *uncharitable interpretation* leads to what is often called the "straw man" fallacy. This involves interpreting your opponent in a way that they would not themselves agree with, in order to make them sound absurd, irrational, or wicked. For example:

P1. Proponents of legalizing marijuana believe that all drugs are harmless and life has no meaning but pleasure.
P2. It is false that all drugs are harmless and life has no meaning but pleasure.
C. It is false that we should legalize marijuana.

(V) The *verification* fallacy is the mistake of concluding that the evidence we use to determine whether or not a proposition is true is the same as what makes it true or false.

P1. We know whether or not someone is in pain by listening to whether they make pain noises or expressions of being in pain.
P2. The actor on stage is making pain noises and expressions of being in pain.
P3. The person being executed by lethal injection is not making pain noises or expressions of being in pain.
C. The actor on stage is in pain, but the person being executed is not.

(W) The *whole-parts* fallacy, sometimes distinguished as the fallacies of composition and division, involve concluding that something is true of the parts because it is true of the whole, or true of the whole because it is true of the parts.

Division:

P1. The statue of liberty is made of copper.
P2. The statue of liberty is a sign of our values as a nation.
C. Copper is a sign of our values as a nation.

Composition:

P1. This corporation is made up of shareholders and employees.
P2. The shareholders and employees of this corporation are all chain smokers.
C. This corporation is a chain smoker.

(X) Fallacies that are inverted forms of traditional argument forms get a big red "X!" For instance, the fallacy of *affirming the consequent* is the reverse of *Modus Ponens*.

P1. If it is raining, then the sidewalk is wet.
P2. The sidewalk is wet.
C. It is raining.

The fallacy of *negating the antecedent* is the reverse of *Modus Tollens*:

P1. If it is raining, then the sidewalk is wet.
P2. It is not raining.
C. The sidewalk is not wet.

To see why both are invalid arguments, consider a sprinkler system used to irrigate a lawn that hits the sidewalk by accident.

(Y) The fallacy of **yearning** involves badly wanting something to be true, or untrue, and concluding that it must be true or untrue as a result. While *denial* is a normal initial stage in the process of grieving a loss, it becomes problematic when carried on for too long.

P1. I don't want it to be true that the climate is changing.
C. The climate is not changing.

Appealing to any emotion such as pity, fear, anger, or worry is problematic in an argument because our emotions do not always line up with the truth. We can feel pity, fear, anger, or worry as much as is justified, without drawing conclusions on how we feel.

P1. This person facing the death penalty is to be pitied.
P2. This person does not want to die.
C. This person should not die.

or

P1. The victims of a crime are to be pitied.
P2. The victims of the crime want this person to die.
C. This person should die.

(Z) Finally, the fallacy of **putting Z before A**, amounts to arguing that because believing something would have negative consequences down the road, the initial belief itself must be false. This is sometimes called *appealing to consequences.*

P1. If I believe that war is approaching, then I will fear losing my investments.
P2. I shouldn't fear losing my investments.
C. War is not approaching.

Of course, there are many other fallacies in reasoning! But reflecting on these common ones can help you see why thinking carefully about arguments is so important

❋ 1.4 Apology ❋
Selections
by Plato
Translated by Benjamin Jowett

✳ ✳

© Nick Pavlakis/Shutterstock.com

Socrates (469–399 B.C.E.) was a Greek philosopher who lived in Athens. Plato was a student of Socrates. Socrates himself wrote nothing, but his ideas were recorded by Plato as a series of dialogues between Socrates and other prominent people of the time. In general it is believed that the earlier dialogues written by Plato give a more accurate picture of what Socrates thought, and the later dialogues represent more heavily the thoughts of Plato himself. This reading contains selections from "The Apology", which is an early dialogue. The *Apology* presents the defense Socrates offered as his trial.

Here are some questions to think about when you read:

* What were the two basic charges against Socrates?

* How did Socrates defend himself against the first charge? How did he defend himself against the second charge? What form of argument is he using?

* What the Oracle say about Socrates? How does Socrates interpret what the Oracle said?

* What was the outcome of the first phase of the trial? What surprised Socrates?

* In Athens, the prosecutor proposed one punishment, and the defendant proposed another, and the jury voted between the two proposals. What punishment did Socrates propose for himself?

* What was the outcome of the punishment phase of the trial?

* After the trial, Socrates's friends devised a way for him to escape punishment, but he refused, and drank the poison willingly. Why do you think Socrates responded as he did?

❀ ❀

The Defense of Socrates

I will begin at the beginning, and ask what the accusation is which has given rise to this slander of me, and which has encouraged Meletus to proceed against me. What do the slanderers say? They shall be my prosecutors, and I will sum up their words in an affidavit.

"Socrates is an evil-doer, and a curious person, who searches into things under the earth and in heaven, and he makes the worse appear the better cause; and he teaches the aforesaid doctrines to others."

That is the nature of the accusation, and that is what you have seen yourselves in the comedy of Aristophanes; who has introduced a man whom he calls Socrates, going about and saying that he can walk in the air, and talking a deal of nonsense concerning matters of which I do not pretend to know either much or little - not that I mean to say anything disparaging of anyone who is a student of natural philosophy. I should be very sorry if Meletus could lay that to my charge. But the simple truth is, O Athenians, that I have nothing to do with these studies. Very many of those here present are witnesses to the truth of this, and to them I appeal. Speak then, you who have heard me, and tell your neighbors whether any of you have ever known me hold forth in few words or in many upon matters of this sort. . . . You hear their answer. And from what they say of this you will be able to judge of the truth of the rest.

As little foundation is there for the report that I am a teacher, and take money; that is no more true than the other. Although, if a man is able to teach, I honor him for being paid. There is Gorgias of Leontium, and Prodicus of Ceos, and Hippias of Elis, who go the round of the cities, and are able to persuade the young men to leave their own citizens, by whom they might be taught for nothing, and come to them, whom they not only pay, but are thankful if they may be allowed to pay them.

. . .

I will refer you to a witness who is worthy of credit, and will tell you about my wisdom - whether I have any, and of what sort - and that witness shall be the god of Delphi. You must have known Chaerephon; he was early a friend of mine, and also a friend of yours, for he shared in the exile of the people, and returned with you. Well, Chaerephon, as you know, was very impetuous in all his doings, and he went to Delphi and boldly asked the oracle to tell him whether - as I was saying, I must beg you not to interrupt - he asked the oracle to tell him whether there was anyone wiser than I was, and the Pythian prophetess answered that there was no man wiser. Chaerephon is dead himself, but his brother, who is in court, will confirm the truth of this story.

Why do I mention this? Because I am going to explain to you why I have such an evil name. When I heard the answer, I said to myself, What can the god mean? and what is the interpretation of this riddle? for I know that I have no wisdom, small or great. What can he mean when he says that I am the wisest of men? And yet he is a god and cannot lie; that would be against his nature.

After a long consideration, I at last thought of a method of trying the question. I reflected that if I could only find a man wiser than myself, then I might go to the god with a refutation in my hand. I should say to him, "Here is a man who is wiser than I am; but you said that I was the wisest." Accordingly I went to one who had the reputation of wisdom, and observed to him - his name I need not mention; he was a politician whom I selected for examination - and the result was as follows: When I began to talk with him, I could not help thinking that he was not really wise, although he was thought wise by many, and wiser still by himself; and I went and tried to explain to him that he thought himself wise, but was not really wise; and the consequence was that he hated me, and his enmity was shared by several who were present and heard me.

❀ ❀

So I left him, saying to myself, as I went away: Well, although I do not suppose that either of us knows anything really beautiful and good, I am better off than he is - for he knows nothing, and thinks that he knows. I neither know nor think that I know. In this latter particular, then, I seem to have slightly the advantage of him. Then I went to another, who had still higher philosophical pretensions, and my conclusion was exactly the same. I made another enemy of him, and of many others besides him.

After this I went to one man after another, being not unconscious of the enmity which I provoked, and I lamented and feared this: but necessity was laid upon me - the word of God, I thought, ought to be considered first. And I said to myself, Go I must to all who appear to know, and find out the meaning of the oracle.

And I swear to you, Athenians, by the dog I swear! - for I must tell you the truth - the result of my mission was just this: I found that the men most in repute were all but the most foolish; and that some inferior men were really wiser and better. I will tell you the tale of my wanderings and of the "Herculean" labors, as I may call them, which I endured only to find at last the oracle irrefutable.

When I left the politicians, I went to the poets; tragic, dithyrambic, and all sorts. And there, I said to myself, you will be detected; now you will find out that you are more ignorant than they are. Accordingly, I took them some of the most elaborate passages in their own writings, and asked what was the meaning of them - thinking that they would teach me something. Will you believe me? I am almost ashamed to speak of this, but still I must say that there is hardly a person present who would not have talked better about their poetry than they did themselves. That showed me in an instant that not by wisdom do poets write poetry, but by a sort of genius and inspiration; they are like diviners or soothsayers who also say many fine things, but do not understand the meaning of them. And the poets appeared

to me to be much in the same case; and I further observed that upon the strength of their poetry they believed themselves to be the wisest of men in other things in which they were not wise. So I departed, conceiving myself to be superior to them for the same reason that I was superior to the politicians.

At last I went to the artisans, for I was conscious that I knew nothing at all, as I may say, and I was sure that they knew many fine things; and in this I was not mistaken, for they did know many things of which I was ignorant, and in this they certainly were wiser than I was. But I observed that even the good artisans fell into the same error as the poets; because they were good workmen they thought that they also knew all sorts of high matters, and this defect in them overshadowed their wisdom - therefore I asked myself on behalf of the oracle, whether I would like to be as I was, neither having their knowledge nor their ignorance, or like them in both; and I made answer to myself and the oracle that I was better off as I was.

This investigation has led to my having many enemies of the worst and most dangerous kind, and has given occasion also to many calumnies, and I am called wise, for my hearers always imagine that I myself possess the wisdom which I find wanting in others: but the truth is, O men of Athens, that God only is wise; and in this oracle he means to say that the wisdom of men is little or nothing; he is not speaking of Socrates, he is only using my name as an illustration, as if he said, He, O men, is the wisest, who, like Socrates, knows that his wisdom is in truth worth nothing. And so I go my way, obedient to the god, and make inquisition into the wisdom of anyone, whether citizen or stranger, who appears to be wise; and if he is not wise, then in vindication of the oracle I show him that he is not wise; and this occupation quite absorbs me, and I have no time to give either to any public matter of interest or to any concern of my own, but I am in utter poverty by reason of my devotion to the god.

❁ ❁

There is another thing: - young men of the richer classes, who have not much to do, come about me of their own accord; they like to hear the pretenders examined, and they often imitate me, and examine others themselves; there are plenty of persons, as they soon enough discover, who think that they know something, but really know little or nothing: and then those who are examined by them instead of being angry with themselves are angry with me: This confounded Socrates, they say; this villainous misleader of youth! - and then if somebody asks them, Why, what evil does he practise or teach? they do not know, and cannot tell; but in order that they may not appear to be at a loss, they repeat the ready-made charges which are used against all philosophers about teaching things up in the clouds and under the earth, and having no gods, and making the worse appear the better cause; for they do not like to confess that their pretence of knowledge has been detected - which is the truth: and as they are numerous and ambitious and energetic, and are all in battle array and have persuasive tongues, they have filled your ears with their loud and inveterate calumnies. And this is the reason why my three accusers, Meletus and Anytus and Lycon, have set upon me; Meletus, who has a quarrel with me on behalf of the poets; Anytus, on behalf of the craftsmen; Lycon, on behalf of the rhetoricians: and as I said at the beginning, I cannot expect to get rid of this mass of calumny all in a moment.

And this, O men of Athens, is the truth and the whole truth; I have concealed nothing, I have dissembled nothing. And yet I know that this plainness of speech makes them hate me, and what is their hatred but a proof that I am speaking the truth? - this is the occasion and reason of their slander of me, as you will find out either in this or in any future inquiry.

I have said enough in my defence against the first class of my accusers; I turn to the second class, who are headed by Meletus, that good and patriotic man, as he calls himself. And now I will try

to defend myself against them: these new accusers must also have their affidavit read. What do they say? Something of this sort: - *That Socrates is a doer of evil, and corrupter of the youth, and he does not believe in the gods of the state, and has other new divinities of his own.* That is the sort of charge; and now let us examine the particular counts.

He says that I am a doer of evil, who corrupt the youth; but I say, O men of Athens, that Meletus is a doer of evil, and the evil is that he makes a joke of a serious matter, and is too ready at bringing other men to trial from a pretended zeal and interest about matters in which he really never had the smallest interest. And the truth of this I will endeavor to prove.

Come hither, Meletus, and let me ask a question of you. You think a great deal about the improvement of youth?

Yes, I do.

Tell the judges, then, who is their improver; for you must know, as you have taken the pains to discover their corrupter, and are citing and accusing me before them. Speak, then, and tell the judges who their improver is. Observe, Meletus, that you are silent, and have nothing to say. But is not this rather disgraceful, and a very considerable proof of what I was saying, that you have no interest in the matter? Speak up, friend, and tell us who their improver is.

The laws.

But that, my good sir, is not my meaning. I want to know who the person is, who, in the first place, knows the laws.

The judges, Socrates, who are present in court.

What do you mean to say, Meletus, that they are able to instruct and improve youth?

Certainly they are.

What, all of them, or some only and not others?

❖ ❖

All of them.

By the goddess Here, that is good news! There are plenty of improvers, then. And what do you say of the audience, - do they improve them?

Yes, they do.

And the senators?

Yes, the senators improve them.

But perhaps the members of the citizen assembly corrupt them? - or do they too improve them?

They improve them.

Then every Athenian improves and elevates them; all with the exception of myself; and I alone am their corrupter? Is that what you affirm?

That is what I stoutly affirm.

I am very unfortunate if that is true. But suppose I ask you a question: Would you say that this also holds true in the case of horses? Does one man do them harm and all the world good? Is not the exact opposite of this true? One man is able to do them good, or at least not many; - the trainer of horses, that is to say, does them good, and others who have to do with them rather injure them? Is not that true, Meletus, of horses, or any other animals? Yes, certainly. Whether you and Anytus say yes or no, that is no matter. Happy indeed would be the condition of youth if they had one corrupter only, and all the rest of the world were their improvers. And you, Meletus, have sufficiently shown that you never had a thought about the young: your carelessness is seen in your not caring about matters spoken of in this very indictment.

And now, Meletus, I must ask you another question: Which is better, to live among bad citizens, or among good ones? Answer, friend, I say; for that is a question which may be easily answered. Do not the good do their neighbors good, and the bad do them evil?

Certainly.

And is there anyone who would rather be injured than benefited by those who live with him? Answer, my good friend; the law requires you to answer - does anyone like to be injured?

Certainly not.

And when you accuse me of corrupting and deteriorating the youth, do you allege that I corrupt them intentionally or unintentionally?

Intentionally, I say.

But you have just admitted that the good do their neighbors good, and the evil do them evil. Now is that a truth which your superior wisdom has recognized thus early in life, and am I, at my age, in such darkness and ignorance as not to know that if a man with whom I have to live is corrupted by me, I am very likely to be harmed by him, and yet I corrupt him, and intentionally, too; - that is what you are saying, and of that you will never persuade me or any other human being. But either I do not corrupt them, or I corrupt them unintentionally, so that on either view of the case you lie. If my offence is unintentional, the law has no cognizance of unintentional offences: you ought to have taken me privately, and warned and admonished me; for if I had been better advised, I should have left off doing what I only did unintentionally - no doubt I should; whereas you hated to converse with me or teach me, but you indicted me in this court, which is a place not of instruction, but of punishment.

I have shown, Athenians, as I was saying, that Meletus has no care at all, great or small, about the matter. But still I should like to know, Meletus, in what I am affirmed to corrupt the young. I suppose you mean, as I infer from your indictment, that I teach them not to acknowledge the gods which the state acknowledges, but some other new divinities or spiritual agencies in their stead. These are the lessons which corrupt the youth, as you say.

Yes, that I say emphatically.

Then, by the gods, Meletus, of whom we are speaking, tell me and the court, in somewhat plainer terms, what you mean! for I do not as yet understand whether you affirm that I teach others to acknowledge some gods, and therefore do believe in gods and am not an entire atheist - this you do not lay to my charge; but only that they are not the same gods which the city recognizes - the charge is that they are different gods. Or, do you mean to say that I am an atheist simply, and a teacher of atheism?

I mean the latter - that you are a complete atheist.

That is an extraordinary statement, Meletus. Why do you say that? Do you mean that I do not believe in the godhead of the sun or moon, which is the common creed of all men?

I assure you, judges, that he does not believe in them; for he says that the sun is stone, and the moon earth.

Friend Meletus, you think that you are accusing Anaxagoras; and you have but a bad opinion of the judges, if you fancy them ignorant to such a degree as not to know that those doctrines are found in the books of Anaxagoras the Clazomenian, who is full of them. And these are the doctrines which the youth are said to learn of Socrates, when there are not unfrequently exhibitions of them at the theatre (price of admission one drachma at the most); and they might cheaply purchase them, and laugh at Socrates if he pretends to father such eccentricities. And so, Meletus, you really think that I do not believe in any god?

I swear by Zeus that you believe absolutely in none at all.

You are a liar, Meletus, not believed even by yourself. For I cannot help thinking, O men of Athens, that Meletus is reckless and impudent, and that he has written this indictment in a spirit of mere wantonness and youthful bravado. Has he not compounded a riddle, thinking to try me? He said to himself: - I shall see whether this wise Socrates will discover my ingenious contradiction, or whether I shall be able to deceive him and the rest of them. For he certainly does appear to me to contradict himself in the indictment as much as if he said that Socrates is guilty of not believing in the gods, and yet of believing in them - but this surely is a piece of fun.

I should like you, O men of Athens, to join me in examining what I conceive to be his inconsistency; and do you, Meletus, answer. And I must remind you that you are not to interrupt me if I speak in my accustomed manner.

Did ever man, Meletus, believe in the existence of human things, and not of human beings? ... I wish, men of Athens, that he would answer, and not be always trying to get up an interruption. Did ever any man believe in horsemanship, and not in horses? or in flute-playing, and not in flute-players? No, my friend; I will answer to you and to the court, as you refuse to answer for yourself. There is no man who ever did. But now please to answer the next question: Can a man believe in spiritual and divine agencies, and not in spirits or demigods?

He cannot.

I am glad that I have extracted that answer, by the assistance of the court; nevertheless you swear in the indictment that I teach and believe in divine or spiritual agencies (new or old, no matter for that); at any rate, I believe in spiritual agencies, as you say and swear in the affidavit; but if I believe in divine beings, I must believe in spirits or demigods; - is not that true? Yes, that is true, for I may assume that your silence gives assent to that. Now what are spirits or demigods? are they not either gods or the sons of gods? Is that true?

Yes, that is true.

❀ ❀

But this is just the ingenious riddle of which I was speaking: the demigods or spirits are gods, and you say first that I don't believe in gods, and then again that I do believe in gods; that is, if I believe in demigods. For if the demigods are the illegitimate sons of gods, whether by the Nymphs or by any other mothers, as is thought, that, as all men will allow, necessarily implies the existence of their parents. You might as well affirm the existence of mules, and deny that of horses and asses. Such nonsense, Meletus, could only have been intended by you as a trial of me. You have put this into the indictment because you had nothing real of which to accuse me. . . .

Someone will say: And are you not ashamed, Socrates, of a course of life which is likely to bring you to an untimely end? To him I may fairly answer: There you are mistaken: a man who is good for anything ought not to calculate the chance of living or dying; he ought only to consider whether in doing anything he is doing right or wrong - acting the part of a good man or of a bad. . . .

Strange, indeed, would be my conduct, O men of Athens, if I who, when I was ordered by the generals whom you chose to command me at Potidaea and Amphipolis and Delium, remained where they placed me, like any other man, facing death; if, I say, now, when, as I conceive and imagine, God orders me to fulfil the philosopher's mission of searching into myself and other men, I were to desert my post through fear of death, or any other fear; that would indeed be strange, and I might justly be arraigned in court for denying the existence of the gods, if I disobeyed the oracle because I was afraid of death: then I should be fancying that I was wise when I was not wise.

For this fear of death is indeed the pretence of wisdom, and not real wisdom, being the appearance of knowing the unknown; since no one knows whether death, which they in their fear apprehend to be the greatest evil, may not be the greatest good. Is there not here conceit of knowledge, which is a disgraceful sort of ignorance? And this is the point in which, as I think, I am superior to men in general, and in which I might perhaps fancy myself wiser than other men, - that whereas I know but little of the world below, I do not suppose that I know: but I do know that injustice and disobedience to a better, whether God or man, is evil and dishonorable, and I will never fear or avoid a possible good rather than a certain evil. And therefore if you let me go now, and reject the counsels of Anytus, who said that if I were not put to death I ought not to have been prosecuted, and that if I escape now, your sons will all be utterly ruined by listening to my words - if you say to me, Socrates, this time we will not mind Anytus, and will let you off, but upon one condition, that are to inquire and speculate in this way any more, and that if you are caught doing this again you shall die; - if this was the condition on which you let me go, I should reply: Men of Athens, I honor and love you; but I shall obey God rather than you, and while I have life and strength I shall never cease from the practice and teaching of philosophy, exhorting anyone whom I meet after my manner, and convincing him, saying:

"O my friend, why do you who are a citizen of the great and mighty and wise city of Athens, care so much about laying up the greatest amount of money and honor and reputation, and so little about wisdom and truth and the greatest improvement of the soul, which you never regard or heed at all? Are you not ashamed of this?"

And if the person with whom I am arguing says: *Yes, but I do care*; I do not depart or let him go at once; I interrogate and examine and cross-examine him, and if I think that he has no virtue, but only says that he has, I reproach him with undervaluing the greater, and overvaluing the less.

And this I should say to everyone whom I meet, young and old, citizen and alien, but especially to

❖ ❖

the citizens, inasmuch as they are my brethren. For this is the command of God, as I would have you know; and I believe that to this day no greater good has ever happened in the state than my service to the God.

For I do nothing but go about persuading you all, old and young alike, not to take thought for your persons and your properties, but first and chiefly to care about the greatest improvement of the soul. I tell you that virtue is not given by money, but that from virtue come money and every other good of man, public as well as private. This is my teaching, and if this is the doctrine which corrupts the youth, my influence is ruinous indeed. But if anyone says that this is not my teaching, he is speaking an untruth. Wherefore, O men of Athens, I say to you, do as Anytus bids or not as Anytus bids, and either acquit me or not; but whatever you do, know that I shall never alter my ways, not even if I have to die many times. . .

And now, Athenians, I am not going to argue for my own sake, as you may think, but for yours, that you may not sin against the God, or lightly reject his boon by condemning me. For if you kill me you will not easily find another like me, who, if I may use such a ludicrous figure of speech, am a sort of gadfly, given to the state by the God; and the state is like a great and noble steed who is tardy in his motions owing to his very size, and requires to be stirred into life. I am that gadfly which God has given the state and all day long and in all places am always fastening upon you, arousing and persuading and reproaching you. And as you will not easily find another like me, I would advise you to spare me. I dare say that you may feel irritated at being suddenly awakened when you are caught napping; and you may think that if you were to strike me dead, as Anytus advises, which you easily might, then you would sleep on for the remainder of your lives, unless God in his care of you gives you another gadfly.

. . . . For if, O men of Athens, by force of persuasion and entreaty, I could overpower your oaths, then I should be teaching you to believe that there are no gods, and convict myself, in my own defence, of not believing in them. But that is not the case; for I do believe that there are gods, and in a far higher sense than that in which any of my accusers believe in them. And to you and to God I commit my cause, to be determined by you as is best for you and me.

[The jury finds Socrates guilty. The Vote is 281–220]

Socrates' Proposal for his Sentence

There are many reasons why I am not grieved, O men of Athens, at the vote of condemnation. I expected it, and am only surprised that the votes are so nearly equal; for I had thought that the majority against me would have been far larger; but now, had thirty votes gone over to the other side, I should have been acquitted. And I may say that I have escaped Meletus. And I may say more; for without the assistance of Anytus and Lycon, he would not have had a fifth part of the votes, as the law requires, in which case he would have incurred a fine of a thousand drachmae, as is evident.

And so he proposes death as the penalty. And what shall I propose on my part, O men of Athens? Clearly that which is my due. And what is that which I ought to pay or to receive?

What shall be done to the man who has never had the wit to be idle during his whole life; but has been careless of what the many care about - wealth, and family interests, and military offices, and speaking in the assembly, and magistracies, and plots, and parties. Reflecting that I was really too honest a man to follow in this way and live, I did not go where I could do no good to you or to myself; but where I could do the greatest good privately to everyone of you, thither I went, and sought to persuade every man among you that he must look to himself, and seek virtue and wisdom before he

❊ ❊

looks to his private interests, and look to the state before he looks to the interests of the state; and that this should be the order which he observes in all his actions. What shall be done to such a one?

Doubtless some good thing, O men of Athens, if he has his reward; and the good should be of a kind suitable to him. What would be a reward suitable to a poor man who is your benefactor, who desires leisure that he may instruct you?

There can be no more fitting reward than maintenance in the Prytaneum, O men of Athens, a reward which he deserves far more than the citizen who has won the prize at Olympia in the horse or chariot race, whether the chariots were drawn by two horses or by many. For I am in want, and he has enough; and he only gives you the appearance of happiness, and I give you the reality. And if I am to estimate the penalty justly, I say that maintenance in the Prytaneum is the just return.

Perhaps you may think that I am braving you in saying this, as in what I said before about the tears and prayers. But that is not the case. I speak rather because I am convinced that I never intentionally wronged anyone, although I cannot convince you of that - for we have had a short conversation only; but if there were a law at Athens, such as there is in other cities, that a capital cause should not be decided in one day, then I believe that I should have convinced you; but now the time is too short. I cannot in a moment refute great slanders; and, as I am convinced that I never wronged another, I will assuredly not wrong myself. I will not say of myself that I deserve any evil, or propose any penalty.

Why should I? Because I am afraid of the penalty of death which Meletus proposes? When I do not know whether death is a good or an evil, why should I propose a penalty which would certainly be an evil? Shall I say imprisonment? And why should I live in prison, and be the slave of the magistrates of the year - of the Eleven? Or shall the penalty be a fine, and imprisonment until the fine is paid? There is the same objection. I should have to lie in prison, for money I have none, and I cannot pay. And if I say exile (and this may possibly be the penalty which you will affix), I must indeed be blinded by the love of life if I were to consider that when you, who are my own citizens, cannot endure my discourses and words, and have found them so grievous and odious that you would fain have done with them, others are likely to endure me. No, indeed, men of Athens, that is not very likely. And what a life should I lead, at my age, wandering from city to city, living in ever-changing exile, and always being driven out! For I am quite sure that into whatever place I go, as here so also there, the young men will come to me; and if I drive them away, their elders will drive me out at their desire: and if I let them come, their fathers and friends will drive me out for their sakes.

Someone will say: Yes, Socrates, but cannot you hold your tongue, and then you may go into a foreign city, and no one will interfere with you? Now I have great difficulty in making you understand my answer to this. For if I tell you that this would be a disobedience to a divine command, and therefore that I cannot hold my tongue, you will not believe that I am serious; and if I say again that the greatest good of man is daily to converse about virtue, and all that concerning which you hear me examining myself and others, and that the life which is unexamined is not worth living - that you are still less likely to believe. And yet what I say is true, although a thing of which it is hard for me to persuade you. Moreover, I am not accustomed to think that I deserve any punishment. Had I money I might have proposed to give you what I had, and have been none the worse. But you see that I have none, and can only ask you to proportion the fine to my means. However, I think that I could afford a minae, and therefore I propose that penalty; Plato, Crito, Critobulus, and Apollodorus, my friends here, bid me say thirty minae, and they will be the

sureties. Well then, say thirty minae, let that be the penalty; for that they will be ample security to you.

[The jury condemns Socrates to death by a vote of 360–141.]

Socrates Comments on his Sentence

Not much time will be gained, O Athenians, in return for the evil name which you will get from the detractors of the city, who will say that you killed Socrates, a wise man; for they will call me wise even although I am not wise when they want to reproach you. If you had waited a little while, your desire would have been fulfilled in the course of nature. For I am far advanced in years, as you may perceive, and not far from death…

The difficulty, my friends, is not in avoiding death, but in avoiding unrighteousness; for that runs faster than death. I am old and move slowly, and the slower runner has overtaken me, and my accusers are keen and quick, and the faster runner, who is unrighteousness, has overtaken them. And now I depart hence condemned by you to suffer the penalty of death, and they, too, go their ways condemned by the truth to suffer the penalty of villainy and wrong; and I must abide by my award - let them abide by theirs. I suppose that these things may be regarded as fated, - and I think that they are well.

…

Let us reflect in another way, and we shall see that there is great reason to hope that death is a good, for one of two things: - either death is a state of nothingness and utter unconsciousness, or, as men say, there is a change and migration of the soul from this world to another.

Now if you suppose that there is no consciousness, but a sleep like the sleep of him who is undisturbed even by the sight of dreams, death will be an unspeakable gain. For if a person were to select the night in which his sleep was undisturbed even by dreams, and were to compare with this the other days and nights of his life, and then were to tell us how many days and nights he had passed in the course of his life better and more pleasantly than this one, I think that any man, I will not say a private man, but even the great king, will not find many such days or nights, when compared with the others. Now if death is like this, I say that to die is gain; for eternity is then only a single night.

But if death is the journey to another place, and there, as men say, all the dead are, what good, O my friends and judges, can be greater than this? If indeed when the pilgrim arrives in the world below, he is delivered from the professors of justice in this world, and finds the true judges who are said to give judgment there, Minos and Rhadamanthus and Aeacus and Triptolemus, and other sons of God who were righteous in their own life, that pilgrimage will be worth making. What would not a man give if he might converse with Orpheus and Musaeus and Hesiod and Homer? Nay, if this be true, let me die again and again. I, too, shall have a wonderful interest in a place where I can converse with Palamedes, and Ajax the son of Telamon, and other heroes of old, who have suffered death through an unjust judgment; and there will be no small pleasure, as I think, in comparing my own sufferings with theirs. Above all, I shall be able to continue my search into true and false knowledge; as in this world, so also in that; I shall find out who is wise, and who pretends to be wise, and is not. What would not a man give, O judges, to be able to examine the leader of the great Trojan expedition; or Odysseus or Sisyphus, or numberless others, men and women too! What infinite delight would there be in conversing with them and asking them questions! For in that world they do not put a man to death for this; certainly not. For besides being happier in that world than in this, they will be immortal, if what is said is true.

Wherefore, O judges, be of good cheer about death, and know this of a truth - that no evil can happen to a good man, either in life or after death. He and

his are not neglected by the gods; nor has my own approaching end happened by mere chance. But I see clearly that to die and be released was better for me; and therefore the oracle gave no sign. For which reason also, I am not angry with my accusers, or my condemners; they have done me no harm, although neither of them meant to do me any good; and for this I may gently blame them.

Still I have a favor to ask of them. When my sons are grown up, I would ask you, O my friends, to punish them; and I would have you trouble them, as I have troubled you, if they seem to care about riches, or anything, more than about virtue; or if they pretend to be something when they are really nothing, - then reprove them, as I have reproved you, for not caring about that for which they ought to care, and thinking that they are something when they are really nothing. And if you do this, I and my sons will have received justice at your hands.

The hour of departure has arrived, and we go our ways—I to die, and you to live. Which is better God only knows.

❀ 1.5 "The Cave" ❀

Selections from The Republic
by Plato
Translated by Benjamin Jowett

✳ ✳

© andreiuc88/Shutterstock.com

Plato's book *The Republic* is a later work by Plato, probably more representative of Plato's views than those of Socrates, even though Socrates is the lead character in the dialogue. One of the most famous selections in the Republic is the allegory of The Cave, which is supposed to be an allegory for what a true philosopher does.

This selection on the Cave is preceded by a selection called "The Divided Line". Socrates uses the metaphor of a line for the relationship between reality and representation. We can see the shadows cast by animals and the animals which cast them; but Socrates thinks that animals we see are themselves the shadows. What are they supposed to be shadows of?

As you read this allegorical story, ask yourself these questions:

* What do you think the people in the cave symbolize?
* What do the shadows on the wall symbolize? What does the fire represent?
* Who does the person who leaves the cave represent?
* What do you think the 'sun' represents? What is the 'world' outside of the cave?
* What happens to the perhaps who returns to the cave? Why? Who might Plato have in mind with this allegory?

❖ ❖

Book VI

The Divided Line

[Socrates, Speaking to Glaucon]

Take a line which has been cut into two unequal parts, and divide each of them again in the same proportion, and suppose the two main divisions to answer, one to the visible and the other to the intelligible, and then compare the subdivisions in respect of their clearness and want of clearness, and you will find that the first section in the sphere of the visible consists of images. And by images I mean, in the first place, shadows, and in the second place, reflections in water and in solid, smooth and polished bodies and the like: Do you understand?

Yes, I understand.

Imagine, now, the other section, of which this is only the resemblance, to include the animals which we see, and everything that grows or is made.

Very good.

Would you not admit that both the sections of this division have different degrees of truth, and that the copy is to the original as the sphere of opinion is to the sphere of knowledge?

Most undoubtedly.

Next proceed to consider the manner in which the sphere of the intellectual is to be divided.

In what manner?

Thus:—There are two subdivisions, in the lower or which the soul uses the figures given by the former division as images; the enquiry can only be hypothetical, and instead of going upwards to a principle descends to the other end; in the higher of the two, the soul passes out of hypotheses, and goes up to a principle which is above hypotheses, making no use of images as in the former case, but proceeding only in and through the ideas themselves.

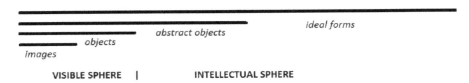

ideal forms

abstract objects

objects

images

VISIBLE SPHERE | **INTELLECTUAL SPHERE**

Book VII

The Cave

[Socrates—GLAUCON]

And now, I said, let me show in a figure how far our nature is enlightened or unenlightened: --Behold! human beings living in a underground den, which has a mouth open towards the light and reaching all along the den; here they have been from their childhood, and have their legs and necks chained so that they cannot move, and can only see before them, being prevented by the chains from turning round their heads. Above and behind them a fire is blazing at a distance, and between the fire and the prisoners there is a raised way; and you will see, if you look, a low wall built along the way, like the screen which marionette players have in front of them, over which they show the puppets.

I see.

And do you see, I said, men passing along the wall carrying all sorts of vessels, and statues and figures of animals made of wood and stone and various materials, which appear over the wall? Some of them are talking, others silent.

You have shown me a strange image, and they are strange prisoners.

Like ourselves, I replied; and they see only their own shadows, or the shadows of one another,

❀ ❀

which the fire throws on the opposite wall of the cave?

True, he said; *how could they see anything but the shadows if they were never allowed to move their heads?*

And of the objects which are being carried in like manner they would only see the shadows?

Yes, he said.

And if they were able to converse with one another, would they not suppose that they were naming what was actually before them?

Very true.

And suppose further that the prison had an echo which came from the other side, would they not be sure to fancy when one of the passers-by spoke that the voice which they heard came from the passing shadow?

No question, he replied.

To them, I said, the truth would be literally nothing but the shadows of the images.

That is certain.

And now look again, and see what will naturally follow it' the prisoners are released and disabused of their error. At first, when any of them is liberated and compelled suddenly to stand up and turn his neck round and walk and look towards the light, he will suffer sharp pains; the glare will distress him, and he will be unable to see the realities of which in his former state he had seen the shadows; and then conceive some one saying to him, that what he saw before was an illusion, but that now, when he is approaching nearer to being and his eye is turned towards more real existence, he has a clearer vision, -what will be his reply? And you may further imagine that his instructor is pointing to the objects as they pass and requiring him to name them, -will he not be perplexed? Will he not fancy that the shadows which he formerly saw are truer than the objects which are now shown to him?

Far truer.

And if he is compelled to look straight at the light, will he not have a pain in his eyes which will make him turn away to take and take in the objects of vision which he can see, and which he will conceive to be in reality clearer than the things which are now being shown to him?

True, he now

And suppose once more, that he is reluctantly dragged up a steep and rugged ascent, and held fast until he 's forced into the presence of the sun himself, is he not likely to be pained and irritated? When he approaches the light his eyes will be dazzled, and he will not be able to see anything at all of what are now called realities.

Not all in a moment, he said.

He will require to grow accustomed to the sight of the upper world. And first he will see the shadows best, next the reflections of men and other objects in the water, and then the objects themselves; then he will gaze upon the light of the moon and the stars and the spangled heaven; and he will see the sky and the stars by night better than the sun or the light of the sun by day?

Certainly.

Last of he will be able to see the sun, and not mere reflections of him in the water, but he will see him in his own proper place, and not in another; and he will contemplate him as he is.

Certainly.

He will then proceed to argue that this is he who gives the season and the years, and is the guardian of all that is in the visible world, and in a certain way the cause of all things which he and his fellows have been accustomed to behold?

Clearly, he said, he would first see the sun and then reason about him.

❀ ❀

And when he remembered his old habitation, and the wisdom of the den and his fellow-prisoners, do you not suppose that he would felicitate himself on the change, and pity them?

Certainly, he would.

And if they were in the habit of conferring honours among themselves on those who were quickest to observe the passing shadows and to remark which of them went before, and which followed after, and which were together; and who were therefore best able to draw conclusions as to the future, do you think that he would care for such honours and glories, or envy the possessors of them? Would he not say with Homer,

"Better to be the poor servant of a poor master, and to endure anything, rather than think as they do and live after their manner?"

Yes, he said, *I think that he would rather suffer anything than entertain these false notions and live in this miserable manner.*

Imagine once more, I said, such an one coming suddenly out of the sun to be replaced in his old situation; would he not be certain to have his eyes full of darkness?

To be sure, he said.

And if there were a contest, and he had to compete in measuring the shadows with the prisoners who had never moved out of the den, while his sight was still weak, and before his eyes had become steady (and the time which would be needed to acquire this new habit of sight might be very considerable) would he not be ridiculous? Men would say of him that up he went and down he came without his eyes; and that it was better not even to think of ascending; and if any one tried to loose another and lead him up to the light, let them only catch the offender, and they would put him to death.

No question, he said.

This entire allegory, I said, you may now append, dear Glaucon, to the previous argument; the prison-house is the world of sight, the light of the fire is the sun, and you will not misapprehend me if you interpret the journey upwards to be the ascent of the soul into the intellectual world according to my poor belief, which, at your desire, I have expressed whether rightly or wrongly God knows. But, whether true or false, my opinion is that in the world of knowledge the idea of good appears last of all, and is seen only with an effort; and, when seen, is also inferred to be the universal author of all things beautiful and right, parent of light and of the lord of light in this visible world, and the immediate source of reason and truth in the intellectual; and that this is the power upon which he who would act rationally, either in public or private life must have his eye fixed.

I agree, he said, *as far as I am able to understand you.*

Moreover, I said, you must not wonder that those who attain to this beatific vision are unwilling to descend to human affairs; for their souls are ever hastening into the upper world where they desire to dwell; which desire of theirs is very natural, if our allegory may be trusted.

Yes, very natural.

And is there anything surprising in one who passes from divine contemplations to the evil state of man, misbehaving himself in a ridiculous manner; if, while his eyes are blinking and before he has become accustomed to the surrounding darkness, he is compelled to fight in courts of law, or in other places, about the images or the shadows of images of justice, and is endeavouring to meet the conceptions of those who have never yet seen absolute justice?

Anything but surprising, he replied.

Any one who has common sense will remember that the bewilderments of the eyes are of two kinds,

and arise from two causes, either from coming out of the light or from going into the light, which is true of the mind's eye, quite as much as of the bodily eye; and he who remembers this when he sees any one whose vision is perplexed and weak, will not be too ready to laugh; he will first ask whether that soul of man has come out of the brighter light, and is unable to see because unaccustomed to the dark, or having turned from darkness to the day is dazzled by excess of light. And he will count the one happy in his condition and state of being, and he will pity the other; or, if he have a mind to laugh at the soul which comes from below into the light, there will be more reason in this than in the laugh which greets him who returns from above out of the light into the den.

That, he said, is a very just distinction.

But then, if I am right, certain professors of education must be wrong when they say that they can put a knowledge into the soul which was not there before, like sight into blind eyes.

They undoubtedly say this, he replied.

Whereas, our argument shows that the power and capacity of learning exists in the soul already; and that just as the eye was unable to turn from darkness to light without the whole body, so too the instrument of knowledge can only by the movement of the whole soul be turned from the world of becoming into that of being, and learn by degrees to endure the sight of being, and of the brightest and best of being, or in other words, of the good.

❧ 1.6 Enthusiasm ❧

Selections from "An Essay Concerning Human Understanding" by John Locke

❋ ❋

© Everett Historical/Shutterstock.com

John Locke (1632–1704) was a British philosopher who, because of his political and religious involvements, spent part of his life in exile in the Netherlands. Among his writings were his *Two Treatises on Government*, which had a significant impact on political thought in the North American colonies which eventually became the United States, as Locke played a role in the administration of these colonies. In addition, he wrote *The Reasonableness of Christianity*, where he argued that religious belief was consistent with rationality, and his *Letters Concerning Toleration*, where he promoted the separation of Church and State. His most influential philosophical work, however, was *An Essay Concerning Human Understanding*, from which this present selection is taken.[1]

By "Enthusiasm", Locke doesn't mean an excited or happy feeling. Instead, he means an individual's claim to know something by direct revelation from God, where the only evidence the individual has that what they have received is a revelation is that they have the belief that they have received a revelation. Locke argues that this violates a basic principle of *Epistemology*, the theory of knowledge. According to this principle, the degree of someone's confidence in a belief should always be in proportion to the degree of his or her evidence for that belief. Someone who has a belief is seeking after the truth, Locke says, so a belief should respond to evidence for what is or isn't true. This principle plays an important role in philosophy.

---

[1] Uzgalis, William, "John Locke", *The Stanford Encyclopedia of Philosophy* (Winter 2014 Edition), Edward N. Zalta (ed.)

Here are some questions to ask yourself as you read:

* What does Locke mean when talking about the love of truth for truth's sake? What is its "unerring mark"?

* What does assuming an authority to dictate the opinions of others indicate?

* Socrates in the Apology concludes that he knows nothing at all. How might Locke use his principle to instead claim that he does know some things after all?

* Why does Locke think his opponent's arguments are circular?

❀ ❀

§ 1. Love of truth necessary.

He that would seriously set upon the search of truth, ought in the first place to prepare his mind with a love of it. For he that loves it not, will not take much pains to get it, nor be much concerned when he misses it.

There is nobody in the commonwealth of learning, who does not profess himself a lover of truth; and there is not a rational creature that would not take it amiss to be thought otherwise of. And yet for all this, one may truly say, that there are very few lovers of truth for truth-sake, even amongst those who persuade themselves that they are so. How a man may know whether he be so in earnest, is worth inquiry: and I think there is one unerring mark of it, viz. the not entertaining any proposition with greater assurance, than the proofs it is built upon will warrant.

Whoever goes beyond this measure of assent, it is plain, receives not truth in the love of it; loves not truth for truth-sake, but for some other by-end. For the evidence that any proposition is true (except such as are self-evident) lying only in the proofs a man has of it, whatsoever degrees of assent he affords it beyond the degrees of that evidence, it is plain that all the surplusage of assurance is owing to some other affection, and not to the love of truth: it being as impossible, that the love of truth should carry my assent above the evidence there is to me that it is true, as that the love of truth should make me assent to any proposition for the sake of that evidence, which it has not, that it is true; which is in effect to love it as a truth, because it is possible or probable that it may not be true.

In any truth that gets not possession of our minds by the irresistible light of self-evidence, or by the force of demonstration, the arguments that gain it assent are the vouchers and gage of its probability to us; and we can receive it for no other, than such as they deliver it to our understandings. Whatsoever credit or authority we give to any proposition, more than it receives from the principles and proofs it supports itself upon, is owing to our inclinations that way, and is so far a derogation from the love of truth as such: which, as it can receive no evidence from our passions or interests, so it should receive no tincture from them.

§ 2. A forwardness to dictate, from whence.

The assuming an authority of dictating to others, and a forwardness to prescribe to their opinions, is a constant concomitant of this bias and corruption of our judgments. For how almost can it be otherwise, but that he should be ready to impose on another's belief, who has already imposed on his own? Who can reasonably expect arguments and conviction from him, in dealing with others, whose understanding is not accustomed to them in his dealing with himself? Who does violence to his own faculties, tyrannizes over his own mind, and usurps the prerogative that belongs to truth alone, which is to command assent by only its own authority, i. e. by and in proportion to that evidence which it carries with it.

§ 3. Force of enthusiasm.

Upon this occasion I shall take the liberty to consider a third ground of assent, which with some men has the same authority, and is as confidently relied on as either faith or reason; I mean enthusiasm: which laying by reason, would set up revelation without it. Whereby in effect it takes away both reason and revelation, and substitutes in the room of it the ungrounded fancies of a man's own brain, and assumes them for a foundation both of opinion and conduct.

§ 4. Reason and revelation.

Reason is natural revelation, whereby the eternal father of light, and fountain of all knowledge, communicates to mankind that portion of truth which he has laid within the reach of their natural faculties: revelation is natural reason enlarged by a new set of discoveries communicated by God immediately, which reason vouches the truth of, by the testimony and proofs it gives, that they come from God. So that he that takes away reason, to make way for revelation, puts out the light of both, and does much-what the same, as if he would persuade a man to put out his eyes, the better to receive the remote light of an invisible star by a telescope.

§ 5. Rise of enthusiasm.

Immediate revelation being a much easier way for men to establish their opinions, and regulate their conduct, than the tedious and not always successful labour of strict reasoning, it is no wonder that some have been very apt to pretend to revelation, and to persuade themselves that they are under the peculiar guidance of heaven in their actions and opinions, especially in those of them which they cannot account for by the ordinary methods of knowledge, and principles of reason.

Hence we see that in all ages, men, in whom melancholy has mixed with devotion, or whose conceit of themselves has raised them into an opinion of a greater familiarity with God, and a nearer admittance to his favour than is afforded to others, have often flattered themselves with a persuasion of an immediate intercourse with the Deity, and frequent communications from the Divine Spirit. God, I own, cannot be denied to be able to enlighten the understanding, by a ray darted into the mind immediately from the fountain of light; this they understand he has promised to do, and who then has so good a title to expect it as those who are his peculiar people, chosen by him, and depending on him?

§ 6. Enthusiasm.

Their minds being thus prepared, whatever groundless opinion comes to settle itself strongly upon their fancies, is an illumination from the spirit of God, and presently of divine authority: and whatsoever odd action they find in themselves a strong inclination to do, that impulse is concluded to be a call or direction from heaven, and must be obeyed; it is a commission from above, and they cannot err in executing it.

§ 7. Enthusiasm Defined

This I take to be properly enthusiasm, which, though founded neither on reason nor divine revelation, but rising from the conceits of a warmed or over-weening brain, works yet, where it once gets footing, more powerfully on the persuasions and actions of men, than either of those two, or both together: men being most forwardly obedient to the impulses they receive from themselves; and the whole man is sure to act more vigorously, where the whole man is carried by a natural motion. For strong conceit, like a new principle, carries all easily with it, when got above common sense, and freed from all restraint of reason, and check of reflection, it is heightened into a divine authority, in concurrence with our own temper and inclination.

§ 8. Enthusiasm mistaken for seeing and feeling.

Though the odd opinions and extravagant actions enthusiasm has run men into, were enough to warn them against this wrong principle, so apt to misguide them both in their belief and conduct; yet the love of something extraordinary, the ease and

❀ ❀

glory it is to be inspired, and be above the common and natural ways of knowledge, so flatters many men's laziness, ignorance, and vanity, that when once they are got into this way of immediate revelation, of illumination without search, and of certainty without proof, and without examination; it is a hard matter to get them out of it. Reason is lost upon them, they are above it: they see the light infused into their understandings, and cannot be mistaken; it is clear and visible there, like the light of bright sunshine; shows itself, and needs no other proof but its own evidence: they feel the hand of God moving them within, and the impulses of the spirit, and cannot be mistaken in what they feel. Thus they support themselves, and are sure reason hath nothing to do with what they see and feel in themselves: what they have a sensible experience of admits no doubt, needs no probation. Would he not be ridiculous, who should require to have it proved to him that the light shines, and that he sees it? It is its own proof, and can have no other. When the spirit brings light into our minds, it dispels darkness. We see it, as we do that of the sun at noon, and need not the twilight of reason to show it us. This light from heaven is strong, clear, and pure, carries its own demonstration with it; and we may as naturally take a glow-worm to assist us to discover the sun, as to examine the celestial ray by our dim candle, reason.

§ 9. Enthusiasm how to be discovered.

This is the way of talking of these men: they are sure, because they are sure: and their persuasions are right, because they are strong in them. For, when what they say is stripped of the metaphor of seeing and feeling, this is all it amounts to: and yet these similies so impose on them, that they serve them for certainty in themselves, and demonstration to others.

§ 10. Sober examination

But to examine a little soberly this internal light, and this feeling on which they build so much. These men have, they say, clear light, and they see; they have awakened sense, and they feel; this cannot, they are sure, be disputed them. For when a man says he sees or feels, nobody can deny it him that he does so. But here let me ask: this seeing, is it the perception of the truth of the proposition, or of this, that it is a revelation from God? This feeling, is it a perception of an inclination or fancy to do something, or of the spirit of God moving that inclination? These are two very different perceptions, and must be carefully distinguished, if we would not impose upon ourselves. I may perceive the truth of a proposition, and yet not perceive that it is an immediate revelation from God. I may perceive the truth of a proposition in Euclid, without its being or my perceiving it to be a revelation: nay, I may perceive I came not by this knowledge in a natural way, and so may conclude it revealed, without perceiving that it is a revelation from God; because there be spirits, which, without being divinely commissioned, may excite those ideas in me, and lay them in such order before my mind, that I may perceive their connexion. So that the knowledge of any proposition coming into my mind, I know not how, is not a perception that it is from God. Much less is a strong persuasion, that it is true, a perception that it is from God, or so much as true. But however it be called light and seeing, I suppose it is at most but belief and assurance: and the proposition taken for a revelation, is not such as they know to be true, but take to be true. For where a proposition is known to be true, revelation is needless: and it is hard to conceive how there can be a revelation to any one of what he knows already. If therefore it be a proposition which they are persuaded, but do not know, to be true, whatever they may call it, it is not seeing, but believing. For these are two ways, whereby truth comes into the mind, wholly distinct, so that one is not the other. What I see I know to be so by the evidence of the thing itself: what I believe I take to be so upon the testimony of another: but this testimony I must know to be given, or else what ground have I of believing? I must see that it is God that reveals this to me, or else I see nothing. The question then here is, how do I know that God is the revealer of this to me; that this impression is made upon my mind by his Holy Spirit, and that therefore I ought to obey it? If I know not this, how great soever the assurance is that I am possessed with, it is groundless; whatever light I pretend to, it is but enthusiasm. For whether the proposition supposed to be revealed, be in itself evidently true, or visibly probable, or by the natural ways of knowledge uncertain, the proposition that must be well grounded, and manifested to be true, is this, that God is the revealer of it, and that what I take to be a revelation is certainly put into my mind by him, and is not an illusion dropped in by some other spirit, or raised by my own fancy. For if I mistake not, these men receive it for true, because they presume God revealed it. Does it not then stand them upon, to examine on what grounds they presume it to be a revelation from God? or else all their confidence is mere presumption: and this light, they are so dazzled with, is nothing but an ignis fatuus that leads them constantly round in this circle; it is a revelation, because they firmly believe it, and they believe it, because it is a revelation.

§ 11. Enthusiasm fails of evidence, that the proposition is from God.

In all that is of divine revelation, there is need of no other proof but that it is an inspiration from God: for he can neither deceive nor be deceived.

But how shall it be known that any proposition in our minds is a truth infused by God; a truth that is revealed to us by him, which he declares to us, and therefore we ought to believe? Here it is that enthusiasm fails of the evidence it pretends to. For men thus possessed boast of a light whereby they say they are enlightened, and brought into the knowledge of this or that truth. But if they know it to be a truth, they must know it to be so, either by its own self-evidence to natural reason, or by the rational proofs that make it out to be so.

If they see and know it to be a truth, either of these two ways, they in vain suppose it to be a revelation. For they know it to be true the same way, that any other man naturally may know that it is so without the help of revelation. For thus all the truths, of what kind soever, that men uninspired are enlightened with, came into their minds, and are established there.

If they say they know it to be true, because it is a revelation from God, the reason is good: but then it will be demanded how they know it to be a revelation from God. If they say, by the light it brings with it, which shines bright in their minds, and they cannot resist: I beseech them to consider whether this be any more than what we have taken notice of already, viz. that it is a revelation, because they strongly believe it to be true.

For all the light they speak of is but a strong, though ungrounded persuasion of their own minds, that it is a truth. For rational grounds from proofs that it is a truth, they must acknowledge to have none; for then it is not received as a revelation, but upon the ordinary grounds that other truths are received: and if they believe it to be true, because it is a revelation, and have no other reason for its being a revelation, but because they are fully persuaded without any other reason that it is true; they believe it to be a revelation, only because they

❖ ❖

strongly believe it to be a revelation; which is a very unsafe ground to proceed on, either in our tenets or actions.

And what readier way can there be to run ourselves into the most extravagant errours and miscarriages, than thus to set up fancy for our supreme and sole guide, and to believe any proposition to be true, any action to be right, only because we believe it to be so?

The strength of our persuasions is no evidence at all of their own rectitude: crooked things may be as stiff and inflexible as straight: and men may be as positive and peremptory in errour as in truth.

How come else the untractable zealots in different and opposite parties? For if the light, which every one thinks he has in his mind, which in this case is nothing but the strength of his own persuasion, be an evidence that it is from God, contrary opinions have the same title to inspirations; and God will be not only the father of lights, but of opposite and contradictory lights, leading men contrary ways; and contradictory propositions will be divine truths, if an ungrounded strength of assurance be an evidence, that any proposition is a divine revelation.

§ 12. Firmness of persuasion no proof that any proposition is from God.

This cannot be otherwise, whilst firmness of persuasion is made the cause of believing, and confidence of being in the right is made an argument of truth. St. Paul himself believed he did well, and that he had a call to it when he persecuted the Christians, whom he confidently thought in the wrong: but yet it was he, and not they, who

were mistaken. Good men are men still, liable to mistakes; and are sometimes warmly engaged in errours, which they take for divine truths, shining in their minds with the clearest light.

§ 13. Light in the mind, what.

Light, true light, in the mind is, or can be nothing else but the evidence of the truth of any proposition; and if it be not a self-evident proposition, all the light it has, or can have, is from the clearness and validity of those proofs, upon which it is received. To talk of any other light in the understanding is to put ourselves in the dark, or in the power of the Prince of darkness, and by our own consent to give ourselves up to delusion to believe a lie. For if strength of persuasion be the light, which must guide us; I ask how shall any one distinguish between the delusions of Satan, and the inspirations of the Holy Ghost? He can transform himself into an angel of light. And they who are led by this son of the morning, are as fully satisfied of the illumination, i. e. are as strongly persuaded, that they are enlightened by the spirit of God, as any one who is so: they acquiesce and rejoice in it, are acted by it: and nobody can be more sure, nor more in the right (if their own strong belief may be judge) than they.

§ 14. Revelation must be judged of by reason.

He therefore that will not give himself up to all the extravagancies of delusion and errour, must bring this guide of his light within to the trial. God, when he makes the prophet, does not unmake the man. He leaves all his faculties in the natural state, to enable him to judge of his inspirations, whether they be of divine original or no. When he illuminates the mind with supernatural light, he does not extinguish that which is natural.

If he would have us assent to the truth of any proposition, he either evidences that truth by the usual methods of natural reason, or else makes it known to be a truth which he would have us assent to, by his authority; and convinces us that it is from him, by some marks which reason cannot be mistaken in. Reason must be our last judge and guide in every thing.

I do not mean that we must consult reason, and examine whether a proposition revealed from God can be made out by natural principles, and if it cannot, that then we may reject it: but consult it we must, and by it examine, whether it be a revelation from God or no. And if reason finds it to be revealed from God, reason then declares for it, as much as for any other truth, and makes it one of her dictates.

Every conceit that thoroughly warms our fancies must pass for an inspiration, if there be nothing but the strength of our persuasions, whereby to judge of our persuasions: if reason must not examine their truth by something extrinsecal to the persuasions themselves, inspirations and delusions, truth and falsehood, will have the same measure, and will not be possible to be distinguished.

§ 15. Belief no proof of revelation.

If this internal light, or any proposition which under that title we take for inspired, be conformable to the principles of reason, or to the word of God, which is attested revelation, reason warrants it, and we may safely receive it for true, and be guided by it

in our belief and actions; if it receive no testimony nor evidence from either of these rules, we cannot take it for a revelation, or so much as for true, till we have some other mark that it is a revelation, besides our believing that it is so. Thus we see the holy men of old, who had revelations from God, had something else besides that internal light of assurance in their own minds, to testify to them that it was from God. They were not left to their own persuasions alone, that those persuasions were from God; but had outward signs to convince them of the author of those revelations. And when they were to convince others, they had a power given them to justify the truth of their commission from heaven, and by visible signs to assert the divine authority of a message they were sent with. Moses saw the bush burn without being consumed, and heard a voice out of it. This was something besides finding an impulse upon his mind to go to Pharaoh, that he might bring his brethren out of Egypt: and yet he thought not this enough to authorize him to go with that message, till God, by another miracle of his rod turned into a serpent, had assured him of a power to testify his mission, by the same miracle repeated before them, whom he was sent to. Gideon was sent by an angel to deliver Israel from the Midianites, and yet he desired a sign to convince him that this commission was from God. These, and several the like instances to be found among the prophets of old, are enough to show that they thought not an inward seeing or persuasion of their own minds, without any other proof, a sufficient evidence that it was from God; though the scripture does not every where mention their demanding or having such proofs.

§ 16. What is not denied

In what I have said I am far from denying that God can, or doth sometimes enlighten men's minds in the apprehending of certain truths, or excite them

❖ ❖

to good actions by the immediate influence and assistance of the holy spirit, without any extraordinary signs accompanying it. But in such cases too we have reason and scripture, unerring rules to know whether it be from God or no.

Where the truth embraced is consonant to the revelation in the written word of God, or the action conformable to the dictates of right reason or holy writ, we may be assured that we run no risk in entertaining it as such; because though perhaps it be not an immediate revelation from God, extraordinarily operating on our minds, yet we are sure it is warranted by that revelation which he has given us of truth . . .

❀ 1.7 Unit 1 Study Guide ❀

* *

History of Western Thought *did not go over*

What did the followers of Confucius teach? How did his virtues differ from Socrates?

What did the Daoists teach? How did they differ from the Confucians?

What did Buddhism teach about the self?

What did Hebrew philosophy teach about God and the world?

Who were the Pre-Socratics?

What is the story of Thales and the olive presses supposed to show?

Who were Plato, Socrates, and Aristotle? How did they know each other? Who wrote what?

What did Stoics, Epicureans, and Skeptics teach?

How did Greek philosophy reach Western Europe after the dark ages?

Who were the major figures in Islamic thought?

In which era were Universities first founded, and why?

What events prompted the Enlightenment?

Who were the major figures in the Enlightenment?

What happened to philosophy after Kant?

How is philosophy different today than it was in the past?

Plato

What happened in the Apology?

How did Socrates defend himself against Meletus?

How did he interpret the words of the Oracle at Delphi?

What punishment did he offer to accept?

What happens in the Allegory of the Cave in the Republic?

Locke

What is "enthusiasm"?

What is the purpose of philosophy?

What's the unerring mark of the lover of truth for truth's sake?

Assuming an authority to dictate the opinions of others is a sign of what?

What is the relationship between "natural reason" and "divine revelation" for Locke?

How does evidence for something's rectitude (or truth) relate to the strength of our persuasions about it?

How should our degree of belief relate to the evidence?

Why does Locke think his opponents' arguments are circular?

How should a statistical average relate to my degree of belief, on Locke's principle?

From Locke's view, what's the best way to develop a character that allows others the freedom to hold their own opinions?

Guide to Philosophical Argument ("The Standard View")

What is and isn't a representation?

How does the meaning of a word relate to concepts?

What's a sentence? What's a proposition?

What is a fact? What is an opinion?

What's the difference between being vague and ambiguous? Vague and relative?

What's the difference between sense and reference?

What sorts of things might make a relative truth true?

How could a word have no referent?

How could a word have no sense?

How would two words have different senses but the same referent?

Why are all opinions either true or false?

If I have so much evidence that I must believe something, why could it still be false?

Harder Questions from the Guide to Philosophical Argument

How would you recognize an inductive argument?

How would you recognize a deductive argument?

How would you recognize an abductive argument?

What are the differences between logical and natural necessity/possibility, or between logical and epistemic necessity/possibility?

What does it mean for an argument to be valid?

What does it mean for an argument to be sound?

Test Yourself

1. Label these three arguments as deductive, inductive, or abductive:

   a. The last five times that it has rained, Jerry has noticed his co-worker Brenda bring a giant umbrella to work. Today, it is raining again. Jerry concludes that Brenda is going to bring a giant umbrella to work today. *inductive*

   b. Jerry notices that his co-worker Brenda keeps bringing an umbrella to work. He concludes that Brenda must be bringing the umbrella because she's worried it will rain, since this best explains his evidence. *~~deductive~~ abductive*

   c. Brenda notices that she has never seen Jerry bring an umbrella to work. She concludes that every time she has seen Jerry come to work, he had no umbrella with him. *deductive*

2. Label these (1) valid and sound; (2) valid but not sound; (3) invalid; or (4) sound, but not valid.

   (Hint: One of these four is impossible. Each of the remaining three will match one of the arguments below.)

   a.
   (P1) A plate of lasagna has more calories than a plate of tacos. (True)
   (P2) A plate of tacos has more calories than a plate of rice cakes. (True)
   (C) A plate of lasagna has more calories than a plate of rice cakes.

   Valid & sound

   b.
   (P1) Everyone in the gym has an iPod. (True)
   (P2) Larry has an iPod. (True)   *could be somewhere else*
   (C) Larry is in the gym.

   Valid & not sound

   c.
   (P1) All cats have worms. (False)
   (P2) Some cats scratch people. (True)
   (C) Some animals with worms scratch people.

   invalid

3. Use two of the following four premises to create a modus ponens argument for the conclusion that "Lily is sleepy".

   It is daytime.

   Lily is a dog.

   If it is daytime, Lily is sleepy.

   Either Lily is sleepy, or Lily is a dog.

Explain why your argument is valid, in terms of the definition of validity.

[Answers to 1: a. inductive, b. abductive, c. deductive. Answers to 2: a. (1), b. (3), c. (2).]

Overview: Unit 2
Knowledge

✳✳

2.1 What Can Be Known?

2.2 Plato, *Meno*, selections

2.3 Rene Descartes, *Meditations*, selections

2.4 John Locke, "Against Innate Ideas" (selections from *An Essay Concerning Human Understanding*)

2.5 David Hume, "The Origins of Ideas" (selections from *An Enquiry Concerning Human Understanding*)

2.6 George Berkeley, *Three Dialogues between Hylas and Philonous*, selections

2.7 Immanuel Kant, *The Critique of Pure Reason*, selections

2.8 Unit 2 Study Guide

In this unit we'll discuss what "knowledge" is, what we can know, and how we come to know it. This will lead us into the question of what our knowledge is about, which we'll follow from the skeptical doubts of Descartes through the Copernican Revolution of Kant.

By the end of this unit, you should be able to:

✳ Define "knowledge".

✳ Evaluate Descartes's doubts about reality and his source of certainty.

✳ Critique Descartes's arguments for the existence of God.

✳ Relate Descartes's belief in God to his solution to his doubts.

✳ Explain the argument for Plato's doctrine of recollection.

✳ Distinguish Empiricism and Rationalism.

* Summarize the views of Locke and Hume on knowledge and identify consequences of Hume's views.

* Define Berkeley's idealism.

* Explain how Kant's "Copernican revolution" in knowledge proposes to resolve the debate between rationalists and empiricists.

* Develop a coherent view on the foundations of knowledge.

❀ 2.1 What Can Be known? ❀

✳✳

In this unit, we'll be studying *Epistemology*, which is the Theory of Knowledge. Epistemology studies two closely related questions: *what do we know*, and *how do we know it*?

Later on in this course, we'll be discussing a number of controversial topics in metaphysics, like whether everything in the world is material or not, whether life after death is possible, whether God exists, whether there is free will, and whether there are any facts about morality. We could simply throw our personal views on these topics back and forth at one another, discussing what seems right to each of us and trying to persuade each other with forceful rhetoric, but that is unlikely to be a very productive conversation. So instead, before we try to tackle these topics, we need to be clear on what we can know, and how we can know it.

We'll begin by trying to come up with a definition of what "knowledge" means, so that we're all on the same page. Then, we'll discuss three major views about how we get knowledge: Rationalism, Empiricism, and Idealism. Finally, we'll see how Immanuel Kant tried to answer these questions, and come to some conclusions about how to answer questions about metaphysics in light of Kant.

A. **Three Types of Knowledge**

B. **How do we Define Knowledge?**

C. **Rationalism**

D. **Foundationalism**

E. **The First Meditation: The Method of Doubt.**

F. **The Second Meditation: The *A Priori***

G. **The Third Meditation—The Degrees of Reality argument**

H. **The Fifth Meditation—The Ontological Argument**

I. **The Fourth and Sixth Meditations—An External World**

J. **Locke's Empiricism**

K. **Hume's Empiricism**

L. **Berkeley's Idealism**

M. **Kant's Revolution**

N. **Metaphysics after Kant**

A. Three Types of Knowledge

The English word "know" has three different senses. Some languages use different words for each sense, but for whatever reason, English combines all three together into one word: knowledge.

The first sense of "know" is **propositional knowledge**, sometimes called "knowing that". For instance, when you say "I know *that* California is the most populous State in the Union" or "I know *that* children are troublesome", what you're claiming to know are propositions: the proposition that "California is the most populous State in the Union" and the proposition that "children are troublesome". These propositions are true or false depending on the facts. This is the kind of knowledge epistemology most often focuses on.

A second sense of "know" is **procedural knowledge**, sometimes called "knowing how". This has to do with knowing a skill or procedure to follow rather that a fact. For instance, when you say "I know how to change a tire" or "I know how to tie my shoes", the "know-how" you're claiming is an *ability* to do something rather than a set of propositions. Procedural knowledge is more than just propositional knowledge: We can imagine a person who reads a book about tires and has a lot of propositional knowledge, but still doesn't know how to change a tire in practice. Propositional knowledge is more than just procedural knowledge: We can imagine a child who knows how to tie his shoes, but who is still learning language and can't claim to know propositions like "the shoe is more secure when tied with a double knot".

A third sense of "know" is **knowledge by acquaintance**. This has to do with having encountered or come into contact with something or someone, rather than knowing facts about that thing or person. Many languages differentiate knowledge by acquaintance from propositional knowledge. In Spanish, for instance, one would use the verb *conocer* for this sense of knowledge, and *saber* for propositional knowledge. For instance, when I say "I know a good restaurant in Kentucky" or "I know Hillary Clinton", I am making a claim to be acquainted with the restaurant or the person, rather than claiming to know a specific proposition. I might know many of the facts about somebody without knowing them, or I might know somebody personally without actually knowing many facts about them.

For the rest of this unit, when talking about "knowledge" we'll be focused entirely on *propositional* knowledge, or "knowing that". However, it is an important distinction to keep in mind.

B. How do we Define Knowledge?

The traditional definitional of propositional knowledge is sometimes called the "JTB" view, because it gives us three *necessary conditions* of knowledge: knowledge must be a Justified True Belief.

The first traditional component of knowledge is **belief**. This might sound unusual to some people. In ordinary language, we usually think of a "belief" as something which *isn't* knowledge. "I believe that the meeting is tomorrow, but I don't know." However, think of

> Knowledge = Justified
> True
> Belief

it this way: In order to know something, I have to *at least* believe that it is true. It seems contradictory to say "I know that Phoenix is the Capital of Arizona, but I don't believe it." Of course, merely believing something isn't enough to count as knowing it: I believe a lot of things that I don't really know for certain. But at a minimum, I must believe it in order to know it.

The second traditional component of knowledge is **truth**. That is, you can't know something that isn't true. You might *think* you know something, and then later learn that it isn't true. For instance, you might think you know that Columbus was the first European to discover North America, and later learn that the Vikings preceded him. But in that case, you'd say "I *thought* I knew, but I didn't *truly* know." This is important to understand, because it means that just because someone says "I know", or people say about someone, "he knows", a person doesn't actually know unless the proposition they believe is true. It can't both be true that "John knows that Mary stole the car" and yet at the same time that "Jim knows that Mary didn't steal the car"—either Jim, or John, or both, merely think they know, but don't really know.

The third traditional component of knowledge is **justification**. This is the most difficult and debatable part of epistemology! Justification has to do with the reasons that someone believes what they do—not the "causes" that produced their belief, but the reasoning that justifies the belief. In order for a belief to be knowledge, it's traditionally held that a person must have sufficient *evidence* in favor of that belief. Think of it this way: Someone who makes a lucky guess, and turns out to be right, has a true belief. But someone who makes a lucky guess doesn't have knowledge. Suppose Hayden believes that a certain horse will win the Kentucky Derby, and places a bet, and wins. Hayden believed that the horse would win, and Hayden's belief was true. But Hayden didn't *know* the horse would win, unless he had special evidence (for instance, evidence that the Derby is rigged, or evidence that the other horses had been injured, or so on). If you don't have enough evidence, you don't have justification, and so you don't have knowledge.

Notice that the traditional definition of knowledge gives only necessary conditions of knowledge, but not sufficient conditions. It's not a complete definition. We know that something is missing, though it's hard to say what it is. Why aren't justification, truth, and belief enough for knowledge by themselves?

Remember the saying that a "stopped watch is right twice a day?" Suppose that the clock on the wall has been running just fine for a long time, but today the battery died. The hands are now stuck in the "11:00 a.m." position. Suppose Aimee walks into the room and sees the clock. Aimee forms the belief that it is 11:00 a.m., and it seems like she's justified in this belief: She has good evidence for it. Suppose also that, by a stroke of good luck, it is in fact 11:00 a.m. Aimee has a justified true belief that it is 11:00 a.m. But does she know that it's 11:00 a.m.? That doesn't seem right. It seems like she'd have believed the same thing even if it were 10:00 a.m.

So, it seems like there's something more to knowledge besides truth, belief, and evidence, like a connection of the right sort between someone's justification for a belief and what makes that belief true, something that rules out the chance of being right by pure luck. It's hard to say exactly what it is, and epistemologists debate it. But for our class, we'll put this issue a side.

Instead, we're going to focus on two key questions about justification:

1. What **kinds of evidence** are there that allow something to count as knowledge?

2. **How certain** does our justification have to be for something to count as knowledge?

We'll start with the first question.

C. Rationalism

Three kinds of evidence are relatively uncontroversial. Most people tend to agree that we can get evidence through perception, memory, and testimony. All three involve some kind of experience we have, either through our senses or through our ability to introspect. These are called **empirical** forms of evidence, meaning that they depend on sensory experience.

> **Empirical** knowledge can only be justified by sensory experience.

* **Perception** includes the evidence we get through sight, hearing, touch, and our sense of our own bodies. For example, when I see a bird flying in the air, this is a good reason to believe that there is a bird flying in the air.

* **Testimony** involves the evidence we get from other people who know something and tell us about it. For example, if someone tells me that they saw a bird outside, then unless I have some reason to think this person is lying to me, I have a good reason to believe that there is a bird outside. Reading a book, like this textbook, also is a source of testimonial evidence.

* **Memory** involves the evidence I get through recollection of something I learned in the past. Most of the knowledge I have depends partly on memory. For instance, I'm not currently looking at the moon, but I have a good reason to believe that the moon exists, because I remember having perceived the moon many times and haven't heard about it from many people.

However, there are many things that people ordinarily claim to know, which it seems hard to justify through perception, memory, or testimony. For example, it seems like we know that it would be unjust to punish someone for a crime she didn't commit, and we know that the fairest way to distribute a pizza with eight equal slices between four people who split the cost of the pizza is to give each person two slices. However, where did we get our understanding of justice and fairness?

Thinking about this question leads many people to become skeptical about moral claims, as we'll see more in Unit 6. However, Plato wanted to say that we knew moral claims, including claims about justice and fairness. So, Plato, through the character Socrates in his dialogue *Meno*, makes a proposal.

Socrates makes an argument to establish that there are some things we all agree that we know, but where our knowledge is potentially independent of sensory experience. Later philosophers will call this *a priori* knowledge, although Plato didn't use this terminology. Instead of being justified by perception, memory or testimony, *a priori* knowledge is justified by a kind of pure reasoning or "rational insight". We know certain things *a priori* simply by reflecting and reasoning logically about the world, and this knowledge is justified in a way that it would be very hard for any empirical evidence to convince us that it is false.

The example which Socrates uses to argue that we must accept that there is knowledge justified independently of sensory experience is our knowledge of mathematics. Nearly everyone agrees that we know truths about geometry and arithmetic. However, what justifies us in thinking we know about them?

> *A Priori* knowledge can be justified independently of sensory experience

Socrates is in a dialogue with Meno, who has a young boy as a slave. Meno's slave had not received any formal education and Meno presumed that the boy knew nothing about geometry. However, through a short conversation with the boy, only asking the boy questions and having the boy reason for himself, Socrates was able to bring the boy to a point where he could deduce basic truths of geometry entirely on his own.

You can substitute Meno's slave in the argument with yourself. You think you know something about mathematics. But what justifies you in believing this?

It can't be perception, because you don't literally see or hear or smell numbers or formulas. You've never seen a perfectly round circle or a square with perfectly straight lines, since there is always a margin in error in drawings. Try to imagine seeing something that would lead you to doubt that 2 + 2 = 4. What could possibly do that? Remember that mathematics doesn't automatically apply to every situation in our physical world. For example, two cups of sugar placed in two cups of boiling water doesn't produce four cups of sugar-water: the sugar dissolves in the water, and the result is closer to three cups. Observing this has never caused humanity to doubt that 2 + 2 = 4; instead, it's caused humanity to develop theories of chemistry. If you saw an experiment that seemed to defy the rules of math, you'd ask about what law of physics explained the relationship, not whether math had been disproven.

It can't be testimony, because even if testimony gives you a reason to believe a mathematical truth at first, *once you understand for yourself* what the mathematical claim means, you no longer rely on the original source of testimony as evidence. Think of it this way. You might think at first that your evidence for mathematical truths is the testimony of your elementary school teachers. But suppose that you were to learn today that the school you went to had been infiltrated by a galactic doomsday cult in order to promote its unusual belief system, according to which the earth was flat and that most events in history were the work of reptilian aliens. On learning this, you might start to wonder about most of the things you learned in school. You might talk to a historian to learn whether Woodrow Wilson really was a shape-shifting lizard person like you were told growing up, and you might even travel around the world to prove to yourself that it was round. But, even though most of the things your teachers said were false and involved indoctrinating you, would you doubt the things they taught you about arithmetic? How would you go about proving to yourself that what they said was right?

The only option remaining is that the evidence your knowledge of mathematics ultimately depends on is memory. But it can't be a memory of some perception or testimony you've had in this life, because we've already seen that your justification depends on neither perception nor testimony. So, Socrates now draws a conclusion about where *a priori* knowledge comes from:

1. All knowledge depends on perception, testimony, and memory.
2. Meno's slave has a knowledge of mathematics.
3. Meno's slave's knowledge of mathematics does not depend on perception.
4. Meno's slave's knowledge of mathematics does not depend on testimony.
5. Meno's slave's knowledge of mathematics does not depend on memories of experiences in this life.

C. Meno's slave's knowledge of mathematics depends on memories of experiences in a previous life.

Plato concludes that prior to this life, our souls lived in the realm of the forms. During this life, we gradually come to recollect what we learned in that prior life—and so when we experience that sudden "aha!" moment of understanding a mathematical principle or geometric theorem for the first time, what is happening is that we are remembering what we previously experienced in the realm of the forms.

If your knowledge of mathematics isn't empirical—or, if it is "empirical" only in the sense that it comes from recollection of a past life, as Socrates thought, but it's unquestionable that you know mathematics, then this makes room for other types of non-empirical knowledge. Socrates concludes that this makes room for knowledge of the nature of justice.

Plato doesn't distinguish between the claim that a belief is *justified* by something other than sensory experience (*a priori*) from the claim that a belief is *caused* by something other than sensory experience (innate knowledge, through recollection of a past life). However, while most contemporary philosophers would reject Plato's story of the soul's pre-existence in the realm of the forms, many would still accept that we have some *a priori* justified knowledge of some things such as mathematics, metaphysics, and morality, since this knowledge can't be empirical.

D. Foundationalism

Plato's offers an answer to our first question, the question about what kinds of evidence there are. Plato arguesis that there is a kind of evidence besides empirical evidence that allows something to count as knowledge—the evidence obtained through pure reasoning, the *a priori*. The second question we wanted to answer was this: how certain does our evidence have to be for something to count as knowledge? Descartes thought that our knowledge had to rest on a basis that was absolutely certain, without any possibility of doubt. This view is called foundationalism.

Remember that on the traditional definition of knowledge, in order to have knowledge, you have to have a justified belief. For a belief to be justified, you have to have a reason for it. Further, your reasons for a belief had better be more certain, not less certain, than the beliefs they justified. You can't, for instance, say that the reason you are 90% sure that Clinton will win the election is that you're 60% sure she'll get the most votes. So:

(1)   If I have knowledge, every belief must be justified by some reason more certain than it.

But what is a reason? The reason I believe that Donald Trump is rich is that I've heard people say that he's rich. But that reason is actually just another belief: I believe that I've heard people say that he's rich. Why do to believe that? Well, the reason is that I remember hearing people say that. But that reason is also a belief: I believe that I remember hearing people say that Donald Trump is rich. Why do I believe that? Well . . . I suppose the reason is that my memory is reliable. But that's also a belief: I believe that my memory is reliable. (But why do I believe that?). In any case, it seems like every reason is a belief:

(2)   Every reason is a belief.

But it also seems like we can potentially go on endlessly through this chain of reasons, asking for the reason for each reason, with no end in sight!

So, we can construct the following argument:

Belief

Reason

(1)   If I have knowledge, every belief must be justified by some reason more certain than it.

(2)   Every reason is a belief.

Reason

(C)   If I have knowledge, every belief must be justified by some belief which is more certain, which is justified by some belief which is yet more certain, and which is justified by some . . . (from 1 and 2).

Reason

The trouble is that none of us has an infinite mind! So it seems really implausible that each of us has an infinite chain of reasons which never ends. The world might contain infinite explanations for why things are the case, but surely our minds don't contain infinite chains of evidence for why we believe what we do. So if our chain of justification isn't going to continue infinitely, it seems like we have two options.

Option 1: Our reasons terminate in a basic *foundational* belief that justifies all other beliefs, or
Option 2: Some of our reasons *justify themselves*—that is, our chain of reasoning is ultimately circular.

Some people accept Option 2, a position called "Coherentism". But many people find it troubling to think that our reasons for believing what we do are ultimately circular. It seems like circular reasoning is supposed to be *bad* reasoning! Those who hold instead that there must be some foundational "rock bottom" to our system of beliefs, which justifies everything else, choose Option 1 and are called "foundationalists".

Now, this foundational set of beliefs that goes on to support and justify all of our other beliefs had better be justified itself. We'd better have more evidence for the foundational belief than for anything else, because if the foundation is uncertain, everything build on it will be too. So the challenge is to answer this question:

What sorts of beliefs do we have the right to be 100% certain about?

This is where we first encounter Rene Descartes, a philosopher who wrote in the seventeenth century, at the end of the Scholastic era of philosophy and the beginning of what is often called the *Enlightenment*. Whereas those before him had rested their foundational beliefs on the authority of tradition handed down from the past, Descartes concluded that the foundation of our knowledge rested on each individual thinking for himself or herself. The work in which he did this, included in your Source Texts for this Unit, is called the *Meditations*.

There are Six Meditations, in which Descartes progresses through his reasoning by engaging in a kind of conversation with himself. Don't be confused by the fact that Descartes seems to disagree with himself in the Meditations! He's carrying on a conversation with himself, playing both roles in the dialogue, inviting you to reason along with him as he comes to his conclusion. In each Meditation, he'll conclude something different, which provides the building block for the next meditation.

E. The First Meditation: The Method of Doubt

In the First Meditation, Descartes begins by trying to doubt everything that he previously thought he knew. Why does he do this? He does this because he wants to discover what the foundation for his knowledge is. Whatever he can't possibly bring himself to doubt will be 100% certain, and that will serve as his new foundation.

He begins by noting that his senses have deceived him. For example, you might have once looked down a long desert highway in the summer and noticed a puddle of water ahead in the distance—but when you got to the spot, the water had "disappeared" and moved on ahead of you. What you saw was a *mirage*. There really was no water. Your senses had deceived you. Now, it's "not prudent to trust those who have deceived us even once", so why do we trust our senses?

However, Descartes notes that this isn't enough reason to doubt everything he knows, because our senses generally only deceive us about things that are very small or far away. Descartes can't doubt that he's seated in his armchair by the fire penning these words at this very moment—that seems impossible to doubt.

Or is it? Descartes then brings to mind that he's had very vivid dreams before—dreams that felt and seemed every bit as real as the experience he's having right now of sitting by the fire. Couldn't he be dreaming all of this up? Couldn't everything in his entire life have been a dream?

However, this still isn't enough reason to doubt everything he knows, Descartes thinks. It's enough reason to doubt *most* of the things he thinks he knows, but not everything. After all, even in his dreams, there are certain fixed truths which it seems impossible to even imagine being false—truths like arithmetic and geometry. Can you imagine a four-sided triangle, or can you imagine five things being six things? Not even in your wildest dreams!

However, then Descartes considers one last possibility, and this leads him to doubt everything he knows. He considers the possibility that his entire existence has been an elaborate act of deception!

Nothing he's encountered in the past, present, or future has been real. Even when he thinks seemingly clear thoughts about mathematics, he's being deceived to think these are certainly true, when they're not. Descartes considers three ways this could be the case:

(a) It could be that an omnipotent god-like being created him, and this being deceives him.

(b) It could be that his mind is the product of random chance events, and thus unreliable.

(c) It could be that an evil demon "of the utmost power and cunning" is deceiving him.

If it helps you to understand Descartes, rather than imagining the evil demon deceiving you about everything and planting thoughts in your head, you might instead imagine the possibility that your mind is plugged into an elaborate simulated reality by some strange alien species that you remain blissfully unaware of (movies with this theme abound). In that world, everything you thought you knew wouldn't be true after all. So you wouldn't really be certain of anything!

Hence, Descartes ends the first meditation by doubting everything he knows. Again, it's important to note that he does *not* do this because he *actually* doubts that there is an external world. Rather, he's using doubt as a *tool* to discover the one thing that he can't doubt.

F. The Second Meditation: The A Priori

In the Second Meditation, Descartes find that one thing he can't doubt. Can you guess out what it is?

Try to go through all of the things you believe. Is there any of them that you can't doubt? Is there any of them which you could still be confident were true even if all of your thoughts actually were implanted by an evil demon, or part of a massive simulation?

What's the one thing you can't doubt?

You can't doubt that you're doubting.

You can't doubt that you're having an experience, right now, of thinking about something. You can doubt that the textbook you're reading is real, that you're really in a philosophy class, that there really ever was a person by the name of "Descartes", or even that *you* really are the sort of person you think you are. But you can't doubt that you're thinking.

So, Descartes has found the foundation of all of his beliefs: *I'm thinking this thought right now.*

From this, something logically follows. If I'm thinking, then of course, I must also *exist.* This is the root of Descartes's famous "Cogito": I think, therefore I am.

Of course, you don't know much about who you are, yet. You might not have been born when you thought you were, or you might not have the body you think you have. You might be 1,000 years old, or 10,000,000 years old. You might not be human. But there is one thing you know about yourself: *you are a thinking thing*.

An "Essential" property of a thing is a property which it is logically necessary that it have. If a property is essential to something, it is logically impossible for it to not have it—a contradiction. What Descartes believes he has found is one of his essential properties. He can't conceive of himself not thinking, and so he concludes it is logically impossible that he is not thinking. So his essential nature is just that: a thinking thing.

Descartes then forms a conclusion about what he is *not.* Consider this argument:

(1) I cannot conceive of myself without a mind.

(2) I can conceive of myself with a different body.

(3) Something is essential to me if and only if I can conceive of myself without it.

(C) I am essentially a mind, not a body.

Descartes's argument is simple. You might think your body is essential to you, but it isn't—you could have had a very different body, or perhaps no body at all. But you mind is essentially to you. Now, you can conceive of a body without a mind, and a mind without a body, Descartes thinks. So being a mind and being a body aren't essentially linked. They're two different fundamental kinds of things—two different *substances*. This view—that the mind and the body are not the same —is called "dualism", and we'll look into it more in Unit 3.

Descartes uses the same method to argue that he knows the essential natures of many other things, *even though he doesn't know whether they actually exist*. Think of it this way: unicorns don't exist. You've never seen one. But you do know something about unicorns: you know that, by definition, unicorns are horse-like creatures with one horn. A two-horned unicorn is a contradiction. So, you know something about the essential nature of unicorns, even though you don't know they exist.

Descartes uses the example of wax. He doesn't know whether the candle in front of him exists or not. But he does know his *idea* of the candle. And from that idea, he knows what's not essential to the candle: its smell, shape, or color. He can imagine the wax in the candle having a different smell, shape, or color. Instead, what is essential to the candle wax is that it takes up space and time, and that it's changeable in shape. He knows this about the essence of wax, even if he doesn't know whether or not wax exists.

This next layer on Descartes's foundation is sometimes called the set of *a priori* truths. *A priori* truths are truths which are supposedly justified by *reason alone*, independent of sensory experience. We can know these truths about the natures of unicorns and wax simply through reasoning about them, even if we don't assume we've actually had experiences of wax or unicorns. This makes Descartes a *rationalist*, which we'll discuss more in a little bit.

This is better than doubting everything. By the end of the Second Meditation, I know that I'm thinking, that I exist, and that I'm a thinking thing, and I know the essences of things—it's still not much. I don't actually know whether there's a real world out there! To prove that, Descartes concludes that the next layer must involve the existence of God.

G. The Third Meditation—The Degrees of Reality argument

Descartes offers two arguments for the existence of God, one in the third meditation, and one in the fifth meditation. The fifth meditation argument is called the "Ontological Argument", and we'll study it in more detail in Unit 5, because it is a very common argument in philosophy for the existence of God. The third meditation argument is much harder to understand, and it is not as common for people to use it.

Notice that Descartes has to argue that God exists without appealing to the existence of anything besides himself. He can't argue that God had to exist to create the world, for instance, because he doesn't know that the world exists yet! Likewise he can't base his argument on something like the belief that the world shows signs of intelligent design, or from the experiences of those in different religions, because these also presuppose that there is a world at all. So, instead, he has to base his argument simply on *a priori*, definitional truths.

The Third Meditation Argument goes like this:

(1) I have the idea of infinite perfection at the highest degree of reality.

(2) Every idea comes from somewhere.

(3) I couldn't get the idea of infinite perfection at the highest degree of reality from anything that wasn't infinite perfection at the highest degree of reality.

(C) I must get the idea of infinite perfection at the highest degree of reality from infinite perfection at the highest degree of reality

Let's consider each premise. In the first premise, Descartes is claiming to have three ideas. First, he's claiming to have the idea of infinite perfection. One component of this is *infinity*, which is an idea that we get from mathematics. The second component is *perfection*, which for Descartes doesn't have to do with "flawlessness" as we might think of perfection, but rather has to do with being "great" in every possible way that a thing can be great. The third is the notion of the *highest degree of reality*. If you think back to Plato's *Republic*, Plato was arguing for a degree of reality higher than our own. Descartes is employing this idea: we can conceive of a reality higher than our own, or even a reality at the highest degree possible.

You may not think that infinite perfection at the highest degree of reality exists. That's fine—Descartes isn't asking you to assume it. He's only asking you to assume that you have the *idea* of infinite perfection at the highest degree of reality. That doesn't require that you be able to have a mental picture of infinite perfection, or that you think you're able to comprehend or grasp infinite perfection—just like one might have the idea of the world's tallest mountain without ever having seen the world's tallest mountain or comprehending much about it. It only requires that you can combine the three ideas together into one idea and say, "I guess I understand that idea."

Someone might say, "I don't think the idea of 'God' is the idea of 'infinite perfection at the highest degree of reality' ". For instance, not everyone might conceive of God in the same way, and not everyone might think of an infinitely perfect being as something they'd call "God". But that wouldn't bother Descartes. He's not concerned with what people *call* "God". He's concerned with whether or not there exists infinite perfection at the highest degree of reality. For simplicity, he'll call this "God", but if it helps to use a different word, that's perfectly fine with him.

The second premise is something Descartes thinks is a logical truth: all ideas must come from *somewhere*. Of course, they might come from the evil demon! But they must come from something.

Let's look at the last premise. Here, Descartes is claiming that this idea couldn't have come from anything else in his experience. Everything he experiences is finite: so where did he get the idea of the infinite? Everything he experiences is imperfect: so where did he get the idea of perfection? Everything he experiences is at this level of reality: so where did he get the idea of something at the highest level of reality?

The last premise is the one most people challenge. Although it might seem *plausible*, that's not good enough for Descartes's standards. Descartes needs a proof for God's existence that can't possibly be doubted. And it does seem like people can doubt the claims in premise 2. We might think that we can get the idea of the infinite from the finite, the idea of the perfect from the imperfect, or the idea of a higher level of reality from our own. If we can doubt premise 2, then Descartes can't use it as a foundation for knowledge.

H. The Fifth Meditation—The Ontological Argument

Because the third meditation argument seems not to meet Descartes's high standard for knowledge—that our foundational knowledge must be absolutely certain—Descartes offers a different argument for the existence of God in the Fifth Meditation. This argument is supposed to be simple and intuitive.

I know the logically necessary properties of things through how I can and can't conceive of them. I know that wax is necessarily material, because I can't conceive of immaterial wax. I know that wax is not necessarily rose-scented, because I can conceive of wax that doesn't smell like roses. I know that I am necessarily a thinking thing, because I can't conceive of myself not thinking. I know that I'm not necessarily 6-feet tall, because I can imagine myself not being 6 feet tall.

Most things in the world, I can conceive of while imagining they don't exist. For example, I can't conceive of a mountain existing without a valley (or other area below it) existing. But I can conceive of a mountain not existing. I can conceive of a valley not existing. I can conceive of a winged horse, but I know winged horses don't exist.

But now, let me try to conceive of an *infinitely perfect being* not existing. Since I have the concept of infinity, and the concept of perfection, I have the concept of an infinitely perfect being. It seems at first like I can imagine such a being not existing, much like the winged horse. However, when I think about it further, I realize that this would be a contradiction. It's more perfect to exist than to not exist. For an infinitely perfect being not to exist would be for an infinitely perfect being not to be perfect—much like a mountain existing without any valley below it. So, I can't conceive of an infinitely perfect being as not existing. This infinitely perfect being necessarily exists. The word "God" is one name we use for this infinitely perfect being.

1. I have the concept of an infinitely perfect being.

2. It is more perfect to exist than not to exist.

3. *Assume it is possible for an infinitely perfect being to not exist.*

4. Then it is possible for an infinitely perfect being to be less perfect than it could be. (1, 2, 3) CONTRADICTION

C. It is not possible for an infinitely perfect being to not exist.

Which premise could we challenge in the argument? The argument is much stronger than the argument Descartes gave in the third meditation. It no longer depends on any premises which seem easy to doubt.

It seems like our only options are to challenge premise 1 or premise 2. Someone might challenge premise 1 by arguing that I don't have a clear and distinct concept of infinite perfection in the way I have a clear concept of a mountain or of wax. What is "perfection"? Is it clear? Alternatively, someone might challenge premise 2 by arguing that some things which don't exist are better for not existing. For example, it seems like it's better for World War III to not exist than for it to exist. Or it seems like we can conceive of a world-wide plague that wipes out half the human population, but it is better for this to not exist than to exist. Finally, some have objected that even though the argument appears both valid and sound, it can't be, because the same style of proof might be used to prove the existence of something Descartes wouldn't accept, like an infinitely wicked being, or an infinitely perfect prime number.

However, if Descartes's argument can be defended from these objections, then Descartes has the proof he needed for the existence of God. Since God is infinitely perfect, God is all powerful, all knowing, and all good. And an all-good being wouldn't want Descartes to be radically deceived about everything, and an all powerful and all knowing being could prevent it, so the existence of God guarantees that Descartes can trust his senses after all.

I. The Fourth and Sixth Meditations—An External World

Now Descartes is ready to build his foundation and reverse all of the doubts he raised in the first Meditation. He intends to prove that we do know that there is an external world outside of our minds after all.

Descartes foundation could be mapped out like this.

I can't doubt that I'm thinking, therefore:

⇒ I know I am thinking.

⇒ I know I exist.

⇒ I know I have the concepts that I have.

⇒ I know the necessary natures of things *a priori* through my concepts.

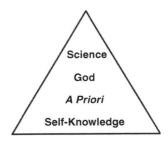

⇒ I know that I have the concept of infinite perfection.

⇒ I know that infinite perfection (God) necessarily exists.

⇒ I know that God is all powerful and all knowing and all good.

⇒ I know that God would not allow me to be deceived by no fault of my own.

⇒ I know that I can trust my senses.

⇒ I know there is an external world.

⇒ the findings of the sciences can be trusted.

How do I know that there is an external world? How do I know that I'm *not* being deceived by an evil demon, and that life is not a dream? According to Descartes, I know these things because I know that an all-good, all-powerful God would not permit me to be deceived this drastically. God might permit me to be deceived in *small* ways, says Descartes. For instance, God might permit me to be deceived in cases where I willingly allow my will to over-reach the scope of my intellect by forming beliefs without adequate reasons for those beliefs. Or, God might permit me to be deceived in a small way in order that some good might come about. But God would not permit me to be radically deceived. My knowledge of God's existence depends only on the *a priori* knowledge I have of my own concepts as a thinking thing, not on any assumptions about an external world.

Descartes has thus achieved a foundation for his scientific knowledge of the external world through his senses. Descartes thought that scientific knowledge wasn't in conflict with believing in God, but in fact was founded on the knowledge that God would not let us be deceived—unless we willingly deceived ourselves by believing more than our evidence justified. He further thought that the foundation of both science and the knowledge of God was rationality—our knowledge of *a priori* truths about the essential natures of things. Finally, all three were founded on our knowledge of ourselves. The individual and his conscious experiences were now at the center of the picture for philosophy.

J. Locke's Empiricism

John Locke objected both to Descartes's Rationalism and to his Foundationalism.

Against Descartes's Rationalism, Locke argued that if we believed there was *a priori* knowledge, then we had to believe there were *innate ideas* which we were born with, independently of experience—but there were no innate ideas.

Against Descartes's Foundationalism, Locke argued that we didn't need a standard of 100% certainty to have knowledge; all we needed was a reasonable probability of being correct.

First, Locke argues that there can be no innate knowledge. His argument is roughly as follows. "Innate knowledge" could mean either (A) knowledge that we know before we know it, or (B) knowledge that is "universally assented" to, so that everyone agrees to it, or (C) knowledge that everyone would agree to under the right circumstances. However:

1. It's contradictory to claim that we know anything before we know it, so (A) is false.
2. There is nothing which is universally assented to, so (B) is false.
3. Empirical knowledge is *also* something that "everyone would agree to under the right circumstances", so (C) is false.
4. If there is innate knowledge then either (A) or (B) or (C) is true.
C. There is no innate knowledge.

Locke thinks that people are speaking thoughtlessly about there being "innate" knowledge, when in fact we don't have a good grasp on what "innate knowledge" even means. Does it mean having knowledge before we're born? How could we have knowledge before existing? Does it mean having knowledge before we become aware that we have knowledge? That would amount to knowing something before we know it.

Perhaps, it means instead that there are some things which *everybody* around the globe and at all ages agrees to. It is hard enough, Locke points out, to find something that every culture and society in the world will agree with maybe certain logical truths like "everything either is or isn't so". But even in those cases, there are some people—children and some people with severe mental disabilities—who won't agree to "everything either is or isn't so".

Maybe we want to say that *under the right conditions*, like being able to understand the meanings of the terms, being of an adequate age, and so on, everyone would agree to these *a priori* claims. However, the same can be said equally of all empirical claims: everyone *in the right conditions* would agree with them. The reason people don't agree on empirical claims is that we aren't all having the same experiences under in the same conditions.

Locke thinks that if we don't have innate knowledge—beliefs that are independent of experience—then we can't have *a priori* knowledge, or justification that is possibly independent of experience. This would undermine Descartes's claim to know truths about the essential natures of things, including God, *a priori*, and so it would undermine his foundationalism also.

But Locke doesn't think that this should worry us. We may not have a single foundation for all of our beliefs—the only foundation for our beliefs is experience of the world around us and our ability to reflect on what we experience. This is less than 100% certain, because we *can* often be deceived by our senses and by what people tell us. However, Locke thinks that knowledge doesn't require 100% certainty. All knowledge requires is *enough* evidence—enough for a strong probability that we are right, even if it is still possible that we are wrong.

Thus, Locke thinks it is possible to know something, and to also know that you could be wrong. Do you think it is possible to truly know something even though your evidence doesn't rule out every chance that you are wrong?

K. Hume's Empiricism

Descartes thought that we knew about the existence of God, of substance, and of a real world outside of our minds *a priori*. Locke also thought that we knew these things, but he thought we knew them empirically. Hume, however, didn't think we could know these things at all.

In fact, many of the things we claim to know, Hume doesn't think we know. According to Hume, we don't know anything through induction, which is the source of most of our scientific knowledge obtained through experimentation. We don't know that we have an essential self, as we'll see Hume argue in Unit 4. There is nothing about the essential natures of things that we now at all; we only know our own words and concepts for things.

The most striking case which Hume gives of something we might think we know, but we don't know empirically, is *causation*. Cause and effect are part of what the sciences are supposed to study. But do we actually *observe* cause and effect relationships? Imagine a case in billiards where the cue ball hits the 8-ball and the 8-ball goes into the pocket.

1. If empiricism is true, then anything we know is either something we directly observe (Hume calls this a "matter of fact") or else it is a logical necessity (Hume calls this a "relation of ideas").

2. The 8-ball logically *could have* started flying when hit by the cue ball, without contradiction, so it is not a logical necessity that it move in the direction the cue ball was going.

3. We do not directly observe the cue ball cause the 8-ball to move forward.

C. We don't know anything about cause and effect.

Premise 1 is just a statement of empiricism, which Locke would agree with. Premise 2 simply states that it is not part of the definition of the terms that a cue ball makes an 8-ball move forward. Premise 3 might seem hard to understand. But think about it: do we literally *see* the cue ball *cause* the 8-ball to move? What does causation smell like, look like, or sound like? What we literally see is just a series of images, like snapshots, almost like an animated film. But the frames in an animated film don't actually cause other events to happen. So how do we know that the cue ball causes the 8-ball to do what it does?

You might reply that we know about cause and effect through inductive arguments. We notice that a certain pattern regularly occurs in the past, and conclude it will happen in the future. But Hume also rejects that we know anything through induction! Inductive arguments aren't cases of logical necessity (they aren't deductively valid), since the future could fail to be like the past without contradiction. And inductive arguments aren't cases where we know something empirically: quite literally, we can't observe the future being like the past, since we can't observe the future!

All that causation means, according to Hume, is that we have a *habit* of expecting that when the cause occurs, it will be regularly followed by the effect at a later time. Not knowledge, just a habit. Not a bad habit, but just a habit.

L. Berkeley's Idealism

Like Locke and Hume, George Berkeley was an empiricist. However, whereas Locke and Hume though that all beliefs depended on experience, and all justification depended on experience, Berkeley went a step farther. Berkeley thought that all truth depended on experience.

Berkeley's view is drastically different from the Standard View discussed in Unit 1. On the Standard View, our ideas *represent* a world which is independent of our ideas. For Berkeley, the notion of a "representation" doesn't make sense at all. Representations are supposed to "correspond to" or "resemble" or "look like" the things they represent. But how can an idea "resemble" anything but another idea? Here is the argument:

1. A represents B if and only if A resembles B.
2. Ideas can only resemble other ideas.
3. "The world" is what our ideas represent.
C. The world is just a collection of ideas.

When we say "my idea of the White House represents the *real* White House", what do we mean? How do we access the "real White House"? What we mean is just that one mental picture of the White House (our concept) looks like another mental picture of the White House (the one we get through perception). How would we ever get beyond perception to things in themselves? That's impossible. So, why insist that real, physical, and material reality exists at all? Wouldn't a simpler theory be that there is no "real", physical world? To exist is simply to be perceived as existing.

You might think, "well, the world is remarkably consistent . . . it isn't like it pops in and out of existence all of the time". Fair enough. But again, it's a very complicated theory to say that the reason our ideas are so consistent is that there is an *invisible and intangible* "real" world of matter, which we can't actually see, which remains even when no one is thinking about it, and which causes our ideas. Why believe in something you can't see, like matter? It's simpler to think that the reason our ideas are consistent is because they continue to be thought about even when we individually aren't thinking about them. That is, in addition to our finite minds, there is an Infinite Mind which is constantly thinking the entire world into existence, and when we have an idea, what we're having is one of the ideas produced by the Infinite Mind. Reality is, for Berkeley, the collection of God's thoughts.

Berkeley's view is called *idealism*. Unlike the standard view on which reality exists independently of our ideas, and our ideas represent reality, an idealist holds that ideas just *are* reality.

M. Kant's Revolution

Although Immanuel Kant never travelled more than 100 miles from his home, he read the works of Locke, Berkeley, Hume, Descartes, and others, and attempted to produce a synthesis of these ideas: a way in which, in some sense, both rationalism, and empiricism, and idealism were correct. Kant called for a "Copernican Revolution" in philosophy. Copernicus had shown that, rather than the sun and the stars revolving around the earth, the earth revolved around the sun. Kant proposed the opposite switch in perspective for philosophy. Instead of assuming that our forms of experience depend on the world, as the Standard View assumes, Kant believed he showed that the world depends upon the forms of our experience.

Kant's philosophy begins by distinguishing two "worlds". There is the world as we experience it, or the *phenomenal* world. "Phenomenal" means "relating to conscious experience": a particular event we experience in perception is called a *phenomenon* and a plurality of events we experience are called *phenomena*. On the other hand, there is Reality in itself, or the *noumenal* world. "Noumenal" means "relating to things as they are in themselves independently of conscious experience", where a singular thing in itself is a *noumenon* and a plurality of things in themselves are *noumena*.

On the Standard View, it is assumed that the phenomenal world, or perception, *represents* the noumenal world, or reality. We can know something about the noumenal world through perception. However, Kant argues as follows:

1. We can only know *p* if there are possible experiences of *p* (phenomena).
2. There is no possible experience of any reality which is independent of experience (noumena).
C. We cannot know any reality which is independent of experience.

In other worlds, no possible phenomenal experience can ever tell us that what we are experiencing is reality in itself independent of experience, because that would be contradictory. Saying that we know the noumenal world through phenomenal experience amounts to saying that our knowledge of reality independent of experience is dependent on experience. So, **all we can know is the phenomenal world; we can't know the noumenal world.**

So, in one way, Kant was like Berkeley, an idealist. Both Kant and Berkeley thought that the only world we could possibly know was the world of ideas and experiences. However, Berkeley thought the only world which *existed at all* was this world of ideas and experiences. Kant, on the other hand, thought that there existed a real world independent of us—reality in itself—and that this the real world caused us to have the experiences we had. It's just that we couldn't *know* this world.

Likewise, in one way, Kant was like Locke and Hume, the empiricists. Kant agreed with the empiricists that all of our knowledge depended on experience. He agreed with Locke that there were no "innate ideas"—every idea we had was generated by the fact that we were having experiences. He disagreed with Socrates and did not believe that we could obtain knowledge of a higher realm of forms through contemplation or recollection of a prior existence.

However, unlike the empiricists, and like the rationalists, Kant thought we *could* have knowledge of *a priori* truths. He developed a unique explanation of how we have *a priori* knowledge *through experience*! Part of knowing our own experiences, says Kant, is knowing the boundary lines of what is and isn't possible to experience. We know the *limits* of possible experience. For instance, we know that we couldn't experience 1+2 not being 3. We know that we couldn't experience a world in which events were not related by cause and effect, no matter how hard Hume tried to get us to imagine differently. We know that we couldn't experience a world without space and time. We know that we couldn't experience a world in which fairness and justice required something different.

Noumena

Reality in Itself
Transcendent

Limits
of
Possible
Experience
a priori

Phenomena

World of Experience
Empirical

You might think, "Wait. People experience time differently. For example, not every society experiences time as involving clocks ticking away the seconds." This is true. For example, other societies may experience time as involving changes in seasons, or cycles of the moon. Kant is not denying this. Rather, consider the following thing which it seems like no one could ever possibly experience: *time progresses forward from what is before to what is after.* You can't imagine time occurring in reverse. You might imagine events going in reverse of what they normally go in, with chickens unhatching and becoming eggs. But the egg in that case would still come *after* the chicken. You can't imagine time stopping. You might imagine events stopping and everyone standing still. However, you'd still be imagining this from a perspective, and for you time would not be stopped—you would be counting away the time as everyone else stood still. Kant develops similar arguments for all of the other *a priori* categories: mathematics (arithmetic and geometry), morality (ethics and justice), and metaphysics (causation, space and time, substance, and reality).

This doesn't mean that our beliefs about mathematics, morality, and metaphysics are justified on the basis of experience. Like Descartes, Kant agrees that our evidence for these things is independent of any particular experience we have. Mathematics, morality, and metaphysics are known *a priori*. However, Kant would say that we're only able to have *a priori* knowledge *because* of experience, since experience tells us the boundary line of what we can't possibly experience any differently.

So, instead of the *a priori* representing necessary truths about the world, the *a priori* represented necessary truths about our way of conceiving and thinking of the world, necessary truths of our psychology. We know that something is true *a priori* for Kant if we cannot possibly conceive of it being otherwise. This doesn't mean guarantee that things in the real world are exactly as we conceive of them. But it does mean that we could never understand or comprehend a reality with a different structure than the one our minds give to it.

N. Metaphysics after Kant

There were some things which Kant thought we *couldn't* know about. These things he called "special metaphysics", and he held that we should be *agnostic* about them—that is, we could not claim to know either way. These topics included whether or not it was possible for the mind (or soul) to be separated from the body, whether or not God exists, and whether or not we have free will. For Kant, these were not truths about our conceptual structure, and so we couldn't know them *a priori*. Instead, they were claims about the noumenal world, which went beyond the boundary of what we could possibly experience. Of course, the remainder of this textbook is occupied with these very issues.

Thus, Kant seemed to leave philosophy with a dilemma. Either:

1. Philosophy can give us knowledge, but this knowledge is only about our own conceptual structure and not any of the classic "philosophical" issues.

2. Philosophy is about the classic "philosophical" issues, but it doesn't qualify as knowledge; it can only describe what it is like to experience life as we do.

Some philosophers in the two centuries after Kant have embraced the first option. They concluded that many of the typical "philosophical" issues like the existence of God, or free will, or the "real" world, or the nature of the self, were either unknowable in principle, or even nonsensical questions that, on reflection, would dissolve away. One of these schools was known as *logical positivism*. Ultimately, what philosophy gave us was a tool for the critical study of our concepts and our shared common language in a clear, rigorous way. Contemporary philosophy found its new role as an aid to modern science. Of course, it would be presumptuous for philosophers to lecture scientists on what "forces" are or what "energy" is. However, philosophers can study what our concepts of "cause" and "effect" are, and so they can inform scientists about what situations it is appropriate to call a relationship between two events a "cause" and "effect" relationship. This can help prevent people who interpret scientific findings from going beyond what the findings actually show. For example, popular science articles regularly proclaim that this-or-that scientific study "proves" or "disproves" the existence of free will. A philosopher might not be able to prove that there is or isn't free will. However, the philosopher understands what we mean by "free will", and so she can explain why the study doesn't prove or disprove "free will", but in fact shows something much weaker.

On this vision of philosophy, it is hard to make any judgments about what is true in the "big picture", but we can be more confident about our judgments in particular cases.

Other philosophers in the two centuries after Kant embraced the second option. They concluded that we could never claim to have knowledge of the truth as it was in itself. However, we can describe the world of experience in which we live as best as we can, and part of our conscious experience includes impressions that we associate with freedom, with our own sense of self, and with the divine. While Kant assumed that the *a priori* involved a necessary conceptual structure that every rational being had in common, other philosophers proposed that what we call "*a priori*" is only a reflection of our historical circumstances, our social context, or even our individual will. For example, *existentialism* argued that our essential nature as human beings was not something given independently of us, but rather something that we actively determined and created. Each of us determines what is within or outside of the bounds of possible experience, and so the essences of things are produced by our own experiences of them. Our existence as conscious beings is prior to our essence. Other philosophers argued in contrast that a necessary part of our experience is that we always experience ourselves as related to some *other* outside ourselves—our sense of self is necessarily produced in opposition to something which is *not* ourselves, or the other person. For these philosophers, my process of interacting with others and gradually bringing myself to see their perspective, and them to see my perspective, is the process that produces the concepts which matter. On this vision of philosophy, we can't trust our judgments about individual cases, since they tend to reflect our own biases and limited experiences. However, we can trust judgments about the "big picture", insofar as this is a case where we can draw on experiences that are common to all of us.

However, the third option is to reject Kant's dilemma in the first place. It is true that we have no guarantee that the way we conceive of the world and divide it up in our minds will line up with the natural boundary markers in the world. It is true that our concepts aren't fixed in stone: they can change over time and history, can be modified in light of new information, and can be adapted through interactions with others. It is also true that our own individual ways of thinking about what words or concepts mean can be wrong, in light of how they are used by our community as a whole.

However, we also can't help but assume that how we think of things *generally does* line up with the way the world is. In order to argue that there is a gap between how we conceive of the world and how the world really is, we have to rely on our concepts to begin with. In a way, thinking that our conceptual structure doesn't "match up" with the "real world", while relying on concepts like "match up" and "real world", is contradicting ourselves—we're acting inconsistently, assuming our conceptual structure does match up in order to assert that it doesn't.

Remember the two questions we started with: *what kinds of evidence* are there, and *how much evidence do we need*? The third approach says that Kant was right that one kind of evidence is empirical, but another kind of evidence is *a priori* knowledge of our own conceptual structure—the way we necessarily must think of the world. However, it rejects the assumption made by Descartes and Kant that we need to have 100% certainty in order to have knowledge. Instead, like Locke, it says that it is enough to have a high probability that we are right.

What is the probability that our whole conceptual structure is entirely wrong about the world? There is a chance, of course—just like there is a chance that our perceptual picture of the world is the product of an evil demon, or a dream. However, it seems unlikely that we would have survived and thrived so far as human beings in an often hostile environment if our concepts were completely and utterly deluded about basic principles of logic and metaphysics. Some of our *particular* concepts may need to be refined through reflecting, listening to others who think differently, and comparison with what we find empirically around us. However, on the whole, it seems like there is a decent probability that the overall structure of our concepts—which we know *a priori*—roughly lines up with the structure of the world.

Our concepts can't tell us whether something actually exists, of course! We can't know from our concept of a unicorn that there are unicorns, and so no one can conclude from their concept of free will that there is actually free will, or from their concept of a god that the god exists. However, our concepts can tell us that something is a logical possibility. Unicorns, for instance, could exist in some possible world very different from our own. When we talk about the "structure" of the world, we mean what is logically possible and what is necessary.

So, as we move forward into these topics in metaphysics—the nature of the mind, the existence of God, and the existence of free will—we'll do so on the assumption that we can get *a priori* evidence in two ways:

> **(C→P) if we can conceive of some scenario, then that is good evidence that the scenario is logically possible.**
>
> **(NC→NP) if we can't conceive of some scenario, then that is good evidence that the scenario is logically impossible.**

Of course, having learned from our trek through epistemology, we'll do this while remaining critical, being aware that it is not always so, and remembering that even if there is *a priori* knowledge, it is not entirely certain to line up with reality in itself.

❀ 2.2 Meno ❀

Selections
by Plato

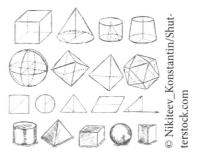

© Nikiteev_Konstantin/Shut-
terstock.com

The *Meno* comes in the middle era of Plato's works. One vexing question is how we can come to have a knowledge of moral truths, such as the nature of justice. It doesn't seem like we observe justice through our senses, and there are no tools we have to scientifically measure justice. So, how do we know what "justice" is?

Plato (that is, Socrates) makes a proposal. First, he will make an argument to establish that there are some things we know where our knowledge is independent of sensory experience. Later philosophers will call this ***a priori*** knowledge, as contrasted with ***empirical*** knowledge which depends on sensory experiences. Then, he'll propose an explanation for how we get this knowledge. Once we know that we obtain some knowledge independently of sensory experience, then there should be nothing strange about justice also being in this category too.

Here are some questions to think about when you read:

* What puzzle is Socrates trying to solve about the boy's knowledge of geometry?

* What answer does Socrates offer to this puzzle?

* What is the 'doctrine of recollection'?

* Plato doesn't distinguish between the claim that a belief is *justified* by something other than sensory experience (*a priori*) from the claim that a belief is *caused* by something other than sensory experience (recollection of a past life). How might this distinction change Plato's argument?

[The Dialogue begins with Meno inquiring of Socrates:

Can you tell me, Socrates, whether virtue is acquired by teaching or by practice; or if neither by teaching nor by practice, then whether it comes to man by nature, or in what other way?

Socrates confesses that he does not know what virtue is, and asks whether Meno knows what virtue is. Meno claims to know what virtue is, and volunteers this answer:

Every age, every condition of life, young or old, male or female, bond or free, has a different virtue: there are virtues numberless, and no lack of definitions of them; for virtue is relative to the actions and ages of each of us in all that we do. And the same may be said of vice, Socrates.

Socrates rebuffs Meno:

When I ask you for one virtue, you present me with a swarm of them which are in your keeping. Suppose that I carry on the figure of the swarm, and ask of you, What is the nature of the bee? and you answer that there are many kinds of bees, and I reply: But do bees differ as bees, because there are many and different kinds of them; or are they not rather to be distinguished by some other quality, as for example beauty, size, or shape? How would you answer me? . . . And so of the virtues, however many and different they may be, they have all a common nature which makes them virtues.

Meno compares Socrates to a torpedo whose touch has taken away his sense and speech. Meno and Socrates then face the question of how one can enquire into the nature of virtue, if one does not already know what virtue is.]

Meno:

And how will you enquire, Socrates, into that which you do not know? What will you put forth as the subject of enquiry? And if you find what you want, how will you ever know that this is the thing which you did not know?

Socrates:

How can you enquire about what you do not know, and if you know why should you enquire?

I know, Meno, what you mean; but just see what a tiresome dispute you are introducing. You argue that a man cannot enquire either about that which he knows, or about that which he does not know; for if he knows, he has no need to enquire; and if not, he cannot; for he does not know the very subject about which he is to enquire.

Men. Well, Socrates, and is not the argument sound?

Soc. I think not.

Men. Why not?

Soc. I will tell you why: I have heard from certain wise men and women who spoke of things divine that—

Men. What did they say?

Soc. They spoke of a glorious truth, as I conceive.

Men. What was it? and who were they?

Soc. The ancient poets tell us that the soul of man is immortal and has a recollection of all that she has ever known in former states of being.

Some of them were priests and priestesses, who had studied how they might be able to give a reason of their profession: there have been poets also, who spoke of these things by inspiration, like Pindar, and many others who were inspired. And they say—mark, now, and see whether their words are true—they say that the soul of man is immortal, and at one time has an end, which is termed dying, and at another time is born again, but is never destroyed. And the moral is, that a man ought to live always in perfect holiness.

❖ ❖

'For in the ninth year Persephone sends the souls of those from whom she has received the penalty of ancient crime back again from beneath into the light of the sun above, and these are they who become noble kings and mighty men and great in wisdom and are called saintly heroes in after ages.'

The soul, then, as being immortal, and having been born again many times, and having seen all things that exist, whether in this world or in the world below, has knowledge of them all; and it is no wonder that she should be able to call to remembrance all that she ever knew about virtue, and about everything; for as all nature is akin, and the soul has learned all things, there is no difficulty in her eliciting or as men say learning, out of a single recollection all the rest, if a man is strenuous and does not faint; for all enquiry and all learning is but recollection.

And therefore we ought not to listen to this sophistical argument about the impossibility of enquiry: for it will make us idle, and is sweet only to the sluggard; but the other saying will make us active and inquisitive. In that confiding, I will gladly enquire with you into the nature of virtue.

Men. Yes, Socrates; but what do you mean by saying that we do not learn, and that what we call learning is only a process of recollection? Can you teach me how this is?

Soc. I told you, Meno, just now that you were a rogue, and now you ask whether I can teach you, when I am saying that there is no teaching, but only recollection; and thus you imagine that you will involve me in a contradiction.

Men. Indeed, Socrates, I protest that I had no such intention. I only asked the question from habit; but if you can prove to me that what you say is true, I wish that you would.

Soc. It will be no easy matter, but I will try to please you to the utmost of my power. Suppose that you call one of your numerous attendants, that I may demonstrate on him.

Men. Certainly. Come hither, *Boy.*

Soc. He is Greek, and speaks Greek, does he not?

Men. Yes, indeed; he was born in the house.

Soc. Attend now to the questions which I ask him, and observe whether he learns of me or only remembers.

Men. I will.

Soc. Tell me, boy, do you know that a figure like this is a square?

Boy. I do.

Soc. And you know that a square figure has these four lines equal?

Boy. Certainly.

Soc. And these lines which I have drawn through the middle of the square are also equal?

Boy. Yes.

Soc. A square may be of any size?

Boy. Certainly.

Soc. And if one side of the figure be of two feet, and the other side be of two feet, how much will the whole be? Let me explain: if in one direction the space was of two feet, and in the other direction of one foot, the whole would be of two feet taken once?

Boy. Yes.

Soc. But since this side is also of two feet, there are twice two feet?

Boy. There are.

Soc. Then the square is of twice two feet?

Boy. Yes.

Soc. And how many are twice two feet? count and tell me.

Boy. Four, Socrates.

Soc. And might there not be another square twice as large as this, and having like this the lines equal?

Boy. Yes.

Soc. And of how many feet will that be?

Boy. Of eight feet.

Soc. And now try and tell me the length of the line which forms the side of that double square: this is two feet—what will that be?

Boy. Clearly, Socrates, it will be double.

Soc. Do you observe, Meno, that I am not teaching the boy anything, but only asking him questions; and now he fancies that he knows how long a line is necessary in order to produce a figure of eight square feet; does he not?

Men. Yes.

Soc. And does he really know?

Men. Certainly not.

Soc. He only guesses that because the square is double, the line is double.

Men. True.

Soc. Observe him while he recalls the steps in regular order. (To the Boy.) Tell me, boy, do you assert that double space comes from a double line? Remember that I am not speaking of an oblong, but of a figure equal every way, and twice the size of this—that is to say of eight feet; and I want to know whether you still say that a double square comes from a double line? . . .

[The boy wrongly assumes that a square with twice the area will have sides of twice the length, and that doubling the length of the sides of a square will only double its area. He is assuming that the pattern he observed in the simple case will continue in the more complex cases. Socrates leads him through questioning to see that this is a mistake, and the boy concludes that he does not know how to do the calculation].

. . .

Soc. Mark now the farther development. I shall only ask him, and not teach him, and he shall share the enquiry with me: and do you watch and see if you find me telling or explaining anything to him, instead of eliciting his opinion. Tell me, boy, is not this a square of four feet which I have drawn?

Boy. Yes.

Soc. And now I add another square equal to the former one?

Boy. Yes.

Soc. And a third, which is equal to either of them?

Boy. Yes.

Soc. Suppose that we fill up the vacant corner?

Boy. Very good.

Soc. Here, then, there are four equal spaces?

Boy. Yes.

Soc. which is, that the square of the diagonal is double the square of the side. And how many times larger is this space than this other?

Boy. Four times.

Soc. But it ought to have been twice only, as you will remember.

Boy. True.

Soc. And does not this line, reaching from corner to corner, bisect each of these spaces?

Boy. Yes.

❖ ❖

Soc. And are there not here four equal lines which contain this space?

Boy. There are.

Soc. Look and see how much this space is.

Boy. I do not understand.

Soc. Has not each interior line cut off half of the four spaces?

Boy. Yes.

Soc. And how many such spaces are there in this section?

Boy. Four.

Soc. And how many in this?

Boy. Two.

Soc. And four is how many times two?

Boy. Twice.

Soc. And this space is of how many feet?

Boy. Of eight feet.

Soc. And from what line do you get this figure?

Boy. From this.

Soc. That is, from the line which extends from corner to corner of the figure of four feet?

Boy. Yes.

Soc. And that is the line which the learned call the diagonal. And if this is the proper name, then you, Meno's slave, are prepared to affirm that the double space is the square of the diagonal?

Boy. Certainly, Socrates.

Soc. What do you say of him, Meno? Were not all these answers given out of his own head?

Men. Yes, they were all his own.

Soc. And yet, as we were just now saying, he did not know?

Men. True.

Soc. But still he had in him those notions of his— had he not?

Men. Yes.

Soc. Then he who does not know may still have true notions of that which he does not know?

Men. He has.

Soc. And at present these notions have just been stirred up in him, as in a dream; but if he were frequently asked the same questions, in different forms, he would know as well as any one at last?

Men. I dare say.

Soc. Without any one teaching him he will recover his knowledge for himself, if he is only asked questions?

Men. Yes.

Soc. And this spontaneous recovery of knowledge in him is recollection?

Men. True.

Soc. And this knowledge which he now has must he not either have acquired or always possessed?

Men. Yes.

Soc. Either this knowledge was acquired by him in a former state of existence, or was always known to him.

But if he always possessed this knowledge he would always have known; or if he has acquired the knowledge he could not have acquired it in this life, unless he has been taught geometry; for he may be made to do the same with all geometry and every other branch of knowledge. Now, has any one ever taught him all this? You must know about him, if, as you say, he was born and bred in your house.

Men. And I am certain that no one ever did teach him.

Soc. And yet he has the knowledge?

Men. The fact, Socrates, is undeniable.

Soc. But if he did not acquire the knowledge in this life, then he must have had and learned it at some other time?

Men. Clearly he must.

Soc. Which must have been the time when he was not a man?

Men. Yes.

Soc. And if there have been always true thoughts in him, both at the time when he was and was not a man, which only need to be awakened into knowledge by putting questions to him, his soul must have always possessed this knowledge, for he always either was or was not a man?

Men. Obviously.

Soc. And if the truth of all things always existed in the soul, then the soul is immortal. Wherefore be of good cheer, and try to recollect what you do not know, or rather what you do not remember.

Men. I feel, somehow, that I like what you are saying.

Soc. Better to enquire than to fancy that there is no such thing as enquiry and no use in it. And I, Meno, like what I am saying. Some things I have said of which I am not altogether confident. But that we shall be better and braver and less helpless if we think that we ought to enquire, than we should have been if we indulged in the idle fancy that there was no knowing and no use in seeking to know what we do not know;—that is a theme upon which I am ready to fight, in word and deed, to the utmost of my power.

Men. There again, Socrates, your words seem to me excellent.

Soc. Then, as we are agreed that a man should enquire about that which he does not know, shall you and I make an effort to enquire together into the nature of virtue?

❁ 2.3 The Meditations ❁

Selections
by Rene Descartes

✳ ✳

© Georgios Kollidas/Shutterstock.com

Rene Descartes (1596–1650) was a French mathematician, scientist, and philosopher. Descartes believed the philosophy which came before him had begun on the wrong foundation, and so he sought to restart philosophy on a new foundation. This new foundation would begin with the experience of being a thinking self. From this, Descartes thought we could derive various logical, rational, and *a priori* truths. From this, Descartes thought we could derive the existence and goodness of a God who could guarantee that our senses would not radically deceive us. And this, Descartes thought, was the foundation of all empirical, scientific knowledge. This is called Descartes's **foundationalism**.

Descartes was writing in an era in which the new modern science, medieval philosophy, and traditional religion were all locked in bitter conflict with one another. By showing the layers of dependence in our knowledge, he sought a kind of reconciliation between them. Descartes's view is a kind of **rationalism** because it holds that some of our knowledge can be justified independently of sensory experience (*a priori*), on the basis of reasoning alone. Descartes's rationalism became the dominant view in European philosophy for a century following his death.

Descartes writes in a *Meditation*, meant to help his readers get into his train of thought. Don't read the Meditation as though it were a treatise or manifesto proposing a particular view from the outset: otherwise, it will seem like Descartes contradicts himself. Instead, read it like a dialogue that Descartes is having with himself. He begins by doubting everything he thought he knew, and uses this process to find the new foundations on which his knowledge depends.

As you read Descartes, here are some questions to ask yourself:

* Why does Descartes begin by trying to doubt everything?

* Which 3 arguments does Descartes offer to lead himself to doubt everything?

* What is the one thing that Descartes can't doubt?

* How does Descartes know about the nature of the wax? How does he know his own nature? What is his nature?

* How does Descartes think he can prove the existence of God a priori?

* How does he use God's existence as a foundation for all other knowledge?

❖ ❖

MEDITATION I.

OF THE THINGS OF WHICH WE MAY DOUBT.

1. SEVERAL years have now elapsed since I first became aware that I had accepted, even from my youth, many false opinions for true, and that consequently what I afterward based on such principles was highly doubtful; and from that time I was convinced of the necessity of undertaking once in my life to rid myself of all the opinions I had adopted, and of commencing anew the work of building from the foundation, if I desired to establish a firm and abiding superstructure in the sciences. But as this enterprise appeared to me to be one of great magnitude, I waited until I had attained an age so mature as to leave me no hope that at any stage of life more advanced I should be better able to execute my design. On this account, I have delayed so long that I should henceforth consider I was doing wrong were I still to consume in deliberation any of the time that now remains for action. To-day, then, since I have opportunely freed my mind from all cares [and am happily disturbed by no passions], and since I am in the secure possession of leisure in a peaceable retirement, I will at length apply myself earnestly and freely to the general overthrow of all my former opinions.

2. But, to this end, it will not be necessary for me to show that the whole of these are false—a point, perhaps, which I shall never reach; but as even now my reason convinces me that I ought not the less carefully to withhold belief from what is not entirely certain and indubitable, than from what is manifestly false, it will be sufficient to justify the rejection of the whole if I shall find in each some ground for doubt. Nor for this purpose will it be necessary even to deal with each belief individually, which would be truly an endless labor; but, as the removal from below of the foundation necessarily involves the downfall of the whole edifice, I will at once approach the criticism of the principles on which all my former beliefs rested.

3. All that I have, up to this moment, accepted as possessed of the highest truth and certainty, I received either from or through the senses. I observed, however, that these sometimes misled us; and it is the part of prudence not to place absolute confidence in that by which we have even once been deceived.

4. But it may be said, perhaps, that, although the senses occasionally mislead us respecting minute objects, and such as are so far removed from us as to be beyond the reach of close observation, there are yet many other of their informations (presentations), of the truth of which it is manifestly impossible to doubt; as for example, that I am in this place, seated by the fire, clothed in a winter dressing gown, that I hold in my hands this piece of paper, with other intimations of the same nature. But how could I deny that I possess these hands and this body, and withal escape being classed with persons in a state of insanity, whose brains are so disordered and clouded by dark bilious vapors as to cause them pertinaciously to assert that they are monarchs when they are in the greatest poverty; or clothed [in gold] and purple when destitute of any covering; or that their head is made of clay, their body of glass, or that they are gourds? I should certainly be not less insane than they, were I to regulate my procedure according to examples so extravagant.

5. Though this be true, I must nevertheless here consider that I am a man, and that, consequently, I am in the habit of sleeping, and representing to myself in dreams those same things, or even sometimes others less probable, which the insane think are presented to them in their waking moments. How often have I dreamt that I was in these familiar circumstances, that I was dressed, and occupied this place by the fire, when I was lying undressed in bed? At the present moment, however, I certainly look upon this paper with eyes wide awake; the head which I now move is not asleep; I extend this hand consciously and with express purpose, and I perceive it; the occurrences in sleep are not so distinct as all this. But I cannot forget that, at other times I have been deceived in sleep by similar illusions; and, attentively considering those cases, I perceive so clearly that there exist no certain marks by which the state of waking can ever be distinguished from sleep, that I feel greatly astonished; and in amazement I almost persuade myself that I am now dreaming.

6. Let us suppose, then, that we are dreaming, and that all these particulars—namely, the opening of the eyes, the motion of the head, the forth- putting of the hands—are merely illusions; and even that we really possess neither an entire body nor hands such as we see. Nevertheless it must be admitted at least that the objects which appear to us in sleep are, as it were, painted representations which could not have been formed unless in the likeness of realities; and, therefore, that those general objects, at all events, namely, eyes, a head, hands, and an entire body, are not simply imaginary, but really existent. For, in truth, painters themselves, even when they study to represent sirens and satyrs by forms the most fantastic and extraordinary, cannot bestow upon them natures absolutely new, but can only make a certain medley of the members of different animals; or if they chance to imagine something so novel that nothing at all similar has ever been seen before, and such as is, therefore, purely fictitious and absolutely false, it is at least certain that the colors of which this is composed are real. And on the same principle, although these general objects, viz. [a body], eyes, a head, hands, and the like, be imaginary, we are nevertheless absolutely necessitated to admit the reality at least of some other objects still more simple and universal than these, of which, just as of certain real colors, all those images of things, whether true and real, or false and fantastic, that are found in our consciousness (cogitatio), are formed.

7. To this class of objects seem to belong corporeal nature in general and its extension; the figure of extended things, their quantity or magnitude, and their number, as also the place in, and the time during, which they exist, and other things of the same sort.

8. We will not, therefore, perhaps reason illegitimately if we conclude from this that Physics, Astronomy, Medicine, and all the other sciences that have for their end the consideration of composite objects, are indeed of a doubtful character; but that Arithmetic, Geometry, and the other sciences of the same class, which regard merely the simplest and most general objects, and scarcely inquire whether or not these are really existent, contain somewhat that is certain and indubitable: for whether I am awake or dreaming, it remains true that two and three make five, and that a square has but four sides; nor does it seem possible that truths so apparent can ever fall under a suspicion of falsity [or incertitude].

9. Nevertheless, the belief that there is a God who is all powerful, and who created me, such as I am, has, for a long time, obtained steady possession of my mind. How, then, do I know that he has not arranged that there should be neither earth, nor sky, nor any extended thing, nor figure, nor magnitude, nor place, providing at the same time, however, for [the rise in me of the perceptions of all these objects, and] the persuasion that these do not exist otherwise than as I perceive them? And further, as I sometimes think that others are in error respecting matters of which they believe themselves to possess a perfect knowledge, how do I know that I am not also deceived each time I add together two and three, or number the sides of a square, or form some judgment still more simple, if more simple indeed can be imagined? But perhaps Deity has not been willing that I should be thus deceived, for he is said to be supremely good. If, however, it were repugnant to the goodness of Deity to have created me subject to constant deception, it would seem

❖ ❖

likewise to be contrary to his goodness to allow me to be occasionally deceived; and yet it is clear that this is permitted.

10. Some, indeed, might perhaps be found who would be disposed rather to deny the existence of a Being so powerful than to believe that there is nothing certain. But let us for the present refrain from opposing this opinion, and grant that all which is here said of a Deity is fabulous: nevertheless, in whatever way it be supposed that I reach the state in which I exist, whether by fate, or chance, or by an endless series of antecedents and consequents, or by any other means, it is clear (since to be deceived and to err is a certain defect) that the probability of my being so imperfect as to be the constant victim of deception, will be increased exactly in proportion as the power possessed by the cause, to which they assign my origin, is lessened. To these reasonings I have assuredly nothing to reply, but am constrained at last to avow that there is nothing of all that I formerly believed to be true of which it is impossible to doubt, and that not through thoughtlessness or levity, but from cogent and maturely considered reasons; so that henceforward, if I desire to discover anything certain, I ought not the less carefully to refrain from assenting to those same opinions than to what might be shown to be manifestly false.

11. But it is not sufficient to have made these observations; care must be taken likewise to keep them in remembrance. For those old and customary opinions perpetually recur— long and familiar usage giving them the right of occupying my mind, even almost against my will, and subduing my belief; nor will I lose the habit of deferring to them and confiding in them so long as I shall consider them to be what in truth they are, viz, opinions to some extent doubtful, as I have already shown, but still highly probable, and such as it is much more reasonable to believe than deny. It is for this reason I am persuaded that I shall not be doing wrong, if, taking an opposite judgment of deliberate design, I become my own deceiver, by supposing, for a time, that all those opinions are entirely false and imaginary, until at length, having thus balanced my old by my new prejudices, my judgment shall no longer be turned aside by perverted usage from the path that may conduct to the perception of truth. For I am assured that, meanwhile, there will arise neither peril nor error from this course, and that I cannot for the present yield too much to distrust, since the end I now seek is not action but knowledge.

12. I will suppose, then, not that Deity, who is sovereignly good and the fountain of truth, but that some malignant demon, who is at once exceedingly potent and deceitful, has employed all his artifice to deceive me; I will suppose that the sky, the air, the earth, colors, figures, sounds, and all external things, are nothing better than the illusions of dreams, by means of which this being has laid snares for my credulity; I will consider myself as without hands, eyes, flesh, blood, or any of the senses, and as falsely believing that I am possessed of these; I will continue resolutely fixed in this belief, and if indeed by this means it be not in my power to arrive at the knowledge of truth, I shall at least do what is in my power, viz, [suspend my judgment], and guard with settled purpose against giving my assent to what is false, and being imposed upon by this deceiver, whatever be his power and artifice. But this undertaking is arduous, and a certain indolence insensibly leads me back to my ordinary course of life; and just as the captive, who, perchance, was enjoying in his dreams an imaginary liberty, when he begins to suspect that it is but a vision, dreads awakening, and conspires with the agreeable illusions that the deception may be prolonged; so I, of my own accord, fall back into the train of my former beliefs, and fear to arouse myself from my slumber, lest the time of laborious wakefulness that would succeed this quiet rest, in place of bringing any light of day, should prove inadequate to dispel the darkness that will arise from the difficulties that have now been raised.

MEDITATION II.

OF THE NATURE OF THE HUMAN MIND; AND THAT IT IS MORE EASILY KNOWN THAN THE BODY.

1. The Meditation of yesterday has filled my mind with so many doubts, that it is no longer in my power to forget them. Nor do I see, meanwhile, any principle on which they can be resolved; and, just as if I had fallen all of a sudden into very deep water, I am so greatly disconcerted as to be unable either to plant my feet firmly on the bottom or sustain myself by swimming on the surface. I will, nevertheless, make an effort, and try anew the same path on which I had entered yesterday, that is, proceed by casting aside all that admits of the slightest doubt, not less than if I had discovered it to be absolutely false; and I will continue always in this track until I shall find something that is certain, or at least, if I can do nothing more, until I shall know with certainty that there is nothing certain. Archimedes, that he might transport the entire globe from the place it occupied to another, demanded only a point that was firm and immovable; so, also, I shall be entitled to entertain the highest expectations, if I am fortunate enough to discover only one thing that is certain and indubitable.

2. I suppose, accordingly, that all the things which I see are false (fictitious); I believe that none of those objects which my fallacious memory represents ever existed; I suppose that I possess no senses; I believe that body, figure, extension, motion, and place are merely fictions of my mind. What is there, then, that can be esteemed true? Perhaps this only, that there is absolutely nothing certain.

3. But how do I know that there is not something different altogether from the objects I have now enumerated, of which it is impossible to entertain the slightest doubt? Is there not a God, or some being, by whatever name I may designate him, who causes these thoughts to arise in my mind?

But why suppose such a being, for it may be I myself am capable of producing them? Am I, then, at least not something? But I before denied that I possessed senses or a body; I hesitate, however, for what follows from that? Am I so dependent on the body and the senses that without these I cannot exist? But I had the persuasion that there was absolutely nothing in the world, that there was no sky and no earth, neither minds nor bodies; was I not, therefore, at the same time, persuaded that I did not exist? Far from it; I assuredly existed, since I was persuaded. But there is I know not what being, who is possessed at once of the highest power and the deepest cunning, who is constantly employing all his ingenuity in deceiving me. Doubtless, then, I exist, since I am deceived; and, let him deceive me as he may, he can never bring it about that I am nothing, so long as I shall be conscious that I am something. So that it must, in fine, be maintained, all things being maturely and carefully considered, that this proposition (pronunciatum) I am, I exist, is necessarily true each time it is expressed by me, or conceived in my mind.

4. But I do not yet know with sufficient clearness what I am, though assured that I am; and hence, in the next place, I must take care, lest perchance I inconsiderately substitute some other object in room of what is properly myself, and thus wander from truth, even in that knowledge (cognition) which I hold to be of all others the most certain and evident. For this reason, I will now consider anew what I formerly believed myself to be, before I entered on the present train of thought; and of my previous opinion I will retrench all that can in the least be invalidated by the grounds of doubt I have adduced, in order that there may at length remain nothing but what is certain and indubitable.

5. What then did I formerly think I was? Undoubtedly I judged that I was a man. But what is a man? Shall I say a rational animal? Assuredly not; for it would be necessary forthwith to inquire into what is meant by animal, and what by rational, and thus,

❖ ❖

from a single question, I should insensibly glide into others, and these more difficult than the first; nor do I now possess enough of leisure to warrant me in wasting my time amid subtleties of this sort. I prefer here to attend to the thoughts that sprung up of themselves in my mind, and were inspired by my own nature alone, when I applied myself to the consideration of what I was. In the first place, then, I thought that I possessed a countenance, hands, arms, and all the fabric of members that appears in a corpse, and which I called by the name of body. It further occurred to me that I was nourished, that I walked, perceived, and thought, and all those actions I referred to the soul; but what the soul itself was I either did not stay to consider, or, if I did, I imagined that it was something extremely rare and subtile, like wind, or flame, or ether, spread through my grosser parts. As regarded the body, I did not even doubt of its nature, but thought I distinctly knew it, and if I had wished to describe it according to the notions I then entertained, I should have explained myself in this manner: By body I understand all that can be terminated by a certain figure; that can be comprised in a certain place, and so fill a certain space as therefrom to exclude every other body; that can be perceived either by touch, sight, hearing, taste, or smell; that can be moved in different ways, not indeed of itself, but by something foreign to it by which it is touched [and from which it receives the impression]; for the power of self-motion, as likewise that of perceiving and thinking, I held as by no means pertaining to the nature of body; on the contrary, I was somewhat astonished to find such faculties existing in some bodies.

6. But [as to myself, what can I now say that I am], since I suppose there exists an extremely powerful, and, if I may so speak, malignant being, whose whole endeavors are directed toward deceiving me? Can I affirm that I possess any one of all those attributes of which I have lately spoken as belonging to the nature of body? After attentively considering them in my own mind, I find none of them that can properly be said to belong to myself. To recount them were idle and tedious. Let us pass, then, to the attributes of the soul. The first mentioned were the powers of nutrition and walking; but, if it be true that I have no body, it is true likewise that I am capable neither of walking nor of being nourished. Perception is another attribute of the soul; but perception too is impossible without the body; besides, I have frequently, during sleep, believed that I perceived objects which I afterward observed I did not in reality perceive. Thinking is another attribute of the soul; and here I discover what properly belongs to myself. This alone is inseparable from me. I am—I exist: this is certain; but how often? As often as I think; for perhaps it would even happen, if I should wholly cease to think, that I should at the same time altogether cease to be. I now admit nothing that is not necessarily true. I am therefore, precisely speaking, only a thinking thing, that is, a mind (mens sive animus), understanding, or reason, terms whose signification was before unknown to me. I am, however, a real thing, and really existent; but what thing? The answer was, a thinking thing.

7. The question now arises, am I aught besides? I will stimulate my imagination with a view to discover whether I am not still something more than a thinking being. Now it is plain I am not the assemblage of members called the human body; I am not a thin and penetrating air diffused through all these members, or wind, or flame, or vapor, or breath, or any of all the things I can imagine; for I supposed that all these were not, and, without changing the supposition, I find that I still feel assured of my existence. But it is true, perhaps, that those very things which I suppose to be non-existent, because they are unknown to me, are not in truth different from myself whom I know. This is a point I cannot determine, and do not now enter into any dispute regarding it. I can only judge of things that are known to me: I am conscious that I exist, and I who know that I exist inquire into what I am. . . .

❂ ❂

8. But what, then, am I? A thinking thing, it has been said. But what is a thinking thing? It is a thing that doubts, understands, [conceives], affirms, denies, wills, refuses; that imagines also, and perceives.

9. Assuredly it is not little, if all these properties belong to my nature. But why should they not belong to it? Am I not that very being who now doubts of almost everything; who, for all that, understands and conceives certain things; who affirms one alone as true, and denies the others; who desires to know more of them, and does not wish to be deceived; who imagines many things, sometimes even despite his will; and is likewise percipient of many, as if through the medium of the senses. Is there nothing of all this as true as that I am, even although I should be always dreaming, and although he who gave me being employed all his ingenuity to deceive me? Is there also any one of these attributes that can be properly distinguished from my thought, or that can be said to be separate from myself? For it is of itself so evident that it is I who doubt, I who understand, and I who desire, that it is here unnecessary to add anything by way of rendering it more clear. And I am as certainly the same being who imagines; for although it may be (as I before supposed) that nothing I imagine is true, still the power of imagination does not cease really to exist in me and to form part of my thought. In fine, I am the same being who perceives, that is, who apprehends certain objects as by the organs of sense, since, in truth, I see light, hear a noise, and feel heat. But it will be said that these presentations are false, and that I am dreaming. Let it be so. At all events it is certain that I seem to see light, hear a noise, and feel heat; this cannot be false, and this is what in me is properly called perceiving (sentire), which is nothing else than thinking.

10. From this I begin to know what I am with somewhat greater clearness and distinctness than heretofore. But, nevertheless, it still seems to me, and I cannot help believing, that corporeal things, whose images are formed by thought [which fall under the senses], and are examined by the same, are known with much greater distinctness than that I know not what part of myself which is not imaginable; although, in truth, it may seem strange to say that I know and comprehend with greater distinctness things whose existence appears to me doubtful, that are unknown, and do not belong to me, than others of whose reality I am persuaded, that are known to me, and appertain to my proper nature; in a word, than myself. But I see clearly what is the state of the case. My mind is apt to wander, and will not yet submit to be restrained within the limits of truth. Let us therefore leave the mind to itself once more, and, according to it every kind of liberty [permit it to consider the objects that appear to it from without], in order that, having afterward withdrawn it from these gently and opportunely [and fixed it on the consideration of its being and the properties it finds in itself], it may then be the more easily controlled.

11. Let us now accordingly consider the objects that are commonly thought to be [the most easily, and likewise] the most distinctly known, viz, the bodies we touch and see; not, indeed, bodies in general, for these general notions are usually somewhat more confused, but one body in particular. Take, for example, this piece of wax; it is quite fresh, having been but recently taken from the beehive; it has not yet lost the sweetness of the honey it contained; it still retains somewhat of the odor of the flowers from which it was gathered; its color, figure, size, are apparent (to the sight); it is hard, cold, easily handled; and sounds when struck upon with the finger. In fine, all that contributes to make a body as distinctly known as possible, is found in the one before us. But, while I am speaking, let it be placed near the fire—what remained of the taste exhales, the smell evaporates, the color changes, its figure is destroyed, its size increases, it becomes liquid, it grows hot, it can hardly be handled, and, although struck upon, it emits no sound. Does the

❖ ❖

same wax still remain after this change? It must be admitted that it does remain; no one doubts it, or judges otherwise. What, then, was it I knew with so much distinctness in the piece of wax? Assuredly, it could be nothing of all that I observed by means of the senses, since all the things that fell under taste, smell, sight, touch, and hearing are changed, and yet the same wax remains.

12. It was perhaps what I now think, viz, that this wax was neither the sweetness of honey, the pleasant odor of flowers, the whiteness, the figure, nor the sound, but only a body that a little before appeared to me conspicuous under these forms, and which is now perceived under others. But, to speak precisely, what is it that I imagine when I think of it in this way? Let it be attentively considered, and, retrenching all that does not belong to the wax, let us see what remains. There certainly remains nothing, except something extended, flexible, and movable. But what is meant by flexible and movable? Is it not that I imagine that the piece of wax, being round, is capable of becoming square, or of passing from a square into a triangular figure? Assuredly such is not the case, because I conceive that it admits of an infinity of similar changes; and I am, moreover, unable to compass this infinity by imagination, and consequently this conception which I have of the wax is not the product of the faculty of imagination. But what now is this extension? Is it not also unknown? for it becomes greater when the wax is melted, greater when it is boiled, and greater still when the heat increases; and I should not conceive [clearly and] according to truth, the wax as it is, if I did not suppose that the piece we are considering admitted even of a wider variety of extension than I ever imagined, I must, therefore, admit that I cannot even comprehend by imagination what the piece of wax is, and that it is the mind alone (mens, Lat., entendement, F.) which perceives it. I speak of one piece in particular; for as to wax in general, this is still more evident. But what is the piece of wax that can be perceived only by the [understanding or] mind? It is certainly the same which I see, touch, imagine; and, in fine, it is the same which, from the beginning, I believed it to be. But (and this it is of moment to observe) the perception of it is neither an act of sight, of touch, nor of imagination, and never was either of these, though it might formerly seem so, but is simply an intuition (inspectio) of the mind, which may be imperfect and confused, as it formerly was, or very clear and distinct, as it is at present, according as the attention is more or less directed to the elements which it contains, and of which it is composed. . . .

14. The man who makes it his aim to rise to knowledge superior to the common, ought to be ashamed to seek occasions of doubting from the vulgar forms of speech: instead, therefore, of doing this, I shall proceed with the matter in hand, and inquire whether I had a clearer and more perfect perception of the piece of wax when I first saw it, and when I thought I knew it by means of the external sense itself, or, at all events, by the common sense (sensus communis), as it is called, that is, by the imaginative faculty; or whether I rather apprehend it more clearly at present, after having examined with greater care, both what it is, and in what way it can be known. It would certainly be ridiculous to entertain any doubt on this point. For what, in that first perception, was there distinct? What did I perceive which any animal might not have perceived? But when I distinguish the wax from its exterior forms, and when, as if I had stripped it of its vestments, I consider it quite naked, it is certain, although some error may still be found in my judgment, that I cannot, nevertheless, thus apprehend it without possessing a human mind.

15. But finally, what shall I say of the mind itself, that is, of myself? for as yet I do not admit that I am anything but mind. What, then! I who seem to possess so distinct an apprehension of the piece of wax, do I not know myself, both with greater truth and certitude, and also much more distinctly and clearly? For if I judge that the wax exists because

I see it, it assuredly follows, much more evidently, that I myself am or exist, for the same reason: for it is possible that what I see may not in truth be wax, and that I do not even possess eyes with which to see anything; but it cannot be that when I see, or, which comes to the same thing, when I think I see, I myself who think am nothing. So likewise, if I judge that the wax exists because I touch it, it will still also follow that I am; and if I determine that my imagination, or any other cause, whatever it be, persuades me of the existence of the wax, I will still draw the same conclusion. And what is here remarked of the piece of wax, is applicable to all the other things that are external to me. And further, if the [notion or] perception of wax appeared to me more precise and distinct, after that not only sight and touch, but many other causes besides, rendered it manifest to my apprehension, with how much greater distinctness must I now know myself, since all the reasons that contribute to the knowledge of the nature of wax, or of any body whatever, manifest still better the nature of my mind? And there are besides so many other things in the mind itself that contribute to the illustration of its nature, that those dependent on the body, to which I have here referred, scarcely merit to be taken into account.

16. But, in conclusion, I find I have insensibly reverted to the point I desired; for, since it is now manifest to me that bodies themselves are not properly perceived by the senses nor by the faculty of imagination, but by the intellect alone; and since they are not perceived because they are seen and touched, but only because they are understood [or rightly comprehended by thought], I readily discover that there is nothing more easily or clearly apprehended than my own mind. But because it is difficult to rid one's self so promptly of an opinion to which one has been long accustomed, it will be desirable to tarry for some time at this stage, that, by long continued meditation, I may more deeply impress upon my memory this new knowledge.

MEDITATION III.

OF GOD: THAT HE EXISTS.

1. I WILL now close my eyes, I will stop my ears, I will turn away my senses from their objects, I will even efface from my consciousness all the images of corporeal things; or at least, because this can hardly be accomplished, I will consider them as empty and false; and thus, holding converse only with myself, and closely examining my nature, I will endeavor to obtain by degrees a more intimate and familiar knowledge of myself. I am a thinking (conscious) thing, that is, a being who doubts, affirms, denies, knows a few objects, and is ignorant of many,—[who loves, hates], wills, refuses, who imagines likewise, and perceives; for, as I before remarked, although the things which I perceive or imagine are perhaps nothing at all apart from me [and in themselves], I am nevertheless assured that those modes of consciousness which I call perceptions and imaginations, in as far only as they are modes of consciousness, exist in me. . . . . .

5. Of my thoughts some are, as it were, images of things, and to these alone properly belongs the name IDEA; as when I think [represent to my mind] a man, a chimera, the sky, an angel or God. Others, again, have certain other forms; as when I will, fear, affirm, or deny, I always, indeed, apprehend something as the object of my thought, but I also embrace in thought something more than the representation of the object; and of this class of thoughts some are called volitions or affections, and others judgments.

6. Now, with respect to ideas, if these are considered only in themselves, and are not referred to any object beyond them, they cannot, properly speaking, be false; for, whether I imagine a goat or chimera, it is not less true that I imagine the one than the other. Nor need we fear that falsity may exist in the will or affections; for, although I may desire objects that are wrong, and even that never existed,

❈ ❈

it is still true that I desire them. There thus only remain our judgments, in which we must take diligent heed that we be not deceived. But the chief and most ordinary error that arises in them consists in judging that the ideas which are in us are like or conformed to the things that are external to us; for assuredly, if we but considered the ideas themselves as certain modes of our thought (consciousness), without referring them to anything beyond, they would hardly afford any occasion of error.

7. But among these ideas, some appear to me to be innate, others adventitious, and others to be made by myself (factitious); for, as I have the power of conceiving what is called a thing, or a truth, or a thought, it seems to me that I hold this power from no other source than my own nature; but if I now hear a noise, if I see the sun, or if I feel heat, I have all along judged that these sensations proceeded from certain objects existing out of myself; and, in fine, it appears to me that sirens, hippogryphs, and the like, are inventions of my own mind. But I may even perhaps come to be of opinion that all my ideas are of the class which I call adventitious, or that they are all innate, or that they are all factitious; for I have not yet clearly discovered their true origin. . . .

14. Now, it is manifest by the natural light that there must at least be as much reality in the efficient and total cause as in its effect; for whence can the effect draw its reality if not from its cause? And how could the cause communicate to it this reality unless it possessed it in itself? And hence it follows, not only that what is cannot be produced by what is not, but likewise that the more perfect, in other words, that which contains in itself more reality, cannot be the effect of the less perfect; and this is not only evidently true of those effects, whose reality is actual or formal, but likewise of ideas, whose reality is only considered as objective. Thus, for example, the stone that is not yet in existence, not only cannot now commence to be, unless it be produced by that which possesses in itself, formally or eminently, all that enters into its composition, [in other words, by that which contains in itself the same properties that are in the stone, or others superior to them]; and heat can only be produced in a subject that was before devoid of it, by a cause that is of an order, [degree or kind], at least as perfect as heat; and so of the others. But further, even the idea of the heat, or of the stone, cannot exist in me unless it be put there by a cause that contains, at least, as much reality as I conceive existent in the heat or in the stone for although that cause may not transmit into my idea anything of its actual or formal reality, we ought not on this account to imagine that it is less real; but we ought to consider that, [as every idea is a work of the mind], its nature is such as of itself to demand no other formal reality than that which it borrows from our consciousness, of which it is but a mode [that is, a manner or way of thinking]. But in order that an idea may contain this objective reality rather than that, it must doubtless derive it from some cause in which is found at least as much formal reality as the idea contains of objective; for, if we suppose that there is found in an idea anything which was not in its cause, it must of course derive this from nothing. But, however imperfect may be the mode of existence by which a thing is objectively [or by representation] in the understanding by its idea, we certainly cannot, for all that, allege that this mode of existence is nothing, nor, consequently, that the idea owes its origin to nothing.

15. Nor must it be imagined that, since the reality which considered in these ideas is only objective, the same reality need not be formally (actually) in the causes of these ideas, but only objectively: for, just as the mode of existing objectively belongs to ideas by their peculiar nature, so likewise the mode of existing formally appertains to the causes of these ideas (at least to the first and principal), by their peculiar nature. And although an idea may give rise to another idea, this regress cannot, nevertheless, be infinite; we must in the end reach a first idea, the cause of which is, as it were, the archetype in which all the reality [or perfection] that is found objectively [or by representation] in these ideas is contained formally [and in act]. I am thus clearly taught by the natural light that ideas exist in me as pictures or images, which may, in truth, readily fall short of the perfection of the objects from which they are taken, but can never contain anything greater or more perfect.

16. And in proportion to the time and care with which I examine all those matters, the conviction of their truth brightens and becomes distinct. But, to sum up, what conclusion shall I draw from it all? It is this: if the objective reality [or perfection] of any one of my ideas be such as clearly to convince me, that this same reality exists in me neither formally nor eminently, and if, as follows from this, I myself cannot be the cause of it, it is a necessary consequence that I am not alone in the world, but that there is besides myself some other being who exists as the cause of that idea; while, on the contrary, if no such idea be found in my mind, I shall have no sufficient ground of assurance of the existence of any other being besides myself, for, after a most careful search, I have, up to this moment, been unable to discover any other ground.

17. But, among these my ideas, besides that which represents myself, respecting which there can be here no difficulty, there is one that represents a God; others that represent corporeal and inanimate things; others angels; others animals; and, finally, there are some that represent men like myself.

18. But with respect to the ideas that represent other men, or animals, or angels, I can easily suppose that they were formed by the mingling and composition of the other ideas which I have of myself, of corporeal things, and of God, although they were, apart from myself, neither men, animals, nor angels.

19. And with regard to the ideas of corporeal objects, I never discovered in them anything so great or excellent which I myself did not appear capable of originating; for, by considering these ideas closely and scrutinizing them individually, in the same way that I yesterday examined the idea of wax, I find that there is but little in them that is clearly and distinctly perceived . . .

20. To ideas of this kind, indeed, it is not necessary that I should assign any author besides myself: for if they are false, that is, represent objects that are unreal, the natural light teaches me that they proceed from nothing; in other words, that they are in me only because something is wanting to the perfection of my nature; but if these ideas are true, yet because they exhibit to me so little reality that I cannot even distinguish the object represented from nonbeing, I do not see why I should not be the author of them.

21. With reference to those ideas of corporeal things that are clear and distinct, there are some which, as appears to me, might have been taken from the idea I have of myself, as those of substance, duration, number, and the like. For when I think that a stone is a substance, or a thing capable of existing of itself, and that I am likewise a substance, although I conceive that I am a thinking and non-extended thing, and that the stone, on the contrary, is extended and unconscious, there being thus the greatest diversity between the two concepts, yet these two ideas seem to have this in common that they both represent substances. In the same way, when I think of myself as now existing, and recollect besides that I existed some time ago, and when I am conscious of various thoughts whose number I know, I then acquire the ideas of duration and number, which I can afterward transfer to as many objects as I please. With respect to the other qualities that go to make up the ideas of corporeal objects, viz, extension, figure, situation, and motion, it is true that they are not formally in me, since I am merely a thinking being; but because they are only certain modes of substance, and because I myself am a substance, it seems possible that they may be contained in me eminently.

❖ ❖

22. There only remains, therefore, the idea of God, in which I must consider whether there is anything that cannot be supposed to originate with myself. By the name God, I understand a substance infinite, [eternal, immutable], independent, all-knowing, all-powerful, and by which I myself, and every other thing that exists, if any such there be, were created. But these properties are so great and excellent, that the more attentively I consider them the less I feel persuaded that the idea I have of them owes its origin to myself alone. And thus it is absolutely necessary to conclude, from all that I have before said, that God exists.

23. For though the idea of substance be in my mind owing to this, that I myself am a substance, I should not, however, have the idea of an infinite substance, seeing I am a finite being, unless it were given me by some substance in reality infinite.

24. And I must not imagine that I do not apprehend the infinite by a true idea, but only by the negation of the finite, in the same way that I comprehend repose and darkness by the negation of motion and light: since, on the contrary, I clearly perceive that there is more reality in the infinite substance than in the finite, and therefore that in some way I possess the perception (notion) of the infinite before that of the finite, that is, the perception of God before that of myself, for how could I know that I doubt, desire, or that something is wanting to me, and that I am not wholly perfect, if I possessed no idea of a being more perfect than myself, by comparison of which I knew the deficiencies of my nature?

25. And it cannot be said that this idea of God is perhaps materially false, and consequently that it may have arisen from nothing [in other words, that it may exist in me from my imperfections as I before said of the ideas of heat and cold, and the like: for, on the contrary, as this idea is very clear and distinct, and contains in itself more objective reality than any other, there can be no one of itself more true, or less open to the suspicion of falsity.

The idea, I say, of a being supremely perfect, and infinite, is in the highest degree true; for although, perhaps, we may imagine that such a being does not exist, we cannot, nevertheless, suppose that his idea represents nothing real, as I have already said of the idea of cold. It is likewise clear and distinct in the highest degree, since whatever the mind clearly and distinctly conceives as real or true, and as implying any perfection, is contained entire in this idea. And this is true, nevertheless, although I do not comprehend the infinite, and although there may be in God an infinity of things that I cannot comprehend, nor perhaps even compass by thought in any way; for it is of the nature of the infinite that it should not be comprehended by the finite; and it is enough that I rightly understand this, and judge that all which I clearly perceive, and in which I know there is some perfection, and perhaps also an infinity of properties of which I am ignorant, are formally or eminently in God, in order that the idea I have of him may be come the most true, clear, and distinct of all the ideas in my mind.

26. But perhaps I am something more than I suppose myself to be, and it may be that all those perfections which I attribute to God, in some way exist potentially in me, although they do not yet show themselves, and are not reduced to act. Indeed, I am already conscious that my knowledge is being increased [and perfected] by degrees; and I see nothing to prevent it from thus gradually increasing to infinity, nor any reason why, after such increase and perfection, I should not be able thereby to acquire all the other perfections of the Divine nature; nor, in fine, why the power I possess of acquiring those perfections, if it really now exist in me, should not be sufficient to produce the ideas of them.

27. Yet, on looking more closely into the matter, I discover that this cannot be; for, in the first place, although it were true that my knowledge daily acquired new degrees of perfection, and although there were potentially in my nature much that was not as yet actually in it, still all these excellences make not the slightest approach to the idea I have of the Deity, in whom there is no perfection merely potentially [but all actually] existent; for it is even an unmistakable token of imperfection in my knowledge, that it is augmented by degrees. Further, although my knowledge increase more and more, nevertheless I am not, therefore, induced to think that it will ever be actually infinite, since it can never reach that point beyond which it shall be incapable of further increase. But I conceive God as actually infinite, so that nothing can be added to his perfection. And, in fine, I readily perceive that the objective being of an idea cannot be produced by a being that is merely potentially existent, which, properly speaking, is nothing, but only by a being existing formally or actually.

28. And, truly, I see nothing in all that I have now said which it is not easy for any one, who shall carefully consider it, to discern by the natural light; but when I allow my attention in some degree to relax, the vision of my mind being obscured, and, as it were, blinded by the images of sensible objects, I do not readily remember the reason why the idea of a being more perfect than myself, must of necessity have proceeded from a being in reality more perfect. On this account I am here desirous to inquire further, whether I, who possess this idea of God, could exist supposing there were no God.

29. And I ask, from whom could I, in that case, derive my existence? Perhaps from myself, or from my parents, or from some other causes less perfect than God; for anything more perfect, or even equal to God, cannot be thought or imagined.

30. But if I [were independent of every other existence, and] were myself the author of my being, I should doubt of nothing, I should desire nothing, and, in fine, no perfection would be awanting to me; for I should have bestowed upon myself every perfection of which I possess the idea, and I should thus be God. And it must not be imagined that what is now wanting to me is perhaps of more difficult acquisition than that of which I am already possessed; for, on the contrary, it is quite manifest that it was a matter of much higher difficulty that I, a thinking being, should arise from nothing, than it would be for me to acquire the knowledge of many things of which I am ignorant, and which are merely the accidents of a thinking substance; and certainly, if I possessed of myself the greater perfection of which I have now spoken [in other words, if I were the author of my own existence], I would not at least have denied to myself things that may be more easily obtained [as that infinite variety of knowledge of which I am at present destitute]. I could not, indeed, have denied to myself any property which I perceive is contained in the idea of God, because there is none of these that seems to me to be more difficult to make or acquire; and if there were any that should happen to be more difficult to acquire, they would certainly appear so to me (supposing that I myself were the source of the other things I possess), because I should discover in them a limit to my power.

31. And though I were to suppose that I always was as I now am, I should not, on this ground, escape the force of these reasonings, since it would not follow, even on this supposition, that no author of my existence needed to be sought after. For the whole time of my life may be divided into an infinity of parts, each of which is in no way dependent on any other; and, accordingly, because I was in existence a short time ago, it does not follow that I must now exist, unless in this moment some cause create me anew as it were, that is, conserve me. In truth, it is perfectly clear and evident to all who will attentively consider the nature of duration, that the conservation of a substance, in each moment of its duration, requires the same power and act that would be necessary to create it, supposing it were not yet in existence; so that it is manifestly a dictate of the natural light that conservation and creation

❖ ❖

differ merely in respect of our mode of thinking [and not in reality].

32. All that is here required, therefore, is that I interrogate myself to discover whether I possess any power by means of which I can bring it about that I, who now am, shall exist a moment afterward: for, since I am merely a thinking thing (or since, at least, the precise question, in the meantime, is only of that part of myself), if such a power resided in me, I should, without doubt, be conscious of it; but I am conscious of no such power, and thereby I manifestly know that I am dependent upon some being different from myself. . . .

37. There remains only the inquiry as to the way in which I received this idea from God; for I have not drawn it from the senses, nor is it even presented to me unexpectedly, as is usual with the ideas of sensible objects, when these are presented or appear to be presented to the external organs of the senses; it is not even a pure production or fiction of my mind, for it is not in my power to take from or add to it; and consequently there but remains the alternative that it is innate, in the same way as is the idea of myself. . . .

39. But before I examine this with more attention, and pass on to the consideration of other truths that may be evolved out of it, I think it proper to remain here for some time in the contemplation of God himself—that I may ponder at leisure his marvelous attributes—and behold, admire, and adore the beauty of this light so unspeakably great, as far, at least, as the strength of my mind, which is to some degree dazzled by the sight, will permit. For just as we learn by faith that the supreme felicity of another life consists in the contemplation of the Divine majesty alone, so even now we learn from experience that a like meditation, though incomparably less perfect, is the source of the highest satisfaction of which we are susceptible in this life.

MEDITATION IIII

OF TRUTH AND ERROR.

1. I HAVE been habituated these bygone days to detach my mind from the senses, and I have accurately observed that there is exceedingly little which is known with certainty respecting corporeal objects, that we know much more of the human mind, and still more of God himself. I am thus able now without difficulty to abstract my mind from the contemplation of [sensible or] imaginable objects, and apply it to those which, as disengaged from all matter, are purely intelligible. And certainly the idea I have of the human mind in so far as it is a thinking thing, and not extended in length, breadth, and depth, and participating in none of the properties of body, is incomparably more distinct than the idea of any corporeal object; and when I consider that I doubt, in other words, that I am an incomplete and dependent being, the idea of a complete and independent being, that is to say of God, occurs to my mind with so much clearness and distinctness, and from the fact alone that this idea is found in me, or that I who possess it exist, the conclusions that God exists, and that my own existence, each moment of its continuance, is absolutely dependent upon him, are so manifest, as to lead me to believe it impossible that the human mind can know anything with more clearness and certitude. And now I seem to discover a path that will conduct us from the contemplation of the true God, in whom are contained all the treasures of science and wisdom, to the knowledge of the other things in the universe.

2. For, in the first place, I discover that it is impossible for him ever to deceive me, for in all fraud and deceit there is a certain imperfection: and although it may seem that the ability to deceive is a mark of subtlety or power, yet the will testifies without doubt of malice and weakness; and such, accordingly, cannot be found in God.

❂ ❂

3. In the next place, I am conscious that I possess a certain faculty of judging [or discerning truth from error], which I doubtless received from God, along with whatever else is mine; and since it is impossible that he should will to deceive me, it is likewise certain that he has not given me a faculty that will ever lead me into error, provided I use it aright.

4. And there would remain no doubt on this head, did it not seem to follow from this, that I can never therefore be deceived; for if all I possess be from God, and if he planted in me no faculty that is deceitful, it seems to follow that I can never fall into error. Accordingly, it is true that when I think only of God (when I look upon myself as coming from God, Fr.), and turn wholly to him, I discover [in myself] no cause of error or falsity: but immediately thereafter, recurring to myself, experience assures me that I am nevertheless subject to innumerable errors. When I come to inquire into the cause of these, I observe that there is not only present to my consciousness a real and positive idea of God, or of a being supremely perfect, but also, so to speak, a certain negative idea of nothing, in other words, of that which is at an infinite distance from every sort of perfection, and that I am, as it were, a mean between God and nothing, or placed in such a way between absolute existence and non-existence, that there is in truth nothing in me to lead me into error, in so far as an absolute being is my creator; but that, on the other hand, as I thus likewise participate in some degree of nothing or of nonbeing, in other words, as I am not myself the supreme Being, and as I am wanting in many perfections, it is not surprising I should fall into error. And I hence discern that error, so far as error is not something real, which depends for its existence on God, but is simply defect; and therefore that, in order to fall into it, it is not necessary God should have given me a faculty expressly for this end, but that my being deceived arises from the circumstance that the power which God has given me of discerning truth from error is not infinite.

5. Nevertheless this is not yet quite satisfactory; for error is not a pure negation, [in other words, it is not the simple deficiency or want of some knowledge which is not due], but the privation or want of some knowledge which it would seem I ought to possess. But, on considering the nature of God, it seems impossible that he should have planted in his creature any faculty not perfect in its kind, that is, wanting in some perfection due to it: for if it be true, that in proportion to the skill of the maker the perfection of his work is greater, what thing can have been produced by the supreme Creator of the universe that is not absolutely perfect in all its parts? And assuredly there is no doubt that God could have created me such as that I should never be deceived; it is certain, likewise, that he always wills what is best: is it better, then, that I should be capable of being deceived than that I should not?

6. Considering this more attentively the first thing that occurs to me is the reflection that I must not be surprised if I am not always capable of comprehending the reasons why God acts as he does; nor must I doubt of his existence because I find, perhaps, that there are several other things besides the present respecting which I understand neither why nor how they were created by him; for, knowing already that my nature is extremely weak and limited, and that the nature of God, on the other hand, is immense, incomprehensible, and infinite, I have no longer any difficulty in discerning that there is an infinity of things in his power whose causes transcend the grasp of my mind: and this consideration alone is sufficient to convince me, that the whole class of final causes is of no avail in physical [or natural] things; for it appears to me that I cannot, without exposing myself to the charge of temerity, seek to discover the [impenetrable] ends of Deity.

7. It further occurs to me that we must not consider only one creature apart from the others, if we wish to determine the perfection of the works of Deity, but generally all his creatures together; for the same

❀ ❀

object that might perhaps, with some show of reason, be deemed highly imperfect if it were alone in the world, may for all that be the most perfect possible, considered as forming part of the whole universe: and although, as it was my purpose to doubt of everything, I only as yet know with certainty my own existence and that of God, nevertheless, after having remarked the infinite power of Deity, I cannot deny that we may have produced many other objects, or at least that he is able to produce them, so that I may occupy a place in the relation of a part to the great whole of his creatures.

8. Whereupon, regarding myself more closely, and considering what my errors are (which alone testify to the existence of imperfection in me), I observe that these depend on the concurrence of two causes, viz, the faculty of cognition, which I possess, and that of election or the power of free choice,—in other words, the understanding and the will. For by the understanding alone, I [neither affirm nor deny anything but] merely apprehend (percipio) the ideas regarding which I may form a judgment; nor is any error, properly so called, found in it thus accurately taken. And although there are perhaps innumerable objects in the world of which I have no idea in my understanding, it cannot, on that account be said that I am deprived of those ideas [as of something that is due to my nature], but simply that I do not possess them, because, in truth, there is no ground to prove that Deity ought to have endowed me with a larger faculty of cognition than he has actually bestowed upon me; and however skillful a workman I suppose him to be, I have no reason, on that account, to think that it was obligatory on him to give to each of his works all the perfections he is able to bestow upon some. Nor, moreover, can I complain that God has not given me freedom of choice, or a will sufficiently ample and perfect, since, in truth, I am conscious of will so ample and extended as to be superior to all limits. And what appears to me here to be highly remarkable is that, of all the other properties

I possess, there is none so great and perfect as that I do not clearly discern it could be still greater and more perfect. For, to take an example, if I consider the faculty of understanding which I possess, I find that it is of very small extent, and greatly limited, and at the same time I form the idea of another faculty of the same nature, much more ample and even infinite, and seeing that I can frame the idea of it, I discover, from this circumstance alone, that it pertains to the nature of God. In the same way, if I examine the faculty of memory or imagination, or any other faculty I possess, I find none that is not small and circumscribed, and in God immense [and infinite]. It is the faculty of will only, or freedom of choice, which I experience to be so great that I am unable to conceive the idea of another that shall be more ample and extended; so that it is chiefly my will which leads me to discern that I bear a certain image and similitude of Deity. For although the faculty of will is incomparably greater in God than in myself, as well in respect of the knowledge and power that are conjoined with it, and that render it stronger and more efficacious, as in respect of the object, since in him it extends to a greater number of things, it does not, nevertheless, appear to me greater, considered in itself formally and precisely: for the power of will consists only in this, that we are able to do or not to do the same thing (that is, to affirm or deny, to pursue or shun it), or rather in this alone, that in affirming or denying, pursuing or shunning, what is proposed to us by the understanding, we so act that we are not conscious of being determined to a particular action by any external force. For, to the possession of freedom, it is not necessary that I be alike indifferent toward each of two contraries; but, on the contrary, the more I am inclined toward the one, whether because I clearly know that in it there is the reason of truth and goodness, or because God thus internally disposes my thought, the more freely do I choose and embrace it; and assuredly divine grace and natural knowledge, very far from diminishing liberty, rather augment and fortify it. But the

❖ ❖

indifference of which I am conscious when I am not impelled to one side rather than to another for want of a reason, is the lowest grade of liberty, and manifests defect or negation of knowledge rather than perfection of will; for if I always clearly knew what was true and good, I should never have any difficulty in determining what judgment I ought to come to, and what choice I ought to make, and I should thus be entirely free without ever being indifferent.

9. From all this I discover, however, that neither the power of willing, which I have received from God, is of itself the source of my errors, for it is exceedingly ample and perfect in its kind; nor even the power of understanding, for as I conceive no object unless by means of the faculty that God bestowed upon me, all that I conceive is doubtless rightly conceived by me, and it is impossible for me to be deceived in it. Whence, then, spring my errors? They arise from this cause alone, that I do not restrain the will, which is of much wider range than the understanding, within the same limits, but extend it even to things I do not understand, and as the will is of itself indifferent to such, it readily falls into error and sin by choosing the false in room of the true, and evil instead of good. . . .

12. But if I abstain from judging of a thing when I do not conceive it with sufficient clearness and distinctness, it is plain that I act rightly, and am not deceived; but if I resolve to deny or affirm, I then do not make a right use of my free will; and if I affirm what is false, it is evident that I am deceived; moreover, even although I judge according to truth, I stumble upon it by chance, and do not therefore escape the imputation of a wrong use of my freedom; for it is a dictate of the natural light, that the knowledge of the understanding ought always to precede the determination of the will. And it is this wrong use of the freedom of the will in which is found the privation that constitutes the form of error. Privation, I say, is found in the act, in so far as it proceeds from myself, but it does not exist in the

faculty which I received from God, nor even in the act, in so far as it depends on him. . . .

17. And since it is in being superior to error that the highest and chief perfection of man consists, I deem that I have not gained little by this day's meditation, in having discovered the source of error and falsity. And certainly this can be no other than what I have now explained: for as often as I so restrain my will within the limits of my knowledge, that it forms no judgment except regarding objects which are clearly and distinctly represented to it by the understanding, I can never be deceived; because every clear and distinct conception is doubtless something, and as such cannot owe its origin to nothing, but must of necessity have God for its author—God, I say, who, as supremely perfect, cannot, without a contradiction, be the cause of any error; and consequently it is necessary to conclude that every such conception [or judgment] is true. Nor have I merely learned today what I must avoid to escape error, but also what I must do to arrive at the knowledge of truth; for I will assuredly reach truth if I only fix my attention sufficiently on all the things I conceive perfectly, and separate these from others which I conceive more confusedly and obscurely; to which for the future I shall give diligent heed.

MEDITATION V

OF THE ESSENCE OF MATERIAL THINGS; AND, AGAIN, OF GOD; THAT HE EXISTS.

1. SEVERAL other questions remain for consideration respecting the attributes of God and my own nature or mind. I will, however, on some other occasion perhaps resume the investigation of these. Meanwhile, as I have discovered what must be done and what avoided to arrive at the knowledge of truth, what I have chiefly to do is to essay to emerge from the state of doubt in which I have for

❀ ❀

some time been, and to discover whether anything can be known with certainty regarding material objects.

2. But before considering whether such objects as I conceive exist without me, I must examine their ideas in so far as these are to be found in my consciousness, and discover which of them are distinct and which confused.

3. In the first place, I distinctly imagine that quantity which the philosophers commonly call continuous, or the extension in length, breadth, and depth that is in this quantity, or rather in the object to which it is attributed. Further, I can enumerate in it many diverse parts, and attribute to each of these all sorts of sizes, figures, situations, and local motions; and, in fine, I can assign to each of these motions all degrees of duration.

4. And I not only distinctly know these things when I thus consider them in general; but besides, by a little attention, I discover innumerable particulars respecting figures, numbers, motion, and the like, which are so evidently true, and so accordant with my nature, that when I now discover them I do not so much appear to learn anything new, as to call to remembrance what I before knew, or for the first time to remark what was before in my mind, but to which I had not hitherto directed my attention.

5. And what I here find of most importance is, that I discover in my mind innumerable ideas of certain objects, which cannot be esteemed pure negations, although perhaps they possess no reality beyond my thought, and which are not framed by me though it may be in my power to think, or not to think them, but possess true and immutable natures of their own. As, for example, when I imagine a triangle, although there is not perhaps and never was in any place in the universe apart from my thought one such figure, it remains true nevertheless that this figure possesses a certain determinate nature, form, or essence, which is immutable and eternal, and not framed by me, nor

in any degree dependent on my thought; as appears from the circumstance, that diverse properties of the triangle may be demonstrated, viz, that its three angles are equal to two right, that its greatest side is subtended by its greatest angle, and the like, which, whether I will or not, I now clearly discern to belong to it, although before I did not at all think of them, when, for the first time, I imagined a triangle, and which accordingly cannot be said to have been invented by me. . . .

7. But now if because I can draw from my thought the idea of an object, it follows that all I clearly and distinctly apprehend to pertain to this object, does in truth belong to it, may I not from this derive an argument for the existence of God? It is certain that I no less find the idea of a God in my consciousness, that is the idea of a being supremely perfect, than that of any figure or number whatever: and I know with not less clearness and distinctness that an [actual and] eternal existence pertains to his nature than that all which is demonstrable of any figure or number really belongs to the nature of that figure or number; and, therefore, although all the conclusions of the preceding Meditations were false, the existence of God would pass with me for a truth at least as certain as I ever judged any truth of mathematics to be.

8. Indeed such a doctrine may at first sight appear to contain more sophistry than truth. For, as I have been accustomed in every other matter to distinguish between existence and essence, I easily believe that the existence can be separated from the essence of God, and that thus God may be conceived as not actually existing. But, nevertheless, when I think of it more attentively, it appears that the existence can no more be separated from the essence of God, than the idea of a mountain from that of a valley, or the equality of its three angles to two right angles, from the essence of a [rectilinear] triangle; so that it is not less impossible to conceive a God, that is, a being supremely perfect, to whom existence is awanting, or who is devoid of a certain perfection, than to conceive a mountain without a valley.

9. But though, in truth, I cannot conceive a God unless as existing, any more than I can a mountain without a valley, yet, just as it does not follow that there is any mountain in the world merely because I conceive a mountain with a valley, so likewise, though I conceive God as existing, it does not seem to follow on that account that God exists; for my thought imposes no necessity on things; and as I may imagine a winged horse, though there be none such, so I could perhaps attribute existence to God, though no God existed.

10. But the cases are not analogous, and a fallacy lurks under the semblance of this objection: for because I cannot conceive a mountain without a valley, it does not follow that there is any mountain or valley in existence, but simply that the mountain or valley, whether they do or do not exist, are inseparable from each other; whereas, on the other hand, because I cannot conceive God unless as existing, it follows that existence is inseparable from him, and therefore that he really exists: not that this is brought about by my thought, or that it imposes any necessity on things, but, on the contrary, the necessity which lies in the thing itself, that is, the necessity of the existence of God, determines me to think in this way: for it is not in my power to conceive a God without existence, that is, a being supremely perfect, and yet devoid of an absolute perfection, as I am free to imagine a horse with or without wings.

11. Nor must it be alleged here as an objection, that it is in truth necessary to admit that God exists, after having supposed him to possess all perfections, since existence is one of them, but that my original supposition was not necessary; just as it is not necessary to think that all quadrilateral figures can be inscribed in the circle, since, if I supposed this, I should be constrained to admit that the rhombus, being a figure of four sides, can be

therein inscribed, which, however, is manifestly false. This objection is, I say, incompetent; for although it may not be necessary that I shall at any time entertain the notion of Deity, yet each time I happen to think of a first and sovereign being, and to draw, so to speak, the idea of him from the storehouse of the mind, I am necessitated to attribute to him all kinds of perfections, though I may not then enumerate them all, nor think of each of them in particular. And this necessity is sufficient, as soon as I discover that existence is a perfection, to cause me to infer the existence of this first and sovereign being; just as it is not necessary that I should ever imagine any triangle, but whenever I am desirous of considering a rectilinear figure composed of only three angles, it is absolutely necessary to attribute those properties to it from which it is correctly inferred that its three angles are not greater than two right angles, although perhaps I may not then advert to this relation in particular. But when I consider what figures are capable of being inscribed in the circle, it is by no means necessary to hold that all quadrilateral figures are of this number; on the contrary, I cannot even imagine such to be the case, so long as I shall be unwilling to accept in thought aught that I do not clearly and distinctly conceive; and consequently there is a vast difference between false suppositions, as is the one in question, and the true ideas that were born with me, the first and chief of which is the idea of God. For indeed I discern on many grounds that this idea is not factitious depending simply on my thought, but that it is the representation of a true and immutable nature: in the first place because I can conceive no other being, except God, to whose essence existence [necessarily] pertains; in the second, because it is impossible to conceive two or more gods of this kind; and it being supposed that one such God exists, I clearly see that he must have existed from all eternity, and will exist to all eternity; and finally, because I apprehend many other properties in God, none of which I can either diminish or change.

❁ ❁

12. But, indeed, whatever mode of probation I in the end adopt, it always returns to this, that it is only the things I clearly and distinctly conceive which have the power of completely persuading me. And although, of the objects I conceive in this manner, some, indeed, are obvious to every one, while others are only discovered after close and careful investigation; nevertheless after they are once discovered, the latter are not esteemed less certain than the former. Thus, for example, to take the case of a right-angled triangle, although it is not so manifest at first that the square of the base is equal to the squares of the other two sides, as that the base is opposite to the greatest angle; nevertheless, after it is once apprehended, we are as firmly persuaded of the truth of the former as of the latter. And, with respect to God if I were not pre-occupied by prejudices, and my thought beset on all sides by the continual presence of the images of sensible objects, I should know nothing sooner or more easily then the fact of his being. For is there any truth more clear than the existence of a Supreme Being, or of God, seeing it is to his essence alone that [necessary and eternal] existence pertains?

13. And although the right conception of this truth has cost me much close thinking, nevertheless at present I feel not only as assured of it as of what I deem most certain, but I remark further that the certitude of all other truths is so absolutely dependent on it that without this knowledge it is impossible ever to know anything perfectly.

14. For although I am of such a nature as to be unable, while I possess a very clear and distinct apprehension of a matter, to resist the conviction of its truth, yet because my constitution is also such as to incapacitate me from keeping my mind continually fixed on the same object, and as I frequently recollect a past judgment without at the same time being able to recall the grounds of it, it may happen meanwhile that other reasons are presented to me which would readily cause me to change my opinion, if I did not know that God existed; and thus I should possess no true and certain knowledge, but merely vague and vacillating opinions. Thus, for example, when I consider the nature of the [rectilinear] triangle, it most clearly appears to me, who have been instructed in the principles of geometry, that its three angles are equal to two right angles, and I find it impossible to believe otherwise, while I apply my mind to the demonstration; but as soon as I cease from attending to the process of proof, although I still remember that I had a clear comprehension of it, yet I may readily come to doubt of the truth demonstrated, if I do not know that there is a God: for I may persuade myself that I have been so constituted by nature as to be sometimes deceived, even in matters which I think I apprehend with the greatest evidence and certitude, especially when I recollect that I frequently considered many things to be true and certain which other reasons afterward constrained me to reckon as wholly false.

15. But after I have discovered that God exists, seeing I also at the same time observed that all things depend on him, and that he is no deceiver, and thence inferred that all which I clearly and distinctly perceive is of necessity true: although I no longer attend to the grounds of a judgment, no opposite reason can be alleged sufficient to lead me to doubt of its truth, provided only I remember that I once possessed a clear and distinct comprehension of it. My knowledge of it thus becomes true and certain. And this same knowledge extends likewise to whatever I remember to have formerly demonstrated, as the truths of geometry and the like: for what can be alleged against them to lead me to doubt of them? Will it be that my nature is such that I may be frequently deceived? But I already know that I cannot be deceived in judgments of the grounds of which I possess a clear knowledge. Will it be that I formerly deemed things to be true and certain which I afterward discovered to be false? But I had no clear and distinct knowledge of any of those things, and, being as yet ignorant of the rule by which I am assured of the truth of a judgment, I was led to give my assent to them on grounds which I afterward discovered were less strong than at the time I imagined them to be. What further objection, then, is there? Will it be said that perhaps I am dreaming (an objection I lately myself raised), or that all the thoughts of which I am now conscious have no more truth than the reveries of my dreams? But although, in truth, I should be dreaming, the rule still holds that all which is clearly presented to my intellect is indisputably true.

16. And thus I very clearly see that the certitude and truth of all science depends on the knowledge alone of the true God, insomuch that, before I knew him, I could have no perfect knowledge of any other thing. And now that I know him, I possess the means of acquiring a perfect knowledge respecting innumerable matters, as well relative to God himself and other intellectual objects as to corporeal nature, in so far as it is the object of pure mathematics [which do not consider whether it exists or not].

MEDITATION VI

OF THE EXISTENCE OF MATERIAL THINGS, AND OF THE REAL DISTINCTION BETWEEN THE MIND AND BODY OF MAN.

1. THERE now only remains the inquiry as to whether material things exist. With regard to this question, I at least know with certainty that such things may exist, in as far as they constitute the object of the pure mathematics, since, regarding them in this aspect, I can conceive them clearly and distinctly. For there can be no doubt that God possesses the power of producing all the objects I am able distinctly to conceive, and I never considered anything impossible to him, unless when I experienced a contradiction in the attempt to conceive it aright. Further, the faculty of imagination which I possess, and of which I am conscious that I

make use when I apply myself to the consideration of material things, is sufficient to persuade me of their existence: for, when I attentively consider what imagination is, I find that it is simply a certain application of the cognitive faculty (facultas cognoscitiva) to a body which is immediately present to it, and which therefore exists.

2. And to render this quite clear, I remark, in the first place, the difference that subsists between imagination and pure intellection [or conception]. For example, when I imagine a triangle I not only conceive (intelligo) that it is a figure comprehended by three lines, but at the same time also I look upon (intueor) these three lines as present by the power and internal application of my mind (acie mentis), and this is what I call imagining. But if I desire to think of a chiliogon, I indeed rightly conceive that it is a figure composed of a thousand sides, as easily as I conceive that a triangle is a figure composed of only three sides; but I cannot imagine the thousand sides of a chiliogon as I do the three sides of a triangle, nor, so to speak, view them as present [with the eyes of my mind]. And although, in accordance with the habit I have of always imagining something when I think of corporeal things, it may happen that, in conceiving a chiliogon, I confusedly represent some figure to myself, yet it is quite evident that this is not a chiliogon, since it in no wise differs from that which I would represent to myself, if I were to think of a myriogon, or any other figure of many sides; nor would this representation be of any use in discovering and unfolding the properties that constitute the difference between a chiliogon and other polygons. But if the question turns on a pentagon, it is quite true that I can conceive its figure, as well as that of a chiliogon, without the aid of imagination; but I can likewise imagine it by applying the attention of my mind to its five sides, and at the same time to the area which they contain. Thus I observe that a special effort of mind is necessary to the act of imagination, which is not required to conceiving or understanding (ad intelligendum);

❀ ❀

and this special exertion of mind clearly shows the difference between imagination and pure intellection (imaginatio et intellectio pura). . . .

23. [It] is quite manifest that, notwithstanding the sovereign goodness of God, the nature of man, in so far as it is composed of mind and body, cannot but be sometimes fallacious. For, if there is any cause which excites, not in the foot, but in some one of the parts of the nerves that stretch from the foot to the brain, or even in the brain itself, the same movement that is ordinarily created when the foot is ill affected, pain will be felt, as it were, in the foot, and the sense will thus be naturally deceived; for as the same movement in the brain can but impress the mind with the same sensation, and as this sensation is much more frequently excited by a cause which hurts the foot than by one acting in a different quarter, it is reasonable that it should lead the mind to feel pain in the foot rather than in any other part of the body. And if it sometimes happens that the parchedness of the throat does not arise, as is usual, from drink being necessary for the health of the body, but from quite the opposite cause, as is the case with the dropsical, yet it is much better that it should be deceitful in that instance, than if, on the contrary, it were continually fallacious when the body is well-disposed; and the same holds true in other cases.

24. And certainly this consideration is of great service, not only in enabling me to recognize the errors to which my nature is liable, but likewise in rendering it more easy to avoid or correct them: for, knowing that all my senses more usually indicate to me what is true than what is false, in matters relating to the advantage of the body, and being able almost always to make use of more than a single sense in examining the same object, and besides this, being able to use my memory in connecting present with past knowledge, and my understanding which

has already discovered all the causes of my errors, I ought no longer to fear that falsity may be met with in what is daily presented to me by the senses. And I ought to reject all the doubts of those bygone days, as hyperbolical and ridiculous, especially the general uncertainty respecting sleep, which I could not distinguish from the waking state: for I now find a very marked difference between the two states, in respect that our memory can never connect our dreams with each other and with the course of life, in the way it is in the habit of doing with events that occur when we are awake. And, in truth, if some one, when I am awake, appeared to me all of a sudden and as suddenly disappeared, as do the images I see in sleep, so that I could not observe either whence he came or whither he went, I should not without reason esteem it either a specter or phantom formed in my brain, rather than a real man. But when I perceive objects with regard to which I can distinctly determine both the place whence they come, and that in which they are, and the time at which they appear to me, and when, without interruption, I can connect the perception I have of them with the whole of the other parts of my life, I am perfectly sure that what I thus perceive occurs while I am awake and not during sleep. And I ought not in the least degree to doubt of the truth of these presentations, if, after having called together all my senses, my memory, and my understanding for the purpose of examining them, no deliverance is given by any one of these faculties which is repugnant to that of any other: for since God is no deceiver, it necessarily follows that I am not herein deceived. But because the necessities of action frequently oblige us to come to a determination before we have had leisure for so careful an examination, it must be confessed that the life of man is frequently obnoxious to error with respect to individual objects; and we must, in conclusion, acknowledge the weakness of our nature.

❧ 2.4 "Against Innate Ideas" ❧
Selections from *An Essay Concerning Human Understanding*
by John Locke

✳ ✳

© Georgios Kollidas/Shutterstock.com

Another section in John Locke's *An Essay Concerning Human Understanding* contains Locke's argument against our having innate ideas. This is central to Locke's *empiricism*, the view that all knowledge is justified by sensory experience alone. Locke's view is opposed to that of Plato and Descartes. Plato believed that some knowledge was "innate" in the sense that it was obtained through recollection of a prior life. Although Descartes did not believe in reincarnation, Descartes did seem to think that our *a priori* knowledge had to be innate knowledge, perhaps imprinted on the soul at birth by God, or perhaps simply part of the physical structure of the body, or perhaps both.

Locke gives several reasons for thinking that nothing is universally assented to—and even if there were something universally assented to, we wouldn't need innate knowledge to explain it. Because of this, he concludes that there is no innate knowledge. If there is no innate knowledge, then Locke thinks it follows that everything we know depends on sensory experience.

Here are some things to think about while reading Locke:

* How does Locke argue against there being anything which is universally assented to?

* Why doesn't Locke think, even if there were universal assent, that innate knowledge would be needed to explain it?

* What is the distinction between 'primary qualities' and 'secondary qualities'?

* How is Locke's standard for knowledge different from Descartes's standard? Why would Descartes doubt that Locke knows empirically the things he claims to know? Why would Locke think this still counts as knowledge?

* How might someone defend that there is some *a priori* knowledge without believing that there is innate knowledge?

❀ ❀

Book I, Chapter II. No Innate Principles in the Mind.

§ 1. The way shewn how we come by any knowledge, sufficient to prove it not innate.

It is an established opinion amongst some men, that there are in the understanding certain innate principles; some primary notions, κοιναὶ ἔννοιαι, characters, as it were, stamped upon the mind of man, which the soul receives in its very first being; and brings into the world with it. It would be sufficient to convince unprejudiced readers of the falseness of this supposition, if I should only shew (as I hope I shall in the following parts of this discourse) how men, barely by the use of their natural faculties, may attain to all the knowledge they have, without the help of any innate impressions; and may arrive at certainty, without any such original notions or principles. For I imagine any one will easily grant, that it would be impertinent to suppose, the ideas of colours innate in a creature, to whom God hath given sight, and a power to receive them by the eyes, from external objects: and no less unreasonable would it be to attribute several truths to the impressions of nature, and innate characters, when we may observe in ourselves faculties, fit to attain as easy and certain knowledge of them, as if they were originally imprinted on the mind.

But because a man is not permitted without censure to follow his own thoughts in the search of truth, when they lead him ever so little out of the common road; I shall set down the reasons that made me doubt of the truth of that opinion, as an excuse for my mistake, if I be in one; which I leave to be considered by those, who, with me, dispose themselves to embrace truth, wherever they find it.

§ 2. General assent the great argument.

There is nothing more commonly taken for granted, than that there are certain principles, both speculative and practical (for they speak of both) universally agreed upon by all mankind: which therefore, they argue, must needs be constant impressions, which the souls of men receive in their first beings, and which they bring into the world with thĕm, as necessarily and really as they do any of their inherent faculties.

§ 3. Universal consent proves nothing innate.

This argument, drawn from universal consent, has this misfortune in it, that if it were true in matter of fact, that there were certain truths, wherein all mankind agreed, it would not prove them innate, if there can be any other way shewn, how men may come to that universal agreement, in the things they do consent in; which I presume may be done.

"What is, is;" and, "it is impossible for the same thing to be, and not to be," not universally assented to.

§ 4. Argument of universal consent

But, which is worse, this argument of universal consent, which is made use of to prove innate principles, seems to me a demonstration that there are none such; because there are none to which all mankind give an universal assent. I shall begin with the speculative, and instance in those magnified principles of demonstration; "whatsoever is, is;" and, "it is impossible for the same thing to be, and not to be;" which, of all others, I think have the most allowed title to innate. These have so settled a reputation of maxims universally received, that it will, no doubt, be thought strange, if any one should seem to question it. But yet I take liberty to say, that these propositions are so far from having an universal assent, that there are a great part of mankind to whom they are not so much as known.

§ 5. Not on the mind naturally imprinted, because not known to children, idiots, &c.

For, first, it is evident, that all children and idiots have not the least apprehension or thought of them; and the want of that is enough to destroy that universal assent, which must needs be the necessary concomitant of all innate truths: it seeming to me near a contradiction, to say, that there are truths imprinted on the soul, which it perceives or understands not; imprinting, if it signify any thing, being nothing else, but the making certain truths to be perceived. For to imprint any thing on the mind, without the mind's perceiving it, seems to me hardly intelligible.

If therefore children and idiots have souls, have minds, with those impressions upon them, they must unavoidably perceive them, and necessarily know and assent to these truths: which since they do not, it is evident that there are no such impressions. For if they are not notions naturally imprinted, how can they be innate? and if they are notions imprinted, how can they be unknown? To say a notion is imprinted on the mind, and yet at the same time to say, that the mind is ignorant of it, and never yet took notice of it, is to make this impression nothing. No proposition can be said to be in the mind, which it never yet knew, which it was never yet conscious of. For if any one may, then, by the same reason, all propositions that are true, and the mind is capable of ever assenting to, may be said to be in the mind, and to be imprinted: since, if any one can be said to be in the mind, which it never yet knew, it must be only, because it is capable of knowing it, and so the mind is of all truths it ever shall know.

Nay, thus truths may be imprinted on the mind, which it never did, nor ever shall know: for a man may live long, and die at last in ignorance of many truths, which his mind was capable of knowing, and that with certainty. So that if the capacity of knowing, be the natural impression contended for, all the truths a man ever comes to know, will, by this account, be every one of them innate; and this great point will amount to no more, but only to a very improper way of speaking; which, whilst it pretends to assert the contrary, says nothing different from those, who deny innate principles. For nobody, I think, ever denied that the mind was capable of knowing several truths. The capacity, they say, is innate, the knowledge acquired. But then to what end such contest for certain innate maxims?

If truths can be imprinted on the understanding without being perceived, I can see no difference there can be, between any truths the mind is capable of knowing, in respect of their original: they must all be innate, or all adventitious: in vain shall a man go about to distinguish them. He therefore, that talks of innate notions in the understanding, cannot (if he intend thereby any distinct sort of truths) mean such truths to be in the understanding, as it never perceived, and is yet wholly ignorant of. For if these words (to be in the understanding) have any propriety, they signify to be understood: so that, to be in the understanding, and not to be understood; to be in the mind, and never to be perceived; is all one, as to say, any thing is, and is not, in the mind or understanding.

If therefore these two propositions, "whatsoever is, is;" and "it is impossible for the same thing to be, and not to be," are by nature imprinted, children cannot be ignorant of them; infants, and all that have souls, must necessarily have them in their understandings, know the truth of them, and assent to it.

§ 6 – 7. *That men know them when they come to the use of reason, answered.*

To avoid this, it is usually answered, That all men know and assent to them, when they come to the use of reason, and this is enough to prove them innate. I answer:

Doubtful expressions that have scarce any signification, go for clear reasons, to those, who being prepossessed, take not the pains to examine, even what they themselves say. For to apply this answer with any tolerable sense to our present purpose, it must signify one of these two things; either, that, as soon as men come to the use of reason, these

❀ ❀

supposed native inscriptions come to be known, and observed by them: or else, that the use and exercise of men's reason assists them in the discovery of these principles, and certainly makes them known to them . . .

§ 9. *It is false that reason discovers them.*

But how can these men think the use of reason necessary, to discover principles that are supposed innate, when reason (if we may believe them) is nothing else but the faculty of deducing unknown truths from principles, or propositions, that are already known? That certainly can never be thought innate, which we have need of reason to discover; unless, as I have said, we will have all the certain truths, that reason ever teaches us, to be innate. We may as well think the use of reason necessary to make our eyes discover visible objects, as that there should be need of reason, or the exercise thereof, to make the understanding see what is originally engraven on it, and cannot be in the understanding before it be perceived by it. So that to make reason discover those truths, thus imprinted, is to say, that the use of reason discovers to a man what he knew before: and if men have those innate impressed truths originally, and before the use of reason, and yet are always ignorant of them, till they come to the use of reason, it is in effect to say, that men know, and know them not, at the same time. . . .

§ 15. *The steps by which the mind attains several truths.*

The senses at first let in particular ideas, and furnish the yet empty cabinet; and the mind by degrees growing familiar with some of them, they are lodged in the memory, and names got to them. Afterwards the mind, proceeding farther, abstracts them, and by degrees learns the use of general names. In this manner the mind comes to be furnished with ideas and language, the materials about which to exercise its discursive faculty: and the use of reason becomes daily more visible, as these materials, that give it employment, increase.

But though the having of general ideas, and the use of general words and reason, usually grow together; yet, I see not, how this any way proves them innate. The knowledge of some truths, I confess, is very early in the mind; but in a way that shows them not to be innate. For, if we will observe, we shall find it still to be about ideas, not innate, but acquired: It being about those first which are imprinted by external things, with which infants have earliest to do, which make the most frequent impressions on their senses. In ideas thus got, the mind discovers that some agree, and others differ, probably as soon as it has any use of memory; as soon as it is able to retain and perceive distinct ideas.

But whether it be then, or no, this is certain, it does so, long before it has the use of words, or comes to that, which we commonly call "the use of reason." For a child knows as certainly, before it can speak, the difference between the ideas of sweet and bitter (i. e. that sweet is not bitter) as it knows afterwards (when it comes to speak) that wormwood and sugar-plums are not the same thing. . . .

Book II, Chapter I. Of Ideas in general, and their Original.

§ 2. *All ideas come from sensation or reflection.*

. . . Let us then suppose the mind to be, as we say, white paper, void of all characters, without any ideas; how comes it to be furnished? Whence comes it by that vast store which the busy and boundless fancy of man has painted on it, with an almost endless variety? Whence has it all the materials of reason and knowledge? To this I answer, in one word, from experience; in all that our knowledge is founded, and from that it ultimately derives itself. Our observation employed either about external sensible objects, or about the internal operations of our minds, perceived and reflected on by ourselves, is that which supplies our understandings with all

❖ ❖

the materials of thinking. These two are the fountains of knowledge, from whence all the ideas we have, or can naturally have, do spring.

§ 3. The objects of sensation one source of ideas.

First, Our senses, conversant about particular sensible objects, do convey into the mind several distinct perceptions of things, according to those various ways wherein those objects do affect them: and thus we come by those ideas we have, of Yellow, White, Heat, Cold, Soft, Hard, Bitter, Sweet, and all those which we call sensible qualities; which when I say the senses convey into the mind, I mean, they from external objects convey into the mind what produces there those perceptions. This great source of most of the ideas we have, depending wholly upon our senses, and derived by them to the understanding, I call sensation.

§ 4. The operations of our minds the other source of them.

Secondly, The other fountain, from which experience furnisheth the understanding with ideas, is the perception of the operations of our own mind within us, as it is employed about the ideas it has got; which operations, when the soul comes to reflect on and consider, do furnish the understanding with another set of ideas, which could not be had from things without; and such are Perception, Thinking, Doubting, Believing, Reasoning, Knowing, Willing, and all the different actings of our own minds; which we being conscious of and observing in ourselves, do from these receive into our understandings as distinct ideas, as we do from bodies affecting our senses. This source of ideas every man has wholly in himself; and though it be not sense, as having nothing to do with external objects, yet it is very like it, and might properly enough be called internal sense. But as I call the other sensation, so I call this reflection, the ideas it affords being such only as the mind gets by reflecting on its own operations within itself. By reflection then, in the following part of this discourse,

I would be understood to mean that notice which the mind takes of its own operations, and the manner of them; by reason whereof there come to be ideas of these operations in the understanding. These two, I say, viz. external material things, as the objects of sensation; and the operations of our own minds within, as the objects of reflection; are to me the only originals from whence all our ideas take their beginnings. The term operations here I use in a large sense, as comprehending not barely the actions of the mind about its ideas, but some sort of passions arising sometimes from them, such as is the satisfaction or uneasiness arising from any thought.

§ 5. All our ideas are of the one or the other of these.

The understanding seems to me not to have the least glimmering of any ideas, which it doth not receive from one of these two. External objects furnish the mind with the ideas of sensible qualities, which are all those different perceptions they produce in us: and the mind furnishes the understanding with ideas of its own operations.

These, when we have taken a full survey of them and their several modes, combinations, and relations, we shall find to contain all our whole stock of ideas; and that we have nothing in our minds which did not come in one of these two ways. . . .

Book II, Chapter VIII. Some farther Considerations concerning our Simple Ideas.

§ 8. Perception

Whatsoever the mind perceives in itself, or is the immediate object of perception, thought, or understanding, that I call idea; and the power to produce any idea in our mind I call quality of the subject wherein that power is. Thus a snow-ball having the power to produce in us the ideas of white, cold, and round, the powers to produce those ideas in us, as they are in the snow-ball, I call qualities; and as they are sensations or perceptions in our understandings, I call them ideas: which ideas, if I speak of sometimes, as in the things themselves, I would be understood to mean those qualities in the objects which produce them in us.

§ 9. *Primary qualities.*

Qualities thus considered in bodies are, first, such as are utterly inseparable from the body, in what estate soever it be; such as in all the alterations and changes it suffers, all the force can be used upon it, it constantly keeps; and such as sense constantly finds in every particle of matter which has bulk enough to be perceived, and the mind finds inseparable from every particle of matter, though less than to make itself singly be perceived by our senses, v. g. Take a grain of wheat, divide it into two parts, each part has still solidity, extension, figure, and mobility; divide it again, and it retains still the same qualities; and so divide it on till the parts become insensible, they must retain still each of them all those qualities. For division (which is all that a mill, or pestle, or any other body does upon another, in reducing it to insensible parts) can never take away either solidity, extension, figure, or mobility from any body, but only makes two or more distinct separate masses of matter, of that which was but one before: all which distinct masses, reckoned as so many distinct bodies, after division make a certain number. These I call original or primary qualities of body, which I think we may observe to produce simple ideas in us, viz. solidity, extension, figure, motion or rest, and number.

§ 10. *Secondary qualities.*

Secondly, such qualities which in truth are nothing in the objects themselves, but powers to produce various sensations in us by their primary qualities, i. e. by the bulk, figure, texture, and motion of their insensible parts, as colours, sounds, tastes, &c. these I call secondary qualities. To these might be added a third sort, which are allowed to be barely powers, though they are as much real qualities in the subject, as those which I, to comply with the common way of speaking, call qualities, but for distinction, secondary qualities. For the power in fire to produce a new colour, or consistency, in wax or clay, by its primary qualities, is as much a quality in fire, as the power it has to produce in me a new idea or sensation of warmth or burning, which I felt not before by the same primary qualities, viz. the bulk, texture, and motion of its insensible parts. . . .

Book IV, Chapter XI. Of our Knowledge of the Existence of other Things.

§ 8. *This certainty is as great as our condition needs.*

. . . . But yet, if after all this any one will be so sceptical, as to distrust his senses, and to affirm that all we see and hear, feel and taste, think and do, during our whole being, is but the series and deluding appearances of a long dream, whereof there is no reality; and therefore will question the existence of all things, or our knowledge of any thing; I must desire him to consider, that if all be a dream, that he doth but dream, that he makes the question; and so it is not much matter, that a waking man should answer him.

But yet, if he pleases, he may dream that I make him this answer, that the certainty of things existing in rerum natura, when we have the testimony of our senses for it, is not only as great as our frame can attain to, but as our condition needs. For our faculties being suited not to the full extent of being, nor to a perfect, clear, comprehensive knowledge of things free from all doubt and scruple; but to the preservation of us, in whom they are; and accommodated to the use of life; they serve to our purpose well enough, if they will but give us certain notice of those things, which are convenient or inconvenient to us. For he that sees a candle burning, and hath

experimented the force of its flame, by putting his finger in it, will little doubt that this is something existing without him, which does him harm, and puts him to great pain: which is assurance enough, when no man requires greater certainty to govern his actions by, than what is as certain as his actions themselves.

And if our dreamer pleases to try, whether the glowing heat of a glass furnace be barely a wandering imagination in a drowsy man's fancy; by putting his hand into it, he may perhaps be wakened into a certainty greater than he could wish, that it is something more than bare imagination. So that this evidence is as great as we can desire, being as certain to us as our pleasure or pain, i. e. happiness or misery; beyond which we have no concernment, either of knowing or being. Such an assurance of the existence of things without us, is sufficient to direct us in the attaining the good, and avoiding the evil, which is caused by them; which is the important concernment we have of being made acquainted with them.

§ 9. But reaches no farther than actual sensation.

In fine then, when our senses do actually convey into our understandings any idea, we cannot but be satisfied that there doth something at that time really exist without us, which doth affect our senses, and by them give notice of itself to our apprehensive faculties, and actually produce that idea which we then perceive: and we cannot so far distrust their testimony, as to doubt, that such collections of simple ideas, as we have observed by our senses to be united together, do really exist together. But this knowledge extends as far as the present testimony of our senses, employed about particular objects that do then affect them, and no farther. For if I saw such a collection of simple ideas, as is wont to be called man, existing together

one minute since, and am now alone, I cannot be certain that the same man exists now, since there is no necessary connexion of his existence a minute since, with his existence now: by a thousand ways he may cease to be, since I had the testimony of my senses for his existence. And if I cannot be certain, that the man I saw last to-day is now in being, I can less be certain that he is so, who hath been longer removed from my senses, and I have not seen since yesterday, or since the last year; and much less can I be certain of the existence of men that I never saw. And therefore though it be highly probable, that millions of men do now exist, yet, whilst I am alone writing this, I have not that certainty of it which we strictly call knowledge; though the great likelihood of it puts me past doubt, and it be reasonable for me to do several things upon the confidence that there are men (and men also of my acquaintance, with whom I have to do) now in the world: but this is but probability, not knowledge.

§ 10. Folly to expect demonstration in every thing.

Whereby yet we may observe, how foolish and vain a thing it is, for a man of a narrow knowledge, who having reason given him to judge of the different evidence and probability of things, and to be swayed accordingly; how vain, I say, it is to expect demonstration and certainty in things not capable of it; and refuse assent to very rational propositions, and act contrary to very plain and clear truths, because they cannot be made out so evident, as to surmount every the least (I will not say reason, but) pretence of doubting. He that in the ordinary affairs of life would admit of nothing but direct plain demonstration, would be sure of nothing in this world, but of perishing quickly. The wholesomeness of his meat or drink would not give him reason to venture on it: and I would fain know, what it is he could do upon such grounds, as are capable of no doubt, no objection.

Book IV, Chapter XV.: Of Probability.

§ 1. Probability is the appearance of agreement upon fallible proofs.

As demonstration is the showing the agreement or disagreement of two ideas, by the intervention of one or more proofs, which have a constant, immutable, and visible connexion one with another; so probability is nothing but the appearance of such an agreement or disagreement, by the intervention of proofs, whose connexion is not constant and immutable, or at least is not perceived to be so, but is, or appears for the most part to be so, and is enough to induce the mind to judge the proposition to be true or false, rather than the contrary. For example: in the demonstration of it a man perceives the certain immutable connexion there is of equality between the three angles of a triangle, and those intermediate ones which are made use of to show their equality to two right ones; and so by an intuitive knowledge of the agreement or disagreement of the intermediate ideas in each step of the progress, the whole series is continued with an evidence, which clearly shows the agreement or disagreement of those three angles in equality to two right ones: and thus he has certain knowledge that it is so. But another man, who never took the pains to observe the demonstration, hearing a mathematician, a man of credit, affirm the three angles of a triangle to be equal to two right ones, assents to it, i. e. receives it for true. In which case the foundation of his assent is the probability of the thing, the proof being such as for the most part carries truth with it: the man, on whose testimony he receives it, not being wont to affirm any thing contrary to, or besides his knowledge, especially in matters of this kind. So that that which causes his assent to this proposition, that the three angles of a triangle are equal to two right ones, that which makes him take these ideas to agree, without knowing them to do so, is the wonted veracity of the speaker in other cases, or his supposed veracity in this.

§ 2. It is to supply the want of knowledge.

Our knowledge, as has been shown, being very narrow, and we not happy enough to find certain truth in every thing which we have occasion to consider; most of the propositions we think, reason, discourse, nay act upon, are such, as we cannot have undoubted knowledge of their truth; yet some of them border so near upon certainty, that we make no doubt at all about them; but assent to them as firmly, and act, according to that assent, as resolutely, as if they were infallibly demonstrated, and that our knowledge of them was perfect and certain. But there being degrees herein from the very neighbourhood of certainty and demonstration, quite down to improbability and unlikeness, even to the confines of impossibility; and also degrees of assent from full assurance and confidence, quite down to conjecture, doubt, and distrust . . .

✾ 2.5 "The Origins of Ideas" ✾

Selections from an Enquiry Concerning Human Understanding by David Hume

✳✳✳

© Georgios Kollidas/Shutterstock.com

David Hume was an empiricist who came a generation later than Locke. But while Locke wanted to try to prove that we can know everything we ordinarily claim to know through sensory experience, without having to appeal to *a priori* knowledge, Hume was more *skeptical* than Locke. Hume thought that many of the things we claim to know would require us to have *a priori* knowledge, which we don't have, so we really don't know much about these things at all. The selection we are reading comes from his *Enquiry Concerning Human Understanding*, published in 1748.

Hume holds that everything we know is either a definitional truth (Hume calls this a "relation of ideas") or else known through empirical observation (Hume calls this a "matter of fact"). Cause and effect relationships are neither definitional truths nor something we observe. So, even though it seems like we do, we don't know anything about cause and effect.

Here are some questions to ask yourself while reading Hume:

* What makes the difference between ideas and impressions?

* Where do we get the idea of causation, according to Hume?

* What does "cause *C* causes effect *E*" really mean, on Hume's account?

* Does Hume's skeptical empiricism seem more right, or Locke's less skeptical empiricism? Or does rationalism seem more right to you?

❂ ❂

. . . Here therefore we may divide all the perceptions of the mind into two classes or species, which are distinguished by their different degrees of force and vivacity. The less forcible and lively are commonly denominated Thoughts or Ideas. The other species want a name in our language, and in most others; I suppose, because it was not requisite for any, but philosophical purposes, to rank them under a general term or appellation. Let us, therefore, use a little freedom, and call them Impressions; employing that word in a sense somewhat different from the usual. By the term impression, then, I mean all our more lively perceptions, when we hear, or see, or feel, or love, or hate, or desire, or will. And impressions are distinguished from ideas, which are the less lively perceptions, of which we are conscious, when we reflect on any of those sensations or movements above mentioned.

Nothing, at first view, may seem more unbounded than the thought of man, which not only escapes all human power and authority, but is not even restrained within the limits of nature and reality. To form monsters, and join incongruous shapes and appearances, costs the imagination no more trouble than to conceive the most natural and familiar objects. And while the body is confined to one planet, along which it creeps with pain and difficulty; the thought can in an instant transport us into the most distant regions of the universe; or even beyond the universe, into the unbounded chaos, where nature is supposed to lie in total confusion. What never was seen, or heard of, may yet be conceived; nor is any thing beyond the power of thought, except what implies an absolute contradiction.

But though our thought seems to possess this unbounded liberty, we shall find, upon a nearer examination, that it is really confined within very narrow limits, and that all this creative power of the mind amounts to no more than the faculty of compounding, transposing, augmenting, or diminishing the materials afforded us by the senses and experience. When we think of a golden mountain, we only join two consistent ideas, gold, and mountain, with which we were formerly acquainted. A virtuous horse we can conceive; because, from our own feeling, we can conceive virtue; and this we may unite to the figure and shape of a horse, which is an animal familiar to us. In short, all the materials of thinking are derived either from our outward or inward sentiment: the mixture and composition of these belongs alone to the mind and will. Or, to express myself in philosophical language, all our ideas or more feeble perceptions are copies of our impressions or more lively ones.

. . . Here, therefore, is a proposition, which not only seems, in itself, simple and intelligible; but, if a proper use were made of it, might render every dispute equally intelligible, and banish all that jargon, which has so long taken possession of metaphysical reasonings, and drawn disgrace upon them. All ideas, especially abstract ones, are naturally faint and obscure: the mind has but a slender hold of them: they are apt to be confounded with other resembling ideas; and when we have often employed any term, though without a distinct meaning, we are apt to imagine it has a determinate idea annexed to it. On the contrary, all impressions, that is, all sensations, either outward or inward, are strong and vivid: the limits between them are more exactly determined: nor is it easy to fall into any error or mistake with regard to them. When we entertain, therefore, any suspicion that a philosophical term is employed without any meaning or idea (as is but too frequent), we need but enquire, from what impression is that supposed idea derived? And if it be impossible to assign any, this will serve to confirm our suspicion. By bringing ideas into so clear a light we may reasonably hope to remove

❖ ❖

all dispute, which may arise, concerning their nature and reality.[1]

But admitting these terms, impressions and ideas, in the sense above explained, and understanding by innate, what is original or copied from no precedent perception, then may we assert that all our impressions are innate, and our ideas not innate.

To be ingenuous, I must own it to be my opinion, that LOCKE was betrayed into this question by the schoolmen, who, making use of undefined terms, draw out their disputes to a tedious length, without ever touching the point in question. A like ambiguity and circumlocution seem to run through that philosopher's reasonings on this as well as most other subjects.

SECTION IV SCEPTICAL DOUBTS CONCERNING THE OPERATIONS OF THE UNDERSTANDING

PART I

ALL the objects of human reason or enquiry may naturally be divided into two kinds, to wit, Relations of Ideas, and Matters of Fact. Of the first kind are the sciences of Geometry, Algebra, and Arithmetic; and in short, every affirmation which is either intuitively or demonstratively certain. That the square of the hypothenuse is equal to the square of the two sides, is a proposition which expresses a relation between these figures. That three times five is equal to the half of thirty, expresses a relation between these numbers. Propositions of this kind are discoverable by the mere operation of thought, without dependence on what is anywhere existent in the universe. Though there never were a circle or triangle in nature, the truths demonstrated by Euclid would for ever retain their certainty and evidence. Matters of fact, which are the second objects of human reason, are not ascertained in the same manner; nor is our evidence of their truth, however great, of a like nature with the foregoing. The contrary of every matter of fact is still possible; because it can never imply a contradiction, and is conceived by the mind with the same facility and distinctness, as if ever so conformable to reality. That the sun will not rise to-morrow is no less intelligible a proposition, and implies no more contradiction than the affirmation, that it will rise. We should in vain, therefore, attempt to demonstrate its falsehood. Were it demonstratively false, it would imply a contradiction, and could never be distinctly conceived by the mind.

It may, therefore, be a subject worthy of curiosity, to enquire what is the nature of that evidence which

---

[1]It is probable that no more was meant by these, who denied innate ideas, than that all ideas were copies of our impressions; though it must be confessed, that the terms, which they employed, were not chosen with such caution, nor so exactly defined, as to prevent all mistakes about their doctrine. For what is meant by innate? If innate be equivalent to natural, then all the perceptions and ideas of the mind must be allowed to be innate or natural, in whatever sense we take the latter word, whether in opposition to what is uncommon, artificial, or miraculous. If by innate be meant, contemporary to our birth, the dispute seems to be frivolous; nor is it worth while to enquire at what time thinking begins, whether before, at, or after our birth. Again, the word idea, seems to be commonly taken in a very loose sense, by LOCKE and others; as standing for any of our perceptions, our sensations and passions, as well as thoughts. Now in this sense, I should desire to know, what can be meant by asserting, that self-love, or resentment of injuries, or the passion between the sexes is not innate?

assures us of any real existence and matter of fact, beyond the present testimony of our senses, or the records of our memory. This part of philosophy, it is observable, has been little cultivated, either by the ancients or moderns; and therefore our doubts and errors, in the prosecution of so important an enquiry, may be the more excusable; while we march through such difficult paths without any guide or direction. They may even prove useful, by exciting curiosity, and destroying that implicit faith and security, which is the bane of all reasoning and free enquiry. The discovery of defects in the common philosophy, if any such there be, will not, I presume, be a discouragement, but rather an incitement, as is usual, to attempt something more full and satisfactory than has yet been proposed to the public.

All reasonings concerning matter of fact seem to be founded on the relation of Cause and Effect. By means of that relation alone we can go beyond the evidence of our memory and senses. If you were to ask a man, why he believes any matter of fact, which is absent; for instance, that his friend is in the country, or in France; he would give you a reason; and this reason would be some other fact; as a letter received from him, or the knowledge of his former resolutions and promises. A man finding a watch or any other machine in a desert island, would conclude that there had once been men in that island. All our reasonings concerning fact are of the same nature. And here it is constantly supposed that there is a connexion between the present fact and that which is inferred from it. Were there nothing to bind them together, the inference would be entirely precarious. The hearing of an articulate voice and rational discourse in the dark assures us of the presence of some person: Why? because these are the effects of the human make and fabric, and closely connected with it. If we anatomize all the other reasonings of this nature, we shall find that they are founded on the relation of cause and effect, and that this relation is either

near or remote, direct or collateral. Heat and light are collateral effects of fire, and the one effect may justly be inferred from the other.

If we would satisfy ourselves, therefore, concerning the nature of that evidence, which assures us of matters of fact, we must enquire how we arrive at the knowledge of cause and effect.

I shall venture to affirm, as a general proposition, which admits of no exception, that the knowledge of this relation is not, in any instance, attained by reasonings a priori; but arises entirely from experience, when we find that any particular objects are constantly conjoined with each other. Let an object be presented to a man of ever so strong natural reason and abilities; if that object be entirely new to him, he will not be able, by the most accurate examination of its sensible qualities, to discover any of its causes or effects. Adam, though his rational faculties be supposed, at the very first, entirely perfect, could not have inferred from the fluidity and transparency of water that it would suffocate him, or from the light and warmth of fire that it would consume him. No object ever discovers, by the qualities which appear to the senses, either the causes which produced it, or the effects which will arise from it; nor can our reason, unassisted by experience, ever draw any inference concerning real existence and matter of fact.

This proposition, that causes and effects are discoverable, not by reason but by experience, will readily be admitted with regard to such objects, as we remember to have once been altogether unknown to us; since we must be conscious of the utter inability, which we then lay under, of foretelling what would arise from them. Present two smooth pieces of marble to a man who has no tincture of natural philosophy; he will never discover that they will adhere together in such a manner as to require great force to separate them in a direct line, while

❖ ❖

they make so small a resistance to a lateral pressure. Such events, as bear little analogy to the common course of nature, are also readily confessed to be known only by experience; nor does any man imagine that the explosion of gunpowder, or the attraction of a loadstone, could ever be discovered by arguments a priori. In like manner, when an effect is supposed to depend upon an intricate machinery or secret structure of parts, we make no difficulty in attributing all our knowledge of it to experience. Who will assert that he can give the ultimate reason, why milk or bread is proper nourishment for a man, not for a lion or a tiger?

But the same truth may not appear, at first sight, to have the same evidence with regard to events, which have become familiar to us from our first appearance in the world, which bear a close analogy to the whole course of nature, and which are supposed to depend on the simple qualities of objects, without any secret structure of parts. We are apt to imagine that we could discover these effects by the mere operation of our reason, without experience. We fancy, that were we brought on a sudden into this world, we could at first have inferred that one Billiard-ball would communicate motion to another upon impulse; and that we needed not to have waited for the event, in order to pronounce with certainty concerning it. Such is the influence of custom, that, where it is strongest, it not only covers our natural ignorance, but even conceals itself, and seems not to take place, merely because it is found in the highest degree.

But to convince us that all the laws of nature, and all the operations of bodies without exception, are known only by experience, the following reflections may, perhaps, suffice. Were any object presented to us, and were we required to pronounce concerning the effect, which will result from it, without consulting past observation; after what manner, I beseech you, must the mind proceed in this operation? It must invent or imagine some

event, which it ascribes to the object as its effect; and it is plain that this invention must be entirely arbitrary. The mind can never possibly find the effect in the supposed cause, by the most accurate scrutiny and examination. For the effect is totally different from the cause, and consequently can never be discovered in it. Motion in the second Billiard-ball is a quite distinct event from motion in the first; nor is there anything in the one to suggest the smallest hint of the other. A stone or piece of metal raised into the air, and left without any support, immediately falls: but to consider the matter a priori, is there anything we discover in this situation which can beget the idea of a downward, rather than an upward, or any other motion, in the stone or metal?

And as the first imagination or invention of a particular effect, in all natural operations, is arbitrary, where we consult not experience; so must we also esteem the supposed tie or connexion between the cause and effect, which binds them together, and renders it impossible that any other effect could result from the operation of that cause. When I see, for instance, a Billiard-ball moving in a straight line towards another; even suppose motion in the second ball should by accident be suggested to me, as the result of their contact or impulse; may I not conceive, that a hundred different events might as well follow from that cause? May not both these balls remain at absolute rest? May not the first ball return in a straight line, or leap off from the second in any line or direction? All these suppositions are consistent and conceivable. Why then should we give the preference to one, which is no more consistent or conceivable than the rest? All our reasonings a priori will never be able to show us any foundation for this preference.

In a word, then, every effect is a distinct event from its cause. It could not, therefore, be discovered in the cause, and the first invention or conception of it, a priori, must be entirely arbitrary.

And even after it is suggested, the conjunction of it with the cause must appear equally arbitrary; since there are always many other effects, which, to reason, must seem fully as consistent and natural. In vain, therefore, should we pretend to determine any single event, or infer any cause or effect, without the assistance of observation and experience.

Hence we may discover the reason why no philosopher, who is rational and modest, has ever pretended to assign the ultimate cause of any natural operation, or to show distinctly the action of that power, which produces any single effect in the universe. It is confessed, that the utmost effort of human reason is to reduce the principles, productive of natural phenomena, to a greater simplicity, and to resolve the many particular effects into a few general causes, by means of reasonings from analogy, experience, and observation. But as to the causes of these general causes, we should in vain attempt their discovery; nor shall we ever be able to satisfy ourselves, by any particular explication of them. These ultimate springs and principles are totally shut up from human curiosity and enquiry. Elasticity, gravity, cohesion of parts, communication of motion by impulse; these are probably the ultimate causes and principles which we shall ever discover in nature; and we may esteem ourselves sufficiently happy, if, by accurate enquiry and reasoning, we can trace up the particular phenomena to, or near to, these general principles. The most perfect philosophy of the natural kind only staves off our ignorance a little longer: as perhaps the most perfect philosophy of the moral or metaphysical kind serves only to discover larger portions of it. Thus the observation of human blindness and weakness is the result of all philosophy, and meets us at every turn, in spite of our endeavours to elude or avoid it. . . .

SECTION V
SCEPTICAL SOLUTION
OF THESE DOUBTS

PART I

. . . Suppose a person, though endowed with the strongest faculties of reason and reflection, to be brought on a sudden into this world; he would, indeed, immediately observe a continual succession of objects, and one event following another; but he would not be able to discover anything farther. He would not, at first, by any reasoning, be able to reach the idea of cause and effect; since the particular powers, by which all natural operations are performed, never appear to the senses; nor is it reasonable to conclude, merely because one event, in one instance, precedes another, that therefore the one is the cause, the other the effect. Their conjunction may be arbitrary and casual. There may be no reason to infer the existence of one from the appearance of the other. And in a word, such a person, without more experience, could never employ his conjecture or reasoning concerning any matter of fact, or be assured of anything beyond what was immediately present to his memory and senses.

Suppose, again, that he has acquired more experience, and has lived so long in the world as to have observed familiar objects or events to be constantly conjoined together; what is the consequence of this experience? He immediately infers the existence of one object from the appearance of the other. Yet he has not, by all his experience, acquired any idea or knowledge of the secret power by which the one object produces the other; nor is it by any process of reasoning, he is engaged to draw this inference. But still he finds himself determined to draw it: and though he should be convinced that his understanding has no part in the operation, he would nevertheless continue in

❀ ❀

the same course of thinking. There is some other principle which determines him to form such a conclusion.

This principle is Custom or Habit. For wherever the repetition of any particular act or operation produces a propensity to renew the same act or operation, without being impelled by any reasoning or process of the understanding, we always say, that this propensity is the effect of Custom. By employing that word, we pretend not to have given the ultimate reason of such a propensity. We only point out a principle of human nature, which is universally acknowledged, and which is well known by its effects. Perhaps we can push our enquiries no farther, or pretend to give the cause of this cause; but must rest contented with it as the ultimate principle, which we can assign, of all our conclusions from experience. It is sufficient satisfaction, that we can go so far, without repining at the narrowness of our faculties because they will carry us no farther. And it is certain we here advance a very intelligible proposition at least, if not a true one, when we assert that, after the constant conjunction of two objects—heat and flame, for instance, weight and solidity— we are determined by custom alone to expect the one from the appearance of the other. This hypothesis seems even the only one which explains the difficulty, why we draw, from a thousand instances, an inference which we are not able to draw from one instance, that is, in no respect, different from them. Reason is incapable of any such variation. The conclusions which it draws from considering one circle are the same which it would form upon surveying all the circles in the universe. But no man, having seen only one body move after being impelled by another, could infer that every other body will move after a like impulse. All inferences from experience, therefore, are effects of custom, not of reasoning.[1]

Custom, then, is the great guide of human life. It is that principle alone which renders our experience useful to us, and makes us expect, for the future, a similar train of events with those which have appeared in the past. Without the influence of custom, we should be entirely ignorant of every matter of fact beyond what is immediately present to the memory and senses. We should never know how to adjust means to ends, or to employ our natural powers in the production of any effect. There would be an end at once of all action, as well as of the chief part of speculation.

But here it may be proper to remark, that though our conclusions from experience carry us beyond our memory and senses, and assure us of matters of fact which happened in the most distant places and most remote ages, yet some fact must always be present to the senses or memory, from which we may first proceed in drawing these conclusions. A man, who should find in a desert country the remains of pompous buildings, would conclude that the country had, in ancient times, been cultivated by civilized inhabitants; but did nothing of this nature occur to him, he could never form such an inference. We learn the events of former ages from history; but then we must peruse the volumes in which this instruction is contained, and thence carry up our inferences from one testimony to another, till we arrive at the eyewitnesses and spectators of these distant events. In a word, if we proceed not upon some fact, present to the memory or senses, our reasonings would be merely hypothetical; and however the particular links might be connected with each other, the whole chain of inferences would have nothing to support it, nor could we ever, by its means, arrive at the knowledge of any real existence. If I ask why you believe any particular matter of fact, which you relate, you must tell me some reason; and this reason will be some other fact, connected with it. But as you

cannot proceed after this manner, in infinitum, you must at last terminate in some fact, which is present to your memory or senses; or must allow that your belief is entirely without foundation.

What, then, is the conclusion of the whole matter? A simple one; though, it must be confessed, pretty remote from the common theories of philosophy. All belief of matter of fact or real existence is derived merely from some object, present to the memory or senses, and a customary conjunction between that and some other object. Or in other words; having found, in many instances, that any two kinds of objects—flame and heat, snow and cold—have always been conjoined together; if flame or snow be presented anew to the senses, the mind is carried by custom to expect heat or cold, and to believe that such a quality does exist, and will discover itself upon a nearer approach. This belief is the necessary result of placing the mind in such circumstances. It is an operation of the soul, when we are so situated, as unavoidable as to feel the passion of love, when we receive benefits; or hatred, when we meet with injuries. All these operations are a species of natural instincts, which no reasoning or process of the thought and understanding is able either to produce or to prevent.

At this point, it would be very allowable for us to stop our philosophical researches. In most questions we can never make a single step farther; and in all questions we must terminate here at last, after our most restless and curious enquiries. But still our curiosity will be pardonable, perhaps commendable, if it carry us on to still farther researches, and make us examine more accurately the nature of this belief, and of the customary conjunction, whence it is derived . . . .

❀ 2.6 "The First Dialogue" ❀

*Selections from Three Dialogues between Hylas and Philonous
by George Berkeley*

* *

© Kritchanut/Shutterstock.com

George Berkeley (1685–1753) was an Anglican Bishop in Ireland. His earliest work was *An Essay Towards a New Theory of Vision*, in which he argued that in perception what we see are not objects and distances, but rather what we see is just an organized field of different colors. This developed later into a theory not only of perception, but of the world itself. Since all we can know of the world through perception are our own perceptions and ideas, it is simpler to believe that all that exists are ideas and perceptions than it is to believe that there is a physical, material world which we can't see.

Like Locke and Hume, Berkeley was an empiricist. But unlike Locke and Hume, Berkeley's empiricism went much farther, into a position called **idealism**. An idealist holds that there is no distinction to be made between our ideas and the "real" world that our ideas are about: the world itself is simply a collection of ideas. For Berkeley, not only does all knowledge depend on experience, but the truth itself depends on experience: all truths are truths of our experience. Berkeley, represents his own views through the character of *Philonous* in this dialogue.

Here are some questions to ask yourself while reading Berkeley:

* Why does Philonous (Berkeley) believe there is no such thing as material substance?
* Why does Hylas think this is an extravagant claim?
* What do we immediately perceive, according to Philonous?
* Who perceives things when we aren't looking at them?

❖❖

THE FIRST DIALOGUE.

Philonous. Good Morrow, Hylas: I did not expect to find you abroad so early.

Hylas. It is indeed something unusual; but my Thoughts were so taken up with a Subject I was discoursing of last Night, that finding I could not sleep, I resolved to rise and take a turn in the Garden. . . .

You were represented in last Night's Conversation, as one who maintained the most extravagant Opinion that ever entered into the Mind of Man, to wit, That there is no such Thing as material Substance in the World.

Phil. That there is no such Thing as what Philosophers call Material Substance, I am seriously persuaded: But if I were made to see any thing absurd or sceptical in this, I should then have the same Reason to renounce this, that I imagine I have now to reject the contrary Opinion.

Hyl. What! can any Thing be more fantastical, more repugnant to common Sense, or a more manifest Piece of Scepticism, than to believe there is no such Thing as Matter?

Phil. Softly, good Hylas. What if it should prove, that you, who hold there is, are by virtue of that Opinion a greater Sceptic, and maintain more Paradoxes and Repugnances to common Sense, than I who believe no such Thing?

Hyl. You may as soon persuade me, The Part is greater than the Whole, as that, in order to avoid Absurdity and Scepticism, I should ever be obliged to give up my Opinion in this Point.

Phil. Well then, are you content to admit that Opinion for true, which upon Examination shall appear most agreeable to common Sense, and remote from Scepticism?

Hyl. With all my Heart. Since you are for raising Disputes about the plainest Things in Nature, I am content for once to hear what you have to say.

Phil. Shall we therefore examine which of us it is that denies the Reality of Sensible Things, or professes the greatest Ignorance of them; since, if I take you rightly, he is to be esteemed the greatest Sceptic?

Hyl. That is what I desire.

Phil. What mean you by Sensible Things?

Hyl. Those Things which are perceived by the Senses. Can you imagine that I mean any thing else?

Phil. Pardon me, Hylas, if I am desirous clearly to apprehend your Notions, since this may much shorten our Inquiry. Suffer me then to ask you this farther Question. Are those Things only perceived by the Senses which are perceived immediately? Or may those Things properly be said to be Sensible, which are perceived mediately, or not without the Intervention of others?

Hyl. I do not sufficiently understand you.

Phil. In reading a Book, what I immediately perceive are the Letters, but mediately, or by means of these, are suggested to my Mind the notions of God, Virtue, Truth, &c. Now, that the Letters are truly Sensible Things, or perceived by Sense, there is no doubt: But I would know whether you take the Things suggested by them to be so too.

Hyl. No certainly, it were absurd to think God or Virtue Sensible Things, though they may be signified and suggested to the Mind by Sensible Marks, with which they have an arbitrary Connexion.

Phil. It seems then, that by Sensible Things you mean those only which can be perceived immediately by Sense.

Hyl. Right.

Phil. Doth it not follow from this, that though I see one part of the Sky Red, and another Blue, and that my Reason doth thence evidently conclude there must be some Cause of that Diversity of Colours,

❖ ❖

yet that Cause cannot be said to be a Sensible Thing, or perceived by the Sense of Seeing?

Hyl. It doth.

Phil. In like manner, though I hear Variety of Sounds, yet I cannot be said to hear the Causes of those Sounds.

Hyl. You cannot.

Phil. And when by my Touch I perceive a Thing to be hot and heavy, I cannot say with any Truth or Propriety, that I feel the Cause of its Heat or Weight.

Hyl. To prevent any more Questions of this kind, I tell you once for all, that by Sensible Things I mean those only which are perceived by Sense, and that in truth the Senses perceive nothing which they do not perceive immediately: for they make no Inferences. The deducing therefore of Causes or Occasions from Effects and Appearances, which alone are perceived by Sense, intirely relates to Reason.

. . .

Hyl. I frankly own, Philonous, that it is in vain to stand out any longer. Colours, Sounds, Tastes, in a word, all those termed Secondary Qualities, have certainly no Existence without the Mind. But by this Acknowledgment I must not be supposed to derogate any thing from the Reality of Matter or external Objects, seeing it is no more than several Philosophers maintain, who nevertheless are the farthest imaginable from denying Matter. For the clearer Understanding of this, you must know sensible Qualities are by Philosophers divided into Primary and Secondary. The former are Extension, Figure, Solidity, Gravity, Motion, and Rest. And these they hold exist really in Bodies. The latter are those above enumerated; or briefly, all sensible Qualities beside the Primary, which they assert are only so many Sensations or Ideas existing no where but in the Mind. But all this, I doubt not, you are already apprised of. For my part, I have been a long time sensible there was such an Opinion current

among Philosophers, but was never thoroughly convinced of its Truth till now.

Phil. You are still then of Opinion, that Extension and Figures are inherent in external unthinking Substances.

. . .

Hyl. I give up the Point for the present, reserving still a Right to retract my Opinion, in case I shall hereafter discover any false Step in my Progress to it.

Phil. That is a Right you cannot be denied. Figures and Extension being dispatched, we proceed next to Motion. Can a real Motion in any external Body be at the same time both very swift and very slow?

Hyl. It cannot.

Phil. Is not the Motion of a Body swift in a reciprocal Proportion to the time it takes up in describing any given Space? Thus a Body that describes a Mile in an Hour, moves three times faster than it would in case it described only a Mile in three Hours.

Hyl. I agree with you.

Phil. And is not Time measured by the Succession of Ideas in our Minds?

Hyl. It is.

Phil. And is it not possible Ideas should succeed one another twice as fast in your Mind, as they do in mine, or in that of some Spirit of another kind?

Hyl. I own it.

Phil. Consequently the same Body may to another seem to perform its Motion over any Space in half the time that it doth to you. And the same Reasoning will hold as to any other Proportion: That is to say, according to your Principles (since the Motions perceived are both really in the Object) it is possible one and the same Body shall be really moved the same way at once, both very swift and very slow. How is this consistent either with common Sense, or with what you just now granted?

Hyl. I have nothing to say to it.

. . .

Phil. Hark; is not this the College-Bell?

Hyl. It rings for Prayers.

Phil. We will go in then if you please, and meet here again to Morrow Morning. In the meantime you may employ your Thoughts on this Morning's Discourse, and try if you can find any Fallacy in it, or invent any new means to extricate yourself.

Hyl. Agreed.

THE SECOND DIALOGUE

Hylas. I beg your Pardon, Philonous, for not meeting you sooner. All this Morning my Head was so filled with our late Conversation, that I had not leisure to think of the Time of the Day, or indeed of any thing else.

Philonous. I am glad you were so intent upon it, in Hopes if there were any Mistakes in your Concessions, or Fallacies in my Reasonings from them, you will now discover them to me.

Hyl. I assure you, I have done nothing ever since I saw you, but search after Mistakes and Fallacies, and with that View have minutely examined the whole Series of Yesterday's Discourse: but all in vain, for the Notions it led me into, upon Review appear still more clear and evident; and the more I consider them, the more irresistibly do they force my Assent.

Phil. And is not this, think you, a Sign that they are genuine, that they proceed from Nature, and are conformable to right Reason? Truth and Beauty are in this alike, that the strictest Survey sets them both off to Advantage. While the false Lustre of Error and Disguise cannot endure being reviewed, or too nearly inspected.

Hyl. I own there is a great deal in what you say. Nor can any one be more intirely satisfied of the Truth of those odd Consequences, so long as I have in View the Reasonings that lead to them. But when these are out of my Thoughts, there seems on the other hand something so satisfactory, so natural and intelligible in the modern way of explaining Things, that I profess I know not how to reject it.

Phil. I know not what way you mean.

Hyl. I mean the way of accounting for our Sensations or Ideas.

Phil. How is that?

Hyl. It is supposed the Soul makes her Residence in some part of the Brain, from which the Nerves take their rise, and are thence extended to all Parts of the Body: And that outward Objects by the different Impressions they make on the Organs of Sense, communicate certain vibrative Motions to the Nerves; and these being filled with Spirits, propagate them to the Brain or Seat of the Soul, which according to the various Impressions or Traces thereby made in the Brain, is variously affected with Ideas.

Phil. And call you this an Explication of the manner whereby we are affected with Ideas?

Hyl. Why not, Philonous, have you any thing to object against it?

Phil. I would first know whether I rightly understand your Hypothesis. You make certain Traces in the Brain to be the Causes or Occasions of our Ideas. Pray tell me, whether by the Brain you mean any sensible Thing?

Hyl. What else think you I could mean?

Phil. Sensible Things are all immediately perceivable; and those Things which are immediately perceivable, are Ideas; and these exist only in the Mind. Thus much you have, if I mistake not, long since agreed to.

Hyl. I do not deny it.

Phil. The Brain therefore you speak of, being a sensible Thing, exists only in the Mind. Now, I would fain know whether you think it reasonable to suppose, that one Idea or Thing existing in the Mind, occasions all other Ideas. And if you think so, pray how do you account for the Origin of that Primary Idea or Brain itself?

Hyl. I do not explain the Origin of our Ideas by that Brain which is perceivable to Sense, this being itself only a Combination of sensible Ideas, but by another which I imagine.

Phil. But are not Things imagined as truly in the Mind as Things perceived?

Hyl. I must confess they are.

Phil. It comes therefore to the same thing; and you have been all this while accounting for Ideas, by certain Motions or Impressions in the Brain, that is, by some Alterations in an Idea, whether sensible or imaginable, it matters not.

Hyl. I begin to suspect my Hypothesis.

Phil. Beside Spirits, all that we know or conceive are our own Ideas. When therefore you say, all Ideas are occasioned by Impressions in the Brain, do you conceive this Brain or no? If you do, then you talk of Ideas imprinted in an Idea, causing that same Idea, which is absurd. If you do not conceive it, you talk unintelligibly, instead of forming a reasonable Hypothesis.

Hyl. I now clearly see it was a mere Dream. There is nothing in it.

Phil. You need not be much concerned at it: for after all, this way of explaining Things, as you called it, could never have satisfied any reasonable Man. What Connvexion is there between a Motion in the Nerves, and the Sensations of Sound or Colour in the Mind? or how is it possible these should be the Effect of that?

Hyl. But I could never think it had so little in it, as now it seems to have.

Phil. Well then, are you at length satisfied that no sensible Things have a real Existence; and that you are in truth an arrant Sceptic?

Hyl. It is too plain to be denied.

Phil. Look! are not the Fields covered with a delightful Verdure? Is there not something in the Woods and Groves, in the Rivers and clear Springs that sooths, that delights, that transports the Soul? At the Prospect of the wide and deep Ocean, or some huge Mountain whose Top is lost in the Clouds, or of an old gloomy Forest, are not our Minds filled with a pleasing Horror? Even in Rocks and Deserts, is there not an agreeable Wildness? How sincere a Pleasure is it to behold the natural Beauties of the Earth! To preserve and renew our Relish for them, is not the Veil of Night alternately drawn over her Face, and doth she not change her Dress with the Seasons? How aptly are the Elements disposed? What Variety and Use in the meanest Productions of Nature? What Delicacy, what Beauty, what Contrivance in animal and vegetable Bodies? How exquisitely are all Things suited, as well to their particular Ends, as to constitute apposite Parts of the Whole! And while they mutually aid and support, do they not also set off and illustrate each other? Raise now your Thoughts from this Ball of Earth, to all those glorious Luminaries that adorn the high Arch of Heaven. The Motion and Situation of the Planets, are they not admirable for Use and Order? Were those (miscalled Erratique) Globes ever known to stray, in their repeated Journeys through the pathless Void? Do they not measure Areas round the Sun ever proportioned to the Times? So fixed, so immutable are the Laws by which the unseen Author of Nature actuates the Universe. How vivid and radiant is the Lustre of the fixed Stars! How magnificent and rich that negligent Profusion, with which they appear to be scattered throughout the whole Azure Vault! Yet if you take the Telescope, it brings into your Sight a new Host of Stars that escape the naked Eye. Here they seem contiguous and minute, but to a nearer View immense Orbs of Light at various Distances, far sunk in the Abyss of Space. Now you must call Imagination to your Aid. The feeble narrow Sense cannot descry innumerable Worlds revolving round the central Fires; and in those Worlds the Energy of an all-perfect Mind displayed in endless Forms. But neither Sense nor Imagination are big enough to comprehend the boundless Extent with all its glittering Furniture. Though the labouring Mind exert and strain each Power to its utmost reach, there still stands out ungrasped a Surplusage immeasurable. Yet all the vast Bodies that compose this mighty Frame, how distant and remote soever, are by some secret Mechanism, some divine Art and Force linked in a mutual Dependence and Intercourse with each other, even with this Earth, which was almost slipt from my Thoughts, and lost in the Croud of Worlds. Is not the whole System immense, beautiful, glorious beyond Expression and beyond Thought! What treatment then do those Philosophers deserve, who would deprive these noble and delightful Scenes of all Reality? How should those Principles be entertained, that lead us to think all the visible Beauty of the Creation a false imaginary Glare? To be plain, can you expect this Scepticism of yours will not be thought extravagantly absurd by all Men of Sense?

Hyl. Other Men may think as they please: But for your part you have nothing to reproach me with. My Comfort is, you are as much a Sceptic as I am.

Phil. There, Hylas, I must beg leave to differ from you.

Hyl. What! have you all along agreed to the Premises, and do you now deny the Conclusion, and leave me to maintain those Paradoxes by myself which you led me into? This surely is not fair.

Phil. I deny that I agreed with you in those Notions that led to Scepticism. You indeed said, the Reality of sensible Things consisted in an absolute Existence out of the Minds of Spirits, or distinct from their being perceived. And pursuant to this Notion of Reality, you are obliged to deny sensible Things any real Existence: That is, according to your own Definition, you profess yourself a Sceptic. But I neither said nor thought the Reality of sensible Things was to be defined after that manner. To me it is evident, for the Reasons you allow of, that sensible Things cannot exist otherwise than in a Mind or Spirit. Whence I conclude, not that they have no real Existence, but that seeing they depend not on my Thought, and have an Existence distinct from being perceived by me, there must be some other Mind wherein they exist. As sure therefore as the sensible World really exists, so sure is there an infinite omnipresent Spirit who contains and supports it.

Hyl. What! this is no more than I and all Christians hold; nay, and all others too who believe there is a God, and that he knows and comprehends all Things.

Phil. Ay, but here lies the Difference. Men commonly believe that all Things are known or perceived by God, because they believe the Being of a God, whereas I on the other side, immediately and necessarily conclude the Being of a God, because all sensible Things must be perceived by him.

Hyl. But so long as we all believe the same thing, what matter is it how we come by that Belief?

Phil. But neither do we agree in the same Opinion. For Philosophers, though they acknowledge all corporeal Beings to be perceived by God, yet they attribute to them an absolute Subsistence distinct from their being perceived by any Mind whatever,

❖ ❖

which I do not. Besides, is there no Difference between saying, There is a God, therefore he perceives all Things: and saying, Sensible Things do really exist: and if they really exist, they are necessarily perceived by an infinite Mind: therefore there is an infinite Mind, or God? This furnishes you with a direct and immediate Demonstration, from a most evident Principle, of the Being of a God. Divines and Philosophers had proved beyond all Controversy, from the Beauty and Usefulness of the several Parts of the Creation, that it was the Workmanship of God. But that setting aside all Help of Astronomy and natural Philosophy, all Contemplation of the Contrivance, Order, and Adjustment of Things, an infinite Mind should be necessarily inferred from the bare Existence of the sensible World, is an Advantage peculiar to them only who have made this easy Reflexion: That the sensible World is that which we perceive by our several Senses; and that nothing is perceived by the Senses beside Ideas; and that no Idea or Archetype of an Idea can exist otherwise than in a Mind. . . .

❀ 2.7 The Critique of Pure Reason ❀

Selections
by Immanuel Kant

* *

Immanuel Kant.

© Nicku/Shutterstock.com

Immanuel Kant (1724–1804) was a German-speaking philosopher who lived in Königsberg, Prussia. Early in his life, Kant was a rationalist, but then he encountered the works of David Hume which "awoke" Kant from his "dogmatic slumber". Kant became convinced that he could develop a *synthesis* of rationalism, empiricism, and idealism – a way to show that all three were, in some way, true.

Kant held that all knowledge depended on experience, and in this sense he was an empiricist. However, he also thought that we could have *a priori* knowledge by reflecting on the *pre-conditions* of experiences. Knowledge was *a priori* when it had to do with how we necessarily experience the world, as a kind of boundary-line or limit to possible experiences we could have. All of our perceptions were filtered through the *a priori* structure of thought.

Here are some questions to ask yourself while reading Kant:

* Why does Kant compare his revolution in Epistemology to Copernicus?

* What can we know, and what can't we know, according to Kant?

* How is Kant's view of the *a priori* an alternative to the one given by Socrates?

* Plato thought the forms were in another reality. Where do you think Kant would say the forms are?

❖ ❖

Preface to the Second Edition

. . . It has hitherto been assumed that our cognition must conform to the objects; but all attempts to ascertain anything about these objects a priori, by means of conceptions, and thus to extend the range of our knowledge, have been rendered abortive by this assumption. Let us then make the experiment whether we may not be more successful in metaphysics, if we assume that the objects must conform to our cognition. This appears, at all events, to accord better with the possibility of our gaining the end we have in view, that is to say, of arriving at the cognition of objects a priori, of determining something with respect to these objects, before they are given to us.

We here propose to do just what Copernicus did in attempting to explain the celestial movements. When he found that he could make no progress by assuming that all the heavenly bodies revolved round the spectator, he reversed the process, and tried the experiment of assuming that the spectator revolved, while the stars remained at rest. We may make the same experiment with regard to the intuition of objects. If the intuition must conform to the nature of the objects, I do not see how we can know anything of them a priori. If, on the other hand, the object conforms to the nature of our faculty of intuition, I can then easily conceive the possibility of such an a priori knowledge. Now as I cannot rest in the mere intuitions, but—if they are to become cognitions—must refer them, as representations, to something, as object, and must determine the latter by means of the former, here again there are two courses open to me. Either, first, I may assume that the conceptions, by which I effect this determination, conform to the object—and in this case I am reduced to the same perplexity as before; or secondly, I may assume that the objects, or, which is the same thing, that experience, in which alone as given objects they are cognized, conform to my

conceptions—and then I am at no loss how to proceed. For experience itself is a mode of cognition which requires understanding. Before objects, are given to me, that is, a priori, I must presuppose in myself laws of the understanding which are expressed in conceptions a priori. To these conceptions, then, all the objects of experience must necessarily conform. Now there are objects which reason thinks, and that necessarily, but which cannot be given in experience, or, at least, cannot be given so as reason thinks them. The attempt to think these objects will hereafter furnish an excellent test of the new method of thought which we have adopted, and which is based on the principle that we only cognize in things a priori that which we ourselves place in them. . . .

Introduction.

I. Of the difference between Pure and Empirical Knowledge

That all our knowledge begins with experience there can be no doubt. For how is it possible that the faculty of cognition should be awakened into exercise otherwise than by means of objects which affect our senses, and partly of themselves produce representations, partly rouse our powers of understanding into activity, to compare to connect, or to separate these, and so to convert the raw material of our sensuous impressions into a knowledge of objects, which is called experience? In respect of time, therefore, no knowledge of ours is antecedent to experience, but begins with it.

But, though all our knowledge begins with experience, it by no means follows that all arises out of experience. For, on the contrary, it is quite possible that our empirical knowledge is a compound of that which we receive through impressions, and that which the faculty of cognition supplies from itself (sensuous impressions giving merely the occasion), an addition which we cannot distinguish from the original element given by sense, till long practice has made us attentive to, and skilful in separating it. It is, therefore, a question which requires close investigation, and not to be answered at first sight, whether there exists a knowledge altogether independent of experience, and even of all sensuous impressions? Knowledge of this kind is called a priori, in contradistinction to empirical knowledge, which has its sources a posteriori, that is, in experience.

But the expression, "a priori," is not as yet definite enough adequately to indicate the whole meaning of the question above started. For, in speaking of knowledge which has its sources in experience, we are wont to say, that this or that may be known a priori, because we do not derive this knowledge immediately from experience, but from a general rule, which, however, we have itself borrowed from experience. Thus, if a man undermined his house, we say, "he might know a priori that it would have fallen;" that is, he needed not to have waited for the experience that it did actually fall. But still, a priori, he could not know even this much. For, that bodies are heavy, and, consequently, that they fall when their supports are taken away, must have been known to him previously, by means of experience.

By the term "knowledge a priori," therefore, we shall in the sequel understand, not such as is independent of this or that kind of experience, but such as is absolutely so of all experience. Opposed to this is empirical knowledge, or that which is possible only a posteriori, that is, through experience. Knowledge a priori is either pure or impure. Pure knowledge a priori is that with which no empirical element is mixed up. For example, the proposition, "Every change has a cause," is a proposition a priori, but impure, because change is a conception which can only be derived from experience.

II. The Human Intellect, even in an Unphilosophical State, is in Possession of Certain Cognitions "a priori".

The question now is as to a criterion, by which we may securely distinguish a pure from an empirical cognition. Experience no doubt teaches us that this or that object is constituted in such and such a manner, but not that it could not possibly exist otherwise. Now, in the first place, if we have a proposition which contains the idea of necessity in its very conception, it is a if, moreover, it is not derived from any other proposition, unless from one equally involving the idea of necessity, it is absolutely priori. Secondly, an empirical judgement never exhibits strict and absolute, but only assumed and comparative universality (by induction); therefore, the most we can say is—so far as we have hitherto observed, there is no exception to this or that rule. If, on the other hand, a judgement carries with it strict and absolute universality, that is, admits of no possible exception, it is not derived from experience, but is valid absolutely a priori.

Empirical universality is, therefore, only an arbitrary extension of validity, from that which may be predicated of a proposition valid in most cases, to that which is asserted of a proposition which holds good in all; as, for example, in the affirmation, "All bodies are heavy." When, on the contrary, strict universality characterizes a judgement, it necessarily indicates another peculiar source of knowledge, namely, a faculty of cognition a priori. Necessity and strict universality, therefore, are infallible tests for distinguishing pure from empirical knowledge, and are inseparably connected with each other. But as in the use of these criteria the empirical limitation is sometimes more easily detected than the contingency of the judgement, or the unlimited universality which we attach to a judgement is often a more convincing proof than its necessity, it

may be advisable to use the criteria separately, each being by itself infallible.

Now, that in the sphere of human cognition we have judgements which are necessary, and in the strictest sense universal, consequently pure a priori, it will be an easy matter to show. If we desire an example from the sciences, we need only take any proposition in mathematics. If we cast our eyes upon the commonest operations of the understanding, the proposition, "Every change must have a cause," will amply serve our purpose. In the latter case, indeed, the conception of a cause so plainly involves the conception of a necessity of connection with an effect, and of a strict universality of the law, that the very notion of a cause would entirely disappear, were we to derive it, like Hume, from a frequent association of what happens with that which precedes; and the habit thence originating of connecting representations—the necessity inherent in the judgement being therefore merely subjective. Besides, without seeking for such examples of principles existing a priori in cognition, we might easily show that such principles are the indispensable basis of the possibility of experience itself, and consequently prove their existence a priori. For whence could our experience itself acquire certainty, if all the rules on which it depends were themselves empirical, and consequently fortuitous? No one, therefore, can admit the validity of the use of such rules as first principles. But, for the present, we may content ourselves with having established the fact, that we do possess and exercise a faculty of pure a priori cognition; and, secondly, with having pointed out the proper tests of such cognition, namely, universality and necessity.

Not only in judgements, however, but even in conceptions, is an a priori origin manifest. For example, if we take away by degrees from our conceptions of a body all that can be referred to mere sensuous experience—colour, hardness or softness, weight, even impenetrability—the body

will then vanish; but the space which it occupied still remains, and this it is utterly impossible to annihilate in thought. Again, if we take away, in like manner, from our empirical conception of any object, corporeal or incorporeal, all properties which mere experience has taught us to connect with it, still we cannot think away those through which we cogitate it as substance, or adhering to substance, although our conception of substance is more determined than that of an object. Compelled, therefore, by that necessity with which the conception of substance forces itself upon us, we must confess that it has its seat in our faculty of cognition a priori. . . .

The light dove cleaving in free flight the thin air, whose resistance it feels, might imagine that her movements would be far more free and rapid in airless space. Just in the same way did Plato, abandoning the world of sense because of the narrow limits it sets to the understanding, venture upon the wings of ideas beyond it, into the void space of pure intellect. He did not reflect that he made no real progress by all his efforts; for he met with no resistance which might serve him for a support, as it were, whereon to rest, and on which he might apply his powers, in order to let the intellect acquire momentum for its progress. It is, indeed, the common fate of human reason in speculation, to finish the imposing edifice of thought as rapidly as possible, and then for the first time to begin to examine whether the foundation is a solid one or no. Arrived at this point, all sorts of excuses are sought after, in order to console us for its want of stability, or rather, indeed, to enable Us to dispense altogether with so late and dangerous an investigation. But what frees us during the process of building from all apprehension or suspicion, and flatters us into the belief of its solidity, is this. A great part, perhaps the greatest part, of the business of our reason consists in the analysation of the conceptions which we already possess of objects. By this means we gain a multitude of cognitions, which although really nothing more than elucidations or explanations of that which (though in a confused manner) was already thought in our conceptions, are, at least in respect of their form, prized as new introspections; whilst, so far as regards their matter or content, we have really made no addition to our conceptions, but only disinvolved them. But as this process does furnish a real priori knowledge, which has a sure progress and useful results, reason, deceived by this, slips in, without being itself aware of it, assertions of a quite different kind; in which, to given conceptions it adds others, a priori indeed, but entirely foreign to them, without our knowing how it arrives at these, and, indeed, without such a question ever suggesting itself. . . . .

SECTION II. Of Time.

SS 5. Metaphysical Exposition of this Conception.

1. Time is not an empirical conception. For neither coexistence nor succession would be perceived by us, if the representation of time did not exist as a foundation a priori. Without this presupposition we could not represent to ourselves that things exist together at one and the same time, or at different times, that is, contemporaneously, or in succession.

2. Time is a necessary representation, lying at the foundation of all our intuitions. With regard to phenomena in general, we cannot think away time from them, and represent them to ourselves as out of and unconnected with time, but we can quite well represent to ourselves time void of phenomena. Time is therefore given a priori. In it alone is all reality of phenomena possible. These may all be annihilated in thought, but time itself, as the universal condition of their possibility, cannot be so annulled. . . .

SS 7. Conclusions from the above Conceptions.

(a) Time is not something which subsists of itself, or which inheres in things as an objective determination, and therefore remains, when abstraction is made of the subjective conditions of the intuition of things. For in the former case, it would be something real, yet without presenting to any power of perception any real object. In the latter case, as an order or determination inherent in things themselves, it could not be antecedent to things, as their condition, nor discerned or intuited by means of synthetical propositions a priori. But all this is quite possible when we regard time as merely the subjective condition under which all our intuitions take place. For in that case, this form of the inward intuition can be represented prior to the objects, and consequently a priori.

(b) Time is nothing else than the form of the internal sense, that is, of the intuitions of self and of our internal state. For time cannot be any determination of outward phenomena. It has to do neither with shape nor position; on the contrary, it determines the relation of representations in our internal state. And precisely because this internal intuition presents to us no shape or form, we endeavour to supply this want by analogies, and represent the course of time by a line progressing to infinity, the content of which constitutes a series which is only of one dimension; and we conclude from the properties of this line as to all the properties of time, with this single exception, that the parts of the line are coexistent, whilst those of time are successive. From this it is clear also that the representation of time is itself an intuition, because all its relations can be expressed in an external intuition.

(c) Time is the formal condition à priori of all phenomena whatsoever. Space, as the pure form of external intuition, is limited as a condition a priori to external phenomena alone. On the other hand, because all representations, whether they have or have not external things for their objects, still in themselves, as determinations of the mind, belong to our internal state; and because this internal state is subject to the formal condition of the internal intuition, that is, to time—time is a condition a priori of all phenomena whatsoever—the immediate condition of all internal, and thereby the mediate condition of all external phenomena. If I can say a priori, "All outward phenomena are in space, and determined a priori according to the relations of space," I can also, from the principle of the internal sense, affirm universally, "All phenomena in general, that is, all objects of the senses, are in time and stand necessarily in relations of time."

. . . . We have now completely before us one part of the solution of the grand general problem of transcendental philosophy, namely, the question: "How are synthetical propositions a priori possible?" That is to say, we have shown that we are in possession of pure a priori intuitions, namely, space and time, in which we find, when in a judgement a priori we pass out beyond the given conception, something which is not discoverable in that conception, but is certainly found a priori in the intuition which corresponds to the conception, and can be united synthetically with it. But the judgements which these pure intuitions enable us to make, never reach farther than to objects of the senses, and are valid only for objects of possible experience.

❊ 2.8 Unit 2 Study Guide ❊

✳✳

Who is Socrates talking to in Plato's Meno?

Meno's slave

What does Socrates hold about learning and recollection?

we learn from memories in a past life

What's Socrates's argument for the doctrine of recollection?

What puzzle is Socrates trying to solve about the boy's knowledge of geometry?

How he retained his knowledge

What answer does Socrates offer to this puzzle?

He learned it from a past life

Why does Socrates argue that Meno's boy slave has *a priori* knowledge?

a priori knowledge comes
from past life

215

rates holds that *a priori* knowledge is justified by what?

Socrates concludes the Meno with what claim about the soul?

How's Plato's epistemology related to empiricism, rationalism, and idealism?

Descartes

First meditation:

Why did Descartes insist that we begin by doubting everything we thought we knew?

What purpose did Descartes have for doubting the existence of the external world?

Which three arguments does Descartes offer in an attempt to lead himself to doubt everything?

Why doesn't the deceitfulness of his senses give Descartes reason to doubt everything?

What never changes in Descartes's dreams?

Second meditation:

What is the one thing that Descartes can't doubt?

that he is doubting

How does Descartes know that he exists?

he is thinking

According to Descartes, what is he?

A thinking thing

Third meditation:

Why does Descartes think that an infinite God must exist?

Fourth meditation:

How does Descartes use God's existence as a foundation for all other knowledge?

What is foundationalism? Why does Descartes hold to it?

Fifth meditation:

Why does Descartes think that the most perfect being conceivable can't fail to exist?

Locke

What is the difference between a "primary quality" and a "secondary quality"?

Where does Locke believe that all of the materials of reason, and all knowledge, come from?

How's Locke's epistemology related to empiricism, rationalism, and idealism?

Hume

What is the difference between ideas and impressions?

Where do we get the idea of causation, according to Hume?

What does "C causes E" mean, on Hume's account?

How's Hume's epistemology related to empiricism, rationalism, and idealism?

What did Hume argue we cannot prove about our experiences and the real world?

What did Hume believe about the laws of nature?

Berkeley:

How's Berkeley's epistemology related to empiricism, rationalism, and idealism?

What did Berkeley believe about the real world and the world of experiences?

What produces our ongoing experiences, according to Berkeley?

Kant

According to Kant, what "world" can we know, and what world can't we know?

What can't any possible phenomenal experience ever tell us, according to Kant?

What does Kant mean by "phenomena?"

According to Kant, how do we have knowledge of *a priori* truths?

Why does Kant compare his "revolution" in philosophy to Copernicus?

How's Kant's epistemology related to empiricism, rationalism, and idealism?

According to the lectures, what is an *a priori* knowledge?

Explain how Kant offers an alternative explanation to *a priori* knowledge to Socrates.

Other points not to miss:

If you know that p, then what must follow about your belief in p?

If you know that p, then what must follow about the truth of p?

What does "justification" mean, and what is its relationship to knowledge?

Can you have a justified true belief without having knowledge?

Can you have knowledge without having a justified true belief?

What are the three types of experiences which can justify beliefs about the external world?

What's a rationalist believe about knowledge? Who were the rationalists?

What's an empiricist believe about knowledge? Who are the empiricists?

What's the difference between local skepticism and global skepticism?

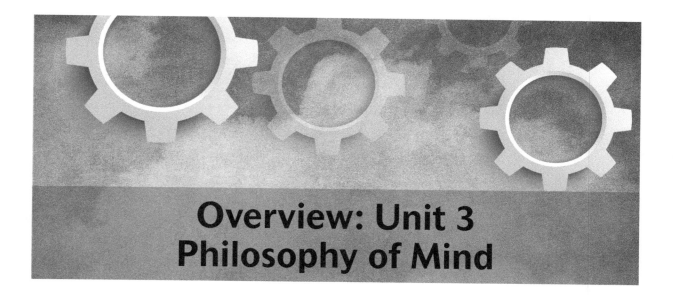

Overview: Unit 3
Philosophy of Mind

＊＊＊

3.1 What Am I?

3.2 Paul Churchland, *Matter and Consciousness*, selections

3.3 Frank Jackson, "What Mary Didn't Know"

3.4 David Chalmers, *The Conscious Mind*, selections

3.5 Thomas Nagel, "What is it like to be a Bat?"

3.6 Alyssa Ney, "Defining Physicalism"

3.7 Aristotle, "The Four Causes"

3.8 Unit 3 Study Guide

In this unit we'll discuss metaphysics, which is the attempt to understand fundamental reality. We'll begin by distinguishing a few different types of explanation. When then turn to a serious problem in metaphysics: what is the nature of this conscious experience which I am having right now? Is its fundamental nature physical, or non-physical? Are 'zombies' possible?

By the end of this Unit, you should be able to:

＊ Identify Aristotle's Four Causes.

＊ Apply the distinction between the four casues to an example from contemporary biology.

＊ Define eliminativist, reductivist, and non-reductivist physicalism; substance dualism and emergentism.

＊ Recognize the roles of religious belief and contemporary neuroscience on the dualist-physicalist debate.

＊ Restate the 'Mary' argument and the 'Zombie' argument for dualism.

＊ Restate and critique common arguments for physicalism.

＊ Formulate compromise positions in the debate between physicalists and dualists.

＊ Develop a coherent view on the nature of the mind.

🌸 3.1 What Am I? 🌸

✳ ✳

Imagine that you are having lunch with a friend, but not a very close friend. Suddenly, you're overcome with a feeling of regret about something you forgot to do yesterday. However, this thing you forgot to do is very embarrassing and even a bit shameful—you don't want your friend to know about it, or even to ask about it, because if your friend found out, your friendship would be threatened. So, you carry on the conversation as though nothing is going on. Inwardly, you feel distressed: you are beating yourself up for being so forgetful, and thinking rapidly through ways that you can fix the problem. Outwardly, however, you are breathing normally, talking at the same pace you talked before, and listening intently to your friend discuss something completely unimportant and trivial. After a few minutes, you make up an excuse and end lunch early. Your excuse sounds convincing, and your friend never knows.

Most of the time, no one else can know as well as you do what you are thinking or feeling or even perceiving. Your *subjectivity* is what separates you from everyone else. The subjective experience you are presently having is what we call your *consciousness*.

A. **What is Consciousness?**

B. **What is Consciousness *not*?**

C. **Dualism and Physicalism**

D. **Defining Physicalism**

E. **Reasons to be a Physicalist**

F. **There is no Telekinesis!**

G. **Dualist Replies**

H. **Mary's Room**

I. **Zombies**

J. **Aristotle's Four Causes**

K. **Dualism, Physicalism, and Middle Ground**

A. What is Consciousness?

Normally we do not think about our own consciousness. Consciousness makes us aware of the world, but we are aware *through* it and not *of* it. We are rarely aware of the fact that we are aware. It is possible to be conscious without being conscious *that* you are conscious, or "self-conscious", and this might be the norm.

My pet dog, for instance, is conscious—she has subjective experiences, unlike a car or a blender that have no experiences. My dog sees and hears and feels hunger and satisfaction and pain and pleasure. The way in which my dog sees is not the same as the way in which the motion detector connected to my burglar alarm "sees": my dog *really sees*, has an experience of seeing. The motion detector does not have an experience when it transmits information: talk of seeing is purely metaphorical. In spite of this, while my dog is conscious, I do not think my dog is self-conscious. When sprawled out on the porch, my dog probably is not reflecting on the fact that she is experiencing the warm sun—rather, she is just experiencing the warm sun. I've laid in the sun before and simply experienced the warmth without the burden of having to think about the fact that I'm experiencing the warmth, and I'd like to think my dog gets to have that experience often. I suppose I could doubt that this is the case, but I trust the experts on animal psychology when they tell me that dogs are conscious, but probably not self-conscious, based on brain structure.

The fact that I just appealed to something about *brains*—dog brains and human brains—to argue for a point about consciousness, raises a question about what connection there might be between consciousness and the brain. Clearly there is *some* connection. Drinking alcohol changes the chemical composition of the blood flowing through one's brain, and this changes the quality of one's subjective experiences. Drinking coffee has a similar but opposite effect. And yet, there are reasons to doubt that the connection between the brain and consciousness is something knowable *a priori*. Through empirical testing we learn of the connections between the mind and the brain. Nothing about the *concept* of consciousness tells us that it is necessarily connected with the brain: someone might never receive any education on anatomy, and so might not know that brains exist, but might still know that he is conscious. Nothing about the *concept* of a brain tells us that it will be conscious: someone might study the brain as a pink and squishy biological and physiological curiosity, without understanding that it is the source of subjective experiences.

Since we can conceive of brains and consciousness independently of each other, we might start to wonder whether *what they are* by nature is independent of each other. What is the relationship between the mind and the body?

This so-called mind-body problem has been a debated issue in Western philosophy since the time of Plato. The concept of consciousness is also at the center of Indian philosophy, and it plays a significant role in thought in Buddhism and Hinduism. While it has a long history, the study of consciousness is one area in which we can say that philosophy has made some progress over the centuries. First, the definition of "consciousness" has gradually become clearer and much more narrower than it was in the past, which distinguishes it from closely related concepts. Second, we've gradually come to understand that there are much more wider variety of nuanced positions to hold about consciousness than the Greeks likely thought there were. Third, contemporary philosophy is able to integrate recent scientific discoveries about the brain to rule out some positions that might have seemed more plausible before we had these discoveries.

Let's begin by talking about the concept of consciousness. What is consciousness *not*, on the "philosophical" definition of consciousness?

B. What is Consciousness *not*?

First, students often confuse the word "consciousness" with the word "conscience". The words sound similar, but mean very different things. Some people believe there is a kind of intuitive moral faculty in our minds, which lets us make quick judgments about whether something is morally right or morally wrong, and they call this "conscience". However, consciousness has to do with having a mind, not necessarily having a sense of morality. While having a mind is obviously a necessary condition of having morality, it is not a sufficient condition: psychopaths and lizards are conscious but do not have a conscience. The only connection is that the words are pronounced similarly, with only a subtle, one-phoneme difference: an 'n' added at the end of conscience, for conscious (kahn'-shuh<u>s</u>) and conscience (kahn'-shuh<u>ns</u>).

Second, our everyday words "conscious" or "consciousness" tend to be used for someone's *behavior* rather than their subjective state. In the everyday sense we would say that someone is conscious if they are awake and *responsive* to stimuli. Someone who has fallen asleep or is in a coma, in the ordinary sense, is unconscious—someone who is moving around and responding to us is conscious. ("Knocking some-one unconscious".) However, on the philosophical definition, we distinguish the subjective experience of consciousness from the ability to respond to stimuli. On the philosophical definition, someone can be responsive but not conscious, or conscious but not responsive. Thus, for most philosophers, a dream is an example of a conscious state: there is something it is like to experience a dream of flying through the sky. If a scan of the brain of a patient in a coma reveals activity much like it occurs in our brains when we are dreaming, then we have reason to believe that the patient in the coma is conscious, on the philosophical definition, even if the patient is unable to interact with us. There is something it is like to be that patient.

Third, because people writing about philosophy tend to use the words "mind" or "mental" and "consciousness" interchangeably, it is easy to confuse "consciousness" with "mental activity" or rational thought. Rational thought involves the conceptual representation of the world—it involves propositions about the world which can be true or false. However, there are many types of conscious experience which can exist without rational thought, on the philosophical definition of "consciousness". A fish may have conscious experiences even though it does not have rational thought. A person in the hospital might be conscious enough to experience a dull aching pain, or a vague sense of pleasure, without yet having rational thoughts about these experiences. Think of it this way: it's undebatable that all *pains* must be con-scious. There is no way in which one can be in pain without being conscious. However, we might debate whether or not all *thoughts* must be conscious. Maybe in the future sophisticated androids with comput-ers for "brains" will be able to engage in convincing conversations with us, and these androids could be said to be "thinking". However, they wouldn't really be conscious.

We can study *cognition*—the mental processing engaged in by rational beings, which corresponds to the transfer of information between different regions of the brain—without our study thereby focus-ing on subjective, qualitative states of consciousness. There exists a science which studies cognition: namely, cognitive science. We are still figuring out what it would mean for there to be a scientific study of consciousness.

Fourth, we should distinguish being conscious or having an experience from being conscious *of* something, or having an experience *of* something. For instance, I am presently having an experience of my computer monitor. However, the way in which the monitor appears to me consciously is not the same as the monitor itself. I might experience the monitor in different ways without the monitor changing—for example, if I were to wear a different pair of glasses.

Finally, we should distinguish being conscious from being able to speak and articulate sentences like "I am conscious". As mentioned earlier, you need not have the ability to reflect upon or think about your own consciousness (you need not have *self*-consciousness) in order to be conscious, let alone the ability to communicate that thought to someone else.

C. Dualism and Physicalism

Remember that in Unit 2, Descartes presented an argument for *dualism*. Descartes's argument went basically like this:

(1) I cannot conceive of myself without a mind.

(2) I can conceive of myself with a different body.

(3) Something is essential to me if and only if I can conceive of myself without it.

(C) I am essentially a mind, not a body.

A **dualist** believes that there are two fundamental kinds of thing in the world—mind and matter. Matter does not have a mind, and the mind is not material. Contrary to this, a **materialist** believes that there is one fundamental kind of thing in the world, the stuff of physics, and if minds exist then they are material objects. The term "materialism" is synonymous with the term **physicalism**: Some authors we read will call themselves "physicalists", and others "materialists", but there is no difference between them for the purpose of our class.

Descartes argued for dualism like this: Because he could conceive of his mind and body existing separately, it was logically possible for them to exist separately. However, since it was logically possible for them to exist separately, they were not essentially the same thing.

Both dualists and physicalists are distinct from **idealists**, like Berkeley (Unit 2). Berkeley held that there was one fundamental kind of thing in the world, namely, mind. "Matter" only existed for Berkeley insofar as someone was consciously experiencing it. Finally, all three are distinct from **panpsychists**. Panpsychists hold that there is one fundamental thing in the world which is both mind and matter—the physical and the mental are two ways of looking at the same substance—and so everything has a degree of consciousness. The consciousness we experience at our level results from the compounding of the consciousness that exists even at the sub-atomic level into conscious cells, which help form a conscious brain. Thomas Nagel, whose work we'll read in this unit, is a panpsychist.

The sharp distinction that Descartes drew between mind and matter has shaped European thought in the centuries after him, and for those who grow up in a Western culture it forms a common cultural meme: *mind over matter!* Descartes's dualism is also found in the works of Plato. However, Ancient and Medieval thinkers in the West did not always so sharply divide the material and the mental. Both Aristotle and Thomas Aquinas, for instance, rejected substance dualism and held that the soul (or mind) was the substantial form of the body, so that the body and soul together composed of one substance—while at the same time holding that the mind and body were distinct. Likewise, many thinkers in Indian philosophy would reject the sharp division between mind and body drawn by Descartes, while at the same time taking consciousness seriously not regarding it as reducible to the material world. So, there is longstanding historical precedent for middle ground between dualism and physicalism, if we can find exactly where that ground is.

Finally, a quick terminological note: Most philosophers now will use the word *mind* to talk about consciousness, but some will follow Descartes in using the word *soul*. The word "soul" in this context, meaning the same thing "mind", is not same as the use of the word "soul" to say things like "the killer has no soul" (meaning he has no conscience), or "this music has no soul" (meaning it has no depth of feeling), or "he must purify his soul" (meaning one's character is morally or religiously defective). It is also different from the use of the word "soul" to talk about what makes someone a unique individual and not someone else, which we'll talk about in Unit 4. Stay focused only on "conscious experience" for the moment and Descartes's idea that there is an immaterial conscious substance independent of the physical world, a kind of ghost.

D. Defining Physicalism

To begin with, we should probably get more precise in how we are defining our terms. We've defined physicalism as the view that there is one fundamental kind of thing in the world, physical stuff. But what is "physical" stuff? How would we define "physical" and "physicalism?

Here is one definition of "physical":

(PHY1) x is physical if and only if x is possibly empirically observable.

We do use the word "physical" in this way in everyday English sometimes: We talk about "emotional pain" as opposed to "physical pain", which makes it misleadingly sound like emotions are not physical processes in the body with effects on heart rate, blood chemistry, and so on. What we mean is that "physical pain" has to do with the observable sorts of damage to the body, whereas "emotional pain" is not observable to others.

The philosopher Thomas Hobbes defined physicalism in terms of (PHY1), and formulated the following argument for physicalism:

1. x is physical if and only if x is possibly empirically observable.
2. We can know that something exists if and only if it is possibly empirically observable.
C. Everything we could ever know exists is physical.

However, this argument shows why definition (PHY1) is problematic. It makes it *trivial* that everything we could ever encounter is physical. Suppose in some possible world that someone were to observe a real ghost—not merely an illusion, but a disembodied spirit. According to Hobbes's definition in premise 1, the ghost would be physical. However, if even ghosts are physical, then what does the term "physical" mean anymore?

Another, more popular approach is to define what's "physical" in terms of the study of physics.

(PHY2) x is physical if and only if x plays a role in theories of Physics.

For instance, quarks and electrons are physical, because they play a role in theories of Physics. Chairs and tables and mountains and trees are physical insofar as they are nothing over and above collections of subatomic particles. Of course, on pain of circularity, we can't then go on to define "physics" as "the study of the physical". So, what then do we mean by "physics?".

In one of our readings, Alyssa Ney discusses a problem known as Hempel's Dilemma. Either by "Physics" we mean our *current* Physics, or else we mean some *future* physics. The following problem follows:

1. Physicalism is the view that everything concrete is by nature physical.
2. x is physical if and only if x plays a role in theories of Physics.
3. "Theories of Physics" means either (a) current physics or (b) future physics.
4. If (a), then physicalism is false.

   5. If (b), then physicalism is unknowable.

   C. Physicalism is either false or unknowable.

Premise four is supposed to follow from the fact that there are undoubtedly concrete things we have not discovered in contemporary physics. Physics changes quickly as we discover new things: the physics of 50 years ago is very different from the physics of today, let alone the physics of 100 or 200 years ago. It would be both pretentious and a tad depressing to suppose that Physics has reached its final theory in our decade, and nothing new will ever be discovered again. Suppose that there is some force or particle we discover in 10 years that we didn't know about today. According to (a), this force or particle will not be physical, since it isn't part of current physics. Physicalism would then seem false, although clearly it shouldn't be made false by discovering something new.

   But suppose instead that we believe (b), then we are referring to an idealized physics in some distant future. Well, we then end up with the same problem that Hobbes's definition had: what if future physics posits that idealism is true and that everything is fundamentally mental—protons and neutrons are made of ghostly intellects. According to (b), ghostly intellects would be physical. In other words, we can't know the future, so on (b) we can never really know what is or isn't physical, and so we can never know if physicalism is true.

   Alyssa Ney attempts to resolve this dilemma by providing a number of alternatives that get around Hempel's dilemma. As you read them, try to think through whether they give a definition of "physical" that is meaningful and substantive without being trivially true.

   For our purposes in this Unit, we'll define "physical" in a purely conventional way. We'll say that by "physical", we mean something that has the same essential nature as the stuff which composes all of the ordinary objects we typically call "physical." So, whatever kind of thing it is that composes of tables and chairs and trees and bodies, physicalism is the claim that everything is essentially that kind of thing.

E. Reasons to be a Physicalist

We should start with three fairly obvious reasons to be a physicalist.

   First of all, if there are souls or immaterial minds, then one must answer how a soul or immaterial mind becomes so strongly associated with one particular physical body. This is the **problem of identification** for substance dualism. How is it that we know that the person we are talking to today has the same mind that he had yesterday? It seems like we use observable material evidence. However, if the mind is not material, then how can material evidence tell us anything about the mind?

   Second, the principle of **Ockham's Razor** says that **if all else is equal, the simpler of two competing hypotheses should be preferred**. If we are able to explain everything which occurs and which we observe by only discussing physical things, then it is unnecessarily extravagant to claim that we also need to invoke the existence of immaterial minds—since immaterial minds wouldn't explain anything further that the physical things don't already explain.

   Third, the **argument from neural dependence** points out that there is a close dependence of our conscious experiences on what is happening to us neurologically in the brain. For example, consider the various medications that might be prescribed by a psychiatrist for depression, bipolar disorder, anxiety disorders, attention deficit disorder, or other mental health problems. No one doubts that these are *physical* medications that affect how the brain transmits certain signals between neurons. However, they have a clear affect on our conscious experiences—people are less depressed or less anxious, for instance. On the other side, consider the effects of drugs such as cocaine, LSD, marijuana, and alcohol. The effects on states of consciousness that these drugs have can range from mild to extreme. However, no one thinks that these substances are anything more than chemical compounds—they contain no ghosts, even if we do sometimes use for alcohol the term *spirits*.

F. There is no Telekinesis!

Another argument for physicalism has its origins in a reply to Descartes by Princess Elizabeth of Bohemia (1618–1680). Elizabeth engaged in an extensive correspondence with Descartes, objecting to his argument on the grounds that he could not explain how immaterial minds could cause material bodies to move. Her **argument from causal dependence** goes like this:

1. If mind and body are wholly distinct, then they are wholly independent.
2. Minds cause bodies to do things.
3. Bodies cause minds to do things.
4. If A causes B, then B partly depends upon A.
5. Mind and Body are not wholly independent. (2,3,4)
C. Mind and body are not wholly distinct.

Premises 1 and 4 are supposed to be definitional claims. Premise 2 says that minds sometimes cause bodies to do things. For instance, sometimes my mental state of deliberating whether to have pizza or tacos for dinner and recognizing that I feel hungry for tacos leads to my physical state of eating tacos. Sometimes my mental state of being afraid that someone is going to break to my house in leads me to engage in the physical action of setting the burglar alarm. Premise 3 says that sometimes bodies cause minds to do things. For instance, when a mosquito bites my body, I consciously experience an itching sensation. When my body is bombarded by the sound-waves and light-waves produced by the car behind me which saw me run a red light, I consciously experience the sound of a police siren, the sight of flashing red and blue lights, and the feeling of intense anxiety.

Here is another way to put the objection to dualism. *Telekinesis* is *the ability to move a physical object with one's mind*: for instance, to stare at a pencil and by willing very hard cause it to levitate. Outside of fantasy and science fiction movies, most people think there is no such thing as telekinesis. However, most people are wrong. In fact, telekinesis happens regularly around the world, all of the time.

Wait. What?

Yes, you heard me. You definitely *can* move some physical objects with your mind. All you have to do is concentrate very hard and will it to happen.

Uh . . .

Hold on. Don't close this book! Trust me. Listen carefully.

I want you to stare at one of your hands very closely. Your hand is an entirely physical object. I want you to imagine that hand levitating upward, extending your arm along with it, until the hand comes to rest on top of your head. Look at it and imagine it happening.

Now—here is the hard part—I want you to will your hand to raise and put it on top of your head. Go on! Will it to happen! If you desire it, nothing can stop you!

Unless you lack motor capacity in your hands, your hand should have moved to the top of your head. You moved a physical object with your mind. Is that telekinesis?

Of course not! Your hand moved through your physical nervous system as a result of activity in your physical brain. There is no need to suppose that something spooky just happened when you moved your hand. Yet, this is what the dualist seemed to be committed to saying: there is widespread and regular telekinesis. Because that is implausible, this is a reason to believe that physicalism is true. If mind and matter are different substances, how does mind cause matter to move?

G. Dualist Replies

However, dualists have a reply to these sorts of arguments for physicalism. First of all, many of the arguments are arguments against Descartes's **substance dualism**, which is the view that mind and body exist wholly independently. What the arguments from neural dependence and causal dependence show is that the mind and the brain are not distinct substances: that is, they exist in dependence on one another, not independently. However, they don't show that the mind and brain (or consciousness and the physical) are identical *in essence*. Two things can be closely related causally and one can depend on the other for its existence, but yet the two things have distinct essences—what it is to be a conscious state is not the same as what it is to be a physical state.

Second, the argument from Ockham's razor only applies if there is nothing that physicalism fails to explain. However, while we may see strong empirical connections between brain events and conscious events that doesn't mean that our understanding of the brain is enough to understand consciousness. If there is something that physicalism does not explain about consciousness, then on Ockham's razor it is perfectly acceptable to invoke the existence of something further to explain it.

Let's start with the obvious differences between the properties of parts of brains, like "being made up of neuron pathways" and "being a centimeter and a half in length", and how different these are from the properties of consciousness, like "tasting like peaches" or "feeling rough like sandpaper". It seems very difficult to reduce the properties in the first category to the properties in the second category. Although we've learned far more about the workings of neurons within the brain over the last several decades, understanding the brain on a smaller scale does not make clear how it is that brains are conscious. Both dualists and physicalists will admit that it is difficult to conceive of a brain as a whole being conscious, and it is equally difficult to conceive of a particular neuron's firing being a thought.

Suppose we eventually gain the ability to predict exactly what someone is thinking by scanning his or her brain. It will still be true that we had to learn about this empirically—we had to *ask* people what they were experiencing or thinking about, and use this to produce a model of what different events in the brain corresponded to. Consciousness is still part of our explanation: We haven't eliminated it from the story. It would be very different if we could, not knowing anything about conscious experiences, simply look at a brain and conclude, "Aha! There must be conscious experiences here!". If minds and brains are identical, it seems surprising that we can learn about one without learning about the other.

Thomas Nagel gives the example of bats. Bats perceive and navigate the world through echolocation, not through vision. We know that bats are conscious, just like we are. But we have no idea what a consciousness that perceives through echolocation *is likely to experience* in comparison to a consciousness that perceives through vision. We can try to imagine it, but our imagination of being a bat will be nothing like the real think. No matter how much we learn about bat brains, it seems unlikely to tell us what it is like to be a bat. It seems unlikely that physical information will ever explain the whole picture of consciousness. Even a computer generated model that purports to be what it is like to be a bat will involve visual stimuli–colors and lines—which may not be anything like how bats perceive their world.

H. Mary's Room

Frank Jackson tells the story of Mary the color scientist. Perhaps, as part of a secretive CIA program, a brilliant child prodigy named Mary spends her life from birth confined in a black and white room, and never sees anything with color in it. While in the room, however, she is trained in neuroscience through the use of black and white computers and black and white textbooks. Gradually she becomes the greatest expert history has every known on color perception: She learns everything to know about neurology, optics, human psychology, the physical processes that occur in the brain when people see color, the way in which information is transferred from the retina to the brain, the way that light waves bounce off of objects . . . and even the poetic and cultural feelings that people associate with certain colors and the things they tend to say about colors. She knows which objects are red and blue and green, even though she's never seen red or blue or green.

Are there any physical facts which Mary doesn't know about color perception? If you can think of one, imagine that she learns that too through the computer monitor. Physical facts are supposed to be quantitative, so it seems like in principle they could all be learned in some way that Mary could access while in her black and white room. Can you think of any exceptions?

One day—perhaps Congress shuts down the CIA program after Mary's situation is reported on WikiLeaks—Mary is released from her colorless room. Suppose she is presented upon release with a bright red rose. This is the first time she has seen red. Does Mary know something new that she didn't know before?

Jackson says that she does. She now knows *what it is like for others to see red*, the qualitative appearance of redness. This leads to the following argument:

1. Mary came to know a new fact about color which she did not know in the room.

2. While she was in the room, Mary knew all of the physical facts about color.

C. The new fact which Mary learned is not a physical fact.

If there are non-physical facts, then physicalism is false, and dualism is true. This doesn't necessarily mean that Cartesian substance dualism is true. Jackson's article only asserts that a weaker form of dualism is true: not the claim that mind and brain exist independently, but only the claim that they are essentially distinct.

How might a physicalist reply to this argument? Think about the three meanings of the notion of "knowledge" we discussed in Unit 2. How might that be applied to offer a rebuttal to this argument?

I. Zombies

Another argument for dualism comes from David Chalmers. Chalmers notes that all physicalists are committed to a claim which he calls supervenience:

Supervenience: *there is no logical possibility of a difference in conscious state without a difference in brain state*

A physicalist holds that every conscious state is identical to some brain state. If two things are one and the same thing, then it is logically impossible for them not to be the same thing. For instance, Mark Twain is the same person as Samuel Clemens. It is not possible for Mark Twain to have been a different person than Samuel Clemens, because these are just two words for the same thing. So, a physicalist has to hold that there is no possible difference in conscious states without a possible difference in brain states.

However, Chalmers presents two arguments against this claim. Both of them may seem to you to involve outlandish scenarios, but remember that Chalmers is not trying to claim that these scenarios are likely or even naturally possible. He is only trying to claim that they are *logically* possible, that they involve no contradiction.

First, Chalmers argues that we can imagine the possibility of an **invert**. Your inverted twin is in the same physical and brain state as you, in the same position, having all of the same beliefs. However, colors look inverted to your twin from what they look like to you. Consider this argument:

1. It is conceivable that you and the invert have identical brain states but different conscious states.

2. If something is conceivable, then it is logically possible.

3. It is logically possible that you and the invert have identical brain states but different conscious states. (1, 2).

4. Supervenience is true if and only if there is no logical possibility of a difference in conscious state without a difference in brain state.

4. Supervenience is not true (3, 4).

5. If physicalism is true, then supervenience is true.

C. Physicalism is not true. (4, 5).

Have you ever wondered if what is blue to you looks red to others, and what's red to you looks blue to them, or if your black is their white and your white is their black? We all use the same words, because we can't peer into one another's minds, but we can imagine our experiences being different. Have you ever looked at the negative of a photograph? What if the way you see the world is the negative image of the colors everyone else sees?

If you can wonder about and imagine these things, then you can conceive of them. However, if you can conceive of them, then

it seems like they are logically possible. But if it is logically possible that there is a difference in color states without a difference in brain states, supervenience is false.

Chalmers's second example involves the idea of a "philosophical zombie". A philosophical zombie is not a brain-eating undead person like the zombies of movies and television. Rather, a philosophical zombie is someone who looks like us, talks like us, laughs like us, cries like us, and in every physical and discernable way is just like us—except there is nothing going on inside of the zombie's consciousness.

Zombies have bodies and brains exactly like we do, down to the tiniest molecule. However, zombies have no consciousness. If we can conceive of your "zombie twin", then we can produce this argument:

1. It is conceivable that you and the zombie have identical brain states but different conscious states.

2. If something is conceivable, then it is logically possible.

3. It is logically possible that you and the zombie have identical brain states but different conscious states. (1, 2)

4. Supervenience is true if and only if there is no logical possibility of a difference in conscious state without a difference in brain state.

4. Supervenience is not true (3, 4).

5. If physicalism is true, then supervenience is true.

C. Physicalism is not true. (4, 5).

How do we know that other people are not zombies? A *behaviorist* holds that we know that other people are conscious because they behave much the same way that we do when we have a conscious experience, such as cowering when feeling pain or hearing a threatening roar. However, does behavior actually reveal all there is to consciousness? Can you actually check to see how much pain someone is in based on how strong the person's pain reactions are? Chalmers would disagree with the behaviorist, and say that he can't check the mind of another person to see if he or she is having an experience like our own when exhibiting some behavior or other, not even by performing a Fourier magnetic resonance imaging (fMRI) scan of the person's brain. The fMRI scan may be paired up with data we have from other people reporting what they were thinking about their brain scans, and this might let us form a conjecture about what the person is thinking. But there is no direct route to go straight from an fMRI to consciousness without going through what people report about consciousness.

Perhaps, we know that other people are not zombies by a kind of analogy to our own experience, or by some kind of direct intuition. In any case, even if we know that the other people around us are not zombies, it does seem like we were able for a moment to clearly conceive and worry about the scenario in which they were zombies. And that suggests that there is some logically possible world—perhaps, with very different laws of nature than our own world—in which zombies exist. However, if it is logically possible for there to be a difference in brain states without a difference in conscious states, then supervenience is false, and physicalism is true.

How do you think a physicalist would respond to Chalmers's argument? Are there cases in which premise 2 might be false? Imagine the world in 1200 AD, before the discovery of modern chemistry. At that time, it was conceivable that water might be any number of substances: an element, a form of carbon, a fusion of lead and gold. However, we now know that water is H_2O. Since water is identical to H_2O, it is not logically possible for water to not be H_2O. In spite of this, it was certainly conceivable that water was not H_2O. So a physicalist might say that we are in the same situation with the brain. Without knowing the whole physical story, zombies are conceivable. However, because every conscious state is identical to a brain state, they aren't possible.

J. Aristotle's Four Causes

We should take a break for a moment to consider a short section of Aristotle's works *Metaphysics* and *Physics* where Aristotle develops an account of four different types of explanation. Although the word "explanation" suggests our practice of explaining things to one another, Aristotle means for these to correspond to actual relationships in the world—was in which one thing can depend upon another. Because "causes" are relationships in the world that ground our explanations, Aristotle's term for "explanation" (αἰτία) is usually translated "cause". Aristotle's four causes are

* **Efficient Causation.** An efficient cause is a past event that produces a future event. It explains why a future event occurs.
  * My belief that I will get a sunburn is an efficient cause of my putting on sunscreen.
  * Drinking alcohol is an efficient cause of drunkenness.
  * The moon is an efficient cause of the tides.
* **Final Causation.** A final cause is a possible future event that gives the reason for a past event. It explains what the event is for.
  * Lions kill their prey so that they eat and survive.
  * The heart exists to pump blood.
  * I dress nicely in order to impress the hiring committee.
  * Seeing is the goal of the eye.
* **Material Causation.** Material causes are the parts of a thing that sustain its existence at a given moment in time. It explains what the object consists in; why the whole is there.
  * A statue is made out of copper.
  * Humans are made out of flesh and blood and lots of water.
  * A chair or table or tree is made out of tiny particles.
* **Formal Causation.** A formal cause is the "real definition", "nature", or "essence" of a thing, that is, what it is to be that thing. It explains why something is what it is.
  * A formal cause of being a bachelor is being unmarried.
  * A formal cause of a being a cat is being a mammal.
  * A formal cause of being a house is being a place in which people might live.

We might think of it this way. Efficient causes explain why something in the future **occurs**. Material causes explain why something at the present **exists**. Final causes explain what the **purpose** of something in the past was. Formal causes explain **what it is to be** a thing.

With this tool in mind, let's return to our debate in the philosophy of mind.

K. Dualism, Physicalism, and Middle Ground

Since there are many different types of explanation, we can now see how middle ground might be possible in the philosophy of mind. Let's have a look at several dualist and physicalist positions which stretch across the full spectrum:

1. Eliminativist Physicalism says that there are no facts about consciousness, and our concept of it is mistaken. Talk about conscious beliefs, feelings, and perceptions ought to be replaced by descriptions of brain states. "Folk psychology" is a fairy tale: there are no thoughts, no minds, no beliefs, and no consciousness. While behaviorism is one type, there are others. Paul Churchland, whose work we read in this unit, advocates this view.

2. Reductive Physicalism says that consciousness is identical to something physical, and fully explained by it. Beliefs, feelings, and perceptions are identical with distinctive types of event in the brain. Perhaps we are not yet able to reduce the mental to the physical, but in some future physics, we will be able to do so.

3. Non-Reductive Physicalism says that our concepts about consciousness are different from our physical concepts, but that they refer to the same particular physical events. Because they are different concepts, we will never be able to understand one in terms of the other: Consciousness is conceptually irreducible to the brain. This explains our intuitions in the case of Mary's Room. However, even though we conceive of them differently, in fact they are identical and it is not possible to have one without the other. A non-reductive physicalist might say that consciousness supervenes on the physical, for instance, but our concept of consciousness isn't physical and hence we can conceive of zombies and inverts, even though they are logically impossible.

4. Emergentist Dualism says that consciousness has its basis in the material world, but isn't a material kind of thing. It depends upon the physical for its existence, but it has an essential nature which is non-physical. So, an emergentist might accept that consciousness supervenes on the physical, but its nature isn't physical. We might put emergentism into Aristotle's terms. The emergentist says that consciousness is explained by the brain in the sense of efficient causation (everything the mind causes, the brain also causes) and material causation (the mind depends on the brain for its existence). However, consciousness is not explained by the brain in the sense of formal causation, since what it is to be in a certain brain state is never what it is to be in a certain conscious state. (Perhaps, also consciousness is not explained by the brain in the sense of final causation, since our conscious states may be *about* certain things which they represent, but brain states are not about other things in this way.)

5. Substance Dualism is the view that consciousness is independent from the physical not only in its nature, but also in its existence and its causal powers—that is, it is independent not only formally, but also materially and efficiently. For the substance dualist, consciousness does not supervene on the physical, and does not depend upon the physical body for its existence. Instead, it is an immaterial substance which interacts with the material world. This is the view which Descartes and Plato held.

As you read through the source texts in this unit, think carefully about what exactly the arguments you hear actually show, and what they don't show. For instance, do the physicalist arguments show that dualism is false, or only the substance dualism is false? Do the dualist arguments show that physicalism is false, or only that reductive physicalism is false? Think carefully about what you read.

Ultimately, the philosophy of mind is an investigation of a very personal question: *what am I?* As you begin reflecting on your own *phenomenology*, becoming conscious of your conscious experience, try to answer that question: what do you think you are?

❈ 3.2 Matter and Consciousness ❈

selections
by Paul Churchland

❋ ❋

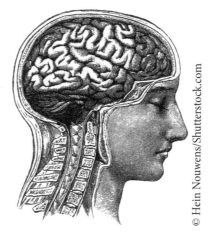

© Hein Nouwens/Shutterstock.com

Paul Churchland (1942 – present) is a Professor of Philosophy and Cognitive Science at the University of California, San Diego. In his book, *Matter and Consciousness*, Churchland defends a materialist view of consciousness. In this selection from a chapter of his book, Churchland first gives a rebuttal to common arguments for *dualism*, the view that consciousness is distinct from any material thing, including the brain. He then proposes reasons that he thinks should lead us to accept physicalism, the view that consciousness is nothing over and above the brain.

Churchland's materialism is distinct from reductive materialism – which says that consciousness can be reduced to something material – and also distinct from non-reductive materialism, which says that consciousness is identical to something material, but our way of understanding it can't be reduced. Instead, Churchland proposes an *eliminative* materialist view, on which our ordinary understanding of consciousness is mistaken and should be replaced with theories derived from neuroscience.

Here are some questions to think about when you read:

* Why does Churchland think that Ockham's razor counts in favor of physicalism?

* How does Churchland respond to the objection that our knowledge of facts about consciousness seems very different from our knowledge of physical facts?

* What empirical evidence does Churchland think there is for materialism?

* How might a dualist interpret this same evidence?

The Ontological Problem (the Mind-Body Problem)[*]

1. Dualism

The dualistic approach to mind encompasses several quite different theories, but they are all agreed that the essential nature of conscious intelligence resides in something *nonphysical*, in something forever beyond the scope of sciences like physics, neurophysiology, and computer science. Dualism is not the most widely held view in the current philosophical and scientific community, but it is the most common theory of mind in the public at large, it is deeply entrenched in most of the world's popular religions, and it has been the dominant theory of mind for most of Western history. It is thus an appropriate place to begin our discussion.

Substance Dualism

The distinguishing claim of this view is that each mind is a distinct nonphysical thing, an individual 'package' of nonphysical substance, a thing whose identity is independent of any physical body to which it may be temporarily 'attached'. Mental states and activities derive their special character, on this view, from their being states and activities of this unique, nonphysical substance.

This leaves us wanting to ask for more in the way of a *positive* characterization of the proposed mind-stuff.

If 'mind-stuff' is so utterly different from 'matter-stuff' in its nature—different to the point that it has no mass whatever, no shape whatever, and no position anywhere in space—then how is it possible for my mind to have any causal influence on my body at all? As Descartes himself was aware (he was one of the first to formulate the law of the conservation of momentum), ordinary matter in space behaves according to rigid laws, and one cannot get bodily movement (= momentum) from nothing. How is this utterly insubstantial 'thinking substance' to have any influence on ponderous matter? How can two such different be in any sort of causal contact?

Such difficulties with Cartesian dualism provide a motive for considering a less radical form of substance dualism, and that is what we find in a view I shall call *popular dualism*. This is the theory that a person is literally a 'ghost in a machine', where the machine is the human body, and the ghost is a spiritual substance, quite unlike physical matter in its internal constitution, but fully possessed of spatial properties even so. In particular, minds are commonly held to be *inside* the bodies they control: inside the head, on most views, in intimate contact with the brain.

This view need not have the difficulties of Descartes'. The mind is right there in contact with the brain,

---

[*] Churchland, Paul M., *Matter and Consciousness*, pp. 7–13, 15–21, 22, 26–29, 32–34, 36–39, 43–45, 47–49, © 1984 Massachusetts Institute of Technology, by permission of The MIT Press.

❊ ❊

and their interaction can perhaps be understood in terms of their exchanging energy of a form that our science has not yet recognized or understood. Ordinary matter, you may recall, is just a form or manifestation of energy. (You may think of a grain of sand as a great deal of energy condensed or frozen into a small package, according to Einstein's relation, $E = mc^2$.) Perhaps mind-stuff is a well-behaved form or manifestation of energy also, but a different form of it. It is thus *possible* that a dualism of this alternative sort be consistent with familiar laws concerning the conservation of momentum and energy. This is fortunate for dualism, since those particular laws are very well established indeed.

This view will appeal to many for the further reason that it at least holds out the possibility (though it certainly does not guarantee) that the mind might survive the death of the body. It does not guarantee the mind's survival because it remains possible that the peculiar form of energy here supposed to constitute a mind can be produced and sustained only in conjunction with the highly intricate form of matter we call the brain, and must disintegrate when the brain disintegrates. So the prospects for surviving death are quite unclear even on the assumption that popular dualism is true. But even if survival were a clear consequence of the theory, there is a pitfall to be avoided here. Its promise of survival might be a reason for *wishing* dualism to be true, but it does not constitute a reason for *believing* that it *is* true. For that, we would need independent empirical evidence that minds do indeed survive the permanent death of the body. Regrettably, and despite the exploitative blatherings of the supermarket tabloids (**TOP DOCS PROVE LIFE AFTER DEATH!!!**), we possess no such evidence.

As we shall see later in this section, when we turn to evaluation, positive evidence for the existence of this novel, nonmaterial, thinking *substance* is in general on the slim side. This has moved many dualists to articulate still less extreme forms of dualism, in hopes of narrowing further the gap between theory and available evidence.

Property Dualism

The basic idea of the theories under this heading is that while there is no *substance* to be dealt with here beyond the physical brain, the brain has a special set of *properties* possessed by no other kind of physical object. It is these special properties that are nonphysical: hence the term *property dualism*. The properties in question are the ones you would expect: the property of having a pain, of having a sensation of red, of thinking that P, of desiring that Q, and so forth. These are the properties that are characteristic of conscious intelligence. They are held to be nonphysical in the sense that they cannot ever be reduced to or explained solely in terms of the concepts of the familiar physical sciences. They will require a wholly new and autonomous science—the 'science of mental phenomena'—if they are ever to be adequately understood.

From here, important differences among the positions emerge. Let us begin with what is perhaps the oldest version of property dualism: *epiphenomenalism*. This term is rather a mouthful, but its meaning is simple. The Greek prefix "epi-" means "above", and the position at issue holds that mental phenomena are not a part of the physical phenomena in the brain that ultimately determine our actions and behavior, but rather ride 'above the fray'. Mental phenomena are thus *epi*phenomena. They are held to just appear or emerge when the growing brain passes a certain level of complexity.

But there is more. The epiphenomenalist holds that while mental phenomena are caused to occur by the various activities of the brain, *they do not have any causal effects in turn*. They are entirely impotent with respect to causal effects on the physical world. They are *mere* epiphenomena. (To fix our ideas, a vague metaphor may be helpful here. Think of our conscious mental states as little sparkles of shimmering light that occur on the wrinkled surface of the brain, sparkles which are caused to occur by physical activity in the brain, but which have no causal effects on the brain in return.) This means that the universal conviction that one's actions are determined by one's desires, decisions, and volitions is false! One's actions are exhaustively determined by physical events in the brain, which events *also* cause the epiphenomena we call desires, decisions, and volitions. There is therefore a constant conjunction between volitions and actions. But according to the epiphenomenalist, it is mere illusion that the former cause the latter.

What could motivate such a strange view? In fact, it is not too difficult to understand why someone might take it seriously. Put yourself in the shoes of a neuroscientist who is concerned to trace the origins of behavior back up the motor nerves to the active cells in the motor cortex of the cerebrum, and to trace in turn their activity into inputs from other parts of the brain, and from the various sensory nerves. She finds a thoroughly physical system of awesome structure and delicacy, and much intricate activity, all of it unambiguously chemical or electrical in nature, and she finds no hint at all of any nonphysical inputs of the kind that substance dualism proposes. What is she to think? From the standpoint of her researches, human behavior is exhaustively a function of the activity of the physical brain. And this opinion is further supported by her confidence that the brain has the behavior-controlling features it does exactly because those features have been ruthlessly selected for during the brain's long evolutionary history. In sum, the seat of human behavior appears entirely physical in its constitution, in its origins, and in its internal activities.

On the other hand, our neuroscientist has the testimony of her own introspection to account for as well. She can hardly deny that she has experiences, beliefs, and desires, nor that they are connected in some way with her behavior. One bargain that can be struck here is to admit the *reality* of mental properties, as nonphysical properties, but demote them to the status of impotent epiphenomena that have nothing to do with the scientific explanation of human and animal behavior. This is the position the epiphenomenalist takes, and the reader can now

perceive the rationale behind it. It is a bargain struck between the desire to respect a rigorously scientific approach to the explanation of behavior, and the desire to respect the testimony of introspection.

The epiphenomenalist's 'demotion' of mental properties—to causally impotent by-products of brain activity—has seemed too extreme for most property dualists, and a theory closer to the convictions of common sense has enjoyed somewhat greater popularity. This view, which we may call *interactionist property dualism*, differs from the previous view in only one essential respect: the interactionist asserts that mental properties do indeed have causal effects on the brain, and thereby, on behavior. The mental properties of the brain are an integrated part of the general causal fray, in systematic interaction with the brain's physical properties. One's actions, therefore, are held to be caused by one's desires and volitions after all.

As before, mental properties are here said to be *emergent* properties, properties that do not appear at all until ordinary physical matter has managed to organize itself, through the evolutionary process, into a system of sufficient complexity. Examples of properties that are emergent in this sense would be the property of being *solid*, the property of being *colored*, and the property of being *alive*. All of these require matter to be suitably organized before they can be displayed. With this much, any materialist will agree. But any property dualist makes the further claim that mental states and properties are *irreducible*, in the sense that they are not just organizational features of physical matter, as are the examples cited. They are said to be novel properties beyond prediction or explanation by physical science.

This last condition—the irreducibility of mental properties—is an important one, since this is what makes the position a dualist position. But it sits poorly with the joint claim that mental properties emerge from nothing more than the organizational achievements of physical matter. If that is how

❖ ❖

mental properties are produced, then one would expect a physical account of them to be possible. The simultaneous claim of evolutionary emergence *and* physical irreducibility is prima facie puzzling.

A property dualist is not absolutely bound to insist on both claims. He could let go the thesis of evolutionary emergence, and claim that mental properties are *fundamental* properties of reality, properties that have been here from the universe's inception, properties on a par with length, mass, electric charge, and other fundamental properties. There is even an historical precedent for a position of this kind. At the turn of this century it was still widely believed that electromagnetic phenomena (such as electric charge and magnetic attraction) were just an unusually subtle manifestation of purely *mechanical* phenomena. Some scientists thought that a reduction of electromagnetics to mechanics was more or less in the bag. They thought that radio waves, for example, would turn out to be just travelling oscillations in a very subtle but jellylike aether that fills space everywhere. But the aether turned out not to exist. So electromagnetic properties turned out to be fundamental properties in their own right, and we were forced to add electric charge to the existing list of fundamental properties (mass, length, and duration).

Perhaps mental properties enjoy a status like that of electromagnetic properties: irreducible, but not emergent. Such a view may be called *elemental-property dualism*, and it has the advantage of clarity over the previous view. Unfortunately, the parallel with electromagnetic phenomena has one very obvious failure. Unlike electromagnetic properties, which are displayed at all levels of reality from the subatomic level on up, mental properties are displayed only in large physical systems that have evolved a very complex internal organization. The case for the evolutionary emergence of mental properties through the organization of matter is extremely strong. They do not appear to be basic or elemental at all. This returns us, therefore, to the issue of their irreducibility. Why should we accept this most basic of the dualist's claims? Why be a dualist?

The argument from introspection is a interesting argument, since it tries to appeal to the direct experience of everyman. But the argument is deeply suspect, in that it assumes that our faculty of inner observation or introspection reveals things as they really are in their innermost nature. This assumption is suspect because we already know that our other forms of observation—sight, hearing, touch, and so on—do no such thing. The red surface of an apple does not *look* like a matrix of molecules reflecting photons at certain critical wavelengths, but that is what it is. The sound of a flute does not *sound* like a sinusoidal compression wave train in the atmosphere, but that is what it is. The warmth of the summer air does not *feel* like the mean kinetic energy of millions of tiny molecules, but that is what it is. If one's pains and hopes and beliefs do not *introspectively* seem like electrochemical states in a neural network, that may be only because our faculty of introspection, like our other senses, is not sufficiently penetrating to reveal such hidden details. Which is just what one would expect anyway. The argument from introspection is therefore entirely without force, unless we can somehow argue that the faculty of introspection is quite different from all other forms of observation.

The argument from irreducibility presents a more serious challenge, but here also its force is less than first impression suggests. Consider first our capacity for mathematical reasoning which so impressed Descartes. The last ten years have made available, to anyone with fifty dollars to spend, electronic calculators whose capacity for mathematical reasoning—the calculational part, at least—far surpasses that of any normal human. The fact is, in the centuries since Descartes' writings, philosophers, logicians, mathematicians, and computer scientists have managed to isolate the general principles of mathematical reasoning, and electronics engineers have created machines that compute in accord with those principles. The result is a hand-held object that would have astonished Descartes. This outcome is impressive not just because machines have proved capable of some of the capacities boasted by human reason, but because some of those achievements invade areas of human reason that past dualistic philosophers have held up as forever closed to mere physical devices.

Although debate on the matter remains open, Descartes' argument from language use is equally dubious. The notion of a *computer language* is by now a commonplace: consider BASIC, PASCAL, FORTRAN, APL, LISP, and so on. Granted, these artificial 'languages' are much simpler in structure and content than human natural language, but the differences may be differences only of degree, and not of kind. As well, the theoretical work of Noam Chomsky and the generative grammar approach to linguistics have done a great deal to explain the human capacity for language use in terms that invite simulation by computers. I do not mean to suggest that truly conversational computers are just around the corner. We have a great deal yet to learn, and fundamental problems yet to solve (mostly having to do with our capacity for inductive or theoretical reasoning). But recent progress here does nothing to support the claim that language use must be forever impossible for a purely physical system. On the contrary, such a claim now appears rather arbitrary and dogmatic.

The next issue is also a live problem: How can we possibly hope to explain or to predict the intrinsic qualities of our sensations, or the meaningful content of our beliefs and desires, in purely physical terms? This is a major challenge to the materialist. But as we shall see in later sections, active research programs are already under way on both problems, and positive suggestions are being explored. It is in fact not impossible to imagine how such explanations might go, though the materialist cannot yet pretend to have solved either problem. Until he does, the dualist will retain a bargaining chip here, but that is about all. What the dualists need in order to establish their case is the conclusion that a physical reduction is outright impossible, and that is a conclusion they have failed to establish. Rhetorical questions, like the one that opens this paragraph, do not constitute arguments. And it is equally difficult, note, to imagine how the relevant phenomena could be explained or predicted solely in terms of the substance dualist's nonphysical mind-stuff. The explanatory problem here is a major challenge to everybody, not just to the materialist. On this issue then, we have a rough standoff.

The final argument in support of dualism urged the existence of parapsychological phenomena such as telepathy and telekinesis, the point being that such mental phenomena are (a) real, and (b) beyond purely physical explanation.

Despite the endless pronouncements and anecdotes in the popular press, and despite a steady trickle of serious research on such things, there is no significant or trustworthy evidence that such phenomena even exist. The wide gap between popular conviction on this matter, and the actual evidence, is something that itself calls for research. For there is not a single parapsychological effect that can be repeatedly or reliably produced in any laboratory suitably equipped to perform and control the experiment. Not one. Honest researchers have been repeatedly hoodwinked by 'psychic' charlatans with skills derived from the magician's trade, and the history of the subject is largely a history of gullibility, selection of evidence, poor experimental controls, and outright fraud by the occasional researcher as well. If someone really does discover a repeatable parapsychological effect, then we shall have to reevaluate the situation, but as things stand, there is nothing here to support a dualist theory of mind.

Upon critical examination, the arguments in support of dualism lose much of their force. But we are not yet done: there are arguments against dualism, and these also require examination.

❖ ❖

Arguments against Dualism

The first argument against dualism urged by the materialists appeals to the greater *simplicity* of their view. It is a principle of rational methodology that, if all else is equal, the simpler of two competing hypotheses should be preferred. This principle is sometimes called "Ockham's Razor"—after William of Ockham, the medieval philosopher who first enunciated it—and it can also be expressed as follows: "Do not multiply entities beyond what is strictly necessary to explain the phenomena." The materialist postulates only one kind of substance (physical matter), and one class of properties (physical properties), whereas the dualist postulates two kinds of matter and/or two classes of properties. And to no explanatory advantage, charges the materialist.

This is not yet a decisive point against dualism, since neither dualism nor materialism can yet explain all of the phenomena to be explained. But the objection does have some force, especially since there is no doubt at all that physical matter exists, while spiritual matter remains a tenuous hypothesis.

If this latter hypothesis brought us some definite explanatory advantage obtainable in no other way, then we would happily violate the demand for simplicity, and we would be right to do so. But it does not, claims the materialist. In fact, the advantage is just the other way around, he argues, and this brings us to the second objection to dualism: the relative *explanatory impotence* of dualism as compared to materialism.

Consider, very briefly, the explanatory resources already available to the neurosciences. We know that the brain exists and what it is made of. We know much of its microstructure: how the neurons are organized into systems and how distinct systems are connected to one another, to the motor nerves going out to the muscles, and to the sensory nerves coming in from the sense organs. We know much of their microchemistry: how the nerve cells fire tiny electrochemical pulses along their various fibers, and how they make other cells fire also, or cease firing. We know some of how such activity processes sensory information, selecting salient or subtle bits to be sent on to higher systems. And we know some of how such activity initiates and coordinates bodily behavior. Thanks mainly to neurology (the branch of medicine concerned with brain pathology), we know a great deal about the correlations between damage to various parts of the human brain, and various behavioral and cognitive deficits from which the victims suffer. There are a great many isolated deficits—some gross, some subtle—that are familiar to neurologists (inability to speak, or to read, or to understand speech, or to recognize faces, or to add/subtract, or to move a certain limb, or to put information into long-term memory, and so on), and their appearance is closely tied to the occurrence of damage to very specific parts of the brain.

Nor are we limited to cataloguing traumas. The growth and development of the brain's microstructure is also something that neuroscience has explored, and such development appears to be the basis of various kinds of learning by the organism. Learning, that is, involves lasting chemical and physical changes in the brain. In sum, the neuroscientist can tell us a great deal about the brain, about its constitution and the physical laws that govern it; he can already explain much of our behavior in terms of the physical, chemical, and electrical properties of the brain; and he has the theoretical resources available to explain a good deal more as our explorations continue. (We shall take a closer look at neurophysiology and neuropsychology in chapter 7.)

Compare now what the neuroscientist can tell us about the brain, and what he can do with that knowledge, with what the dualist can tell us about spiritual substance, and what he can do with those assumptions. Can the dualist tell us anything about the internal constitution of mind-stuff? Of the

❀ ❀

nonmaterial elements that make it up? Of the laws that govern their behavior? Of the mind's structural connections with the body? Of the manner of its operations? Can he explain human capacities and pathologies in terms of its structures and its defects? The fact is, the dualist can do none of these things, because no detailed theory of mind-stuff has ever been formulated. Compared to the rich resources and explanatory successes of current materialism, dualism is less a theory of mind than it is an empty space waiting for a genuine theory of mind to be put in it.

Thus argues the materialist. But again, this is not a completely decisive point against dualism. The dualist can admit that the brain plays a major role in the administration of both perception and behavior—on his view the brain is the *mediator* between the mind and the body—but he may attempt to argue that the materialist's current successes and future explanatory prospects concern only the mediative functions of the brain, not the *central* capacities of the nonphysical mind, capacities such as reason, emotion, and consciousness itself. On these latter topics, he may argue, both dualism *and* materialism currently draw a blank.

But this reply is not a very good one. So far as the capacity for reasoning is concerned, machines already exist that execute in minutes sophisticated deductive and mathematical calculations that would take a human a lifetime to execute. And so far as the other two mental capacities are concerned, studies of such things as depression, motivation, attention, and sleep have revealed many interesting and puzzling facts about the neurochemical and neurodynamical basis of both emotion and consciousness. The *central* capacities, no less than the peripheral, have been addressed with profit by various materialist research programs.

In any case, the (substance) dualist's attempt to draw a sharp distinction between the unique 'mental'

capacities proper to the nonmaterial mind, and the merely mediative capacities of the brain, prompts an argument that comes close to being an outright refutation of (substance) dualism. If there really is a distinct entity in which reasoning, emotion, and consciousness take place, and if that entity is dependent on the brain for nothing more than sensory experiences as input and volitional executions as output, *then one would expect reason, emotion, and consciousness to be relatively invulnerable to direct control or pathology by manipulation or damage to the brain*. But in fact the exact opposite is true. Alcohol, narcotics, or senile degeneration of nerve tissue will impair, cripple, or even destroy one's capacity for rational thought. Psychiatry knows of hundreds of emotion-controlling chemicals (lithium, chlorpromazine, amphetamine, cocaine, and so on) that do their work when vectored into the brain. And the vulnerability of consciousness to the anesthetics, to caffeine, and to something as simple as a sharp blow to the head, shows its very close dependence on neural activity in the brain. All of this makes perfect sense if reason, emotion, and consciousness are activities of the brain itself. But it makes very little sense if they are activities of something else entirely.

We may call this the argument from the *neural dependence* of all known mental phenomena. Property dualism, note, is not threatened by this argument, since, like materialism, property dualism reckons the brain as the seat of all mental activity. We shall conclude this section, however, with an argument that cuts against both varieties of dualism: the argument from *evolutionary history*.

What is the origin of a complex and sophisticated species such as ours? What, for that matter, is the origin of the dolphin, the mouse, or the housefly? Thanks to the fossil record, comparative anatomy, and the biochemistry of proteins and nucleic acids, there is no longer any significant doubt on this matter. Each existing species is a surviving type

❀ ❀

from a number of variations on an earlier type of organism; each earlier type is in turn a surviving type from a number of variations on a still earlier type of organism; and so on down the branches of the evolutionary tree until, some three billion years ago, we find a trunk of just one or a handful of very simple organisms. These organisms, like their more complex offspring, are just self-repairing, self-replicating, energy-driven molecular structures. (That evolutionary trunk has its own roots in an earlier era of purely chemical evolution, in which the molecular elements of life were themselves pieced together.) The mechanism of development that has structured this tree has two main elements: (1) the occasional blind variation in types of reproducing creature, and (2) the selective survival of some of these types due to the relative reproductive advantage enjoyed by individuals of those types. Over periods of geological time, such a process can produce an enormous variety of organisms, some of them very complex indeed.

For purposes of our discussion, the important point about the standard evolutionary story is that the human species and all of its features are the wholly physical outcome of a purely physical process. Like all but the simplest of organisms, we have a nervous system. And for the same reason: a nervous system permits the discriminative guidance of behavior. But a nervous system is just an active matrix of cells, and a cell is just an active matrix of molecules. We are notable only in that our nervous system is more complex and powerful than those of our fellow creatures. Our inner nature differs from that of simpler creatures in degree, but not in kind.

If this is the correct account of our origins, then there seems neither need, nor room, to fit any nonphysical substances or properties into our theoretical account of ourselves. We are creatures of matter. And we should learn to live with that fact.

Suggested Readings

Popper, Sir Karl, *The Self and Its Brain*, with Sir John C. Eccles (New York: Springer-Verlag, 1977).

Margolis, Joseph, *Persons and Minds: The Prospects of Nonreductive Materialism* (Dordrecht-Holland: Reidel, 1978).

Jackson, Frank, "Epiphenomenal Qualia," *The Philosophical Quarterly*, vol. 32, no. 127 (April, 1982).

Nagel, Thomas, "What Is It Like to Be a Bat?" *Philosophical Review*, vol. LXXXIII (1974). Reprinted in *Readings in Philosophy of Psychology*, vol. I, ed. N. Block (Cambridge, MA: Harvard University Press, 1980).

3. Reductive Materialism (the Identity Theory)

Reductive materialism, more commonly known as *the identity theory*, is the most straightforward of the several materialist theories of mind. Its central claim is simplicity itself: Mental states *are* physical states of the brain. That is, each type of mental state or process is *numerically identical with* (is one and the very same thing as) some type of physical state or process within the brain or central nervous system. At present we do not know enough about the intricate functionings of the brain actually to state the relevant identities, but the identity theory is committed to the idea that brain research will eventually reveal them.

Historical Parallels

As the identity theorist sees it, the result here predicted has familiar parallels elsewhere in our scientific history. Consider sound. We now know that sound is just a train of compression waves traveling through the air, and that the property of being high pitched is identical with the property of having a high oscillatory frequency. We have

❖ ❖

learned that light is just electromagnetic waves, and our best current theory says that the color of an object is identical with a triplet of reflectance efficiencies the object has, rather like a musical chord that it strikes, though the 'notes' are struck in electromagnetic waves instead of in sound waves. We now appreciate that the warmth or coolness of a body is just the energy of motion of the molecules that make it up: warmth is identical with high average molecular kinetic energy, and coolness is identical with low average molecular kinetic energy. We know that lightning is identical with a sudden large-scale discharge of electrons between clouds, or between the atmosphere and the ground. What we now think of as 'mental states,' argues the identity theorist, are identical with brain states in exactly the same way.

Intertheoretic Reduction

These illustrative parallels are all cases of successful *intertheoretic reduction*. That is, they are all cases where a new and very powerful theory turns out to entail a set of propositions and principles that mirror perfectly (or almost perfectly) the propositions and principles of some older theory or conceptual framework. The relevant principles entailed by the new theory have the same structure as the corresponding principles of the old framework, and they apply in exactly the same cases. The only difference is that where the old principles contained (for example) the notions of "heat", "is hot", and "is cold", the new principles contain instead the notions of "total molecular kinetic energy", "has a high mean molecular kinetic energy", and "has a low mean molecular kinetic energy".

If the new framework is far better than the old at explaining and predicting phenomena, then we have excellent reason for believing that the theoretical terms of the *new* framework are the terms that describe reality correctly. But if the old framework worked adequately, so far as it went, and if it parallels a portion of the new theory in the systematic way described, then we may properly conclude that the old terms and the new terms refer to the very same things, or express the very same properties. We conclude that we have apprehended the very same reality that is incompletely described by the old framework, but with a new and more penetrating conceptual framework. And we announce what philosophers of science call "intertheoretic identities": light *is* electromagnetic waves, temperature *is* mean molecular kinetic energy, and so forth.

The examples of the preceding two paragraphs share one more important feature in common. They are all cases where the things or properties on the receiving end of the reduction are *observable* things and properties within our *common-sense* conceptual framework. They show that intertheoretic reduction occurs not only between conceptual frameworks in the theoretical stratosphere: common-sense observables can also be reduced. There would therefore be nothing particularly surprising about a reduction of our familiar introspectible mental states to physical states of the brain. All that would be required would be that an explanatorily successful neuroscience develop to the point where it entails a suitable 'mirror image' of the assumptions and principles that constitute our common-sense conceptual framework for mental states, an image where brain-state terms occupy the positions held by mental-state terms in the assumptions and principles of common sense. If this (rather demanding) condition were indeed met, then, as in the historical cases cited, we would be justified in announcing a reduction, and in asserting the identity of mental states with brain states.

Arguments for the Identity Theory

What reasons does the identity theorist have for believing that neuroscience will eventually achieve the strong conditions necessary for the reduction of our 'folk' psychology? There are at least four reasons, all directed at the conclusion that the correct account of human-behavior-and-its-causes must reside in the physical neurosciences.

We can point first to the purely physical origins and ostensibly physical constitution of each individual human. One begins as a genetically programmed monocellular organization of molecules (a fertilized ovum), and one develops from there by the accretion of further molecules whose structure and integration is controlled by the information coded in the DNA molecules of the cell nucleus. The result of such a process would be a purely physical system whose behavior arises from its internal operations and its interactions with the rest of the physical world. And those behavior-controlling internal operations are precisely what the neurosciences are about.

This argument coheres with a second argument. The origins of each *type* of animal also appear exhaustively physical in nature. The argument from evolutionary history discussed earlier (p. 20) lends further support to the identity theorist's claim, since evolutionary theory provides the only serious explanation we have for the behavior-controlling capacities of the brain and central nervous system. Those systems were selected for because of the many advantages (ultimately, the reproductive advantage) held by creatures whose behavior was thus controlled. Again our behavior appears to have its basic causes in neural activity.

The identity theorist finds further support in the argument, discussed earlier, from the neural dependence of all known mental phenomena (see p. 20). This is precisely what one should expect, if the identity theory is true. Of course, systematic neural dependence is also a consequence of property dualism, but here the identity theorist will appeal to considerations of simplicity. Why admit two radically different classes of properties and operations if the explanatory job can be done by one?

A final argument derives from the growing success of the neurosciences in unraveling the nervous systems of many creatures and in explaining their behavioral capacities and deficits in terms of the structures discovered. The preceding arguments all suggest that neuroscience should be successful in this endeavor, and the fact is that the continuing history of neuroscience bears them out. Especially in the case of very simple creatures (as one would expect), progress has been rapid. And progress has also been made with humans, though for obvious moral reasons exploration must be more cautious and circumspect. In sum, the neurosciences have a long way to go, but progress to date provides substantial encouragement to the identity theorist.

Even so, these arguments are far from decisive in favor of the identity theory. No doubt they do provide an overwhelming case for the idea that the causes of human and animal behavior are essentially physical in nature, but the identity theory claims more than just this. It claims that neuroscience will discover a taxonomy of neural states that stand in a one-to-one correspondence with the mental states of our common-sense taxonomy. Claims for intertheoretic identity will be justified only if such a match-up can be found. But nothing in the preceding arguments guarantees that the old and new frameworks will match up in this way, even if the new framework is a roaring success at explaining and predicting our behavior. Furthermore, there are arguments from other positions within the materialist camp to the effect that such convenient match-ups are rather unlikely. Before exploring those, however, let us look at some more traditional objections to the identity theory.

Arguments against the Identity Theory

We may begin with the argument from introspection discussed earlier. Introspection reveals a domain of thoughts, sensations, and emotions, not

❁ ❁

a domain of electrochemical impulses in a neural network. Mental states and properties, as revealed in introspection, appear radically different from any neurophysiological states and properties. How could they possibly be the very same things?

1. My mental states are introspectively known by me as states of my conscious self.

2. My brain states are *not* introspectively known by me as states of my conscious self.

   Therefore, by Leibniz' Law (that numerically identical things must have exactly the same properties),

3. My mental states are not identical with my brain states.

This, in my experience, is the most beguiling form of the argument from introspection, seductive of freshmen and faculty alike. But it is a straightforward instance of a well-known fallacy, which is clearly illustrated in the following parallel arguments:

1. Muhammad Ali is widely known as a heavyweight champion.

2. Cassius Clay is *not* widely known as a heavyweight champion.

   Therefore, by Leibniz' Law,

3. Muhammad Ali is not identical with Cassius Clay.

or,

1. Aspirin is recognized by John to be a pain reliever.

2. Acetylsalicylic acid is *not* recogized by John to be a pain reliever.

   Therefore, by Leibniz' Law,

3. Aspirin is not identical with acetylsalicylic acid.

Despite the truth of the relevant premises, both conclusions are false: the identities are wholly genuine. Which means that both arguments

are invalid. The problem is that the 'property' ascribed in premise (1), and withheld in premise (2), consists only in the subject item's being *recognized, perceived*, or *known* as something-or-other. But such apprehension is not a genuine property of the item itself, fit for divining identities, since one and the same subject may be successfully recognized under one name or description, and yet fail to be recognized under another (accurate, coreferential) description. Bluntly, Leibniz' Law is not valid for these bogus 'properties'. The attempt to use them as above commits what logicians call an *intensional* fallacy. The premises may reflect, not the failure of certain objective identities, but only our continuing failure to appreciate them.

A different version of the preceding argument must also be considered, since it may be urged that one's brain states are more than merely not (yet) known by introspection: they are not know*able* by introspection under any circumstances. Thus,

1. My mental states are knowable by introspection.

2. My brain states are *not* knowable by introspection.

   Therefore, by Leibniz' Law,

3. My mental states are not identical with my brain states.

Here the critic will insist that being know*able* by introspection *is* a genuine property of a thing, and that this modified version of the argument is free of the 'intensional fallacy' discussed above.

And so it is. But now the materialist is in a position to insist that the argument contains a false premise—premise (2). For if mental states are indeed brain states, then it is really brain states we have been introspecting all along, though without fully appreciating what they are. And if we can learn to think of and recognize those states under mentalistic descriptions, as we all have, then we can certainly learn to think of and recognize them

❖ ❖

under their more penetrating neurophysiological descriptions. At the very least, premise (2) simply begs the question against the identity theorist. The mistake is amply illustrated in the following parallel argument:

1. Temperature is knowable by feeling.
2. Mean molecular kinetic energy is *not* knowable by feeling.

   Therefore, by Leibniz' Law,

3. Temperature is not identical with mean molecular kinetic energy.

This identity, at least, is long established, and this argument is certainly unsound: premise (2) is false. Just as one can learn to feel that the summer air is about 70°F, or 21°C, so one can learn to feel that the mean KE of its molecules is about 6.2×10^{-21} joules, for whether we realize it or not, that is what our discriminatory mechanisms are keyed to. Perhaps our brain states are similarly accessible. The introspectibility of brain states is addressed again in chapter 8.

Consider now a final argument, again based on the introspectible qualities of our sensations. Imagine a future neuroscientist who comes to know everything there is to know about the physical structure and activity of the brain and its visual system, of its actual and possible states. If for some reason she has never actually *had* a sensation-of-red (because of color blindness, say, or an unusual environment), then there will remain something she does *not* know about certain sensations: *what it is like to have a sensation-of-red*. Therefore, complete knowledge of the physical facts of visual perception and its related brain activity still leaves something out. Accordingly, materialism cannot give an adequate account of all mental phenomena, and the identity theory must be false.

The identity theorist can reply that this argument exploits an unwitting equivocation on the term "know". Concerning our neuroscientist's utopian knowledge of the brain, "knows" means something

like "has mastered the relevant set of neuroscientific propositions". Concerning her (missing) knowledge of what it is like to have a sensation-of-red, "knows" means something like "has a prelinguistic representation of redness in her mechanisms for noninferential discrimination". It is true that one might have the former without the latter, but the materialist is not committed to the idea that having knowledge in the former sense automatically constitutes having knowledge in the second sense. The identity theorist can admit a duality, or even a plurality, of different *types of knowledge* without thereby committing himself to a duality in *types of things known*. The difference between a person who knows all about the visual cortex but has never enjoyed the sensation-of-red, and a person who knows no neuroscience but knows well the sensation-of-red, may reside not in *what* is respectively known by each (brain states by the former, nonphysical *qualia* by the latter), but rather in the different *type*, or *medium*, or *level* of representation each has of exactly the same thing: brain states.

In sum, there are pretty clearly more ways of 'having knowledge' than just having mastered a set of sentences, and the materialist can freely admit that one has 'knowledge' of one's sensations in a way that is independent of the neuroscience one may have learned. Animals, including humans, presumably have a prelinguistic mode of sensory representation. This does not mean that sensations are beyond the reach of physical science. *It just means that the brain uses more modes and media of representation than the mere storage of sentences.* All the identity theorist needs to claim is that those other modes of representation will also yield to neuroscientific explanation.

The identity theory has proved to be very resilient in the face of these predominantly antimaterialist objections. But further objections, rooted in competing forms of materialism, constitute a much more serious threat, as the following sections will show.

4. Functionalism

According to *functionalism*, the essential or defining feature of any type of mental state is the set of causal relations it bears to (1) environmental effects on the body, (2) other types of mental states, and (3) bodily behavior. Pain, for example, characteristically results from some bodily damage or trauma; it causes distress, annoyance, and practical reasoning aimed at relief; and it causes wincing, blanching, and nursing of the traumatized area. Any state that plays exactly that functional role is a pain, according to functionalism. Similarly, other types of mental states (sensations, fears, beliefs, and so on) are also defined by their unique causal roles in a complex economy of internal states mediating sensory inputs and behavioral outputs.

Imagine a being from another planet, says the functionalist, a being with an alien physiological constitution, a constitution based on the chemical element silicon, for example, instead of on the element carbon, as ours is. The chemistry and even the physical structure of the alien's brain would have to be systematically different from ours. But even so, that alien brain could well sustain a functional economy of internal states whose mutual *relations* parallel perfectly the mutual relations that define our own mental states. The alien may have an internal state that meets all the conditions for being a pain state, as outlined earlier. That state, considered from a purely physical point of view, would have a very different makeup from a human pain state, but it could nevertheless be identical to a human pain state from a purely functional point of view. And so for all of his functional states.

If the alien's functional economy of internal states were indeed *functionally isomorphic* with our own internal economy—if those states were causally connected to inputs, to one another, and to behavior in ways that parallel our own internal connections—then the alien would have pains, and desires, and hopes, and fears just as fully as we,

despite the differences in the physical system that sustains or realizes those functional states. What is important for mentality is not the matter of which the creature is made, but the structure of the internal activities which that matter sustains.

If we can think of one alien constitution, we can think of many, and the point just made can also be made with an artificial system. Were we to create an electronic system—a computer of some kind—whose internal economy were functionally isomorphic with our own in all the relevant ways, then it too would be the subject of mental states.

What this illustrates is that there are almost certainly many more ways than one for nature, and perhaps even for man, to put together a thinking, feeling, perceiving creature. And this raises a problem for the identity theory, for it seems that there is no single type of physical state to which a given type of mental state must always correspond. Ironically, there are *too many* different kinds of physical systems that can realize the functional economy characteristic of conscious intelligence. If we consider the universe at large, therefore, and the future as well as the present, it seems quite unlikely that the identity theorist is going to find the one-to-one match-ups between the concepts of our common-sense mental taxonomy and the concepts of an overarching theory that encompasses all of the relevant physical systems. But that is what intertheoretic reduction is standardly said to require. The prospects for universal identities, between types of mental states and types of brain states, are therefore slim.

If the functionalists reject the traditional 'mental-type = physical type' identity theory, virtually all of them remain committed to a weaker 'mental token = physical token' identity theory, for they still maintain that each *instance* of a given type of mental state is numerically identical with some specific physical state in some physical system or other. It is only universal (type/type) identities that are rejected. Even so, this rejection is typically taken to support the claim that the science of psychology is or should be *methodologically autonomous* from the various physical sciences such as physics, biology, and even neurophysiology. Psychology, it is claimed, has its own irreducible laws and its own abstract subject matter.

As this book is written, functionalism is probably the most widely held theory of mind among philosophers, cognitive psychologists, and artificial intelligence researchers.

5. Eliminative Materialism

The identity theory was called into doubt not because the prospects for a materialist account of our mental capacities were thought to be poor, but because it seemed unlikely that the arrival of an adequate materialist theory would bring with it the nice one-to-one match-ups, between the concepts of folk psychology and the concepts of theoretical neuroscience, that intertheoretic reduction requires. The reason for that doubt was the great variety of quite different physical systems that could instantiate the required functional organization. *Eliminative materialism* also doubts that the correct neuroscientific account of human capacities will produce a neat reduction of our common-sense framework, but here the doubts arise from a quite different source.

As the eliminative materialists see it, the one-to-one match-ups will not be found, and our common-sense psychological framework will not enjoy an intertheoretic reduction, *because our common-sense psychological framework is a false and radically misleading conception of the causes of human behavior and the nature of cognitive activity*. On this view, folk psychology is not just an incomplete representation of our inner natures; it is an outright *mis*representation of our internal states and activities. Consequently, we cannot expect a truly adequate neuroscientific account of our inner lives to provide theoretical categories that match up nicely with the categories of our common-sense framework. Accordingly, we must expect that the older framework will simply be eliminated, rather than be reduced, by a matured neuroscience.

Historical Parallels

As the identity theorist can point to historical cases of successful inter-theoretic reduction, so the eliminative materialist can point to historical cases of the outright elimination of the ontology of an older theory in favor of the ontology of a new and superior theory. For most of the eighteenth and nineteenth centuries, learned people believed that heat was a subtle *fluid* held in bodies, much in the way water is held in a sponge. A fair body of moderately successful theory described the way this fluid substance—called "caloric"—flowed within a body, or from one body to another, and how it produced thermal expansion, melting, boiling, and so forth. But by the end of the last century it had become abundantly clear that heat was not a substance at all, but just the energy of motion of the trillions of jostling molecules that make up the heated body itself. The new theory—the "corpuscular/kinetic theory of matter and heat"—was much more successful than the old in explaining and predicting the thermal behavior of bodies. And since we were unable to *identify* caloric fluid with kinetic energy (according to the old theory, caloric is a material *substance*; according to the new theory, kinetic energy is a form of *motion*), it was finally agreed that there is *no such thing* as caloric. Caloric was simply eliminated from our accepted ontology.

A second example. It used to be thought that when a piece of wood burns, or a piece of metal rusts, a spiritlike substance called "phlogiston" was being released: briskly, in the former case, slowly in the latter. Once gone, that 'noble' substance left only a base pile of ash or rust. It later came to be appreciated that both processes involve, not the loss of something, but the *gaining* of a substance taken from the atmosphere: oxygen. Phlogiston emerged, not as an

incomplete description of what was going on, but as a radical misdescription. Phlogiston was therefore not suitable for reduction to or identification with some notion from within the new oxygen chemistry, and it was simply eliminated from science.

Admittedly, both of these examples concern the elimination of something nonobservable, but our history also includes the elimination of certain widely accepted 'observables'. Before Copernicus' views became available, almost any human who ventured out at night could look up at *the starry sphere of the heavens*, and if he stayed for more than a few minutes he could also see that it *turned*, around an axis through Polaris. What the sphere was made of (crystal?) and what made it turn (the gods?) were theoretical questions that exercised us for over two millennia. But hardly anyone doubted the existence of what everyone could observe with their own eyes. In the end, however, we learned to reinterpret our visual experience of the night sky within a very different conceptual framework, and the turning sphere evaporated.

Witches provide another example. Psychosis is a fairly common affliction among humans, and in earlier centuries its victims were standardly seen as cases of demonic possession, as instances of Satan's spirit itself, glaring malevolently out at us from behind the victims' eyes. That witches exist was not a matter of any controversy. One would occasionally see them, in any city or hamlet, engaged in incoherent, paranoid, or even murderous behavior. But observable or not, we eventually decided that witches simply do not exist. We concluded that the concept of a witch is an element in a conceptual framework that misrepresents so badly the phenomena to which it was standardly applied that literal application of the notion should be permanently withdrawn. Modern theories of mental dysfunction led to the elimination of witches from our serious ontology.

The concepts of folk psychology—belief, desire, fear, sensation, pain, joy, and so on—await a similar fate,

according to the view at issue. And when neuroscience has matured to the point where the poverty of our current conceptions is apparent to everyone, and the superiority of the new framework is established, we shall then be able to set about *reconceiving* our internal states and activities, within a truly adequate conceptual framework at last. Our explanations of one another's behavior will appeal to such things as our neuropharmacological states, the neural activity in specialized anatomical areas, and whatever other states are deemed relevant by the new theory. Our private introspection will also be transformed, and may be profoundly enhanced by reason of the more accurate and penetrating framework it will have to work with—just as the astronomer's perception of the night sky is much enhanced by the detailed knowledge of modern astronomical theory that he or she possesses.

The magnitude of the conceptual revolution here suggested should not be minimized: it would be enormous. And the benefits to humanity might be equally great. If each of us possessed an accurate neuroscientific understanding of (what we now conceive dimly as) the varieties and causes of mental illness, the factors involved in learning, the neural basis of emotions, intelligence, and socialization, then the sum total of human misery might be much reduced. The simple increase in mutual understanding that the new framework made possible could contribute substantially toward a more peaceful and humane society. Of course, there would be dangers as well: increased knowledge means increased power, and power can always be misused.

Arguments against Eliminative Materialism

The initial plausibility of this rather radical view is low for almost everyone, since it denies deeply entrenched assumptions. That is at best a question-begging complaint, of course, since those assumptions are precisely what is at issue. But the following line of thought does attempt to mount a real argument.

Eliminative materialism is false, runs the argument, because one's introspection reveals directly the existence of pains, beliefs, desires, fears, and so forth. Their existence is as obvious as anything could be.

The eliminative materialist will reply that this argument makes the same mistake that an ancient or medieval person would be making if he insisted that he could just see with his own eyes that the heavens form a turning sphere, or that witches exist. The fact is, all observation occurs within some system of concepts, and our observation judgments are only as good as the conceptual framework in which they are expressed. In all three cases—the starry sphere, witches, and the familiar mental states—precisely what is challenged is the integrity of the background conceptual frameworks in which the observation judgments are expressed. To insist on the validity of one's experiences, *traditionally interpreted*, is therefore to beg the very question at issue. For in all three cases, the question is whether we should *re*conceive the nature of some familiar observational domain.

A second criticism attempts to find an incoherence in the eliminative materialist's position. The bald statement of eliminative materialism is that the familiar mental states do not really exist. But that statement is meaningful, runs the argument, only if it is the expression of a certain *belief*, and an *intention* to communicate, and a *knowledge* of the language, and so forth. But if the statement is true, then no such mental states exist, and the statement is therefore a meaningless string of marks or noises, and cannot be true. Evidently, the assumption that eliminative materialism is true entails that it cannot be true.

The hole in this argument is the premise concerning the conditions necessary for a statement to be meaningful. It begs the question. If eliminative materialism is true, then meaningfulness must have some different source. To insist on the 'old' source is to insist on the validity of the very framework at issue. Again, an historical parallel may be helpful here. Consider the medieval theory that being biologically *alive* is a matter of being ensouled by an immaterial *vital spirit*. And consider the following response to someone who has expressed disbelief in that theory.

> My learned friend has stated that there is no such thing as vital spirit. But this statement is incoherent. For if it is true, then my friend does not have vital spirit, and must therefore be *dead*. But if he is dead, then his statement is just a string of noises, devoid of meaning or truth. Evidently, the assumption that antivitalism is true entails that it cannot be true! Q.E.D.

This second argument is now a joke, but the first argument begs the question in exactly the same way.

A final criticism draws a much weaker conclusion, but makes a rather stronger case. Eliminative materialism, it has been said, is making mountains out of molehills. It exaggerates the defects in folk psychology, and underplays its real successes. Perhaps the arrival of a matured neuroscience will require the elimination of the occasional folk-psychological concept, continues the criticism, and a minor adjustment in certain folk-psychological principles may have to be endured. But the large-scale elimination forecast by the eliminative materialist is just an alarmist worry or a romantic enthusiasm.

Perhaps this complaint is correct. And perhaps it is merely complacent. Whichever, it does bring out the important point that we do not confront two simple and mutually exclusive possibilities here: pure reduction versus pure elimination. Rather, these are the end points of a smooth

❁ ❁

spectrum of possible outcomes, between which there are mixed cases of partial elimination and partial reduction. Only empirical research can tell us where on that spectrum our own case will fall. Perhaps we should speak here, more liberally, of "revisionary materialism", instead of concentrating on the more radical possibility of an across-the-board elimination. Perhaps we should. But it has been my aim in this section to make it at least intelligible to you that our collective conceptual destiny lies substantially toward the revolutionary end of the spectrum.

Suggested Readings

Feyerabend, Paul, "Comment: 'Mental Events and the Brain,'" *Journal of Philosophy*, vol. LX (1963). Reprinted in *The Mind/Brain Identity Theory*, ed. C. V. Borst (London: Macmillan, 1970).

Feyerabend, Paul, "Materialism and the Mind-Body Problem," *Review of Metaphysics*, vol. XVII (1963). Reprinted in *The Mind/Brain Identity Theory*, ed. C. V. Borst (London: Macmillan, 1970).

Rorty, Richard, "Mind-Body Identity, Privacy, and Categories," *Review of Metaphysics*, vol. XIX (1965). Reprinted in *Materialism and the Mind-Body Problem*, ed. D. M. Rosenthal (Englewood Cliffs, NJ: Prentice-Hall, 1971).

Rorty, Richard, "In Defense of Eliminative Materialism," *Review of Metaphysics*, vol. XXIV (1970). Reprinted in *Materialism and the Mind-Body Problem*, ed. D. M. Rosenthal (Englewood Cliffs, NJ: Prentice-Hall, 1971).

Churchland, Paul, "Eliminative Materialism and the Propositional Attitudes," *Journal of Philosophy*, vol. LXXVIII, no. 2 (1981).

Dennett, Daniel, "Why You Can't Make a Computer that Feels Pain," in *Brainstorms* (Montgomery, VT: Bradford, 1978; Cambridge, MA: MIT Press).

Churchland, Paul, "Some Reductive Strategies in Cognitive Neurobiology," *Mind*, vol. 95, no. 379 (1986).

❊ 3.3 What Mary Didn't Know ❊

selections
by Frank Jackson

✳✳

Frank Jackson (1943-present) is a Professor of philosophy at Australian National University. In the early 1980's, Jackson developed The Knowledge Argument for dualism about consciousness. The knowledge argument notes that how we know about consciousness seems very different from the way we know about other things. It seems like we could know everything about how brain states work without knowing *what it is like* to be the person who is in that brain state.

Jackson presents a thought-experiment involving Mary, a color scientist, who grows up in a colorless room. She never experiences the color red, but she knows everything about how the brain and underlying neurons work, how light waves work, how the process of perception works in translating light waves into brain states, how human psychology works, and so on. Yet, when she leaves the colorless room and sees red for the first time, she learns something new: what it's like for others to see red.

Here are some questions to think about when you read:

* Why does Mary's knowing all the physical facts, but not knowing what it's like to see red, seem to entail dualism?

* Some people suggest that what Mary doesn't know is *how* to recognize red, which is a skill rather than a fact. How does Jackson respond?

* Some people have suggested that what Mary doesn't know is red itself – that is, she's not personally acquainted with red. How does Jackson respond?

* Roughly 15 years after writing this piece, Jackson ceased to be a dualist and became a physicalist. What considerations might have influenced him to change his mind?

Epiphenomenal Qualia*

I. THE KNOWLEDGE ARGUMENT FOR QUALIA

People vary considerably in their ability to discriminate colours. Suppose that in an experiment to catalogue this variation Fred is discovered. Fred has better colour vision than anyone else on record; he makes every discrimination that anyone has ever made, and moreover he makes one that we cannot even begin to make. Show him a batch of ripe tomatoes and he sorts them into two roughly equal groups and does so with complete consistency. That is, if you blindfold him, shuffle the tomatoes up, and then remove the blindfold and ask him to sort them out again, he sorts them into exactly the same two groups.

We ask Fred how he does it. He explains that all ripe tomatoes do not look the same colour to him, and in fact that this is true of a great many objects that we classify together as red. He sees two colours where we see one, and he has in consequence developed for his own use two words 'red$_1$' and 'red$_2$' to mark the difference. Perhaps he tells us that he has often tried to teach the difference between red$_1$ and red$_2$ to his friends but has got nowhere and has concluded that the rest of the world is red$_1$-red$_2$ colour-blind —or perhaps he has had partial success with his children, it doesn't matter. In any case he explains to us that it would be quite wrong to think that because 'red' appears in both 'red$_1$' and 'red$_2$' that the two colours are shades of the one colour. He only uses the common term 'red' to fit more easily into our restricted usage. To him red$_1$ and red$_2$ are as different from each other and all the other colours as yellow is from blue. And his discriminatory behaviour bears this out: he sorts red$_1$ from red$_2$ tomatoes with the greatest of ease in a wide variety of viewing circumstances. Moreover, an investigation of the physiological basis of Fred's exceptional ability reveals that Fred's optical system is able to separate out two groups of wave-lengths in the red spectrum as sharply as we are able to sort out yellow from blue.

I think that we should admit that Fred can see, really see, at least one more colour than we can; red$_1$ is a different colour from red$_2$. We are to Fred as a totally red-green colour-blind person is to us. H. G. Wells' story "The Country of the Blind" is about a sighted person in a totally blind community. This person never manages to convince them that he can see, that he has an extra sense. They ridicule this sense as quite inconceivable, and treat his capacity to avoid falling into ditches, to win fights and so on as precisely that capacity and nothing more. We would be making their mistake if we refused to allow that Fred can see one more colour than we can.

* From *The Philosophical Quarterly*, Volume 32 (127), pp. 127–136, April 1982, by Frank Jackson. Copyright 1982 Scots Philosophical Association and the University of St. Andrews. Reprinted by permission of Oxford University Press.

What kind of experience does Fred have when he sees red_1 and red_2? What is the new colour or colours like? We would dearly like to know but do not; and it seems that no amount of physical information about Fred's brain and optical system tells us. We find out perhaps that Fred's cones respond differentially to certain light waves in the red section of the spectrum that make no difference to ours (or perhaps he has an extra cone) and that this leads in Fred to a wider range of those brain states responsible for visual discriminatory behaviour. But none of this tells us what we really want to know about his colour experience. There is something about it we don't know. But we know, we may suppose, everything about Fred's body, his behaviour and dispositions to behaviour and about his internal physiology, and everything about his history and relation to others that can be given in physical accounts of persons. We have all the physical information. Therefore, knowing all this is *not* knowing everything about Fred. It follows that Physicalism leaves something out.

To reinforce this conclusion, imagine that as a result of our investigations into the internal workings of Fred we find out how to make everyone's physiology like Fred's in the relevant respects; or perhaps Fred donates his body to science and on his death we are able to transplant his optical system into someone else—again the fine detail doesn't matter. The important point is that such a happening would create enormous interest. People would say, "At last we will know what it is like to see the extra colour, at last we will know how Fred has differed from us in the way he has struggled to tell us about for so long". Then it cannot be that we knew all along all about Fred. But *ex hypothesi* we did know all along everything about Fred that features in the physicalist scheme; hence the physicalist scheme leaves something out.

Put it this way. *After* the operation, we will know *more* about Fred and especially about his colour experiences. But beforehand we had all the physical information we could desire about his body and brain, and indeed everything that has ever featured in physicalist accounts of mind and consciousness. Hence there is more to know than all that. Hence Physicalism is incomplete.

Fred and the new colour(s) are of course essentially rhetorical devices. The same point can be made with normal people and familiar colours. Mary is a brilliant scientist who is, for whatever reason, forced to investigate the world from a black and white room *via* a black and white television monitor. She specialises in the neurophysiology of vision and acquires, let us suppose, all the physical information there is to obtain about what goes on when we see ripe tomatoes, or the sky, and use terms like 'red', 'blue', and so on. She discovers, for example, just which wave-length combinations from the sky stimulate the retina, and exactly how this produces *via* the central nervous system the contraction of the vocal chords and expulsion of air from the lungs that results in the uttering of the sentence 'The sky is blue'. (It can hardly be denied that it is in principle possible to obtain all this physical information from black and white television, otherwise the Open University would of *necessity* need to use colour television.)

What will happen when Mary is released from her black and white room or is given a colour television monitor? Will she *learn* anything or not? It seems just obvious that she will learn something about the world and our visual experience of it. But then it is inescapable that her previous knowledge was incomplete. But she had *all* the physical information. *Ergo* there is more to have than that, and Physicalism is false.

Clearly the same style of Knowledge argument could be deployed for taste, hearing, the bodily sensations and generally speaking for the various mental states which are said to have (as it is variously put) raw feels, phenomenal features or qualia. The conclusion in each case is that the qualia are left out of the physicalist story. And the polemical strength of the Knowledge argument is that it is so hard to deny the central claim that one can have all the physical information without having all the information there is to have.

What Mary Didn't Know^{**}

WHAT MARY DIDN'T KNOW[*]

MARY is confined to a black-and-white room, is educated through black-and-white books and through lectures relayed on black-and-white television. In this way she learns everything there is to know about the physical nature of the world. She knows all the physical facts about us and our environment, in a wide sense of 'physical' which includes everything in *completed* physics, chemistry, and neurophysiology, and all there is to know about the causal and relational facts consequent upon all this, including of course functional roles. If physicalism is true, she knows all there is to know. For to suppose otherwise is to suppose that there is more to know than every physical fact, and that is just what physicalism denies.

Physicalism is not the noncontroversial thesis that the actual world is largely physical, but the challenging thesis that it is entirely physical. This is why physicalists must hold that complete physical knowledge is complete knowledge simpliciter. For suppose it is not complete: then our world must differ from a world, $W(P)$, for which it is complete, and the difference must be in nonphysical facts; for our world and $W(P)$ agree in all matters physical. Hence, physicalism would be false at our world [though contingently so, for it would be true at $W(P)$].[1]

It seems, however, that Mary does not know all there is to know. For when she is let out of the black-and-white room or given a color television, she will learn what it is like to see something red, say. This is rightly described as *learning*—she will not say "ho, hum." Hence, physicalism is false. This is the knowledge argument against physicalism in one of its manifestations.[2] This note is a reply to three objections to it mounted by Paul M. Churchland.[†]

---

[*] I am much indebted to discussions with David Lewis and with Robert Pargetter.

[1] The claim here is not that, if physicalism is true, only what is expressed in explicitly physical language is an item of knowledge. It is that, if physicalism is true, then if you know everything expressed or expressible in explicitly physical language, you know everything. *Pace* Terence Horgan, "Jackson on Physical Information and Qualia," *Philosophical Quarterly*, XXXIV, 135 (April 1984): 147–152.

[2] Namely, that in my "Epiphenomenal Qualia," *ibid.*, XXXII, 127 (April 1982): 127–136. See also Thomas Nagel, "What Is It Like to Be a Bat?", *Philosophical Review*, LXXXIII, 4 (October 1974): 435–450, and Howard Robinson, *Matter and Sense* (New York: Cambridge, 1982).

^{**} From *The Journal of Philosophy*, Volume 83, No. 5, May 1986 by Frank Jackson. Copyright © 1986 by Journal of Philosphy. Reprinted by permission.

[†] "Reduction, Qualia, and the Direct Introspection of Brain States," this JOURNAL, LXXXII, 1 (January 1985): 8–28. Unless otherwise stated, future page references are to this paper.

I. THREE CLARIFICATIONS

The knowledge argument does not rest on the dubious claim that logically you cannot imagine what sensing red is like unless you have sensed red. Powers of imagination are not to the point. The contention about Mary is not that, despite her fantastic grasp of neurophysiology and everything else physical, she *could not imagine* what it is like to sense red; it is that, as a matter of fact, she *would not know*. But if physicalism is true, she would know; and no great powers of imagination would be called for. Imagination is a faculty that those who *lack* knowledge need to fall back on.

Secondly, the intensionality of knowledge is not to the point. The argument does not rest on assuming falsely that, if *S* knows that *a* is *F* and if *a* = *b*, then *S* knows that *b* is *F*. It is concerned with the nature of Mary's total body of knowledge before she is released: is it complete, or do some facts escape it? What is to the point is that *S* may know that *a* is *F* and *know* that *a* = *b*, yet arguably not know that *b* is *F*, by virtue of not being sufficiently logically alert to follow the consequences through. If Mary's lack of knowledge were at all like this, there would be no threat to physicalism in it. But it is very hard to believe that her lack of knowledge could be remedied merely by her explicitly following through enough logical consequences of her vast physical knowledge. Endowing her with great logical acumen and persistence is not in itself enough to fill in the gaps in her knowledge. On being let out, she will not say "I could have worked all this out before by making some more purely logical inferences."

Thirdly, the knowledge Mary lacked which is of particular point for the knowledge argument against physicalism is *knowledge about the experiences of others*, not about her own. When she is let out, she has new experiences, color experiences she has never had before. It is not, therefore, an objection to physicalism that she learns *something* on being let out. Before she was let out, she could not have

known facts about her experience of red, for there were no such facts to know. That physicalist and nonphysicalist alike can agree on. After she is let out, things change; and physicalism can happily admit that she learns this; after all, some physical things will change, for instance, her brain states and their functional roles. The trouble for physicalism is that, after Mary sees her first ripe tomato, she will realize how impoverished her conception of the mental life of *others* has been *all along*. She will realize that there was, all the time she was carrying out her laborious investigations into the neurophysiologies of others and into the functional roles of their internal states, something about these people she was quite unaware of. All along their experiences (or many of them, those got from tomatoes, the sky, . . .) had a feature conspicuous to them but until now hidden from her (in fact, not in logic). But she knew all the physical facts about them all along; hence, what she did not know until her release is not a physical fact about their experiences. But it is a fact about them. That is the trouble for physicalism.

Churchland's first objection is that the knowledge argument contains a defect that "is simplicity itself" (23). The argument equivocates on the sense of 'knows about'. How so? Churchland suggests that the following is "a conveniently tightened version" of the knowledge argument:

(1) Mary knows everything there is to know about brain states and their properties.

(2) It is not the case that Mary knows everything there is to know about sensations and their properties.

Therefore, by Leibniz's law,

(3) Sensations and their properties ≠ brain states and their properties (23).

Churchland observes, plausibly enough, that the type or kind of knowledge involved in premise 1 is distinct from the kind of knowledge involved in premise 2. We might follow his lead and tag the first 'knowledge by description', and the second

❀ ❀

'knowledge by acquaintance'; but, whatever the tags, he is right that the displayed argument involves a highly dubious use of Leibniz's law.

My reply is that the displayed argument may be convenient, but it is not accurate. It is not the knowledge argument. Take, for instance, premise 1. The whole thrust of the knowledge argument is that Mary (before her release) does *not* know everything there is to know about brain states and their properties, because she does not know about certain qualia associated with them. What is complete, according to the argument, is her knowledge of matters physical. A convenient and accurate way of displaying the argument is:

(1)' Mary (before her release) knows everything physical there is to know about other people.

(2)' Mary (before her release) does not know everything there is to know about other people (because she *learns* something about them on her release).

Therefore,

(3)' There are truths about other people (and herself) which escape the physicalist story.

What is immediately to the point is not the kind, manner, or type of knowledge Mary has, but *what* she knows. What she knows beforehand is ex hypothesi everything physical there is to know, but is it everything there is to know? That is the crucial question.

There is, though, a relevant challenge involving questions about kinds of knowledge. The challenge, mounted by David Lewis and Laurence Nemirow, is that on her release Mary does *not* learn something or acquire knowledge in the relevant sense. What Mary acquires when she is released is a certain representational or imaginative ability; it is knowledge how rather than knowledge that. Hence, a physicalist can admit that Mary acquires something very significant of a knowledge kind—which can hardly be denied—without admitting that this shows that her earlier factual knowledge is defective. She knew all *that* there was to know about the experiences of others beforehand, but lacked an ability until after her release.[3]

Now it is certainly true that Mary will acquire abilities of various kinds after her release. She will, for instance, be able to imagine what seeing red is like, be able to remember what it is like, and be able to understand why her friends regarded her as so deprived (something which, until her release, had always mystified her). But is it plausible that that is *all* she will acquire? Suppose she received a lecture on skepticism about other minds while she was incarcerated. On her release she sees a ripe tomato in normal conditions, and so has a sensation of red. Her first reaction is to say that she now knows more about the kind of experiences others have when looking at ripe tomatoes. She then remembers the lecture and starts to worry. Does she really know more about what their experiences are like, or is she indulging in a wild generalization from one case? In the end she decides she does know, and that skepticism is mistaken (even if, like so many of us, she is not sure how to demonstrate its errors). What was she to-ing and fro-ing about—her abilities? Surely not; her representational abilities were a known constant throughout. What else then was she agonizing about than whether or not she had gained factual knowledge of others? There would

---

[3] See Laurence Nemirow, review of Thomas Nagel, *Mortal Questions, Philosophical Review*, LXXXIX, 3 (July 1980): 473–477, and David Lewis, "Postscript to 'Mad Pain and Martian Pain,'" *Philosophical Papers*, vol. 1 (New York: Oxford, 1983). Churchland mentions both Nemirow and Lewis, and it may be that he intended his objection to be essentially the one I have just given. However, he says quite explicitly (bottom of p. 23) that his objection does not need an "ability" analysis of the relevant knowledge.

❖ ❖

be nothing to agonize about if ability was *all* she acquired on her release.

I grant that I have no *proof* that Mary acquires on her release, as well as abilities, factual knowledge about the experiences of others —and not just because I have no disproof of skepticism. My claim is that the knowledge argument is a valid argument from highly plausible, though admittedly not demonstrable, premises to the conclusion that physicalism is false. And that, after all, is about as good an objection as one could expect in this area of philosophy.

❁ 3.4 The Conscious Mind ❁

selections
David Chalmers

✳✳✳

© Jeff Thrower/Shutterstock.com

David Chalmers (1966 – present) is an Australian philosopher, a Professor of philosophy at Australian National University and at New York University. Chalmers writes on Metaphysics and the Philosophy of Language, but is best known for bringing to light the "Hard Problem" of consciousness – understanding how *"what it is like"* experiences are generated from brain states – as distinct from the "Easy" problem of finding correlations between brain states and conscious states.

In this selection, Chalmers offers an argument for a kind of dualism. Although Chalmers believes that the laws of nature in our world necessitate that consciousness arise from brain states, he offers reason to doubt that it is a *logical necessity* that consciousness arise from brain states in every possible world. The two examples he gives are the conceivability of *Inverts* and *Zombies*. An *invert* is someone who is just like us in every way physically, but whose color experiences are inverted from our own, so that white is black and black is white. A *zombie* in the philosophical sense is not a flesh-eating monster, but rather someone who looks and talks and acts like us, and has a brain like us, but has no conscious experience inside.

Here are some questions to think about when you read:

* What is meant by "supervenience"?

* Why is the conceivability of zombies supposed to imply the logical possibility of zombies?

* Why is the logical possibility of zombies supposed to entail that consciousness is not identical to an event in the brain?

* Does Chalmers's argument seem strong enough to support dualism? If so, what form of dualism? If not, which premises would you reject?

Can Consciousness be Reductively Explained?

To make our case against reductive explanation, we need to show that consciousness is not logically supervenient on the physical . . .

Let us consider my zombie twin. This creature is molecule for molecule identical to me, and identical in all the low-level properties postulated by a completed physics, but he lacks conscious experience entirely...

What is going on in my zombie twin? He is physically identical to me, and we may as well suppose that he is embedded in an identical environment. He will certainly be identical to me functionally: he will be processing the same sort of information, reacting in a similar way to inputs, with ... indistinguishable behavior resulting. ... He will be awake, able to report the contents of his internal states, able to focus attention in various places, and so on. It is just that none of this functioning will be accompanied by any real conscious experience. There will be no phenomenal feel. There is nothing it is like to be a zombie....

As long as some positive fact about experience in our world does not hold in a physically identical world, then consciousness does not logically supervene.

It is therefore enough to note that one can coherently imagine a physically identical world in which conscious experiences are inverted, or ... *imagine a being physically identical to me but with inverted conscious experiences. One might imagine, for example, that where I have a red experience, my inverted twin has a blue experience, and vice-versa.*

You can access the full text through the ASU Library!

See Chapter 3, "Can Consciousness be Reductively Explained?" in the e-book linked below:

http://site.ebrary.com.ezproxy1.lib.asu.edu/lib/asulib/reader.action?docID=10279015

ASU Login required.

Citation: Chalmers, David. "Can Consciousness be Reductively Explained?" Chapter 3 in *The Conscious Mind: In Search of a Fundamental Theory.* Oxford University Press. 1996, pp 94-123.

✿ 3.5 What Is It Like to Be a Bat? ✿

selections
by Thomas Nagel

✳✳

© lineartestpilot/Shutterstock.com

Thomas Nagel (1937 – Present) is an American philospher currently teaching at New York University. Nagel is known for developing thought experiments which challenge common assumptions in philosophy. He advocates panpsychism, which is the view that being conscious and being material are two mutually irreducible aspects of the very same thing at the most basic level of the universe – because of this, everything has a degree of consciousness.

Bats are like us in being mammals with highly developed brains and complex sensory systems. They are almost certainly conscious, just as we are. They feel pain and have experiences. However, bats are unlike us in that their perceptual systems are entirely different. They "see" with their ears, using echolocation to navigate where objects are. While we can try to imagine some of the experiences of bats – hanging upside down, maybe – we can't even begin to imagine what it is like to perceive the shapes of objects around us through hearing. While studies of the brains and behavior of bats will reveal a great deal about their psychology, it will never put us in a position to imagine what the subjective experience of a bat is like.

Here are some questions to think about when you read:

* Why can't we know what it is like to be a bat, according to Nagel?

* What is this supposed to tell us about the nature of consciousness?

* How is this argument similar to Jackson's Argument? How is it different?

* How is this argument similar to Chalmers's argument? How is it different?

267

WHAT IS IT LIKE TO BE A BAT?

❋ ❋

CONSCIOUSNESS is what makes the mind-body problem really intractable. Perhaps that is why current discussions of the problem give it little attention or get it obviously wrong. The recent wave of reductionist euphoria has produced several analyses of mental phenomena and mental concepts designed to explain the possibility of some variety of materialism, psychophysical identification, or reduction.[1] But the problems dealt with are those common to this type of reduction and other types, and what makes the mind-body problem unique, and unlike the water-H_2O problem or the Turing machine-IBM machine problem or the lightning-electrical discharge problem or the gene-DNA problem or the oak tree-hydrocarbon problem, is ignored.

Every reductionist has his favorite analogy from modern science. It is most unlikely that any of these unrelated examples of successful reduction will shed light on the relation of mind to brain. But philosophers share the general human weakness for explanations of what is incomprehensible in terms suited for what is familiar and well understood, though entirely different. This has led to the acceptance of implausible accounts of the mental largely because they would permit familiar kinds of reduction. I shall try to explain why the usual examples do not help us to understand the relation between mind and body— why, indeed, we have at present no conception of what an explanation of the physical nature of a mental phenomenon would be. Without consciousness the mind-body problem would be much less interesting. With consciousness it seems hopeless. The most important and characteristic feature of conscious mental phenomena is very poorly understood. Most reductionist theories do not even try to explain it. And careful examination will show that no currently available concept of reduction is applicable to it. Perhaps a new theoretical form can be devised for the purpose, but such a solution, if it exists, lies in the distant intellectual future.

---

[1] Examples are J. J. C. Smart, *Philosophy and Scientific Realism* (London, 1963); David K. Lewis, "An Argument for the Identity Theory," *Journal of Philosophy*, LXIII (1966), reprinted with addenda in David M. Rosenthal, *Materialism & the Mind-Body Problem* (Englewood Cliffs, N. J., 1971); Hilary Putnam, "Psychological Predicates" in Capitan and Merrill, *Art, Mind, & Religion* (Pittsburgh, 1967), reprinted in Rosenthal, *op. cit.*, as "The Nature of Mental States"; D. M. Armstrong, *A Materialist Theory of the Mind* (London, 1968); D. C. Dennett, *Content and Consciousness* (London, 1969). I have expressed earlier doubts in "Armstrong on the Mind," *Philosophical Review*, LXXIX (1970), 394–403; "Brain Bisection and the Unity of Consciousness," *Synthèse*, 22 (1971); and a review of Dennett, *Journal of Philosophy*, LXIX (1972). See also Saul Kripke, "Naming and Necessity" in Davidson and Harman, *Semantics of Natural Language* (Dordrecht, 1972), esp. pp. 334–342; and M. T. Thornton, "Ostensive Terms and Materialism," *The Monist*, 56 (1972).

❀ ❀

Conscious experience is a widespread phenomenon. It occurs at many levels of animal life, though we cannot be sure of its presence in the simpler organisms, and it is very difficult to say in general what provides evidence of it. (Some extremists have been prepared to deny it even of mammals other than man.) No doubt it occurs in countless forms totally unimaginable to us, on other planets in other solar systems throughout the universe. But no matter how the form may vary, the fact that an organism has conscious experience *at all* means, basically, that there is something it is like to *be* that organism. There may be further implications about the form of the experience; there may even (though I doubt it) be implications about the behavior of the organism. But fundamentally an organism has conscious mental states if and only if there is something that it is like to *be* that organism—something it is like *for* the organism.

We may call this the subjective character of experience. It is not captured by any of the familiar, recently devised reductive analyses of the mental, for all of them are logically compatible with its absence. It is not analyzable in terms of any explanatory system of functional states, or intentional states, since these could be ascribed to robots or automata that behaved like people though they experienced nothing.[2] It is not analyzable in terms of the causal role of experiences in relation to typical human behavior—for similar reasons.[3] I do not deny that conscious mental states and events cause behavior, nor that they may be given functional characterizations. I deny only that this kind of thing exhausts their analysis. Any reductionist program has to to

be based on an analysis of what is to be reduced. If the analysis leaves something out, the problem will be falsely posed. It is useless to base the defense of materialism on any analysis of mental phenomena that fails to deal explicitly with their subjective character. For there is no reason to suppose that a reduction which seems plausible when no attempt is made to account for consciousness can be extended to include consciousness. Without some idea, therefore, of what the subjective character of experience is, we cannot know what is required of a physicalist theory.

While an account of the physical basis of mind must explain many things, this appears to be the most difficult. It is impossible to exclude the phenomenological features of experience from a reduction in the same way that one excludes the phenomenal features of an ordinary substance from a physical or chemical reduction of it—namely, by explaining them as effects on the minds of human observers.[4] If physicalism is to be defended, the phenomenological features must themselves be given a physical account. But when we examine their subjective character it seems that such a result is impossible. The reason is that every subjective phenomenon is essentially connected with a single point of view, and it seems inevitable that an objective, physical theory will abandon that point of view.

Facts about what it is like to be an *X* are very peculiar, so peculiar that some may be inclined to doubt their reality, or the significance of claims about them. To illustrate the connection between

---

[2] Perhaps there could not actually be such robots. Perhaps anything complex enough to behave like a person would have experiences. But that, if true, is a fact which cannot be discovered merely by analyzing the concept of experience.

[3] It is not equivalent to that about which we are incorrigible, both because we are not incorrigible about experience and because experience is present in animals lacking language and thought, who have no beliefs at all about their experiences.

[4] Cf. Richard Rorty, "Mind-Body Identity, Privacy, and Categories," *The Review of Metaphysics,* XIX (1965), esp. 37–38.

subjectivity and a point of view, and to make evident the importance of subjective features, it will help to explore the matter in relation to an example that brings out clearly the divergence between the two types of conception, subjective and objective.

I assume we all believe that bats have experience. After all, they are mammals, and there is no more doubt that they have experience than that mice or pigeons or whales have experience. I have chosen bats instead of wasps or flounders because if one travels too far down the phylogenetic tree, people gradually shed their faith that there is experience there at all. Bats, although more closely related to us than those other species, nevertheless present a range of activity and a sensory apparatus so different from ours that the problem I want to pose is exceptionally vivid (though it certainly could be raised with other species). Even without the benefit of philosophical reflection, anyone who has spent some time in an enclosed space with an excited bat knows what it is to encounter a fundamentally *alien* form of life.

I have said that the essence of the belief that bats have experience is that there is something that it is like to be a bat. Now we know that most bats (the microchiroptera, to be precise) perceive the external world primarily by sonar, or echolocation, detecting the reflections, from objects within range, of their own rapid, subtly modulated, high-frequency shrieks. Their brains are designed to correlate the outgoing impulses with the subsequent echoes, and the information thus acquired enables bats to make precise discriminations of distance, size, shape, motion, and texture comparable to those we make by vision. But bat sonar, though clearly a form of perception, is not similar in its operation to any sense that we possess, and there is no reason to suppose that it is subjectively like anything we can experience or imagine. This appears to create difficulties for the notion of what it is like to be a bat. We must consider whether any method will permit us to extrapolate to the inner life of the bat from our own case,[5] and if not, what alternative methods there may be for understanding the notion.

Our own experience provides the basic material for our imagination, whose range is therefore limited. It will not help to try to imagine that one has webbing on one's arms, which enables one to fly around at dusk and dawn catching insects in one's mouth; that one has very poor vision, and perceives the surrounding world by a system of reflected high-frequency sound signals; and that one spends the day hanging upside down by one's feet in an attic. In so far as I can imagine this (which is not very far), it tells me only what it would be like for *me* to behave as a bat behaves. But that is not the question. I want to know what it is like for a *bat* to be a bat. Yet if I try to imagine this, I am restricted to the resources of my own mind, and those resources are inadequate to the task. I cannot perform it either by imagining additions to my present experience, or by imagining segments gradually subtracted from it, or by imagining some combination of additions, subtractions, and modifications.

To the extent that I could look and behave like a wasp or a bat without changing my fundamental structure, my experiences would not be anything like the experiences of those animals. On the other hand, it is doubtful that any meaning can be attached to the supposition that I should possess the internal neurophysiological constitution of a bat. Even if I could by gradual degrees be transformed into a bat, nothing in my present constitution enables me to imagine what the experiences of such a future stage of myself thus metamorphosed would be like. The

---

[5] By "our own case" I do not mean just "my own case," but rather the mentalistic ideas that we apply unproblematically to ourselves and other human beings.

best evidence would come from the experiences of bats, if we only knew what they were like.

So if extrapolation from our own case is involved in the idea of what it is like to be a bat, the extrapolation must be incompletable. We cannot form more than a schematic conception of what it *is* like. For example, we may ascribe general *types* of experience on the basis of the animal's structure and behavior. Thus we describe bat sonar as a form of three-dimensional forward perception; we believe that bats feel some versions of pain, fear, hunger, and lust, and that they have other, more familiar types of perception besides sonar. But we believe that these experiences also have in each case a specific subjective character, which it is beyond our ability to conceive. And if there is conscious life elsewhere in the universe, it is likely that some of it will not be describable even in the most general experiential terms available to us.[6] (The problem is not confined to exotic cases, however, for it exists between one person and another. The subjective character of the experience of a person deaf and blind from birth is not accessible to me, for example, nor presumably is mine to him. This does not prevent us each from believing that the other's experience has such a subjective character.)

This brings us to the edge of a topic that requires much more discussion than I can give it here: namely, the relation between facts on the one hand and conceptual schemes or systems of representation on the other. My realism about the subjective domain in all its forms implies a belief in the existence of facts beyond the reach of human concepts.

Certainly it is possible for a human being to believe that there are facts which humans never *will* possess the requisite concepts to represent or comprehend. Indeed, it would be foolish to doubt this, given the finiteness of humanity's expectations. After all, there would have been transfinite numbers even if everyone had been wiped out by the Black Death before Cantor discovered them. But one might also believe that there are facts which *could* not ever be represented or comprehended by human beings, even if the species lasted forever—simply because our structure does not permit us to operate with concepts of the requisite type. This impossibility might even be observed by other beings, but it is not clear that the existence of such beings, or the possibility of their existence, is a precondition of the significance of the hypothesis that there are humanly inaccessible facts. (After all, the nature of beings with access to humanly inaccessible facts is presumably itself a humanly inaccessible fact.) Reflection on what it is like to be a bat seems to lead us, therefore, to the conclusion that there are facts that do not consist in the truth of propositions expressible in a human language. We can be compelled to recognize the existence of such facts without being able to state or comprehend them.

If we acknowledge that a physical theory of mind must account for the subjective character of experience, we must admit that no presently available conception gives us a clue how this could be done. The problem is unique. If mental processes are indeed physical processes, then there is something it is like, intrinsically,[7] to undergo certain physical

---

[6] Therefore the analogical form of the English expression "what it is *like*" is misleading. It does not mean "what (in our experience) it *resembles*," but rather "how it is for the subject himself."

[7] The relation would therefore not be a contingent one, like that of a cause and its distinct effect. It would be necessarily true that a certain physical state felt a certain way. Saul Kripke (*op. cit.*) argues that causal behaviorist and related analyses of the mental fail because they construe, e.g., "pain" as a merely contingent name of pains. The subjective character of an experience ("its immediate phenomenological quality" Kripke calls it [p. 340]) is the essential property left out by such analyses, and the one in virtue of which it is, necessarily, the experience it is. My view is closely related to his. Like Kripke, I find the hypothesis that a certain brain state should *necessarily* have a certain subjective character incomprehensible without further explanation.

❀ ❀

processes. What it is for such a thing to be the case remains a mystery.

What moral should be drawn from these reflections, and what should be done next? It would be a mistake to conclude that physicalism must be false. Nothing is proved by the inadequacy of physicalist hypotheses that assume a faulty objective analysis of mind. It would be truer to say that physicalism is a position we cannot understand because we do not at present have any conception of how it might be true. Perhaps it will be thought unreasonable to require such a conception as a condition of understanding. After all, it might be said, the meaning of physicalism is clear enough: mental states are states of the body; mental events are physical events. We do not know *which* physical states and events they are, but that should not prevent us from understanding the hypothesis. What could be clearer than the words "is" and "are"?

But I believe it is precisely this apparent clarity of the word "is" that is deceptive. Usually, when we are told that X is Y we know *how* it is supposed to be true, but that depends on a conceptual or theoretical background and is not conveyed by the "is" alone. We know how both "X" and "Y" refer, and the kinds of things to which they refer, and we have a rough idea how the two referential paths might converge on a single thing, be it an object, a person, a process, an event, or whatever. But when the two terms of the identification are very disparate it may not be so clear how it could be true. We may not have even a rough idea of how the two referential paths could converge, or what kind of things they might converge on, and a theoretical framework may have to be supplied to enable us to understand this. Without the framework, an air of mysticism surrounds the identification.

This explains the magical flavor of popular presentations of fundamental scientific discoveries, given

out as propositions to which one must subscribe without really understanding them. For example, people are now told at an early age that all matter is really energy. But despite the fact that they know what "is" means, most of them never form a conception of what makes this claim true, because they lack the theoretical background.

At the present time the status of physicalism is similar to that which the hypothesis that matter is energy would have had if uttered by a pre-Socratic philosopher. We do not have the beginnings of a conception of how it might be true. In order to understand the hypothesis that a mental event is a physical event, we require more than an understanding of the word "is." The idea of how a mental and a physical term might refer to the same thing is lacking, and the usual analogies with theoretical identification in other fields fail to supply it. They fail because if we construe the reference of mental terms to physical events on the usual model, we either get a reappearance of separate subjective events as the effects through which mental reference to physical events is secured, or else we get a false account of how mental terms refer (for example, a causal behaviorist one).

Strangely enough, we may have evidence for the truth of something we cannot really understand. Suppose a caterpillar is locked in a sterile safe by someone unfamiliar with insect metamorphosis, and weeks later the safe is reopened, revealing a butterfly. If the person knows that the safe has been shut the whole time, he has reason to believe that the butterfly is or was once the caterpillar, without having any idea in what sense this might be so. (One possibility is that the caterpillar contained a tiny winged parasite that devoured it and grew into the butterfly.)

It is conceivable that we are in such a position with regard to physicalism.

❊ 3.6 Defining Physicalism ❊

selections
Alyssa Ney

❊ ❊

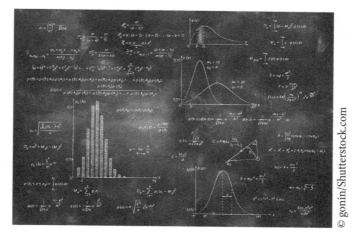

© gonin/Shutterstock.com

Alyssa Ney is a Professor of philosophy at the University of Rochester, who writes on topics in Metaphysics and the Philosophy of Science. Ney, a physicalist, is attempting to better define what physicalism means in order to be able to defend it. "Physicalism" is supposed to be a theory of *ontology*, or the theory of what exists: everything which exists in concrete reality is Physical. But what does "Physical" mean?

A common way to define "Physical" is in terms of the physical sciences. Something is "Physical" if it is the kind of thing which Physicists study or which plays a role in the theories of Physics. However, what "Physics" do we mean? Physics has changed significantly between the 17th century and today. How do we know it won't change drastically in the future?

Here are some questions to think about when you read:

* What is "Hempel's Dilemma" and why is it a problem for physicalism?
* Why not define physicalism in terms of present physics?
* Why not define physicalism in terms of future physics?
* Why does Ney think her proposal avoids Hempel's dilemma?
* Are there are other ways one could defining physicalism?

Defining Physicalism

Alyssa Ney presents 'Hempel's Dilemma':

When the physicalist says that the world contains just what physics says it contains, does she mean what current physics says it contains or what some future, ideal or completed physics will say it contains? If physicalism is the view that the world contains just what current physics says it contains, then surely physicalism is false..... if physicalism is defined in terms of future, completed physics, physicalism might be true in epistemically possible scenarios in which it is intuitively false. For example, suppose physicists in the end posit fundamental mental entities as part of the true, final theory. . . . if physicalism is the view that the world contains just what a future, completed physics says it contains, then this is a scenario compatible with the truth of physicalism. . . .

She then proposes solutions, including one of her own:

Bas van Fraassen has argued that it is wrong to think of physicalism as a doctrine, i.e., a contentful claim that may be taken as true or false. Rather, physicalism should be viewed as a stance one takes toward the world. [I develop] a proposal similar to this position arguing that physicalism is a specific attitude one takes towards forming one's ontological commitments. One is a physicalist in so far as one is disposed to believe in all and only those entities which (current) physics says exists. This understanding of physicalism avoids Hempel's Dilemma since physicalism so construed is not the type of thing to be true, false, or trivial. Instead, like other stances or attitudes, it may be justified or not justified.

You can access the full text through the ASU Library!

http://ejournals.ebsco.com.ezproxy1.lib.asu.edu/direct.asp?ArticleID=4248B9927E1A02561359

ASU Login required.

Alyssa Ney . Defining Physicalism. *Philosophy Compass*, Volume 3, Number 5 (September 2008), pp. 1033–1048.

❧ 3.7 The Four Causes ❧
selections from Metaphysics, Book V and Physics, Book III, Part 3
by Aristotle

* *

©veronchick84/Shutterstock.com

Aristotle attempts in this selection to define a number of basic terms in metaphysics, including "Nature" and "Cause". Aristotle holds that there are four distinct senses of the word *aitia*, or "cause", which we might better translate "four types of reasons", or "four types of answers to the question *why?*" These are known as efficient, final, formal, and material causes.

Here are some questions to think about when you read:

* How does the definition of "nature" relate to the four causes?

* Can any one of the causes be reduced to the others? What do you think?

* Can any of the causes be understood without understanding the others? What do you think?

* How do we get knowledge about each of the four causes? Which causes does it seem like we are able to study using measurement and experimentation? Which ones can't we study in this way?

* When someone says that the mind wholly depends upon the brain, what sort of causation do they have in mind to affirm? When someone says that the mind is the very same thing as the brain, what sort of causation do they have in mind to deny?

Metaphysics, Book V, Sections 1-5

Section 1

'BEGINNING' means (1) that part of a thing from which one would start first, e.g a line or a road has a beginning in either of the contrary directions. (2) That from which each thing would best be originated, e.g. even in learning we must sometimes begin not from the first point and the beginning of the subject, but from the point from which we should learn most easily. (3) That from which, as an immanent part, a thing first comes to be, e,g, as the keel of a ship and the foundation of a house, while in animals some suppose the heart, others the brain, others some other part, to be of this nature. (4) That from which, not as an immanent part, a thing first comes to be, and from which the movement or the change naturally first begins, as a child comes from its father and its mother, and a fight from abusive language. (5) That at whose will that which is moved is moved and that which changes changes, e.g. the magistracies in cities, and oligarchies and monarchies and tyrannies, are called arhchai, and so are the arts, and of these especially the architectonic arts. (6) That from which a thing can first be known, -this also is called the beginning of the thing, e.g. the hypotheses are the beginnings of demonstrations. (Causes are spoken of in an equal number of senses; for all causes are beginnings.) It is common, then, to all beginnings to be the first point from which a thing either is or comes to be or is known; but of these some are immanent in the thing and others are outside. Hence the nature of a thing is a beginning, and so is the element of a thing, and thought and will, and essence, and the final cause-for the good and the beautiful are the beginning both of the knowledge and of the movement of many things.

Section 2

'Cause' means (1) that from which, as immanent material, a thing comes into being, e.g. the bronze is the cause of the statue and the silver of the saucer, and so are the classes which include these. (2) The form or pattern, i.e. the definition of the essence, and the classes which include this (e.g. the ratio 2:1 and number in general are causes of the octave), and the parts included in the definition. (3) That from which the change or the resting from change first begins; e.g. the adviser is a cause of the action, and the father a cause of the child, and in general the maker a cause of the thing made and the change-producing of the changing. (4) The end,

The Works of Aristotle, Volume 8: Metaphysics 2E: Book 5, translated and edited by W.D. Ross (1928): Sections 1–2, 4–5 - 2,351 words "By permission of Oxford University Press."

i.e. that for the sake of which a thing is; e.g. health is the cause of walking. For 'Why does one walk?' we say; 'that one may be healthy'; and in speaking thus we think we have given the cause. The same is true of all the means that intervene before the end, when something else has put the process in motion, as e.g. thinning or purging or drugs or instruments intervene before health is reached; for all these are for the sake of the end, though they differ from one another in that some are instruments and others are actions.

These, then, are practically all the senses in which causes are spoken of, and as they are spoken of in several senses it follows both that there are several causes of the same thing, and in no accidental sense (e.g. both the art of sculpture and the bronze are causes of the statue not in respect of anything else but qua statue; not, however, in the same way, but the one as matter and the other as source of the movement), and that things can be causes of one another (e.g. exercise of good condition, and the latter of exercise; not, however, in the same way, but the one as end and the other as source of movement). -Again, the same thing is the cause of contraries; for that which when present causes a particular thing, we sometimes charge, when absent, with the contrary, e.g. we impute the shipwreck to the absence of the steersman, whose presence was the cause of safety; and both-the presence and the privation-are causes as sources of movement.

All the causes now mentioned fall under four senses which are the most obvious. For the letters are the cause of syllables, and the material is the cause of manufactured things, and fire and earth and all such things are the causes of bodies, and the parts are causes of the whole, and the hypotheses are causes of the conclusion, in the sense that they are that out of which these respectively are made; but of these some are cause as the substratum (e.g. the parts), others as the essence (the whole, the synthesis, and the form). The semen, the physician, the adviser, and in general the agent, are all sources of change or of rest. The remainder are causes as the end and the good of the other things; for that

for the sake of which other things are tends to be the best and the end of the other things; let us take it as making no difference whether we call it good or apparent good.

These, then, are the causes, and this is the number of their kinds, but the varieties of causes are many in number, though when summarized these also are comparatively few. Causes are spoken of in many senses, and even of those which are of the same kind some are causes in a prior and others in a posterior sense, e.g. both 'the physician' and 'the professional man' are causes of health, and both 'the ratio 2:1' and 'number' are causes of the octave, and the classes that include any particular cause are always causes of the particular effect. Again, there are accidental causes and the classes which include these; e.g. while in one sense 'the sculptor' causes the statue, in another sense 'Polyclitus' causes it, because the sculptor happens to be Polyclitus; and the classes that include the accidental cause are also causes, e.g. 'man'-or in general 'animal'-is the cause of the statue, because Polyclitus is a man, and man is an animal. Of accidental causes also some are more remote or nearer than others, as, for instance, if 'the white' and 'the musical' were called causes of the statue, and not only 'Polyclitus' or 'man'. But besides all these varieties of causes, whether proper or accidental, some are called causes as being able to act, others as acting; e.g. the cause of the house's being built is a builder, or a builder who is building.-The same variety of language will be found with regard to the effects of causes; e.g. a thing may be called the cause of this statue or of a statue or in general of an image, and of this bronze or of bronze or of matter in general; and similarly in the case of accidental effects. Again, both accidental and proper causes may be spoken of in combination; e.g. we may say not 'Polyclitus' nor 'the sculptor' but 'Polyclitus the sculptor'. Yet all these are but six in number, while each is spoken of in two ways; for (A) they are causes either as the individual, or as the genus, or as the accidental, or as the genus that includes the accidental, and these either as combined, or as taken simply; and (B) all may be taken as acting or as having a capacity. But they differ inasmuch as the acting causes, i.e. the individuals, exist, or do not exist, simultaneously with the things of which they are causes, e.g. this particular man who is healing, with this particular man who is recovering health, and this particular builder with this particular thing that is being built; but the potential causes are not always in this case; for the house does not perishat the same time as the builder.

[…]

Section 4

'Nature' means (1) the genesis of growing things-the meaning which would be suggested if one were to pronounce the 'u' in phusis long. (2) That immanent part of a growing thing, from which its growth first proceeds. (3) The source from which the primary movement in each natural object is present in it in virtue of its own essence. Those things are said to grow which derive increase from something else by contact and either by organic unity, or by organic adhesion as in the case of embryos. Organic unity differs from contact; for in the latter case there need not be anything besides the contact, but in organic unities there is something identical in both parts, which makes them grow together instead of merely touching, and be one in respect of continuity and quantity, though not of quality.-(4) 'Nature' means the primary material of which any natural object consists or out of which it is made, which is relatively unshaped and cannot be changed from its own potency, as e.g. bronze is said to be the nature of a statue and of bronze utensils, and wood the nature of wooden things; and so in all other cases; for when a product is made out of these materials, the first matter is preserved throughout. For it is in this way that people call the elements of natural objects also their nature, some naming fire, others earth, others air, others water, others something else of the sort, and some naming more than one of these, and others all of them.-(5) 'Nature' means the essence of natural objects, as with those who say the

nature is the primary mode of composition, or as Empedocles says:—

Nothing that is has a nature,
But only mixing and parting of the mixed,
And nature is but a name given them by men.

Hence as regards the things that are or come to be by nature, though that from which they naturally come to be or are is already present, we say they have not their nature yet, unless they have their form or shape. That which comprises both of these exists by nature, e.g. the animals and their parts; and not only is the first matter nature (and this in two senses, either the first, counting from the thing, or the first in general; e.g. in the case of works in bronze, bronze is first with reference to them, but in general perhaps water is first, if all things that can be melted are water), but also the form or essence, which is the end of the process of becoming.-(6) By an extension of meaning from this sense of 'nature' every essence in general has come to be called a 'nature', because the nature of a thing is one kind of essence.

From what has been said, then, it is plain that nature in the primary and strict sense is the essence of things which have in themselves, as such, a source of movement; for the matter is called the nature because it is qualified to receive this, and processes of becoming and growing are called nature because they are movements proceeding from this. And nature in this sense is the source of the movement of natural objects, being present in them somehow, either potentially or in complete reality.

Section 5

We call 'necessary' (1) (a) that without which, as a condition, a thing cannot live; e.g. breathing and food are necessary for an animal; for it is incapable of existing without these; (b) the conditions without which good cannot be or come to be, or without which we cannot get rid or be freed of evil; e.g. drinking the medicine is necessary in order that we may be cured of disease, and a man's sailing to Aegina is necessary in order that he may get his money.-(2) The compulsory and compulsion, i.e. that which impedes and tends to hinder, contrary to impulse and purpose. For the compulsory is called necessary (whence the necessary is painful, as Evenus says: 'For every necessary thing is ever irksome'), and compulsion is a form of necessity, as Sophocles says: 'But force necessitates me to this act'. And necessity is held to be something that cannot be persuaded-and rightly, for it is contrary to the movement which accords with purpose and with reasoning.-(3) We say that that which cannot be otherwise is necessarily as it is. And from this sense of 'necessary' all the others are somehow derived; for a thing is said to do or suffer what is necessary in the sense of compulsory, only when it cannot act according to its impulse because of the compelling forces-which implies that necessity is that because of which a thing cannot be otherwise; and similarly as regards the conditions of life and of good; for when in the one case good, in the other life and being, are not possible without certain conditions, these are necessary, and this kind of cause is a sort of necessity. Again, demonstration is a necessary thing because the conclusion cannot be otherwise, if there has been demonstration in the unqualified sense; and the causes of this necessity are the first premisses, i.e. the fact that the propositions from which the syllogism proceeds cannot be otherwise.

Now some things owe their necessity to something other than themselves; others do not, but are themselves the source of necessity in other things. Therefore the necessary in the primary and strict sense is the simple; for this does not admit of more states than one, so that it cannot even be in one state and also in another; for if it did it would already be in more than one. If, then, there are any things that are eternal and unmovable, nothing compulsory or against their nature attaches to them.

CHAPTER III.

THESE things being defined, let us consider, with respect to causes, what they are, and how many there are in number: for since this treatise is for the sake of knowing natural things, and we do not think that we know any thing, till we are in possession of the cause on account of which that thing subsists, (and this is to be in possession of the first cause) this also must be done by us in discoursing concerning generation and corruption, and all physical mutation; that knowing the principles of these, we may endeavour to refer to them each of the objects of investigation.

Cause, therefore, is after one manner said to be that, from which, being inherent, something is produced: as, for instance, brass is the cause of the statue, silver of the bowl, and the genera of these. But after another manner cause is form and paradigm (and this is the definition of the essence of a thing) and the genera of this. Thus, for instance, the form of the diapason is two to one, and in short number, and the parts which are contained in the definition. Further, still, cause is that whence the first principle of mutation or rest is derived. Thus he who consults is a cause of this kind, and a father of his child, and, in short, the maker of that which is made, and that which changes of that which is changed. Again, cause is as the end; and this is that for the sake of which; as health of walking: for why

does he walk? We say, that he may be in health; and having thus said, we think that we have assigned the cause. This cause also is seen in such things as are for the sake of the end, when something else moves which has an intermediate subsistence. Thus, leanness, or purgation, or medicines, or instruments, are for the sake of health: for all these are for the sake of the end. They differ, however, from each other, because some of them are works, and others instruments. Causes, therefore, are *nearly* predicated in so many ways.

Again: since natural and generated form is a participation of form in matter, but all participation is a resemblance of that which is participated, it is entirely necessary that there should be a paradigmatic cause of material natures. But that which makes, either makes rashly and by chance, or has some purpose in view, and establishes an end of its production, for the sake of which the maker makes, and that which is generated, is generated. But if that which makes primarily and properly makes rashly and by chance, what will there be among makers which will will make for the sake of good? It is necessary, therefore, that the first maker should make for the sake of something, and should have for his end that for the sake of which he makes. And thus also the final cause will become apparent to us from the first maker, who is established as the object of desire to the other producing causes. And that these, indeed, are the causes of generated

❀ ❀

natures, is evident. But that there are only these, may be seen from division: for that which is generated, which we call natural and a composite, is a certain subject, is in a subject, and is nothing else. It is likewise either self-subsistent, or derives its being from some other. If, therefore, it is self-subsistent, it is impossible that it should be generated in a part of time, and that it should be corporeal and divisible. Hence, it must have some other producing cause beside itself; and this must either be moved, or immoveable. And if moved, it must either be moved by itself, or by another. But that which is moved by another does not primarily move. And that which is moved by itself, either in one part moves, and in another is moved, or it moves and is moved according to the whole of itself, as is the soul, according to Plato. But this is the principle of motion and generation. It does not, however, impart the never-failing, so far as it is moved, nor is it perfectly the primary leader of motion, so far as it has a certain duplicity of that which moves and that which is moved. The immoveable, therefore, is the first principle of motion, subsisting as a *properly* producing principle, and as eternally motive. But that which at some particular time is generated and moved, cannot proximately be generated and moved by an eternal and immoveable principle: for such a principle is productive, and motive of things eternal. But that which is eternally moved by it, according to the different conditions of itself, is the cause, as an instrument, of things which are generated and moved at some particular time, because it moves being moved. And if every material form is either the first, or from the first, and with reference to the first, but nothing material is the first, being a participation,— there is something first to which it is assimilated. And if that which properly makes, either makes rashly and casually, or looking to a definite scope, and if it is impossible it should make casually, it is necessary that there should always be a certain end, and that for the sake of which a thing energizes or subsists.

But it happens, since causes are multifariously predicated, that there are also many causes of the same thing, and this not from accident. Thus the statuary's art and the brass are causes of the statue, not according to any thing else, but so far as it is a statue; yet not after the same manner; but the one is a cause, as matter, and the other as that whence motion is derived. Some things also are the causes of each other. Thus labour is the cause of a good habit of body, and a good habit of body, of labour; though not after the same manner; but the one as the end; and the other as the principle of motion. Again, the same thing is the cause of contraries: for that which when present is the cause of this effect, is sometimes, when absent, said by, us to be the cause of a contrary effect. Thus we say that the absence of the pilot is the cause of the loss of the ship, the presence of whom is the cause of its safety. But all the causes which we have now enumerated fall into four most manifest modes: for letters are the causes of syllables; matter is the cause of things which consist from workmanship; fire, and things of this kind, are the causes of body; parts of the whole, and hypotheses of the conclusion; all which are causes as that from which a thing proceeds. Of these causes, however, some are as a subject, as, for instance, parts; but others as essences, viz. whole, composition, and form. But seed, a physician, he who consults, and, in short, he who makes, are all of them causes, as that whence the principle of mutation, or permanency, or motion is derived. Others again are causes as the end, and the good of other things: for that for the sake of which a thing subsists, ranks as that which is best, and the end of other things. It makes, however, no difference whether we say the end is good itself, or apparent good. Such, therefore, and so many are the species of causes.

The modes of causes, however, are many in number, but they will be fewer when collected into a sum: for causes are multifariously predicated; and of those which are of a similar species, one is prior and posterior to another. Thus the physician and the artist are the causes of health; the double and number, of the diapason; and always things which contain are thus related with respect to particulars. Causes also are predicated as accidents, and the genera of these. Thus Polycletus is in one way the cause of the statue, and in another way the statuary, because it happens to the statuary to be Polycletus. Those things, likewise, which contain accident are called causes; as if man, or, in short, animal should be the cause of a statue. Of accidents, also, some are more remote and proximate than others; as if, for instance, something white and a musician should be said to be the cause of a statue. But, besides all these causes, and those which are denominated according to accident, some things are called causes from the power which they possess, and others from the energy which they exert. Thus the builder is the cause of the house being built, or the builder when building. The like also may be said in those things of which the causes are such as we have above enumerated. Thus, for instance, there is a cause of this particular statue, or of statue, or, in short, of image. There is also a cause of this brass, or of brass, or, in short, of matter; and in a similar manner with respect to accidents. These too and those are denominated connectedly; for instance, not Polycletus nor a statuary, but Polycletus the statuary. At the same time, however, all these are in multitude six; but they are predicated in a twofold respect: for they are predicated either as particulars, or as genus, or as subsisting according to accident, or as the genus of accident; and either as these connectedly, or simply considered. All these, too, subsist either energizing, or according to capacity. They so far, however, differ, that the energizers of particulars at the same time exist and cease to be with the things of which they are the causes. Thus this man who heals is contemporary with him who is healed, and this builder with the building. But causes which are denominated according to capacity, do not always subsist together: for the house

and the builder do not perish at one and the same time. It is, however, necessary always to investigate the supreme cause of every thing, as in our investigations of other things. Thus, for instance, a man builds because he is a builder; but he is a builder according to the building art. Thus, therefore, is the prior cause; and so in every thing. Further, still, it is necessary to investigate the genera of genera; and particulars of particulars: as a statuary is the cause of a statue; but this statuary is the cause of this statue. We should also explore the capacities of capabilities, and the energizers of things effected by energy. How many causes, therefore, there are, and after what manner they are causes, let it be considered as sufficiently defined by us.

CHAPTER IV.

FORTUNE, also, and chance, are said to be in the number of causes; and many things are said both to be, and to be produced through fortune and chance. Let us consider, therefore, after what manner fortune and chance subsist in these causes, and whether the former of these is the same with or different from the latter, and, in short, what each of them is: for with some it is dubious whether these things have a subsistence or not. For, say they, nothing is produced from fortune, but there is a certain definite cause of all such things as we say are produced from chance or fortune. Thus, for instance, the cause of a man fortuitously coming into the forum, and there finding what he wished indeed to find, but did not think he should, is the wish of buying something when he came into the forum. In like manner, in other things which are said to originate from fortune, some cause may always be assigned, and not fortune. For if fortune were any thing, it would truly appear to be absurd; and some one might doubt why no one of the ancient wise men, when assigning the causes of generation and corruption, has ever defined any thing concerning

fortune. As it seems, however, they did not think that any thing is produced from fortune. But this is wonderful. For many things are produced, and have a subsistence, from fortune and chance; and though they were not ignorant that each of these may be referred to a certain cause of things which are generated, according to the ancient assertion which subverts fortune, yet at the same time they all say that some of these are from fortune, and others not. Hence, some mention should have been made by them of fortune. They did not, however, think that fortune was any thing belonging either to friendship or strife, or fire, or intellect, or any thing else of things of this kind. They are chargeable, therefore, with absurdity, whether they did not conceive that it had a subsistence, or whether fancying that it had, they omitted it; especially since it was sometimes employed by them. Thus Empedocles says that the air is not always separated in the highest place, but just as it may *happen*: for in his Cosmopoeia he says:

Thus it then chanc'd to run, tho' varying oft.

❊ 3.8 Unit 3 Study Guide ❊

✳✳

Aristotle

Should be able to define and recognize examples of:

material causes

formal causes

efficient causes

final causes

What are the ways in which Aristotle defines "nature"?

Which sense of "necessary" does Aristotle say is the one from which all of the others are somehow derived?

What do Aristotle's four causes have in common?

Frank Jackson

Who is Mary?

What was the new fact that Mary the color scientist learned?

How does she learn it?

Why is the "Mary" argument a challenge to physicalism?

David Chalmers

What arguments does Chalmers offer against materialism?

What is a Zombie?

Chalmers's "Zombie" argument depends on inferring _____ possibility from _____ possibility.

Why would the logical possibility of Zombies demonstrate that mental–physical supervenience is false?

Paul Churchland

What does the principle of "Ockham's Razor" say?

How does Churchland's argument appeal to the effects of lithium, alcohol, and cocaine?

How does Churchland's argument appeal to trauma or damage to the brain?

What is the "Problem of Identification"?

Points not to Miss

What does a substance dualist believe about consciousness?

What does an emergentist dualist believe about the mind?

What does a panpsychist believe about the mind?

What does a reductive physicalist believe about the mind?

What does a non-reductive physicalist believe about the mind?

What does an eliminativist believe about the mind?

In the dualist-materialist debate, one property x supervenes on another y when …

What is your "subjectivity"?

What are the different senses of "consciousness"?

What can and can't be consciouson the philosophical definition?

How does the philosophical definition of consciousness relate to

other senses of the word "consciousness"?

self-consciousness?

brains?

the properties of brains?

souls and how they relate to bodies?

our knowledge of the contents of other people's minds?

bats?

Questions for further thought

How do you think future discoveries in the scientific study of the brain might inform the debates between dualism and physicalism?

How do you think religious belief relates to the debate between dualists and physicalists?

Test Yourself

1. Exposure to radiation can produce health problems years later. In the sense in which the radiation exposure explains why the health problems occur, the radiation is a _____ of the health problems.
   a. material cause
   b. formal cause
   c. efficient cause
   d. final cause

2. A Senator is defined as a member of the upper house of Congress. In the sense in which being a Congressman partly explains why a Senator is what he or she is, being a Congressman is a _____ of being a Senator.
   a. material cause
   b. formal cause
   c. efficient cause
   d. final cause

3. Ice sculptures are made out of frozen water. In the sense in which the water explains why the ice sculpture is there, the water is a _____ of the ice sculpture.
   a. material cause
   b. formal cause
   c. efficient cause
   d. final cause

4. Wombats burrow in order to avoid predators. In the sense in which avoiding predators explains why Wombats burrow, avoiding predators is a _____ of Wombats' burrowing.
   a. material cause
   b. formal cause
   c. efficient cause
   d. final cause

[answers: c, b, a, d]

Overview: Unit 4
Personal Identity

* *

4.1 Who Am I?

4.2 John Locke, "On Identity and Diversity" (selections from *An Essay Concerning Human Understanding*)

4.3 Derek Parfit & Godfrey Vesey, "Personal Identity", selections

4.4 David Hume, "On Personal Identity" (selections from *A Treatise of Human Nature*)

4.5 Charles Daniels, "Personal Identity", selections

4.6 Plato, *Phaedo*, selections

4.7 Unit 4 Study Guide

In this unit we'll consider the nature of personal identity. Although I ought to understand myself better than I understand anything else, it is difficult to say what it is that makes me myself and not you or someone else. We'll look at many different attempts to come up with a definition of the self and the difficulties that arise with them.

By the end of this unit, you should be able to:

* Identify major arguments for and against the possibility of survival after death.

* Summarize Locke's problem of personal identity.

* Summarize Hume's account of personal identity.

* Explain the problems of fission and fusion for personal identity.

* Explain the problems of reincarnation and teleportation for personal identity.

* Develop a coherent view on the nature of the self.

❀ 4.1 Who Am I? ❀

✳ ✳

In our last unit, we tried to answer the question *what am I?*, about the nature of conscious experience. However, in this Unit we will try to answer a different question, *who am I?*

You might think that this is an easy question, not a difficult philosophical question. Each of us consider certain aspects about ourselves more central to our identity, and other aspects of ourselves less central. So, you might think that all there is to figuring out personal identity is figuring out which aspects of yourself you want to consider more important or central, and which ones you're more willing to be flexible about. Maybe you're open to changing your political party someday, but not open to changing the primary language you speak, or vice-versa.

However, the question of personal identity is more difficult than that. The question isn't about the characteristics which the self *has*, but about what the self *is* which has them. Who is that?

- **A. The Problem of Diachronic Identity**
- **B. The Problem of Synchronic Identity**
- **C. Qualitative and Numerical Identity**
- **D. Defining Yourself: An Exercise**
- **E. Locke against the Physical Substance and Immaterial Substance Theories**
- **F. Locke's Memory Theory**
- **G. Daniels's Objections**
- **H. Derek Parfit on Split Brains**
- **I. Hume's Skepticism about the Self**
- **J. Survival**
- **K. Conclusions**

A. The Problem of Diachronic Identity

The majority of College Students take out student loans in order to finance their education. Their hope is that the money borrowed now, to help pay for tuition and expenses while pursuing a degree, will be paid off in the future when they have better employment opportunities afforded by a college degree. However, it's not always easy to keep in mind the interests of the future person who will have to pay off these loans.

Sometimes borrowers tend to dissociate their *present self*, who enjoys the borrowed money today, from their *future self* who will bear the burden of paying the loan off. This is one reason that it's easy for many people to take out more debt than they should.

But think about this for a moment. Why should I think of that future person making student loan payments 10 years from now as *myself*? People change a lot over the course of 10 years. A 30-year-old often doesn't have the same interests, values, or beliefs as the 20-year-old who took out the loans. The 20-year-old might be interested in seeing the world or expressing artistic talents while the 30-year-old might be interested in paying bills and feeding a child. Why say that the 20-year-old and the 30-year old are the *same person*? Why should the 30-year-old feel responsible for paying the debts of the 20-year-old, and why should the 20-year-old feel concerned about what happens to the 30-year-old?

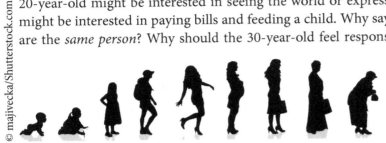

© majivecka/Shutterstock.com

This raises the first problem of personal identity, which we might call the **diachronic** problem of personal identity. *Dia* is Greek for "through", and *chronos* for "time", so this is the problem of why we should think of there as being a stable personal identity through time. Why think that a 5-year-old running around wildly in 1935 is the *same person* as the 85-year-old in 2015 who has difficulty walking? Why think that I'm the same person today as I was yesterday?

B. The Problem of Synchronic Identity

The difficulty is that any way of answering the *diachronic* problem of personal identity, by giving a *definition* of the "self" in terms of necessary and sufficient conditions, seems to create a new problem of **synchronic** personal identity. *Syn* is Greek for "with", and so by "synchronic" we mean *at the same time*, as in *synchronized* swimming or keeping in *synch* with a bit of music. The synchronic problem of personal identity asks this question: what makes me *myself* right now, as opposed to *you* right now? Why am I Jeff and not someone else?

Imagine if you say, for instance, that what makes my 20-year-old self the same person as my 30-year-old self is that both of us have certain physical characteristics or events in our life history in common: We both have a certain hair and skin color, a certain overall bodily structure, were born on a certain day in

© Zarya Maxim Alexandrovich/Shutterstock.com

a certain place, and so on. But then, this raises a problem of synchronic personal identity: There are many different bodies and birthplaces in the world, and why is it that I should have the one I do and not another?

We're often asked to imagine or dream about being very different that we are right now. This sort of reflection seems important to ethical thinking. "How would you feel if you were them?", someone might say. Before I judge too harshly a student who cheats on an exam, for instance, someone might tell me to ask, "what would life be like in their shoes?"

Whenever someone asks me to imagine myself "in someone else's shoes", they're *not* just asking me to imagine myself transported into someone else's immediate circumstances. It seems clear enough that we wouldn't all do the same thing in the same immediate circumstances. We have different personalities and temperaments: One person might respond to being underprepared for an exam by cheating, another by trying to cram at the last minute, another by taking the low grade and hoping to make it up later, another by withdrawing from the class, another by becoming despondent and missing the exam, another by making up an excuse to take it late, another by reflecting on the fact that, really, grades don't matter that much . . . Rather, in order to understand another person's point of view, I have to imagine myself having the same life history, the same biological and psychological composition, including the same body and the same personality, the same memories and life circumstances, the same background, and anything else which is at all relevant to being that person. I'm asked to simulate in my own mind what it must be like to be them.

Yet, this seems to raise a question: why is it the case that I have *this* personality, memory, background, life history, and physical characteristics, and not *that* one that the other person has?

Imagine yourself switching not just bodies and roles, but *thoughts* with another student in your class, or the person teaching your class. If you can imagine that, it suggests that it is possible. But then this raises the question: why are you not that other person?

C. Qualitative and Numerical Identity

Before we go much further, we should clear up an important distinction between two senses of the words "same" or "identical". Consider that in one sense, everyone else in the class has *the same* textbook as you do: that is, the textbook they have is similar in every relevant way. However, in another sense, you don't all have the same textbook: that is, you're hopefully not sharing a textbook! Similarly, say that, living in Arizona, I drive a Honda Civic, and my friend who lives in Florida also drives a Honda Civic. The sense in which my friend and I drive the same car is not the same as the sense in which my spouse and I drive the same car.

This first sense of "same" we'll call *qualitative* identity: that is, two things are qualitatively identical when they have all of the relevant qualities (or properties) in common. The second sense of "same" we'll call *numerical* identity: that is, "two" things are numerically identical when they are really one and the same thing (and so, not really two things after all).

Questions about personal identity are questions about *numerical* identity. I want to know why, despite the fact that we're not qualitatively identical, my future self, present self, and past self are numerically identical. Likewise, I want to know why I am numerically *distinct* from other people, which is a difficult question that can't be answered simply by appealing to the fact that we are qualitatively different.

We should also note that what both of these identity relations have in common is a set of three important properties.

© YAKOBCHUK VASYL/Shutterstock.com

These properties apply to every *equivalence* relation, such as "x is equal to y", "x is the same size as y", and "x is just as heavy as y". So they also apply to the relationship "x is qualitatively identical to y" and to the relationship "x is numerically identical to y":

(i) **Reflexivity**: for all x, x = x. In other words everything is identical to itself!

(ii) **Symmetry**: for all x and y, if x = y then y = x. In other words, if A is the same as B, the B is the same as A.

(iii) **Transitivity**: for all x, y, and z, if x = y and y = z, then x = z. In other words, if A is the same as B, and B is the same as C, then A is the same as C.

D. Defining yourself: An Exercise

To see why it is so difficult to answer these questions of personal identity, you might try this exercise. Remember that the qualities of a good philosophical definition are that the definition gives *necessary and sufficient conditions* and that it *is not circular*. Now try, for a moment, to write out a definition of your essential self.

At first, you might reach for certain properties you have which seem very important to your sense of who you are, or which you feel make you different and unique compared to other people. For instance, you might write on your list:

* Past events that have strongly influenced your course of life

* Relationships that you find it hard to imagine yourself apart from

* A set of beliefs about the world that are important to your identity

* A community or group of people that you consider yourself part of

* Personality traits that tend to set you apart from others

* Physical characteristics that most others don't share, like your DNA

There is one sense of the word "self" in which these things are part of what makes up someone's "self". We might call this sense the *self-as-it-has*. Everything on this list will be properties which I *have*. But precisely because they are what I have, they can't be what I *am*: that is, the thing which has the properties cannot be a property of itself. We might also call this sense the *accidental self*, as opposed to the *essential self*, because all of these properties are properties that I *could have failed to have*, which means I could still have existed without them.

To understand why this is, go through the list you just wrote and cross out anything on the list that is not a *necessary condition* for being yourself. If you *could have existed*, in some very different possible world, without that property, then it isn't a necessary condition. For instance:

* My birth could have occurred at a different place or time.

* The various influential events in my life might have simply failed to occur.

© Derek Hatfield/Shutterstock.com

* I might have still existed even with different beliefs, or a drastically different personality, speaking another language or with different tastes in music.
* For any physical characteristic I have, there is a possible world where it is different. My brain might have been injured, for instance, or deformed.

It's true that this wouldn't be the same *accidental* self. That is, *qualitatively* these people are completely unlike me, so that I might even say "that's not even me anymore". But in these possible scenarios I'd still exist as *numerically* one and the same person. That is, my essential self would be unchanged.

When you're done taking off everything on your list which isn't a necessary condition, then cross off anything which isn't a *sufficient* condition of your identity. If *nothing else* could exist and meet that condition, without being you, then something is a sufficient condition.

Notice that many of the other things on your list might disappear. Consider that:

* Someone else might have had exactly similar life circumstances as you; perhaps, in a different world, someone else grew up with your parents, went to your school, had your friends, and experienced exactly similar events.
* Other people are members of the same community or group of people, and share similar personality traits and tastes without being you.
* A possible or actual sibling has the same parents as you.
* Someone else might have the same DNA as you; for instance, your clone.

© Sangoiri/Shutterstock.com

Finally, remember that definitions cannot be circular. That is, you can't appeal to the thing you are trying to define in the definition. Consider the following definitions:

* Having my body
* Having my mind
* Having my exact location in space and time

It's true, of course, that no one could possibly have *my* body, *my* mind, or *my* exact location in space and time. But that is because I've written *my*self into the definition: I'm appealing to a notion of "me" in order to define myself in this way. But this is circular. Given all of the bodies in the world, or all of the minds, how would we pick out one as *me* if we weren't already given which person I was? Imagine if we remove the circularity from these definitions:

* Having a body like such-and-such
* Having a mind like such-and-such
* Having such-and-such a location in space and time

Now it's clear that these won't be necessary conditions anymore: I might have had a different sort of body, mind, or location. They also won't be sufficient conditions anymore: in a different world, someone else might have had a body like mine, a mind like mine, or the location in space and time which I had in this world.

E. Locke against the Physical Substance and Immaterial Substance Theories

So, now you can see the challenge in defining the "self"! Let's take a look at what a number of philosophers have written about personal identity, starting with John Locke.

In the selection in this textbook, Locke begins by arguing against two of the most common theories of personal identity. These are:

The *physical substance* theory, which says that being the same person means having the same physical substance: in other words, the same body.

The *immaterial substance* (or "soul") theory, which says that being the same person means having the same immaterial thinking substance: in other words, the same "soul", as Descartes and Plato defined the soul.

Locke's four arguments against these theories all have the same basic structure. All four appeal to the principle (C→P) that, if a difference is conceivable, then that difference is logically possible. Let's look at them one at a time.

4a. Against Physical Substance Theory Part 1

P1. It is possible to have one physical substance with two persons.

P2. Two things can't possibly be numerically identical to one thing.

C. Persons are not numerically identical with physical substances.

Premise 2 is simply the definition of numerical identity given earlier. Premise 1 says that it is possible to have one body with two persons in it. This is only about what is *possible*, not about what is probable or likely. Locke doesn't need to prove that there are actual cases where two people share a body, but only that there are possible, imaginable cases. For instance, it is possible that in a genuine case of multiple personality disorder, where there are two distinct people sharing a body, taking turns. What other cases can you imagine in support of Premise 1?

4b. Against Physical Substance Theory Part 2

P1. It is possible to have two physical substances with one person.

P2. Two things can't possibly be numerically identical to one thing.

C. Persons are not numerically identical with physical substances.

Now the scenario has switched: we're considering the possibility of one person having two different bodies. For instance, it seems like we can imagine a person undergoing a complicated operation in which their consciousness is "downloaded" from an old body to an identical clone body; perhaps, this could be a case of one person with two bodies. Locke gives the example of the religious doctrine of the resurrection of the dead: On this view, at the end of time, people who had previously died will be raised back to life, but they will have new bodies. Locke doesn't require his reader to believe this doctrine: It's enough for premise 1 if it can be imagined without contradiction. What other cases can you imagine in support of Premise 1?

4c. Against Immaterial Substance Theory Part 1

P1. It is possible to have one immaterial substance with two persons.

P2. Two things can't possibly be numerically identical to one thing.

C. Persons are not numerically identical with immaterial substances.

What Locke means here by "immaterial mental substance" or "conscious substance" is Descartes's idea of the "thinking thing", the non-physical substance in which thoughts, perceptions, and conscious experience occur, sometimes called a "soul". (Note the use of the word "soul" here is not the same as the use of the word "soul" simply to mean "self", or the use of "soul" to mean someone's character or emotional core, or a certain religious use of the word "soul" to discuss the passions or purification of the soul.) What would an example be in which there was one soul, but two distinct persons?

Locke offers the doctrine of reincarnation, which is taught in Hinduism and was also held by some of the ancient Greek philosophers. According to reincarnation, after death the soul moves into a different body and experiences a new life. This process may continue for a very long time, so that the soul of a person alive today may have also been the soul of a person living 400 or even 4000 years ago. What's important is that even though these two people would have the same soul, they would be *different people*. Locke doesn't require his reader to hold that reincarnation is true, but only that it is logically possible without contradiction. If it's possible, that's enough to support Premise 1.

4d. Against Immaterial Substance Theory Part 2

P1. It is possible to have two immaterial substances with one person.

P2. Two things can't possibly be numerically identical to one thing.

C. Persons are not numerically identical with immaterial substances.

Finally, Locke considers the possibility that we change souls during our sleep, so that every time we awaken, we awaken with a new soul. Someone might hold that this doesn't happen: for instance, maybe God would not allow an overnight switch of souls. However, if it is a logical possibility, that is enough for Premise 1.

Locke himself was neutral between physicalism and dualism in his *Essay Concerning Human Understanding*. What's interesting is that Locke's arguments seem to show that questions of Personal Identity are *independent* of the debate between Dualists and Physicalists we discussed in Unit 3. Even if physicalists are right that the mind is physical, Locke says the self can't be identical with a physical substance. Even if dualists are right that the mind is non-physical, Locke says the self can't be identical with a non-physical substance.

F. Locke's Memory Theory

So, if personal identity isn't about having the same *body* or the same *soul*, what is it about?

Locke asks us to consider an example where a finger is accidentally cut off of a living body. Normally, we'd expect consciousness to stay with the body. But suppose

© Wanchai Orsuk/Shutterstock.com

instead that it went along with the finger: Suppose that the next thing I knew, I had the perspective of a finger laying on the ground. We'd say in that instance that personal identity had to do with where consciousness went, not where the majority of the body was.

So, personal identity has to do with *consciousness*. But I'm only conscious of this moment, in a sense. I'm not actually currently experiencing my past conscious self or my future conscious self. Locke needs a way in which we can speak of consciousness *extended* backward into the past as well as into the future. There is, Locke says, a sense in which I am conscious of events in the past: I *remember* my past conscious experiences of those events. Likewise, there is a sense in which consciousness extends into the future: I anticipate that there will be a person in the future who remembers my present conscious experiences.

It does seem like personal identity has a close connection to memory. Locke asks us to consider an example of someone who claimed to be the reincarnation of Socrates, or the reincarnation of someone who was a witness present at the battle of Troy or the deluge of Noah. Such a person would presumably have the same *soul* (or immaterial substance) as these people. But that wouldn't make them the same *person*. In order to establish that they were the same person, we'd demand to know something more: we'd want to know whether or not they *remembered* firsthand the trial in Athens, the battle of Troy, or the flood of Noah.

Likewise, it seems like we only praise and blame people for things they actually remember doing. We don't hold someone accountable for a crime in the same way if they don't remember what they did wrong, or if they were in a very different psychological state. For instance, if someone slipped Charlie a drug without his knowing that caused him to act out of character and say insulting things, we wouldn't blame Charlie as much for the things he did under the influence of the drug. (Of course, if he took the drug willingly, we'd blame him all the more for taking it in the first place). Thus, Locke says that we do not punish the madman for the sober person's actions, nor the sober person for the madman's actions.

So, this might be a tempting theory of personal identity:

(M1) A is the same person as B if and only if A remembers being B or B remembers being A.

However, there is a problem with (M1). What is it?

Clearly I don't remember *everything* about my past self. I remember a few events that happened when I was 12 years old, but I don't remember every event that happened at age 12. In fact, I can be surprised at learning from someone else that I did or said something at that age because I don't remember it now. Does that mean that any part of my past which I don't remember didn't happen to *me*, but instead happened to someone else? If I don't remember this present moment in the future, does that mean I'm dead? Does forgetfulness kill?

Of course not, Locke would say. Instead, we should think in terms of a *chain* of memories linking up these different events. It's true that I don't remember everything at age 12, but let's suppose I do remember 1 particular event that year. At the time of that event (*t*), if you had asked my 12-year-old self, he would have remembered other events that year which I've now forgotten, including what happened just the moment before (*t-1*). And at that time (*t-1*) he would have remembered the moment before that (*t-2*), and so on, continuing backward. So instead, we could say:

(M2)   A is the same person as B if and only if A remembers being B, or A remembers being C and C remembers being B, or A remembers being D and D remembers being C and C remembers being B, or . . . [repeated endlessly] . . . or B remembers being A, or B remembers being C and C remembers being A, or B remembers being D and D remembers being C and C remembers being A, or . . . [repeated endlessly].

So, Locke concludes that personal identity over time consists in being linked by a chain of memory. Unfortunately, there are some potential objections to Locke's view. We'll first consider two objections from Charles Daniels, then one from Derek Parfit, and lastly one from David Hume.

G. Daniels's Objections

Charles Daniels offers two cases that seem to undermine the view that personal identity can be defined in terms of memory. For Daniels it is important to distinguish *how we know* that something is the case, from what in fact *makes it the case*. It might be that, most of the time, we use information about someone's body, for instance, to know that they are the same person as before. This doesn't work in every conceivable case, because bodily identity alone doesn't *make* personal identity, but it is one way we know about it. Likewise, it might be that, most of the time, we use information about someone's memories to determine that they are the same person as before: certainly this is the case when we think about ourselves. But while this gives us information about them being the same person, it isn't sufficient for being the same person.

Consider the following example: suppose that a new form of "transportation" is developed in which a machine records all of the information about your exact physical structure down to the smallest particle, including your brain. It then disintegrates you. This information is then transmitted to a new city, and in this new city, a similar device reconstitutes a body with the same exact structure and brain yours has. (Assume that reproducing your brain will reproduce your mind and memories exactly.) Because travel is instantaneous, this becomes a popular way to travel.

© serazetdinov/Shutterstock.com

In science fiction, this idea is usually called "teleportation". We're usually willing to grant that someone who is teleported is still the same person as they were before they were teleported. Certainly Locke would have to agree that you remain the same person after teleportation: you have all of the same memories as before.

However, suppose that there is a dirty secret behind these machines: instead of disintegrating the original body as promised in advertising, they wait until the new body is created, and then drop the old body into a pit full of sadists who torture it for pleasure.

Would you travel by these machines, if you new this? If you did travel by one of them, expecting to arrive in Tokyo, and found yourself in the pit of sadists, what complaint would you have? After all, if you weren't in the pit of sadists, you would simply have been disintegrated. But, supposedly, this isn't 'you' at all: supposedly, you (or rather, your clone) is in Tokyo totally oblivious to your fate.

It seems like on Locke's theory, you're *both* the person in the pit of sadists and the person in Tokyo. Both of them remember being you just a moment ago. But to Daniels this is clearly false. Two people can't be one person. Is it much consolation to you, in the pit of sadists, that "you" are in Tokyo having a good time?

Another example Daniels gives involves the case of his friend Dokes, who claims to remember being Henry Morgan the Pirate in a past life, centuries ago. Suppose that Dokes in fact does know a lot of personal details about Henry Morgan the Pirate that no history book has ever recorded. He knows where Captain Morgan buried his hidden treasure before he died, and takes you to the spot, and you dig it up together. Would you conclude that Dokes was in fact the same person as Morgan?

Daniels says that in this bizarre and outlandish situation you'd probably want to distinguish two conceivable possibilities. The first possibility is that, despite everything you believed before about the world, your friend Dokes really does remember being Henry Morgan. The second possibility, also in spite of everything you believed before, is that your friend Dokes is experiencing some sort of psychic Clairvoyance, which makes it seem like he remembers being Morgan, and transmits Morgan's thoughts to him, but isn't in fact *memory*.

The reason you can distinguish these, says Daniels, is because *remembering an experience presupposes that you are identical to the person who had the experience.* If you aren't identical, you don't *really* remember, you only seem to remember. In other words, part of the definition of "memory" is personal identity.

Similarly, in the teleportation case, there is a difference between you *really* remembering stepping into the machine before finding yourself in the pit of sadists, and your clone's *false* memory of having stepped into the machine before coming into existence for the first time in Tokyo.

Of course, this is a huge problem for Locke! If Locke can't distinguish real memories from false memories without appealing to personal identity, it means that defining personal identity in terms of memory is circular. His theory got it backward: the nature of personal identity is what grounds the nature of memory.

H. Derek Parfit on Split Brains

Derek Parfit has proposed another example that seems to go against Locke's memory theory. The example sounds very much like something out of science fiction, but it is clearly conceivable, which suggests that it is at least *logically* possible. For that matter, Parfit thinks it is a natural possibility, with technology progressing at the rate it does; it is entirely feasible that the example will be a real worry for people in the future.

Some psychological studies have suggested that each hemisphere of the brain (left and right) can or does give rise to a distinct center of consciousness. A surgery known as *corpus callosotomy* is sometimes performed to help patients with severe epilepsy, which involves severing the corpus callosum that links together the right and left hemispheres of the brain, greatly reducing the communication between each half of the brain. People who have had this surgery generally function normally, but suffer some speech difficulties and, in certain experimental conditions, seem to behave in ways that suggest that the two sides of the brain are acting independently—for instance, the patient may begin moving one hand, and then the other hand may stop the first hand from moving, or the patient may be able to act on spoken directions with one hand but not with the other.

Suppose that, someday, scientists develop a procedure by which it is possible not only to divide the two halves of the brain, but to transplant them independently into separate bodies. We'll suppose for simplicity that it is also possible to clone or duplicate exactly, down to the molecule, every aspect of the body. The left half of the brain is placed in body L, and the right half of the brain is placed in body R. If it makes things simpler, suppose that the missing half of the brain—the right half of L's brain and the left half of R's brain—has been duplicated and is hooked up again to the half which had been removed. This process of *fission* produces two bodies out of one. We can also imagine the reverse process, or *fusion*: where half of the brain of each person is placed into a new body, and the two halves fused together.

Suppose that you are the patient in the fission case. Which person will you wake up as? There seem to be four conceivable scenarios:

a. You will wake up as R.

b. You will wake up as L.

c. You will wake up as both R and L.

d. You will wake up as neither R nor L: you'll be dead.

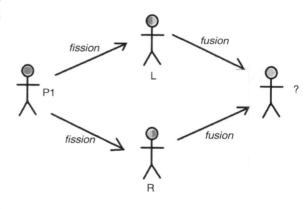

The trouble with options (a) and (b) is that they seem excessively arbitrary. Why would you wake up as (a) rather than (b)? If you think that there is something special about one half of the brain—say, the language centers of the brain in the left hemisphere—and this leads you to think you will wake up as L, recall that these parts have been duplicated and fused to the right half of the brain in R.

You might think that you'll be identical to both R and L in the future. However, this violates the rule of transitivity: **if A is identical to B, and B is identical to C, then A is identical to C:**

1. You = R

2. You = L

3. If x = y and y = z then x = z

C. R = L

But R and L are clearly *not* the same person. They will wake up with the same memories—both will remember the same moment of going into surgery—but they will not be the same person. They are two different people, with different futures ahead of them. Locke's memory theory can't be right.

This leaves us with option (d): You are not identical to R and you are not identical to L. They are different people from you. Does this mean that the surgery which was supposed to duplicate you instead kills you? If someone committed a murder and then had this surgery, would it be impossible to prosecute either person who woke up for the murder—even though both remembered doing it?

Parfit says no. Instead, he says that we need to distinguish *identity* from *survival* (which he calls *q-identity*). Strictly speaking, neither R nor L is identical to you. But strictly speaking, even if you don't have the surgery, your "self" 3 days from now isn't truly identical to you either. The reasons that personal identity matters are survival and responsibility. Your self 3 days from now *survives* you because your self 3 days from now is *psychologically continuous* with you—that is, they have the same memories, likes, hopes, fears, thought patterns, personality, and goals as you do, except for small and gradual changes. Likewise, both R and L survive you, because they are both psychologically continuous with you. All that *matters* for personal identity, insofar as personal identity matters, is psychological continuity.

I. Hume's Skepticism about the Self

A third challenge to Locke's memory theory came from David Hume. Remember that Hume was an empiricist. Hence, he thought that the only things were could know were relations of ideas (definitional truths) and matters of fact (empirical truths).

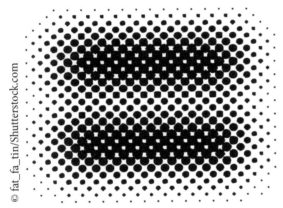

Consider first the person who just started reading this sentence right now, and then consider the person who just finished reading this sentence right now. It is obvious that these are the same person. But how do we know that they are the same person? Nothing in the definition of "person who started reading sentence S at time t" entails that this person is identical to "person who finished reading sentence S at time $t+1$". So it isn't a definitional truth. Is it empirical? Did I observe that the person who started reading was the same as the person who finished reading? How so? The entire time, all that I saw was the text. I never saw the reader of the text.

Have you ever seen yourself? You've seen many images, and perhaps some of those images you associate with yourself more closely than others. However, anything that you have seen is something that *you* have seen—which means that you were looking at the thing seen and not at the thing that was doing the seeing. You observe, but you never observe *the observer*.

For Hume, the notion of "self" is the notion of *whatever* is having this perception at this moment, but we have no way of knowing that whatever is perceiving one moment is the perceiver of the next. Instead, we bundle together a series of perceptions and call that bundle a "self".

Did you ever make a "flipbook" in elementary school? That is, a booklet where on each page you draw one image, and slightly change it on the next page, so that when you flip through the pages it creates an animated "movie", and it looks like the characters are moving? This is, of course, how an animated film works: Each frame of the film has an image that has been drawn separately, but which is only slightly different from the previous image, creating the illusion that there is *one* character moving instead of many different images.

On Hume's view, that's roughly what is happening with you. You tell a story that bundles together all of these images, creating the perception of a continuous "self". But your knowledge of this "self" is simply knowledge of a *fiction*, a character that you invented, with nothing real behind it.

© Memo Angeles/Shutterstock.com

J. Survival

We began with a very practical question: Who is going to be responsible for paying off your student loans? We've seen several answers so far. However, personal identity also matters for a far more existential sort of question: what happens after you die?

Plato's Arguments

Plato's *Phaedo* contains a very early set of arguments given by Socrates that the essential self or soul will survive death. However, most of these arguments seem more perplexing than persuasive. For example:

1. The soul guides and leads the body.
2. The gods guide and lead the world.
3. The soul is similar to the gods (by 1, 2).
4. The gods are immortal.
C. The soul is immortal.

This is an argument by analogy, but it's perplexing to see why being god-like in directing the body would entail being god-like in immortality. Another example:

1. Philosophy involves separating the soul (intellect) from the body (emotion).
2. Death involves separating the soul from the body.
3. Philosophy is a preparation for death (1, 2).
4. Preparing the soul for death is pointless if the soul does not survive death.
5. Philosophy is not pointless.
C. The soul survives death.

While one can see why Socrates's argument would appeal to a philosopher's sense of purpose in his or her life, but why assume that every philosopher thinks that what they are doing is a preparation for dying, as opposed to an active engagement in the questions of life?

Arguments from Inconceivability

Perhaps, we could argue that there must be life after death because we simply can't imagine not continuing to exist. Consider the following argument, which many people initially find plausible:

1. I can't conceive of myself ceasing to exist.
2. If something is not conceivable, then it isn't logically possible.
C. It is not logically possible that I cease to exist.

The argument is valid. However, premise 1 is deceptive. There is a sense in which I can't conceive of *myself* not existing. Trying to imagine myself and then imagine not existing applied to myself just won't work. Any time I imagine a situation, *I* show up in that situation as the one imagining it.

However, this is not a good reason to conclude that I exist necessarily both infinitely in the past and infinitely into the future! Instead, we need to reformulate what we're trying to conceive of. I *can* conceive a time in the past in which *the world didn't yet have me in it*, and so similarly I can conceive of a world in the future which no longer has me in it. In other words, I can *objectively* conceive of a possible future in which I no longer exist, even though *subjectively* I can't put myself into that future, since I don't exist in it.

Perhaps, the issue instead is that I can't imagine any *transition* between consciously existing and not consciously existing. Which leads to a different argument:

1. For any moment T1 at which I exist, and T2 at which I don't exist, I must conceive of the moment *immediately before* I cease to exist at T2 as occurring after T1. Call this T1.5

2. For any moment T1.5 at which I exist, and T2 at which I don't exist, I must conceive of the moment *immediately before* I cease to exist at T2 as occurring after T1.5. Call this T1.75

3. For any moment T1.75 at which I exist, and T2 at which I don't exist, I must conceive of the moment *immediately before* I cease to exist at T2 as occurring after T1.75. Call this T1.825

4. For any moment T1.875 at which I exist, and T2 at which I don't exist, I must conceive of the moment *immediately before* I cease to exist at T2 as occurring after T1.875. Call this T1.9375 and so on . . .

The argument makes use of the fact that we can always imagine another moment between any two moments in time. For any two times you name, one at which I am conscious and one at which I am not, I will always be able to conceive of a moment between them. So, I can never conceive of there as being a final moment of my existence, because I will always conceive of existing the moment afterward. Existing or not existing seems like a clear-cut property. But there may be no clear borderline that can be drawn between when I consciously exist and when I have entirely ceased to consciously exist. Even after my last coherent thought, how many sensations will I feel before I'm not feeling any more?

However this is still not a good argument that I can't cease to exist. The same type of argument was used by Zeno of Elea to prove that nothing could *move*: in taking one step, I am in some sense performing an infinite series of actions, first moving half of the way, but before that a quarter of the way, but before that an eighth of the way . . . but never reaching the end. Yet clearly something is wrong with the argument, since I do move. The same argument could be used to prove that I never fall asleep!

Arguments from Experience

Perhaps, there are no *a priori* arguments that there is life after death. But couldn't someone offer empirical argument, from experience?

Of course, presumably, most of us don't know from experience what the process of dying is like. Our experiences as living bodies may be very different from the experiences of someone in a dying body. Even in everyday experience, the subjective experience of time does not always line up with the way time works objectively, and our experiences in dreams do not resemble our experiences while awake.

Some people who have been near the point of death, or who were dead by clinical standards of brain and heart function but who were successfully resuscitated, report memories of intense experiences during the period they were "dead". These experiences might involve intense feelings and dramatic visions of a supernatural quality that change the person's outlook on life.

This is shaky as evidence for life continuing outside of the body after death, however. First, physiological accounts (in terms of neurological processes) and psychological accounts (in terms of false memories) have been offered for these experiences. So there may be no need to invoke a further supernatural explanation for near-death experiences unless we are already inclined to do so by pre-existing beliefs about the supernatural. Second, it's not clear that first-hand reports from someone who went unconscious under traumatic circumstances will be more reliable as a guide to the nature of reality in itself than a dream.

Of course, for someone who has had such an experience, it may be impossible not to think of it as real. However, for those who haven't, perhaps, the safest way to interpret reports of these experiences is not as evidence about what *being dead* is like (or that there is something it is like to be dead), but rather as potential evidence about what *the process of dying* is like and what feelings and experiences might accompany it.

Charting the Possibilities

It appears that *a priori* reasoning can't tell us whether or not there is life after death, and no experience can tell us what death is like, since none of us is currently dead. However, philosophical reasoning can still tell us what is logically possible or impossible. So, philosophy can tell us what conditions would have obtain in order for someone to survive death. That can't tell us how probable surviving or not surviving death is, or whether it actually occurs, only what would count as surviving death.

However, we might group the remaining theories of personal identity in this Unit into three categories. First, there is the *bodily* theory of identity which Locke attacked; second, there are the *psychological* theories of identity which Locke and Parfit held in different forms; third, there are *further fact* theories of identity on which neither memory nor bodily identity are sufficient.

Thinking next about the theories of the mind in Unit 3, we might group them into *substance dualism*, on which I am essentially a non-physical mental substance, not a functioning physical body, and into *physical-dependence* views, including both physicalism and emergentist dualism, on which my conscious experiences essentially depend on a functioning physical body. Physical dependence views seem to account for the ability of changes in the bodily, like ingesting a mood-altering drug, to produce changes in our conscious experiences.

This gives us six possible combinations of views. What would have to be the case, in each situation, for someone to count as having survived death?[1] See the Chart Below:

---

[1] Note: there are other possible views about personal identity which we haven't charted here, of course. For instance, if Hume is right about personal identity, there is no fact of the matter about whether there is life after death. Perhaps I tell a story in which the experiences of someone in the future are really me, or perhaps I don't; this is up to me.

Case 1. If **Substance Dualism** is correct, and the **Bodily Theory** of identity is true, then I will live after death if and only if my soul is reunited with the exact same body. If someone were to reconstruct my body without my soul returning to it, I would not survive. If my soul were to move on to some other body or plane of existence, or if my soul were to die when my body died, I would not survive.	**Case 2.** If **Substance Dualism** is correct, and the **Psychological Theory** of identity is true, then I will live after death if and only if my memories and personality traits remain with my soul even when my brain dies. If my soul lived on but forgot about the events in this life, then this would not count as living after death.	**Case 3.** If **Substance Dualism** is correct, and the **Further Fact** theory of identity is true, then I will live after death if and only if my soul continues to remain alive after my body dies and that further fact—whatever it is—doesn't change. Even if I had no memories after death, and never had a body again, perhaps, I would still survive.
Case 4. If **Physical-Dependence** is correct, and the **Bodily Theory** of identity is true, then I will live after death if and only if this same body is brought back to life or reconstituted in its current form. Even if a different body were to be built, and my memories and psychology were put into it, this wouldn't count as life after death. On the other hand, if my body were brought back to life, then this would count as life after death, even if that person had no memories.	**Case 5.** If **Physical-Dependence** is correct, and the **Psychological Theory** of identity is true, then I will live after death if and only if some body or other is brought into being in the future which maintains the continuous stream of my memories, likes and dislikes, and personality. Even if this future body is very different from my current body, or removed from it in space and time, provided that my psychology is duplicated in this body, that will be sufficient for survival.	**Case 6.** If **Physical-Dependence** is correct, and the **Further Fact** theory of identity is true, then I will live after death if and only if somebody or other comes into being in the future to which this further fact applies. This body might be drastically different physically and psychologically and far removed from the original, provided that the further fact (whatever it is) might still apply to it.

Is Death a Bad thing?

The question of whether it is possible to survive death remains a nagging one. But one question we've seemed to presuppose without taking a critical eye to it is whether death is a bad thing. Clearly someone's death is bad for the friends and family left behind who grieve their loss. However, is death bad for the person who dies?

The ancient Greek philosopher Epicurus held that there was nothing bad about death at all. First, he proposed that something can be bad for us only if we experience it. If death means that all experiences cease, then no one experiences being dead. In that case, being dead is no worse than being in a dreamless sleep, or going under anesthesia. Second, he held that our attitudes of fear and regret toward death were irrational and inconsistent. Why do we regret that we won't live forever, when we don't regret that we weren't born earlier? After all, none of us experienced a time before we were alive, but we don't get upset that we missed out on years we could have lived. Why think it would be good for us to live an extra 20 years in the future, but not that it would be good for us to have lived 20 extra years in the past?

On the other hand, if someone holds that death is bad for the person who dies, then they hold that a world in which there is life after death is better than a world in which there is not life after death. The question then arises: Is the world we live in the better world, or the worse world? If God exists, then that gives us some reason to think that we live in the better world, and that God can bring the relevant scenario in Case 1–Case 6 about. However, if reflecting on the world leads to the conclusion that it is the worse world, and not the better one, then one may doubt God exits, and doubt that any of Case 1–Case 6 would ever occur. We'll investigate this question more as we move on into Unit 5.

K. Conclusions

Defining your essential self—giving necessary and sufficient conditions for what it is to be *you*—is extremely difficult, as we have seen in this unit. However, it might be a surprise to learn that there are four ways in which one *can* give a definition with necessary and sufficient conditions for the self, without circularity.

(1) I = Jeff

(2) I = the *actual* teacher of this class

(3) I = *that* guy

(4) $I_{\text{spoken by me}}$ = $you_{\text{spoken by you to me}}$

Why are these good definitions? Well, it takes a bit of background to understand it. There are two ways words can refer to something.

1. **Words can refer through a description**. A description represents an object or a state of affairs, so to determine what a description refers to, we find whichever object matches that description. For instance, "the President of the United States in 2014" refers to Barack Obama, or "the first man on the moon" refers to Neil Armstrong. Notice that descriptions can refer to one thing in one possible world, and another thing in another possible world. For instance, it could have been that Mitt Romney was the president of the United States in 2014, and it could have been that Yuri Gargarin was the first man on the moon.

2. **Words can refer through direct reference.** Some words and phrases do not refer by means of a description–instead, they refer directly. For instance, the name "Jeff" refers directly to me, this particular person. The name "Jeff" does not stand for some complex description, like "the person teaching Introduction to Philosophy who was born in Tucson Arizona . . ." because someone could know who Jeff was without knowing these descriptive facts about Jeff. Rather, the name Jeff necessarily refers to the particular it does—me—in every possible world. The name "Jeff" has no other content besides the person it refers to.

Because of this, **proper names** like "Jeff" are commonly called rigid designators—that is, they designate the same object in every possible world. There is a possible world where someone else is teaching Introduction to Philosophy, and a possible world where I wasn't born in Tucson, Arizona. There's also a possible world in which I was named "Jacob", not "Jeff". However, there's no possible world in which I am not Jeff.

Another way to create a rigid designator is to add the word "**actual**" to a description. The word "actual" rules out explicitly any other possibility but the actual world. For instance, while it is possible that someone else could be teaching our class, it is not possible that someone else could *actually* be teaching our class. I could have been born in Phoenix instead of Tucson, but I couldn't have actually been born in Phoenix instead of Tucson, because I was actually born in Tucson.

A third way to directly refer is by means of a **demonstrative**. Demonstratives include the words "that" or "this" when used to refer directly to a particular. For instance, while someone else could be *the guy who is teaching our class*, no one else could be *that* guy. When someone else uses a demonstrative like this to pick out a particular, it's almost like they're creating a name for the particular they're referring to.

The Fourth way to directly refer is by means of an **indexical** word like "I" or "you". What indexicals refer to depends on the context in which they are spoken. However, once given a context, they refer directly. For instance, when *you* use the word "you" to refer to me, you refer to this particular who I am, and your use of "you" couldn't have referred to anyone else. You might use the word "you" to refer to someone else on a different occasion, in a different context.

Why does this matter? Well, perhaps, here is the lesson we should learn from this exploration of personal identity.

There may be some types of questions, like "who am I?" or "what makes me myself?" which simply can't be given an answer in terms of a description. The word *I* will necessarily refer to the same person in every possible world, but a description like *the teacher of introduction to philosophy* will refer to me in one world and not in others. Every description I give in an attempt to answer the question "Who am I?" will raise the same question all over again! It becomes circular.

However, these types of questions *can* be given an answer by referring directly. We might say that these types of questions are such that their answers cannot be represented (on pain of circularity), and also their answers are external to themselves. For instance, in defining myself as "you [spoken by you]" or "*that* guy [spoken by a third person]" I define myself by someone outside myself. In defining myself as "the actual such-and-such", I define myself by a wolrd outside myself. Since representing something is not a necessary condition of referring to something, we can meaningfully talk about and refer to the answers to these questions even though we can't meaningfully represent or describe them.

❋ 4.2 On Identity and Diversity ❋

Selections from *An Essay Concerning Human Understanding* by John Locke

✳✳

© Kenshi991/Shutterstock.com

no invisible Egyptians indissoluble

In Unit 1 and Unit 2 we discussed two sections of John Locke's *Essay Concerning Human Understanding*. Another section, which we haven't looked at yet, addresses questions of personal identity. Locke wanted to show that regardless of which view we took in the philosophy of mind—dualism or physicalism— neither would answer questions about personal identity. Being the same person couldn't be defined in terms of being the same soul *or* being the same body.

Instead, Locke proposed a *memory theory* of personal identity. On this theory, what makes you identical to a person in the past is that you remember having been that person, and what makes you identical to a person in the future is that the future person will remember having been you.

Here are some questions to think about as you read:

* Why do questions about personal identity matter to Locke?

* How does being the same man or human differ from being the same person?

* What examples does he give? What is each example suppose to illustrate?

* How does Locke relate his theory to our reasons for punishing or excusing someone?

* Can you think of an objection to Locke's theory? Why might it be problematic?

Of Identity and Diversity

§ 6. Identity of man

... This also shows wherein the identity of the same man consists: viz. in nothing but a participation of the same continued life, by constantly fleeting particles of matter, in succession vitally united to the same organized body. He that shall place the identity of man in any thing else, but like that of other animals in one fitly organized body, taken in any one instant, and from thence continued under one organization of life in several successively fleeting particles of matter united to it, will find it hard to make an embryo, one of years, mad and sober, the same man, by any supposition, that will not make it possible for Seth, Ismael, Socrates, Pilate, St. Austin, and Cæsar Borgia, to be the same man. For if the identity of soul alone makes the same man, and there be nothing in the nature of matter why the same individual spirit may not be united to different bodies, it will be possible that those men living in distant ages, and of different tempers, may have been the same man: which way of speaking must be, from a very strange use of the word man, applied to an idea, out of which body and shape are excluded. And that way of speaking would agree yet worse with the notions of those philosophers who allow of transmigration, and are of opinion that the souls of men may, for their miscarriages, be detruded into the bodies of beasts, as fit habitations, with organs suited to the satisfaction of their brutal inclinations. But yet I think nobody, could

he be sure that the soul of Heliogabalus were in one of his hogs, would yet say that hog were a man or Heliogabalus.

§ 7. Identity suited to the idea

It is not therefore unity of substance that comprehends all sorts of identity, or will determine it in every case: but to conceive and judge of it aright, we must consider what idea the word it is applied to stands for; it being one thing to be the same substance, another the same man, and a third the same person, if person, man, and substance, are three names standing for three different ideas; for such as is the idea belonging to that name, such must be the identity: which, if it had been a little more carefully attended to, would possibly have prevented a great deal of that confusion which often occurs about this matter, with no small seeming difficulties, especially concerning personal identity, which therefore we shall, in the next place, a little consider.

§ 8. Personal identity

This being premised, to find wherein personal identity consists, we must consider what person stands for; which, I think, is a thinking intelligent being, that has reason and reflection, and can consider itself as itself, the same thinking thing in different

✿ ✿

times and places; which it does only by that consciousness which is inseparable from thinking, and, as it seems to me, essential to it: it being impossible for any one to perceive, without perceiving that he does perceive. When we see, hear, smell, taste, feel, meditate, or will any thing, we know that we do so. Thus it is always as to our present sensations and perceptions: and by this every one is to himself that which he calls self; it not being considered in this case whether the same self be continued in the same or divers substances. For since consciousness always accompanies thinking, and it is that which makes every one to be what he calls self, and thereby distinguishes himself from all other thinking things; in this alone consists personal identity, i. e. the sameness of a rational being: and as far as this consciousness can be extended backwards to any past action or thought, so far reaches the identity of that person; it is the same self now it was then; and it is by the same self with this present one that now reflects on it, that that action was done.

§ 9. Consciousness makes personal identity

But it is farther inquired, whether it be the same identical substance? This few would think they had reason to doubt of, if these perceptions, with their consciousness, always remained present in the mind, whereby the same thinking thing would be always consciously present, and, as would be thought, evidently the same to itself. But that which seems to make the difficulty is this, that this consciousness being interrupted always by forgetfulness, there being no moment of our lives wherein we have the whole train of all our past actions before our eyes in one view, but even the best memories losing the sight of one part whilst they are viewing another; and we sometimes, and that the greatest part of our lives, not reflecting on our past selves, being intent on our present thoughts, and in sound sleep having no thoughts at all, or at least none

with that consciousness which remarks our waking thoughts: I say, in all these cases, our consciousness being interrupted, and we losing the sight of our past selves, doubts are raised whether we are the same thinking thing, i. e. the same substance or no. Which however reasonable or unreasonable, concerns not personal identity at all: the question being, what makes the same person, and not whether it be the same identical substance, which always thinks in the same person; which in this case matters not at all: different substances, by the same consciousness (where they do partake in it), being united into one person, as well as different bodies by the same life are united into one animal, whose identity is preserved, in that change of substances, by the unity of one continued life. For it being the same consciousness that makes a man be himself to himself, personal identity depends on that only, whether it be annexed solely to one individual substance, or can be continued in a succession of several substances. For as far as any intelligent being can repeat the idea of any past action with the same consciousness it had of it at first, and with the same consciousness it has of any present action; so far it is the same personal self. For it is by the consciousness it has of its present thoughts and actions, that it is self to itself now, and so will be the same self, as far as the same consciousness can extend to actions past or to come; and would be by distance of time, or change of substance, no more two persons, than a man be two men by wearing other clothes to-day than he did yesterday, with a long or a short sleep between: the same consciousness uniting those distant actions into the same person, whatever substances contributed to their production.

§ 10. Personal identity in change of substances

That this is so, we have some kind of evidence in our very bodies, all whose particles, whilst vitally united to this same thinking conscious self, so that we feel when they are touched, and are affected by, and conscious of good or harm that happens to them, are a part of ourselves; i. e. of our thinking conscious self. Thus the limbs of his body are to every one a part of himself; he sympathizes and is concerned for them. Cut off a hand, and thereby separate it from that consciousness he had of its heat, cold, and other affections, and it is then no longer a part of that which is himself, any more than the remotest part of matter. Thus we see the substance, whereof personal self consisted at one time, may be varied at another, without the change of personal identity; there being no question about the same person, though the limbs which but now were a part of it, be cut off.

§ 11. Whether in the change of thinking substances

But the question is, "whether if the same substance which thinks, be changed, it can be the same person; or, remaining the same, it can be different persons?"

And to this I answer, first, This can be no question at all to those who place thought in a purely material animal constitution, void of an immaterial substance. For whether their supposition be true or no, it is plain they conceive personal identity preserved in something else than identity of substance; as animal identity is preserved in identity of life, and not of substance. And therefore those who place thinking in an immaterial substance only, before they can come to deal with these men, must show why personal identity cannot be preserved in the change of immaterial substances, or variety of particular immaterial substances, as well as animal identity is preserved in the change of material substances, or variety of particular bodies: unless they will say, it is one immaterial spirit that makes the same life in brutes, as it is one immaterial spirit that makes the same person in men; which the Cartesians at least will not admit, for fear of making brutes thinking things too.

§ 12. Whether if the same thinking substance be changed, it can be the same person

But next, as to the first part of the question, "whether if the same thinking substance (supposing immaterial substances only to think) be changed, it can be the same person?" I answer, that cannot be resolved, but by those who know what kind of substances they are that do think, and whether the consciousness of past actions can be transferred from one thinking substance to another. I grant, were the same consciousness the same individual action, it could not: but it being a present representation of a past action, why it may not be possible, that that may be represented to the mind to have been, which really never was, will remain to be shown. And therefore how far the consciousness of past actions is annexed to any individual agent, so that another cannot possibly have it, will be hard for us to determine, till we know what kind of action it is that cannot be done without a reflex act of perception accompanying it, and how performed by thinking substances, who cannot think without being conscious of it. But that which we call the same consciousness, not being the same individual act, why one intellectual substance may not have represented to it, as done by itself, what it never did, and was perhaps done by some other agent; why, I say, such a representation may not possibly be without reality of matter of fact, as well as several representations in dreams are, which yet whilst dreaming we take for true, will be difficult to conclude from the nature of things. And that it never is so, will by us, till we have clearer views of the nature of thinking substances, be best resolved into the goodness of God, who as far as the happiness or misery of any of his sensible creatures is concerned in it, will not by a fatal errour of theirs transfer from one to another that consciousness which draws reward or punishment with it. How far this may be an argument against those who would place thinking in a system of fleeting animal spirits, I leave to be considered. But yet to return to the question before us, it must be allowed, that if the same consciousness (which, as has been shown, is quite a different thing from the same numerical figure or motion in body) can be transferred from one thinking substance to another, it will be possible that two thinking substances may make but one person. For the same consciousness being preserved, whether in the same or different substances, the personal identity is preserved.

§ 13. Whether the same immaterial substance remaining, there may be two distinct persons

As to the second part of the question, "whether the same immaterial substance remaining, there may be two distinct persons?" which question seems to me to be built on this, whether the same immaterial being, being conscious of the action of its past duration, may be wholly stripped of all the consciousness of its past existence, and lose it beyond the power of ever retrieving again; and so as it were beginning a new account from a new period, have a consciousness that cannot reach beyond this new state. All those who hold pre-existence are evidently of this mind, since they allow the soul to have no remaining consciousness of what it did in that pre-existent state, either wholly separate from body, or informing any other body; and if they should not, it is plain, experience would be against them. So that personal identity reaching no farther than consciousness reaches, a preexistent spirit not having continued so many ages in a state of silence, must needs make different persons. Suppose a Christian, Platonist, or Pythagorean should,

upon God's having ended all his works of creation the seventh day, think his soul hath existed ever since; and would imagine it has revolved in several human bodies, as I once met with one, who was persuaded his had been the soul of Socrates; (how reasonably I will not dispute; this I know, that in the post he filled, which was no inconsiderable one, he passed for a very rational man, and the press has shown that he wanted not parts or learning) would any one say, that he being not conscious of any of Socrates's actions or thoughts, could be the same person with Socrates? Let any one reflect upon himself, and conclude that he has in himself an immaterial spirit, which is that which thinks in him, and in the constant change of his body keeps him the same; and is that which he calls himself: Let him also suppose it to be the same soul that was in Nestor or Thersites, at the siege of Troy (for souls being, as far as we know any thing of them in their nature, indifferent to any parcel of matter, the supposition has no apparent absurdity in it), which it may have been, as well as it is now the soul of any other man: but he now having no consciousness of any of the actions either of Nestor or Thersites, does or can he conceive himself the same person with either of them? can he be concerned in either of their actions? attribute them to himself, or think them his own more than the actions of any other men that ever existed? So that this consciousness not reaching to any of the actions of either of those men, he is no more one self with either of them, than if the soul or immaterial spirit that now informs him, had been created, and began to exist, when it began to inform his present body; though it were ever so true, that the same spirit that informed Nestor's or Thersites's body, were numerically the same that now informs his. For this would no more make him the same person with Nestor, than if some of the particles of matter that were once a part of Nestor, were now a part of this man; the same immaterial substance, without the same consciousness, no more making

❀ ❀

the same person by being united to any body, than the same particle of matter, without consciousness united to any body, makes the same person. But let him once find himself conscious of any of the actions of Nestor, he then finds himself the same person with Nestor.

§ 14. The same person at the resurrection

And thus we may be able, without any difficulty, to conceive the same person at the resurrection, though in a body not exactly in make or parts the same which he had here, the same consciousness going along with the soul that inhabits it. But yet the soul alone, in the change of bodies, would scarce to any one, but to him that makes the soul the man, be enough to make the same man. For should the soul of a prince, carrying with it the consciousness of the prince's past life, enter and inform the body of a cobler, as soon as deserted by his own soul, every one sees he would be the same person with the prince, accountable only for the prince's actions: but who would say it was the same man? The body too goes to the making the man, and would, I guess, to every body determine the man in this case; wherein the soul, with all its princely thoughts about it, would not make another man: but he would be the same cobler to every one besides himself. I know that, in the ordinary way of speaking, the same person, and the same man, stand for one and the same thing. And indeed every one will always have a liberty to speak as he pleases, and to apply what articulate sounds to what ideas he thinks fit, and change them as often as he pleases. But yet when we will inquire what makes the same spirit, man, or person, we must fix the ideas of spirit, man, or person in our minds; and having resolved with ourselves what we mean by them, it will not be hard to determine in either of them, or the like, when it is the same, and when not.

§ 15. Consciousness makes the same person

But though the same immaterial substance or soul does not alone, wherever it be, and in whatsoever state, make the same man; yet it is plain consciousness, as far as ever it can be extended, should it be to ages past, unites existences and actions, very remote in time, into the same person, as well as it does the existences and actions of the immediately preceding moment; so that whatever has the consciousness of present and past actions, is the same person to whom they both belong. Had I the same consciousness that I saw the ark and Noah's flood, as that I saw an overflowing of the Thames last winter, or as that I write now; I could no more doubt that I who write this now, that saw the Thames overflowed last winter, and that viewed the flood at the general deluge, was the same self, place that self in what substance you please, than that I who write this am the same myself now whilst I write (whether I consist of all the same substance, material or immaterial, or no) that I was yesterday. For as to this point of being the same self, it matters not whether this present self be made up of the same or other substances; I being as much concerned, and as justly accountable for any action that was done a thousand years since, appropriated to me now by this self-consciousness, as I am for what I did the last moment.

§ 16. Self depends on consciousness

Self is that conscious thinking thing, whatever substance made up of (whether spiritual or material, simple or compounded, it matters not), which is sensible, or conscious of pleasure and pain, capable of happiness or misery, and so is concerned for itself, as far as that consciousness extends. Thus every one finds, that whilst comprehended under that consciousness, the little finger is as much a part of himself as what is most so. Upon separation of this little finger, should this consciousness go along with the little finger, and leave the rest of the body, it is evident the little finger would be the person, the same person; and self then would have nothing to do with the rest of the body. As in this case it is the consciousness that goes along with the substance, when one part is separate from another, which makes the same person, and constitutes this inseparable self; so it is in reference to substances remote in time. That with which the consciousness of this present thinking thing can join itself, makes the same person, and is one self with it, and with nothing else; and so attributes to itself, and owns all the actions of that thing as its own, as far as that consciousness reaches, and no farther; as every one who reflects will perceive.

§ 17. Objects of reward and punishment

In this personal identity, is founded all the right and justice of reward and punishment; happiness and misery being that for which every one is concerned for himself, and not mattering what becomes of any substance not joined to, or affected with that consciousness. For as it is evident in the instance I gave but now, if the consciousness went along with the little finger when it was cut off, that would be the same self which was concerned for the whole body yesterday, as making part of itself, whose actions then it cannot but admit as its own now. Though if the same body should still live, and immediately, from the separation of the little finger, have its own peculiar consciousness, whereof the little finger knew nothing; it would not at all be concerned for it, as a part of itself, or could own any of its actions, or have any of them imputed to him.

§ 18. Identity of consciousness

This may show us wherein personal identity consists; not in the identity of substance, but, as I have said, in the identity of consciousness; wherein, if Socrates and the present mayor of Queenborough agree, they are the same person: if the same Socrates waking and sleeping do not partake of the same consciousness, Socrates waking and sleeping is not the same person. And to punish Socrates waking for what sleeping Socrates thought, and waking Socrates was never conscious of; would be no more of right, than to punish one twin for what his brother-twin did, whereof he knew nothing, because their outsides were so like, that they could not be distinguished; for such twins have been seen.

§ 19. Loss of memory

But yet possibly it will still be objected, suppose I wholly lose the memory of some parts of my life beyond a possibility of retrieving them, so that perhaps I shall never be conscious of them again; yet am I not the same person that did those actions, had those thoughts that I once was conscious of, though I have now forgot them? To which I answer, that we must here take notice what the word I is applied to: which, in this case, is the man only. And the same man being presumed to be the same person, I is easily here supposed to stand also for the same person. But if it be possible for the same man to have distinct incommunicable consciousness at different times, it is past doubt the same man would at different times make different persons; which, we see, is the sense of mankind in the solemnest declaration of their opinions; human laws not punishing the mad man for the sober man's actions, nor the sober man for what the mad man did, thereby making them two persons: which is somewhat explained by our way of speaking in English, when we say such an one is not himself, or is beside himself; in which phrases it is insinuated, as if those who now, or at least first used them, thought that self was changed, the self-same person was no longer in that man.

§ 20. Difference between identity of man and person

But yet it is hard to conceive that Socrates, the same individual man, should be two persons. To help us a little in this, we must consider what is meant by Socrates, or the same individual man.

First, it must be either the same individual, immaterial, thinking substance; in short, the same numerical soul, and nothing else.

Secondly, or the same animal, without any regard to an immaterial soul.

Thirdly, or the same immaterial spirit united to the same animal.

Now take which of these suppositions you please, it is impossible to make personal identity to consist in any thing but consciousness, or reach any farther than that does.

For by the first of them, it must be allowed possible that a man born of different women, and in distant times, may be the same man. A way of speaking, which whoever admits, must allow it possible for the same man to be two distinct persons, as any two that have lived in different ages, without the knowledge of one another's thoughts.

By the second and third, Socrates in this life, and after it, cannot be the same man any way, but by the same consciousness; and so making human identity to consist in the same thing wherein we place personal identity, there will be no difficulty to allow the same man to be the same person. But then they who place human identity in consciousness only, and not in something else, must consider how they will make

the infant Socrates the same man with Socrates after the resurrection. But whatsoever to some men makes a man, and consequently the same individual man, wherein perhaps few are agreed, personal identity can by us be placed in nothing but consciousness (which is that alone which makes what we call self) without involving us in great absurdities.

§ 21. Drunk and sober, same man

But is not a man drunk and sober the same person? Why else is he punished for the fact he commits when drunk, though he be never afterwards conscious of it? Just as much the same person as a man, that walks, and does other things in his sleep, is the same person, and is answerable for any mischief he shall do in it. Human laws punish both, with a justice suitable to their way of knowledge; because in these cases, they cannot distinguish certainly what is real, what counterfeit: and so the ignorance in drunkenness or sleep is not admitted as a plea. For though punishment be annexed to personality, and personality to consciousness, and the drunkard perhaps be not conscious of what he did; yet human judicatures justly punish him, because the fact is proved against him, but want of consciousness cannot be proved for him. But in the great day, wherein the secrets of all hearts shall be laid open, it may be reasonable to think, no one shall be made to answer for what he knows nothing of; but shall receive his doom, his conscience accusing or excusing him.

§ 22. Consciousness alone makes self

Nothing but consciousness can unite remote existences into the same person, the identity of substance will not do it. For whatever substance there is, however framed, without consciousness there is no person: and a carcase may be a person, as well as any sort of substance be so without consciousness.

❀ ❀

Could we suppose two distinct incommunicable consciousnesses acting the same body, the one constantly by day, the other by night; and, on the other side, the same consciousness acting by intervals two distinct bodies: I ask in the first case, whether the day and the night man would not be two as distinct persons, as Socrates and Plato? And whether, in the second case, there would not be one person in two distinct bodies, as much as one man is the same in two distinct cloathings? Nor is it at all material to say, that this same, and this distinct consciousness, in the cases above mentioned, is owing to the same and distinct immaterial substances, bringing it with them to those bodies; which, whether true or no, alters not the case: since it is evident the personal identity would equally be determined by the consciousness, whether that consciousness were annexed to some individual immaterial substance or no. For granting, that the thinking substance in man must be necessarily supposed immaterial, it is evident that immaterial thinking thing may sometimes part with its past consciousness, and be restored to it again, as appears in the forgetfulness men often have of their past actions: and the mind many times recovers the memory of a past consciousness, which it had lost for twenty years together. Make these intervals of memory and forgetfulness, to take their turns regularly by day and night, and you have two persons with the same immaterial spirit, as much as in the former instance two persons with the same body. So that self is not determined by identity or diversity of substance, which it cannot be sure of but only by identity of consciousness.

§ 23. Unity of physical substance without unity of consciousness

Indeed it may conceive the substance, whereof it is now made up, to have existed formerly, united in the same conscious being: but consciousness removed, that substance is no more itself, or makes no more a part of it than any other substance; as is evident in the instance we have already given of a limb cut off, of whose heat, or cold, or other affections, having no longer any consciousness, it is no more of a man's self, than any other matter of the universe. In like manner it will be in reference to any immaterial substance, which is void of that consciousness whereby I am myself to myself: if there be any part of its existence, which I cannot upon recollection join with that present consciousness whereby I am now myself, it is in that part of its existence no more myself, than any other immaterial being. For whatsoever any substance has thought or done, which I cannot recollect, and by my consciousness make my own thought and action, it will no more belong to me, whether a part of me thought or did it, than if it had been thought or done by any other immaterial being any where existing.

§ 24. Self as the object of unique concern

I agree, the more probable opinion is, that this consciousness is annexed to, and the affection of one individual immaterial substance.

But let men, according to their diverse hypotheses, resolve of that as they please, this every intelligent being, sensible of happiness or misery, must grant, that there is something that is himself that he is concerned for, and would have happy: that this self has existed in a continued duration more than one instant, and therefore it is possible may exist, as it has done, months and years to come, without any certain bounds to be set to its duration, and may be the same self, by the same consciousness continued on for the future. And thus, by this consciousness, he finds himself to be the same self which did such or such an action some years since, by which he comes to be happy or miserable now. In all which account of self, the same numerical substance is not considered as making the same self; but the

❀ ❀

same continued consciousness, in which several substances may have been united, and again separated from it; which, whilst they continued in a vital union with that, wherein this consciousness then resided, made a part of that same self. Thus any part of our bodies vitally united to that which is conscious in us, makes a part of ourselves: but upon separation from the vital union, by which that consciousness is communicated, that which a moment since was part of ourselves, is now no more so, than a part of another man's self is a part of me: and it is not impossible, but in a little time may become a real part of another person. And so we have the same numerical substance become a part of two different persons; and the same person preserved under the change of various substances. Could we suppose any spirit wholly stripped of all its memory or consciousness of past actions, as we find our minds always are of a great part of ours, and sometimes of them all; the union or separation of such a spiritual substance would make no variation of personal identity, any more than that of any particle of matter does. Any substance vitally united to the present thinking being, is a part of that very same self which now is: any thing united to it by a consciousness of former actions, makes also a part of the same self, which is the same both then and now.

§ 25. Person a forensick term

Person, as I take it, is the name for this self. Wherever a man finds what he calls himself, there I think another may say is the same person. It is a forensick term appropriating actions and their merit; and so belongs only to intelligent agents capable of a law, and happiness and misery. This personality extends itself beyond present existence to what is past, only by consciousness, whereby it becomes concerned and accountable, owns and imputes to itself past actions, just upon the same ground, and for the

same reason that it does the present. All which is founded in a concern for happiness, the unavoidable concomitant of consciousness; that which is conscious of pleasure and pain, desiring that that self that is conscious should be happy. And therefore whatever past actions it cannot reconcile or appropriate to that present self by consciousness, it can be no more concerned in, than if they had never been done: and to receive pleasure or pain, i. e. reward or punishment, on the account of any such action, is all one as to be made happy or miserable in its first being, without any demerit at all. For supposing a man punished now for what he had done in another life, whereof he could be made to have no consciousness at all, what difference is there between that punishment, and being created miserable? And therefore conformable to this the apostle tells us, that at the great day, when every one shall "receive according to his doings, the secrets of all hearts shall be laid open." The sentence shall be justified by the consciousness all persons shall have, that they themselves, in what bodies soever they appear, or what substances soever that consciousness adheres to, are the same that committed those actions, and deserve that punishment for them.

§ 26. Unity of immaterial and material susbtance not necessary

I am apt enough to think I have, in treating of this subject, made some suppositions that will look strange to some readers, and possibly they are so in themselves. But yet, I think, they are such as are pardonable in this ignorance we are in of the nature of that thinking thing that is in us, and which we look on as ourselves. Did we know what it was, or how it was tied to a certain system of fleeting animal spirits; or whether it could or could not perform its operations of thinking and memory out of a body organized as ours is: and whether it has pleased God, that no one such spirit shall ever be united to any one but such body, upon the right constitution of whose organs its memory should depend: we might see the absurdity of some of those suppositions I have made. But taking, as we ordinarily now do, (in the dark concerning these matters) the soul of a man, for an immaterial substance, independent from matter, and indifferent alike to it all, there can from the nature of things be no absurdity at all to suppose, that the same soul may, at different times, be united to different bodies, and with them make up, for that time, one man: as well as we suppose a part of a sheep's body yesterday should be a part of a man's body to-morrow, and in that union make a vital part of Meliboeus himself, as well as it did of his ram.

§ 27. The difficulty from ill use of names

To conclude: Whatever substance begins to exist, it must, during its existence, necessarily be the same: whatever compositions of substances begin to exist, during the union of those substances the concrete must be the same: whatsoever mode begins to exist, during its existence it is the same: and so if the composition be of distinct substances and different modes, the same rule holds. Whereby it will appear, that the difficulty or obscurity that has been about this matter, rather rises from the names ill used, than from any obscurity in things themselves. For whatever makes the specifick idea to which the name is applied, if that idea be steadily kept to, the distinction of any thing into the same and divers will easily be conceived, and there can arise no doubt about it.

❧ 4.3 Personal Identity ❧

Selections
by Derek Parfit & Godfrey Vesey

❋❋

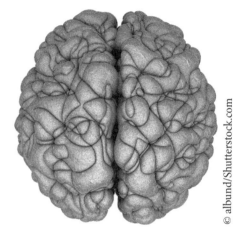

© albund/Shutterstock.com

Derek Parfit (1942—present) is a British philosopher at Oxford University known for his works on Ethics. Parfit raises a problem for the concept of "personal identity" itself. Parfit brings up hypothetical cases in which a person's brain is split in two and placed in two distinct bodies. In these cases, it seems like a person could *survive* this operation as both people, but the person couldn't be *identical* to both people, since they are not identical to each other. As a result, Parfit thinks that we should conclude that the important questions—questions about personal responsibility, or about surviving death—don't depend on personal identity at all, but instead on a different relation, which he calls *psychological continuity*.

Parfit's notion of psychological continuity is like Locke's memory theory, but richer since it also involves aspects like a person's personality and temperament. For Parfit, we can survive as a future person despite forgetting things or differences in personality, so long as the change happens gradually and our future self is adequately similar to and connected with the psychology our past self had. This means there is the hypothetical possibility not only of *fission* of one person into two persons, but the *fusion* of two people into one person.

In this selection, Derek Parfit is interviewed about his views by Godfrey Vesey, who was the founding Professor of Philosophy of the Open University of the United Kingdom.

323

Here are some questions to think about as you read:

* What is all there is to personal identity, for Parfit?

* How does he argue for his view?

* Why isn't this "real" personal identity? Why it not matter? What's wrong with our "real" common sense concept of personal identity?

* How is the identity of a person like the identity of a business or corporation? How is it like the identity of a piece of furniture?

* How do you think this view applies to issues in criminal justice?

Brain Transplants and Personal Identity*

BRAIN TRANSPLANTS

In 1973 in the *Sunday Times* there was a report of how a team from the Metropolitan Hospital in Cleveland under Dr R. J. White had successfully transplanted a monkey's head on to another monkey's body.[1] Dr White was reported as having said, 'Technically a human head transplant is possible', and as hoping that 'it may be possible eventually to transplant *parts* of the brain or other organs inside the head'.

The possibility of brain transplants gives rise to a fascinating philosophical problem. Imagine the following situation:

> Two men, a Mr Brown and a Mr Robinson, had been operated on for brain tumours and brain extractions had been performed on both of them. At the end of the operations, however, the assistant inadvertently put Brown's brain in Robinson's head, and Robinson's brain in Brown's head. One of these men immediately dies, but the other, the one with Robinson's body and Brown's brain, eventually regains consciousness. Let us call the latter 'Brownson'. Upon regaining

consciousness Brownson exhibits great shock and surprise at the appearance of his body. Then, upon seeing Brown's body, he exclaims incredulously 'That's me lying there!' Pointing to himself he says 'This isn't my body; the one over there is!' When asked his name he automatically replies 'Brown'. He recognizes Brown's wife and family (whom Robinson had never met), and is able to describe in detail events in Brown's life, always describing them as events in his own life. Of Robinson's past life he evinces no knowledge at all. Over a period of time he is observed to display all of the personality traits, mannerisms, interests, likes and dislikes, and so on, that had previously characterized Brown, and to act and talk in ways completely alien to the old Robinson.[2]

The next step is to suppose that Brown's brain is not simply transplanted whole into someone else's brainless head, but is divided in two and half put into each of *two* other people's brainless heads. The same memory having been coded in many parts of the cortex, they *both* then say they are Brown, are able to describe events in Brown's life

---

[1] *Sunday Times*, 9 December, 1973, p. 13.
[2] Shoemaker (1963) pp. 23–4.

as if they are events in their own lives, etc. What should we say now?

The implications of this case for what we should say about personal identity are considered by Derek Parfit in a paper entitled 'Personal Identity'. Parfit's own view is expressed in terms of a relationship he calls 'psychological continuity'. He analyses this relationship partly in terms of what he calls '*q*-memory' ('*q*' stands for 'quasi'). He sketches a definition of '*q*-memory' as follows:

> I am *q*-remembering an experience if (1) I have a belief about a past experience which seems in itself like a memory belief, (2) someone did have such an experience, and (3) my belief is dependent upon this experience in the same way (whatever that is) in which a memory of an experience is dependent upon it.[3]

Parfit's thesis is that there is nothing more to personal identity than this 'psychological continuity'. This is *not* to say that whenever there is a sufficient degree of psychological continuity there is personal identity, for psychological continuity could be a one-two, or 'branching', relationship, and we are able to speak of 'identity' only when there is a one-one relationship. It *is* to say that a common belief—in the special nature of personal identity—is mistaken.

In the discussion that follows I began by asking Parfit what he thinks of this common belief. Derek Parfit is a Fellow of All Souls, Oxford.

PERSONAL IDENTITY

VESEY Derek, can we begin with the belief that you claim most of us have about personal identity? It's this: whatever happens between now and some future time either I shall still exist or I shan't. And any future experience will either be my experience

or it won't. In other words, personal identity is an all or nothing matter: either I survive or I don't. Now what do you want to say about that?

PARFIT It seems to me just false. I think the true view is that we can easily describe and imagine large numbers of cases in which the question, 'Will that future person be me—or someone else?', is both a question which doesn't have any answer at all, and there's no puzzle that there's no answer.

VESEY Will you describe one such case.

PARFIT One of them is the case discussed in the correspondence material, the case of division in which we suppose that each half of my brain is to be transplanted into a new body and the two resulting people will both seem to remember the whole of my life, have my character and be psychologically continuous with me in every way. Now in this case of division there were only three possible answers to the question, 'What's going to happen to *me*?' And all three of them seem to me open to very serious objections. So the conclusion to be drawn from the case is that the question of what's going to happen to me, just doesn't have an answer. I think the case also shows that that's not mysterious at all.

VESEY Right, let's deal with these three possibilities in turn.

PARFIT Well, the first is that I'm going to be both of the resulting people. What's wrong with that answer is that it leads very quickly to a contradiction.

VESEY How?

PARFIT The two resulting people are going to be different people from each other. They're going to live completely different lives. They're going to be as different as any two people are. But if they're different people from each other it can't be the case that I'm going to be both of them. Because if I'm both of them, then one of the resulting people is going to be the same person as the other.

---

[3] Parfit (1971) p. 15.

❖ ❖

VESEY Yes. They can't be different people and be the same person, namely me.

PARFIT Exactly. So the first answer leads to a contradiction.

VESEY Yes. And the second?

PARFIT Well, the second possible answer is that I'm not going to be both of them but just one of them. This doesn't lead to a contradiction, it's just wildly implausible. It's implausible because my relation to each of the resulting people is exactly similar.

VESEY Yes, so there's no reason to say that I'm one rather than the other?

PARFIT It just seems absurd to suppose that, when you've got exactly the same relation, one of them is identity and the other is nothing at all.

VESEY It does seem absurd, but there are philosophers who would say that sort of thing. Let's go on to the third.

PARFIT Well, the only remaining answer, if I'm not going to be both of them or only one of them, is that I'm going to be neither of them. What's wrong with this answer is that it's grossly misleading.

VESEY Why?

PARFIT If I'm going to be neither of them, then there's not going to be anyone in the world after the operation who's going to be me. And that implies, given the way we now think, that the operation is as bad as death. Because if there's going to be no one who's going to be me, then I cease to exist. But it's obvious on reflection that the operation isn't as bad as death. It isn't bad in any way at all. That this is obvious can be shown by supposing that when they do the operation only one of the transplants succeeds and only one of the resulting people ever comes to consciousness again.

VESEY Then I think we would say that this person is me. I mean we'd have no reason to say that he wasn't.

PARFIT On reflection I'm sure we would all think that I would survive as that one person.

VESEY Yes.

PARFIT Yes. Well, if we now go back to the case where both operations succeed . . .

VESEY Where there's a double success . . .

PARFIT It's clearly absurd to suppose that a double success is a failure.

VESEY Yes.

PARFIT So the conclusion that I would draw from this case is firstly, that to the question, 'What's going to happen to me?', there's no true answer.

VESEY Yes.

PARFIT Secondly, that if we decide to say one of the three possible answers, what we say is going to obscure the true nature of the case.

VESEY Yes.

PARFIT And, thirdly, the case isn't in any way puzzling. And the reason for that is this. My relation to each of the resulting people is the relation of full psychological continuity. When I'm psychologically continuous with only one person, we call it identity. But if I'm psychologically continuous with two future people, we can't call it identity. It's not puzzling because we know exactly what's going to happen.

VESEY Yes, could I see if I've got this straight? Where there is psychological continuity in a one-one case, this is the sort of case which we'd ordinarily talk of in terms of a person having survived the operation, or something like that.

PARFIT Yes,

VESEY Now what about when there is what you call psychological continuity—that's to say, where the people seem to remember having been me and so on—in a one-two case? Is this survival or not?

PARFIT Well, I think it's just as good as survival, but the block we have to get over is that we can't say that anyone in the world after the operation is going to be me.

VESEY No.

PARFIT Well, we can say it but it's very implausible. And we're inclined to think that if there's not going to be anyone who is me tomorrow, then I don't survive. What we need to realize is that my relation to each of those two people is just as good as survival. Nothing is missing at all in my relation to both of them, as compared with my relation to myself tomorrow.

VESEY Yes.

PARFIT So here we've got survival without identity. And that only seems puzzling if we think that identity is a further fact over and above psychological continuity.

VESEY It is very hard not to think of identity being a further fact, isn't it?

PARFIT Yes, I think it is. I think that the only way to get rid of our temptation to believe this is to consider many more cases than this one case of division. Perhaps I should give you another one. Suppose that the following is going to happen to me. When I die in a normal way, scientists are going to map the states of all the cells in my brain and body and after a few months they will have constructed a perfect duplicate of me out of organic matter. And this duplicate will wake up fully psychologically continuous with me, seeming to remember my life with my character, etc.

VESEY Yes.

PARFIT Now in this case, which is a secular version of the Resurrection, we're very inclined to think that the following question arises and is very real and very important. The question is, 'Will that person who wakes up in three months be me or will he be some quite other person who's merely artificially made to be exactly like me?'

VESEY It does seem to be a real question. I mean in the one case, if it is going to be me, then I have expectations and so on, and in the other case, where it isn't me, I don't.

PARFIT I agree, it seems as if there couldn't be a bigger difference between it being me and it being someone else.

VESEY But you want to say that the two possibilities are in fact the same?

PARFIT I want to say that those two descriptions, 'It's going to be me' and 'It's going to be someone who is merely exactly like me', don't describe different outcomes, different courses of events, only one of which can happen. They are two ways of describing one and the same course of events. What I mean by that perhaps could be shown if we take an exactly comparable case involving not a person but something about which I think we're not inclined to have a false view.

VESEY Yes.

PARFIT Something like a club. Suppose there's some club in the nineteenth century...

VESEY The Sherlock Holmes Club or something like that?

PARFIT Yes, perhaps. And after several years of meeting it ceases to meet. The club dies.

VESEY Right.

PARFIT And then two of its members, let's say, have emigrated to America, and after about fifteen years they get together and they start up a club. It has exactly the same rules, completely new membership except for the first two people, and they give it the same name. Now suppose someone came along and said: 'There's a real mystery here, because the following question is one that must have an answer. But how can we answer it?' The question is, 'Have they started up the very same club—is it the same club as the one they belonged to in England—or is it a completely new club that's just exactly similar?'

VESEY Yes.

PARFIT Well, in that case we all think that this man's remark is absurd; there's no difference at all. Now that's my model for the true view about the case where they make a duplicate of me. It seems that there's all the difference in the world between its being me and its being this other person who's exactly like me. But if we think there's no difference at all in the case of the clubs, why do we think there's a difference in the case of personal identity, and how can we defend the view that there's a difference?

VESEY I can see how some people would defend it. I mean, a dualist would defend it in terms of a soul being a simple thing, but . . .

PARFIT Let me try another case which I think helps to ease us out of this belief we're very strongly inclined to hold.

VESEY Go on.

PARFIT Well, this isn't a single case, this is a whole range of cases. A whole smooth spectrum of different cases which are all very similar to the next one in the range. At the start of this range of cases you suppose that the scientists are going to replace one per cent of the cells in your brain and body with exact duplicates.

VESEY Yes.

PARFIT Now if that were to be done, no one has any doubt that you'd survive. I think that's obvious because after all you can *lose* one per cent of the cells and survive. As we get further along the range they replace a larger and larger percentage of cells with exact duplicates, and of course at the far end of this range, where they replace a hundred per cent, then we've got my case where they just make a duplicate out of wholly fresh matter.

VESEY Yes.

PARFIT Now on the view that there's all the difference in the world between its being me and its being this other person who is exactly like me, we ought in consistency to think that in some case in the middle of that range, where, say, they're going to replace fifty per cent, the same question arises: is it going to be me or this completely different character? I think that even the most convinced dualist who believes in the soul is going to find this range of cases very embarrassing, because he seems committed to the view that there's some crucial percentage up to which it's going to be him and after which it suddenly ceases to be him. But I find that wholly unbelievable.

VESEY Yes. He's going to have to invent some sort of theory about the relation of mind and body to get round this one. I'm not quite sure how he would do it. Derek, could we go on to a related question? Suppose that I accepted what you said, that is, that there isn't anything more to identity than what you call psychological continuity in a one-one case. Suppose I accept that, then I would want to go on and ask you, well, what's the philosophical importance of this?

PARFIT The philosophical importance is, I think, that psychological continuity is obviously, when we think about it, a matter of degree. So long as we think that identity is a further fact, one of the things we're inclined to think is that it's all or nothing, as you said earlier. Well, if we give up that belief and if we realize that what matters in my continued existence is a matter of degree, then this does make a difference in actual cases. All the cases that I've considered so far are of course bizarre science fiction cases. But I think that in actual life it's obvious on reflection that, to give an example, the relations between me now and me next year are much closer in every way than the relations between me now and me in twenty years. And the sorts of relations that I'm thinking of are relations

❀ ❀

of memory, character, ambition, intention—all of those. Next year I shall remember much more of this year than I will in twenty years. I shall have a much more similar character. I shall be carrying out more of the same plans, ambitions and, if that is so, I think there are various plausible implications for our moral beliefs and various possible effects on our emotions.

VESEY For our moral beliefs? What have you in mind?

PARFIT Let's take one very simple example. On the view which I'm sketching it seems to me much more plausible to claim that people deserve much less punishment, or even perhaps no punishment, for what they did many years ago as compared with what they did very recently. Plausible because the relations between them now and them many years ago when they committed the crime are so much weaker.

VESEY But they are still the people who are responsible for the crime.

PARFIT I think you say that because even if they've changed in many ways, after all it was just as much they who committed the crime. I think that's true, but on the view for which I'm arguing, we would come to think that it's a completely trivial truth. It's like the following truth: it's like the truth that all of my relatives are just as much my relatives. Suppose I in my will left more money to my close relatives and less to my distant relatives; a mere pittance to my second cousin twenty-nine times removed. If you said, 'But that's clearly unreasonable because all of your relatives are just as much your relatives', there's a sense in which that's true but it's obviously too trivial to make my will an unreasonable will. And that's because what's involved in kinship is a matter of degree.

VESEY Yes.

PARFIT Now, if we think that what's involved in its being the same person now as the person who committed the crime is a matter of degree, then the truth that it was just as much him who committed the crime, will seem to us trivial in the way in which the truth that all my relatives are equally my relatives is trivial.

VESEY Yes. So you think that I should regard myself in twenty years' time as like a fairly distant relative of myself?

PARFIT Well, I don't want to exaggerate; I think the connections are much closer.

VESEY Suppose I said that this point about psychological continuity being a matter of degree—suppose I said that this isn't anything that anybody denies?

PARFIT I don't think anybody does on reflection deny that psychological continuity is a matter of degree. But I think what they may deny, and I think what may make a difference to their view, if they come over to the view for which I'm arguing —what they may deny is that psychological continuity is all there is to identity. Because what I'm arguing against is this further belief which I think we're all inclined to hold even if we don't realize it. The belief that however much we change, there's a profound sense in which the changed us is going to be just as much us. That even if some magic wand turned me into a completely different sort of person—a prince with totally different character, mental powers—it would be just as much me. That's what I'm denying.

VESEY Yes. This is the belief which I began by stating, and I think that if we did lose that belief that would be a change indeed.

PERSONAL IDENTITY AND PSYCHOLOGICAL CONTINUITY

The discussion I had with Parfit was very much a one-sided affair. The object was for him to make reasonably clear what his views are, and my job

❈ ❈

was to feed him the right questions. There was no more than a hint ('*Suppose* that I accepted what you said . . . ' etc.) that I had some reservations about his argument.

Let us reconsider what he calls 'a secular version of the Resurrection'. Suppose scientists do as Parfit suggests. That is, they 'map the states of all the cells in my brain and body' and construct 'a perfect duplicate of me out of organic matter'. But suppose they do it while I am still alive. Certainly people might mistake the duplicate for me, just as they sometimes mistake identical twins for one another. But there is nothing in this to tempt *me* to say that I am identical with the duplicate, any more than there is a temptation to say that identical twins are numerically identical. Suppose, next, that I die. We shall then have a case of one-one psychological continuity (me before death being psychologically continuous with my duplicate after my death). By Parfit's reckoning my duplicate will then qualify for the description of being identical with me. But why should the fact of my having died mean that someone who, prior to my death, was not me should now be me? Does not the idea that my duplicate becomes me on my death contradict what we ordinarily mean by personal identity?

The crucial question is: what *do* we ordinarily mean by personal identity? Is there just one thing we mean?

Wittgenstein writes:

> Our actual use of the phrase 'the same person' and of the name of a person is based on the fact that many characteristics which we use as the criteria for identity coincide in the vast majority of cases . . . . This can best be seen by imagining unreal cases which show us what different 'geometries' we would be inclined to use if facts were different. . . . Imagine a man whose memories on the even days of his life comprise the events

of all these days, skipping entirely what happened on the odd days. On the other hand, he remembers on an odd day what happened on previous odd days, but his memory then skips the even days without a feeling of discontinuity. If we like we can also assume that he has alternating appearances and characteristics on odd and even days. Are we bound to say that here two persons are inhabiting the same body? That is, is it right to say that there are, and wrong to say that there aren't, or vice versa? Neither. For the *ordinary* use of the word 'person' is what one might call a composite use suitable under the ordinary circumstances. If I assume, as I do, that these circumstances are changed, the application of the term 'person' or 'personality' has thereby changed; and if I wish to preserve this term and give it a use analogous to its former use, I am at liberty to choose between many uses, that is, between many different kinds of analogy. One might say in such a case that the term 'personality' hasn't got one legitimate heir only.[4]

What Wittgenstein says enables us to see why we can be led to say that a duplicate of me is, or is not, me. It depends on which of the 'many characteristics which we use as the criteria for identity' is uppermost in our minds when we consider the case. Recognition that 'the *ordinary* use of the word "person" is what one might call a composite use suitable under the ordinary circumstances' enables us to deal with the problem cases in another way than that of saying that the duplicate is, or is not, me. We can say: the question cannot be answered in terms of the ordinary use of the phrase 'the same person'.

---

[4] Wittgenstein (1958) pp. 61–2.

❀ ❀

But does not Parfit say as much? He does. He says that we can imagine cases in which the question 'Will that future person be me?' is a question which does not have any answer. But he also says that the belief most of us have about personal identity—that whatever happens between now and some future time either I shall still exist or I shall not—is false. It is this last way of putting it, in terms of *belief*, that is confusing. It is confusing because we expect questions about belief to be ones *employing* concepts rather than ones *about* concepts. Whereas the question 'In these changed circumstances would our ordinary concept of personal identity still be applicable?' is obviously a question *about* a concept, the question 'If this were to happen is it true that I would either exist or not?' has the appearance of being a question *employing* the concept.

If one mistook the question about the concept for one employing the concept then one would be likely to think of whatever concept one adopted to fit the changed circumstances as being the original concept and not a new one, one of its 'heirs'. I am prepared to accept that the concept of 'one-one psychological continuity' is one of the heirs of our ordinary concept of personal identity. Another heir would be that of bodily continuity. The point is that, as Wittgenstein puts it, 'the term "personality" hasn't got one legitimate heir only'. Parfit, I feel, gives the impression that it has one legitimate heir only.

There is a reference in the last part of our discussion to the implications of Parfit's views for our moral beliefs. These are interestingly developed in a paper he has written, 'Later Selves and Moral Principles'.[5] Two other philosophers with a special interest in personal identity are Sydney Shoemaker, from whose book *Self-Knowledge and Self-Identity*[6] I quoted earlier, and Bernard Williams, whose book is entitled *Problems of the Self*.[7]

---

[5] Parfit (1973).
[6] Shoemaker (1963).
[7] Williams (1973).

❀ 4.4 Personal Identity ❀

Selections from A Treatise of Human Nature
by David Hume

© Ann Precious/Shutterstock.com

David Hume, as discussed in Unit 2, was an Empiricist. He believed that we could only know empirical truths (matters of fact) and definitional truths (relations of ideas). However, how do I know myself? My self isn't something I understand through the definition of the word "self" or "me", because what's that say about me? But I also don't observe myself. I observe events and experiences, but I never observe the *observer* of these experiences.

Hume concludes that there is no true "self" over time at all. What I mean by the "self" is the subject having of my experiences at this moment, but I have no reason to think that there is something which makes this subject right now the same as the one a moment ago or a moment from now. The only thing which links these is the *story* that I tell which links together my series of perceptions in continuing succession. Imagine an animated film on a film-strip. Why think the character in the first frame is the same as the character in the next frame? When we watch the film go by, it looks like there is one character, moving—but really, there are many different characters, each at a different point in time. Similarly, the notion of a consistent self is a *fiction* which we invent.

Here are some questions to think about as you read:

* Why would Hume reject the theory that identity involves sameness of body or soul?
* Why would Hume reject Locke's theory?
* How does this relate to Hume's account of causation?
* Where does the concept of identity come from?
* If you are a fiction, then who is telling the story?

Personal Identity

There are some philosophers, who imagine we are every moment intimately conscious of what we call our Self; that we feel its existence and its continuance in existence; and are certain, beyond the evidence of a demonstration, both of its perfect identity and simplicity. The strongest sensation, the most violent passion, say they, instead of distracting us from this view, only fix it the more intensely, and make us consider their influence on self either by their pain or pleasure. To attempt a farther proof of this were to weaken its evidence; since no proof can be deriv'd from any fact, of which we are so intimately conscious; nor is there any thing, of which we can be certain, if we doubt of this.

Unluckily all these positive assertions are contrary to that very experience, which is pleaded for them, nor have we any idea of self, after the manner it is here explain'd. For from what impression cou'd this idea be deriv'd? This question 'tis impossible to answer without a manifest contradiction and absurdity; and yet 'tis a question, which must necessarily be answer'd, if we wou'd have the idea of self pass for clear and intelligible. It must be some one impression, that gives rise to every real idea. But self or person is not any one impression, but that to which our several impressions and ideas are suppos'd to have a reference. If any impression gives rise to the idea of self, that impression must continue invariably the same, thro' the whole course of our lives; since self is suppos'd to exist after that

manner. But there is no impression constant and invariable. Pain and pleasure, grief and joy, passions and sensations succeed each other, and never all exist at the same time. It cannot, therefore, be from any of these impressions, or from any other, that the idea of self is deriv'd; and consequently there is no such idea.

But farther, what must become of all our particular perceptions upon this hypothesis? All these are different, and distinguishable, and separable from each other, and may be separately consider'd, and may exist separately, and have no need of any thing to support their existence. After what manner, therefore, do they belong to self; and how are they connected with it? For my part, when I enter most intimately into what I call myself, I always stumble on some particular perception or other, of heat or cold, light or shade, love or hatred, pain or pleasure. I never can catch myself at any time without a perception, and never can observe any thing but the perception. When my perceptions are remov'd for any time, as by sound sleep; so long am I insensible of myself, and may truly be said not to exist. And were all my perceptions remov'd by death, and cou'd I neither think, nor feel, nor see, nor love, nor hate after the dissolution of my body, I shou'd be entirely annihilated, nor do I conceive what is farther requisite to make me a perfect non-entity. If any one upon serious and unprejudic'd reflexion, thinks he has

335

❀ ❀

a different notion of himself, I must confess I can reason no longer with him. All I can allow him is, that he may be in the right as well as I, and that we are essentially different in this particular. He may, perhaps, perceive something simple and continu'd, which he calls himself; tho' I am certain there is no such principle in me.

But setting aside some metaphysicians of this kind, I may venture to affirm of the rest of mankind, that they are nothing but a bundle or collection of different perceptions, which succeed each other with an inconceivable rapidity, and are in a perpetual flux and movement. Our eyes cannot turn in their sockets without varying our perceptions. Our thought is still more variable than our sight; and all our other senses and faculties contribute to this change; nor is there any single power of the soul, which remains unalterably the same, perhaps for one moment. The mind is a kind of theatre, where several perceptions successively make their appearance; pass, re-pass, glide away, and mingle in an infinite variety of postures and situations. There is properly no simplicity in it at one time, nor identity in different; whatever natural propension we may have to imagine that simplicity and identity. The comparison of the theatre must not mislead us. They are the successive perceptions only, that constitute the mind; nor have we the most distant notion of the place, where these scenes are represented, or of the materials, of which it is compos'd.

What then gives us so great a propension to ascribe an identity to these successive perceptions, and to suppose ourselves possest of an invariable and uninterrupted existence thro' the whole course of our lives? In order to answer this question, we must distinguish betwixt personal identity, as it regards our thought or imagination, and as it regards our passions or the concern we take in ourselves. The first is our present subject; and to explain it perfectly we must take the matter pretty deep, and account for that identity, which we attribute to plants and animals; there being a great analogy betwixt it, and the identity of a self or person.

We have a distinct idea of an object, that remains invariable and uninterrupted thro' a suppos'd variation of time; and this idea we call that of identity or sameness. We have also a distinct idea of several different objects existing in succession, and connected together by a close relation; and this to an accurate view affords as perfect a notion of diversity, as if there was no manner of relation among the objects. But tho' these two ideas of identity, and a succession of related objects be in themselves perfectly distinct, and even contrary, yet 'tis certain, that in our common way of thinking they are generally confounded with each other. That action of the imagination, by which we consider the uninterrupted and invariable object, and that by which we reflect on the succession of related objects, are almost the same to the feeling, nor is there much more effort of thought requir'd in the latter case than in the former. The relation facilitates the transition of the mind from one object to another, and renders its passage as smooth as if it contemplated one continu'd object. This resemblance is the cause of the confusion and mistake, and makes us substitute the notion of identity, instead of that of related objects. However at one instant we may consider the related succession as variable or interrupted, we are sure the next to ascribe to it a perfect identity, and regard it as invariable and uninterrupted. Our propensity to this mistake is so great from the resemblance above-mention'd, that we fall into it before we are aware; and tho' we incessantly correct ourselves by reflexion, and return to a more accurate method of thinking, yet we cannot long sustain our philosophy, or take off this biass from the imagination. Our last resource is to yield to it, and boldly assert that these different related objects are in effect the same, however interrupted and variable. In order to justify to ourselves this absurdity, we often feign some new and unintelligible principle, that connects the objects together, and prevents their interruption or variation.

❖ ❖

Thus we feign the continu'd existence of the perceptions of our senses, to remove the interruption; and run into the notion of a soul, and self, and substance, to disguise the variation. But we may farther observe, that where we do not give rise to such a fiction, our propension to confound identity with relation is so great, that we are apt to imagine1 something unknown and mysterious, connecting the parts, beside their relation; and this I take to be the case with regard to the identity we ascribe to plants and vegetables. And even when this does not take place, we still feel a propensity to confound these ideas, tho' we are not able fully to satisfy ourselves in that particular, nor find any thing invariable and uninterrupted to justify our notion of identity.

Thus the controversy concerning identity is not merely a dispute of words. For when we attribute identity, in an improper sense, to variable or interrupted objects, our mistake is not confin'd to the expression, but is commonly attended with a fiction, either of something invariable and uninterrupted, or of something mysterious and inexplicable, or at least with a propensity to such fictions. What will suffice to prove this hypothesis to the satisfaction of every fair enquirer, is to shew from daily experience and observation, that the objects, which are variable or interrupted, and yet are suppos'd to continue the same, are such only as consist of a succession of parts, connected together by resemblance, contiguity, or causation. . . . .

A ship, of which a considerable part has been chang'd by frequent reparations, is still consider'd as the same; nor does the difference of the materials hinder us from ascribing an identity to it. The common end, in which the parts conspire, is the same under all their variations, and affords an easy transition of the imagination from one situation of the body to another . . . . .

. . . Every one must allow, that in a very few years both vegetables and animals endure a total change, yet we still attribute identity to them, while their form, size, and substance are entirely alter'd. An oak, that grows from a small plant to a large tree, is still the same oak; tho' there be not one particle of matter, or figure of its parts the same. An infant becomes a man, and is sometimes fat, sometimes lean, without any change in his identity.

We may also consider the two following phænomena, which are remarkable in their kind. The first is, that tho' we commonly be able to distinguish pretty exactly betwixt numerical and specific identity, yet it sometimes happens, that we confound them, and in our thinking and reasoning employ the one for the other.

Thus a man, who hears a noise, that is frequently interrupted and renew'd, says, it is still the same noise; tho' 'tis evident the sounds have only a specific identity or resemblance, and there is nothing numerically the same, but the cause, which produc'd them. In like manner it may be said without breach of the propriety of language, that such a church, which was formerly of brick, fell to ruin, and that the parish rebuilt the same church of freestone, and according to modern architecture. Here neither the form nor materials are the same, nor is there any thing common to the two objects, but their relation to the inhabitants of the parish; and yet this alone is sufficient to make us denominate them the same. But we must observe, that in these cases the first object is in a manner annihilated before the second comes into existence; by which means, we are never presented in any one point of time with the idea of difference and multiplicity; and for that reason are less scrupulous in calling them the same . . . .

The whole of this doctrine leads us to a conclusion, which is of great importance in the present affair, viz. that all the nice and subtile questions concerning personal identity can never possibly be decided, and are to be regarded rather as grammatical than as philosophical difficulties.

❋ 4.5 Personal Identity ❋

Selections
by Charles Daniels

❋ ❋

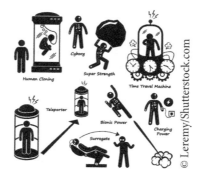

Charles B. Daniels (1934–2012) was a Professor of Philosophy at the University of Victoria, in British Columbia, Canada.[1] He wrote on topics including ethics, ancient philosophy, perception, and personal identity. This selection is taken from an article called "Personal Identity", published in the *American Philosophical Quarterly* (1969).

Daniels offers two vivid thought experiments which pose a challenge to Locke's theory of personal identity. Both raise the question of what exactly counts as a "memory", and reveal that the nature of memory seems to by grounded in the nature of personal identity, not the other way around.

Here are some questions to think about as you read:

* What happens in the example involving a new mode of transportation? What is it supposed to show?

* What happens in the example of Dokes and Morgan? What is it supposed to show?

* Why does Daniels think we need both memory and bodily identity as evidence of personal identity?

* Daniels died after a long struggle with Alzheimer's, but people who knew him spoke of his optimism and courage in the face of his disease. The loss of memory which accompanies Alzheimer's raises many questions about personal identity. How do you think the views on personal identity we've read about would address Alzheimer's patients?

---

[1] Charles Daniels, obituary. *The Vancouver Sun*, September 8, 2012.

Personal Identity

"A machine is built that will, when a person enters it, record the type and position of each molecule in his body and then disintegrate him. The process takes a few seconds and ends with a pile of debris on the floor of the recording chamber. The tape containing the recorded information can then be fed back into the machine; and . . . the machine will fabricate a person who not only looks and talks exactly like the one who first entered the machine, but also believes that he is that person . . .

"A horrible rumor has begun to circulate about the entrepreneurs who control these machines . . . What really happens, once the tape is made, is that a trap door opens in the bottom of the recording chamber, and the unsuspecting soul inside falls into the basement, where he is seized by a band of sadists . . . so the duplicate is merely a duplicate.. . .

"Suppose my oldest friend awakes one morning thoroughly convinced that he is Henry Morgan, the pirate . . . He seems to know vastly more about the intimate details of Morgan's sordid life than the John Dokes I have known could possibly be in a position to know . . . he pointed [us] to a spot where we dug up a treasure and the bones of the men he claimed he had murdered . . .

"We might account for Dokes's strange insight in other ways than by calling it remembering. Dokes might simply have clairvoyant knowledge of what Morgan did, felt, thought, etc. . . . "

Read the Full Text through the ASU Library!

Citation: Daniels, Charles B. "Personal Identity", *American Philosophical Quarterly*, Vol. 6, No. 3 (Jul., 1969), 226–232

❋ 4.6 Phaedo ❋

*Selections
by Plato*

* *

© agsandrew/Shutterstock.com

The *Phaedo* is a dialogue written by Plato during his middle period around the same time as the *Meno*, before the *Republic* but after the *Apology*. While the *Apology* was an account of Socrates's trial, the *Phaedo* gives an account of Socrates's last discussion with his friends before his death. Socrates said he was not afraid of death, even though his friends urged him to take an opportunity to escape. In the *Phaedo*, Socrates offers arguments to think that the soul will survive the death of the body, and life will continue.

Here are some questions to think about as you read:

* ∗ How does the *Phaedo* rely on conclusions we read about in the *Meno*?

* ∗ How does Socrates think about philosophy?

* ∗ Why is the corruptibility of the body supposed to show that the soul will survive?

* ∗ How does Plato's concept of a 'soul' seem different or similar to various religious accounts of the soul? How does Plato's concept of a 'soul' seem different or similar to various dualist accounts of the conscious mind given in Unit 3?

* ∗ How might Locke, Hume, or Parfit respond to Plato's view of personal identity?

Phaedo

[Socartes is speaking to Simmias]

. . .What again shall we say of the actual acquirement of knowledge?-is the body, if invited to share in the inquiry, a hinderer or a helper? I mean to say, have sight and hearing any truth in them? Are they not, as the poets are always telling us, inaccurate witnesses? and yet, if even they are inaccurate and indistinct, what is to be said of the other senses?-for you will allow that they are the best of them?

Certainly, he replied.

Then when does the soul attain truth?-for in attempting to consider anything in company with the body she is obviously deceived.

Yes, that is true.

Then must not existence be revealed to her in thought, if at all?

Yes.

And thought is best when the mind is gathered into herself and none of these things trouble her-neither sounds nor sights nor pain nor any pleasure-when she has as little as possible to do with the body, and has no bodily sense or feeling, but is aspiring after being?

That is true.

And in this the philosopher dishonors the body; his soul runs away from the body and desires to be alone and by herself?

That is true.

Well, but there is another thing, Simmias: Is there or is there not an absolute justice?

Assuredly there is.

And an absolute beauty and absolute good?

Of course.

But did you ever behold any of them with your eyes?

Certainly not.

Or did you ever reach them with any other bodily sense? (and I speak not of these alone, but of absolute greatness, and health, and strength, and of the essence or true nature of everything). Has the reality of them ever been perceived by you through the bodily organs? or rather, is not the nearest approach to the knowledge of their several natures made by him who so orders his intellectual vision as to have the most exact conception of the essence of that which he considers?

Certainly.

And he attains to the knowledge of them in their highest purity who goes to each of them with the mind alone, not allowing when in the act of thought the intrusion or introduction of sight or any other sense in the company of reason, but with the very light of the mind in her clearness penetrates into

the very fight of truth in each; he has got rid, as far as he can, of eyes and ears and of the whole body, which he conceives of only as a disturbing element, hindering the soul from the acquisition of knowledge when in company with her-is not this the sort of man who, if ever man did, is likely to attain the knowledge of existence?

There is admirable truth in that, Socrates, replied Simmias.

And when they consider all this, must not true philosophers make a reflection, of which they will speak to one another in such words as these: We have found, they will say, a path of speculation which seems to bring us and the argument to the conclusion that while we are in the body, and while the soul is mingled with this mass of evil, our desire will not be satisfied, and our desire is of the truth. For the body is a source of endless trouble to us by reason of the mere requirement of food; and also is liable to diseases which overtake and impede us in the search after truth: and by filling us so full of loves, and lusts, and fears, and fancies, and idols, and every sort of folly, prevents our ever having, as people say, so much as a thought. For whence come wars, and fightings, and factions? whence but from the body and the lusts of the body? For wars are occasioned by the love of money, and money has to be acquired for the sake and in the service of the body; and in consequence of all these things the time which ought to be given to philosophy is lost. Moreover, if there is time and an inclination toward philosophy, yet the body introduces a turmoil and confusion and fear into the course of speculation, and hinders us from seeing the truth: and all experience shows that if we would have pure knowledge of anything we must be quit of the body, and the soul in herself must behold all things in themselves: then I suppose that we shall attain that which we desire, and of which we say that we are lovers, and that is wisdom, not while we live, but after death, as the argument shows; for if while in company with the body the soul cannot have pure

knowledge, one of two things seems to follow-either knowledge is not to be attained at all, or, if at all, after death. For then, and not till then, the soul will be in herself alone and without the body. In this present life, I reckon that we make the nearest approach to knowledge when we have the least possible concern or interest in the body, and are not saturated with the bodily nature, but remain pure until the hour when God himself is pleased to release us. And then the foolishness of the body will be cleared away and we shall be pure and hold converse with other pure souls, and know of ourselves the clear light everywhere; and this is surely the light of truth. For no impure thing is allowed to approach the pure. These are the sort of words, Simmias, which the true lovers of wisdom cannot help saying to one another, and thinking. You will agree with me in that?

Certainly, Socrates.

But if this is true, O my friend, then there is great hope that, going whither I go, I shall there be satisfied with that which has been the chief concern of you and me in our past lives. And now that the hour of departure is appointed to me, this is the hope with which I depart, and not I only, but every man who believes that he has his mind purified.

Certainly, replied Simmias.

And what is purification but the separation of the soul from the body, as I was saying before; the habit of the soul gathering and collecting herself into herself, out of all the courses of the body; the dwelling in her own place alone, as in another life, so also in this, as far as she can; the release of the soul from the chains of the body?

Very true, he said.

And what is that which is termed death, but this very separation and release of the soul from the body?

To be sure, he said.

And the true philosophers, and they only, study and are eager to release the soul. Is not the separation and release of the soul from the body their especial study?

That is true.

And as I was saying at first, there would be a ridiculous contradiction in men studying to live as nearly as they can in a state of death, and yet repining when death comes.

Certainly.

Then, Simmias, as the true philosophers are ever studying death, to them, of all men, death is the least terrible. Look at the matter in this way: how inconsistent of them to have been always enemies of the body, and wanting to have the soul alone, and when this is granted to them, to be trembling and repining; instead of rejoicing at their departing to that place where, when they arrive, they hope to gain that which in life they loved (and this was wisdom), and at the same time to be rid of the company of their enemy. Many a man has been willing to go to the world below in the hope of seeing there an earthly love, or wife, or son, and conversing with them. And will he who is a true lover of wisdom, and is persuaded in like manner that only in the world below he can worthily enjoy her, still repine at death? Will he not depart with joy? Surely he will, my friend, if he be a true philosopher. For he will have a firm conviction that there only, and nowhere else, he can find wisdom in her purity. And if this be true, he would be very absurd, as I was saying, if he were to fear death.

He would, indeed, replied Simmias.

And when you see a man who is repining at the approach of death, is not his reluctance a sufficient proof that he is not a lover of wisdom, but a lover of the body, and probably at the same time a lover of either money or power, or both?

That is very true, he replied.

There is a virtue, Simmias, which is named courage. Is not that a special attribute of the philosopher?

Certainly.

Again, there is temperance. Is not the calm, and control, and disdain of the passions which even the many call temperance, a quality belonging only to those who despise the body and live in philosophy?

That is not to be denied. . . .

[Cebes takes over the discussion with Socrates]

Cebes answered: *I agree, Socrates, in the greater part of what you say. But in what relates to the soul, men are apt to be incredulous; they fear that when she leaves the body her place may be nowhere, and that on the very day of death she may be destroyed and perish-immediately on her release from the body, issuing forth like smoke or air and vanishing away into nothingness. For if she could only hold together and be herself after she was released from the evils of the body, there would be good reason to hope, Socrates, that what you say is true. But much persuasion and many arguments are required in order to prove that when the man is dead the soul yet exists, and has any force of intelligence.*

True, Cebes, said Socrates; and shall I suggest that we talk a little of the probabilities of these things?

I am sure, said Cebes, *that I should gready like to know your opinion about them.*

. . . Yet once more consider the matter in this light: When the soul and the body are united, then nature orders the soul to rule and govern, and the body to obey and serve. Now which of these two functions is akin to the divine? and which to the mortal? Does not the divine appear to you to be that which naturally orders and rules, and the mortal that which is subject and servant?

True.

And which does the soul resemble?

❖ ❖

The soul resembles the divine and the body the mortal-there can be no doubt of that, Socrates.

Then reflect, Cebes: is not the conclusion of the whole matter this?-that the soul is in the very likeness of the divine, and immortal, and intelligible, and uniform, and indissoluble, and unchangeable; and the body is in the very likeness of the human, and mortal, and unintelligible, and multiform, and dissoluble, and changeable. Can this, my dear Cebes, be denied?

No, indeed.

But if this is true, then is not the body liable to speedy dissolution? And is not the soul almost or altogether indissoluble?

Certainly.

And do you further observe, that after a man is dead, the body, which is the visible part of man, and has a visible framework, which is called a corpse, and which would naturally be dissolved and decomposed and dissipated, is not dissolved or decomposed at once, but may remain for a good while, if the constitution be sound at the time of death, and the season of the year favorable? For the body when shrunk and embalmed, as is the custom in Egypt, may remain almost entire through infinite ages; and even in decay, still there are some portions, such as the bones and ligaments, which are practically indestructible. You allow that?

Yes.

And are we to suppose that the soul, which is invisible, in passing to the true Hades, which like her is invisible, and pure, and noble, and on her way to the good and wise God, whither, if God will, my soul is also soon to go-that the soul, I repeat, if this be her nature and origin, is blown away and perishes immediately on quitting the body as the many say? That can never be, dear Simmias and Cebes. The truth rather is that the soul which is pure at departing draws after her no bodily taint, having never voluntarily had connection with the body, which she is ever avoiding, herself gathered into herself (for such abstraction has been the study of her life). And what does this mean but that she has been a true disciple of philosophy and has practised how to die easily? And is not philosophy the practice of death?

Certainly.

That soul, I say, herself invisible, departs to the invisible world to the divine and immortal and rational: thither arriving, she lives in bliss and is released from the error and folly of men, their fears and wild passions and all other human ills, and forever dwells, as they say of the initiated, in company with the gods. Is not this true, Cebes?

Yes, said Cebes, beyond a doubt.

But the soul which has been polluted, and is impure at the time of her departure, and is the companion and servant of the body always, and is in love with and fascinated by the body and by the desires and pleasures of the body, until she is led to believe that the truth only exists in a bodily form, which a man may touch and see and taste and use for the purposes of his lusts-the soul, I mean, accustomed to hate and fear and avoid the intellectual principle, which to the bodily eye is dark and invisible, and can be attained only by philosophy-do you suppose that such a soul as this will depart pure and unalloyed?

❀ 4.7 Unit 4 Study Guide ❀

✳✳✳

Plato's *Phaedo*

What is Socrates's view of the soul?

What arguments does Socrates give for the possibility of surviving death?

How does Socrates use the claim that "Philosophers are Wise"?

How does Socrates use the claim that there is *a priori* knowledge?

How does Socrates argue from the corruptibility of the body?

How does Socrates use the premise that the soul "rules and leads"?

What does Socrates think will happen to the soul after death?

Locke

Why does personal identity matter? What does the concept of a person include?

What would have to be true for Locke to say that you were the same person as someone who fought in the Trojan wars?

Why doesn't Locke think personal identity has anything to do with physical substance?

Why doesn't Locke think personal identity has anything to do with non-physical, conscious substance?

On Locke's theory, what is personal identity determined by?

According to Locke, why can't Dualist or Materialist accounts of conscious substance tell us what personal identity consists in?

What examples does Locke give where physical identity differs from personal identity?

What examples does Locke give where identity of conscious substance (or soul) differs from personal identity?

According to Locke, the same man at different times could be different persons. How does he use this to explain a feature of "human laws"?

What is the difference between "same man [or human]" and "same person"?

Hume

What does Hume's account of the "self" say?

What are you, according to Hume's account?

Does Hume think there are souls?

Does Hume think the essential self remains constant?

According to Hume, where does the concept of identity come from?

Parfit

All there is to personal identity, for Parfit, is _____ _____.
What does the two-word phrase you wrote in the blanks above mean?

Because the question, "will that future person be me—or someone else?" is a question which no amount of further information can answer, what should we do?

According to Parfit's split brain thought experiment, if I had the surgery, would I *survive* as L, R, neither, or both? Would I be *identical* to L, R, neither, or both?

What's wrong with our common sense concept of personal identity?

What is the example involving the split-brain case and the brain transplant supposed to show about survival and personal identity? (Think of the three aspects of all identity relations.)

In Parfit's "Secular version of the Ressurection", what happens?

Parft discusses the case of a club which meets in England for many years, disbands, and re-forms. What is this example supposed to show?

What view does Parfit take of punishment, given his view that personal identity is a matter of degree?

Be able to explain the problem of split brains for personal identity, including the scenario that is supposed to be a problem, what theories it is a problem for, and what you think we should conclude from it.

Daniels

Could there be a fact of the matter about personal identity, if no one could know it?

What is the example of Dokes and Morgan supposed to show?

What example does Daniels give involving a new mode of transportation?

Daniels gives an example involving a new mode of transportation—with a horrible twist. What's the horrible twist?

How does Daniels argue against Locke's memory theory of personal identity?

When two people fall in love with one person, with Daniels's machine, what happens?

Be able to explain the problem of teleportation for personal identity, including the scenario which is supposed to be a problem, what theories it is a problem for, and what you think we should conclude from it.

Points not to Miss

What are the two senses of "same"?

What's the difference between qualitative identity and numerical identity?

How might two things be qualitatively but not numerically identical, or vice-versa?

Three aspects of identity relations:

>   What does the transitivity of identity mean?

>   What does the symmetry of identity mean?

>   What does the reflexivity of identity mean?

Why are questions about personal identity relevant?

What, if anything, would the logical possibility of surviving death tell us about its probability?

I can't conceive of myself existing and then ceasing to exist. However, this doesn't guarantee that I will survive death. Why not?

The existence of God would guarantee that all moral agents survive death only if certain conditions and assumptions were to hold. What are those conditions and assumptions?

If I am essentially a non-physical mental substance, not a functioning physical body, and at death, nothing about me will change except that my functioning physical body will cease to exist, then when my body is dead, what will happen to me?

If I am identical to a functioning physical substance, and that functioning physical substance will cease forever to exist at death, then at death, what will happen to me?

Assume I am essentially a functioning physical substance, my body. How might I survive death?

Assume I am essentially a non-physical mental substance (or soul). Why might I nonetheless cease to exist when my body ceases to exist?

Overview: Unit 5
Philosophy of Religion

✳ ✳

In this unit, we'll complete our discussion of metaphysics with what is either the most important or least important question of all: Why does anything exist at all? Does the existence of God explain the cosmos? What reasons might there be for believing that God exists? If God does exist, then why is there so much evil in the world?

By the end of this unit, you should be able to:

✳ Restate and critique the ontological argument for the existence of God.

✳ Restate and critique the teleological argument for the existence of God.

✳ Outline arguments within Broad's discussion of religious experience.

✳ Explain and evaluate a variety of cosmological arguments for the existence of God.

✳ Explain the problem of evil.

✳ Evaluate major responses to the problem of evil.

✳ Develop your own views in the philosophy of religion.

❀ 5.1 Does God Exist? ❀

✳ ✳

The philosophy of religion involves trying to address traditionally religious questions philosophically—that is, by thinking clearly and carefully about them. Philosophy is neither inherently opposed to nor supportive of any particular religion. However, many of the questions that religious beliefs attempt to answer are the very sort of difficult questions which philosophy is about: Does the universe have a cause? Is there life after death? What is the self? So, insofar as religions make claims about the answers to these questions, it makes sense to evaluate these religious claims philosophically.

This Unit deals with a major question in the philosophy of religion: does God exist? This is not the only question in the philosophy of religion. We might ask instead about the relationship between the natural environment and humankind, for example, or about whether history is an endless cycle, or about whether God can have multiple human avatars, only one, or none at all. However, we only have time and space here to discuss one question. Many of the world's major religions claim that God exists. Whether one thinks God exists or not seems to have consequences for how one will approach other areas of philosophy—recall that Descartes made this the foundation of his epistemology, and some people think this is important to ethics. So, this is why we will concern ourselves with the question of whether God exists.

A. What do philosophers mean by "God"?

B. Positive Arguments from Religious Experience

C. Negative Arguments from Religious Experience

D. Does Everything Have an Explanation?

E. The Paradox of Sufficient Reason

F. The Cosmological Argument

G. Varieties of Cosmological Argument

H. The Alternative Deities Objection

I. Denying the Need for Explanation

J. The Teleological Argument

K. A Modern Ontological Argument

L. Anselm's Ontological Argument

M. Benefits of the Ontological Argument

N. The Problem of Evil—The First Version

O. Why Doesn't God Intervene?—The Second Version

A. What do philosophers mean by "God"?

Discussion of God in philosophy is usually conducted in a monotheistic context. *Theism* (from the Greek *theos*, or "god") is the view that either God or gods exist; *atheism* (for the Greek *a-*, or "without") holds that neither God nor gods exist. A related position, known as *agnosticism* (from the Greek *a-* or without and *gnosis* or knowledge, "without knowledge"), holds that one cannot know that God exists or not.

Judaism, Christianity, Islam, Zoroastrianism, and Sikhism are all *monotheistic* religions, which all claim that exactly one God exists, and that God is distinct from the world. This distinguishes them from *polytheistic* religions, which holds that multiple gods exist, and from *pantheistic* religions, which holds that the world itself is God.[1]

The monotheistic religions do not all make the same claims about God, of course–they differ quite drastically in their *theology*, or teachings about God. It may be tempting to say that they do not mean the same thing by "God" at all, or that the "God" of one monotheistic religion is not the same as the "God" of another.

However, recall that in Unit 1 we distinguished between the *sense* of a word, and the *referent* of that word. We might say that the word "God" has different senses, depending on which religion's theology one is working from. However, if any supreme being exists at all, then this being will necessarily be the *referent* of all of these different senses of the word "God".

Here is a simpler way to put the same point. Suppose that Sam, Todd, and Quinn belong to different religions. Todd says, "God is one, and has no partners". Sam says, "No, God is three distinct persons, unified." Quinn says, "God has many manifestations." Clearly, Quinn and Todd and Sam do not believe the same things about God. However, the fact that they are *disagreeing* reveals that they must believe they are referring to the same thing. Or, suppose that Quinn says of God "She is our mother", and Sam says "No, He is our father" and Todd says "God has no gender at all." Clearly, Sam, Quinn, and Todd do not have the same idea or *sense* in mind when they use the word "God". However, if there is a God, then Sam, Quinn, and Todd have referred to the same God, even if they have made claims about God which can't all be true at once.

So, what we're after in philosophy is a very **minimal definition** of the word "God". It will not include most of the things people believe about God, or what they think of when they hear the word "God", but it

---

[1] Hinduism is complex; since there are many gods in its pantheon, it is usually interpreted by Westerners as polytheistic—holding that there are multiple gods—much like the ancient religions of Europe were polytheistic. However, Hinduism is composed of many sects with differing beliefs, with some holding that one particular god is the Supreme God over others, others believing that the gods are aspects of one Supreme God, Brahman, and others holding a pantheistic view.

will include the basic claim which monotheistic religions have in common. This minimal definition will apply without regard to whether any particular religion is correct about God. This minimal definition will be the thing that we can engage in philosophical argument about. Here are the three claims that we'll take as a minimal definition of what the philosophers we read in this unit will mean by "God":

1. **God is the reason that the world is there.** God is supposed to be the ultimate *creator* of the world, the Ultimate Explainer of the whole cosmos and all of space and time, the "because" which answers the biggest "why" question. God is the reason for everything which exists in the world, including the world itself.

2. **God is a transcendent being and not a part of the world.** God is supposed to be distinct from the world. The world is what is real and capable of representation, but God is supposed to be real yet not capable of representation. This means that God can't be described, imagined, or conceived of in any literal sense. For any "mental picture" someone associates with God, God is nothing like the mental picture.

3. **God is the greatest possible being.** God is supposed to be great, so great that nothing else could possibly be greater. God is supposed to have the greatest possible power (*omnipotence*), to have the greatest possible knowledge (*omniscience*), and to have the greatest possible moral goodness (*omnibenevolence*). God is supposed to exist *necessarily* rather than contingently.

So, why think that God exists at all? Although many people in the world think God exists, there are also very many people in the world who have no belief in God at all, including people who used to believe God exists but now don't. So, why believe one way or another?

B. Positive Arguments from Religious Experience

Very few of the people who believe that God exists do so because they were persuaded by an argument they heard in a philosophy class. Instead, they would say that their belief in God comes from a kind of religious experience they've had.

* In a few cases this might be a very dramatic mystical experience, like a shocking vision of a reality which seemed *more* real than our reality, or an insight into our own reality through a different lens, or a feeling of inward conversion or transformation.

* For most people, it is likely to involve a less dramatic religious experience, like a feeling that there is another presence in the room, or that one's prayers are being heard, or that an idea comes from someplace outside of one's own head.

* Religious experiences can include even the very ordinary sort of experience, like the experience of being part of a community and tradition, or the experience of repeating a daily or weekly or yearly rhythm, or the experience of feeling loved, or the experience of having family or friends who are sincere and seek to share and pass on a belief in God.

* People who are part of a religious group often share their experiences with one another and see themselves as connected to the experiences of a community in the distant past, which have been handed down and entrusted to them.

Likewise, very few of the people who *don't* believe that God exists hold this belief as a result of taking a philosophy class and listening to arguments.

* First, some people simply do not have a word in their language or culture which corresponds to anything like the word "God" defined above. Some religions, like Buddhism, include a concept of supernatural beings, but not of any all-powerful God. Some religions, like Confucianism, are not particularly concerned with the supernatural at all. The concept of "God" may seem like an imported, foreign concept.

* Second, many people who have the word "God" in their language nonetheless do not believe that God exists, because of experiences with religion which they have or haven't had. Religious experiences can be negative as well as positive: religious communities sometimes exercise control over their members, isolate them from the world, or seek internal conformity to the point of limiting the freedom to think outside of certain boundaries. Uncovering secretive or deceptive practices within a religion, or learning facts about the religion's founding or texts, or learning about the sordid or even violent history of a religion, can easily leave someone dubious that the religion is of divine origin.

* Finally, many religious claims about the supernatural seem to go contrary to everyday experience for most people, such as claims about miracles. Just like a person's belief that he has experienced a miraculous event gives him a reason to believe in the supernatural, a person's experiencing no miraculous events would give reason to doubt the supernatural.

Let's try to formalize these arguments for a moment.

Argument 1

1. Angie had a religious experience that makes it seem as though God exists.
2. Angie's experience accurately represents reality.
C. God exists.

Argument 2

1. Bertie had a religious experience that makes it seem as though God does not exist.
2. Bertie's experience accurately represents reality.
C. God does not exist.

We can see immediately the weakness in both of these arguments. The second premise of each argument assumes that the individual's experience accurately reflects reality as a whole. But how can we be confident of this?

Now, it may be that it's not possible for Angie to imagine her experience not reflecting reality—her experience is simply too real for her to doubt, although she can't make others have that experience. And it may be that it's not possible for Bertie to imagine his experience not reflecting reality, and hence he finds it hard to take any talk of God seriously. So, it may be that Angie and Bertie are both justified in holding their own beliefs as a result of their own experiences.

However, our method in philosophy is to engage in dialogue with each other. That means we must appeal to reasoning that others besides us can understand and to experiences that everyone has in common. What can we say about Angie's and Bertie's experiences?

C. D. Broad's article on the Argument from Religious Experience helps us to consider both the possibility that someone like Angie's religious experiences are accurate, and that they are inaccurate. One possibility is that Angie's experiences do not in fact reflect the existence of God, but instead they reflect something which has gone wrong in her brain chemistry, or a product of social psychology or social pressure, or simply a product of Angie's desire for an orderly and meaningful universe. Another possibility is that Angie's experiences do reflect reality. Broad suggests that perhaps religious experience is something like musical ability—some people are dramatic musical geniuses, most people have an ordinary level of musical ability, and a few people are simply tone deaf. However, since we can imagine both possibilities, we can't clearly say whether premise 2 is true or false.

Likewise, we can imagine both the possibility that Bertie's experiences are accurate, and that they are inaccurate. The fact that Bertie has had negative experiences with a religious group is perfectly compatible with the existence of a transcendent creator—God might exist, but not be associated with the particular religious group Bertie had experiences with, or with any religion. Bertie's experience—or his readings in the history of religion—may simply reflect the reality of human social behavior in any group, not something about humanity being alone in the cosmos. On the other hand, Bertie's experiences could accurately reflect a world without a God, since someone might *expect* that God would give Bertie a different set of experiences, or produce a history of the world different than the one we have.

C. Negative Arguments from Religious Experience

Of course the *absence* of a certain experience can be as much a reason to believe or disbelieve in God as the presence of some experience. For instance, someone might reason that *if* God exists, then God would be capable of giving him or her the very sorts of religious experiences which other people claim lead them to believe that God exists, and God would want people to believe that God exists, so that the absence of any such experience in one's life becomes a reason to believe that God does not exist:

Argument 3

1. If God exists, then Darla will have a religious experience of God.
2. Darla does not have a religious experience of God.
C. God does not exist.

To resist this argument, a theist would need to give Darla a satisfying explanation for why God couldn't or wouldn't give Darla a religious experience of this sort. What might a theist propose? Do you think this would satisfy Darla?

On the other hand, someone might believe in God because there is a certain experience they expect to have in the world around them, which they *don't* have. Their reasoning goes like this: if God exists, then God has the highest degree of importance, to the point that God alone is worthy of what is called "worship", an attitude one has in the face of something of the greatest worth and importance. However, if God does not exist, then *something else* necessarily must be of the highest degree of importance, and thus worthy of the attitude one has toward things of the greatest worth and importance, worship. But I've never encountered anything in the world which has the highest degree of importance to me, to the point where I would worship that thing. Even things which I think are very important, like my family and friends, I don't think should be worshipped. So, since something must be of the highest importance to me, and nothing in the world fits the bill, something outside of the world, God, must be of the highest importance to me.

Argument 4

1. Clyde has not had the experience of finding anything which is of the highest importance to him in the world.

2. If there were something of the highest importance to him in the world, Clyde would have found it.

C. What's of the highest importance to Clyde is outside of the world, God.

To resist this argument, what could an atheist propose? Do you think this would satisfy Clyde?

The one thing that we can say about all of these arguments is that they will only be appealing to the extent that a person has had the experiences (or absences of experiences) described in each of them. What they don't offer, however, are any *a priori* reasons, independent of experience and common to everyone, to think that God exists or does not exist.

But some philosophers have argued that there *are* arguments which can be given for or against the existence of God which appeal to reasons and principles that we should all hold in common. We'll start with arguments given *for* God's existence—the cosmological, ontological, and teleological arguments— and then turn to an argument *against* God's existence.

D. Does Everything Have an Explanation?

Does everything have an explanation?

Remember that Unit 4 ended with the suggestion that there are some questions about personal identity which in principle can't be answered. We can discuss psychological continuity and use this to answer questions about personal identity over time. But it seems like we can't answer the question, "why am I this person and not that person?". Trying to give an answer to this question simply raises the same question again. So, this might suggest that there are some things which don't have an explanation.

However, one of the features of the world we live in is that we can comprehend and understand and explain it to an impressive degree. Indeed, our scientific understanding of the world has advanced the most over the last 500 years precisely by assuming that everything does in fact have an explanation, and seeking out those explanations rigorously. Further, if something were not even in principle capable of explanation, would it be part of the world at all? Remember that by "the world", as we defined it in Unit 1, we don't mean "the earth" or even "the universe at this moment"; rather, by "the world" we mean all of space, all of time, and all of reality (including anything which does not exist in space and time) *which can be represented* in some manner or other. Anything which couldn't be represented would be *transcendent*, not part of the world at all. If something can't be explained, it can't be represented. So it seems like, by definition, everything in the world must have an explanation; otherwise we couldn't really represent it at all.

E. The Paradox of Sufficient Reason

So, let's work on the assumption for a moment that everything does in fact have an explanation. It follows that everything which is explained is explained by something else, which in turn must have an explanation of its own. For example, the boiling of water in a tea kettle can be explained by the heat of the water, which can be explained by the stove on which the kettle sits, which can be explained by the gas or electricity which runs the stove, which in turn will have an explanation of its own, and so on. Imagine the chain of explanations which there must be, starting with an original event E1 and working backward, so that E2 explains E1, E3 explains E2, and so on:

$$\ldots \rightarrow E5 \rightarrow E4 \rightarrow E3 \rightarrow E2 \rightarrow E1$$

Where does this series stop?

Well, it seems as though there are three possibilities. The first possibility is that the series stops with some original, basic explainer. The second possibility is that the series continues on infinitely. The third possibility is that somewhere along the way the chain of explanations loops back around upon itself.

The third possibility would be a circular explanation. In a circular explanation, something ultimately explains itself. For instance, if I said "the tea kettle is boiling because of the heat of the water, which is hot because of the stove, which is hot because of the electric current, where is there because the tea kettle is boiling . . .", then I would have given a circular explanation. However, most people find it hard to make sense of what it would be for something to explain itself. This is why circular explanations are generally thought to be bad explanations.

> 1. Explanation stops with an original, basic explainer, or
> 2. Explanation continues infinitely, or
> 3. Explanations are circular

The second possibility, that the series continues on infinitely, might arguably make sense. On the one hand, it is hard to fathom a series of reasons going backward infinitely, and none of us could ever understand or articulate an infinite chain of explanations. This seems to be outside of the bounds of what we could represent. But, on the other hand, why are we entitled to assume that the series simply must stop somewhere, and not go on forever? That said, we're working on the assumption that *everything* has an explanation. So, if there could be such a thing as an infinitely long chain of explanations, then *the infinite chain itself* would be a thing which requires an explanation at a higher order. Suppose there were an infinite number of infinite chains of explanation, if this makes any sense at all. Then this too would need an explanation. And so on.

So, this leaves us with the first possibility. Suppose that the chain of explanations in the world ends somewhere, at some original, bedrock, basic starting point which explains everything else. Call it "B". B is the thing which explains everything else. What can we say about B? Isn't it something also? So, wouldn't it also need an explanation, given our assumption that everything has an explanation? However, if B has an explanation, then it isn't really the basic starting point and explainer of everything after all. So the first possibility is self-contradictory and not a possibility at all.

At this point, it seems like our starting assumption, that *everything* has an explanation, is what got us into trouble. In order to hold on to this assumption, we seem to be forced to call some things "explanations", like infinitely infinite chains or circular explanations, which many people wouldn't normally regard as explanations at all. So, perhaps it is better to conclude that not everything has an explanation.

F. The Cosmological Argument

If we conclude this, then we seem to face a paradox. On the one hand, it can't be that everything must have an explanation, because whatever explains everything will be part of the everything which must be explained. On the other hand, everything we can possibly think about, talk about, understand, or otherwise represent must have an explanation. If something didn't have an explanation, it wouldn't be a think we could talk about.

One proposal to resolve the paradox is this: whatever it is that explains everything else is transcendent. Something transcendent can't itself be represented, understood, or explained. Everything that *can* be represented has an explanation, but at the end of the chain of explanations is something that *can't* be represented and couldn't have an explanation. That is, on this proposal, there is some part of reality which is not part of the world that we can represent, which explains the world that we can represent. It is more basic than the world, and the ultimate cause of it.

So, everything in the world must in principle have an explanation, but there is something outside of the world which can't in principle have an explanation. This argument has come to be known as the "Cosmological Argument" for the existence of God.

A basic cosmological argument can be formalized as follows:

1. Everything representable has an explanation (The Principle of Sufficient Reason)

2. Explanations cannot be circular (The Principle of Non-Circularity)

C. There is something transcendent that explains everything

Since something infinite can be represented, even an infinite series of explanations would itself need an explanation. So, the ultimate explainer of everything must be a transcendent being, which cannot be represented.

G. Varieties of Cosmological Argument

That said, it is better to think of the Cosmological Argument as a *type* of argument, rather than a specific argument. The proposal that the world has a transcendent Ultimate Explainer has been influential in Western philosophy since Aristotle. Aristotle argued that there must be a "prime mover" or "first cause" of some sort which started the world. Aristotle's idea was later adapted by a number of Islamic philosophers, most notable Ibn Sina (Avicenna), who used it to argue for the existence of God, or Allah, as the ultimate explainer of the world. Versions of Avicenna's argument were then adapted by the Jewish philosopher Maimonides and the Christian scholastic philosopher Thomas Aquinas.

There are a wide variety of ways in which one can run the cosmological argument. For instance:

* The efficient causal version: every event in the world must have a cause. Any series of events is itself an event. But what is the cause of the series of events in the world, whether this series goes infinitely backward in time or begins in a moment with a Big Bang? The cause can't itself be an event in the world.

* The material causal version: everything in the world at this very moment depends for its existence on something more basic. My body depends for its existence on cells, which depend on atoms, which depend on sub-atomic particles. Whatever is at the bottom level (quarks, branes, fields, strings?) depends for its existence on something more basic. So there must be some fundamental being on which everything depends for its being.

* The teleological version: everything in the world happens for some greater purpose. So there must be an ultimate purpose behind all of the purposes in the world, which is the will of God.

* The personal identity version: it is a fact of the matter that I'm *me* and not *you*. But this fact can't be explained by any property that you or I have in relation to the world. So there must be something outside of this world which makes me *me* and not *you*.

* The Argument from Contingency: our world is contingent, just one of the many possible worlds which could have been actualized. Why is this world that we are in the actual world, and not one of the others? Nothing within the actual world can explain this, since its actuality is precisely what needs explained. So there must be something which exists necessarily, which isn't a contingent part of the world, which explains why we are in this world and not another.

To see how these arguments could be written out formally:

1. Every part of the world has an explanation.
2. Explanations are not circular.
C. The world must have an explanation which is not part of the world.

One of the source texts in this unit comes from Thomas Aquinas's *Five Ways*, which presents five different forms of the Cosmological argument. One of these is the Argument from Contingency.

The Argument from Contingency (Aquinas)

1. Everything which could have been otherwise has an explanation.
2. The actual world is not necessarily the world; the world could have been otherwise.
C. That the world is actual must have an explanation which is necessary.

Another source text in this unit is William Lane Craig's *Kalam Cosmological Argument*, a modern-day variation on an early Islamic version of the causal argument.

The Causal Argument (Craig)

1. Every event in the world in time has a cause.
2. There does not exist an infinite series of causes.
C. The series of events in time in the world must have a first cause which is not in time.

All of the arguments have in common three key elements:

1. Some *type of explanation* which is supposed to be required of everything in the world.
2. The conclusion that some Ultimate Explainer explains the world.
3. The conclusion that this Ultimate Explainer is transcendent, outside of the world.

The world's three major Abrahamic religious traditions, Islam, Judaism, and Christianity, historically have held that God meets the criteria in #2 and #3. That is, God is traditionally said to be the creator of the world, and God is also traditionally said to be transcendent or outside of the realm of things that can be represented and explained by something else, such that representing God in pictures or images is considered idolatry. (Christianity might add that God can be represented by himself, but not by anything else.)

However, many thinkers in history have not believed that God exists and do not accept that the cosmological argument is sound. Famous philosophers who defended atheism or agnosticism include Bertrand Russell and David Hume. Many of the philosophers we've read in this course so far, such as David Chalmers and Derek Parfit, are atheists. So, let's look at the number of objections to the Cosmological Argument that could be raised on behalf of the atheist.

H. The Alternative Deities Objection

One way to resist a Cosmological Argument is to argue that it something else besides the traditional conception of God could fulfill the role of Ultimate Explainer. The argument, it is thought, proves *too much*, since it could apply to many other things as well.

For instance, someone might propose that a Magical Pink Unicorn is the reason that the world exists. Or, someone might propose that the world is an egg laid by the Great Penguin, and so the Great Penguin is the Ultimate Explainer. Or, one of the gods, like Zeus or Woden or Jupiter, or a monster made of pasta, might be the Ultimate explainer.

However, a Magical Pink Unicorn is not transcendent: we can imagine a pink unicorn and can represent it quite clearly. A Magical Pink Unicorn, hence, falls into the category of things we can understand, which are part of the world that needs explanation. Likewise, even if it is true that our cosmos is an egg laid by the Great Penguin, the Great Penguin is a representable part of the world, and so the Great Penguin would also need an explanation. The same applies to the various gods; if one holds that the gods live on Mount Olympus or engage in romantic relationships with other gods, then one holds that the gods can be represented, and so they are not transcendent, and hence they need an explanation. In contrast, the Ultimate Explainer of the Cosmological argument is not the sort of thing which can be represented in this way.

In general, the chief mark of the cosmological argument is that it makes a sharp distinction between the category of things which require explanation (contingent, representable beings) and the Ultimate Explainer (a necessary, transcendent being), to make clear why the Ultimate Explainer doesn't itself need explanation. The advantage of this argument for the traditional monotheist is that it is not an argument that any old god or "creator being" started it all (often conceived of anthropomorphically), but an argument that the explainer of the universe is the transcendent God of traditional monotheism, necessarily existing outside of time and space, beyond conception and understanding, to which our human categories apply only metaphorically. As such, it escapes the common "but what created God?" objection, since one can't sensibly ask for an explanation of something which is by definition inexplicable.

That said, this line of argument does show that the Cosmological Argument only supports a very general conclusion—a transcendent, unexplainable, ultimate explainer—and says nothing more about whether this explainer is perfect or even morally good, cares for the world, or has any connection to the various events which religious traditions associate with God. One might readily use another word instead of "God" without a loss of meaning. So, while this line of argument doesn't undermine the Cosmological Argument, it does reveal that it is an argument for the existence of "God" only in a very general sense. It does not give us reason to think that God is perfect—so far as this version of the cosmological argument is concerned soon, the Ultimate Explainer might be neither good nor bad.

I. Denying the Need for Explanation

Another way to resist a Cosmological Argument is to hold that the particular type of explanation it calls for is unnecessary. In some cases, it may be easier to see how someone would do this than others. For instance, it's easy to see how someone might resist the teleological version: The argument that everything in the world must have some purpose, so the world as a whole must have an ultimate purpose. How do we know that everything must have a purpose? Many people have doubted that. Likewise, following Hume, we might hold that there are no real facts about personal identity, and so resist any cosmological argument making use of personal identity.

One can resist the causal version of the Cosmological Argument by arguing that **causation requires time**. Causes must always occur before their effects in time: future events can't cause past events (there is no 'backward causation'), and something outside of time can't cause events in time. So, asking for the cause of the Big Bang (if time has a beginning), or the cause of the Infinite history of the world (if time has no beginning), is demanding the impossible: These things can't have a cause, because there is nothing prior to them in time.

A more difficult version of the Cosmological Argument to resist is the actuality version. This argument doesn't demand an explanation of any particular event in the universe, but only asks for an explanation of the universe as a whole. Given all of the logically possible universes, including ones in which you and I never existed, or ones in which earth never existed, why is it this universe and not another which is actual?

It is true, of course, that we would ask the same question in any other universe we ended up in. So we're not asking why the earth is so green and the water so blue, as opposed to a world where earth is pink and water black; it's not some particular feature of this world we're asking about. Inside, we're asking why this world we are in is actual and not merely possible.

Some philosophers and some scientists hold that **many universes besides ours are real**. That is, they believe that, in addition to our universe, there exist other universes like ours: Perhaps, a parallel one which has an earth like ours and a sun like ours, but in which something has gone differently at the level studied by quantum mechanics, and as a result many things in that world are different. This might seem to reduce the pressure of the Cosmological Argument at first, since it would mean that some, or perhaps all, of the other possible worlds are as real as our world. Nonetheless, you and I are present now in only one of these worlds, the actual world. Perhaps we have counterparts in parallel universes. But these counterparts aren't you and I right now; I'm not experiencing what they're experiencing. So, the question remains: why are we experiencing this world, and not another? Why is our world actual, and not another?

Conversely, the philosopher Baruch Spinoza held that there are **no other logically possible worlds besides our own**. Our world was *necessarily* the case, and so it needed no further explanation. Although all events within the world have explanations and can be understood, the world as a whole does not have an explanation, and goes beyond what we can understand. On this view, the world itself meets many of the criteria associated with God: It exists independently without explanation, beyond our understanding, and yet it is the ultimate explanation for everything else besides itself. So, Spinoza concluded that the world itself was God, a view called *pantheism* (from Greek *pan-* or "all").

Alternatively, an atheist might accept that our world is contingent, and yet nonetheless deny the claim that the world's being actual rather than possible requires some further sort of explanation. We might **reject the principle of sufficient reason** entirely, and hold that some things do not have any explanation. Or we might reject that the principle of sufficient reason applies to the world as a whole, even if one thinks that it applies to parts of the world. Likewise, we can reject that principle of non-circularity applies to the world as a whole: perhaps it is true that no part of the world explains itself, but the world as a whole does explain itself.

Or perhaps the question "why is this world actual, and not another?", while it might seem at first to make sense, is **a nonsensical question**. We think that we can imagine another possible world as though it were actual and not merely possible. But this is sort of like trying to imagine yourself being Hillary

Clinton. Perhaps, you can imagine yourself having many of the properties Hillary Clinton has, but you can't actually *be* somebody you're *not*: that's a contradiction. So, perhaps, we can imagine the world we live in being very different than it is. But we can't imagine the world we live in not being the world we live in; this is confused.

This is perhaps the basic point where theists and atheists simply disagree. Both agree that not everything has an explanation, but one holds that it is God which has no explanation, and the other that it is the world as a whole which has no explanation. Both agree that the question "why this world?" isn't something that we can understand the answer to, but one holds that this is because the question itself is confused and has no answer, while the other holds that the question makes sense, but the answer is a being beyond understanding.

J. The Teleological Argument

Even if it is sound, which is debatable, the cosmological argument does not appear to establish that God is the greatest possible being, or even good. A very different argument was proposed by William Paley, in one of our source texts, to try to establish both the existence and perfection of God. This is sometimes called the "teleological argument", or the argument from design.

The cosmological argument is about *that the world is*, the teleological argument is about *how the world is*. Instead of asking why a world exists at all, or why this world of the many possible worlds is actual, the teleological argument asks us to focus on observable features of our world—beauty, order, the functioning of all of the pieces into a grand whole. The cosmological argument is *a priori*, but the teleological argument is empirical.

The Watchmaker

Consider an ecosystem like the tropical rain forest. Every part of the rain forest is interdependent on all of the other parts. The smaller plants at the lower levels depend on the shade provided by the tall trees. The plants depend on insects for pollination, and the insects depend on the plants for food. The smaller animals depend on the insects for food, and the larger animals on the smaller animals and the plants for food. The delicate balances between prey and predator, or between two cooperating species, can be upset easily by human intervention—hunting of predators leads to overpopulation of the prey, which destroys the plant life in the forest, which leads the prey to die off. The entire system is a delicately balanced, organized whole. And this rainforest as a whole depends upon the climate systems on earth—the forest depends upon the regular flow of rains, which are produced by the evaporation of tropical waters. And the climate systems on earth depend on factors like our precise distance from the sun, and the precise balance of oxygen and carbon and other gasses in our atmosphere—changing this distribution of gasses could raise or lower the temperature. And the distribution of these gasses in turn depends upon plants like those in the rain forest!

This finely tuned order requires some sort of explanation. The best explanation for this order, says Paley, is that it was fine-tuned by an intelligent and good being, like God. Paley compares the world to the intricate mechanism found inside of a watch. (Think of a mechanical, Swiss watch with many gears, not an electronic watch). If we observed a watch, we'd conclude it had a designer. So, on observing the world, we should conclude it had a designer. The world has a "watchmaker."

The "God of the Gaps" objection

One criticism of Paley's argument is that it appeals to a "God of the gaps" strategy. The existence of God is invoked to "fill in the gaps" where science can't explain something at the time—the reason for the order in the world—but as science progresses and the gaps get smaller, God is less useful as a hypothesis. When we didn't know the origins of tides or lightening, the existence of God seemed like an obvious necessity; when we found other explanations for these things, the existence of God was invoked to explain something else, like the existence of biological life; when we found explanations for life, God was invoked to explain something else.

And, in fact, scientists in our own day—two centuries after Paley—do actively offer models that seek to explain how complex ecosystems work, and the many other systems which advocates of the teleological argument believe require design. These models rely on constraints upon randomness rather than design: for example, the constraint that living organisms either survive long enough to reproduce within the environment they are in, or die out. Since these models give an explanation that doesn't require the existence of God, we don't need to appeal to a divine designer to explain the order and complexity in our world.

While there will inevitably be many "gaps" remaining in our current scientific knowledge of the world, and there are things for which we do not have any good explanation, perhaps it's wiser to bet that in the future we *will* find an explanation, rather than that only God can provide this explanation. There may be features of our cosmos which are objectively "improbable"—for instance, that the earth has just the right balance to support life. However, when we consider that any alternative would have been equally improbable, perhaps the need for explanation is reduced—it is "improbable" to pull out a Jack of Spades out of a randomly shuffled deck of cards, but all of the other cards are equally improbable.

Note that the "God of the gaps" objection doesn't apply to the cosmological argument, since the cosmological argument is not seeking an explanation of some "gap" in our understanding of how the world works which could in principle be explained by something in the world, but instead is seeking an explanation which even in principle nothing in the world could explain. It applies to the teleological argument because it is not clear why only the existence of God could explain the order, beauty, purposefulness, and appearance of design noted in the teleological argument. Saving the teleological argument from this objection requires showing that there is something about the *type* of explanation involved in explaining why we live in a world like ours, which nothing but a divine designer could even conceivably explain.

Hume's Objection

David Hume raises an objection to the teleological argument which goes a very different route. Instead, Hume points out that even if the teleological argument is right, and that we know that the world has a designer, we would know very little about this designer on the basis of the creation. The designer must be fairly intelligent—but not necessarily omniscient. The designer must be as powerful as a god—but not necessarily an all-powerful God. The designer might be one god, but could also be many gods, or even a whole team of gods. There is no reason to suppose, says Hume, that the designer isn't a physical being with hands and feet. The designer might be an alien race. The designer might be imperfect: This world might only be the rough draft of a better world, or one of many worlds this designer or other designers made. And while the designer made some good things in the world, this isn't proof that the designer is good—the designer might have made the world with bad intentions.

If we take the analogy to the "watchmaker" very far, says Hume, what we end up with is an anthropomorphic notion of God—not a transcendent being, but a being who is simply an idealized version of ourselves. Some religions would accept the existence of a designer of this sort. However, the traditional monotheistic religions would not.

Perhaps what we are looking for in the teleological argument is an explanation, not of the world, but of ourselves. *We* seem extremely lucky to be in this world, since we would not have existed in a world ever so slightly different than the one we live in. The claim that "our world could not exist merely by chance" is not at its core about the rain forests or the order found in nature. Rather, it is an expression of a much deeper conviction that *I* could not exist merely by chance.

K. A Modern Ontological Argument

In contrast to the teleological argument, which rests on empirical premises, the ontological argument is an attempt to prove that God exists with purely definitional premises. If the ontological argument is correct, the existence of God is a *theorem*, a proof with no premises, alongside the theorems of logic like the theorem *P or not-P* or the theorem *If P or Q and not Q, then P*. The proof has the structure of a *Reductio* argument. In a Reductio argument, you assume the *opposite* of what you want to prove, show that a contradiction follows from this assumption, and conclude that your assumption must have been false. For example:

1. Triangles have more sides than squares do (assume).
2. Triangles have 3 sides (definition).
3. Squares have 4 sides (definition).
4. 3 sides is more than 4 sides (from premises 1, 2, and 3).
5. 3 sides is not more than 4 sides (mathematical truth).
6. Contradiction! (4, 5).
C. Triangles <u>do not</u> have more sides than squares do.

In the ontological argument, our starting assumption will be that:

1. A greatest possible being does not necessarily exist. (assume)

Remember that we defined "God" earlier, in philosophical discussions, as the "Greatest possible being", meaning a being which is great in every possible way in which something can be great: more powerful than anything else is or could be, knowing more than anything else does or could know, morally better than anything else is or could be, and so on. Premise 1 is the assumption that this being at least *might* not exist. Premise 1 doesn't actually assume that there is or isn't such a being; rather, it assumes it at least might not exist—that there is at least one possible world in which the being does not exist.

Our next step in the argument is supposed to simply be a definitional truth.

2. A being which necessarily exists is greater than a being which does not necessarily exist. (definition)

Something which does not necessarily exist either exists contingently, or is impossible. Something which exists *contingently* is something which exists, but which could cease to exist or fail to have ever existed.

For example, horses exist contingently. In our world, there are horses, but in another world, there might not have been horses. Unicorns also exist contingently. In other possible worlds there are unicorns, but not in our world. On the other hand, something which exists necessarily could not possibly cease to exist or fail to have ever existed. Numbers, for instance, exist necessarily, since in every possible world $2 + 2 = 4$ is a fact.

Something which exists necessarily seems greater than something which exists only contingently, or which doesn't exist at all. Just like knowing everything is greater than knowing only some things and not others, and being able to do anything is greater than being able to do only some things but not others, it would seem like existing in every possible world is greater than existing only in some possible worlds but not others—that just what "greater" means.

However, from step 2 and our assumption in 1, something troubling follows in step 3:

3. A being which necessarily exists is greater than the greatest possible being. (1,2)

If a necessarily existing being is greater than a non-necessarily existing being, and the greatest possible being is a non-necessarily existing being, then a necessary being is greater than the greatest possible being.

But nothing could possibly be greater than the greatest possible being! Line 3 is a contradiction! And so, we get this argument, by Reductio.

1. A greatest possible being does not necessarily exist. (assume)
2. A being which necessarily exists is greater than a being which does not necessarily exist.
3. A being which necessarily exists is greater than the greatest possible being. (1,2)
4. Contradiction! (3)
C. A greatest possible being does necessarily exist.

Since our assumption on line 1 lead to a contradiction, we must conclude that our assumption on line 1 was false: and so, a greatest possible being *does* necessarily exist. That is, as we defined "God" earlier, God necessarily exists.

It is difficult to object to this modern version of the ontological argument. There are, roughly, two ways of going about it. The harder way is to challenge the logic of "necessary" and "possible" used in the proof, which would take us into modal logic, and outside the scope of this class. However, the easier way is to deny that line 2 is really a definitional claim, like "triangles have three sides". Instead, it could be thought to be a claim we can investigate and wonder about. *Is necessarily existing necessarily greater than not necessarily existing?* Couldn't it be that some necessarily existing things are greater than some contingent things, but some contingent things are greater than some necessary things? There's very little we can use as a guide as to whether existing in all possible worlds is greater than only existing in a few. The notion of "greatness" here might be a reflection of a certain temperament which not all people share—perhaps other people don't have this same concept of "greatness"?

L. Anselm's Ontological Argument

To understand this "modern" version of the ontological argument it will help to look at an older version of the ontological argument and many of the objections which were raised against it, which applied to the original but not to the modern version.

Anselm, the archbishop of Canterbury, first developed the ontological argument. His original version goes as follows:

1. A being than which none greater can be conceived exists only in conception but not in reality. (assume)

2. A being which exists in reality is greater than a being which exists only in conception.

3. We can conceive of a being which exists in reality and is greater than a being than which none greater can be conceived.

4. Contradiction! (3)

C. There exists a being than which none greater can be conceived.

Notice that Anselm's argument does not actually say that we can conceive of this being, only that we can't conceive of anything greater than this being. So, Anselm's argument does not require that someone have a concept of "God" or a concept of "the greatest being", but only that this person have a concept of some things being greater than others.

An initial objection to Anselm, provided by his fellow monk Gaunilo, was that the argument proves too much. Can't it also be used to prove the existence of a greatest conceivable island?

1. An island than which none greater can be conceived exists only in conception but not in reality. (assume)

2. An island which exists in reality is greater than one which exists only in conception.

3. We can conceive of an island which exists in reality and is greater than an island than which none greater can be conceived.

4. Contradiction! (3)

C. There exists an island than which none greater can be conceived.

It's absurd that a "greatest conceivable island" exists, so we can't use the same form of argument to "prove" that a "greatest conceivable being" exists.

Another objection, raised by Immanuel Kant, is that "exists" is not a property. Things which exist have properties which can be added or taken away, but existing itself is not something which can be added or taken away—a thing cannot both exist and fail to have the property of existence! So it is not as though there is a thing called "existing in reality" which one being has and the other lacks in premise 3.

A final objection is that it isn't clear why premise 2 is true. Is existing in reality *always* better than existing only in the conception? Surely, World War III is better existing only in the conception and not in reality.

The modern version of the ontological argument addresses all three objections, however. On the modern version, what the greatest possible being has is *necessary* existence, not mere existence. Necessarily existing means existing in all possible worlds, not simply our own world. So:

* While it is possible for a greatest possible island to exist, it is not possible for a greatest possible island to *necessarily* exist. Islands are, by definition, concrete contingent objects. Contingent objects exist in some possible worlds, but not others. So, a "necessarily existing greatest possible island" could not exist, whereas a "necessarily existing greatest possible being" could.

* While we might question whether "existing" is a property, "necessarily existing" is clearly a property. That is, it is something which a thing can fail to have. A thing can both exist and

yet fail to have the property of necessarily existing. (You and I, for example, exist, but don't necessarily exist).

* While it's plausible that existing in reality is sometimes worse than existing only in conception, *necessarily existing* in all possible worlds does seem like a perfection which makes a thing greater, much like being omnipotent (all powerful) and omniscient (all knowing).

M. Benefits of the Ontological Argument

Many people doubt that the Ontological argument is sound, even though it is very difficult to say why it is unsound. However, those who accept the ontological argument find it beneficial for supporting traditional theism. If a greatest possible being necessarily exists, and we define "God" as "the greatest possible being", then God necessarily exists. Saying "God is the greatest possible being" is not a substantive claim, like "Bachelors are messy." Rather, it is a definitional claim—the word "God" just *means* "greatest possible being", much like "bachelor" just means "unmarried male".

A greatest possible being will have all of the "perfections"—that is, for all of the ways in which a thing can be great, God will be the greatest in that respect. The three perfections which are the focus of the philosophy of religion are:

Omniscience	all-knowing, knowing all of the facts
Omnipotence	all-powerful, able to do whatever is logically possible
Omnibenevolence	all-good, incapable of doing evil

To these are often added:

Omnipresence	all-present; present at all points in space
Eternal	present at all points in time
Immutability	unchanging; always constant
Freedom	independent of outside forces
Self-existing	not created by or dependent on anything else for existence

However, these "benefits" of the ontological argument at expressing the traditional notion of God are also its greatest costs. If God is all-powerful, all-knowing, and all-good, then why is there so much evil in the world? This will become one of the most persuasive arguments for atheism.

N. The Problem of Evil: The First Version

Notice that all of the arguments for the existence of God are ones in which God explains why we are in the world that we are in. The Teleological argument says that God *designed* our world. The Cosmological argument says that God chose to actualize our world out of the many possible worlds which could have been. The Ontological argument says that God is omnipotent—that is, God has the power to make our world however God pleases. It would seem natural to suppose that God, being the greatest possible being, would make the best of all possible worlds.

However, the world that we are in is not a good world. Instead, we live in a world which is often unjust and in which there is tremendous suffering with no apparent purpose. In one of our readings, B. C. Johnson tells the story of a young child caught in a burning building. In another of our readings, Dostoevsky's character Ivan Karamazov relates the story of a child hunted down by a wealthy landowner and mauled by his dogs while his mother watched, a crime for which the wealthy landowner is never punished. Our world produces a regular supply of war, genocide, slavery, and complete indifference. Even when people manage to be on their best behavior, they are prone to get sick from diseases and plagues, suffer from famines and droughts, and have their lives turned upside down by earthquakes, floods, and other natural disasters.

We might construct a *Reductio* argument against the existence of God by this method.

Argument 5.1N–Version 1

1. God exists (assumption).
2. If God exists, then God is all-good.
3. God is ultimately responsible for everything which occurs.
4. An all-good being cannot be ultimately responsible for evil.
5. Evil events do occur.
6. Contradiction! (3, 4)
C. God does not exist.

Premises 2 and 3 come from the definition of God. Since God is the Ultimate Explainer of our world, it follows that God is Ultimately Responsible for what happens in the world, including the evil events which happened. After all, God could have brought into existence a different world, without those same evil events.

However, recall the *dialectic* of our argument: that is, who is on the offense, and who is on the defense. Earlier, when arguments for the existence of God were given, the theist was on the offense, and the atheist was on the defense. This meant that the atheist was entitled to make assumptions which the theist disagreed with without having to offer proof for them, since the burden of proof was on the theist. For example, an atheist does not have to know personally how to provide an explanation for every complex and orderly phenomenon in nature in order to resist the teleological argument, but only has to show that it is plausible enough that these things might be explained without God. Likewise, an atheist does not have to come up with a complete explanation for the religious experiences of those who claim to have them, but only has to show it is plausible enough that there could be an alternative explanation.

However, in this case, the theist is on the defense. The theist only needs to show that it is plausible enough to think that one of the premises is false. When on the defensive, the theist is entitled to make assumptions about God or the world without having to prove them—by appealing, for instance traditional religious teachings. A very common teaching in monotheistic religions is that our world is not, in fact, the world which God created. Rather, while God originally created humans to live in a perfect Eden or Paradise, it is said that humans fell from that world to Earth as a result of a free choice to act wrongly. Because of this, Earth is an imperfect world defined by suffering and death, a world which is only partly the product of divine design, and which is partly the product of human wrongdoing:

> Allah said, "Descend, being to one another enemies. And for you on the earth is a place of settlement and enjoyment for a time." He said, "Therein you will live, and therein you will die, and from it you will be brought forth." (Quran 7:24–25).
>
> And unto Adam he said, . . . "cursed is the earth for thy sake; in sorrow shalt thou eat of it all the days of thy life . . . And the Lord God sent him forth from the garden of Eden." (Genesis 3:17,23)

At this point, the theist may appeal to a common principle of legal responsibility known as the "Doctrine of Double Effect"—one may foresee an evil effect resulting from one's actions, but not be responsible for the evil effect, provided that one did not intend the evil effect to happen—for instance, if it happens because of the intentions of someone else. Suppose a professor allows for a take-home essay exam, knowing that some students will use the opportunity to cheat, but most students will benefit from the time to work on the exam. The professor is not responsible for the cheating, even though she knew it would occur—the student caught cheating bears full responsibility. Similarly, while God, being omniscient, must foreknow that the evil events in the world would occur, God would not be ultimately responsible for the evil events if they are unintended consequences, resulting not from God's intentions but from the intentions of humans.

O. Why Doesn't God Intervene?—The Second Version

However, even if the theist can hold that God is not strictly *responsible* for causing the evil in the world, it seems like the theist must still admit that God *allows* evil, and *fails to prevent* the evil from occurring. If I know that my neighbor intends to murder someone, and I have the power to stop him by calling the police, then I still have a responsibility to call the police and stop the murder, even if I would not be responsible for the murder itself. Likewise, suppose I am walking down the street when I happen to come across a man drowning a child in a swimming pool. If I simply walk on by, or stop to observe the scene indifferently, then my failure to intervene seems morally wrong. I may not be responsible for the drowning in the way the man who drowns the child is, but neither can I be excused for my inaction.

Yet this seems like what the theist must say about God: that God, having the power to intervene at any moment to prevent the many tragic events in our world, simply watches them happen without doing anything about it. The revised argument goes like this:

Argument 5.1O–Version 2

1. God exists, and is all-good, all-knowing, and all-powerful. (assumption)
2. If someone all-good knows an evil event will occur and has the power to prevent the evil, then that person will intervene to prevent the evil event and the evil event won't occur.
3. God intervenes to prevent evil events and evil events do not occur. (From 1, 2)

4. Evil events do occur.

5. Contradiction! (3, 4)

C. God does not exist.

The traditional theist is not able to reject the first premise, since it follows from the definition of God as the "greatest possible being". Someone might hold to a non-traditional form of theism and accept an all-powerful, all-knowing god who is not perfectly good, but who is either morally neutral, or careless and prone to mistakes, or simply evil. However, such a god would not be worthy of the worship or praise usually attributed to God. Someone might hold that God is not all-powerful, or not all-knowing, while still accepting a version of the teleological argument, but this person could not accept the cosmological or ontological argument.

Someone might accept that God is all-knowing, but might hold (contrary to the Standard View) that there are no facts about the future, and so nothing can be known about them. If true, this would explain why God does not always prevent evil before it starts. However, it seems like some evils may occur for an extended period of time before a stop is put to them—again, genocides may last for months or years, and the practice of slavery lasted for centuries. Within that time period, surely God could have intervened.

Likewise, it would be difficult for the traditional theist to reject the forth premise. Someone who holds that there are no facts about morality and that nothing is objectively "good" or "evil"—that "good" and "evil" are determined by what someone subjectively believes about them–would deny the forth premise. So, in order to argue against the existence of God using this argument, someone must accept that there are objective truths about morality independent of what people believe about them, a position we'll discuss in Unit 6 known as Moral Objectivism. Some theists instead hold to a kind of moral subjectivism. They might hold that morality is an expression of our social practices, feelings, desires, or will, for example, saying something is "evil" is simply saying that one feels unhappy about it and desires that it not exist. Or they might hold that moral truths depend upon on the will and commands of God— that is, not that God commands and wills according to what is intrinsically good, but that God makes something "good" or "evil" by commanding or willing it to be so.

If this were true, then it would be a definitional truth that there would not exist anything truly "evil" in the world, since even things which appear like great evils to us—the black plague, for instance—are only "evil" in the sense that we desire that they not exist. But, on this view, we are confused: Since God has willed these things to exist, they are good. However, while traditional theists hold that morality depends on God ontologically, that is, the nature of God is what grounds the nature of the good—they do not generally hold that morally depends on God volitionally: that is, that morality is independent of God's nature and depends instead on some arbitrary act of will.

So, the best option for the traditional theist is to reject premise 2: *If someone all-good knows an evil event will occur and has the power to prevent the evil, then that person will intervene to prevent the evil event and the evil event won't occur.* And, thinking about this premise, we can think of many counterexamples. For example, a good person can allow a lesser evil event to occur in order to prevent a greater evil, or allow it for a greater good which outweighs the evil. For example, a government might impose a quarantine on a few people infected with a highly contagious and deadly disease in order to protect everyone else from contracting it.

So, premise 2 seems false. A good person *can* know an evil event will occur and fail to intervene to prevent the evil, *if that person has a sufficiently good reason to do so.* The existence of God is compatible with the existence of evil, provided that God has a good reason to allow the evil. But what sort of reason could be good enough to explain the sort of evil we see in the world?

P. No Sufficiently Good Reason—The Third Version

Because it isn't obvious what sorts of reasons would justify the great degree of evil we see in the world, we can formulate a revised version of the argument.

Argument 5.1P – Version 3

1. God exists, and is all-good, all-knowing, and all-powerful. (assumption)
2. If someone all-good knows an evil event will occur and has the power to prevent the evil, then that person will intervene to prevent the evil event and the evil event won't occur, <u>unless that person has a sufficiently good reason to do so.</u>
3. God intervenes to prevent evil events and evil events do not occur unless god has a sufficiently good reason to allow the evil. (1, 2)
4. Evil events do occur.
5. For at least some evil events, <u>God has no sufficiently good reason to allow the evil.</u>
6. Contradiction! (3, 4, 5)
C. God does not exist.

If the theist says that God allows evil for a reason, then it seems legitimate for us to ask what that reason is. The possible reasons God could have for allowing evil seem to fall into two categories:

Contingent Reasons: It might be that an evil event occurs in order to bring about some good event. For example, someone might break a leg and be sent to the hospital, and while in the hospital might meet someone and find true love. Or, someone might lose their life in order to save others. Or, someone might make a painful mistake, but learn and be stronger from the experience. Or, experiencing suffering might lead someone to become a better person, or to stop doing greater moral evil.

Necessary Reasons: It might be that there was no way in which God allow any less evil in the world without sacrificing some greater good. For instance, perhaps there is a logically necessary cosmic balance of good and evil, and for God to reduce the evil at one place and time would cause evil at another place and time. Or, perhaps without the degree of evil we have, it would be impossible to appreciate the goodness of the good.

However, since God is capable of bringing about any logically possible world, then the reasons God has for allowing evil cannot be contingent reasons. God is supposed to be all-powerful. That means that God could have brought about a world with the same positive outcomes without using the negative as a means to achieve it. For instance, there is no necessary connection between breaking a leg and meeting the love of one's life. God could have brought about another possible world in which the same two people found each other and fell in love without the broken leg. Rather than requiring one soldier to give his life by jumping on a grenade to save others, God could have prevented the grenade from exploding entirely. That is what *omnipotent* means! It seems reasonable to think that God could have someone learn a lesson without the painful experience, or become a better person without experiencing suffering—for instance, by surrounding them with people who have a positive influence on them. Further, there seem like many cases where suffering occurs without any beneficial effect. For instance, many people suffer and only become more bitter and impatient, not more kind, through the experience.

Thus, the only reasons which God would have to allow evil are necessary reasons—the evil in our world must be the minimum amount which is logically unavoidable in order to achieve our degree of good. However, it seems like the theist owes some explanation of what these reasons could be.

The most common reason offered for the evil in the world is that evil is necessary for *free will*.

Q. The Free Will Defense

The theist can claim that all of the evil which God allows in the world, God allows out of deference to human free will, because free will is such a great good that it outweighs much evil. While there can be moral *value* without free will—some things might be intrinsically good even in a deterministic world—perhaps there can't be morally praiseworthy *actions* without free will, since we can only praise someone for doing something that they had the option not to do. So someone could see how free will is necessary for the highest good—the choices made by a good will—and hence worth the cost of permitting people to also choose evil.

Again, the theist does not have to prove that free will exists—the theist is on the defense, not the offense. The theist also does not need to prove that free will is a great moral good. Some students have a strong intuition that it would be a better world if God simply created people so that they were incapable of doing wrong, since it would be better to avoid evil altogether. However, other students have a strong intuition that eliminating evil in this way would also eliminate the good, since there is nothing worth praising in doing good if you can't help but do it. Some students feel revolted at the idea of being made into a "robot", while other students feel like it would be a great relief to not have free will. The feeling that one has free will can be both exhilarating and frightening, much like the feeling one gets when standing on the edge of a tall building without a guard rail, aware that at any moment one could choose to jump. However, the theist is on defense, so the theist may simply assume that free will is a great moral good.

The free will defense against the problem of evil reveals that we've not yet defined what we mean by *evil*. The word is ambiguous, as Swinburne points out, between two senses:

active evil, or *moral evil*, which has to do with an agent's evil intentions, such as the evil of intending to cause someone else to fail in order to gloat at their failure, or the evil of intending to hurt someone in an act of revenge.

passive evil, or suffering, which has to do with negative experiences that we would rather not have, such as the evil of failing, or the evil or being hurt. Included in this category are both physical and emotional pain, as well as *natural evils* such as cancer or heart disease, or losing one's home or one's family in a catastrophic flood.

A simple example to draw the distinction is this. Suppose that a sadist is torturing an innocent person for fun. Active evil is what the torturer is doing. Passive evil is what the tortured person experiences.

Swinburne holds that the free will defense applies only to active evil, not to passive evil. Perhaps God can't prevent active evil without eliminating free will. However, it seems as though God could prevent or reduce the suffering in the world without taking away free will. No one can claim that a child who has cancer has it because the child chose to have cancer. Nothing about free will is involved in a catastrophic flood. Again, God is omnipotent. God could have allowed active evils without allowing the suffering which accompanies those evils. God could have made a world, for instance, in which sadists thought that they were torturing their victims, but God arranged things so that the torture victim actually experienced bliss.

R. The Argument from Pointless Suffering—The Fourth Version

A simpler word for "passive evil" is simply *suffering*. The problem is that at least some suffering in our world seems pointless. So, we might reformulate the problem of evil by replacing the word "evil" with "suffering".

Argument 5.1R – Version 4

1. God exists, and is all-good, all-knowing, and all-powerful. (assumption)
2. If someone all-good knows <u>suffering</u> will occur and has the power to prevent the suffering, then that person will intervene to prevent the suffering and the suffering won't occur, unless that person has a sufficiently good reason to do so.
3. God intervenes to prevent suffering, and suffering does not occur unless God has a sufficienlty good reason to allow it. (1, 2)
4. <u>Suffering</u> does occur.
5. For at least some suffering, God has no sufficiently good reason to allow the <u>suffering</u>.
6. Contradiction! (3, 4, 5)
C. God does not exist

The most controversial premise will be premise 5, of course. What reasons could God have to allow suffering? Swinburne, a theist, proposes that God made the world incomplete, so that we could join him in the work of completing it. Our experiences of suffering are simply our being aware of the incompleteness of the world, and this feeling of suffering gives us an incentive to try to complete or finish the world. It is not that any sort of evil exists in our world, but only an absence of good—much as cold is the absence of heat. Suffering is not evil in itself, but it is simply a representation of an absence of good—suffering is an awareness of what is lacking. Creating us so that we didn't suffer at all would require creating us ignorant of the kind of world we lived in and indifferent to it. And it is a greater good for God to allow this incomplete world, so that we can participate in its creation, than it would be for God to simply create us in a ready-made paradise from the start.

Still, even if one accepts Swinburne's account for suffering *in general*, there seem like many *specific* cases of suffering we can think of where it seems like God could effectively prevent that suffering without removing our ability to "complete" the world. Suffering often seems pointless.

Maybe there is no good explanation for suffering at all. In fact, the attempt to try to explain suffering and justify it seems almost like an insult to the person who has been through it—part of the experience of suffering is the experience of pointlessness. In the Jewish scriptures, a man named Job endures intense suffering, symbolic of the suffering of the Jewish people themselves during the Babylonian exile, and in other eras. In the book, God condemns those who try to justify or explain away this suffering as somehow Job's fault or something Job deserved. Instead, the answer to suffering is that God's ways are higher than man's ways, and unknowable from a human perspective—and God has reasons for allowing suffering that are beyond our understanding.

Perhaps all of the evil events in our world culminate in some grand picture we can't appreciate from our point of view. The evil moments are the dissonant notes in a larger harmony which is more perfect and more beautiful because of them, but the song stretches so far beyond our lifetimes that we can't really hear it.

Suppose that this is the right response. Suppose that God allows evil for reasons beyond our "ken" (or understanding). We might then ask ourselves, suggests B. C. Johnson, whether we find more consistent with our evidence the hypothesis that:

(a) Suffering has no purpose.

(b) Suffering has a purpose which we can't understand.

If we already believe that God exists, then perhaps (b) is plausible. However, if we don't assume from the beginning that God exists, and we interpret our observations through that lens, Johnson thinks that hypothesis (a) seems to better explain our evidence than hypothesis (b), so we should conclude that premise 5 is true.

S. Dostoevsky's Argument—the Fifth Version

Unfortunately, the preceding discussion of the problem of evil makes it sounds like a debate over whether or not God has made a mistake about economics. Russell asserts that the amount of suffering in the world isn't worth whatever value that God has produced through it, and his opponent argues that it's silly to think that we could possibly know what's ultimately valuable to God. But this misses the point. The real debate is not about whether God has placed a good trade or not. The debate is whether any sort of trade is acceptable to begin with.

There is something unsettling about the idea of using someone's suffering as a means to an end. Treating someone else's pain as a means to achieving some higher goal of ours, no matter how lofty our goal might be, is treating them as deserving of less dignity and worth than we have.

Dostoevsky, through the character of Ivan, urges us to consider whether the suffering of even one child could be justified for a sufficiently lofty goal. Suppose that after death God unites everyone together in heaven, and all people enjoy completely harmonious relationships with one another and the highest feeling of blissfulness. All of the highest pleasure for all of eternity would seem to outweigh whatever unpleasantness we experienced on earth. However, suppose that in order to achieve this heavenly state for the human race, it was necessary that one young child at one point in time be tortured to death and never enter heaven. Would a good God allow the child to be tortured for the greater good?

For Dostoevsky, the answer is definitively *no!* Ivan states that he would rather "return his ticket" to this heavenly state than be part of the torture of that child. A god who allowed that wouldn't be good.

Much like the term "evil" in our argument was ambiguous and needed clarification, the term "good" in our argument also seems to need clarification. What does it mean to say that God is all-good?

We could mean that God is *good for us*. However, it's not clear why being the most perfect possible being would require being good for humans. Defining the goodness of God in terms of the value God provides to humans seems a little bit backward. Why think that our suffering is at all significant or worthy of attention in the scope of the universe?

We might mean that God is *exalted*. God might be "perfect" in the way that a "perfect" triangle has three equal sides and three equal angles, that is, God's perfection involves being infinitely above everything else and completely self-contained, dependent on nothing. The Stoics conceived of moral goodness in this way: the morally good life was the life of perfect freedom and detachment, where one was affected by nothing and unmoved even by the suffering one saw. If God is good in the Stoic sense, then it would be a *defect* for God to be particularly concerned with human affairs and suffering.

However, in assuming that being all-good requires preventing suffering, we seem to be appealing to a notion of "goodness" that involves not simply being great and exalted, and not simply fulfilling one's duty, and certainly not simply engaging in an economic transaction to maximize gain, but, rather, something more like being *compassionate*. Compassion for the good that God is supposed to haveseems to be inconsistent with allowing unnecessary suffering:

Argument 5.1S – Version 5

1. God exists, and is <u>all compassionate</u>, all-knowing, and all-powerful. (assumption)
2. If someone <u>all-compassionate</u> knows suffering will occur and has the power to prevent the suffering, then that person will intervene to prevent the suffering and the suffering won't occur, unless that person has a sufficiently good reason to do so.

3. God intervenes to prevent suffering and suffering does not occur unless God has a sufficiently good reason to allow it. (1, 2)

4. Suffering does occur.

5. For at least some suffering, God has no sufficiently good reason to allow the suffering.

6. Contradiction! (3, 4, 5)

C. God does not exist

The problem of evil for Dostoevsky is the problem of how God can look in on the suffering in the world, not intervening to prevent it, and yet still be truly compassionate rather than the Stoic ideal. Suffering is inherently pointless—the attempt to give suffering a higher meaning or purpose in a divine economy turns God into some sort of stock trader. The question isn't whether suffering has a point, but whether God is compassionate if God doesn't stop it.

Why is it that we think premise 2 is true? The term "compassionate" literally means "feeling with" someone—the Greek equivalent is "sympathy". We associate someone being compassionate or sympathetic with that person trying to make life better for the person they feel compassion toward. When I feel badly for a student in the midst of a personal crisis, for example, I try to do what little I can by extending deadlines, because I feel compassion. However, does this mean that an all-compassionate being would stop all suffering before it starts?

Consider that sometimes our compassion is not so selfless as we pretend it to be. Seeing someone who is suffering makes me very uncomfortable. One way to relieve that discomfort is to try to resolve it by doing something for the person who is suffering. However, an equally effective way is to simply stop seeing the person who is suffering—to put them out of sight. Our society is content with suffering in prisons, for instance, provided that it doesn't appear too vividly on television. Sometimes our sense of "compassion" can drive us to want to intervene where we ought not to intervene. An eagerness to solve everyone else's problems leads quickly to failing to respect their autonomy and distinctness from myself: much like an army invading other nations in order to save their people from corrupt governments finds that the local inhabitants do not particularly want to be "saved" by the foreign invaders, other people are likely to be unhappy with my "sympathy" if I take it to mean that I must always save them.

For example, it might be easier to give someone who is going through withdrawal from an addiction the thing they crave, or easier to cut oneself off from them entirely; it is much harder to go through the experience with them. It might be easier to try to make a grieving person feel better than it is to sit with them in their grief. The desire to make someone else's suffering disappear can often be selfishness disguised as compassion—what I want is for my own discomfort to go away, for the suffering person to go away, so that I don't have to feel compassion any longer.

Dostoevsky was a theist, and Dostoevsky's own response to this argument would be to deny premise 2. Instead of preventing suffering, which can be done without compassion, what compassion requires is experiencing the suffering of someone else. So, for Dostoevsky, the omni-benevolence of God requires that God experiences the full sum of human suffering, as vividly as those suffering it experience it. Suffering obtains meaning as a kind of religious experience of what it is like to be God. However, the experience of suffering is essentially an experience of being imperfect, limited, and weak, and this may seem hard to reconcile with the perfection and power of God.

There are other arguments for atheism besides the problem of evil. For example, it is sometimes argued that the traditional theist's definition of God is incoherent and self-contradictory; for instance, being omnipresent might be thought to conflict with being transcendent and outside the world, or being immutable might be thought to conflict with having freedom. Others argue that theism is simply an empty and meaningless hypothesis, since it seems hard to say what difference we would see in the world to tell us whether God existed or not. By the theist's own admission, God is transcendent and indescribable, so one might doubt that any talk about "God" is meaningful. Several arguments for theism depend on an assumption that we have some *a priori* knowledge of the Principle of Sufficient Reason, but empiricists will deny that we have this knowledge. Others argue that theism conflicts with some other claim that the theist typically holds, such as the existence of free will. All of these are arguments that can be offered for atheism. However, the problem of evil is the argument which most immediately demands a response from the theist.

T. Conclusions

Many students find it refreshing to discuss religious topics like the existence of God outside of the usual context, in a philosophical context. We've focused on logical arguments for both sides and have, I hope, avoided common stereotypes.

Theists tend to be stereotyped as pulled by strong emotions into making "leaps of faith" against reason; but in our discussion, it is the theist's commitment to reason, and to a reasonable universe, which have been the basis for theism. Atheists tend to be stereotyped as skeptical about morality and breaking with moral conventions; but in our discussion, it is the atheist's commitment to morality, and to refusing to ignore and excuse injustice, which have been the basis for atheism.

Of course, there are aspects of religion which do not involve making claims about the world—rather, they form part of a way of life. The practices of meditating, worshipping, fasting, praying, offering a sacrifice, taking a vow, giving a blessing, volunteering time to serve a cause, or making a pilgrimage—these are activities, not assertions. Knowing a way of life is not a matter of knowing the conclusion to an argument. However, understanding the arguments on both sides will certainly make a difference to how one creates a way of life.

❋ 5.2 "The Ontological Argument" ❋

selections from Prosolgium
by Anselm of Canterbury

❋ ❋

© Mirages.nl/Shutterstock.com

St. Anselm (1033–1109) was a monk and philosopher who served as the Archbishop of Canterbury. Anselm is the first known to have developed the Ontological Argument for the existence of God. Anselm's argument is a predecessor of Descartes's argument.

Anselm argued that we can prove the existence of God by definition, using logic alone. His argument is a type of *Reductio*: assume that a *being than which none greater can be conceived* does not exist. It follows that there is a being greater than it which does exist, which is a contradiction. So, there exists a being than which none greater can be conceived; which is what we mean by "God".

Anselm's argument is typically printed alongside a response by the monk Gaunilo, who objected to Anselm's argument, and Anselm's response to Gaunilo.

Here are some questions to think about as you read:

* Why does the argument assume that God *doesn't* exist?

* How is existing supposed to follow from the definition of God?

* Why doesn't defining God amount to assuming that God exists?

* Why does Anselm say "being than which none greater can be conceived", rather than "greatest being which can be conceived"?

* How did Gaunilo object to Anselm?

* How did Anselm respond?

Proslogion

CHAPTER II.

. . . AND so, Lord, do you, who do give understanding to faith, give me, so far as you knowest it to be profitable, to understand that you are as we believe; and that you are that which we believe. And indeed, we believe that you are a being than which nothing greater can be conceived. Or is there no such nature, since the fool has said in his heart, there is no God? (Psalms xiv. 1). But, at any rate, this very fool, when he hears of this being of which I speak —a being than which nothing greater can be conceived —understands what be hears, and what he understands is in his understanding; although he does not understand it to exist.

For, it is one thing for an object to be in the understanding, and another to understand that the object exists. When a painter first conceives of what he will afterwards perform, he has it in his understanding, but be does not yet understand it to be, because he has not yet performed it. But after he has made the painting, be both has it in his understanding, and he understands that it exists, because he has made it.

Hence, even the fool is convinced that something exists in the understanding, at least, than which nothing greater can be conceived. For, when he hears of this, he understands it. And whatever is understood, exists in the understanding. And assuredly that, than which nothing greater can be conceived, cannot exist in the understanding alone. For, suppose it exists in the understanding alone: then it can be conceived to exist in reality; which is greater.

Therefore, if that, than which nothing greater can be conceived, exists in the understanding alone, the very being, than which nothing greater can be conceived, is one, than which a greater can be conceived. But obviously this is impossible. Hence, there is doubt that there exists a being, than which nothing greater can be conceived, and it exists both in the understanding and in reality.

CHAPTER III.

God cannot be conceived not to exist. —God is that, than which nothing greater can be conceived. —That which can be conceived not to exist is not God.

AND it assuredly exists so truly, that it cannot be conceived not to exist. For, it is possible to conceive of a being which cannot be conceived not to exist; and this is greater than one which can be conceived not to exist. Hence, if that, than which nothing greater can be conceived, can be conceived not to exist, it is not that, than which nothing greater can be conceived. But this is an irreconcilable contradiction. There is, then, so truly a being than which nothing greater can be conceived to exist, that it cannot even be conceived not to exist;. and this being you are, O Lord, our God.

So truly, therefore, do you exist, O Lord, my God, that you can not be conceived not to exist; and rightly. For, if a mind could conceive of a being better than you, the creature would rise above the Creator; and this is most absurd. And, indeed, whatever else there is, except you alone, can be conceived not to exist. To you alone, therefore, it belongs to exist more truly than all other beings, and hence in a higher degree than all others. For, whatever else exists does not exist so truly, and hence in a less degree it belongs to it to exist. Why, then, has the fool said in his heart, there is no God (Psalms xiv. 1), since it is so evident, to a rational mind, that you do exist in the highest degree of all? Why, except that he is dull and a fool?

CHAPTER IV.

How the fool has said in his heart what cannot be conceived. –*A thing may be conceived in two ways: (1) when the word signifying it is conceived; (2) when the thing itself is understood As far as the word goes, God can be conceived not to exist; in reality he cannot.*

BUT how has the fool said in his heart what he could not conceive; or how is it that he could not conceive what he said in his heart? since it is the same to say in the heart, and to conceive.

But, if really, nay, since really, he both conceived, because he said in his heart; and did not say in his heart, because he could not conceive; there is more than one way in which a thing is said in the heart or conceived. For, in one sense, an object is conceived, when the word signifying it is conceived; and in another, when the very entity, which the object is, is understood.

In the former sense, then, God can be conceived not to exist; but in the latter, not at all. For no one who understands what fire and water are can conceive fire to be water, in accordance with the nature of the facts themselves, although this is possible according

to the words. So, then, no one who understands what God is can conceive that God does not exist; although he says these words in his heart, either without any or with some foreign, signification. For, God is that than which a greater cannot be conceived. And he who thoroughly understands this, assuredly understands that this being so truly exists, that not even in concept can it be non-existent. Therefore, he who understands that God so exists, cannot conceive that he does not exist.

I thank you, gracious Lord, I thank you; because what I formerly believed by your bounty, I now so understand by your illumination, that if I were unwilling to believe that you do exist, I should not be able not to understand this to be true.

CHAPTER V.

God is whatever it is better to be than not to be; and he, as the only self-existent being, creates all things from nothing.

WHAT are you, then, Lord God, than whom nothing greater can be conceived? But what are you, except that which, as the highest of all beings, alone exists through itself, and creates all other things from nothing? For, whatever is not this is less than a thing which can be conceived of. But this cannot be conceived of you. What good, therefore, does the supreme Good lack, through which every good is? Therefore, you are just, truthful, blessed, and whatever it is better to be than not to be. For it is better to be just than not just; better to be blessed than not blessed.

CHAPTER VI.

How God is sensible (sensibilis) although he is not a body. —God is sensible, omnipotent, compassionate, passionless; for it is better to be these than not be. He who in any way knows, is not improperly said in some sort to feel.

❀ ❀

BUT, although it is better for you to be sensible, omnipotent, compassionate, passionless, than not to be these things; how are you sensible, if you are not a body; or omnipotent, if you has not all powers; or at once compassionate and passionless? For, if only corporeal things are sensible, since the senses encompass a body and are in a body, how are you sensible, although you are not a body, but a supreme Spirit, who is superior to body? But, if feeling is only cognition, or for the sake of cognition, —for he who feels obtains knowledge in accordance with the proper functions of his senses; as through sight, of colors; through taste, of flavors, —whatever in any way cognises is not inappropriately said, in some sort, to feel.

Therefore, O Lord, although you are not a body yet you are truly sensible in the highest degree in respect of this, that you do cognise all things in the highest degree; and not as an animal cognises, through a corporeal sense.

CHAPTER VII.

How he is omnipotent, although there are many things of which he is not capable. —To be capable of being corrupted, or of lying, is not power, but impotence. God can do nothing by virtue of impotence, and nothing has power against him.

BUT how are you omnipotent, if you are not capable of all things? Or, if you can not be corrupted, and can not lie, nor make what is true, false —as, for example, if you should make what has been done not to have been done, and the like. —how are you capable of all things? Or else to be capable of these things is not power, but impotence. For, he who is capable of these things is capable of what is not for his good, and of what he ought not to do; and the more capable of them he is, the more power have adversity and perversity against him; and the less has he himself against these.

He, then, who is thus capable is so not by power, but by impotence. For, he is not said to be able because he is able of himself, but because his impotence gives something else power over him. Or, by a figure of speech, just as many words are improperly applied, as when we use "to be" for "not to be," and "to do" for what is really not to do, "or to do nothing." For, often we say to a man who denies the existence of something: "It is as you say it to be," though it might seem more proper to say, "It is not, as you say it is not." In the same way, we say, "This man sits just as that man does," or, "This man rests just as that man does"; although to sit is not to do anything, and to rest is to do nothing.

So, then, when one is said to have the power of doing or experiencing what is not for his good, or what he ought not to do, impotence is understood in the word power. For, the more he possesses this power, the more powerful are adversity and perversity against him, and the more powerless is he against them.

Therefore, O Lord, our God, the more truly are you omnipotent, since you are capable of nothing through impotence, and nothing has power against you.

CHAPTER VIII.

How he is compassionate and passionless. God is compassionate, in terms of our experience, because we experience the effect of compassion. God is not compassionate, in terms of his own being, because he does not experience the feeling (affectus) of compassion.

BUT how are you compassionate, and, at the same time, passionless? For, if you are passionless, you do not feel sympathy; and if you do not feel sympathy, your heart is not wretched from sympathy for the wretched ; but this it is to be compassionate. But if you are not compassionate, whence comes so great consolation to the wretched? How, then, are you compassionate and not compassionate, O Lord, unless because you are compassionate in terms of our experience, and not compassionate in terms of your being.

Truly, you are so in terms of our experience, but you are not so in terms of your own. For, when you behold us in our wretchedness, we experience the effect of compassion, but you do not experience the feeling. Therefore, you are both compassionate, because you do save the wretched, and spare those who sin against you; and not compassionate because you are affected by no sympathy for wretchedness.

IN BEHALF OF THE FOOL.

AN ANSWER TO THE ARGUMENT OF ANSELM IN THE PROSLOGIUM BY GAUNILO, A MONK OF MARMOUTIER

Gaunilon's Argument against Anselm

It is said that somewhere in the ocean is an island, which, because of the difficulty, or rather the impossibility, of discovering what does not exist, is called the lost island. And they say that this island has an inestimable wealth of all manner of riches and delicacies in greater abundance than is told of the Islands of the Blest; and that having no owner or inhabitant, it is more excellent than all other countries, which are inhabited by mankind, in the abundance with which it is stored.

Now if some one should tell me that there is such an island, I should easily understand his words, in which there is no difficulty. But suppose that he went on to say, as if by a logical inference: "You can no longer doubt that this island which is more excellent than all lands exists somewhere, since you have no doubt that it is in your understanding. And since it is more excellent not to be in the understanding alone, but to exist both in

the understanding and in reality, for this reason it must exist. For if it does not exist, any land which really exists will be more excellent than it; and so the island already understood by you to be more excellent will not be more excellent."

If a man should try to prove to me by such reasoning that this island truly exists, and that its existence should no longer be doubted, either I should believe that he was jesting, or I know not which I ought to regard as the greater fool: myself, supposing that I should allow this proof; or him, if he should suppose that he had established with any certainty the existence of this island. For he ought to show first that the hypothetical excellence of this island exists as a real and indubitable fact, and in no wise as any unreal object, or one whose existence is uncertain, in my understanding. . . .

Anselm's Reply to Gaunilon

. . . . BUT, you say, it is as if one should suppose an island in the ocean, which surpasses all lands in its fertility, and which, because of the difficulty, or the impossibility, of discovering what does not exist, is called a lost island; and should say that there be no doubt that this island truly exists in reality, for this reason, that one who hears it described easily understands what he hears.

Now I promise confidently that if any man shall devise anything existing either in reality or in concept alone (except that than which a greater be conceived) to which he can adapt the sequence of my reasoning, I will discover that thing, and will give him his lost island, not to be lost again.

But it now appears that this being than which a greater is inconceivable cannot be conceived not to be, because it exists on so assured a ground of truth; for otherwise it would not exist at all.

Hence, if any one says that he conceives this being not to exist, I say that at the time when he conceives of this either he conceives of a being than which a greater is inconceivable, or he does not

conceive at all. If he does not conceive, he does not conceive of the non-existence of that of which he does not conceive. But if he does conceive, he certainly conceives of a being which cannot be even conceived not to exist. For if it could be conceived not to exist, it could be conceived to have a beginning and an end. But this is impossible.

He, then, who conceives of this being conceives of a being which cannot be even conceived not to exist; but he who conceives of this being does not conceive that it does not exist; else he conceives what is inconceivable. The non-existence, then, of that than which a greater cannot be conceived is inconceivable. . . . .

You say, moreover, that whereas I assert that this supreme being cannot be conceived not to exist, it might better be said that its non-existence, or even the possibility of its non-existence, cannot be understood.

But it was more proper to say, it cannot be conceived. For if I had said that the object itself cannot be understood not to exist, possibly you yourself, who say that in accordance with the true meaning of the term what is unreal cannot be understood, would offer the objection that nothing which is can be understood not to be, for the non-existence of what exists is unreal: hence God would not be the only being of which it could be said, it is impossible to understand its non-existence. For thus one of those beings which most certainly exist can be understood not to exist in the same way in which certain other real objects can be understood not to exist.

But this objection, assuredly, cannot be urged against the term conception, if one considers the matter well. For although no objects which exist can be understood not to exist, yet all objects, except that which exists in the highest degree, can be conceived not to exist. For all those objects, and those alone, can be conceived not to exist, which have a beginning or end or composition of parts: also, as I have already said, whatever at any place or at any time does not exist as a whole.

That being alone, on the other hand, cannot be conceived not to exist, in which any conception discovers neither beginning nor end nor composition of parts, and which any conception finds always and everywhere as a whole.

Be assured, then, that you can conceive of your own non-existence, although you are most certain that you exist. I am surprised that you should have admitted that you are ignorant of this. For we conceive of the non-existence of many objects which we know to exist, and of the existence of many which we know not to exist; not by forming the opinion that they so exist, but by imagining that they exist as we conceive of them.

And indeed, we can conceive of the non-existence of an object, although we know it to exist, because at the same time we can conceive of the former and know the latter. And we cannot conceive of the nonexistence of an object, so long as we know it to exist, because we cannot conceive at the same time of existence and non-existence.

If, then, one will thus distinguish these two senses of this statement, he will understand that nothing, so long as it is known to exist, can be conceived not to exist; and that whatever exists, except that being than which a greater cannot be conceived, can be conceived not to exist, even when it is known to exist.

So, then, of God alone it can be said that it is impossible to conceive of his non-existence; and yet many objects, so long as they exist, in one sense cannot be conceived not to exist. But in what sense God is to be conceived not to exist, I think has been shown clearly enough in my book.

❊ 5.3 "The Five Ways" ❊

selections from Summa Theologica
by Thomas Aquinas

✳ ✳

© Tupungato/Shutterstock.com

St. Thomas Aquinas (1225–1274) was a monk, philosopher and theologian. Following the model of the Muslim philosopher Averroes, Aquinas attempted to reconcile Aristotle's philosophy with his own Christian faith, pushing for a rational investigation. His *Summa Theologica* is primarily a theological work, but it deals also with ethics, and politics, and law. "The Five Ways", is a small but famous selection of that work.

Aquinas develops five different versions of the Cosmological argument for the existence of God. Cosmological arguments begin with some general feature of our world which needs explanation, like the fact that the world actually exists, and then argue that the chain of explanation must terminate with something that is outside of the realm of explanation, a kind of Ultimate Explainer.

Here are some questions to think about as you read:

* Which of the five arguments seems strongest to you? Which seems weakest? Why?

* Which arguments involve features of the world which science can now explain?

* Which arguments involve features of the world which science could never explain?

* How do all of Aquinas's arguments rely on the assumption that everything has an explanation?

* How do all of Aquinas's arguments rely on the assumption that nothing in our world explains itself?

389

The Five Ways

by *Thomas Aquinas*
Translated by Laurence Shapcote

The First Way: The Argument From Change

The existence of God can be shown in five ways. The first and clearest is taken from the idea of motion.

(1) Now it is certain, and our senses corroborate it, that some things in this world are in motion.

(2) But everything which is in motion is moved by something else.

(3) For nothing is in motion except in so far as it is in potentiality in relation to that towards which it is in motion.

(4) Now a thing causes movement in so far as it is in actuality. For to cause movement is nothing else than to bring something from potentiality to actuality; but a thing cannot be brought from potentiality to actuality except by something which exists in actuality, as, for example, that which is hot in actuality, like fire, makes wood, which is only hot in potentiality, to be hot in actuality, and thereby causes movement in it and alters it.

(5) But it is not possible that the same thing should be at the same time in actuality and potentiality in relation to the same thing, but only in relation to different things; for what is hot in actuality cannot at the same time be hot in potentiality, though it is at the same time cold in potentiality.

(6) It is impossible, therefore, that in relation to the same thing and in the same way anything should both cause movement and be caused, or that it should cause itself to move.

(7) Everything therefore that is in motion must be moved by something else. If therefore the thing which causes it to move be in motion, this too must be moved by something else, and so on.

(8) But we cannot proceed to infinity in this way, because in that case there would be no first mover, and in consequence, neither would there be any other mover; for secondary movers do not cause movement except they be moved by a first mover, as, for example, a stick cannot cause movement unless it is moved by the hand. Therefore it is necessary to stop at some first mover which is moved by nothing else. And this is what we all understand God to be.

The Second Way: The Argument From Causation

The Second Way is taken from the idea of the Efficient Cause.

(1) For we find that there is among material things a regular order of efficient causes.

(2) But we do not find, nor indeed is it possible, that anything is the efficient cause of itself,

for in that case it would be prior to itself, which is impossible.

(3) Now it is not possible to proceed to infinity in efficient causes.

(4) For if we arrange in order all efficient causes, the first is the cause of the intermediate, and the intermediate the cause of the last, whether the intermediate be many or only one.

(5) But if we remove a cause the effect is removed; therefore, if there is no first among efficient causes, neither will there be a last or an intermediate.

(6) But if we proceed to infinity in efficient causes there will be no first efficient cause, and thus there will be no ultimate effect, nor any intermediate efficient causes, which is dearly false. Therefore it is necessary to suppose the existence of some first efficient cause, and this men call God.

The Third Way: The Argument From Contingency

The Third Way rests on the idea of the "contingent" and the "necessary" and is as follows:

(1) Now we find that there are certain things in the Universe which are capable of existing and of not existing, for we find that some things are brought into existence arid then destroyed, and consequently are capable of being or not being.

(2) But it is impossible for all things which exist to be of this kind, because anything which is capable bf not existing, at some time or other does not exist.

(3) If therefore all things are capable of not existing, there was a time when nothing existed in the Universe.

(4) But if this is true there would also be nothing in existence now; because anything that does

not exist cannot begin to exist except by the agency of something which has existence. If therefore there was once nothing which existed, it would have been impossible for anything to begin to exist, and so nothing would exist now.

(5) This is clearly false. Therefore all things are not contingent, and there must be something which is necessary in the Universe.

(6) But everything which is necessary either has or has not the cause of its necessity from an outside source. Now it is not possible to proceed to infinity in necessary things which have a cause of their necessity, as has been proved in the case of efficient causes. Therefore it is necessary to suppose the existence of something which is necessary in itself, not having the cause of its necessity from any outside source, but which is the cause of necessity in others. And this "something" we call God.

The Fourth Way: The Argument From Degrees Of Excellence

The Fourth Way is taken from the degrees which are found in things.

(1) For among different things we find that one is more or less good or true or noble; and likewise in the case of other things of this kind.

(2) But the words "more" or "less" are used of different things in proportion as they approximate in their different ways to something which has the particular quality in the highest degree-e.g., we call a thing hotter when it approximates more nearly to that which is hot in the highest degree. There is therefore something which is true in the highest degree, good in the highest degree and noble in the highest degree;

❖ ❖

(3) and consequently there must be also something which has being in the highest degree. For things which are true in the highest degree also have being in the highest degree (see Aristotle, Metaphysics, 2).

(4) But anything which has a certain quality of any kind in the highest degree is also the cause of all things of that kind, as, for example, fire which is hot in the highest degree is the cause of all hot things (as is said in the same book).

(5) Therefore there exists something which is the cause of being, and goodness, and of every perfection in all existing things; and this we call God.

The Fifth Way: The Argument From Harmony

The Fifth Way is taken from the way in which nature is governed.

(1) For we observe that certain things which lack knowledge, such as natural bodies, work for an End. This is obvious, because they always, or at any rate very frequently, operate in the same way so as to attain the best possible result.

(2) Hence it is clear that they do not arrive at their goal by chance, but by purpose.

(3) But those things which have no knowledge do not move towards a goal unless they are guided by someone or something which does possess knowledge and intelligence-e.g., an arrow by an archer. Therefore, there does exist something which possesses intelligence by which all natural things are directed to their goal; and this we call God.

❈ 5.4 "Professor Mackie and the Kalam Cosmological Argument" ❈

selections
by William Craig

✳✳

William Craig (1949–present) is a theologian and philosopher of religion who teaches at Biola University. Craig defends a variation of the Cosmological argument first developed by the Kalam school in Islamic thought. Whereas Aquinas's argument seeks to explain the *contingency* of the world by a necessary being, Craig's argument seeks to explain the *causal origin* of the universe by a being outside of time. Craig argues that the universe must have had a beginning at some point in time, perhaps 13.8 billion years ago. Since whatever begins to exist has a cause of its existence, the universe must have a cause of its existence, and that cause must be something which had no beginning.

J. L. Mackie (1917–1981) was an Australian skeptic and philosopher who had challenged the Kalam Cosmological argument, arguing that the universe might extend back in time infinitely. Craig presents his argument, then presents Mackie's objection, and lastly provides his own reply to Mackie's objection.

Here are some questions to think about as you read:

* What are the premises of Craig's argument?
* Which of them are controversial, and which uncontroversial?
* What is an "actual infinite"? Why does Mackie think it can exist?
* Why does Craig think it can't exist?
* Why does Craig thinks he escapes the objection that God must have had a beginning?

393

PROFESSOR MACKIE AND THE KALAM COSMOLOGICAL ARGUMENT*

INTRODUCTION

I should like to focus on Mackie's analysis of one particular argument, the kalam cosmological argument. For his discussion at this point seems to me to be superficial, and I think it can be shown that he has failed to provide any compelling or even intuitively appealing objection against the argument.

The kalam argument is simply the old first cause cosmological argument based on impossibility of an infinite temporal regress of events. It may be schematized:

1. Whatever begins to exist has a cause of its existence.
2. The universe began to exist.
   2.1 Argument based on the impossibility of an actual infinite:
      2.11 An actual infinite cannot exist.
      2.12 An infinite temporal regress of events is an actual infinite.
      2.13 Therefore, an infinite temporal regress of events cannot exist.
   2.2 Argument based on the impossibility of the formation of an actual infinite by successive addition:
      2.21 A collection formed by successive addition cannot be actually infinite.
      2.22 The temporal series of past events is a collection formed by successive addition.
      2.23 Therefore, the temporal series of past events cannot be actually infinite.
3. Therefore, the universe has a cause of its existence.

Since the universe is the temporal series of events, the proof that that series had a beginning is taken to show that the universe began to exist. This conclusion has, as Mackie notes, received strong empirical support from cosmological research in astronomy and astrophysics during the last fifty years. Since the universe began to exist a finite time ago, it must have been brought into being by a reality *extra se* [outside itself].

MACKIE 'S CRITIQUE

Mackie objects to both premises of the kaldm cosmological argument. Turning his attention first to (2), Mackie asserts that (2.2) 'just expresses a prejudice against an actual infinity'. In the medieval versions of the argument, (2.2) was often portrayed as the impossibility of traversing the infinite. Since an infinite distance cannot be crossed, if the past were infinite, then today would never arrive. But this is obviously absurd, since today has arrived. Therefore, the past must be finite. Against this version of the argument, Mackie objects that it illicitly assumes an infinitely distant starting point for the temporal series and then pronounces it impossible to traverse the distance from that point to today. If we take the notion of infinity seriously, however, we must say that in an infinite past there would be no starting point whatever, even an infinitely distant one. Thus, from any specific point in past time there is only a finite stretch that needs to be traversed to reach the present.

Mackie finds (2.I) to be a more ingenious argument, but none the less fallacious. He contends that a proper understanding of the principles employed in infinite set theory enables us to see that the alleged absurdities entailed by the existence of an actual infinite (for example, infinities of different sizes), to which the proponent of the kalam argument appeals as evidence for (2. I I), in fact involve no real contradiction. This is because our normal criteria for smaller than and equal to fail to be mutually exclusive for infinite groups. For finite groups to be smaller than means that the members of one group can be correlated one to one with a proper part of another group; to be equal to means that the members of the two groups can be exactly matched in a one to one correlation. These two criteria are mutually exclusive for all finite groups, but not for infinite groups. Once we understand this relation between the two criteria, we see that there is no real contradiction.

Mackie admits, however, that many people still harbour doubts about the existence of an actual infinite in the real world and that not all mathematicians or philosophers are ready to accept the actual infinite even in the mathematical realm. Moreover, current astronomy supports a finite past history for the universe. But, he continues, even if we grant (2) that the universe began to exist, there is no good reason to accept (I). For ' . . . there is a priori no good reason why a sheer origination of things, not determined by anything, should be unacceptable,

whereas the existence of a god [sic] with the power to create something out of nothing is acceptable." Indeed, creatio ex nihilo raises problems.

(i) If God began to exist at a point in time, then this is as great a puzzle as the sheer origination of a material world.

(ii) If God has existed for infinite time, this would raise again the problem of the actual infinite.

(iii) If God's existence is not in time at all, this would be a complete mystery.

Suppose someone sought to escape these difficulties by proving the beginning of the universe by empirical evidence alone, not appealing to the philosophical arguments concerning the actual infinite, and then fastening on (ii). In that case, Mackie rejoins, he is still using the crucial assumptions that God's existence and power are self-explanatory, but that the unexplained origination of a material world is unintelligible. But this first assumption borrows from the ontological argument the notion of a being whose existence is self-explanatory because its non-existence is impossible, a notion that is indefensible. And as for the second assumption, there is no good ground for an a priori certainty that the beginning of things could not have been sheerly inexplicable. If we do find this origin of something from nothing improbable, then it should only serve to cast doubt on the interpretation of the big bang as an absolute beginning. Thus, the idea of creation is vaguely explanatory, apparently satisfying, until, that is, we take a hard look at it and try to formulate the suggestion precisely. Therefore, the kalam cosmological argument fails.

RESPONSE

As I said, it seems to me that none of Mackie's objections is cogently proved or even intuitively appealing. To see this, let us retrace our steps, examining Mackie's refutations as we go. With regard to (2.2) he is mistaken to call this a prejudice against the actual infinite, for the argument does not deny, as does (2.I) that an actual infinite can exist, but only that it can be formed by successive addition, or to use the medieval idiom, that it can be traversed.

Mackie's objection that this impossibility is based on the assumption of an infinitely distant starting point is entirely groundless. I know of no proponent of the kalam argument who made such an assumption; on the contrary, the beginningless character of an infinite temporal series serves only to underscore the difficulty of its formation by successive addition. For in this case the past would be like the second version of Zeno's Dichotomy paradox, in which Achilles to reach a certain point must have travelled across an infinite series of intervals from the beginningless and open end, with this exception: in the case of the past, unlike the case of the stadium, the intervals are actual and equal. The fact that there is no beginning at all, not even an infinitely distant one, makes the difficulty worse, not better. It is not the proponent of the kalam argument who fails to take infinity seriously . . . .

Turning to (2.I), Mackie has only succeeded in specifying some of the conditions which give rise to the absurdities entailed in the existence of an actual infinite, but he has done nothing to justify the assumption that those conditions may hold in the real world. He asserts, in effect, that both the Euclidean principle that the whole is greater than its part and the Cantorian principle of correspondence hold for finite collections, but that they are incompatible when applied to infinite collections. Infinite set theory therefore maintains logical consistency by abandoning the Euclidean principle. But the question is not whether infinite set theory, granted its conventions and axioms, constitutes an internally logically consistent system. The issue is whether such a system can be instantiated or obtain in the real world. Rather than alleviating the difficulties entailed therein, Mackie has merely specified an aspect of that system which supplies

the conditions which, if instantiated in the real world, would spawn the absurdities like Hilbert's Hotel or Russell's Tristram Shandy paradox. The price paid for abandoning the Euclidean principle with regard to infinite collections in favour of the principle of correspondence would be being saddled with all the absurd situations which would be entailed if an infinite collection could exist in reality. Thus, Mackie has said nothing to resolve the absurdities or to commend to our thinking the real existence of an actual infinite.

Professor Mackie's attempts to refute (2), therefore, seem to fall far short of the mark. He himself recognizes that some thinkers question even the legitimacy of the actual infinite in mathematics and that (2) is probable on scientific grounds alone. Therefore, it is incumbent upon him to turn back the force of (i) Whatever begins to exist has a cause of its existence. Rather than refute the principle, however, he simply demands what good reason there is apriori to accept it. He writes, 'As Hume pointed out, we can certainly conceive an uncaused beginning-to-be of an object; if what we can thus conceive is nevertheless in some way impossible, this still requires to be shown.'" But as has been often pointed out, Hume's argument in no way makes it plausible to think that something could really come into existence without a cause. As G. E. M. Anscombe observes, Hume asks us to envision a picture, as it were, of something coming into being without a cause and to title the picture 'x coming into being without a cause'. She comments 'Indeed I can form an image and give my picture that title. But from my being able to do that, nothing whatever follows about what is possible to suppose "without contradiction or absurdity" as holding in reality'.

What the defender of the kalam argument maintains is that it is really impossible for something to come from nothing. But how can this be shown? I think that one could produce arguments for the principle, but that since the principle is so intuitively obvious in itself, it would be perhaps unwise to do so, for one ought not to try to prove the obvious via the less obvious. After all, does anyone sincerely think that things can pop into existence uncaused out of nothing? Does he believe that it is really possible that, say, a raging tiger should suddenly come into existence uncaused out of nothing in the room in which he is now reading this article? How much the same would this seem to apply to the entire universe! If there were originally absolute nothingness - no God, no space, no time–how could the universe possibly come to exist?

THE UNINTELLIGIBILITY OBJECTION

So why not accept the truth of (i) as plausible and reasonable, at least more so than its opposite? Because, Mackie responds, in this context the theism implied in granting the principle is even more unintelligible than the denial of the principle. But is this the case? Certainly the proponent of the kalam argument would not hold to Mackie's option (i). Nor would he hold to (ii) if he regarded the philosophical arguments for (2) as cogent, for God without the creation would have to exist changelessly, if one is to avoid an infinite regress of events in God's life. Therefore, he holds quite happily to some version of (iii), most plausibly, I would argue, by maintaining that God without creation exists changelessly and timelessly with an eternal determination for the creation of a temporal world and that with creation God enters into temporal relationships with the universe, time arising concomitantly with the first event. This may

be mysterious in the sense of being wonderful or awesome, which indeed it is, but it is not so far as I can see unintelligible, as is something's coming into being uncaused out of nothing.

What is Mackie's counsel? 'We should infer that the universe must have had some physical antecedents, even if the big bang has to be taken as a discontinuity so radical that we cannot explain it, because we can find no laws which we can extrapolate backwards through this discontinuity.' Here I think we see more clearly than ever the quasi-religious character of Mackie's atheism. Either we believe that the universe came to exist uncaused out of nothing or else no matter what the empirical evidence for an absolute beginning, no matter how deep a caesura we have to carve in nature, we should infer that the universe must be eternal. The existence of a creator God is not even an alternative. The theist can hardly be blamed for not impaling himself on the horns of this dilemma. On the contrary, in light of the foregoing discussion, of the three options, theism seems the most plausible route to take. In conclusion, Professor Mackie's objections to the kalam argument appear to be unsound. His objection against (2.2), when relevant, only strengthened the argument therein, while his analysis of (2.I) merely drew our attention to the conditions which generate the absurdities in question. He provided no good reason to doubt the truth of (i) per se, a truth which is intuitively appealing and which he admits to be confirmed in our experience. His attempts to undermine (i) in this special context failed to show any unintelligibility either in God's relation to the world or in His mode of existence. Hence, neither premise of the argument appears to have been successfully refuted.

❀ 5.5 "The Watchmaker" ❀

selections from Natural Theology
by William Paley

✳✳✳

© Gitanna/Shutterstock.com

William Paley (1743–1805) was a philosopher and member of the clergy in the Church of England who wrote several books, the last of which was *Natural Theology*. Paley sought to base religious belief on an empirical foundation, rather than *a priori* proofs of the existence of God. The existence of God was a hypothesis that needed confirmation just like any other hypothesis, and Paley thought he had found that confirmation in the order and structure of the world. The world, like a well-designed watch, must have an intelligent designer. This is called the *teleological* argument.

Paley's book became very popular after his death, and changed popular thinking about how people were to know that God existed; his work even influenced a young Charles Darwin to pursue biology. However, Darwin's later development of the theory of evolution later was widely seen as refuting Paley's argument: we suddenly had a simpler, materialistic explanation for the order in the world. Paley had proposed a "god of the gaps", meant to explain what we currently don't know, and the gap had closed.

Here are some questions to think about as you read:

* What analogies does Paley use in his argument?

* Why does he think these analogies hold?

* What would it take to show Paley correct? What would it take to refute Paley?

* Why do you think Paley wanted an empirical rather than an *a priori* foundation for his religious belief? Why might many of his fellow clergy have opposed this?

* Do you the teleological argument loses its persuasiveness given the evolutionary accounts offered for complex biological systems?

NATURAL THEOLOGY

CHAPTER I.

STATE OF THE ARGUMENT.

IN crossing a heath, suppose I pitched my foot against a stone, and were asked how the stone came to be there; I might possibly answer, that, for any thing I knew to the contrary, it had lain there for ever: nor would it perhaps be very easy to show the absurdity of this answer. But suppose I had found a watch upon the ground, and it should be inquired how the watch happened to be in that place; I should hardly think of the answer which I had before given, that, for any thing I knew, the watch might have always been there. Yet why should not this answer serve for the watch as well as for the stone? why is it not as admissible in the second case, as in the first? For this reason, and for no other, viz. that, when we come to inspect the watch, we perceive (what we could not discover in the stone) that its several parts are framed and put together for a purpose, e. g. that they are so formed and adjusted as to produce motion, and that motion so regulated as to point out the hour of the day; that, if the different parts had been differently shaped from what they are, of a different size from what they are, or placed after any other manner, or in any other order, than that in which they are placed, either no motion at all would have been carried on in the machine, or none which would have answered the use that is now served by it. To reckon up a few of the plainest of these parts, and of their offices, all tending to one result:—We see a cylindrical box containing a coiled elastic spring, which, by its endeavour to relax itself, turns round the box. We next observe a flexible chain (artificially wrought for the sake of flexure), communicating the action of the spring from the box to the fusee. We then find a series of wheels, the teeth of which catch in, and apply to, each other, conducting the motion from the fusee to the balance, and from the balance to the pointer; and at the same time, by the size and shape of those wheels, so regulating that motion, as to terminate in causing an index, by an equable and measured progression, to pass over a given space in a given time. We take notice that the wheels are made of brass in order to keep them from rust; the springs of steel, no other metal being so elastic; that over the face of the watch there is placed a glass, a material employed in no other part of the work, but in the room of which, if there had been any other than a transparent substance, the hour could not be seen without opening the case. This mechanism being observed (it requires indeed an examination of the instrument, and perhaps some previous knowledge of the subject, to perceive and understand it; but being once, as we have said, observed and understood), the inference, we think, is inevitable, that the watch must have had a maker: that there must have existed, at some time, and at some place or other, an artificer or artificers who formed it for the purpose which we find it actually to answer; who

❖ ❖

comprehended its construction, and designed its use.

I. Nor would it, I apprehend, weaken the conclusion, that we had never seen a watch made; that we had never known an artist capable of making one; that we were altogether incapable of executing such a piece of workmanship ourselves, or of understanding in what manner it was performed; all this being no more than what is true of some exquisite remains of ancient art, of some lost arts, and, to the generality of mankind, of the more curious productions of modern manufacture. Does one man in a million know how oval frames are turned? Ignorance of this kind exalts our opinion of the unseen and unknown artist's skill, if he be unseen and unknown, but raises no doubt in our minds of the existence and agency of such an artist, at some former time, and in some place or other. Nor can I perceive that it varies at all the inference, whether the question arise concerning a human agent, or concerning an agent of a different species, or an agent possessing, in some respects, a different nature.

II. Neither, secondly, would it invalidate our conclusion, that the watch sometimes went wrong, or that it seldom went exactly right. The purpose of the machinery, the design, and the designer, might be evident, and in the case supposed would be evident, in whatever way we accounted for the irregularity of the movement, or whether we could account for it or not. It is not necessary that a machine be perfect, in order to show with what design it was made: still less necessary, where the only question is, whether it were made with any design at all.

III. Nor, thirdly, would it bring any uncertainty into the argument, if there were a few parts of the watch, concerning which we could not discover, or had not yet discovered, in what manner they conduced to the general effect; or even some parts, concerning which we could not ascertain, whether they conduced to that effect in any manner whatever. For, as to the first branch of the case; if by the loss, or disorder, or decay of the parts in question, the movement of the watch were found in fact to be stopped, or disturbed, or retarded, no doubt would remain in our minds as to the utility or intention of these parts, although we should be unable to investigate the manner according to which, or the connexion by which, the ultimate effect depended upon their action or assistance; and the more complex is the machine, the more likely is this obscurity to arise. Then, as to the second thing supposed, namely, that there were parts which might be spared, without prejudice to the movement of the watch, and that we had proved this by experiment,—these superfluous parts, even if we were completely assured that they were such, would not vacate the reasoning which we had instituted concerning other parts. The indication of contrivance remained, with respect to them, nearly as it was before.

IV. Nor, fourthly, would any man in his senses think the existence of the watch, with its various machinery, accounted for, by being told that it was one out of possible combinations of material forms; that whatever he had found in the place where he found the watch, must have contained some internal configuration or other; and that this configuration might be the structure now exhibited, viz. of the works of a watch, as well as a different structure.

V. Nor, fifthly, would it yield his inquiry more satisfaction to be answered, that there existed in things a principle of order, which had disposed the parts of the watch into their present form and situation. He never knew a watch made by the principle of order; nor can he even form to himself an idea of what is meant by a principle of order, distinct from the intelligence of the watch-maker.

VI. Sixthly, he would be surprised to hear that the mechanism of the watch was no proof of contrivance, only a motive to induce the mind to think so:

VII. And not less surprised to be informed, that the watch in his hand was nothing more than the result of the laws of metallicnature. It is a perversion of language to assign any law, as the efficient, operative cause of any thing. A law presupposes an agent; for it is only the mode, according to which an agent proceeds: it implies a power; for it is the order, according to which that power acts. Without this agent, without this power, which are both distinct from itself, the law does nothing; is nothing. The expression, "the law of metallic nature," may sound strange and harsh to a philosophic ear; but it seems quite as justifiable as some others which are more familiar to him, such as "the law of vegetable nature," "the law of animal nature," or indeed as "the law of nature" in general, when assigned as the cause of phænomena, in exclusion of agency and power; or when it is substituted into the place of these.

VIII. Neither, lastly, would our observer be driven out of his conclusion, or from his confidence in its truth, by being told that he knew nothing at all about the matter. He knows enough for his argument: he knows the utility of the end: he knows the subserviency and adaptation of the means to the end. These points being known, his ignorance of other points, his doubts concerning other points, affect not the certainty of his reasoning. The consciousness of knowing little, need not beget a distrust of that which he does know.

❁ 5.6 "The Teleological Argument Critiqued" ❁

selections from Dialogues Concerning Natural Religion by David Hume

* *

© Patricia Hofmeester/Shutterstock.com

David Hume believed the idea of God was best explained by tendencies in human psychology, not by rational proofs or supernatural intervention. An agnostic, he wrote extensively during his life raising skeptical objections to religion. *Dialogues Concerning Natural Religion*, from which this selection is taken, contains Hume's most forceful attack on religious beliefs in God. Concerned about arousing public anger, his friends persuaded him not to have it published until after his death.

Although David Hume lived before William Paley, Hume's objections in this selection clearly apply to Paley's argument. Hume argues that the appearance of design tells us nothing meaningful about the nature of the designer.

Hume wrote a dialogue between three characters. *Cleanthes* represents the proponent of the teleological argument, someone like Paley who believes that the appearance of design in nature offers empirical evidence of God's existence and nature. *Demea* represents the traditional view of Aquinas and Anselm that God's existence is known *a priori*, and his nature is unknowable. *Philo* represents the voice of Hume's own skepticism towards religion and lack of a belief in God.

Here are some questions to think about as you read:

* Why doesn't Hume think the teleological argument shows that there is only one designer, or the designer is perfect, or that our world is the best possible world?
* Why doesn't the argument show that the designer is immaterial, all-powerful, or all-knowing?
* What does Demea think we should conclude from these objections to the argument?
* What does Philo think we should conclude from these objections to the argument?

Dialogues Concerning Natural Religion

Characters:

Cleanthes
Demea
Philo

Not to lose any time in circumlocutions, said Cleanthes, addressing himself to Demea, much less in replying to the pious declamations of Philo; I shall briefly explain how I conceive this matter. Look round the world: contemplate the whole and every part of it: you will find it to be nothing but one great machine, subdivided into an infinite number of lesser machines, which again admit of subdivisions to a degree beyond what human senses and faculties can trace and explain. All these various machines, and even their most minute parts, are adjusted to each other with an accuracy which ravishes into admiration all men who have ever contemplated them. The curious adapting of means to ends, throughout all nature, resembles exactly, though it much exceeds, the productions of human contrivance; of human designs, thought, wisdom, and intelligence. Since, therefore, the effects resemble each other, we are led to infer, by all the rules of analogy, that the causes also resemble; and that the Author of Nature is somewhat similar to the mind of man, though possessed of much larger faculties, proportioned to the grandeur of the work which he has executed. By this argument a posteriori, and by this argument alone, do we prove at once the existence of a Deity, and his similarity to human mind and intelligence.

I shall be so free, Cleanthes, said Demea, as to tell you, that from the beginning, I could not approve of your conclusion concerning the similarity of the Deity to men; still less can I approve of the mediums by which you endeavour to establish it. What! No demonstration of the Being of God! No abstract arguments! No proofs a priori! Are these, which have hitherto been so much insisted on by philosophers, all fallacy, all sophism? Can we reach no further in this subject than experience and probability? I will not say that this is betraying the cause of a Deity: but surely, by this affected candour, you give advantages to Atheists, which they never could obtain by the mere dint of argument and reasoning.

. . .

What I chiefly scruple in this subject, said Philo, is not so much that all religious arguments are by Cleanthes reduced to experience, as that they appear not to be even the most certain and irrefragable of that inferior kind. That a stone will fall, that fire will burn, that the earth has solidity, we have observed a thousand and a thousand times; and when any new instance of this nature is presented, we draw without hesitation the accustomed inference. The exact similarity of the cases gives us a perfect assurance of a similar event; and a stronger evidence is never desired nor sought after. But wherever you depart, in the least, from the similarity of the cases, you diminish proportionably the

❈ ❈

evidence; and may at last bring it to a very weak analogy, which is confessedly liable to error and uncertainty. After having experienced the circulation of the blood in human creatures, we make no doubt that it takes place in Titius and Maevius. But from its circulation in frogs and fishes, it is only a presumption, though a strong one, from analogy, that it takes place in men and other animals. The analogical reasoning is much weaker, when we infer the circulation of the sap in vegetables from our experience that the blood circulates in animals; and those, who hastily followed that imperfect analogy, are found, by more accurate experiments, to have been mistaken.

If we see a house, Cleanthes, we conclude, with the greatest certainty, that it had an architect or builder; because this is precisely that species of effect which we have experienced to proceed from that species of cause. But surely you will not affirm, that the universe bears such a resemblance to a house that we can with the same certainty infer a similar cause, or that the analogy is here entire and perfect. The dissimilitude is so striking, that the utmost you can here pretend to is a guess, a conjecture, a presumption concerning a similar cause; and how that pretension will be received in the world, I leave you to consider.

It would surely be very ill received, replied Cleanthes; and I should be deservedly blamed and detested, did I allow, that the proofs of a Deity amounted to no more than a guess or conjecture. But is the whole adjustment of means to ends in a house and in the universe so slight a resemblance? The economy of final causes? The order, proportion, and arrangement of every part? Steps of a stair are plainly contrived, that human legs may use them in mounting; and this inference is certain and infallible. Human legs are also contrived for walking and mounting; and this inference, I allow, is not altogether so certain, because of the dissimilarity which you remark; but does it, therefore, deserve the name only of presumption or conjecture?

. . .

Good God! cried Demea, interrupting him, where are we? Zealous defenders of religion allow, that the proofs of a Deity fall short of perfect evidence! And you, Philo, on whose assistance I depended in proving the adorable mysteriousness of the Divine Nature, do you assent to all these extravagant opinions of Cleanthes? For what other name can I give them? or, why spare my censure, when such principles are advanced, supported by such an authority, before so young a man as Pamphilus?

You seem not to apprehend, replied Philo, that I argue with Cleanthes in his own way; and, by shewing him the dangerous consequences of his tenets, hope at last to reduce him to our opinion. But what sticks most with you, I observe, is the representation which Cleanthes has made of the argument a posteriori; and finding that that argument is likely to escape your hold and vanish into air, you think it so disguised, that you can scarcely believe it to be set in its true light. Now, however much I may dissent, in other respects, from the dangerous principles of Cleanthes, I must allow that he has fairly represented that argument; and I shall endeavour so to state the matter to you, that you will entertain no further scruples with regard to it.

Were a man to abstract from every thing which he knows or has seen, he would be altogether incapable, merely from his own ideas, to determine what kind of scene the universe must be, or to give the preference to one state or situation of things above another. For as nothing which he clearly conceives could be esteemed impossible or implying a contradiction, every chimera of his fancy would be upon an equal footing; nor could he assign any just reason why he adheres to one idea or system, and rejects the others which are equally possible.

Again; after he opens his eyes, and contemplates the world as it really is, it would be impossible for him at first to assign the cause of any one event, much

❀ ❀

less of the whole of things, or of the universe. He might set his fancy a rambling; and she might bring him in an infinite variety of reports and representations. These would all be possible; but being all equally possible, he would never of himself give a satisfactory account for his preferring one of them to the rest. Experience alone can point out to him the true cause of any phenomenon.

. . .

Now, according to this method of reasoning, Demea, it follows, (and is, indeed, tacitly allowed by Cleanthes himself,) that order, arrangement, or the adjustment of final causes, is not of itself any proof of design; but only so far as it has been experienced to proceed from that principle. For ought we can know a priori, matter may contain the source or spring of order originally within itself as well as mind does; and there is no more difficulty in conceiving, that the several elements, from an internal unknown cause, may fall into the most exquisite arrangement, than to conceive that their ideas, in the great universal mind, from a like internal unknown cause, fall into that arrangement. The equal possibility of both these suppositions is allowed. But, by experience, we find, (according to Cleanthes,) that there is a difference between them. Throw several pieces of steel together, without shape or form; they will never arrange themselves so as to compose a watch. Stone, and mortar, and wood, without an architect, never erect a house. But the ideas in a human mind, we see, by an unknown, inexplicable economy, arrange themselves so as to form the plan of a watch or house. Experience, therefore, proves, that there is an original principle of order in mind, not in matter. From similar effects we infer similar causes. The adjustment of means to ends is alike in the universe, as in a machine of human contrivance. The causes, therefore, must be resembling.

I was from the beginning scandalized, I must own, with this resemblance, which is asserted, between

the Deity and human creatures; and must conceive it to imply such a degradation of the Supreme Being as no sound Theist could endure. With your assistance, therefore, Demea, I shall endeavour to defend what you justly call the adorable mysteriousness of the Divine Nature, and shall refute this reasoning of Cleanthes, provided he allows that I have made a fair representation of it.

. . .

When Cleanthes had assented, Philo, after a short pause, proceeded in the following manner.

That all inferences, Cleanthes, concerning fact, are founded on experience; and that all experimental reasonings are founded on the supposition that similar causes prove similar effects, and similar effects similar causes; I shall not at present much dispute with you. But observe, I entreat you, with what extreme caution all just reasoners proceed in the transferring of experiments to similar cases. Unless the cases be exactly similar, they repose no perfect confidence in applying their past observation to any particular phenomenon. Every alteration of circumstances occasions a doubt concerning the event; and it requires new experiments to prove certainly, that the new circumstances are of no moment or importance. A change in bulk, situation, arrangement, age, disposition of the air, or surrounding bodies; any of these particulars may be attended with the most unexpected consequences: and unless the objects be quite familiar to us, it is the highest temerity to expect with assurance, after any of these changes, an event similar to that which before fell under our observation. The slow and deliberate steps of philosophers here, if any where, are distinguished from the precipitate march of the vulgar, who, hurried on by the smallest similitude, are incapable of all discernment or consideration.

But can you think, Cleanthes, that your usual phlegm and philosophy have been preserved in so wide a step as you have taken, when you

❖ ❖

compared to the universe houses, ships, furniture, machines, and, from their similarity in some circumstances, inferred a similarity in their causes? Thought, design, intelligence, such as we discover in men and other animals, is no more than one of the springs and principles of the universe, as well as heat or cold, attraction or repulsion, and a hundred others, which fall under daily observation. It is an active cause, by which some particular parts of nature, we find, produce alterations on other parts. But can a conclusion, with any propriety, be transferred from parts to the whole? Does not the great disproportion bar all comparison and inference? From observing the growth of a hair, can we learn any thing concerning the generation of a man? Would the manner of a leaf's blowing, even though perfectly known, afford us any instruction concerning the vegetation of a tree?

. . .

But, allowing that we were to take the operations of one part of nature upon another, for the foundation of our judgment concerning the origin of the whole, (which never can be admitted,) yet why select so minute, so weak, so bounded a principle, as the reason and design of animals is found to be upon this planet? What peculiar privilege has this little agitation of the brain which we call thought, that we must thus make it the model of the whole universe? Our partiality in our own favour does indeed present it on all occasions; but sound philosophy ought carefully to guard against so natural an illusion.

So far from admitting, continued Philo, that the operations of a part can afford us any just conclusion concerning the origin of the whole, I will not allow any one part to form a rule for another part, if the latter be very remote from the former. Is there any reasonable ground to conclude, that the inhabitants of other planets possess thought, intelligence, reason, or any thing similar to these faculties in men? When nature has so extremely diversified her manner of operation in this small globe, can we imagine that she incessantly copies herself throughout so immense a universe? And if thought, as we may well suppose, be confined merely to this narrow corner, and has even there so limited a sphere of action, with what propriety can we assign it for the original cause of all things? The narrow views of a peasant, who makes his domestic economy the rule for the government of kingdoms, is in comparison a pardonable sophism.

But were we ever so much assured, that a thought and reason, resembling the human, were to be found throughout the whole universe, and were its activity elsewhere vastly greater and more commanding than it appears in this globe; yet I cannot see, why the operations of a world constituted, arranged, adjusted, can with any propriety be extended to a world which is in its embryo state, and is advancing towards that constitution and arrangement. By observation, we know somewhat of the economy, action, and nourishment of a finished animal; but we must transfer with great caution that observation to the growth of a foetus in the womb, and still more in the formation of an animalcule in the loins of its male parent. Nature, we find, even from our limited experience, possesses an infinite number of springs and principles, which incessantly discover themselves on every change of her position and situation. And what new and unknown principles would actuate her in so new and unknown a situation as that of the formation of a universe, we cannot, without the utmost temerity, pretend to determine.

A very small part of this great system, during a very short time, is very imperfectly discovered to us; and do we then pronounce decisively concerning the origin of the whole?

Admirable conclusion! Stone, wood, brick, iron, brass, have not, at this time, in this minute globe of earth, an order or arrangement without human art and contrivance; therefore the universe could

not originally attain its order and arrangement, without something similar to human art. But is a part of nature a rule for another part very wide of the former? Is it a rule for the whole? Is a very small part a rule for the universe? Is nature in one situation, a certain rule for nature in another situation vastly different from the former?

And can you blame me, Cleanthes, if I here imitate the prudent reserve of Simonides, who, according to the noted story, being asked by Hiero, What God was? desired a day to think of it, and then two days more; and after that manner continually prolonged the term, without ever bringing in his definition or description? Could you even blame me, if I answered at first, that I did not know, and was sensible that this subject lay vastly beyond the reach of my faculties? You might cry out sceptic and rallier, as much as you pleased: but having found, in so many other subjects much more familiar, the imperfections and even contradictions of human reason, I never should expect any success from its feeble conjectures, in a subject so sublime, and so remote from the sphere of our observation. When two species of objects have always been observed to be conjoined together, I can infer, by custom, the existence of one wherever I see the existence of the other; and this I call an argument from experience. But how this argument can have place, where the objects, as in the present case, are single, individual, without parallel, or specific resemblance, may be difficult to explain. And will any man tell me with a serious countenance, that an orderly universe must arise from some thought and art like the human, because we have experience of it? To ascertain this reasoning, it were requisite that we had experience of the origin of worlds; and it is not sufficient, surely, that we have seen ships and cities arise from human art and contrivance. . . .

The discoveries by microscopes, as they open a new universe in miniature, are still objections, according to you, arguments, according to me. The further we push our researches of this kind, we are still led to infer the universal cause of all to be vastly different from mankind, or from any object of human experience and observation.

And what say you to the discoveries in anatomy, chemistry, botany? . . . . .

These surely are no objections, replied Cleanthes; they only discover new instances of art and contrivance. It is still the image of mind reflected on us from innumerable objects. Add, a mind like the human, said Philo. I know of no other, replied Cleanthes. And the liker the better, insisted Philo. To be sure, said Cleanthes.

Now, Cleanthes, said Philo, with an air of alacrity and triumph, mark the consequences. First, By this method of reasoning, you renounce all claim to infinity in any of the attributes of the Deity. For, as the cause ought only to be proportioned to the effect, and the effect, so far as it falls under our cognizance, is not infinite; what pretensions have we, upon your suppositions, to ascribe that attribute to the Divine Being? You will still insist, that, by removing him so much from all similarity to human creatures, we give in to the most arbitrary hypothesis, and at the same time weaken all proofs of his existence.

Secondly, You have no reason, on your theory, for ascribing perfection to the Deity, even in his finite capacity, or for supposing him free from every error, mistake, or incoherence, in his undertakings. There are many inexplicable difficulties in the works of Nature, which, if we allow a perfect author to be proved a priori, are easily solved, and become only seeming difficulties, from the narrow capacity of man, who cannot trace infinite relations. But according to your method of reasoning, these difficulties become all real; and perhaps will be insisted on, as new instances of likeness to human art and contrivance. At least, you must acknowledge, that it is impossible for us to tell, from our limited views, whether this system contains any great faults, or deserves any considerable praise, if compared to

❀ ❀

other possible, and even real systems. Could a peasant, if the Aeneid were read to him, pronounce that poem to be absolutely faultless, or even assign to it its proper rank among the productions of human wit, he, who had never seen any other production?

. . .

But were this world ever so perfect a production, it must still remain uncertain, whether all the excellences of the work can justly be ascribed to the workman. If we survey a ship, what an exalted idea must we form of the ingenuity of the carpenter who framed so complicated, useful, and beautiful a machine? And what surprize must we feel, when we find him a stupid mechanic, who imitated others, and copied an art, which, through a long succession of ages, after multiplied trials, mistakes, corrections, deliberations, and controversies, had been gradually improving? Many worlds might have been botched and bungled, throughout an eternity, ere this system was struck out; much labour lost, many fruitless trials made; and a slow, but continued improvement carried on during infinite ages in the art of world-making. In such subjects, who can determine, where the truth; nay, who can conjecture where the probability lies, amidst a great number of hypotheses which may be proposed, and a still greater which may be imagined?

And what shadow of an argument, continued Philo, can you produce, from your hypothesis, to prove the unity of the Deity? A great number of men join in building a house or ship, in rearing a city, in framing a commonwealth; why may not several deities combine in contriving and framing a world? This is only so much greater similarity to human affairs. By sharing the work among several, we may so much further limit the attributes of each, and get rid of that extensive power and knowledge, which must be supposed in one deity, and which, according to you, can only serve to weaken the proof of his existence. And if such foolish, such vicious creatures as man, can yet often unite in framing and executing one plan, how much more those deities or demons, whom we may suppose several degrees more perfect!

. . .

To multiply causes without necessity, is indeed contrary to true philosophy: but this principle applies not to the present case. Were one deity antecedently proved by your theory, who were possessed of every attribute requisite to the production of the universe; it would be needless, I own, (though not absurd,) to suppose any other deity existent. But while it is still a question, Whether all these attributes are united in one subject, or dispersed among several independent beings, by what phenomena in nature can we pretend to decide the controversy? Where we see a body raised in a scale, we are sure that there is in the opposite scale, however concealed from sight, some counterpoising weight equal to it; but it is still allowed to doubt, whether that weight be an aggregate of several distinct bodies, or one uniform united mass. And if the weight requisite very much exceeds any thing which we have ever seen conjoined in any single body, the former supposition becomes still more probable and natural. An intelligent being of such vast power and capacity as is necessary to produce the universe, or, to speak in the language of ancient philosophy, so prodigious an animal exceeds all analogy, and even comprehension.

But further, Cleanthes: men are mortal, and renew their species by generation; and this is common to all living creatures. The two great sexes of male and female, says Milton, animate the world. Why must this circumstance, so universal, so essential, be excluded from those numerous and limited deities? Behold, then, the theogony of ancient times brought back upon us.

And why not become a perfect Anthropomorphite? Why not assert the deity or deities to be corporeal, and to have eyes, a nose, mouth, ears, etc.? Epicurus maintained, that no man had ever seen reason but in a human figure; therefore the gods must have a human figure. And this argument, which is deservedly so much ridiculed by Cicero, becomes, according to you, solid and philosophical.

In a word, Cleanthes, a man who follows your hypothesis is able perhaps to assert, or conjecture, that the universe, sometime, arose from something like design: but beyond that position he cannot ascertain one single circumstance; and is left afterwards to fix every point of his theology by the utmost license of fancy and hypothesis. This world, for aught he knows, is very faulty and imperfect, compared to a superior standard; and was only the first rude essay of some infant deity, who afterwards abandoned it, ashamed of his lame performance: it is the work only of some dependent, inferior deity; and is the object of derision to his superiors: it is the production of old age and dotage in some superannuated deity; and ever since his death, has run on at

adventures, from the first impulse and active force which it received from him. You justly give signs of horror, Demea, at these strange suppositions; but these, and a thousand more of the same kind, are Cleanthes's suppositions, not mine. From the moment the attributes of the Deity are supposed finite, all these have place. And I cannot, for my part, think that so wild and unsettled a system of theology is, in any respect, preferable to none at all.

. . .

These suppositions I absolutely disown, cried Cleanthes: they strike me, however, with no horror, especially when proposed in that rambling way in which they drop from you. On the contrary, they give me pleasure, when I see, that, by the utmost indulgence of your imagination, you never get rid of the hypothesis of design in the universe, but are obliged at every turn to have recourse to it. To this concession I adhere steadily; and this I regard as a sufficient foundation for religion.

❃ 5.7 "Religious Experience" ❃
selections from Arguments for the Existence of God II
C. D. Broad

✳ ✳

©Artemiy Bogdanoff/Shutterstock.com

C. D. Broad (1887–1971) was an English philosopher at Cambridge University. Broad was an atheist who investigated claims people made about having had religious experiences. In this selection, he wonders whether the variety of religious experiences reported by people across cultures and centuries give a reason to believe in the supernatural.

"Religious experience" is a broad term meant to include everything from mystical visions of another world, to feeling a sense of peace or a supernatural presence. The central question about religious experience for Broad is whether it represents the world and thus counts as a type of perception. Broad notes that even if many such experiences are mere hallucinations, a perceptual system which sometimes gets it wrong must also sometimes get it right.

Here are some questions to think about as you read:

* What is the musical metaphor meant to show about degrees of religious experience?

* If religious experiences were a form of perception, what would this entail?

* Why might extreme religious experiences be connected to psychological problems? Why doesn't Broad think this is enough to dismiss these religious experiences?

* What is testimony about a religious experience evidence of, and to whom? What is it not evidence of, for Broad?

411

Religious Experience[*]

ARGUMENTS FOR THE EXISTENCE OF GOD. II

I shall therefore confine myself in this article to specifically religious experience and the argument for the existence of God which has been based on it.

This argument differs in the following important respect from the other two empirical types of argument. The Argument from Design and the arguments from ethical premises start from facts which are common to every one. But some people seem to be almost wholly devoid of any specifically religious experience; and among those who have it the differences of kind and degree are enormous. Founders of religions and saints, e.g., often claim to have been in direct contact with God, to have seen and spoken with Him, and so on. An ordinary religious man would certainly not make any such claim, though he might say that he had had experiences which assured him of the existence and presence of God. So the first thing that we have to notice is that capacity for religious experience is in certain respects like an ear for music. There are a few people who are unable to recognize and distinguish the simplest tune. But they are in a minority, like the people who have absolutely no kind of religious experience. Most people have some slight appreciation of music. But the differences of degree in this respect are enormous, and those who have not much gift for music have to take the statements of accomplished musicians very largely on trust. Let us, then, compare tone-deaf persons to those who have no recognizable religious experience at all; the ordinary followers of a religion to men who have some taste for music but can neither appreciate the more difficult kinds nor compose; highly religious men and saints to persons with an exceptionally fine ear for music who may yet be unable to compose it; and the founders of religions to great musical composers, such as Bach and Beethoven.

This analogy is, of course, incomplete in certain important respects. Religious experience raises three problems, which are different though closely interconnected.

i. What is the psychological analysis of religious experience? Does it contain factors which are present also in certain experiences which are not religious? Does it contain any factor which never occurs in any other kind of experience? If it contains no such factor, but is a blend of elements each of which can occur separately or in non-religious experiences, its psychological peculiarity

[*] From *Journal of Theological Studies*, Volume os-XL, Issue 2, January 1939, pages 156–167. Reprinted by permission of Oxford University Press.

must consist in the characteristic way in which these elements are blended in it. Can this peculiar structural feature of religious experience be indicated and described?

ii. What are the genetic and causal conditions of the existence of religious experience? Can we trace the origin and development of the disposition to have religious experiences

    a. in the human race, and

    b. in each individual?

Granted that the disposition is present in nearly all individuals at the present time, can we discover and state the variable conditions which call it into activity on certain occasions and leave it in abeyance on others?

iii. Part of the content of religious experience is alleged knowledge or well-founded belief about the nature of reality, e.g., that we are dependent on a being who loves us and whom we ought to worship, that values are somehow conserved in spite of the chances and changes of the material world at the mercy of which they seem prima facie to be, and so on. Therefore there is a third problem. Granted that religious experience exists, that it has such-and-such a history and conditions, that it seems vitally important to those who have it, and that it produces all kinds of effects which would not otherwise happen, is it veridical? Are the claims to knowledge or well-founded belief about the nature of reality, which are an integral part of the experience, true or probable? Now, in the case of musical experience, there are analogies to the psychological problem and to the genetic or causal problem, but there is no analogy to the epistemological problem of validity. For, so far as I am aware, no part of the content of musical experience is alleged knowledge about the nature of reality; and therefore no question of its being veridical or delusive can arise.

Since both musical experience and religious experience certainly exist, any theory of the universe which was incompatible with their existence would be false, and any theory which failed to show the connexion between their existence and the other facts about reality would be inadequate. So far the two kinds of experience are in exactly the same position. But a theory which answers to the condition that it allows of the existence of religious experience and indicates the connexion between its existence and other facts about reality may leave the question as to its validity quite unanswered. Or, alternatively, it may throw grave doubt on its cognitive claims, or else it may tend to support them. Suppose, e.g., that it could be shown that religious experience contains no elements which are not factors in other kinds of experience. Suppose further it could be shown that this particular combination of factors tends to originate and to be activated only under certain conditions which are known to be very commonly productive of false beliefs held with strong conviction. Then a satisfactory answer to the questions of psychological analysis and causal antecedents would have tended to answer the epistemological question of validity in the negative On the other hand, it might be that the only theory which would satisfactorily account for the origin of the religious disposition and for the occurrence of actual religious experiences under certain conditions was a theory which allowed some of the cognitive claims made by religious experience to be true or probable. Thus the three problems, though entirely distinct from each other, may be very closely connected; and it is the existence of the third problem in connexion with religious experience which puts it, for the present purpose, in a different category from musical experience.

In spite of this essential difference the analogy is not to be despised, for it brings out at least one important point. If a man who had no ear for music were to give himself airs on that account, and were to talk de haut en bas about those who can appreciate music and think it highly important, we should

❀ ❀

regard him, not as an advanced thinker, but as a self-satisfied Philistine. And, even if he did not do this but only propounded theories about the nature and causation of musical experience, we might think it reasonable to feel very doubtful whether his theories would be adequate or correct. In the same way, when persons without religious experience regard themselves as being on that ground superior to those who have it, their attitude must be treated as merely silly and offensive. Similarly, any theories about religious experience constructed by persons who have little or none of their own should be regarded with grave suspicion. (For that reason it would be unwise to attach very much weight to anything that the present writer may say on this subject.)

On the other hand, we must remember that the possession of a great capacity for religious experience, like the possession of a great capacity for musical appreciation and composition, is no guarantee of high general intelligence. A man may be a saint or a magnificent musician and yet have very little common sense, very little power of accurate introspection or of seeing causal connexions, and scarcely any capacity for logical criticism. He may also be almost as ignorant about other aspects of reality as the non-musical or non-religious man is about musical or religious experience. If such a man starts to theorize about music or religion, his theories may be quite as absurd, though in a different way, as those made by persons who are devoid of musical or religious experience. Fortunately it happens that some religious mystics of a high order have been extremely good at introspecting and describing their own experiences. And some highly religious persons have had very great critical and philosophical abilities. St. Teresa is an example of the first, and St. Thomas Aquinas of the second.

Now I think it must be admitted that, if we compare and contrast the statements made by religious mystics of various times, races, and religions, we find a common nucleus combined with very great differences of detail. Of course the interpretations which they have put on their experiences are much more varied than the experiences themselves. It is obvious that the interpretations will depend in a large measure on the traditional religious beliefs in which various mystics have been brought up. I think that such traditions probably act in two different ways.

(i) The tradition no doubt affects the theoretical interpretation of experiences which would have taken place even if the mystic had been brought up in a different tradition. A feeling of unity with the rest of the universe will be interpreted very differently by a Christian who has been brought up to believe in a personal God and by a Hindu mystic who has been trained in a quite different metaphysical tradition.

(ii) The traditional beliefs, on the other hand, probably determine many of the details of the experience itself. A Roman Catholic mystic may have visions of the Virgin and the saints, whilst a Protestant mystic pretty certainly will not.

Thus the relations between the experiences and the traditional beliefs are highly complex. Presumably the outlines of the belief are determined by the experience. Then the details of the belief are fixed for a certain place and period by the special peculiarities of the experiences had by the founder of a certain religion. These beliefs then become traditional in that religion. Thenceforth they in part determine the details of the experiences had by subsequent mystics of that religion, and still more do they determine the interpretations which these mystics will put upon their experiences. Therefore, when a set of religious beliefs has once been established, it no doubt tends to produce experiences which can plausibly be taken as evidence for it. If it is a tradition in a certain religion that one can communicate with saints, mystics of that religion will seem to see and to talk with saints in their mystical visions; and this fact will be taken as further evidence for the belief that one can communicate with saints.

Much the same double process of causation takes place in sense-perception. On the one hand, the beliefs and expectations which we have at any moment largely determine whatinterpretation we shall put on a certain sensation which we should in any case have had then. On the other hand, our beliefs and expectations do to some extent determine and modify some of the sensible characteristics of the sensa themselves. When I am thinking only of diagrams a certain visual stimulus may produce a sensation of a sensibly flat sensum; but a precisely similar stimulus may produce a sensation of a sensibly solid sensum when I am thinking of solid objects.

Such explanations, however, plainly do not account for the first origin of religious beliefs, or for the features which are common to the religious experiences of persons of widely different times, races, and traditions.

Now, when we find that there are certain experiences which, though never very frequent in a high degree of intensity, have happened in a high degree among a few men at all times and places; and when we find that, in spite of differences in detail which we can explain, they involve certain fundamental conditions which are common and peculiar to them; two alternatives are open to us. (i) We may suppose that these men are in contact with an aspect of reality which is not revealed to ordinary persons in their everyday experience. And we may suppose that the characteristics which they agree in ascribing to reality on the basis of these experiences probably do belong to it. Or (ii) we may suppose that they are all subject to a delusion from which other men are free. In order to illustrate these alternatives it will be useful to consider three partly analogous cases, two of which are real and the third imaginary.

   a. Most of the detailed facts which biologists tell us about the minute structure and changes in cells can be perceived only by persons who have had a long training in the use of the microscope. In this case we believe that the agreement among trained microscopists really does correspond to facts which untrained persons cannot perceive.

   b. Persons of all races who habitually drink alcohol to excess eventually have perceptual experiences in which they seem to themselves to see snakes or rats crawling about their rooms or beds. In this case we believe that this agreement among drunkards is merely a uniform hallucination.

   c. Let us now imagine a race of beings who can walk about and touch things but cannot see. Suppose that eventually a few of them developed the power of sight. All that they might tell their still blind friends about colour would be wholly unintelligible to and unverifiable by the latter. But they would also be able to tell their blind friends a great deal about what the latter would feel if they were to walk in certain directions. These statements would be verified. This would not, of course, prove to the blind ones that the unintelligible statements about colour correspond to certain aspects of the world which they cannot perceive. But it would show that the seeing persons had a source of additional information about matters which the blind ones could understand and test for themselves. It would not be unreasonable then for the blind ones to believe that probably the seeing ones are also able to perceive other aspects of reality which they are describing correctly when they make their unintelligible statements containing colour-names. The question then is whether it is reasonable to regard the agreement between the experiences of religious mystics as more like the agreement among trained microscopists about the minute structure of

cells, or as more like the agreement among habitual drunkards about the infestation of their rooms by pink rats or snakes, or as more like the agreement about colours which the seeing men would express in their statements to the blind men.

Why do we commonly believe that habitual excess of alcohol is a cause of a uniform delusion and not a source of additional information? The main reason is as follows. The things which drunkards claim to perceive are not fundamentally different in kind from the things that other people perceive. We have all seen rats and snakes, though the rats have generally been grey or brown and not pink. Moreover the drunkard claims that the rats and snakes which he sees are literally present in his room and on his bed, in the same sense in which his bed is in his room and his quilt is on his bed. Now we may fairly argue as follows. Since these are the sort of things which we could see if they were there, the fact that we cannot see them makes it highly probable that they are not there. Again, we know what kinds of perceptible effect would generally follow from the presence in a room of such things as rats or snakes. We should expect fox-terriers or mongooses to show traces of excitement, cheese to be nibbled, corn to disappear from bins, and so on. We find that no such effects are observed in the bedrooms of persons suffering from delirium tremens. It therefore seems reasonable to conclude that the agreement among drunkards is a sign, not of a revelation, but of a delusion.

Now the assertions in which religious mystics agree are not such that they conflict with what we can perceive with our senses. They are about the structure and organization of the world as a whole and about the relations of men to the rest of it. And they have so little in common with the facts of daily life that there is not much chance of direct collision. I think that there is only one important point on which there is conflict. Nearly all mystics seem to be agreed that time and change and unchanging

duration are unreal or extremely superficial, whilst these seem to plain men to be the most fundamental features of the world. But we must admit, on the one hand, that these temporal characteristics present very great philosophical difficulties and puzzles when we reflect upon them. On the other hand, we may well suppose that the mystic finds it impossible to state clearly in ordinary language what it is that he experiences about the facts which underlie the appearance of time and change and duration. Therefore it is not difficult to allow that what we experience as the temporal aspect of reality corresponds in some sense to certain facts, and yet that these facts appear to us in so distorted a form in our ordinary experience that a person who sees them more accurately and directly might refuse to apply temporal names to them.

Let us next consider why we feel fairly certain that the agreement among trained microscopists about the minute structure of cells expresses an objective fact, although we cannot get similar experiences. One reason is that we have learned enough, from simpler cases of visual perception, about the laws of optics to know that the arrangement of lenses in a microscope is such that it will reveal minute structure, which is otherwise invisible, and will not simply create optical delusions. Another reason is that we know of other cases in which trained persons can detect things which untrained people will overlook, and that in many cases the existence of these things can be verified by indirect methods. Probably most of us have experienced such results of training in our own lives.

Now religious experience is not in nearly such a strong position as this. We do not know much about the laws which govern its occurrence and determine its variations. No doubt there are certain standard methods of training and meditation which tend to produce mystical experiences. These have been elaborated to some extent by certain Western mystics and to a very much greater extent by Eastern Yogis. But I do not think that we can see here as we can in the case of microscopes and the training which is required to make the best use of them, any conclusive reason why these methods should produce veridical rather than delusive experiences. Uniform methods of training and meditation would be likely to produce more or less similar experiences, whether these experiences were largely veridical or wholly delusive.

Is there any analogy between the facts about religious experience and the fable about the blind men some of whom gained the power of sight? It might be said that many ideals of conduct and ways of life, which we can all recognize now to be good and useful, have been introduced into human history by the founders of religions. These persons have made actual ethical discoveries which others can afterwards recognize to be true. It might be said that this is at least roughly analogous to the case of the seeing men telling the still blind men of facts which the latter could and did verify for themselves. And it might be said that this makes it reasonable for us to attach some weight to what founders of religions tell us about things which we cannot understand or verify for ourselves; just as it would have been reasonable for the blind men to attach some weight to the unintelligible statements which the seeing men made to them about colours.

I think that this argument deserves a certain amount of respect, though I should find it hard to estimate how much weight to attach to it. I should be inclined to sum up as follows. When there is a nucleus of agreement between the experiences of men in different places, times, and traditions, and when they all tend to put much the same kind of interpretation on the cognitive content of these experiences, it is reasonable to ascribe this agreement to their all being in contact with a certain objective aspect of reality unless there be some positive reason to think otherwise. The practical postulate which we go upon everywhere else is to treat cognitive claims as veridical unless there be some positive reason to think them delusive. This, after all, is our only guarantee

for believing that ordinary sense-perception is veridical. We cannot prove that what people agree in perceiving really exists independently of them; but we do always assume that ordinary waking sense-perception is veridical unless we can produce some positive ground for thinking that it is delusive in any given case. I think it would be inconsistent to treat the experiences of religious mystics on different principles. So far as they agree they should be provisionally accepted as veridical unless there be some positive ground for thinking that they are not. So the next question is whether there is any positive ground for holding that they are delusive.

There are two circumstances which have been commonly held to cast doubt on the cognitive claims of religious and mystical experience

(i) it is alleged that founders of religions and saints have nearly always had certain neuropathic symptoms or certain bodily weaknesses, and that these would be likely to produce delusions. Even if we accept the premises, I do not think that this is a very strong argument.

a. It is equally true that many founders of religions and saints have exhibited great endurance and great power of organization and business capacity which would have made them extremely successful and competent in secular affairs. There are very few offices in the cabinet or in the highest branches of the civil service which St. Thomas Aquinas could not have held with conspicuous success. I do not, of course, regard this as a positive reason for accepting the metaphysical doctrines which saints and founders of religions have based on their experiences; but it is relevant as a rebuttal of the argument which we are considering.

b. Probably very few people of extreme genius in science or art are perfectly normal mentally or physically, and some

❀ ❀

of them are very crazy and eccentric indeed. Therefore it would be rather surprising if persons of religious genius were completely normal, whether their experiences be veridical or delusive.

c. Suppose, for the sake of argument, that there is an aspect of the world which remains altogether outside the ken of ordinary persons in their daily life. Then it seems very likely that some degree of mental and physical abnormality would be a necessary condition for getting sufficiently loosened from the objects of ordinary sense-perception to come into cognitive contact with this aspect of reality. Therefore the fact that those persons who claim to have this peculiar kind of cognition generally exhibit certain mental and physical abnormalities is rather what might be anticipated if their claims were true. One might need to be slightly 'cracked' in order to have some peep-holes into the super-sensible world.

d. If mystical experience were veridical, it seems quite likely that it would produce abnormalities of behaviour in those who had it strongly. Let us suppose, for the sake of argument, that those who have religious experience are in frequent contact with an aspect of reality of which most men get only rare and faint glimpses. Then such persons are, as it were, living in two worlds, while the ordinary man is living in only one of them. Or, again, they might be compared to a man who has to conduct his life with one ordinary eye and another of a telescopic kind. Their behaviour may be appropriate to the aspect of reality which they alone perceive and think all-important; but, for that very reason,

it may be inappropriate to those other aspects of reality which are all that most men perceive or judge to be important and on which all our social institutions and conventions are built.

(ii) A second reason which is commonly alleged for doubt about the claims of religious experience is the following. It is said that such experience always originates from and remains mixed with certain other factors, e.g., sexual emotion, which are such that experiences and beliefs that arise from them are very likely to be delusive. I think that there are a good many confusions on this point, and it will be worth while to begin by indicating some of them.

When people say that B 'originated from' A, they are liable to confuse at least three different kinds of connexion between A and B.

v. It might be that A is a necessary but insufficient condition of the existence of B.

vi. It might be that A is a necessary and sufficient condition of the existence of B. Or

vii. it might be that B simply is A in a more complex and disguised form.

Now, when there is in fact evidence only for the first kind of connexion, people are very liable to jump to the conclusion that there is the third kind of connexion. It may well be the case, e.g., that no one who was incapable of strong sexual desires and emotions could have anything worth calling religious experience. But it is plain that the possession of a strong capacity for sexual experience is not a sufficient condition of having religious experience; for we know that the former quite often exists in persons who show hardly any trace of the latter. But, even if it could be shown that a strong capacity for sexual desire and emotion is both necessary and sufficient to produce religious experience, it would not follow that the latter is just the former

in disguise. In the first place, it is not at all easy to discover the exact meaning of this metaphorical phrase when it is applied to psychological topics. And, if we make use of physical analogies, we are not much helped. A mixture of oxygen and hydrogen in presence of a spark is necessary and sufficient to produce water accompanied by an explosion. But water accompanied by an explosion is not a mixture of oxygen and hydtogen and a spark 'in a disguised form', whatever that may mcan.

Now I think that the present rather vaguely formulated objection to the validity of the claims of religious experience might be stated somewhat as follows. 'In the individual religious experience originates from, and always remains mixed with, sexual desires and emotions. The other generative factor of it is the religious tradition of the society in which he lives, the teachings of his parents, nurses, schoolmasters, etc. In the race religious experience originated from a mixture of false beliefs about nature and man, irrational fears, sexual and other impulses, and so on. Thus the religious tradition arose from beliefs which we now recognize to have been false and from emotions which we now recognize to have been irrelevant and misleading. It is now drilled into children by those who are in authority over them at a time of life when they are intellectually and emotionally at much the same stage as the primitive savages among whom it originated. It is, therefore, readily accepted, and it determines beliefs and emotional dispositions which persist long after the child has grown up and acquired more adequate knowledge of nature and of himself.'

Persons who use this argument might admit that it does not definitely prove that religious beliefs are false and groundless. False beliefs and irrational fears in our remote ancestors might conceivably be the origin of true beliefs and of an appropriate feeling of awe and reverence in ourselves. And, if sexual desires and emotions be an essential condition and constituent of religious experience, the experience may nevertheless be veridical in important respects. We might merely have to rewrite one of the beatitudes and say 'Blessed are the impure in heart, for they shall see God'. But, although it is logically possible that such causes should produce such effects, it would be said that they are most unlikely to do so. They seem much more likely to produce false beliefs and misplaced emotions.

It is plain that this argument has considerable plausibility. But it is worth while to remember that modern science has almost as humble an ancestry as contemporary religion. If the primitive witch-smeller is the spiritual progenitor of the Archbishop of Canterbury, the primitive rain-maker is equally the spiritual progenitor of the Cavendish Professor of Physics. There has obviously been a gradual refinement and purification of religious beliefs and concepts in the course of history, just as there has been in the beliefs and concepts of science. Certain persons of religious genius, such as some of the Hebrew prophets and the founders of Christianity and of Buddhism, do seem to have introduced new ethico-religious concepts and beliefs which have won wide acceptance, just as certain men of scientific genius, such as Galileo, Newton, and Einstein, have done in the sphere of science. It seems somewhat arbitrary to count this process as a continual approximation to true knowledge of the material aspect of the world in the case of science, and to refuse to regard is as at all similar in thc case of religion. Lastly, we must remember that all of us have accepted the current common-sense and scientific view of the material world on the authority of our parents, nurses, masters, and companions at a time when we had neither the power nor the inclination to criticize it. And most of us accept, without even understanding, the more recondite doctrines of contemporary physics simply on the authority of those whom we have been taught to regard as experts.

On the whole, then, I do not think that what we know of the conditions under which religious

beliefs and emotions have arisen in the life of the individual and the race makes it reasonable to think that they are specially likely to be delusive or misdirected. At any rate any argument which starts from that basis and claims to reach such a conclusion will need to be very carefully handled if its destructive effects are to be confined within the range contemplated by its users. It is reasonable to think that the concepts and beliefs of even the most perfect religions known to us are extremely inadequate to the facts which they express; that they are highly confused and are mixed up with a great deal of positive error and sheer nonsense; and that, if the human race goes on and continues to have religious experiences and to reflect on them, they will be altered and improved almost out of recognition. But all this could be said, mutatis mutandis, of scientific concepts and theories.

The claim of any particular religion or sect to have complete or final truth on these subjects seems to me to be too ridiculous to be worth a moment's consideration.

But the opposite extreme of holding that the whole religious experience of mankind is a gigantic system of pure delusion seems to me to be almost (though not quite) as far-fetched.

❀ 5.8 "Can Evil ever Be Justified?" ❀

selections from Brothers Karamazov
by Fyodor Dostoevsky

✳ ✳

© Zadiraka Engenii/Shutterstock.com

Fyodor Dostoevsky (1821-1881) was a Russian novelist who opposed both rationalistic theism and materialistic empiricism. His novels influenced the growth of existentialism in philosophy. Dostoevsky was part of the Russian Orthodox church, and his novels reflect a concern with issues of suffering and redemption.

In this selection from *The Brothers Karamazov*, Alyosha, a novice monk, seeks an explanation from his brother Ivan, an atheist. Ivan vividly presents the problem of evil, and he argues against the possibility of any *theodicy*–an attempt to reconcile the justice of God with the evil in the world. According to Ivan, no goodness, no matter how good, would ever be sufficient to justify the suffering of one innocent child. Compassion would refuse to use an individual's suffering as a means to achieving some other purpose, no matter how great and beautiful the purpose was.

Here are some questions to think about as you read:

* Aside from being graphic, what does the example of the child mauled by dogs show?

* Why would "God turned the suffering of the child into a greater good" not be an acceptable answer to Dostoevsky?

* Why would "God eventually punished the child's killer, and the child lived in joy eternally in heaven" not be an acceptable answer to Dostoevsky?

* Why does Ivan say he would return his "ticket"?

* Dostoevsky's response to the problem of evil elsewhere in his work was that God experienced all suffering and evil, so experiencing suffering was experiencing God. What might Ivan have said if Alyosha had proposed this?

Rebellion

Ivan's Conversation with Alyosha

Do you understand that, friend and brother, you pious and humble novice? Do you understand why this infamy must be and is permitted? Without it, I am told, man could not have existed on earth, for he could not have known good and evil. Why should he know that diabolical good and evil when it costs so much? Why, the whole world of knowledge is not worth that child's prayer to dear, kind God'! I say nothing of the sufferings of grown-up people, they have eaten the apple, damn them, and the devil take them all! But these little ones! I am making you suffer, Alyosha, you are not yourself. I'll leave off if you like."

"Nevermind. I want to suffer too," muttered Alyosha.

"One picture, only one more, because it's so curious, so characteristic, and I have only just read it in some collection of Russian antiquities. I've forgotten the name. I must look it up. It was in the darkest days of serfdom at the beginning of the century, and long live the Liberator of the People! There was in those days a general of aristocratic connections, the owner of great estates, one of those men—somewhat exceptional, I believe, even then—who, retiring from the service into a life of leisure, are convinced that they've earned absolute power over the lives of their subjects. There were such men then. So our general, settled on his property of two thousand souls, lives in pomp, and domineers over his poor neighbours as though they were dependents and buffoons. He has kennels of hundreds of hounds and nearly a hundred dog-boys—all mounted, and in uniform. One day a serf-boy, a little child of eight, threw a stone in play and hurt the paw of the general's favourite hound. 'Why is my favourite dog lame?' He is told that the boy threw a stone that hurt the dog's paw. 'So you did it.' The general looked the child up and down. 'Take him.' He was taken—taken from his mother and kept shut up all night. Early that morning the general comes out on horseback, with the hounds, his dependents, dog-boys, and huntsmen, all mounted around him in full hunting parade. The servants are summoned for their edification, and in front of them all stands the mother of the child. The child is brought from the lock-up. It's a gloomy, cold, foggy, autumn day, a capital day for hunting. The general orders the child to be undressed; the child is stripped naked. He shivers, numb with terror, not daring to cry. . . . 'Make him run,' commands the general. 'Run! run!' shout the dog-boys. The boy runs. . . . 'At him!' yells the general, and he sets the whole pack of hounds on the child. The hounds catch him, and tear him to pieces before his mother's eyes! . . . I believe the general was

❖ ❖

afterwards declared incapable of administering his estates. Well — what did he deserve? To be shot? To be shot for the satisfaction of our moral feelings? Speak, Alyosha!

"To be shot," murmured Alyosha, lifting his eyes to Ivan with a pale, twisted smile.

"Bravo!" cried Ivan delighted. "If even you say so . . . You're a pretty monk! So there is a little devil sitting in your heart, Alyosha Karamazov!"

"What I said was absurd, but-"

"That's just the point, that 'but'!" cried Ivan. "Let me tell you, novice, that the absurd is only too necessary on earth. The world stands on absurdities, and perhaps nothing would have come to pass in it without them. We know what we know!"

"What do you know?"

"I understand nothing," Ivan went on, as though in delirium. "I don't want to understand anything now. I want to stick to the fact. I made up my mind long ago not to understand. If I try to understand anything, I shall be false to the fact, and I have determined to stick to the fact."

"Why are you trying me?" Alyosha cried, with sudden distress. "Will you say what you mean at last?"

"Of course, I will; that's what I've been leading up to. You are dear to me, I don't want to let you go, and I won't give you up to your Zossima."

Ivan for a minute was silent, his face became all at once very sad.

"Listen! I took the case of children only to make my case clearer. Of the other tears of humanity with which the earth is soaked from its crust to its centre, I will say nothing. I have narrowed my subject on purpose. I am a bug, and I recognise in all humility that I cannot understand why the world is arranged as it is. Men are themselves to blame, I suppose; they were given paradise, they wanted freedom, and stole fire from heaven, though they knew they would become unhappy, so there is no need to pity them. With my pitiful, earthly, Euclidian understanding, all I know is that there is suffering and that there are none guilty; that cause follows effect, simply and directly; that everything flows and finds its level—but that's only Euclidian nonsense, I know that, and I can't consent to live by it! What comfort is it to me that there are none guilty and that cause follows effect simply and directly, and that I know it?—I must have justice, or I will destroy myself. And not justice in some remote infinite time and space, but here on earth, and that I could see myself. I have believed in it. I want to see it, and if I am dead by then, let me rise again, for if it all happens without me, it will be too unfair. Surely I haven't suffered simply that I, my crimes and my sufferings, may manure the soil of the future harmony for somebody else. I want to see with my own eyes the hind lie down with the lion and the victim rise up and embrace his murderer. I want to be there when everyone suddenly understands what it has all been for. All the religions of the world are built on this longing, and I am a believer. But then there are the children, and what am I to do about them? That's a question I can't answer. For the hundredth time I repeat, there are numbers of questions, but I've only taken the children, because in their case what I mean is so unanswerably clear. Listen! If all must suffer to pay for the eternal harmony, what have children to do with it, tell me, please? It's beyond all comprehension why they should suffer, and why they should pay for the harmony. Why should they, too, furnish material to enrich the soil for the harmony of the future? I understand solidarity in sin among men. I understand solidarity in retribution, too; but there can be no such solidarity with children. And if it is really true that they must share responsibility for all their fathers' crimes, such a truth is not of this world and is beyond my comprehension. Some jester will say, perhaps, that the

❖ ❖

child would have grown up and have sinned, but you see he didn't grow up, he was torn to pieces by the dogs, at eight years old. Oh, Alyosha, I am not blaspheming! I understand, of course, what an upheaval of the universe it will be when everything in heaven and earth blends in one hymn of praise and everything that lives and has lived cries aloud: 'Thou art just, O Lord, for Thy ways are revealed.' When the mother embraces the fiend who threw her child to the dogs, and all three cry aloud with tears, 'Thou art just, O Lord!' then, of course, the crown of knowledge will be reached and all will be made clear. But what pulls me up here is that I can't accept that harmony. And while I am on earth, I make haste to take my own measures. You see, Alyosha, perhaps it really may happen that if I live to that moment, or rise again to see it, I, too, perhaps, may cry aloud with the rest, looking at the mother embracing the child's torturer, 'Thou art just, O Lord!' but I don't want to cry aloud then. While there is still time, I hasten to protect myself, and so I renounce the higher harmony altogether. It's not worth the tears of that one tortured child who beat itself on the breast with its little fist and prayed in its stinking outhouse, with its unexpiated tears to 'dear, kind God'! It's not worth it, because those tears are unatoned for. They must be atoned for, or there can be no harmony. But how? How are you going to atone for them? Is it possible? By their being avenged? But what do I care for avenging them? What do I care for a hell for oppressors? What good can hell do, since those children have already been tortured? And what becomes of harmony, if there is hell? I want to forgive. I want to embrace. I don't want more suffering. And if the sufferings of children go to swell the sum of sufferings which was necessary to pay for truth, then I protest that the truth is not worth such a price. I don't want the mother to embrace the oppressor who threw her son to the dogs! She dare not forgive him! Let her forgive him for herself, if she will, let her forgive the torturer for the immeasurable suffering of her mother's heart. But the sufferings of her tortured child she has no right to forgive; she dare not forgive the torturer, even if the child were to forgive him! And if that is so, if they dare not forgive, what becomes of harmony? Is there in the whole world a being who would have the right to forgive and could forgive? I don't want harmony. From love for humanity I don't want it. I would rather be left with the unavenged suffering. I would rather remain with my unavenged suffering and unsatisfied indignation, even if I were wrong. Besides, too high a price is asked for harmony; it's beyond our means to pay so much to enter on it. And so I hasten to give back my entrance ticket, and if I am an honest man I am bound to give it back as soon as possible. And that I am doing. It's not God that I don't accept, Alyosha, only I most respectfully return him the ticket."

"That's rebellion," murmered Alyosha, looking down.

"Rebellion? I am sorry you call it that," said Ivan earnestly. "One can hardly live in rebellion, and I want to live. Tell me yourself, I challenge your answer. Imagine that you are creating a fabric of human destiny with the object of making men happy in the end, giving them peace and rest at last, but that it was essential and inevitable to torture to death only one tiny creature — that baby beating its breast with its fist, for instance — and to found that edifice on its unavenged tears, would you consent to be the architect on those conditions? Tell me, and tell the truth."

"No, I wouldn't consent," said Alyosha softly.

"And can you admit the idea that men for whom you are building it would agree to accept their happiness on the foundation of the unexpiated blood of a little victim? And accepting it would remain happy for ever?"

"No, I can't admit it. Brother," said Alyosha suddenly, with flashing eyes, "you said just now, is there a being in the whole world who would have the right to forgive and could forgive? But there is a Being and He can forgive everything, all and for all, because He gave His innocent blood for all and everything. You have forgotten Him, and on Him is built the edifice, and it is to Him they cry aloud, 'Thou art just, O Lord, for Thy ways are revealed!'

"Ah! the One without sin and His blood! No, I have not forgotten Him; on the contrary I've been wondering all the time how it was you did not bring Him in before, for usually all arguments on your side put Him in the foreground.

❄ 5.9 "Why Doesn't God Intervene to Prevent Evil?" ❄

selections
by B.C. Johnson

✳✳✳

© Everett Historical/Shutterstock.com

B.C. Johnson argues that even if it may be *logically possible* that God has a higher purpose for evil which is beyond our understanding, nonetheless it is far more probable that evil has no purpose at all, rather than that evil has a purpose we can't understand. So, the existence of evil is evidence against the existence of God.

Consider the immense evil and suffering which occurred during the holocaust. Either this evil had no purpose, or it had a purpose we can understand, or it has a purpose that we can't understand. There is no purpose we can understand for the holocaust–it is an insult to the victims and their families to even entertain the idea that it was justified by any good effects which followed. So, we have to decide whether it is more likely that the evil had no purpose and God does not exist, or more likely that the evil had a purpose we can't understand, and God does exist.

Here are some questions to think about as you read:

* When is not seeing something a reason to believe it isn't there? When is not seeing something *not* a reason to believe it isn't there?

* Why does Johnson think that the best explanation for why we don't see God intervening to stop evil is that God isn't there?

* Part of the experience for victims of great evils is the meaninglessness and purposelessness of their suffering; insisting that their suffering had a higher purpose seems like minimizing the suffering. Does this give an *a priori* reason to reject any higher purpose for suffering?

* Could God allow pointless suffering?

God and the Problem of Evil

B. C. JOHNSON

B. C. Johnson is a pen name for the author, who wishes to remain anonymous. In this essay, Johnson compares God's behavior with that of a morally good person. If you know that a six-month-old baby is in a burning building and you have the opportunity to save it without undue risk to your life, you would no doubt save it. Of course, if you couldn't save it, you would be excused. The question is "Why doesn't God intervene to save not just babies who are caught in fires but people everywhere who are suffering and in great need of help?" Johnson considers various "excuses" the theist might claim for God and argues that they all fail. His conclusion is that if there is a God, he or she is probably either evil or both good and evil.

Study Questions

1. What, according to Johnson, are some of the bad explanations for God not intervening to prevent evil?

2. How is God like a bystander who, though he didn't start the fire, refuses to help save the baby, even when he could easily do so.

3. How does Johnson respond to the suggestion that it is best for us to face disaster without assistance?

4. What does Johnson say to the objection that God's intervention would destroy a considerable amount of moral urgency?

5. What does Johnson say about the claim that evil is a necessary by-product of the laws of nature, so that it would be irrational for God to interfere every time a disaster happens?

6. What do people mean when they say that God has a "higher morality" than we have, so that we cannot apply our standards to him? What is Johnson's response to this defense of theism?

7. What are the three possibilities concerning God's moral character? Which does Johnson argue for? Do you agree?

HERE IS A COMMON SITUATION: A house catches on fire and a six-month-old baby is painfully burned to death. Could we possibly describe as "good" any person who had the power to save this child and yet refused to do so? God undoubtedly has this power and yet in many cases of this sort he has refused to help. Can we call God "good"? Are there adequate excuses for his behavior?

❀ ❀

First, it will not do to claim that the baby will go to heaven. It was either necessary for the baby to suffer or it was not. If it was not, then it was wrong to allow it. The child's ascent to heaven does not change this fact. If it was necessary, the fact that the baby will go to heaven does not explain why it was necessary, and we are still left without an excuse for God's inaction.

It is not enough to say that the baby's painful death would in the long run have good results and therefore should have happened, otherwise God would not have permitted it. For if we know this to be true, then we know—just as God knows—that every action successfully performed must in the end be good and therefore the right thing to do, otherwise God would not have allowed it to happen. We could deliberately set houses ablaze to kill innocent people and if successful we would then know we had a duty to do it. A defense of God's goodness which takes as its foundation duties known only after the fact would result in a morality unworthy of the name. Furthermore, this argument does not explain why God allowed the child to burn to death. It merely claims that there is some reason discoverable in the long run. But the belief that such a reason is within our grasp must rest upon the additional belief that God is good. This is just to counter evidence against such a belief by assuming the belief to be true. It is not unlike a lawyer defending his client by claiming that the client is innocent and therefore the evidence against him must be misleading—that proof vindicating the defendant will be found in the long run. No jury of reasonable men and women would accept such a defense and the theist cannot expect a more favorable outcome.

The theist often claims that man has been given free will so that if he accidentally or purposefully causes fires, killing small children, it is his fault alone. Consider a bystander who had nothing to do with starting the fire but who refused to help even though he could have saved the child with no harm to himself. Could such a bystander be called good? Certainly not. If we would not consider a mortal human being good under these circumstances, what grounds could we possibly have for continuing to assert the goodness of an all-powerful God?

The suggestion is sometimes made that it is best for us to face disasters without assistance, otherwise we would become dependent on an outside power for aid. Should we then abolish modern medical care or do away with efficient fire departments? Are we not dependent on their help? Is it not the case that their presence transforms us into soft, dependent creatures? The vast majority are not physicians or firemen. These people help in their capacity as professional outside sources of aid in much the same way that we would expect God to be helpful. Theists refer to aid from firemen and physicians as cases of man helping himself. In reality, it is a tiny minority of men helping a great many. We can become just as dependent on them as we can on God. Now the existence of this kind of outside help is either wrong or right. If it is right, then God should assist those areas of the world which do not have this kind of help. In fact, throughout history, such help has not been available. If aid ought to have been provided, then God should have provided it. On the other hand, if it is wrong to provide this kind of assistance, then we should abolish the aid altogether. But we obviously do not believe it is wrong.

Similar considerations apply to the claim that if God interferes in disasters, he would destroy a considerable amount of moral urgency to make things right. Once again, note that such institutions as modern medicine and fire departments are relatively recent. They function irrespective of whether we as individuals feel any moral urgency to support them. To the extent that they help others, opportunities to feel moral urgency are destroyed because they reduce the number of cases which appeal to us for help. Since we have not always had such institutions, there must have been a time when there was greater moral urgency than there is now.

❈ ❈

If such a situation is morally desirable, then we should abolish modern medical care and fire departments. If the situation is not morally desirable, then God should have remedied it.

Besides this point, we should note that God is represented as one who tolerates disasters, such as infants burning to death, in order to create moral urgency. It follows that God approves of these disasters as a means to encourage the creation of moral urgency. Furthermore, if there were no such disasters occurring, God would have to see to it that they occur. If it so happened that we lived in a world in which babies never perished in burning houses, God would be morally obliged to take an active hand in setting fire to houses with infants in them. In fact, if the frequency of infant mortality due to fire should happen to fall below a level necessary for the creation of maximum moral urgency in our real world, God would be justified in setting a few fires of his own. This may well be happening right now, for there is no guarantee that the maximum number of infant deaths necessary for moral urgency are occurring.

All of this is of course absurd. If I see an opportunity to create otherwise nonexistent opportunities for moral urgency by burning an infant or two, then I should *not* do so. But if it is good to maximize moral urgency, then I *should* do so. Therefore, it is not good to maximize moral urgency. Plainly we do not in general believe that it is a good thing to maximize moral urgency. The fact that we approve of modern medical care and applaud medical advances is proof enough of this.

The theist may point out that in a world without suffering there would be no occasion for the production of such virtues as courage, sympathy, and the like. This may be true, but the atheist need not demand a world without suffering. He need only claim that there is suffering which is in excess of that needed for the production of various virtues. For example, God's active attempts to save six-month-old infants from fires would not in itself create a world without suffering. But no one could sincerely doubt that it would improve the world.

The two arguments against the previous theistic excuse apply here also. "Moral urgency" and "building virtue" are susceptible to the same criticisms. It is worthwhile to emphasize, however, that we encourage efforts to eliminate evils; we approve of efforts to promote peace, prevent famine, and wipe out disease. In other words, we do value a world with fewer or (if possible) no opportunities for the development of virtue (when "virtue" is understood to mean the reduction of suffering). If we produce such a world for succeeding generations, how will they develop virtues? Without war, disease, and famine, they will not be virtuous. Should we then cease our attempts to wipe out war, disease, and famine? If we do not believe that it is right to cease attempts at improving the world, then by implication we admit that virtue-building is not an excuse for God to permit disasters. For we admit that the development of virtue is no excuse for permitting disasters.

It might be said that God allows innocent people to suffer in order to deflate man's ego so that the latter will not be proud of his apparently deserved good fortune. But this excuse succumbs to the arguments used against the preceding excuses and we need discuss them no further.

Theists may claim that evil is a necessary by-product of the laws of nature and therefore it is irrational for God to interfere every time a disaster happens. Such a state of affairs would alter the whole causal order and we would then find it impossible to predict anything. But the death of a child caused by an electrical fire could have been prevented by a miracle and no one would ever have known. Only a minor alteration in electrical equipment would have been necessary. A very large disaster could have been avoided simply by producing in Hitler a miraculous heart attack— and no one would have known it was a miracle. To argue that continued miraculous intervention by God would be wrong is like insisting that one should never use salt because ingesting five pounds of it would be fatal. No one is requesting that God interfere all of the time. He should, however, intervene to prevent especially horrible disasters. Of course, the question arises: where does one draw the line? Well, certainly the line should be drawn somewhere this side of infants burning to death. To argue that we do not know where the line should be drawn is no excuse for failing to interfere in those instances that would be called clear cases of evil.

It will not do to claim that evil exists as a necessary contrast to good so that we might know what good is. A very small amount of evil, such as a toothache, would allow that. It is not necessary to destroy innocent human beings.

The claim could be made that God has a "higher morality" by which his actions are to be judged. But it is a strange "higher morality" which claims that what we call "bad" is good and what we call "good" is bad. Such a morality can have no meaning to us. It would be like calling black "white" and white "black." In reply the theist may say that God is the wise Father and we are ignorant children. How can we judge God any more than a child is able to judge his parent? It is true that a child may be puzzled by his parents' conduct, but his basis for deciding that their conduct is nevertheless good would be the many instances of good behavior he has observed. Even so, this could be misleading. Hitler, by all accounts, loved animals and children of the proper race; but if Hitler had had a child, this off-spring would hardly have been justified in arguing that his father was a good man. At any rate, God's "higher morality," being the opposite of ours, cannot offer any grounds for deciding that he is somehow good.

Perhaps the main problem with the solutions to the problem of evil we have thus far considered is

that no matter how convincing they may be in the abstract, they are implausible in certain particular cases. Picture an infant dying in a burning house and then imagine God simply observing from afar. Perhaps God is reciting excuses in his own behalf. As the child succumbs to the smoke and flames, God may be pictured as saying: "Sorry, but if I helped you I would have considerable trouble deflating the ego of your parents. And don't forget I have to keep those laws of nature consistent. And anyway if you weren't dying in that fire, a lot of moral urgency would just go down the drain. Besides, I didn't start this fire, so you can't blame *me*."

It does no good to assert that God may not be all-powerful and thus not able to prevent evil. He can create a universe and yet is conveniently unable to do what the fire department can do— rescue a baby from a burning building. God should at least be as powerful as a man. A man, if he had been at the right place and time, could have killed Hitler. Was this beyond God's abilities? If God knew in 1910 how to produce polio vaccine and if he was able to communicate with somebody, he should have communicated this knowledge. He must be incredibly limited if he could not have managed this modest accomplishment. Such a God if not dead, is the next thing to it. And a person who believes in such a ghost of a God is practically an atheist. To call such a thing a god would be to strain the meaning of the word.

The theist, as usual, may retreat to faith. He may say that he has faith in God's goodness and therefore the Christian Deity's existence has not been disproved. "Faith" is here understood as being much like confidence in a friend's innocence despite the evidence against him. Now in order to have confidence in a friend one must know him well enough to justify faith in his goodness. We cannot have justifiable faith in the supreme goodness of strangers. Moreover, such confidence must come not just from a speaking acquaintance. The friend may continually assure us with his words that he is good

but if he does not act like a good person, we would have no reason to trust him. A person who says he has faith in God's goodness is speaking as if he had known God for a long time and during that time had never seen Him do any serious evil. But we know that throughout history God has allowed numerous atrocities to occur. No one can have justifiable faith in the goodness of such a God.

This faith would have to be based on a close friendship wherein God was never found to do anything wrong. But a person would have to be blind and deaf to have had such a relationship with God. Suppose a friend of yours had always claimed to be good yet refused to help people when he was in a position to render aid. Could you have justifiable faith in his goodness?

You can of course say that you trust God anyway — that no arguments can undermine your faith. But this is just a statement describing how stubborn you are; it has no bearing whatsoever on the question of God's goodness.

The various excuses theists offer for why God has allowed evil to exist have been demonstrated to be inadequate. However, the conclusive objection to these excuses does not depend on their inadequacy.

First, we should note that every possible excuse making the actual world consistent with the existence of a good God could be used in reverse to make that same world consistent with an evil God. For example, we could say that God is evil and that he allows free will so that we can freely do evil things, which would make us more truly evil than we would be if forced to perform evil acts. Or we could say that natural disasters occur in order to make people more selfish and bitter, for most people-tend to have a "me-first" attitude in a disaster (note, for example, stampedes to leave burning buildings). Even though some people achieve virtue from disasters, this outcome is necessary if persons are to react freely to disaster—necessary

if the development of moral degeneracy is to continue freely. But, enough; the point is made. Every excuse we could provide to make the world consistent with a good God can be paralleled by an excuse to make the world consistent with an evil God. This is so because the world is a mixture of both good and bad.

Now there are only three possibilities concerning God's moral character. Considering the world as it actually is, we may believe: (*a*) that God is more likely to be all evil than he is to be all good; (*b*) that God is less likely to be all evil than he is to be all good; or (*c*) that God is equally as likely to be all evil as he is to be good. In case (*a*) it would be admitted that God is unlikely to be all good. Case (*b*) cannot be true at all, since—as we have seen—the belief that God is all evil can be justified to precisely the same extent as the belief that God is all good. Case (*c*) leaves us with no reasonable excuses for a good God to permit evil. The reason is as follows: if an excuse is to be a reasonable excuse, the circumstances it identifies as excusing conditions must be actual. For example, if I run over a pedestrian and my excuse is that the brakes failed because someone tampered with them, then the facts had better bear this out. Otherwise the excuse will not hold. Now if case (*c*) is correct and, given the facts of the actual world, God is as likely to be all evil as he is to be all good, then these facts do not support the excuses which could be made for a good God permitting evil. Consider an analogous example. If my excuse for running over the pedestrian is that my brakes were tampered with, and if the actual facts lead us to believe that it is no more likely that they were tampered with than that they were not, the excuse is no longer reasonable. To make good my excuse, I must show that it is a fact or at least highly probable that my brakes were tampered with—not that it is just a possibility. The same point holds for God. His excuse must not be a possible excuse, but an actual one. But case (*c*), in maintaining that it is just as likely that God is all evil as that he is all good, rules this out. For if case

❖ ❖

(*c*) is true, then the facts of the actual world do not make it any more likely that God is all good than that he is all evil. Therefore, they do not make it any more likely that his excuses are good than that they are not. But, as we have seen, good excuses have a higher probability of being true.

Cases (*a*) and (*c*) conclude that it is unlikely that God is all good, and case (*b*) cannot be true. Since these are the only possible cases, there is no escape from the conclusion that it is unlikely that God is all good. Thus the problem of evil triumphs over traditional theism.

For Further Reflection

1. Do you find Johnson's arguments cogent? How might a theist reply to them?

2. Some theologians have argued that the biblical picture of God is not the same as the philosopher's. The philosopher pictures God as being all-powerful, while the Bible sees God as very powerful but still limited: He cannot prevent all evils. Would this revision of theism be an acceptable way to get around the problem of evil? Why or why not?

3. Suppose someone objects to the way the problem of evil is set forth, arguing that the problem is unjustifiably anthropomorphic. As someone said, "Who put human beings at the center of the definition of evil?" Should we take a more global view of evil, considering the harm done to animals and the environment? Is it a self-serving bias (sometimes called *speciesism*) that makes humanity the ultimate object of concern here?

❊ 5.10 "The Problem of Evil" ❊

selections from Reason and Religion
Richard Swinburne

❊❊❊

© De Visu/Shutterstock.com

Richard Swinburne (1934–Present) is a Professor of Philosophy at the University of Oxford. Swinburne has published several books on the philosophy of religion. Swinburne argues here that the existence of God is probable even given the existence of evil.

Swinburne begins by distinguishing *active evil*, which is the evil of the immoral intentions and desires behind an act, and *passive evil*, which is the evil of painful feelings and emotions. He presents the *free will defense* to explain the existence of active evil: God does not stop us from intending to do evil or desiring to do evil, even though these are morally bad, because this would requiring taking away our free will. However, explaining the existence of passive evil is more difficult. Swinburne suggests that God created the world "unfinished", and gave us the task of completing it, and painful feelings and emotions are to help us complete the task.

Here are some questions to think about as you read:

* Who is the *theodicist*? Who is the *antitheodicist*?

* What answer to passive evil does Swinburne attribute to Plantinga?

* Why does Swinburne think God could not prevent humans from intending or desiring evil without removing their free will? Why think God could prevent humans from actually carrying out their evil intentions without removing their free will?

* Why does Swinburne think God had to create humans with pain? Why couldn't God create a "finished" universe? Why couldn't God create an unfinished universe without pain?

435

The Problem of Evil*

RICHARD SWINBURNE

God is, by definition, omniscient, omnipotent, and perfectly good. By "omniscient" I understand "one who knows all true propositions". By "omnipotent" I understand "able to do anything logically possible".[1] By "perfectly good" I understand "one who does no morally bad action", and I include among actions omissions to perform some action. The problem of evil is then often stated as the problem whether the existence of God is compatible with the existence of evil. Against the suggestion of compatibility, an atheist often suggests that the existence of evil entails the nonexistence of God. For, he argues, if God exists, then being omniscient, he knows under what circumstances evil will occur, if he does not act; and being omnipotent, he is able to prevent its occurrence. Hence, being perfectly good, he will prevent its occurrence and so evil will not exist. Hence the existence of God entails the nonexistence of evil. Theists have usually attacked this argument by denying the claim that necessarily a perfectly good being, foreseeing the occurrence of evil and able to prevent it, will prevent it. And indeed, if evil is understood in the very wide way in which it normally is understood in this context, to include physical pain of however slight a degree, the cited claim is somewhat implausible. For it implies that if through my neglecting frequent warnings to go to the dentist, I find myself one morning with a slight toothache, then necessarily, there does not exist a perfectly good being who foresaw the evil and was able to have prevented it. Yet it seems fairly obvious that such a being might well choose to allow me to suffer some mild consequences of my folly—as a lesson for the future which would do me no real harm.

The threat to theism seems to come, not from the existence of evil as such, but rather from the existence of evil of certain kinds and degrees—severe undeserved physical pain or mental anguish, for example. I shall therefore list briefly the kinds of evil which are evident in our world, and ask whether their existence in the degrees in which we find them is compatible with the existence of God. I shall call the man who argues for compatibility the theodicist, and his opponent the antitheodicist. The theodicist will claim that it is not morally wrong for God to create or

[1] This account of omnipotence will do for present purposes. But a much more careful account is needed to deal with other well-known difficulties. I have attempted to provide such an account in my "Omnipotence," *American Philosophical Quarterly*, 10 (1973), 231–237.

permit the various evils, normally on the grounds that doing so is providing the logically necessary conditions of greater goods. The antitheodicist denies these claims by putting forward moral principles which have as consequences that a good God would not under any circumstances create or permit the evils in question. I shall argue that these moral principles are not, when carefully examined, at all obvious, and indeed that there is a lot to be said for their negations. Hence I shall conclude that it is plausible to suppose that the existence of these evils is compatible with the existence of God.[2]

Since I am discussing only the compatibility of various evils with the existence of God, I am perfectly entitled to make occasionally some (nonself-contradictory) assumption, and argue that if it was true, the compatibility would hold. For if p is compatible with q, given r (where r is not self-contradictory), then p is compatible with q simpliciter. It is irrelevant to the issue of compatibility whether these assumptions are true. If, however, the assumptions which I make are clearly false, and if also it looks as if the existence of God is compatible with the existence of evil *only* given those assumptions, the formal proof of compatibility will lose much of interest. To avoid this danger, I shall make only such assumptions as are not clearly false—and also in fact the ones which I shall make will be ones to which many theists are already committed for entirely different reasons.

What then is wrong with the world? First, there are painful sensations, felt both by men, and, to a lesser extent, by animals. Second, there are painful emotions, which do not involve pain in the literal sense of this word—for example, feelings of loss and failure and frustration. Such suffering exists mainly among men, but also, I suppose, to some small extent among animals too. Third, there are evil and undesirable states of affairs, mainly states of men's minds, which do not involve suffering. For example, there are the states of mind of hatred and envy; and such states of the world as rubbish tipped over a beauty spot. And fourth, there are the evil actions of men, mainly actions having as foreseeable consequences evils of the first three types, but perhaps other actions as well—such as lying and promise breaking with no such foreseeable consequences. As before, I include among actions, omissions to perform some actions. If there are rational agents other than men and God (if he exists), such as angels or devils or strange beings on distant planets, who suffer and perform evil actions, then their evil feelings, states, and actions must be added to the list of evils.

I propose to call evil of the first type physical evil, evil of the second type mental evil, evil of the third type state evil, and evil of the fourth type moral evil. Since there is a clear contrast between evils of the first three types, which are evils that happen to men or animals or the world, and evils of the fourth type which are evils that men do, there is an advantage in having one name for evils of any of the first three types—I shall call these passive evils.[3] I distinguish evil from mere absence of good. Pain is not simply the absence of pleasure. A headache is a pain, whereas not having the sensation of drinking whiskey is, for many people, mere absence of pleasure. Likewise, the feeling of loss in bereavement is an evil involving suffering, to be contrasted with the mere absence of the pleasure of companionship. Some thinkers have, of course, claimed that a good God would create a "best of

---

[2.] Some of what I have to say will not be especially original. The extensive writing on this subject has of course been well described in John Hick, *Evil and the God of Love* (London, 1966).

[3.] In discussion of the problem of evil, terminology has not always been very clear or consistent. See Gerald Wallace, "The Problems of Moral and Physical Evil," *Philosophy*, 46 (1971), 349–351.

all (logically) possible worlds"[4] (i.e., a world than which no better is logically possible), and for them the mere absence of good creates a problem since it looks as if a world would be a better world if it had that good. For most of us, however, the mere absence of good seems less of a threat to theism than the presence of evil, partly because it is not at all clear whether any sense can be given to the concept of a best of all possible worlds (and if it cannot then of logical necessity there will be a better world than any creatable world) and partly because even if sense can be given to this concept it is not at all obvious that God has an obligation to create such a world[5]—to whom would he be doing an injustice if he did not? My concern is with the threat to theism posed by the existence of evil.

Now much of the evil in the world consists of the evil actions of men and the passive evils brought about by those actions. (These include the evils brought about intentionally by men, and also the evils which result from long years of slackness by many generations of men. Many of the evils of 1975 are in the latter category, and among them many state evils. The hatred and jealousy which many men and groups feel today result from an upbringing consequent on generations of neglected opportunities for reconciliations.) The antitheodicist suggests as a moral principle (P1) that a creator able to do so ought to create only creatures such that necessarily they do not do evil actions. From this it follows that God would not have made men who do evil actions. Against this suggestion the theodicist naturally deploys the free-will defense,

elegantly expounded in recent years by Alvin Plantinga.[6] This runs roughly as follows it is not logically possible for an agent to make another agent such that necessarily he freely does only good actions. Hence if a being G creates a free agent, he gives to the agent power of choice between alternative actions, and how he will exercise that power is something which G cannot control while the agent remains free. It is a good thing that there exist free agents, but a logically necessary consequence of their existence is that their power to choose to do evil actions may sometimes be realized. The price is worth paying, however, for the existence of agents performing free actions remains a good thing even if they sometimes do evil. Hence it is not logically possible that a creator create free creatures "such that necessarily they do not do evil actions". But it is not a morally bad thing that he create free creatures, even with the possibility of their doing evil. Hence the cited moral principle is implausible.

The free-will defense as stated needs a little filling out. For surely there could be free agents who did not have the power of moral choice, agents whose only opportunities for choice were between morally indifferent alternatives—between jam and marmalade for breakfast, between watching the news on BBC 1 or the news on ITV. They might lack this power either because they lacked the power of making moral judgments (i.e., lacked moral discrimination); or because all their actions which were morally assessable were caused by factors outside their control; or because they saw with complete clarity what was right and wrong and had

---

[4.] Indeed they have often made the even stronger claim that a good God would create *the* best of all (logically) possible worlds—implying that necessarily there was just one possible world better than all others. There seem to me no grounds at all for adopting this claim.

[5.] That he has no such obligation is very well argued by Robert Merrihew Adams, "Must God Create the Best?" *Philosophical Review*, 81 (1972), 317–332.

[6.] See Alvin Plantinga, "The Free Will Defence," in Max Black, ed., *Philosophy in America* (London, 1965); *God and Other Minds* (Ithaca, N.Y., and London, 1967), chaps. 5 and 6; and *The Nature of Necessity* (Oxford, 1974), chap. 9.

❖ ❖

no temptation to do anything except the right.[7] The free-will defense must claim, however, that it is a good thing that there exist free agents with the power and opportunity of choosing between morally good and morally evil actions, agents with sufficient moral discrimination to have some idea of the difference and some (though not overwhelming) temptation to do other than the morally good. Let us call such agents humanly free agents. The defense must then go on to claim that it is not logically possible to create humanly free agents such that necessarily they do not do morally evil actions. Unfortunately, this latter claim is highly debatable, and I have no space to debate it.[8] I propose therefore to circumvent this issue as follows. I shall add to the definition of humanly free agents, that they are agents whose choices do not have fully deterministic precedent causes. Clearly then it will not be logically possible to create humanly free agents whose choices go one way rather than another, and so not logically possible to create humanly free agents such that necessarily they do not do evil actions. Then the free-will defense claims that (P1) is not universally true; it is not morally wrong to create humanly free agents—despite the real possibility that they will do evil. Like many others who have discussed this issue, I find this a highly plausible suggestion. Surely as parents we regard it as a good thing that our children have power to do free actions of moral significance—even if the consequence is that they sometimes do evil actions. This conviction is likely to be stronger, not weaker, if we hold that the free actions with which we are concerned are ones which do not have fully deterministic precedent causes. In this way we show the existence of God to be compatible with the existence of moral evil—but only subject to a very big assumption—that men are humanly free agents. If they are not, the compatibility shown by the free will defense is of little interest. For the agreed exception to (P1) would not then justify a creator making men who did evil actions; we should need a different exception to avoid incompatibility. The assumption seems to me not clearly false, and is also one which most theists affirm for quite other reasons. Needless to say, there is no space to discuss the assumption here.

All that the free-will defense has shown so far, however (and all that Plantinga seems to show) is grounds for supposing that the existence of moral evil is compatible with the existence of God. It has not given grounds for supposing that the existence of evil consequences of moral evils is compatible with the existence of God. In an attempt to show an incompatibility, the antitheodicist may suggest instead of (P1), (P2)— that a creator able to do so ought always to ensure that any creature whom he creates does not cause passive evils, or at any rate passive evils which hurt creatures other than himself. For could not God have made a world where there are humanly free creatures, men with the power to do evil actions, but where those actions do not have evil consequences, or at any rate evil consequences which affect others—e.g., a world where men cannot cause pain and distress to other men? Men might well do actions which are evil either because they were actions which they believed would have evil consequences or because they were evil for some other reason (e.g., actions which involved promise breaking) without them in fact having any passive evils as consequences.

[7.] In the latter case they would have, in Kant's terminology, holy wills. I argue that God must be such an agent in my "Duty and the Will of God," *Canadian Journal of Philosophy*, 4 (1974), 213–227.

[8.] For the debate see Antony Flew, "Divine Omnipotence and Human Freedom," in Antony Flew and Alasdair MacIntyre, eds., *New Essays in Philosophical Theology*; John L. Mackie, "Evil and Omnipotence," *Mind*, 64 (1955), 200–212 and Plantinga, "Free Will Defence."

❀ ❀

Agents in such a world would be like men in a simulator training to be pilots. They can make mistakes, but no one suffers through those mistakes. Or men might do evil actions which did have the evil consequences which were foreseen but which damaged only themselves. Some philosophers might hold that an action would not be evil if its foreseen consequences were ones damaging only to the agent, since, they might hold, no one has any duties to himself. For those who do not hold this position, however, there are some plausible candidates for actions evil solely because of their foreseeable consequences for the agent—e.g., men brooding on their misfortunes in such a way as foreseeably to become suicidal or misanthropic.

I do not find (P2) a very plausible moral principle. A world in which no one except the agent was affected by his evil actions might be a world in which men had freedom but it would not be a world in which men had responsibility. The theodicist claims that it would not be wrong for God to create interdependent humanly free agents, a society of such agents responsible for each other's well-being, able to make or mar each other.

Fair enough, the antitheodicist may again say. It is not wrong to create a world where creatures have responsibilities for each other. But might not those responsibilities simply be that creatures had the opportunity to benefit or to withhold benefit from each other, not a world in which they had also the opportunity to cause each other pain? One answer to this is that if creatures have only the power to benefit and not the power to hurt each other, they obviously lack any very strong responsibility for each other. To bring out the point by a caricature—a world in which I could choose whether or not to give you sweets, but not whether or not to break your leg or make you unpopular, is not a world in which I have a very strong influence on your destiny, and so not a world in which I have a very full responsibility for you. Further, however, there is a point which will depend on an argument

which I will give further on. In the actual world very often a man's withholding benefits from another is correlated with the latter's suffering some passive evil, either physical or mental. Thus if I withhold from you certain vitamins, you will suffer disease. Or if I deprive you of your wife by persuading her to live with me instead, you will suffer grief at the loss. Now it seems to me that a world in which such correlations did not hold would not necessarily be a better world than the world in which they do. The appropriateness of pain to bodily disease or deprivation, and of mental evils to various losses or lacks of a more spiritual kind, is something for which I shall argue in detail a little later.

So then the theodicist objects to (P2) on the grounds that the price of possible passive evils for other creatures is a price worth paying for agents to have great responsibilities for each other. It is a price which (logically) must be paid if they are to have those responsibilities. Here again a reasonable antitheodicist may see the point. In bringing up our own children, in order to give them responsibility, we try not to interfere too quickly in their quarrels—even at the price, sometimes, of younger children getting hurt physically. We try not to interfere, first, in order to train our children for responsibility in later life and second because responsibility here and now is a good thing in itself. True, with respect to the first reason, whatever the effects on character produced by training, God could produce without training. But if he did so by imposing a full character on a humanly free creature, this would be giving him a character which he had not in any way chosen or adopted for himself. Yet it would seem a good thing that a creator should allow humanly free creatures to influence by their own choices the sort of creatures they are to be, the kind of character they are to have. That means that the creator must create them immature, and allow them gradually to make decisions which affect the sort of beings they will be. And one of the greatest privileges which a creator can give to a creature is to allow him to help in the process of education, in putting alternatives before his fellows.

Yet though the antitheodicist may see the point, in theory, he may well react to it rather like this. "Certainly some independence is a good thing. But surely a father ought to interfere if his younger son is really getting badly hurt. The ideal of making men free and responsible is a good one, but there are limits to the amount of responsibility which it is good that men should have, and in our world men have too much responsibility. A good God would certainly have intervened long ago to stop some of the things which happen in our world." Here, I believe, lies the crux—it is simply a matter of quantity. The theodicist says that a good God could allow men to do to each other the hurt they do, in order to allow them to be free and responsible. But against him the antitheodicist puts forward as a moral principle (*P3*) that a creator able to do so ought to ensure that any creature whom he creates does not cause passive evils as many and as evil as those in our world. He says that in our world freedom and responsibility have gone too far—produced too much physical and mental hurt. God might well tolerate a boy hitting his younger brother, but not Belsen.

The theodicist is in no way committed to saying that a good God will not stop things getting too bad. Indeed, if God made our world, he has clearly done so. There are limits to the amount and degree of evil which are possible in our world. Thus there are limits to the amount of pain which a person can suffer—persons live in our world only so many years and the amount which they can suffer at any given time (if mental goings-on are in any way correlated with bodily ones) is limited by their physiology. Further, theists often claim that from time to time God intervenes in the natural order which he has made to prevent evil which would otherwise occur. So the theodicist can certainly claim that a good God stops too much suffering—it is just that he and his opponent draw the line in different places. The issue as regards the passive evils caused by men turns ultimately on the quantity of evil. To this crucial matter I shall return toward the end of the paper.

We shall have to turn next to the issue of passive evils not apparently caused by men. But, first, I must consider a further argument by the theodicist in support of the free-will defense and also an argument of the antitheodicist against it. The first is the argument that various evils are logically necessary conditions for the occurrence of actions of certain especially good kinds. Thus for a man to bear his suffering cheerfully there has to be suffering for him to bear. There have to be acts which irritate for another to show tolerance of them. Likewise it is often said, acts of forgiveness, courage, self-sacrifice, compassion, overcoming temptation, etc., can be performed only if there are evils of various kinds. Here, however, we must be careful. One might reasonably claim that all that is necessary for some of these good acts (or acts as good as these) to be performed is belief in the existence of certain evils, not their actual existence. You can show compassion toward someone who appears to be suffering, but is not really; you can forgive someone who only appeared to insult you, but did not really. But if the world is to be populated with imaginary evils of the kind needed to enable creatures to perform acts of the above specially good kinds, it would have to be a world in which creatures are generally and systematically deceived about the feelings of their fellows—in which the behavior of creatures generally and unavoidably belies their feelings and intentions. I suggest, in the tradition of Descartes (*Meditations* 4, 5 and 6), that it would be a morally wrong act of a creator to create such a deceptive world. In that case, given a creator, then, without an immoral act on his part, for acts of courage, compassion, etc., to be acts open to men to perform, there have to be various evils. Evils give men the opportunity to perform those acts which show men at their best. A world without evils would be a world in which men could show no forgiveness, no compassion, no self-sacrifice. And men without that opportunity are deprived of the opportunity to show themselves at their noblest. For this reason God might well allow some of his creatures to perform evil acts with passive evils as consequences, since these provide the opportunity for especially noble acts.

Against the suggestion of the developed free-will defense that it would be justifiable for God to permit a creature to hurt another for the good of his or the other's soul, there is one natural objection which will surely be made. This is that it is generally supposed to be the duty of men to stop other men hurting each other badly. So why is it not God's duty to stop men hurting each other badly? Now the theodicist does not have to maintain that it is never God's duty to stop men hurting each other; but he does have to maintain that it is not God's duty in circumstances where it clearly is our duty to stop such hurt if we can—e.g., when men are torturing each other in mind or body in some of the ways in which they do this in our world and when, if God exists, he does not step in.

Now different views might be taken about the extent of our duty to interfere in the quarrels of others. But the most which could reasonably be claimed is surely this—that we have a duty to interfere in three kinds of circumstances— (1) if an oppressed person asks us to interfere and it is probable that he will suffer considerably if we do not, (2) if the participants are children or not of sane mind and it is probable that one or other will suffer considerably if we do not interfere, or (3) if it is probable that considerable harm will be done to others if we do not interfere. It is not very plausible to suppose that we have any duty to interfere in the quarrels of grown sane men who do not wish us to do, unless it is probable that the harm will spread. Now note that in the characterization of each of the circumstances in which we would have a duty to interfere there occurs the word "probable", and

it is being used in the 'epistemic' sense—as "made probable by the total available evidence". But then the "probability" of an occurrence varies crucially with which community or individual is assessing it, and the amount of evidence which they have at the time in question. What is probable relative to your knowledge at t_1 may not be at all probable relative to my knowledge at t_2. Hence a person's duty to interfere in quarrels will depend on their probable consequences relative to that person's knowledge. Hence it follows that one who knows much more about the probable consequences of a quarrel may have no duty to interfere where another with less knowledge does have such a duty—and conversely. Hence a God who sees far more clearly than we do the consequences of quarrels may have duties very different from ours with respect to particular such quarrels. He may know that the suffering that A will cause B is not nearly as great as B's screams might suggest to us and will provide (unknown to us) an opportunity to C to help B recover and will thus give C a deep responsibility which he would not otherwise have. God may very well have reason for allowing particular evils which it is our bounden duty to attempt to stop at all costs simply because he knows so much more about them than we do. And this is no ad hoc hypothesis—it follows directly from the characterization of the kind of circumstances in which persons have a duty to interfere in quarrels.

We may have a duty to interfere in quarrels when God does not for a very different kind of reason. God being our creator, the source of our beginning and continuation of existence, has rights over us which we do not have over our fellow-men. To allow a man to suffer for the good of his or someone else's soul one has to stand in some kind of parental relationship toward him. I don't have the right to let some stranger Joe Bloggs suffer for the good of his soul or of the soul of Bill Snoggs, but I do have *some* right of this kind in respect of my own children. I may let the younger son suffer *somewhat* for the good of his and his brother's soul. I have this right because in small part I am responsible for his existence, its beginning and continuance. If this is correct, then a fortiori, God who is, ex hypothesi, so much more the author of our being than are our parents, has so many more rights in this respect. God has rights to allow others to suffer, while I do not have those rights and hence have a duty to interfere instead. In these two ways the theodicist can rebut the objection that if we have a duty to stop certain particular evils which men do to others, God must have this duty too.

In the free-will defense, as elaborated above, the theist seems to me to have an adequate answer to the suggestion that necessarily a good God would prevent the occurrence of the evil which men cause—if we ignore the question of the quantity of evil, to which I will return at the end of my paper. But what of the passive evil apparently not due to human action? What of the pain caused to men by disease or earthquake or cyclone, and what too of animal pain which existed before there were men? There are two additional assumptions, each of which has been put forward to allow the free-will defense to show the compatibility of the existence of God and the existence of such evil. The first is that, despite appearances, men are ultimately responsible for disease, earthquake, cyclone, and much animal pain. There seem to be traces of this view in Genesis 3:16–20. One might claim that God ties the goodness of man to the well-being of the world and that a failure of one leads to a failure of the other. Lack of prayer, concern, and simple goodness lead to the evils in nature. This assumption, though it may do some service for the free-will defense, would seem unable to account for the animal pain which existed before there were men. The other assumption is that there exist humanly free creatures other than men, which we may call fallen angels, who have chosen to do evil, and have brought about the passive evils not brought about by men. These were given the care of much of the

material world and have abused that care. For reasons already given, however, it is not God's moral duty to interfere to prevent the passive evils caused by such creatures. This defense has recently been used by, among others, Plantinga. This assumption, it seems to me, will do the job, and is not *clearly* false. It is also an assumption which was part of the Christian tradition long before the free-will defense was put forward in any logically rigorous form. I believe that this assumption may indeed be indispensable if the theist is to reconcile with the existence of God the existence of passive evils of certain kinds, e.g., certain animal pain. But I do not think that the theodicist need deploy it to deal with the central cases of passive evils not caused by men—mental evils and the human pain that is a sign of bodily malfunctioning. Note, however, that if he does not attribute such passive evils to the free choice of some other agent, the theodicist must attribute them to the direct action of God himself, or rather, what he must say is that God created a universe in which passive evils must necessarily occur in certain circumstances, the occurrence of which is necessary or at any rate not within the power of a humanly free agent to prevent. The antitheodicist then naturally claims, that although a creator might be justified in allowing free creatures to produce various evils, nevertheless (P4) a creator is never justified in creating a world in which evil results except by the action of a humanly free agent. Against this the theodicist tries to sketch reasons which a good creator might have for creating a world in which there is evil not brought about by humanly free agents. One reason which he produces is one which we have already considered earlier in the development of the free-will defense. This is the reason that various evils are logically necessary conditions for the occurrence of actions of certain especially noble kinds. This was adduced earlier as a reason why a creator might allow creatures to perform evil acts with passive evils as consequences. It can also be adduced as a reason why he might himself bring about passive

❀ ❀

evils—to give further opportunities for courage, patience, and tolerance. I shall consider here one further reason that, the theodicist may suggest, a good creator might have for creating a world in which various passive evils were implanted, which is another reason for rejecting (*P4*). It is, I think, a reason which is closely connected with some of the other reasons which we have been considering why a good creator might permit the existence of evil.

A creator who is going to create humanly free agents and place them in a universe has a choice of the kind of universe to create. First, he can create a finished universe in which nothing needs improving. Humanly free agents know what is right, and pursue it; and they achieve their purposes without hindrance. Second, he can create a basically evil universe, in which everything needs improving, and nothing can be improved. Or, third, he can create a basically good but half-finished universe—one in which many things need improving, humanly free agents do not altogether know what is right, and their purposes are often frustrated; but one in which agents can come to know what is right and can overcome the obstacles to the achievement of their purposes. In such a universe the bodies of creatures may work imperfectly and last only a short time; and creatures may be morally ill-educated, and set their affections on things and persons which are taken from them. The universe might be such that it requires long generations of cooperative effort between creatures to make perfect. While not wishing to deny the goodness of a universe of the first kind, I suggest that to create a universe of the third kind would be no bad thing, for it gives to creatures the privilege of making their own universe. Genesis 1 in telling of a God who tells men to "subdue" the earth pictures the creator as creating a universe of this third kind; and fairly evidently—given that men are humanly free agents—our universe is of this kind.

Now a creator who creates a half-finished universe of this third kind has a further choice as to how he molds the humanly free agents which it contains. Clearly he will have to give them a nature of some kind, that is, certain narrow purposes which they have a natural inclination to pursue until they choose or are forced to pursue others—e.g., the immediate attainment of food, sleep, and sex. There could hardly be humanly free agents without some such initial purposes. But what is he to do about their knowledge of their duty to improve the world—e.g., to repair their bodies when they go wrong, so that they can realize long-term purposes, to help others who cannot get food to do so, etc.? He could just give them a formal hazy knowledge that they had such reasons for action without giving them any strong inclination to pursue them. Such a policy might well seem an excessively laissez-faire one. We tend to think that parents who give their children no help toward taking the right path are less than perfect parents. So a good creator might well help agents toward taking steps to improve the universe. We shall see that he can do this in one of two ways.

An action is something done for a reason. A good creator, we supposed, will give to agents some reasons for doing right actions—e.g., that they are right, that they will improve the universe. These reasons are ones of which men can be aware and then either act on or not act on. The creator could help agents toward doing right actions by making these reasons more effective causally; that is, he could make agents so that by nature they were inclined (though not perhaps compelled) to pursue what is good. But this would be to impose a moral character on agents, to give them wide general purposes which they naturally pursue, to make them naturally altruistic, tenacious of purpose, or strong-willed. But to impose a character on creatures might well seem to take away from creatures the privilege of developing their own characters and those of their fellows. We tend to think that parents who try too forcibly to impose a character, however good a character, on their children, are less than perfect parents.

The alternative way in which a creator could help creatures to perform right actions is by sometimes providing additional reasons for creatures to do what is right, reasons which by their very nature have a strong causal influence. Reasons such as improving the universe or doing one's duty do not necessarily have a strong causal influence, for as we have seen creatures may be little influenced by them. Giving a creature reasons which by their nature were strongly causally influential on a particular occasion on any creature whatever his character would not impose a particular character on a creature. It would, however, incline him to do what is right on that occasion and maybe subsequently too. Now if a reason is by its nature to be strongly causally influential it must be something of which the agent is aware which causally inclines him (whatever his character) to perform some action, to bring about some kind of change. What kind of reason could this be except the existence of an unpleasant feeling, either a sensation such as a pain or an emotion such as a feeling of loss or deprivation. Such feelings are things of which agents are conscious, which cause them to do whatever action will get rid of those feelings, and which provide reason for performing such action. An itch causally inclines a man to do whatever will cause the itch to cease, e.g., scratch, and provides a reason for doing that action. Its causal influence is quite independent of the agent—saint or sinner, strong-willed or weak-willed, will all be strongly inclined to get rid of their pains (though some may learn to resist the inclination). Hence a creator who wished to give agents some inclination to improve the world without giving them a character, a wide set of general purposes which they naturally pursue, would tie some of the imperfections of the world to physical or mental evils.

To tie desirable states of affairs to pleasant feelings would not have the same effect. Only an existing feeling can be causally efficacious. An agent could be moved to action by a pleasant feeling only when he had it, and the only action to which he could be moved would be to keep the world as it is, not to improve it. For men to have reasons which move men of any character to actions of perfecting the world, a creator needs to tie its imperfections to unpleasant feelings, that is, physical and mental evils.

There is to some considerable extent such tie-up in our universe. Pain normally occurs when something goes wrong with the working of our body which is going to lead to further limitation on the purposes which we can achieve; and the pain ends when the body is repaired. The existence of the pain spurs the sufferer, and others through the sympathetic suffering which arises when they learn of the sufferer's pain, to do something about the bodily malfunctioning. Yet giving men such feelings which they are inclined to end involves the imposition of no character. A man who is inclined to end his toothache by a visit to the dentist may be saint or sinner, strong-willed or weak-willed, rational or irrational. Any other way of which I can conceive of giving men an inclination to correct what goes wrong, and generally to improve the universe, would seem to involve imposing a character. A creator could, for example, have operated exclusively by threats and promises, whispering in men's ears, "unless you go to the dentist, you are going to suffer terribly", or "if you go to the dentist, you are going to feel wonderful". And if the order of nature is God's creation, he does indeed often provide us with such threats and promises—not by whispering in our ears but by providing inductive evidence. There is plenty of inductive evidence that unattended cuts and sores will lead to pain; that eating and drinking will lead to pleasure. Still, men do not always respond to threats and promises or take the trouble to notice inductive evidence (e.g., statistics showing the correlation between smoking and cancer). A creator could have made men so that they naturally took more account of inductive evidence. But to do so would be to impose character. It would be to make men, apart from any choice of theirs, rational and strong-willed.

Many mental evils too are caused by things going wrong in a man's life or in the life of his fellows and often serve as a spur to a man to put things right, either to put right the cause of the particular mental evil or to put similar things right. A man's feeling of frustration at the failure of his plans spurs him either to fulfill those plans despite their initial failure or to curtail his ambitions. A man's sadness at the failure of the plans of his child will incline him to help the child more in future. A man's grief at the absence of a loved one inclines him to do whatever will get the loved one back. As with physical pain, the spur inclines a man to do what is right but does so without imposing a character—without, say, making a man responsive to duty, or strong-willed.

Physical and mental evils may serve as spurs to long-term co-operative research leading to improvement of the universe. A feeling of sympathy for the actual and prospective suffering of many from tuberculosis or cancer leads to acquisition of knowledge and provision of cure for future sufferers. Cooperative and long-term research and cure is a very good thing, the kind of thing toward which men need a spur. A man's suffering is never in vain if it leads through sympathy to the work of others which eventually provides a long-term cure. True, there could be sympathy without a sufferer for whom the sympathy is felt. Yet in a world made by a creator, there cannot be sympathy on the large scale without a sufferer, for whom the sympathy is felt, unless the creator planned for creatures generally to be deceived about the feelings of their fellows; and that, we have claimed, would be morally wrong.

So generally many evils have a biological and psychological utility in producing spurs to right action without imposition of character, a goal which it is hard to conceive of being realized in any other way. This point provides a reason for the rejection of

(P4). There are other kinds of reason which have been adduced reasons for rejecting (P4)— e.g., that a creator could be justified in bringing about evil as a punishment—but I have no space to discuss these now. I will, however, in passing, mention briefly one reason why a creator might make a world in which certain mental evils were tied to things going wrong. Mental suffering and anguish are a man's proper tribute to losses and failures, and a world in which men were immunized from such reactions to things going wrong would be a worse world than ours. By showing proper feelings a man shows his respect for himself and others. Thus a man who feels no grief at the death of his child or the seduction of his wife is rightly branded by us as insensitive, for he has failed to pay the proper tribute of feeling to others, to show in his feeling how much he values them, and thereby failed to value them properly—for valuing them properly involves having proper reactions of feeling to their loss. Again, only a world in which men feel sympathy for losses experienced by their friends, is a world in which love has full meaning.

So, I have argued, there seem to be kinds of justification for the evils which exist in the world, available to the theodicist. Although a good creator might have very different kinds of justification for producing, or allowing others to produce, various different evils, there is a central thread running through the kind of theodicy which I have made my theodicist put forward. This is that it is a good thing that a creator should make a half-finished universe and create immature creatures, who are humanly free agents, to inhabit it; and that he should allow them to exercise some choice over what kind of creatures they are to become and what sort of universe is to be (while at the same time giving them a slight push in the direction of doing what is right); and that the creatures should have power to affect not only the development of the inanimate universe but the well-being and moral character of their fellows, and that there should be opportunities for creatures to develop noble characters and do especially noble actions. My theodicist has argued that if a creator is to make a universe of this kind, then evils of various kinds may inevitably—at any rate temporarily—belong to such a universe; and that it is not a morally bad thing to create such a universe despite the evils.

Now a morally sensitive antitheodicist might well in principle accept some of the above arguments. He may agree that in principle it is not wrong to create humanly free agents, despite the possible evils which might result, or to create pains as biological warnings. But where the crunch comes, it seems to me is in the amount of evil which exists in our world. The antitheodicist says, all right, it would not be wrong to create men able to harm each other, but it would be wrong to create men able to put each other in Belsen. It would not be wrong to create backaches and headaches, even severe ones, as biological warnings, but not the long severe incurable pain of some diseases. In reply the theodicist must argue that a creator who allowed men to do little evil would be a creator who gave them little responsibility; and a creator who gave them only coughs and colds, and not cancer and cholera would be a creator who treated men as children instead of giving them real encouragement to subdue the world. The argument must go on with regard to particular cases. The antitheodicist must sketch in detail and show his adversary the horrors of particular wars and diseases. The theodicist in reply must sketch in detail and show his adversary the good which such disasters make possible. He must show to his opponent men working together for good, men helping each other to overcome disease and famine; the heroism of men who choose the good in spite of temptation, who help others not merely by giving them food but who teach them right and wrong, give them something to live for and something to die for. A world in which this is possible can only be a world in which there is much evil as

well as great good. Interfere to stop the evil and you cut off the good.

Like all moral arguments this one can be settled only by each party pointing to the consequences of his opponent's moral position and trying to show that his opponent is committed to implausible consequences. They must try, too, to show that each other's moral principles do or do not fit well with other moral principles which each accepts. The exhibition of consequences is a long process, and it takes time to convince an opponent even if he is prepared to be rational, more time than is available in this paper. All that I claim to have *shown* here is that there is no *easy proof* of incompatibility between the existence of evils of the kinds we find around us and the existence of God. Yet my sympathies for the outcome of any more detailed argument are probably apparent, and indeed I may have said enough to convince some readers as to what that outcome would be.

My sympathies lie, of course, with the theodicist. The theodicist's God is a god who thinks the higher goods so worthwhile that he is prepared to ask a lot of man in the way of enduring evil. Creatures determining in cooperation their own character and future, and that of the universe in which they live, coming in the process to show charity, forgiveness, faith, and self-sacrifice is such a worthwhile thing that a creator would not be unjustified in making or permitting a certain amount of evil in order that they should be realized. No doubt a good creator would put a limit on the amount of evil in the world and perhaps an end to the struggle with it after a number of years. But if he allowed creatures to struggle with evil, he would allow them a real struggle with a real enemy, not a parlor game. The antitheodicist's mistake lies in extrapolating too quickly from *our* duties when faced with evil to the duties of a creator, while ignoring the enormous differences in the circumstances of each. Each of us at one time can make the existing universe better or worse only in a few particulars. A creator can choose the kind of universe and the kind of creatures there are to be. It seldom becomes us in our ignorance and weakness to do anything more than remove the evident evils—war, disease, and famine. We seldom have the power or the knowledge or the right to use such evils to forward deeper and longer-term goods. To make an analogy, the duty of the weak and ignorant is to eliminate cowpox and not to spread it, while the doctor has a duty to spread it (under carefully controlled conditions). But a creator who made or permitted his creatures to suffer much evil and asked them to suffer more is a very demanding creator, one with high ideals who expects a lot. For myself I can say that I would not be too happy to worship a creator who expected too little of his creatures. Nevertheless such a God does ask a lot of creatures. A theodicist is in a better position to defend a theodicy such as I have outlined if he is prepared also to make the further additional claim—that God knowing the worthwhileness of the conquest of evil and the perfecting of the universe by men, shared with them this task by subjecting himself as man to the evil in the world. A creator is more justified in creating or permitting evils to be overcome by his creatures if he is prepared to share with them the burden of the suffering and effort.

5.11 Unit 5 Study Guide

* *

Anselm

How does the ontological argument define God?

What premises does the ontological argument depend upon?

Why does the Ontological argument assume that God does not exist?

What is Gaunilo's critique of the Ontological argument?

Are ontological arguments *a priori* or empirical?

Aquinas

Which of the four arguments is Aquinas's paper relevant to?

What are Aquinas's "Five Ways"? (know their names and their summaries)

Why does the Cosmological Argument make it difficult to talk about God? How does Aquinas resolve this?

Craig

What are the premises of Craig's argument?

Why does Craig think we must believe that the universe began to exist?

What was Mackie's critique? How does Craig respond?

Paley and Hume on the Teleological Argument

What are the premises in the Teleological argument?

What analogy does the teleological argument rely on?

How are intentions related to the teleological argument?

Are teleological arguments *a priori* or empirical?

What does "God of the gaps" mean?

Must a theist believe the world shows evidence of God's design?

Must an atheist deny that there is order or purpose in nature?

How does Hume critique the teleological argument?

How does Hume suggest the analogy in the teleological argument should be taken farther?

C. D. Broad

Which of the arguments for God's existence is Broad's paper relevant to?

What is the analogy C. D. Broad begins with, involving degrees?

What analogy does C. D. Broad suggest better describes religious experiences?

What attitude does Broad think those who have no religious experiences should have toward those who do have them?

How does Broad think religious traditions shape religious experiences?

How does Broad think psychological problems relate to religious experiences?

Dostoevsky

How does Ivan respond to the claim that God allows evil for some the greater good?

How does Ivan respond to the claim that God will make everything right in the end, and all will be reconciled in universal harmony?

What is "Dostoevsky's Response" to the Problem of Evil?

Johnson

Why does Johnson reject the claim that the evil in the world for reasons we could possibly understand?

When is our failure to see something evidence that it isn't there at all, according to Johnson?

Why does the absence of a miraculous response to evil suggest that there isn't a God?

Why does Johnson reject the claim that the evil in the world is permitted for reasons 'beyond our understanding'?

Swinburne

What is the distinction between active evil and passive evil?

When a sadist tortures an innocent person, what's the active evil, and what's the passive evil?

Why doesn't the Free Will defense resolve the Problem of Evil?

How does Swinburne suggest that the problem of evil needs to be reformulated, given the distinction between active evil and passive evil?

Why does Swinburne suggest God might have created an imperfect world?

Points not to Miss

What are the major views in the philosophy of religion?

What does a theist believe?

What does an agnostic believe?

What does a "soft" atheist believe?

What does a "hard" atheist believe?

What does a polytheist believe?

What does a pantheist believe?

What does a monotheist believe?

What does an Abrahamic monotheist believe?

What three attributes are traditionally associated with God in Western Philosophy?

What attributes do some theists believe God has that aren't shown *a priori* by the arguments given in class?

What is the argument for atheism from Occam's Razor?

What are the four types of arguments for the Existence of God?

Ontological arguments argue from _____ to the conclusion that _____.

Cosmological arguments argue from _____ to the conclusion that _____.

Teleological arguments argue from _____ to the conclusion that _____.

Experiential arguments argue from _____ to the conclusion that _____.

What is the "ethical argument" for belief in God? Why is it not an argument that God actually exists?

The Problem of Evil

In what situations might someone all-good know an evil event will occur and have the power to prevent it, yet decline to intervene to prevent the evil event?

Why does it seem that God is still responsible for the evil in the world, even if God didn't create the evil in the world (or didn't create this evil world)?

How does the problem of evil ultimately need to define "evil"?

How does the problem of evil ultimately need to define "good"?

Cosmological Argument

According to the Cosmological argument, why can't the question "why is this the actual world?" be answered by appealing to some feature of the actual world?

What responses can an atheist give to cosmological arguments?

What are the various premises which feature in versions of the Cosmological argument?

Why doesn't the theist consider "what caused God?" to be a valid objection to the causal version of the Cosmological argument?

What rebuttal can an atheist offer of the claim that, because every event in our world has a prior cause, God must exist to cause the first event that caused everything in our world?

What does "orthodgonal" mean? What issues are *orthogonal* to the cosmological argument?

Difficult Questions

Explain two different versions of the cosmological argument for the existence of God, including

the contingent feature of the universe;

why a theist believes the existence of God is needed to explain it; and

how an atheist might respond.

Explain two different responses to the problem of evil which a theist might offer, including

what premises of the original argument they reject;

what the strengths of the response are;

what the weaknesses of the response are;

Overview: Unit 6
Ethics and Free Will

✳ ✳

6.1 What Is My Responsibility?

6.2 Immanuel Kant, *Fundamental Principles for the Metaphysics of Morals*, selections

6.3 J. S. Mill, *Utilitarianism*, selections

6.4 Aristotle, *The Nicomachean Ethics*, selections

6.5 Baron d'Holbach, "Determinism" (selections from *The System of Nature*)

6.6 Richard Taylor, "Libertarianism" (selections from *Metaphysics*)

6.7 Selections on Compatibilism

6.8 Judith Jarvis Thomson, "The Trolley Problem"

6.9 Unit 6 Study Guide

We'll finish the class with a consideration of moral philosophy. Are claims about what you morally ought to do objectively true, relatively true, or neither true nor false? How can anyone be held morally responsible for their actions if the world works in a deterministic way?

By the end of this unit, you should be able to:

✳ Distinguish moral realism and anti-realism; objectivism and relativism; and situationalism and absolutism.

✳ Restate arguments for and against moral realism and objectivism.

✳ Distinguish consequentialism, deontology, virtue ethics, and other normative ethical systems.

✳ Relate normative ethical systems to contemporary debates in applied ethics.

459

* Restate, contrast, and evaluate competing definitions of Libertarianism; Determinism; and Compatibilism.
* Restate arguments for Libertarianism; Determinism; Compatibilism.
* Relate debates about free will to questions of moral responsibility.
* Explain competing definitions of free will and of possibility.
* Justify a position on a contemporary moral debate.

✿ 6.1 What is my Responsibility? ✿

✳ ✳

So far in this class, we've considered questions about what we can know, or "epistemology", and questions about the structure of reality, or "metaphysics". Now we'll turn to questions in the third major branch of philosophy, questions about Ethics.

- **A. How do People Think about Ethics?**
- **B. The First Problem: Skepticism about Moral Truths**
- **C. Responses to Skepticism about Moral Truths**
- **D. How to Reject the Verification Principle**
- **E. Kant: Morality as Non-Contradiction**
- **F. Mill: Morality as Maximizing Utility**
- **G. Aristotle: It's who you are, not what you do.**
- **H. The Second Problem: Determinism**
- **I. A Thought Experiment**
- **J. Defining Free Will**
- **K. Free Will as Agent Causation**
- **L. Free Will as the Ability to Do Otherwise**
- **M. Free Will as Acting for One's Own Reasons**
- **N. Conclusion**

A. How do People Think about Ethics?

When philosophers talk about "ethics" or "morality", they usually use these words interchangeably. The word "morality" might have a more somber and solemn tone to it, and the word "ethics" might have more of a professional and academic tone. However, both words seem to be basically about the same thing: questions about what one ought or ought not to do, about what should and should not be the case, and about who one should and should not strive to be like. These are sometimes called *normative* questions or *prescriptive* questions, because they go beyond describing how the world is, and say something about how the world should be.

Ethical questions tend to be highly controversial, because there is no universally agreed upon way to think about ethics. Consider how many different ways that human societies on our planet think about ethical questions:

* Some people think of ethics in terms of being *healthy* or maintaining a state of *purity*. For instance, some people think
  * one shouldn't eat dead animals.
  * one shouldn't despoil the natural environment.
  * one should avoid contact with bad places, people, or things.
  * one should live in harmony with the higher pattern of nature.
  * one should avoid sexual relationships with relatives.

* Some people think in ethics in terms of the development of inner *character* or *virtue*. For instance, some people think
  * one should strive to be brave, generous, witty, and tasteful.
  * one should strive to be compassionate, meek, and humble.
  * one should strive to be wise, educated, and reflective.
  * one should strive to be bold, dramatic, and influential.

* Some people think of ethics in terms of *reciprocity* and *loyalty* to one's family, friends, or community. For instance, some people think
  * one should be careful to always repay gifts and favors.
  * one should take care of one's family and relatives before strangers.
  * one should never abandon a friend in danger or need.
  * one should never give aid to the enemies of one's people.

* Some people think of ethics in terms of an obligation to give *obedience* to the commands of a legitimate *authority*. For instance, some people think
  * one should obey the law.
  * one should submit to the wishes of parents and elders.
  * one should follow the commandments of God.
  * one should respect the outcomes of democratic elections.

* Some people think of ethics in terms of a duty to act on *principles* that are *just*, fair to everyone, and preserve everyone's moral *rights*. For instance, some people think
  * one should tell the truth in every situation.
  * one should never steal what belongs to someone else.
  * one should never intentionally kill an innocent person.
  * one should donate a percentage of income to charity.

* Some people think of ethics in terms of bringing about the most *good* or *happiness* in the world while minimizing the amount of badness or pain. For instance, some people think
  * one should try to increase the quality of life for everyone in society.
  * one should try to reduce the amount of suffering from disease and famine.
  * one should not torture someone else simply for a laugh.
  * one should not prolong the misery of a dying person or animal.

* Some people think of ethics in terms of exercising one's own *freedom* as an agent, never being forced to act by compulsion or coercion. For instance, some people think:

- ◆ one should arrive at decisions in a detached and dispassionate way.
- ◆ one should act on one's own well-considered reasons.
- ◆ one shouldn't act out of anger or impatience.
- ◆ one shouldn't act out of a sense of social pressure or obligation.

* Some people think of ethics in terms of maintaining the right qualities in relationships with *others*. For instance, some people think

- ◆ one should seek to care for other people and meet their needs.
- ◆ one should be patient with other people when they are difficult.
- ◆ one should not judge others for the things they do wrong.
- ◆ one should not think of others as tools to get what one wants.

* Finally, some people think of ethics as closely tied to the idea of a meaningful life, which may require an individual to go over and above what most people are required to do. For instance, someone might think that he or she

- ◆ should sacrifice happiness for the sake of art, music, or academic work.
- ◆ should dedicate life to protesting injustice while knowing nothing will change.
- ◆ has a special calling from God to live a life of simplicity and poverty.
- ◆ has a special role in society to be the "gadfly" who asks difficult questions.
- ◆ must voluntarily go without food certain times of year to share in human suffering.

Of course, there's nothing incompatible about these various ways of thinking about ethics. Most people think of ethics as some mixture of many or most of these categories. Perhaps, these are different ways of thinking about the same thing, or perhaps there are a variety of very different normative properties in the world which we lump together and call "ethics". In any case, there isn't enough space in this textbook to cover all of them! So, by the end of this unit, we'll only have had a chance to talk about three of them: ethics as acting on just *principles*, ethics as bringing about good *outcomes*, and ethics as *character*.

Before we do that, however, we should notice that all of these ways of thinking of ethics share two assumptions in common:

1. They assume there are *facts* of the matter about what one should or shouldn't do or be and we can actually *know* something about these facts.

2. They assume that someone can be held *personally responsible* for meeting or not meeting the standard of what they should or shouldn't do or be.

Now, both of these assumptions are something that can be seriously questioned. So, before discuss different theories of ethics, we'll first need to respond to questions that people have raised about these two assumptions.

B. The First Problem: Skepticism about Moral Truths

First, someone might be skeptical about whether there are moral truths. How we could ever claim to *know* something about morality? After all, when reading the list of examples above of what people believe about morality, it's quite likely that you agreed with some of the things on the list, but disagreed with others.

Not everyone believes that eating meat is wrong, for example. People disagree pretty dramatically about many moral issues. For everything you agree with, there's likely someone who disagrees with it, and for everything you disagree with, there's likely someone who agrees with it. How can we think there are facts about morality, if humans understand morality in so many different ways?

Of course, there are other topics that people disagree about, but this disagreement doesn't lead us to believe that no one could ever hope to know the answer. For instance, some people disagree about whether global climate change is being produced by human-caused increased emissions of CO_2 gasses. However, either one side or the other must be right, and it seems like there is ample evidence which can help resolve the question. Likewise, many people disagree about what caused the extinction of the dinosaurs. But again, seeing that people disagree about this doesn't cause anyone to doubt that there's a fact of the matter about what caused it or good evidence about the answer to the question.

What's different about moral disagreement is that it isn't easy to see what sort of evidence could prove that one side is correct and the other incorrect. What sort of experiment would one conduct to show that lying is wrong?

Consider the following argument:

Argument 6.1.1

1. There is a fact of the matter about S if and only if there is some possible method of verifying through observation that S is true or false.

2. There is no possible method of verifying through observation whether moral claims are true or false.

C. There is no fact of the matter about whether moral claims are true or false.

Premise 1 gives a principle—call it the *verification principle*—which says that there can only be a fact of the matter about some subject matter ("S" is a variable, representing any subject matter) only in those cases where topics about that subject matter can be shown to be true. For instance, suppose that someone walked up to you and claimed that "each of us has an inner *auraton* which is *taintificated* when we come in contact with *aethereal sprytes*". To try to understand what this person even meant by "inner auraton", "taintificated", and "aethereal sprytes", it seems like it would be reasonable to ask them how one is to determine that one is in contact with an aethereal spryte, and how one is to determine that one's inner auraton has been taintificated.

Suppose this person gives an answer like this: "symptoms of a taintificated inner auraton include nausea, anxiety, and depression", and "a sure sign that one is in the presence of an aethereal spryte is that one feels a tingling sensation up one's spine". Well, now, even if you don't yourself believe in auratons and sprytes, you can at least start to make sense of what these words mean, and you can acknowledge that the other person is making a claim that can be tested and its truth or falsity objectively measured: is feeling a tingling sensation up one's spine a reliable pre-cursor to nausea, anxiety, and depression?

But suppose instead that this person gives an answer like this: "there's no tool for measuring whether or not you're in the presence of a spryte" and "people with a taintificated auraton have the same experiences as those without one." Now it doesn't seem like they're really discussing a fact in the world at all. If someone disagreed with them, insisting that it is the *absence* rather than the presence of sprytes which leads to taintification, how would anyone ever resolve that question?

The problem is that, according to Premise 2 of the argument, morality is just like that. How would you measure the badness or goodness of an action? What do you see or hear that can confirm or disconfirm moral claims like "treat the elderly with respect" or "pay back what you owe someone else"? Does murder smell or taste different than killing in self-defense? What weights and measures would one use for rightness and wrongness?

None, of course! You can't measure morality. There is something fundamentally different about moral terms like *should* and *shouldn't*. It doesn't seem like one can demonstrate facts about *should* and *shouldn't* through measurements of how things *are.* We might rephrase the argument slightly:

Argument 6.1.2

1. There is a fact of the matter about S if and only if there is some possible method of verifying through observation that S is true or false.

2. There is no possible method of verifying through observation whether claims about what one should or shouldn't do are true or false.

C. There is no fact of the matter about what one should or shouldn't do.

If someone accepts premises 1 and 2, then the conclusion follows: there are no facts about morality. This position is called moral anti-realism.

C. Responses to Skepticism about Moral Truths

This graphic illustrates the possible responses to skepticism about moral truths.

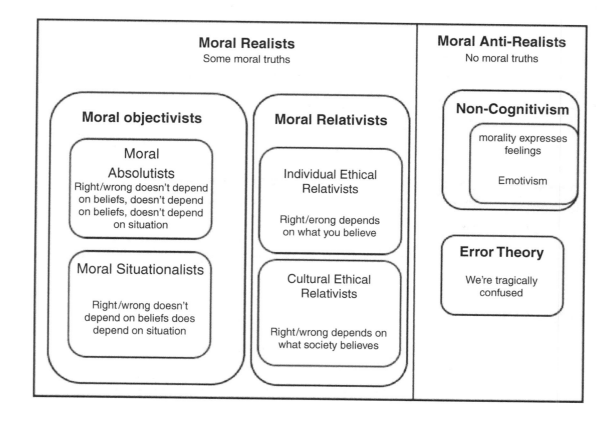

A **moral anti-realist** is someone who believes there are no statements about morality which are true or false because of the way reality is.

An **error theorist** thinks we are tragically confused: it seems like there are facts about morality, but there really aren't. A non-cognitivist, on the other hand, thinks that the reason there are no facts about morality is because sentences about what we "ought" to do or "should" do don't express propositions.

Remember that not all sentences express propositions. Commands like "please pass the salt" are neither true nor false. According to a **non-cognitivism**, a sentence like "you shouldn't cheat on tests" is more like the expression "boo cheating!", or the command "don't cheat on tests!", or a fictional sentence like "Spock is wise". They may be sincere or insincere, but they are neither true nor false. What's really going on when someone says something like "You shouldn't do that!" is more like expressing their authority over another person and ability to tell them what to do, or expressing a feeling that they would like the other person to adopt. This view is sometimes called "emotivism" because it means that morality is an expression of how we want others to feel.

> ### Example: Anti-Realist Error Theory
> There is no fact of the matter about whether a bicycle is happy or unhappy.
> There is no fact of the matter about whether the number 5 is lucky or unlucky.
> Morality is like this: it sounds like something that can be true or false, and we all believe it is true or false (and maybe we must), but there is no truth or falsity behind it.

> ### Example: Anti-Realist Non-Cognitivism
> There's no fact of the matter about whether "Oh yeah baby! ASU rocks!" is true.
> There's no fact of the matter about whether "Shut your mouth, loser!" is true.
> Morality is like this: some other kind of activity rather than describing the world.

A **moral realist** is someone who believes that there are some statements about morality which are true or false because of the way reality is. A sentence like "you shouldn't cheat on tests" is true, just like it's true that the earth is round and it's true that 2+2=4. However, moral realists disagree on how best to respond to the argument for moral skepticism.

A **moral relativist** rejects premise 2 of the skeptic's argument. There *is* a possible method of confirming through observation whether claims about what one should or shouldn't do are true or false, an empirical test for morality. Take a poll! Learning what is morally right and wrong is just a matter of asking other people what they think is morally right and wrong. A moral relativist believes that statements about morality depend on what someone or some group of people believes about morality. For instance, a moral relativist about cheating believes that whether "you shouldn't cheat on tests" is true or not is relative to who is speaking and what that person believes about cheating, much like "chocolate is tastier than vanilla" is relative to the person is speaking.

There are two types of moral relativism.

Subjectivism, also called **Individual Ethical Relativism**, is the view that that what is right or wrong is relative to each individual. "You shouldn't cheat on tests" may be true relative to me (because I think cheating is wrong), but not true relative to you (because you think cheating is okay). Is murder wrong?

It depends who you ask. Murder is wrong for you if you believe it is wrong, but it isn't wrong for you if you don't believe it is wrong.

If you ask an individual ethical relativist "why do you believe that your spouse lying to you is wrong?", then that person can only reply "my spouse lying to me is wrong to me because I believe it is wrong, so I believe it is wrong because I know that I believe that it is wrong; of course it may not be wrong relative to my spouse to lie to me, because my spouse seems not to believe that it is wrong . . . "

> **Example: Subjectivism**
> Some people think that cilantro is tasty
> Some people think that cilantro is gross
> What makes cilantro tasty or gross is that the individual who's talking believes it is tasty or gross
> Morality is like this: what makes something right is that you believe it is right

The difficulty with subjectivism is that it means that, when you believe that something is morally wrong, what you believe is *that you believe that something is morally wrong*. But this leads to an infinite regress. What you believe is that you believe that you believe that you believe . . . and so on. This makes the belief that something is wrong almost trivial. Think of it this way: if two people get into an argument about whether something is right or wrong, relativism says that there are confused. Their views do not actually conflict with one another.

Conventionalism, also called **Cultural Ethical Relativism**, is the view that what is right or wrong is relative to each culture or society. "You shouldn't cheat on tests" may be true relative to American academic culture, but not relative to the culture of a very different society and time. What's right or wrong can always change from society to society, or from the past to the present: slavery is immoral now, but it was morally acceptable in the past. Individuals can be wrong about morality when they get the

> **Example: Conventionalism**
> Some societies believe that mullets are cool
> Some societies believe that mullets are not cool
> What makes a mullet cool (here) is that this society here believes they are cool.
> Moral claims are like this: something is right or wrong because a society believes it to be right or wrong.

standards of their culture wrong: for example, if John believes that lying to his spouse is morally right, but he lives in a culture where that is considered wrong, then he's wrong to lie to his spouse. If enough of my neighbors agree that something is wrong, then for the cultural relativist, it's immoral for me to do it.

Conventionalism helps explain why there are so many different ways that humans think about morality. However, it entails that there is no such thing as moral progress in a society. The abolition of slavery, the prohibition of child abuse, the increased acceptance of people who are different than us, even tolerance for other cultures—all of these are cultural values of our time and place. For the conventionalist, a society with these values is not objectively better than a society which practices slavery and child abuse, or a society which believes that it has the duty to conquer the world to impose its culture and values on all people.

Moral Objectivists hold instead that some moral truths are true or false *independent of whether anybody believes that they are true or false*. A moral objectivist about cheating believes that "you shouldn't cheat on tests" is true, even if you and I, or our culture, or everybody in the world believed that you should cheat on tests.

Of course, someone can be a moral objectivist about some things and a cultural relativist about others. For example, you might think that murder is wrong no matter what anybody believes, but believe whether or not picking your nose is wrong depends on what your culture believes.

Just because objectivists believe that morality is not relative to what an individual or culture believes, that doesn't mean that objectivists can't believe that morality depends partly on the situation. Some objectivists believe that the same moral truths apply to all situations, whereas others think that results matter to what is right or wrong.

An **Absolutist** is a kind of moral objectivist who also believes that there are some moral truths which are universal and do not vary across situations. For example, a moral absolutist might believe that lying is always wrong *no matter what the consequences*. A person could be a moral objectivist but not a moral absolutist—they could believe that lying is wrong whether anyone believes it is wrong or not, but that lying is only wrong when it causes someone harm.

A **Situationalist** is someone who believes morality changes from situation to situation, but doesn't depend on anyone's beliefs. A situationalist is a moral objectivist, but not a moral absolutist. For example, it might be wrong to lie in some situations, but morally acceptable in the case of a "white lie", or in a case where it saves a life. It might be wrong to kill in some situations, but acceptable in defense of the life of someone else.

> **Example: Absolutism**
> Believing "some cows aren't cows" is contradicting yourself.
> Wanting to have your cake and eat it too is contradicting yourself.
> Nothing about your situation, or your other beliefs, or your society, or your tastes changes that this is a contradiction.
> Morality is like this: the fact of the matter is universal across all possible situations

> **Example: Situationalism**
> Sometimes you should take the Loop 101 to the Loop 202 to the I-10 to get to downtown Phoenix.
> Sometimes you should take the US 60 to the 1-17 to get to downtown Phoenix.
> Morality is like this: there is a fact of the matter, but it depends on details of the situation.

D. How to Reject the Verification Principle

All moral objectivists have to reject premise 1 of the Skeptic's Argument, the verification principle. They hold that there are facts of the matter which we can know, even though our way of knowing them doesn't involve any empirical observation of the world. Instead, we know these facts a priori, through pure reason.

Examples given in Unit 2 of truths which were supposed to be justified *a priori* included mathematical truths and logical truths. So, could moral truths also be *a priori*, alongside math and logic?

It may not be easy at first to see how moral truths would be anything like logical truths. Moral truths say things like "don't harm people if you don't have to." Logical truths say things like "if A or B, and not B, then A."

More significantly, *no one disagrees* about logical and mathematical truths. Everyone who understands what is meant by them agrees to them. If you understand what "2+2" means, you understand that it is 4. But morality isn't like that! There are many ways of thinking about morality, and people fight and disagree over ethics. Simply understanding what someone means by "you shouldn't allow assisted suicide" doesn't resolve the question of whether you should or shouldn't allow it. So, how is morality in any way like logic?

However, consider for a moment a valid argument: an argument where, if the premises were true, then the conclusion would necessarily be true. For instance, Argument 6.1.2 again:

1. There is a fact of the matter about *S* if and only if there is some possible method of verifying through observation that *S* is true or false.

2. There is no possible method of verifying through observation whether claims about what one should or shouldn't do are true or false.

C. There is no fact of the matter about what one should or shouldn't do.

Given that the argument is valid, and one believes the premises, one is supposed to do with the conclusion?

. . . One is supposed to believe it.

Why?

. . . Because to believe the premises of a valid argument, but not believe the conclusion, is to believe a contradiction.

And why shouldn't one believe a contradiction?

. . . Because the most basic, most foundational principle of logic is the principle of non-contradiction: *don't contradict yourself*. You shouldn't hold beliefs in a self-contradictory way.

Now, the principle of non-contradiction is not controversial, and it's not the sort of thing that people who are skeptical about morality are typically skeptical of. However, notice that it is a *normative* principle: it's a principle about what one should and shouldn't do. One *should* believe the conclusion of a valid argument if one believes the premises, because one *shouldn't* contradict oneself, on pain of irrationality.

However, it seems like this puts the moral anti-realist in a bit of a bind. Suppose someone makes an argument for moral anti-realism. In doing so, this person takes for granted that the person they are speaking to believes that the principle of non-contradiction is true; otherwise, there'd be no point in arguing with them. So, in order to argue for moral anti-realism, one is committed to there being at least one fact about what one should or shouldn't do; namely, it's a fact that one shouldn't believe contradictions. However, the argument for moral anti-realism concludes that:

C. There is no fact of the matter about what one should or shouldn't do.

So in order to argue for moral anti-realism, the moral anti-realist must contradict himself or herself. He or she must hold that there *is* a fact of the matter about what one should do (one shouldn't believe a contradiction) and yet that there is not a fact of the matter about what one should do (given the conclusion). But this itself is arguing in a self-contradictory way.

Here is another way to view it. Remember the verification principle, which says that

1. There is a fact of the matter about *S* if and only if there is some possible method of verifying through observation that *S* is true.

Why should someone believe the verification principle? It's not empirical: how would we observe that the verification principle is true? What test would we run? Is it *a priori*? Well, maybe, but if so, then there's no possible method of verifying it through observation, so according to the verification principle, the verification principle is false. It's certainly every bit as controversial as moral claims are.

Further, isn't the moral anti-realist claiming that the verification principle is something we *should believe*, and claiming that we *shouldn't* believe in anything for which there is no possible method of verifying its truth? That is, wouldn't it be legitimate to write the argument this way:

1. We should believe there is a fact of the matter about *S* if and only if there is some possible method of verifying through observation that *S* is true or false.

2. There is no possible method of verifying through observation whether claims about what one should or shouldn't do are true or false.

C. We should not believe there is a fact of the matter about what one should or shouldn't do.

Now, this is obviously self-contradictory! According to the conclusion, we shouldn't believe the first premise! So, the argument for moral anti-realism fails by its own standards.

E. Kant: Morality as Non-Contradiction

This is good news for the moral realist, because it says that in order to engage in any sort of reasoning or argumentation, one is at least committed to the existence of some facts about what one should or shouldn't do. Someone who denies this can't very well argue or speak at all. It leaves some hope that we can know something about morality.

But it doesn't give us much to work with. There seems like quite a gap between "you should not believe anything is both true and false at the same time" and the claim that, say, "you should love your neighbor as yourself".

However, one philosopher, Immanuel Kant, believed that this gap could be bridged. In reality, morality was just a specialized type of logic: Both were applications of the principle of non-contradiction.

The reason I shouldn't believe that something is both true and false, or believe a contradiction, is that *I shouldn't act in a contradictory way, period.* Now, consider some other ways I might contradict myself:

* I might tell a lie. In order to lie, I have to rely on my words being accepted as truth; yet I know my words aren't true.

* I might steal something and try to sell it at a pawn shop. I have to act as though no one has a right to their property in order to take the item, and yet I have to consider myself to have a right to the stolen property in order to get paid for it at the pawn shop.

* I might borrow money not intending to pay it back. Calling it "borrowing" instead of "stealing" means I do intend to pay it back, yet I don't.

* I might attempt suicide in order to spare myself further pain. In order to have this motive for suicide, I have to consider myself intrinsically valuable and worth sparing pain; yet in order to take my own life, I have to not consider myself intrinsically valuable.

These are examples of cases where moral truths can be explained as truths of logic for Kant, cases where we can't act on a self-contradictory principle. In fact, Kant thinks all of morality can be explained in this way. Moral truths are true whenever they follow from the principle that we shouldn't contradict ourselves, which is a principle that every rational being must hold. Of course, to get this to work, Kant needs to add something controversial. He has to claim that:

(Not-Special)

Whatever set of principles I apply to myself I also must intend to apply to all other rational beings like myself.

The (Not-Special) principle claims that I am not special. There is nothing that distinguishes me from everyone else when it comes to matters of morality. Because of this, it would be a contradiction for me to act on one principle for others, and a different principle when dealing with myself. Instead, I must act as though same principles apply to everyone; Kant calls this a "universal law". He adapts this into what he calls the **First Formulation of the Categorical Imperative**:

act only on that maxim which you can always and at the same time will to be a universal law

Consider some examples:

* I have a duty to tell the truth when testifying in court, because if I testified falsely in court, then I would have to will that everyone should testify falsely in court, but then it would be impossible to give false testimony.
* I have a duty to be charitable and generous at least some times in life, because if I was never generous, then I would have to will that no one ever be generous with those in need, but then I would have to will that no one would never give anything to me when I was in need, but I could never will for that to happen.

Kant thought a **Second Formulation of the Categorical Imperative** was equivalent to the first.

act so as always to treat the humanity in yourself and others at least partly an end in itself, never merely as a means to an end.

A "means" is a way of getting something. An "end" is a goal. It would be contradictory for me to treat myself as merely a means to my ends—that is, to treat myself as a merely tool to getting what I want. In pursuing what I want, I'm treating myself as an end in itself. But I'm not special. So, it's also contradictory of me to treat someone else as only a means to getting what I want, without regarding what they want, and without viewing them as an end in themselves. Kant imagines morality as a kind of universal government run by all rational beings, a "kingdom of ends", enacting only those laws which everyone could agree to consistently follow. Here are two examples:

* I have a duty to treat my employees with respect, because if I was disrespectful to one of them, then I would be treating them as lacking inherent dignity and not being an end in themselves, but then I would have to will that others treat me as something other than an end in itself, but I could never will to be treated in that way.
* Although I'm allowed to use my waiter at a restaurant as a means to getting what I want—namely, food—I can't use my waiter as *merely* a means to getting what I want. I also have to treat him like a human being, look him in the eyes like a real person, say "please" and "thank you" rather than giving orders and, most importantly, I'm obliged to leave a generous tip, even though I'll be out of the restaurant before he notices that I didn't leave one.

With the second formulation, Kant has captured a widely shared view about ethics that one should act toward one's neighbors in the same way that one would have one's neighbors act toward oneself.

F. Mill: Morality as Maximizing Utility

Kant's view is absolutist. It is also a **deontological** view of morality. That means that it is actions themselves and the intentions behind them which matter for morality, not the consequences of those actions. However, this can seem like a very rigid system. Aren't there exceptions to every rule? Aren't there cases where we have to choose the lesser of two evils?

A **consequentialist** holds that what ultimately matters in morality are the consequences of our actions for everyone affected by them, rather than actions themselves. A consequentialist is a type of situationalist. John Stuart Mill was a consequentialist, and the particular view he advocated for is called Utilitarianism. Mill proposed the "Greatest Happiness Principle", which says:

> actions are right in proportion as they tend to promote happiness; wrong as they tend to promote unhappiness.

So, we might define Utilitarianism as the Combination of two claims:

Consequentialism says that the right action is one that produces a higher balance of good minus bad which results from the action, for all people affected by it, than any alternative act, regardless of someone's intentions or motives.

Hedonism[1], which says that good consists in happiness and bad consists in pain; though the pleasure and pain of everyone matters equally, not just my own pleasure and pain.

To calculate what action you should perform, a Utilitarian uses this formula:

1. For the action you are considering, take all the pleasures produced as a result of the action, multiplied by their intensity, multiplied by every person experiencing them, multiplied by the duration of time each pleasure lasts.

2. Also take all the pains produced as a result of the action, multiplied by their intensity, multiplied by every person experiencing them, multiplied by the duration of time each pain lasts.

3. Subtract 2 from 1. Call the result "Utility", pleasure minus pain.

4. Repeat Steps #1–3 for *every possible action* you might take in this situation.

5. Pick the action you find in #4 which brings about the greatest Utility.

For example, suppose you are contemplating whether to tell a lie to your boss cover up something illegal a co-worker did at work that would get him fired. The rule "do not lie" generally serves the greater good, so almost all of the time one should not lie. But there are situations where it is okay to lie, like withholding information from someone who will use it to harm others, or protecting someone who is very ill from hearing something that will worsen his condition. What would you need to consider in this situation?

---

[1] The word "hedonist" normally means a person who pursues pleasure for themselves. However, in philosophy it means a person who thinks pleasure is the one intrinsically valuable thing—not only pleasure for themselves, but for others. So a Utilitarian might be a "hedonist", but they nonetheless might believe they are obligated to go through some pain or trouble in order to bring pleasure or happiness to someone else.

What are the most likely consequences for everyone involved of telling the lie to your boss? What are the most likely consequences for everyone involved of not telling the lie? What's the better result?

A good example to help clearly distinguish Kant from Mill is self-sacrifice. Many people believe self-sacrifice, for a worthy goal, is a praiseworthy thing to do. For example, Gandhi fasted for a long period of time as a public protest, in an attempt to free India from British rule peacefully rather than through violence. Mother Theresa spent her life serving the sick and dying in Calcutta. If these sacrifices are praiseworthy, then why is this so?

* Immanuel Kant would have to claim there was a universal rule that applied in all situations, like "always sacrifice yourself selflessly for the sake of others". But a rule like this could never be applied to everyone at all times—it could never be a universal law! If everyone sacrificed themselves selflessly, who would be left to sacrifice for? This would be treating yourself as a means to an end, and not respecting yourself as an end in itself.

* John Stuart Mill argues instead that self-sacrifice isn't praiseworthy *because* it is a sacrifice, but rather that the worthiness of a sacrifice is the contribution it makes to the happiness in the world as a whole. The suffering of Gandhi and Mother Teresa was small compared to the reduction of suffering in the world they achieved through it.

In Mill's day, people tended to think of Utilitarianism as a cold, grey view on which morality was simply a matter of crunching numbers and being practical. Mill wrote against this view, arguing that Utilitarianism had room for the "higher pleasures", including things that were beautiful, ornamental, and merely amusing. He argued that:

* "Utility" doesn't mean the rejection of beauty, ornament, or amusement. It doesn't mean barren or mechanical or efficient, the way the word "Utilitarian" sometimes is used in English. In fact, beauty, ornamentation, amusement, and richer and deeper things are included in the definition of utility, because they cause pleasure too.

* The "higher pleasures", like enjoying a good novel, were valued more highly by those who experienced them than the "lower pleasures", like eating delicious food. So, saying that pleasure was the only good didn't entail that Utilitarianism was merely a "pig philosophy" that turned people into mere animals.

* Often people are tempted by the lower pleasures to sacrifice the higher ones, but they always feel bad afterward—to give a modern example, missing out on quality time with your wife and children to play an engrossing computer game is something you will eventually regret, since it means sacrificing a higher pleasure for a lower one. People lose their higher aspirations quite easy, and can be brought down from a life seeking higher pleasures to a life seeking lower pleasures through bad experiences, becoming more cynical with age, bad relationships or opportunities in life. So a Utilitarian should try to encourage people's higher aspirations over basic pleasures and give everyone an opportunity to experience the higher pleasures through providing education.

Why think that Utilitarianism is correct that only utility (pleasure–pain) is valuable? Mill says we have to actually look at the real world to decide what people prefer and value, not just reflect in our armchairs about what people should value. Pleasure is a subjective thing, but it's also universally valued across all humanity, and pain is universally disvalued. Anything else that people value, they typically value *because* it tends to produce pleasure or reduce pain. So, that makes utility the ultimate value.

Of course, there are many objections to Mill. Someone might object that pain and pleasure are reliable *indicators* of whether something is good or bad for us, but they don't function correctly all the time: there can be illusory pleasures which are actually bad for us, for instance. Or, suppose that it would make one person—call her Martha—immensely happy if the rest of us tattooed her name to our foreheads, so happy that it would outweigh the displeasure and annoyance the rest of us felt. Mill's view would say that we are required to tattoo "Martha" onto our foreheads.

Another objection, raised by the American philosopher John Rawls (1921–2002), is that utilitarianism leaves out justice and any consideration of people's rights. For example, a Utilitarian seems to have to say that when we can't find the person guilty of committing a crime, it might be acceptable to frame an innocent person for the crime and punish them in a brutal way, if people in society get enough pleasure over watching the brutal punishment of someone they believe to be guilty to outweigh the pain of the person being punished.

Finally, an objection Mill himself considered and recognized is that no one can possibly know all of the possible consequences of their actions! However, he has a response to this objection.

Mill points out that Utilitarianism isn't meant to be an infallible way to make everyday decisions, but just an answer to the question of what makes something right or wrong. Overall experience over the course of time and history have given us a good sense for what *tends* to make people unhappy or happy, and that's what we should work with when making decisions. Often everyday moral rules are useful to that end, so there's no reason to throw them out. Rules like "don't lie", "don't murder", "don't steal", "don't commit adultery", and so on tend to promote the general happiness. Utilitarianism just helps us know when there are exceptions to the rules.

For Mill, the intentions you have behind your actions don't matter. You could do the right thing entirely by accident, or out of selfish motives; the right thing could be done by an evil person, and the wrong thing by a completely innocent person. Mill says that morality is about what actions are right or wrong, not about how you evaluate people. The Utilitarian is just establishing which actions are right and wrong in the situation, not how people should be judged.

G. Aristotle: It's who you are, not what you do

Unlike Mill, for Aristotle the focus is not on evaluating actions, but on evaluating people. For Aristotle, it's not what you do that matters, but who you are. There isn't much we can say about what actions are right or wrong in all situations. Every situation is different. It takes practical wisdom to discern what to do in each new situation, not blind adherence to rules. The goal of morality is to develop one's state of character (habits, desires, and dispositions) to become more inclined to virtue and less to vice.

Aristotle begins by setting out to find what "the good" for a human life is. He concludes that whatever is ultimately good for us must be good for its own sake and good entirely on its own. Aristotle finds one thing that meets this category: happiness. People want to be happy for their own sake, and not as a means to something else. And happiness is enough on its own to be good; it doesn't need something else to make it good. It's our ability to reason, our rational nature that makes us distinctly human. So what is good for a human life—the "happy life" for a human—must be a life which is consistent with our rational nature.

Everything that has an end or purpose has a **virtue** for achieving that end. For instance, it is a knife's virtue for a knife to be sharp, a soup's virtue for the soup to be hot, an eye's virtue for the eye to see accurately and clearly, and a dog's virtue to be obedient and friendly. Virtues are relative to functions. If the function of human beings is to be rational, then there are certain virtues that fit that. What's it mean to live in a rational way?

Aristotle says that the rational way to live is to have a disposition to choose the mean. By "the mean", Aristotle means a kind of idealized half-way point between two extremes. One extreme is being too cowardly: being afraid of small things or too afraid to act when it is time to act. Another extreme is being too brash: rushing out into harm's way without a care in the world. The rational person seeks moderation. Moderation means feeling the right things at the right times, with the right people, in the right way, with the right motive, with respect to the right objects

Here are some examples of what Aristotle considered Virtues.

VICE/TOO MUCH	VIRTUE/MEAN	VICE/TOO LITTLE
Excessive fearlessness	Courage	Cowardice
Rashness	Confidence	Cowardice
Self-Indulgence	Temperance	Insensibility (to pleasure)
Prodigality	Liberality	Meanness
Tastelessness/Vulgarity	Magnificence	Niggardliness
Empty Vanity	Proper Pride	Undue Humility
Ambitiousness	Proper desire of Honor	Unambitiousness
Irascibility	Good-Temperedness	Unirascibility
Boastfulness	Truthfulness	Mock-Modesty
Buffoonery	Ready-Wittedness	Boorishness
Flattery/Obsequiousness	Friendliness	Quarrelsomeness

Unlike Deontology and Utilitarianism, Virtue Ethics doesn't specify a right decision in every situation. The point isn't to always do the right thing, since it's often hard to say what the right thing is. Instead, the point is to become a good person. A person who is good internally will tend to do the right things externally, even if they sometimes make mistakes.

What makes an action a "just action" or a "temperate action"? There's no formula for figuring this out—you have to look instead to a kind of perfect example. *Actions are called just and temperate when they are such as the just or temperate man would do*, and a person is just and temperate when he does these things the way the ideal just and temperate person would do them.

Like Utilitarianism, virtue does have something to do with pleasure and pains, but it doesn't involve math. The virtuous person feels pleasure in the right circumstances, in the right way, at the right times, and so on—and pain in the right circumstances, in the right way, and at the right times. One *uses* pleasures and pains in order to achieve virtue and happiness, but they aren't in themselves good or bad for us.

Aristotle's Virtue Ethics has attracted the attention of contemporary philosophers as an alternative to consequentialism and deontology. Contemporary Virtue Ethicists do not follow Aristotle's particular list of virtues, since some items on Aristotle's list reflected his biases against slaves, women, foreigners, and peasants. However, Virtue Ethicists may use Aristotle's theory to develop a different set of virtues such as compassion, fairness, patience, and caring.

Finally, notice that for Aristotle, moral virtue is a habit that comes as a result of training. Becoming virtuous requires receiving a moral education from a young age. By being forced to perform virtuous actions externally (even though they don't come naturally at first), Aristotle thinks a person will be developed internally (their state of character) into the sort of person who has a habit of performing virtuous actions. These habits then produce more virtuous actions externally, and the process reinforces itself.

For example, if you respond with anger at a small insult, then you build the habit in yourself of always responding with anger to small insults. The next time you are insulted, you feel angrier than you would have otherwise. But if you get used to responding calmly to small insults, you make yourself more resilient to larger insults in the future.

H. The Second Problem: Determinism

We've now taken a look at three approaches to Ethics, one in terms of principles, one in terms of results, and one in terms of character. Each of them has a response to problem of skepticism. For Kant, moral rightness and wrongness is known the way we know logic. For Mill, we know moral goodness and badness through immediate experience, like pleasure and pain. For Aristotle, we know about morality through understanding our own nature as rational human beings.

All of these views seem to be committed to the idea that a person can be held morally *responsible* or *blamed* for doing the wrong thing or having a corrupt character. We generally blame people only when they had control over what they did wrong. To take a simple example, imagine that you spill a can of soda on your friend's carpet. If you spill the soda because you were negligent and careless, you will be blamed a little. If you spill the soda deliberately, in an act of spite, then you will be blamed a lot. But if you spill the soda because your friend tackled you and knocked over the cat, or because there was an earthquake, or because the can of soda had a defect in it that caused it to leak, then you won't be blamed at all, because it wasn't under your control.

We believe that there are differences in how much control we have, and so there are differences in how much blame we deserve when something goes wrong. But the question is this: Are any of our actions *really* under our control at all? Can we be blamed for them? Or does this assume a kind of free will which is at odds with our living in a physical universe? Consider this argument:

Argument 6.1.3

1. Every action I take, I either do for a reason or for no reason.
2. The reasons for an action are a cause of that action.
3. If I take an action for no reason, then that action is random.
4. Anything which is random not under my control.
5. If I take an action for a reason, then either that reason is under my control or not under my control.
6. Even if the immediate cause of my action is under my control, it is fully determined by ultimate causes outside myself which are not under my control.
7. If my action or its ultimate causes are not under my control, then my action is not free.
C. No action I take is free.
8. If I don't act freely, I can't be blamed for what I do.
C2. I can't be blamed for anything I do.

All of the premises of the argument seem initially plausible and hard to dispute. Premises 1 & 5 are logical truths, and Premise 3 seems to be a definitional truth. Premise 2 says that the reason for my action—say, my desire to bring something about—is a cause of it. Premise 7 says that freedom has to do with having control over what one does. So, I don't do anything freely, because I don't ultimately have control over my actions. But it seems like we can't blame someone if they have no control over what they do. So it seems like we can't blame anyone for anything.

Premise 6 is the only somewhat controversial premise: it is a claim that *determinism* is true. Determinism is a statement about the completeness of the physical world and my membership in the physical world. Everything in the physical world is determined by the way matter and energy behave, subject to the laws of nature. It's possible that my reason for choosing to act is the result of another choice I made earlier. But eventually this chain of causes is going to end with something outside myself that I didn't have any choice over, such as my circumstances, my genetic composition, my upbringing, and so on.

If this argument is correct, I do nothing freely, and there is no free will. If there is no free will, then no one can be blamed for doing the wrong thing, acting on a contradictory principle, or failing to maximize utility. No one can be blamed for having a corrupt character. How would someone resist this argument?

I. A Thought Experiment

Suppose an evil villain has kidnapped you and hooked you up to a device which measured your breathing. On the other end of the device are a number of helpless people trapped in a box over a cliff, who will plunge to their deaths on the 10th breath you take. You try very hard to conserve your first nine breaths, drawing them out as long as possible, moving as little as possible, and becoming light-headed and nearly fainting each time. When it comes time for that deadly 10th breath, you hold your breath with all of your strength for two and a half minutes . . . three minutes . . . but, at last, you reach a point where you simply can't hold your breath anymore. The instinctive pull in your body is simply too strong, and you take a breath. The people plunge helplessly to their deaths below. You faint in horror.

The next thing you know, you find yourself safe and comfortable in a hospital room . . . in jail. The evil villain, now defeated, sleeps in the bed on the other side of the room. A prosecutor approaches you: *accessory to murder*, the charges read. "You caused the deaths of those innocent people by taking your 10th breath," the prosecutor grimly declared "and so you are responsible for them".

Now, obviously, this isn't what should happen! You aren't responsible for what happened, the evil villain is. But why aren't you responsible for what happened? *Your action caused these people to die.*

Well, the obvious answer is that, while you did breathe, and your breathing caused people to die, *something else caused you to breathe*. Instinct caused you to breathe. Some semi-autonomous features of your nervous system located in your brain caused you to breathe. Breathing is innate, not something you can simply turn off. You didn't breathe as a matter of your own free will. It's not as though you could have simply held your breath forever, at least not in a world like ours. You can't be held responsible for something if you couldn't have done any differently.

However, while you are resentfully mulling this over in your head, thinking through how you'll defend yourself from these absurd charges, you overhear the evil villain's defense attorney talking to her client. He says:

"Don't worry about a thing, boss. We've got the perfect defense. You are the child of two evil villains, and you likely inherited the villainy gene from your parents. Further, they raised you in a villain commune, and from an early age you learned to do acts of villainy, removing any conscience you might have had. Of course, your life up to this point has offered you no real opportunities to leave the world of villainy to live a normal life, since the world has fixed your identity as "evil villain" with no opportunity to change, breeding a deep sense of hatred and resentment. You have, as every psychologist would agree, some serious psychological problems and a lack of impulse control. All of this compounded to produce the state in your brain that caused you to kidnap and kill those innocent people. So, really, a number of factors outside of your control caused you to kill those people. You didn't act of your own free will and aren't to blame."

Suddenly, your defense is in trouble. If "I didn't do this of my own free will" is a good defense for you, then it looks like it is a good defense for the evil villain. But you don't want to let the evil villain off the hook! He kidnapped you and hooked you up to the device and put you through the horror of watching these people die. However, if it's not a good defense for the evil villain that something else caused him to act, then it's not a good defense for you that something else caused you to breathe.

Fortunately, just as you are beginning to worry, your defense attorney shows up. She was a philosophy major.

J. Defining Free Will

Your defense attorney notices how you're implicitly defining "Free Will". Right now, both you and the evil villain are defining free will this way:

Free Will—Implausible Definition
An agent's action *A* is free if and only if it has no causes outside of the agent's control.

Your action of breathing had a cause outside yourself, and villain's action had causes outside himself, so on definition A neither of you had free will. However, she points out that this is an absurd definition of free will. If this definition were true, then no human could ever have free will! Consider that *every* event has a number of causes outside of the agent's control. An event is a cause of some effect whenever, had the event gone differently, the effect wouldn't have occurred as it did. Consider that the following are then causes of your being at the present moment right now, doing whatever you are doing (presumably, reading this book):

* you were born
* people provided you with enough food, so that you survived
* people helped you learn English well enough to read this text
* your body has fought off diseases well enough to keep you alive so far
* an asteroid did not destroy the earth five years ago
* someone published this book and got a copy to you

Knowing your own individual situation, you can certainly think of other causes of your being where you are right now, reading this book. Does the fact that you were born mean you aren't freely reading this book right now? Does the fact that you couldn't read this book if no one had published it imply that you didn't really, freely choose to read this book?

That would be silly, your lawyer says. In fact, *all* of our choices have at least some causes which are outside of our control. Some people have called this "determinism":

Determinism—Trivial Definition
An event is determined if and only if it has a cause at a prior point in time.

However, this way of defining "determinism" is nearly a trivial truth. It doesn't say anything interesting or substantial about the human condition. It is very difficult to imagine an event which doesn't have a cause. So, merely being caused can't be an excuse that lets either you or the evil villain off the hook for what you did.

What your lawyer says you need to find is a way of defining "Free Will" and "Determinism" so that the evil villain can still be said to have acted of his own "free will", but your breathing will instead qualify as something "Determined", which is not of your own free will.

Unfortunately, she is a public defender. This means that she can only spend a brief moment with each of her long list of clients before moving on to the next client, since she is paid by the state to represent those who can't afford to hire a lawyer of their own. So, she leaves you with three texts to read. Each text defines free will differently. Your job is to pick the one which you think the court is most likely to believe.

Here are some options:

K. Free Will as Agent Causation

Richard Taylor argues that free-will involves a distinctive type of causation that only agents—rational beings capable of free choice—can make. Taylor would reject the premise that the reasons for an action must be causes of that action. Even though I perform actions for reasons, and reasons have causes outside of myself, my action is not caused by my reasons. In fact, my action isn't caused by anything or event at all! It is caused by *me*.

What is it for *me* to cause an event directly—not events in my brain, but me? On Taylor's view, there is an ordinary type of causation called *event causation*, which holds only between one event and another, and a different type of causation, called *agent* causation, which holds between an agent and an action. Free will involves the agent cause of an action. What do we mean by agent cause?

To illustrate, suppose I go out to a bowling alley, bowl a few games, and eat pizza. Here are some sentences I could say:

(a) I eat pizza.
(b) I eat.
(c) *Pizza eats.
(d) I roll the ball down the lane.
(e) *I roll down the lane.
(f) The ball rolls down the lane.

Notice that (b) is grammatical, but (e) is not, and (f) is grammatical, but (c) is not. When the verb "roll" is used in (f), "the ball" is the subject of the verb, indicating that it is the thing rolling but *not* the *agent* which does the rolling. However, in (d) "I" am the subject of the sentence, indicating now not that I am the thing rolled but rather that I am the *agent* behind the rolling, and the ball is suddenly the object of the sentence, even though it's actually the thing rolling.

Verbs like "eat" or "push" or "pull" all require a subject which is an agent: I pull the door closed, the door does not pull closed. Verbs like "roll" and "drop" change their meaning depending on whether the subject is an agent: I drop the glass on the floor, which means that the glass drops on the floor, not that I drop on the floor.

This is what we mean by an "agent": Being an agent is being like the person rolling the bowling ball rather than being like the bowling ball which is rolled. The concept of agency is deeply embedded in how we ordinarily think about action; some languages mark the distinction between agents and non-agents more explicitly than English does.

Now compare:

(g) I knocked the pins down.
(h) The ball knocked the pins down.

Both (g) and (h) are true. But in (g) the type of causation we are discussing is agent causation, whereas in (h) the type of causation is merely event causation. We'd say that (g) describes an action, but (h) only describes an event. With this in mind, here is how the agent causal libertarian defines free will:

Free Will—Agent Causation
An agent's action *A* is free if and only if it was self-determined by an agent instead of determined by outside forces or indeterministic chance.

The downside of this definition of free will is that it requires swallowing some serious consequences. Physics only studies events, not human agency. So, this definition seems to commit us to a view that there is a special type of causation which doesn't fall under the ordinary laws of physics.

Note that a very weak form of determinism is compatible even with a view on which we ourselves are causes of our own choices. Call this "emergentist determinism".

Determinism—Emergentist Definition
An event is determined if and only if it and only if nothing more is required for the event to occur than prior states of the world and laws of nature.

On this definition, the physical world is enough to bring about our minds, choices, and actions, but our minds and choices are still distinct from the physical world, and they still count as causes of our actions. We may not be the *only* causes of our actions, but this doesn't rule out our being *one* of the causes of our actions.

How do you think this would apply to your defense?

L. Free Will as the Ability to Do Otherwise

A weaker definition of free-will comes from Gottfried Leibniz (1646–1716). Leibniz writes:

> An act necessarily follows from a volition to do it and the ability to do it. When all the conditions for willing to do something are matched by equally strong conditions against willing to do it, no volition occurs. Rather there is indifference.

> If complete indifference is required for freedom, then there is scarcely ever a free act, since I think it hardly ever happens that everything on both sides is equal. . . . I don't think examples can be found in which the will chooses—that is, where it arbitrarily breaks a deadlock by just choosing—because there is always some reason for choosing one alternative rather than the other.[2]

---

[2] From Leibniz, "Freedom and Possibility" (1680), Translated by Jonathan Bennett (2015).

For Leibniz, there will always be enough reasons to push us in one direction or another. Free will doesn't require us to be indifferent between choices or even to deliberate between choices. All that free will requires, according to Leibniz, is the logical possibility of doing differently.

David Hume held a similar view. Hume held that all of our actions were caused by forces outside of us, and so our actions were in principle predictable. However, because causes don't necessitate their effects, we still had the capability of acting otherwise, and had free will.

Leibniz notes that if having free will meant our choices weren't fully caused by reasons, then even God would not have free will, since God always chooses what is best. However, Leibniz argues that God does have free will in the sense that it would not be a *contradiction* for God to fail to choose what is best. It is only "necessary" that God choose the best in the sense of being a moral necessity, given that God never acts arbitrarily, but not in the sense of being a logical necessity.

> Rather is it true freedom, and the most perfect, to be able to make the best use of one's free will, and always to exercise this power, without being turned aside either by outward force or by inward passions, whereof the one enslaves our bodies and the other our souls. There is nothing less servile and more befitting the highest degree of freedom than to be always led toward the good, and always by one's own inclination, without any constraint and without any displeasure . . .

> This necessity is called moral, because for the wise what is necessary and what is owing are equivalent things; and when it is always followed by its effect, as it indeed is in the perfectly wise, that is, in God, one can say that it is a happy necessity. The more nearly creatures approach this, the closer do they come to perfect felicity. Moreover, necessity of this kind is not the necessity one endeavors to avoid, and which destroys morality, reward and commendation. For that which it brings to pass does not happen whatever one may do and whatever one may will, but because one desires it. A will to which it is natural to choose well deserves most to be commended; and it carries with it its own reward, which is supreme happiness . . .

> But a will that would always drift along at random would scarcely be any better for the government of the universe than the fortuitous concourse of corpuscles . . .[3]

Even if one does not believe in God, one can read Leibniz as making a conceptual point that also applies to human beings. It is only "necessary" that we choose what we do in the sense that we have a complete set of reasons for our actions, and we never act randomly or indeterminately, but not in the sense that it is impossible for us to do otherwise. We can then define free will this way:

Free Will—Non-Agent-Causal Libertarianism
An action is free if and only if it was a natural possibility for one to do otherwise, given prior events occurring as they did.

Notice this definition of free will is *compatible* with—that is, it can be true at the same time as—a certain form of determinism:

Determinism—Causal Exclusive Determinism
An event is determined if and only if it is *only* caused by prior events outside of our control.

---

[3] From Leibniz, "Theodicy" (1710). Translated by E. M. Huggard (1875–1890).

One downside is that non-agent-causal libertarianism seems to say that we have free will only because we *could have* acted randomly, even though we didn't—our choices are still caused by events outside our control. Is this enough for free will?

How do you think this would apply to your situation, defending yourself from the unjust charge?

M. Free Will as Acting for One's Own Reasons

Paul-Henri Thiry, the Baron of Holbach (1723–1789), was a French philosopher who argued that free will was an illusion. For Holbach, every action we take is determined by prior events, such that there is no natural possibility of us doing otherwise—that is, doing otherwise would violate the laws of nature in some way.

We might call this *logical entailment determinism* because it envisions cause and effect as working like a kind of logical argument, where the premises are causes (initial conditions) and laws of nature, and the conclusion is the effect of those causes. For example:

1. The ball is in motion at t_1. (Initial Condition)
2. No opposing force acts on the ball between t_1 and t_2. (Initial Condition)
3. Everything in motion remains in motion without an opposing force. (Law)
C. The ball is in motion at t_2. (Effect)

The argument is valid. Given prior states of world and the laws of nature, it is not a natural possibility for future events to go any differently than they do.

Determinism—Logical Entailment Determinism
An event is determined if and only if there is no natural possibility of it occurring otherwise, given prior events.

If this is true then, in principle, if a perfect reasoner had access to all of the initial conditions in the physical world at time t_1, and knew all of the laws of nature, then this reasoner could determine exactly what would happen at time t_2—including your choices. Your will is determined by the various objects which act on your senses and by the processes in your brain, so there is no possibility that you could have chosen any differently than you did. For you to have chosen differently, something else at t_2 would have had to be different in the physical world.

Some people doubt whether Holbach is right about the physical world. We might doubt whether causation works like a logical deduction, for instance. Concerns about indeterminacy within physics might make us suspicious that anyone could ever deduce the future state of the world from a past state of the world. Holbach's determinism is the most extreme form of determinism, and it is questionable whether we could ever have empirical evidence for it. While we might have empirical evidence that all events are entirely caused by prior events, we can't have empirical evidence that there is *no possible world* in which something went differently. We can't observe other possible worlds.

However, even if Holbach's determinism is true, there may be a way to hold that we nonetheless have free will. W. T. Stace reminds us that speaking of actions as "free" or not is something people did long before philosophers came around to worry about it. Instead of assuming that philosophers have access to a special notion called "free will", we should instead look at how people actually use phrases like "freedom" or "free will" in ordinary language. We should let people define what "free will" means by observing how they actually use that phrase in practice.

Stace brings up a number of examples which suggest that when people say someone has "free will", or "acts freely", then they mean the action's immediate causes are psychological states in the agent. In other words, I act freely when I act for my own reasons. On the other hand, we say that someone does not have free will when he or she seems to be compelled to act by outside forces. For instance, if someone is ordered at gunpoint to do something, that person isn't free, because the immediate cause of the action is *someone else's* psychological states, which are external to that agent.

Free Will—Compatibilism

An action is free if and only if it an agent performs it for her own reasons; that is, if its immediate causes are psychological states of the agent, not external force or compulsion.

This way of defining free will has the advantage of being compatible with *any* form of determinism! Stace says that questions about whether someone should be blamed or held responsible don't require us to figure out whether every event in the world has a sufficient cause, or whether another world in which we acted differently is logically possible, or whether there is a special kind of causation that only applies to agents, or whether any other type of determinism is true or not. Instead, that matters is whether or not someone acted because they *wanted to* or whether someone was, say kidnapped and forced into it by the mafia.

Now that you've seen all the options, which set of definitions do you think would be most helpful to your case?

N. Conclusion

Now, as you begin to read Unit 6 source texts, think about how each thinker is trying to resolve a question at the foundation of Ethics. Kant, Mill, and Aristotle are trying to explain how we can know something about morality. Taylor and Stace are trying to show that we can be morally blameworthy for our actions, and Baron d'Holbach concludes that we cannot.

After you read, it's your turn to decide what you think. What positions do you hold on topics in ethics? Do you think we have free will? Do you think free will is compatible with determinism? How would you argue for your positions? How might someone object to your arguments? How would you respond?

❁ 6.2 Fundamental Principles for the Metaphysics of Morals ❁
Selections
by Immanuel Kant

❋❋

© Boris15/Shutterstock.com

Immanuel Kant (1724–1804) was a Prussian philosopher who wrote at the end of the Enlightenment era in Europe. We've already looked at Kant's Epistemology in Unit 2. In the era prior to Kant, moral philosophy focused on issues of having the appropriate emotions and sentiments. In the *Groundwork* (or "Fundamental Principles") *for the Metaphysics of Morals*, Kant argues that morality is grounded not in feeling, but in logic. We should do our duty because it's our duty, not because we feel a certain way, and not because of what the consequences might be for ourselves or others. Kant's view is a type of **deontology**.

A basic principle of logic is that a contradiction can't be true, and arguments appeal to the principle that one should not believe a contradiction. Kant turns this into a moral general principle that one should not act in a self-contradictory way. Further, since there is nothing special about *me*, I should only act on rules that could be consistently followed by everybody. The result is the First Formulation of Kant's Categorical Imperative: a*ct only on that maxim whereby thou canst at the same time wil that it should become a universal law.*

By grounding morality in logic, Kant avoided the skepticism about morality raised by moral anti-realists. For Kant, morality is *a priori synthetic* knowledge, and we know it the same way we know about metaphysics and mathematics: we know about morality not through experience and observation, but through pure reasoning. However, one might question if unemotional obedience to duty for the sake of duty is really a sign of good moral character.

Here are some questions to think about when you read:

* What is the only thing which can be called good without qualification?
* What does the moral worth of an action lie in? What doesn't it lie in?
* What does each word in each version of the Categorical Imperative mean?
* What examples does Kant use to illustrate his Categorical Imperative?
* What examples can you think of which would illustrate Kant's Categorical Imperative in practice?

The Categorical Imperative

The Good Will

Nothing can possibly be conceived in the world, or even out of it, which can be called good, without qualification, except a good will. Intelligence, wit, judgement, and the other talents of the mind, however they may be named, or courage, resolution, perseverance, as qualities of temperament, are undoubtedly good and desirable in many respects; but these gifts of nature may also become extremely bad and mischievous if the will which is to make use of them, and which, therefore, constitutes what is called character, is not good. It is the same with the gifts of fortune. Power, riches, honour, even health, and the general well-being and contentment with one's condition which is called happiness, inspire pride, and often presumption, if there is not a good will to correct the influence of these on the mind, and with this also to rectify the whole principle of acting and adapt it to its end. The sight of a being who is not adorned with a single feature of a pure and good will, enjoying unbroken prosperity, can never give pleasure to an impartial rational spectator. Thus a good will appears to constitute the indispensable condition even of being worthy of happiness.

There are even some qualities which are of service to this good will itself and may facilitate its action, yet which have no intrinsic unconditional value, but always presuppose a good will, and this qualifies the esteem that we justly have for them and does not permit us to regard them as absolutely good. Moderation in the affections and passions, self-control, and calm deliberation are not only good in many respects, but even seem to constitute part of the intrinsic worth of the person; but they are far from deserving to be called good without qualification, although they have been so unconditionally praised by the ancients. For without the principles of a good will, they may become extremely bad, and the coolness of a villain not only makes him far more j5, but also directly makes him more abominable in our eyes than he would have been without it.

A good will is good not because of what it performs or effects, not by its aptness for the attainment of some proposed end, but simply by virtue of the volition; that is, it is good in itself, and considered by itself is to be esteemed much higher than all that can be brought about by it in favour of any inclination, nay even of the sum total of all inclinations. Even if it should happen that, owing to special disfavour of fortune, or the niggardly provision of a step-motherly nature, this will should wholly lack power to accomplish its purpose, if with its greatest efforts it should yet achieve nothing, and there should remain only the good will (not, to be sure, a mere wish, but the summoning of all means in our power), then, like a jewel, it would still shine by its own light, as a thing which has its whole value in itself. Its usefulness or fruitfulness can neither add nor take away anything from this value. It would be, as it were, only the setting to enable us to handle it the more conveniently in common commerce, or to attract to it the attention of those who are not yet connoisseurs, but not to recommend it to true connoisseurs, or to determine its value . . . .

Consequences not Relevant

[An] action done from duty derives its moral worth, not from the purpose which is to be attained by it, but from the maxim by which it is determined, and therefore does not depend on the realization of the object of the action, but merely on the principle of volition by which the action has taken place, without regard to any object of desire. It is clear from what precedes that the purposes which we may have in view in our actions, or their effects regarded as ends and springs of the will, cannot give to actions any unconditional or moral worth. In what, then, can their worth lie, if it is not to consist in the will and in reference to its expected effect? It cannot lie anywhere but in the principle of the will without regard to the ends which can be attained by the action. For the will stands between its a priori principle, which is formal, and its a posteriori spring, which is material, as between two roads, and as it must be determined by something, it that it must be determined by the formal principle of volition when an action is done from duty, in which case every material principle has been withdrawn from it . . . .

Duty is the necessity of acting from respect for the law. I may have inclination for an object as the effect of my proposed action, but I cannot have respect for it, just for this reason, that it is an effect and not an energy of will. Similarly I cannot have respect

for inclination, whether my own or another's; I can at most, if my own, approve it; if another's, sometimes even love it; i.e., look on it as favourable to my own interest. It is only what is connected with my will as a principle, by no means as an effect—what does not subserve my inclination, but over-powers it, or at least in case of choice excludes it from its calculation—in other words, simply the law of itself, which can be an object of respect, and hence a command. Now an action done from duty must wholly exclude the influence of inclination and with it every object of the will, so that nothing remains which can determine the will except objectively the law, and subjectively pure respect for this practical law, and consequently the maxim[1] that I should follow this law even to the thwarting of all my inclinations.

Thus the moral worth of an action does not lie in the effect expected from it, nor in any principle of action which requires to borrow its motive from this expected effect. For all these effects—agreeableness of one's condition and even the promotion of the happiness of others—could have been also brought about by other causes, so that for this there would have been no need of the will of a rational being; whereas it is in this alone that the supreme and unconditional good can be found. The pre-eminent good which we call moral can therefore consist in nothing else than the conception of law in itself, which certainly is only possible in a rational being, in so far as this conception, and not the expected effect, determines the will. This is a good which is already present in the person who acts accordingly, and we have not to wait for it to appear first in the result.

---

[1]A maxim is the subjective principle of volition. The objective principle (i.e., that which would also serve subjectively as a practical principle to all rational beings if reason had full power over the faculty of desire) is the practical law.

❖ ❖

A Universal Law

But what sort of law can that be, the conception of which must determine the will, even without paying any regard to the effect expected from it, in order that this will may be called good absolutely and without qualification? As I have deprived the will of every impulse which could arise to it from obedience to any law, there remains nothing but the universal conformity of its actions to law in general, which alone is to serve the will as a principle, i.e., I am never to act otherwise than so that I could also will that my maxim should become a universal law. Here, now, it is the simple conformity to law in general, without assuming any particular law applicable to certain actions, that serves the will as its principle and must so serve it, if duty is not to be a vain delusion and a chimerical notion. The common reason of men in its practical judgements perfectly coincides with this and always has in view the principle here suggested. Let the question be, for example: May I when in distress make a promise with the intention not to keep it? I readily distinguish here between the two significations which the question may have: Whether it is prudent, or whether it is right, to make a false promise? The former may undoubtedly be the case. I see clearly indeed that it is not enough to extricate myself from a present difficulty by means of this subterfuge, but it must be well considered whether there may not hereafter spring from this lie much greater inconvenience than that from which I now free myself, and as, with all my supposed cunning, the consequences cannot be so easily foreseen but that credit once lost may be much more injurious to me than any mischief which I seek to avoid at present, it should be considered whether it would not be more prudent to act herein according to a universal maxim and to make it a habit to promise nothing except with the intention of keeping it. But it is soon clear to me that such a maxim will still only be based on the fear of consequences. Now it is a wholly different thing to be truthful from duty

and to be so from apprehension of injurious consequences. In the first case, the very notion of the action already implies a law for me; in the second case, I must first look about elsewhere to see what results may be combined with it which would affect myself. For to deviate from the principle of duty is beyond all doubt wicked; but to be unfaithful to my maxim of prudence may often be very advantageous to me, although to abide by it is certainly safer. The shortest way, however, and an unerring one, to discover the answer to this question whether a lying promise is consistent with duty, is to ask myself, "Should I be content that my maxim (to extricate myself from difficulty by a false promise) should hold good as a universal law, for myself as well as for others? And should I be able to say to myself, "Every one may make a deceitful promise when he finds himself in a difficulty from which he cannot otherwise extricate himself?" Then I presently become aware that while I can will the lie, I can by no means will that lying should be a universal law. For with such a law there would be no promises at all, since it would be in vain to allege my intention in regard to my future actions to those who would not believe this allegation, or if they over hastily did so would pay me back in my own coin. Hence my maxim, as soon as it should be made a universal law, would necessarily destroy itself.

I do not, therefore, need any far-reaching penetration to discern what I have to do in order that my will may be morally good. Inexperienced in the course of the world, incapable of being prepared for all its contingencies, I only ask myself: Canst thou also will that thy maxim should be a universal law? If not, then it must be rejected, and that not because of a disadvantage accruing from it to myself or even to others, but because it cannot enter as a principle into a possible universal legislation, and reason extorts from me immediate respect for such legislation. I do not indeed as yet discern on what this respect is based (this the philosopher may inquire), but at least I understand this, that it

is an estimation of the worth which far outweighs all worth of what is recommended by inclination, and that the necessity of acting from pure respect for the practical law is what constitutes duty, to which every other motive must give place, because it is the condition of a will being good in itself, and the worth of such a will is above everything.

Thus, then, without quitting the moral knowledge of common human reason, we have arrived at its principle. And although, no doubt, common men do not conceive it in such an abstract and universal form, yet they always have it really before their eyes and use it as the standard of their decision. . . .

The Categorical Imperative

On the other hand, the question how the imperative of morality is possible, is undoubtedly one, the only one, demanding a solution, as this is not at all hypothetical, and the objective necessity which it presents cannot rest on any hypothesis, as is the case with the hypothetical imperatives. Only here we must never leave out of consideration that we cannot make out by any example, in other words empirically, whether there is such an imperative at all, but it is rather to be feared that all those which seem to be categorical may yet be at bottom hypothetical. For instance, when the precept is: "Thou shalt not promise deceitfully"; and it is assumed that the necessity of this is not a mere counsel to avoid some other evil, so that it should mean: "Thou shalt not make a lying promise, lest if it become known thou shouldst destroy thy credit," but that an action of this kind must be regarded as evil in itself, so that the imperative of the prohibition is categorical; then we cannot show with certainty in any example that the will was determined merely by the law, without any other spring of action, although it may appear to be so. For it is always possible that fear of disgrace, perhaps also obscure dread of other

dangers, may have a secret influence on the will. Who can prove by experience the non-existence of a cause when all that experience tells us is that we do not perceive it? But in such a case the so-called moral imperative, which as such appears to be categorical and unconditional, would in reality be only a pragmatic precept, drawing our attention to our own interests and merely teaching us to take these into consideration. . . .

When I conceive a hypothetical imperative, in general I do not know beforehand what it will contain until I am given the condition. But when I conceive a categorical imperative, I know at once what it contains. For as the imperative contains besides the law only the necessity that the maxims* shall conform to this law, while the law contains no conditions restricting it, there remains nothing but the general statement that the maxim of the action should conform to a universal law, and it is this conformity alone that the imperative properly represents as necessary.

There is therefore but one categorical imperative, namely, this: Act only on that maxim whereby thou canst at the same time will that it should become a universal law.

Now if all imperatives of duty can be deduced from this one imperative as from their principle, then, although it should remain undecided what is called duty is not merely a vain notion, yet at least we shall be able to show what we understand by it and what this notion means.

Since the universality of the law according to which effects are produced constitutes what is properly called nature in the most general sense (as to form), that is the existence of things so far as it is determined by general laws, the imperative of duty may be expressed thus: Act as if the maxim of thy action were to become by thy will a universal law of nature.

Examples

We will now enumerate a few duties, adopting the usual division of them into duties to ourselves and to others, and into perfect and imperfect duties.

1. A man reduced to despair by a series of misfortunes feels wearied of life, but is still so far in possession of his reason that he can ask himself whether it would not be contrary to his duty to himself to take his own life. Now he inquires whether the maxim of his action could become a universal law of nature. His maxim is: "From self-love I adopt it as a principle to shorten my life when its longer duration is likely to bring more evil than satisfaction." It is asked then simply whether this principle founded on self-love can become a universal law of nature. Now we see at once that a system of nature of which it should be a law to destroy life by means of the very feeling whose special nature it is to impel to the improvement of life would contradict itself and, therefore, could not exist as a system of nature; hence that maxim cannot possibly exist as a universal law of nature and, consequently, would be wholly inconsistent with the supreme principle of all duty.

2. Another finds himself forced by necessity to borrow money. He knows that he will not be able to repay it, but sees also that nothing will be lent to him unless he promises stoutly to repay it in a definite time. He desires to make this promise, but he has still so much conscience as to ask himself: "Is it not unlawful and inconsistent with duty to get out of a difficulty in this way?" Suppose however that he resolves to do so: then the maxim of his action would be expressed thus: "When I think myself in want of money, I will borrow money and promise to repay it, although I know that I never can do so." Now this principle of self-love or of one's own advantage may perhaps be consistent with my whole future welfare; but the question now is, "Is it right?" I change then the suggestion of self-love into a universal law, and state the question thus: "How would it be if my maxim were a universal law?" Then I see at once that it could never hold as a universal law of nature, but would necessarily contradict itself. For supposing it to be a universal law that everyone when he thinks himself in a difficulty should be able to promise whatever he pleases, with the purpose of not keeping his promise, the promise itself would become impossible, as well as the end that one might have in view in it, since no one would consider that anything was promised to him, but would ridicule all such statements as vain pretences.

3. A third finds in himself a talent which with the help of some culture might make him a useful man in many respects. But he finds himself in comfortable circumstances and prefers to indulge in pleasure rather than to take pains in enlarging and improving his happy natural capacities. He asks, however, whether his maxim of neglect of his natural gifts, besides agreeing with his inclination to indulgence, agrees also with what is called duty. He sees then that a system of nature could indeed subsist with such a universal law although men (like the South Sea islanders) should let their talents rest and resolve to devote their lives merely to idleness, amusement, and propagation of their species—in a word, to enjoyment; but he cannot possibly will that this should be a universal law of nature, or be implanted in us as such by a natural instinct. For, as a rational being, he necessarily wills that his faculties be developed, since they serve him and have been given him, for all sorts of possible purposes.

4. A fourth, who is in prosperity, while he sees that others have to contend with great wretchedness and that he could help them, thinks: "What concern is it of mine? Let everyone be as happy as Heaven pleases, or as he can make himself; I will take nothing from him nor even envy him, only I do not wish to contribute anything to his welfare or to his assistance in distress!" Now no doubt if such a mode of thinking were a universal law, the

human race might very well subsist and doubtless even better than in a state in which everyone talks of sympathy and good-will, or even takes care occasionally to put it into practice, but, on the other side, also cheats when he can, betrays the rights of men, or otherwise violates them. But although it is possible that a universal law of nature might exist in accordance with that maxim, it is impossible to will that such a principle should have the universal validity of a law of nature. For a will which resolved this would contradict itself, inasmuch as many cases might occur in which one would have need of the love and sympathy of others, and in which, by such a law of nature, sprung from his own will, he would deprive himself of all hope of the aid he desires. . . .

An End in Himself

Now I say: man and generally any rational being exists as an end in himself, not merely as a means to be arbitrarily used by this or that will, but in all his actions, whether they concern himself or other rational beings, must be always regarded at the same time as an end. All objects of the inclinations have only a conditional worth, for if the inclinations and the wants founded on them did not exist, then their object would be without value. But the inclinations, themselves being sources of want, are so far from having an absolute worth for which they should be desired that on the contrary it must be the universal wish of every rational being to be wholly free from them. Thus the worth of any object which is to be acquired by our action is always conditional. Beings whose existence depends not on our will but on nature's, have nevertheless, if they are irrational beings, only a relative value as means, and are therefore called things; rational beings, on the contrary, are called persons, because their very nature points them out as ends in themselves, that is as something which must not be used merely as

means, and so far therefore restricts freedom of action (and is an object of respect). These, therefore, are not merely subjective ends whose existence has a worth for us as an effect of our action, but objective ends, that is, things whose existence is an end in itself; an end moreover for which no other can be substituted, which they should subserve merely as means, for otherwise nothing whatever would possess absolute worth; but if all worth were conditioned and therefore contingent, then there would be no supreme practical principle of reason whatever. . . .

To abide by the previous examples:

Firstly, under the head of necessary duty to oneself: He who contemplates suicide should ask himself whether his action can be consistent with the idea of humanity as an end in itself. If he destroys himself in order to escape from painful circumstances, he uses a person merely as a mean to maintain a tolerable condition up to the end of life. But a man is not a thing, that is to say, something which can be used merely as means, but must in all his actions be always considered as an end in himself. I cannot, therefore, dispose in any way of a man in my own person so as to mutilate him, to damage or kill him. (It belongs to ethics proper to define this principle more precisely, so as to avoid all misunderstanding, e. g., as to the amputation of the limbs in order to preserve myself, as to exposing my life to danger with a view to preserve it, etc. This question is therefore omitted here.)

Secondly, as regards necessary duties, or those of strict obligation, towards others: He who is thinking of making a lying promise to others will see at once that he would be using another man merely as a mean, without the latter containing at the same time the end in himself. For he whom I propose by such a promise to use for my own purposes cannot possibly assent to my mode of acting towards him and, therefore, cannot himself contain the end of this action. This violation of the principle of humanity in other men is more obvious if we take in examples of attacks on the freedom and property of others. For then it is clear that he who transgresses the rights of men intends to use the person of others merely as a means, without considering that as rational beings they ought always to be esteemed also as ends, that is, as beings who must be capable of containing in themselves the end of the very same action.

Thirdly, as regards contingent (meritorious) duties to oneself: It is not enough that the action does not violate humanity in our own person as an end in itself, it must also harmonize with it. Now there are in humanity capacities of greater perfection, which belong to the end that nature has in view in regard to humanity in ourselves as the subject: to neglect these might perhaps be consistent with the maintenance of humanity as an end in itself, but not with the advancement of this end.

Fourthly, as regards meritorious duties towards others: The natural end which all men have is their own happiness. Now humanity might indeed subsist, although no one should contribute anything to the happiness of others, provided he did not intentionally withdraw anything from it; but after all this would only harmonize negatively not positively with humanity as an end in itself, if every one does not also endeavour, as far as in him lies, to forward the ends of others. For the ends of any subject which is an end in himself ought as far as possible to be my ends also, if that conception is to have its full effect with me. . . . .

The Kingdom of Ends

By a kingdom I understand the union of different rational beings in a system by common laws.

Now since it is by laws that ends are determined as regards their universal validity, hence, if we abstract from the personal differences of rational beings and likewise from all the content of their private ends, we shall be able to conceive all ends combined in a systematic whole (including both rational beings as ends in themselves, and also the special ends which each may propose to himself), that is to say, we can conceive a kingdom of ends, which on the preceding principles is possible.

For all rational beings come under the law that each of them must treat itself and all others never merely as means, but in every case at the same time as ends in themselves. Hence results a systematic union of rational being by common objective laws, i.e., a kingdom which may be called a kingdom of ends, since what these laws have in view is just the relation of these beings to one another as ends and means. It is certainly only an ideal.

A rational being belongs as a member to the kingdom of ends when, although giving universal laws in it, he is also himself subject to these laws. He belongs to it as sovereign when, while giving laws, he is not subject to the will of any other.

A rational being must always regard himself as giving laws either as member or as sovereign in a kingdom of ends which is rendered possible by the freedom of will. He cannot, however, maintain the latter position merely by the maxims of his will, but only in case he is a completely independent being without wants and with unrestricted power adequate to his will.

Morality consists then in the reference of all action to the legislation which alone can render a kingdom of ends possible.

❀ 6.3 Utilitarianism ❀

Selections
by J. S. Mill

✳ ✳

© Everett Historical/Shutterstock.com

John Stuart Mill (1806-1873) was an English philosopher who is best known for his works on Ethics (*Utiliarianism*) and Political Philosophy (*On Liberty*), although he also wrote books on other philosophical topics (*A System of Logic*). Mill was a bit of a child prodigy, and he was raised by parents who were followers of Jeremy Bentham, the founder of Utilitarianianism. They put a great deal of pressure on him as a young child to become the next great Utilitarian philosopher. Mill suffered a mental breakdown as a young man, unable to bear the pressure. However, he ultimately did fulfill the destiny his parents designed for him, producing a reformed version of Utiliarianism.

Utilitarianism consists of two principles, *hedonism*, which says that good consists in happiness and bad consists in pain, and *consequentialism*, which says that the right action is the one which produces a higher balance of good–bad. Mill summarizes Utilitarianism using the Greatest Happiness Principle, that:

> "*Actions are right in proportion as they tend to promote happiness; wrong as they tend to promote unhappiness.*"

Here are some questions to think about when you read:

* What makes one pleasure more valuable than another?
* Does Mill think that Utilitarianism is about being practical and useful?
* Is it possible to act morally for selfish reasons? Why or why not?
* What do you think Mill would say about the death penalty?

Utilitarianism

The Greatest Happiness Principle

. . . The creed which accepts as the foundation of morals, Utility, or the Greatest Happiness Principle, holds that actions are right in proportion as they tend to promote happiness, wrong as they tend to produce the reverse of happiness. By happiness is intended pleasure, and the absence of pain; by unhappiness, pain, and the privation of pleasure. To give a clear view of the moral standard set up by the theory, much more requires to be said; in particular, what things it includes in the ideas of pain and pleasure; and to what extent this is left an open question. But these supplementary explanations do not affect the theory of life on which this theory of morality is grounded—namely, that pleasure, and freedom from pain, are the only things desirable as ends; and that all desirable things (which are as numerous in the utilitarian as in any other scheme) are desirable either for the pleasure inherent in themselves, or as means to the promotion of pleasure and the prevention of pain.

Now, such a theory of life excites in many minds, and among them in some of the most estimable in feeling and purpose, inveterate dislike. To suppose that life has (as they express it) no higher end than pleasure—no better and nobler object of desire and pursuit—they designate as utterly mean and grovelling; as a doctrine worthy only of swine, to whom the followers of Epicurus were, at a very early period, contemptuously likened; and modern holders of the doctrine are occasionally made the subject of equally polite comparisons by its German, French, and English assailants.

When thus attacked, the Epicureans have always answered, that it is not they, but their accusers, who represent human nature in a degrading light; since the accusation supposes human beings to be capable of no pleasures except those of which swine are capable. If this supposition were true, the charge could not be gainsaid, but would then be no longer an imputation; for if the sources of pleasure were precisely the same to human beings and to swine, the rule of life which is good enough for the one would be good enough for the other. The comparison of the Epicurean life to that of beasts is felt as degrading, precisely because a beast's pleasures do not satisfy a human being's conceptions of happiness. Human beings have faculties more elevated than the animal appetites, and when once made conscious of them, do not regard anything as happiness which does not include their gratification. I do not, indeed, consider the Epicureans to have been by any means faultless in drawing out their scheme of consequences from the utilitarian principle. To do this in any sufficient manner, many Stoic, as well as Christian elements require to be included. But there is no known Epicurean theory of life which does not

❖ ❖

assign to the pleasures of the intellect; of the feelings and imagination, and of the moral sentiments, a much higher value as pleasures than to those of mere sensation. It must be admitted, however, that utilitarian writers in general have placed the superiority of mental over bodily pleasures chiefly in the greater permanency, safety, uncostliness, &c., of the former—that is, in their circumstantial advantages rather than in their intrinsic nature. And on all these points utilitarians have fully proved their case; but they might have taken the other, and, as it may be called, higher ground, with entire consistency. It is quite compatible with the principle of utility to recognise the fact, that some kinds of pleasure are more desirable and more valuable than others. It would be absurd that while, in estimating all other things, quality is considered as well as quantity, the estimation of pleasures should be supposed to depend on quantity alone.

Qualities of Pleasure

If I am asked, what I mean by difference of quality in pleasures, or what makes one pleasure more valuable than another, merely as a pleasure, except its being greater in amount, there is but one possible answer. Of two pleasures, if there be one to which all or almost all who have experience of both give a decided preference, irrespective of any feeling of moral obligation to prefer it, that is the more desirable pleasure. If one of the two is, by those who are competently acquainted with both, placed so far above the other that they prefer it, even though knowing it to be attended with a greater amount of discontent, and would not resign it for any quantity of the other pleasure which their nature is capable of, we are justified in ascribing to the preferred enjoyment a superiority in quality, so far outweighing quantity as to render it, in comparison, of small account.

Now it is an unquestionable fact that those who are equally acquainted with, and equally capable of appreciating and enjoying, both, do give a most marked preference to the manner of existence which employs their higher faculties. Few human creatures would consent to be changed into any of the lower animals, for a promise of the fullest allowance of a beast's pleasures; no intelligent human being would consent to be a fool, no instructed person would be an ignoramus, no person of feeling and conscience would be selfish and base, even though they should be persuaded that the fool, the dunce, or the rascal is better satisfied with his lot than they are with theirs. They would not resign what they possess more than he, for the most complete satisfaction of all the desires which they have in common with him. If they ever fancy they would, it is only in cases of unhappiness so extreme, that to escape from it they would exchange their lot for almost any other, however undesirable in their own eyes. A being of higher faculties requires more to make him happy, is capable probably of more acute suffering, and is certainly accessible to it at more points, than one of an inferior type; but in spite of these liabilities, he can never really wish to sink into what he feels to be a lower grade of existence. We may give what explanation we please of this unwillingness; we may attribute it to pride, a name which is given indiscriminately to some of the most and to some of the least estimable feelings of which mankind are capable; we may refer it to the love of liberty and personal independence, an appeal to which was with the Stoics one of the most effective means for the inculcation of it; to the love of power, or to the love of excitement, both of which do really enter into and contribute to it: but its most appropriate appellation is a sense of dignity, which all human beings possess in one form or other, and in some, though by no means in exact, proportion to their higher faculties, and which is so essential a part of the happiness of those in whom it is strong, that nothing which conflicts with it could be, otherwise than momentarily, an object of desire to them. Whoever supposes that this preference takes place at a sacrifice of happiness-that the superior being, in anything like equal circumstances, is not happier than the inferior-confounds the two very different ideas, of happiness, and content. It is indisputable that the being whose capacities of enjoyment are low, has the greatest chance of having them fully satisfied; and a highly-endowed being will always feel that any happiness which he can look for, as the world is constituted, is imperfect. But he can learn to bear its imperfections, if they are at all bearable; and they will not make him envy the being who is indeed unconscious of the imperfections, but only because he feels not at all the good which those imperfections qualify. It is better to be a human being dissatisfied than a pig satisfied; better to be Socrates dissatisfied than a fool satisfied. And if the fool, or the pig, is of a different opinion, it is because they only know their own side of the question. The other party to the comparison knows both sides.

An Objection

It may be objected, that many who are capable of the higher pleasures, occasionally, under the influence of temptation, postpone them to the lower. But this is quite compatible with a full appreciation of the intrinsic superiority of the higher. Men often, from infirmity of character, make their election for the nearer good, though they know it to be the less valuable; and this no less when the choice is between two bodily pleasures, than when it is between bodily and mental. They pursue sensual indulgences to the injury of health, though perfectly aware that health is the greater good. It may be further objected, that many who begin with youthful enthusiasm for everything noble, as they advance in years sink into indolence and selfishness. But I do not believe that those who undergo this very common change, voluntarily choose the lower description of pleasures in preference to the higher. I believe that before they devote themselves exclusively to the one, they have already become incapable of the other. Capacity for the nobler feelings is in most natures a very tender plant, easily killed, not only by hostile influences, but by mere want of sustenance; and in the majority of young persons it speedily dies away if the occupations to which their position in life has devoted them, and the society into which it has thrown them, are not favourable to keeping that higher capacity in exercise. Men lose their high aspirations as they lose their intellectual tastes, because they have not time or opportunity for indulging them; and they addict themselves to inferior pleasures, not because they deliberately prefer them, but because they are either the only ones to which they have access, or the only ones which they are any longer capable of enjoying. It may be questioned whether any one who has remained equally susceptible to both classes of pleasures, ever knowingly and calmly preferred the lower; though many, in all ages, have broken down in an ineffectual attempt to combine both.

From this verdict of the only competent judges, I apprehend there can be no appeal. On a question which is the best worth having of two pleasures, or which of two modes of existence is the most grateful to the feelings, apart from its moral attributes and from its consequences, the judgment of those who are qualified by knowledge of both, or, if they differ, that of the majority among them, must be admitted as final. And there needs be the less hesitation to accept this judgment respecting the quality of pleasures, since there is no other tribunal to be referred to even on the question of quantity. What means are there of determining which is the acutest of two pains, or the intensest of two pleasurable sensations, except the general suffrage of those who are familiar with both? Neither pains nor pleasures are homogeneous, and pain is always heterogeneous with pleasure. What is there to decide whether a particular pleasure is worth purchasing at the cost of a particular pain, except the feelings and judgment of the experienced? When, therefore, those feelings and judgment declare the pleasures derived from the higher faculties to be preferable in kind, apart from the question of intensity, to those of which the animal nature, disjoined from the higher faculties, is susceptible, they are entitled on this subject to the same regard.

Not the Agent's own Happiness

I have dwelt on this point, as being a necessary part of a perfectly just conception of Utility or Happiness, considered as the directive rule of human conduct. But it is by no means an indispensable condition to the acceptance of the utilitarian standard; for that standard is not the agent's own greatest happiness, but the greatest amount of happiness altogether; and if it may possibly be doubted whether a noble character is always the happier for its nobleness, there can be no doubt that it makes other people happier, and that the world in general is immensely a gainer by it. Utilitarianism, therefore, could only attain its end by the general cultivation of nobleness of character, even if each individual were only benefited by the nobleness of others, and his own, so far as happiness is concerned, were a sheer deduction from the benefit. But the bare enunciation of such an absurdity as this last, renders refutation superfluous.

According to the Greatest Happiness Principle, as above explained, the ultimate end, with reference to and for the sake of which all other things are desirable (whether we are considering our own good or that of other people), is an existence exempt as far as possible from pain, and as rich as possible in enjoyments, both in point of quantity and quality; the test of quality, and the rule for measuring it against quantity, being the preference felt by those who, in their opportunities of experience, to which must be added their habits of self-consciousness and self-observation, are best furnished with the means of comparison. This, being, according to

the utilitarian opinion, the end of human action, is necessarily also the standard of morality; which may accordingly be defined, the rules and precepts for human conduct, by the observance of which an existence such as has been described might be, to the greatest extent possible, secured to all mankind; and not to them only, but, so far as the nature of things admits, to the whole sentient creation.

Can We Do without Happiness?

And this leads to the true estimation of what is said by the objectors concerning the possibility, and the obligation, of learning to do without happiness. Unquestionably it is possible to do without happiness; it is done involuntarily by nineteen-twentieths of mankind, even in those parts of our present world which are least deep in barbarism; and it often has to be done voluntarily by the hero or the martyr, for the sake of something which he prizes more than his individual happiness. But this something, what is it, unless the happiness of others, or some of the requisites of happiness? It is noble to be capable of resigning entirely one's own portion of happiness, or chances of it: but, after all, this self-sacrifice must be for some end; it is not its own end; and if we are told that its end is not happiness, but virtue, which is better than happiness, I ask, would the sacrifice be made if the hero or martyr did not believe that it would earn for others immunity from similar sacrifices? Would it be made, if he thought that his renunciation of happiness for himself would produce no fruit for any of his fellow creatures, but to make their lot like his, and place them also in the condition of persons who have renounced happiness? All honour to those who can abnegate for themselves the personal enjoyment of life, when by such renunciation they contribute worthily to increase the amount of happiness in the world; but he who does it, or professes to do it, for any other purpose, is no more deserving of admiration than the ascetic mounted on his pillar. He may be an inspiriting proof of what men can do, but assuredly not an example of what they should.

Though it is only in a very imperfect state of the world's arrangements that any one can best serve the happiness of others by the absolute sacrifice of his own, yet so long as the world is in that imperfect state, I fully acknowledge that the readiness to make such a sacrifice is the highest virtue which can be found in man. I will add, that in this condition of the world, paradoxical as the assertion may be, the conscious ability to do without happiness gives the best prospect of realizing such happiness as is attainable. For nothing except that consciousness can raise a person above the chances of life, by making him feel that, let fate and fortune do their worst, they have not power to subdue him: which, once felt, frees him from excess of anxiety concerning the evils of life, and enables him, like many a Stoic in the worst times of the Roman Empire, to cultivate in tranquillity the sources of satisfaction accessible to him, without concerning himself about the uncertainty of their duration, any more than about their inevitable end.

Meanwhile, let utilitarians never cease to claim the morality of self-devotion as a possession which belongs by as good a right to them, as either to the Stoic or to the Transcendentalist. The utilitarian morality does recognise in human beings the power of sacrificing their own greatest good for the good of others. It only refuses to admit that the sacrifice is itself a good. A sacrifice which does not increase, or tend to increase, the sum total of happiness, it considers as wasted. The only self-renunciation which it applauds, is devotion to the happiness, or to some of the means of happiness, of others; either of mankind collectively, or of individuals within the limits imposed by the collective interests of mankind. . . .

On the Absence of Proof

OF WHAT SORT OF PROOF THE PRINCIPLE OF UTILITY IS SUSCEPTIBLE

It has already been remarked, that questions of ultimate ends do not admit of proof, in the ordinary acceptation of the term. To be incapable of proof by reasoning is common to all first principles; to the first premises of our knowledge, as well as to those of our conduct. But the former, being matters of fact, may be the subject of a direct appeal to the faculties which judge of fact—namely, our senses, and our internal consciousness. Can an appeal be made to the same faculties on questions of practical ends? Or by what other faculty is cognizance taken of them?

Questions about ends are, in other words, questions what things are desirable. The utilitarian doctrine is, that happiness is desirable, and the only thing desirable, as an end; all other things being only desirable as means to that end. What ought to be required of this doctrine—what conditions is it requisite that the doctrine should fulfil—to make good its claim to be believed?

The only proof capable of being given that an object is visible, is that people actually see it. The only proof that a sound is audible, is that people hear it: and so of the other sources of our experience. In like manner, I apprehend, the sole evidence it is possible to produce that anything is desirable, is that people do actually desire it. If the end which the utilitarian doctrine proposes to itself were not, in theory and in practice, acknowledged to be an end, nothing could ever convince any person that it was so. No reason can be given why the general happiness is desirable, except that each person, so far as he believes it to be attainable, desires his own happiness. This, however, being a fact, we have not

❀ ❀

only all the proof which the case admits of, but all which it is possible to require, that happiness is a good: that each person's happiness is a good to that person, and the general happiness, therefore, a good to the aggregate of all persons. Happiness has made out its title as one of the ends of conduct, and consequently one of the criteria of morality.

But it has not, by this alone, proved itself to be the sole criterion. To do that, it would seem, by the same rule, necessary to show, not only that people desire happiness, but that they never desire anything else. Now it is palpable that they do desire things which, in common language, are decidedly distinguished from happiness. They desire, for example, virtue, and the absence of vice, no less really than pleasure and the absence of pain. The desire of virtue is not as universal, but it is as authentic a fact, as the desire of happiness. And hence the opponents of the utilitarian standard deem that they have a right to infer that there are other ends of human action besides happiness, and that happiness is not the standard of approbation and disapprobation.

But does the utilitarian doctrine deny that people desire virtue, or maintain that virtue is not a thing to be desired? The very reverse. It maintains not only that virtue is to be desired, but that it is to be desired disinterestedly, for itself. Whatever may be the opinion of utilitarian moralists as to the original conditions by which virtue is made virtue; however they may believe (as they do) that actions and dispositions are only virtuous because they promote another end than virtue; yet this being granted, and it having been decided, from considerations of this description, what is virtuous, they not only place virtue at the very head of the things which are good as means to the ultimate end, but they also recognise as a psychological fact the possibility of its being, to the individual, a good in itself, without looking to any end beyond it; and hold, that the mind is not in a right state, not in a state conformable to Utility, not in the state most conducive to the general happiness, unless it does love virtue in this manner—as a thing desirable in itself, even although, in the individual instance, it should not produce those other desirable consequences which it tends to produce, and on account of which it is held to be virtue. This opinion is not, in the smallest degree, a departure from the Happiness principle. The ingredients of happiness are very various, and each of them is desirable in itself, and not merely when considered as swelling an aggregate. The principle of utility does not mean that any given pleasure, as music, for instance, or any given exemption from pain, as for example health, are to be looked upon as means to a collective something termed happiness, and to be desired on that account. They are desired and desirable in and for themselves; besides being means, they are a part of the end. Virtue, according to the utilitarian doctrine, is not naturally and originally part of the end, but it is capable of becoming so; and in those who love it disinterestedly it has become so, and is desired and cherished, not as a means to happiness, but as a part of their happiness.

❋ 6.4 The Nicomachean Ethics ❋

Selections
by Aristotle

❋❋❋

© Lefteris Papaulakis/Shutterstock.com

Aristotle, who lived in ancient Athens, was a student of Plato. We discussed his Metaphysics in Unit 3. The Nicomachean Ethics are a compilation of lecture notes from a series of talks Aristotle gave his students. Aristotle focused on what it meant to live a happy life.

Aristotle's Ethics is very different from that of Kant and Mill. Kant and Mill were both seeking to determine what made an action right or wrong. However, Aristotle didn't think philosophers could develop rules for what actions were right and wrong that didn't have exceptions. Instead he attempted to determine what made a person's character good or bad as a whole. A person with good moral character, Aristotle thought, would know how to act appropriately in any new situation he was thrown into.

Virtues are the good states of character a person should seek to develop. For Aristotle virtues are founded on the distinctive function of human beings which separates us from animals: the ability to reason. A reasonable person avoids extremes, and so Aristotle believed virtue lies in the mean between extremes. For instance, bravery is a virtue because it is the mean between the extreme of cowardice and the extreme of rushing mindlessly into danger. The supreme good in life, happiness, was achieved through a life of virtue. Aristotle's view is known as Virtue Ethics.

Here are some questions to think about when you read:

* How do we obtain virtue, according to Aristotle?

* What does he mean by calling virtue a "trained faculty"?

* Many hold that determining the right action is a matter of contemplation, thinking about the action itself (Kant) or about its consequences (Mill). What does Aristotle think?

* Would you say that our motives or intentions matter to Aristotle? How? Does this make him more similar to Kant or to Mill?

Nicomachean Ethics

The Good

Every art and every kind of inquiry, and likewise every act and purpose, seems to aim at some good: and so it has been well said that the good is that at which everything aims.

But a difference is observable among these aims or ends. What is aimed at is sometimes the exercise of a faculty, sometimes a certain result beyond that exercise. And where there is an end beyond the act, there the result is better than the exercise of the faculty.

Now since there are many kinds of actions and many arts and sciences, it follows that there are many ends also; e.g. health is the end of medicine, ships of shipbuilding, victory of the art of war, and wealth of economy.

But when several of these are subordinated to some one art or science,—as the making of bridles and other trappings to the art of horsemanship, and this in turn, along with all else that the soldier does, to the art of war, and so on,—then the end of the master-art is always more desired than the ends of the subordinate arts, since these are pursued for its sake. And this is equally true whether the end in view be the mere exercise of a faculty or something beyond that, as in the above instances.

If then in what we do there be some end which we wish for on its own account, choosing all the others as means to this, but not every end without exception as a means to something else (for so we should go on ad infinitum, and desire would be left void and objectless),—this evidently will be the good or the best of all things. And surely from a practical point of view it much concerns us to know this good; for then, like archers shooting at a definite mark, we shall be more likely to attain what we want.

If this be so, we must try to indicate roughly what it is, and first of all to which of the arts or sciences it belongs.

It would seem to belong to the supreme art or science, that one which most of all deserves the name of master-art or master-science.

Now Politics seems to answer to this description. For it prescribes which of the sciences a state needs, and which each man shall study, and up to what point; and to it we see subordinated even the highest arts, such as economy, rhetoric, and the art of war.

Since then it makes use of the other practical sciences, and since it further ordains what men are to do and from what to refrain, its end must include the ends of the others, and must be the proper good of man.

For though this good is the same for the individual and the state, yet the good of the state seems a grander and more perfect thing both to attain and to secure; and glad as one would be to do this service for a single individual, to do it for a people and for a number of states is nobler and more divine.

This then is the aim of the present inquiry, which is a sort of political inquiry . . . .

Notions of Happiness

It seems that men not unreasonably take their notions of the good or happiness from the lives actually led, and that the masses who are the least refined suppose it to be pleasure, which is the reason why they aim at nothing higher than the life of enjoyment.

For the most conspicuous kinds of life are three: this life of enjoyment, the life of the statesman, and, thirdly, the contemplative life.

The mass of men show themselves utterly slavish in their preference for the life of brute beasts, but their views receive consideration because many of those in high places have the tastes of Sardanapalus.

Men of refinement with a practical turn prefer honour; for I suppose we may say that honour is the aim of the statesman's life.

But this seems too superficial to be the good we are seeking: for it appears to depend upon those who give rather than upon those who receive it; while we have a presentiment that the good is something that is peculiarly a man's own and can scarce be taken away from him.

Moreover, these men seem to pursue honour in order that they may be assured of their own excellence,—at least, they wish to be honoured by men of sense, and by those who know them, and on the ground of their virtue or excellence. It is plain, then, that in their view, at any rate, virtue or excellence is better than honour; and perhaps we should take this to be the end of the statesman's life, rather than honour.

But virtue or excellence also appears too incomplete to be what we want; for it seems that a man might have virtue and yet be asleep or be inactive all his life, and, moreover, might meet with the greatest disasters and misfortunes; and no one would maintain that such a man is happy, except for argument's sake. But we will not dwell on these matters now, for they are sufficiently discussed in the popular treatises.

The third kind of life is the life of contemplation: we will treat of it further on.

As for the money-making life, it is something quite contrary to nature; and wealth evidently is not the good of which we are in search, for it is merely useful as a means to something else. So we might rather take pleasure and virtue or excellence to be ends than wealth; for they are chosen on their own account. But it seems that not even they are the end, though much breath has been wasted in attempts to show that they are.

Happiness the End

Leaving these matters, then, let us return once more to the question, what this good can be of which we are in search.

It seems to be different in different kinds of action and in different arts,—one thing in medicine and another in war, and so on. What then is the good in each of these cases? Surely that for the sake of which all else is done. And that in medicine is health, in war is victory, in building is a house,—a different thing in each different case, but always, in whatever we do and in whatever we choose, the end. For it is always for the sake of the end that all else is done.

If then there be one end of all that man does, this end will be the realizable good,—or these ends, if there be more than one.

By this generalization our argument is brought to the same point as before. This point we must try to explain more clearly.

❀ ❀

We see that there are many ends. But some of these are chosen only as means, as wealth, flutes, and the whole class of instruments. And so it is plain that not all ends are final.

But the best of all things must, we conceive, be something final.

If then there be only one final end, this will be what we are seeking,—or if there be more than one, then the most final of them.

Now that which is pursued as an end in itself is more final than that which is pursued as means to something else, and that which is never chosen as means than that which is chosen both as an end in itself and as means, and that is strictly final which is always chosen as an end in itself and never as means.

Happiness seems more than anything else to answer to this description: for we always choose it for itself, and never for the sake of something else; while honour and pleasure and reason, and all virtue or excellence, we choose partly indeed for themselves (for, apart from any result, we should choose each of them), but partly also for the sake of happiness, supposing that they will help to make us happy. But no one chooses happiness for the sake of these things, or as a means to anything else at all.

We seem to be led to the same conclusion when we start from the notion of self-sufficiency.

The final good is thought to be self-sufficing [or all-sufficing]. In applying this term we do not regard a man as an individual leading a solitary life, but we also take account of parents, children, wife, and, in short, friends and fellow-citizens generally, since man is naturally a social being. Some limit must indeed be set to this; for if you go on to parents and descendants and friends of friends, you will never come to a stop. But this we will consider further on: for the present we will take self-sufficing to mean what by itself makes life desirable and in want of nothing. And happiness is believed to answer to this description.

And further, happiness is believed to be the most desirable thing in the world, and that not merely as one among other good things: if it were merely one among other good things [so that other things could be added to it], it is plain that the addition of the least of other goods must make it more desirable; for the addition becomes a surplus of good, and of two goods the greater is always more desirable.

Thus it seems that happiness is something final and self-sufficing, and is the end of all that man does . . .

Moral Excellences

Excellence, then, being of these two kinds, intellectual and moral intellectual excellence owes its birth and growth mainly to instruction, and so requires time and experience, while moral excellence is the result of habit or custom (ἔθος), and has accordingly in our language received a name formed by a slight change from ἔθος.

From this it is plain that none of the moral excellences or virtues is implanted in us by nature; for that which is by nature cannot be altered by training. For instance, a stone naturally tends to fall downwards, and you could not train it to rise upwards, though you tried to do so by throwing it up ten thousand times, nor could you train fire to move downwards, nor accustom anything which naturally behaves in one way to behave in any other way.

The virtues, then, come neither by nature nor against nature, but nature gives the capacity for acquiring them, and this is developed by training.

Again, where we do things by nature we get the power first, and put this power forth in act afterwards: as we plainly see in the case of the senses; for it is not by constantly seeing and hearing that we acquire those faculties, but, on the contrary, we had the power first and then used it, instead of acquiring the power by the use. But the virtues we acquire by doing the acts, as is the case with the arts too. We learn an art by doing that which we wish to do when we have learned it; we become builders by building, and harpers by harping. And so by doing just acts we become just, and by doing acts of temperance and courage we become temperate and courageous.

This is attested, too, by what occurs in states; for the legislators make their citizens good by training; i.e. this is the wish of all legislators, and those who do not succeed in this miss their aim, and it is this that distinguishes a good from a bad constitution.

Again, both the moral virtues and the corresponding vices result from and are formed by the same acts; and this is the case with the arts also. It is by harping that good harpers and bad harpers alike are produced: and so with builders and the rest; by building well they will become good builders, and bad builders by building badly. Indeed, if it were not so, they would not want anybody to teach them, but would all be born either good or bad at their trades. And it is just the same with the virtues also. It is by our conduct in our intercourse with other men that we become just or unjust, and by acting in circumstances [36]of danger, and training ourselves to feel fear or confidence, that we become courageous or cowardly. So, too, with our animal appetites and the passion of anger; for by behaving in this way or in that on the occasions with which these passions are concerned, some become temperate and gentle, and others profligate and ill-tempered. In a word, acts of any kind produce habits or characters of the same kind.

Hence we ought to make sure that our acts be of a certain kind; for the resulting character varies as they vary. It makes no small difference, therefore, whether a man be trained from his youth up in this way or in that, but a great difference, or rather all the difference.

The Golden Mean

But our present inquiry has not, like the rest, a merely speculative aim; we are not inquiring merely in order to know what excellence or virtue is, but in order to become good; for otherwise it would profit us nothing. We must ask therefore about these acts, and see of what kind they are to be; for, as we said, it is they that determine our habits or character.

First of all, then, that they must be in accordance with right reason is a common characteristic of them, which we shall here take for granted, reserving for future discussion the question what this right reason is, and how it is related to the other excellences.

But let it be understood, before we go on, that all reasoning on matters of practice must be in outline merely, and not scientifically exact: for, as we said at starting, the kind of reasoning to be demanded varies with the subject in hand; and in practical matters and questions of expediency there are no invariable laws, any more than in questions of health.

And if our general conclusions are thus inexact, still more inexact is all reasoning about particular cases; for these fall under no system of scientifically established rules or traditional maxims, but the agent must always consider for himself what the special occasion requires, just as in medicine or navigation.

But though this is the case we must try to render what help we can.

First of all, then, we must observe that, in matters of this sort, to fall short and to exceed are alike fatal. This is plain (to illustrate what we cannot see by what we can see) in the case of strength and health. Too much and too little exercise alike destroy strength, and to take too much meat and drink, or to take too little, is equally ruinous to health, but the fitting amount produces and increases and

preserves them. Just so, then, is it with temperance also, and courage, and the other virtues. The man who shuns and fears everything and never makes a stand, becomes a coward; while the man who fears nothing at all, but will face anything, becomes foolhardy. So, too, the man who takes his fill of any kind of pleasure, and abstains from none, is a profligate, but the man who shuns all (like him whom we call a "boor") is devoid of sensibility. Thus temperance and courage destroyed both by excess and defect, but preserved by moderation.

Moderation

We have thus found the genus to which virtue belongs; but we want to know, not only that it is a trained faculty, but also what species of trained faculty it is.

We may safely assert that the virtue or excellence of a thing causes that thing both to be itself in good condition and to perform its function well. The excellence of the eye, for instance, makes both the eye and its work good; for it is by the excellence of the eye that we see well. So the proper excellence of the horse makes a horse what he should be, and makes him good at running, and carrying his rider, and standing a charge.

If, then, this holds good in all cases, the proper excellence or virtue of man will be the habit or trained faculty that makes a man good and makes him perform his function well.

How this is to be done we have already said, but we may exhibit the same conclusion in another way, by inquiring what the nature of this virtue is.

Now, if we have any quantity, whether continuous or discrete, it is possible to take either a larger [or too large], or a smaller [or too small], or an equal [or fair] amount, and that either absolutely or relatively to our own needs.

By an equal or fair amount I understand a mean amount, or one that lies between excess and deficiency.

By the absolute mean, or mean relatively to the thing itself, I understand that which is equidistant from both extremes, and this is one and the same for all.

By the mean relatively to us I understand that which is neither too much nor too little for us; and this is not one and the same for all.

For instance, if ten be larger [or too large] and two be smaller [or too small], if we take six we take the mean relatively to the thing itself [or the arithmetical mean]; for it exceeds one extreme by the same amount by which it is exceeded by the other extreme: and this is the mean in arithmetical proportion.

Virtue, then, is a kind of moderation (μεσότης τις),* inasmuch as it aims at the mean or moderate amount (τὸ μέσον).

Again, there are many ways of going wrong (for evil is infinite in nature, to use a Pythagorean figure, while good is finite), but only one way of going right; so that the one is easy and the other hard—easy to miss the mark and hard to hit. On this account also, then, excess and deficiency are characteristic of vice, hitting the mean is characteristic of virtue:

"Goodness is simple, ill takes any shape."

The Definition of Virtue

Virtue, then, is a habit or trained faculty of choice, the characteristic of which lies in moderation or observance of the mean relatively to the persons concerned, as determined by reason, i.e. by the reason by which the prudent man would determine it. And it is a moderation, firstly, inasmuch as it comes

in the middle or mean between two vices, one on the side of excess, the other on the side of defect; and, secondly, inasmuch as, while these vices fall short of or exceed the due measure in feeling and in action, it finds and chooses the mean, middling, or moderate amount.

Regarded in its essence, therefore, or according to the definition of its nature, virtue is a moderation or middle state, but viewed in its relation to what is best and right it is the extreme of perfection.

But it is not all actions nor all passions that admit of moderation; there are some whose very names imply badness, as malevolence, shamelessness, envy, and, among acts, adultery, theft, murder. These and all other like things are blamed as being bad in themselves, and not merely in their excess or deficiency. It is impossible therefore to go right in them; they are always wrong: rightness and wrongness in such things (e.g. in adultery) does not depend upon whether it is the right person and occasion and manner, but the mere doing of any one of them is wrong.

It would be equally absurd to look for moderation or excess or deficiency in unjust cowardly or profligate conduct; for then there would be moderation in excess or deficiency, and excess in excess, and deficiency in deficiency.

The fact is that just as there can be no excess or deficiency in temperance or courage because the mean or moderate amount is, in a sense, an extreme, so in these kinds of conduct also there can be no moderation or excess or deficiency, but the acts are wrong however they be done. For, to put it generally, there cannot be moderation in excess or deficiency, nor excess or deficiency in moderation.

The Several Virtues

But it is not enough to make these general statements [about virtue and vice]: we must go on and apply them to particulars [i.e. to the several virtues and vices]. For in reasoning about matters of conduct general statements are too vague, and do not convey so much truth as particular propositions. It is with particulars that conduct is concerned: our statements, therefore, when applied to these particulars, should be found to hold good.

These particulars then [i.e. the several virtues and vices and the several acts and affections with which they deal], we will take from the following table.

Moderation in the feelings of fear and confidence is courage: of those that exceed, he that exceeds in fearlessness has no name (as often happens), but he that exceeds in confidence is foolhardy, while he that exceeds in fear, but is deficient in confidence, is cowardly.

Moderation in respect of certain pleasures and also (though to a less extent) certain pains is temperance, while excess is profligacy. But defectiveness in the matter of these pleasures is hardly ever found, and so this sort of people also have as yet received no name: let us put them down as "void of sensibility."

In the matter of giving and taking money, moderation is liberality, excess and deficiency are prodigality and illiberality. But both vices exceed and fall short in giving and taking in contrary ways: the prodigal exceeds in spending, but falls short in taking; while the illiberal man exceeds in taking, but falls short in spending. (For the present we are but giving an outline or summary, and aim at nothing more; we shall afterwards treat these points in greater detail.)

But, besides these, there are other dispositions in the matter of money: there is a moderation which is called magnificence (for the magnificent is not the same as the liberal man: the former deals with large sums, the latter with small), and an excess which is called bad taste or vulgarity, and a deficiency which is called meanness; and these vices differ from those which are opposed to liberality: how they differ will be explained later.

With respect to honour and disgrace, there is a moderation which is high-mindedness, an excess which may be called vanity, and a deficiency which is little-mindedness.

But just as we said that liberality is related to magnificence, differing only in that it deals with small sums, so here there is a virtue related to high-mindedness, and differing only in that it is concerned with small instead of great honours. A man may have a due desire for honour, and also more or less than a due desire: he that carries this desire to excess is called ambitious, he that has not enough of it is called unambitious, but he that has the due amount has no name. There are also no abstract names for the characters, except "ambition," corresponding to ambitious. And on this account those who occupy the extremes lay claim to the middle place. And in common parlance, too, the moderate man is sometimes called ambitious and sometimes unambitious, and sometimes the ambitious man is praised and sometimes the unambitious. Why this is we will explain afterwards; for the present we will follow out our plan and enumerate the other types of character.

In the matter of anger also we find excess and deficiency and moderation. The characters themselves hardly have recognized names, but as the moderate man is here called gentle, we will call his character gentleness; of those who go into extremes, we may take the term wrathful for him who exceeds, with wrathfulness for the vice, and wrathless for him who is deficient, with wrathlessness for his character.

Besides these, there are three kinds of moderation, bearing some resemblance to one another, and yet different. They all have to do with intercourse in speech and action, but they differ in that one has to do with the truthfulness of this intercourse, while the other two have to do with its pleasantness—one of the two with pleasantness in matters of amusement, the other with pleasantness in all the relations of life. We must therefore speak of these qualities also in order that we may the more plainly see how, in all cases, moderation is praiseworthy, while the extreme courses are neither right nor praiseworthy, but blamable.

In these cases also names are for the most part wanting, but we must try, here as elsewhere, to coin names ourselves, in order to make our argument clear and easy to follow.

In the matter of truth, then, let us call him who observes the mean a true [or truthful] person, and observance of the mean truth [or truthfulness]: pretence, when it exaggerates, may be called boasting, and the person a boaster; when it understates, let the names be irony and ironical.

With regard to pleasantness in amusement, he who observes the mean may be called witty, and his character wittiness; excess may be called buffoonery, and the man a buffoon; while boorish may stand for the person who is deficient, and boorishness for his character.

With regard to pleasantness in the other affairs of life, he who makes himself properly pleasant may be called friendly, and his moderation friendliness; he that exceeds may be called obsequious if he have no ulterior motive, but a flatterer if he has an eye to his own advantage; he that is deficient in this respect, and always makes himself disagreeable, may be called a quarrelsome or peevish fellow.

Moreover, in mere emotions and in our conduct with regard to them, there are ways of observing the mean; for instance, shame (αἰδώς), is not a virtue, but yet the modest (αἰδήμων) man is praised. For in these matters also we speak of this man as observing the mean, of that man as going beyond it (as the shame-faced man whom the least thing makes shy), while he who is deficient in the feeling, or lacks it altogether, is called shameless; but the term modest (αἰδήμων) is applied to him who observes the mean.

❀ ❀

Righteous indignation, again, hits the mean between envy and malevolence. These have to do with feelings of pleasure and pain at what happens to our neighbours. A man is called righteously indignant when he feels pain at the sight of unde-served prosperity, but your envious man goes beyond him and is pained by the sight of any one in prosperity, while the malevolent man is so far from being pained that he actually exults in the misfor-tunes of his neighbours.

But we shall have another opportunity of discuss-ing these matters.

As for justice, the term is used in more senses than one; we will, therefore, after disposing of the above questions, distinguish these various senses, and show how each of these kinds of justice is a kind of moderation.

And then we will treat of the intellectual virtues in the same way.

Deficiency and Excess

There are, as we said, three classes of disposition, viz. two kinds of vice, one marked by excess, the other by deficiency, and one kind of virtue, the observance of the mean. Now, each is in a way opposed to each, for the extreme dispositions are opposed both to the mean or moderate disposition and to one another, while the moderate disposition is opposed to both the extremes. Just as a quantity which is equal to a given quantity is also greater when compared with a less, and less when com-pared with a greater quantity, so the mean or mod-erate dispositions exceed as compared with the defective dispositions, and fall short as compared with the excessive dispositions, both in feeling and in action; e.g. the courageous man seems fool-hardy as compared with the coward, and cowardly as compared with the foolhardy; and similarly the temperate man appears profligate in comparison with the insensible, and insensible in compari-son with the profligate man; and the liberal man appears prodigal by the side of the illiberal man, and illiberal by the side of the prodigal man.

And so the extreme characters try to displace the mean or moderate character, and each represents him as falling into the opposite extreme, the coward calling the courageous man foolhardy, the foolhardy calling him coward, and so on in other cases.

But while the mean and the extremes are thus opposed to one another, the extremes are strictly contrary to each other rather than to the mean; for they are further removed from one another than from the mean, as that which is greater than a given magnitude is further from that which is less, and that which is less is further from that which is greater, than either the greater or the less is from that which is equal to the given magnitude.

Sometimes, again, an extreme, when compared with the mean, has a sort of resemblance to it, as foolhardiness to courage, or prodigality to liberal-ity; but there is the greatest possible dissimilarity between the extremes.

Again, "things that are as far as possible removed from each other" is the accepted definition of con-traries, so that the further things are removed from each other the more contrary they are.

In comparison with the mean, however, it is some-times the deficiency that is the more opposed, and sometimes the excess; e.g. foolhardiness, which is excess, is not so much opposed to courage as cow-ardice, which is deficiency; but insensibility, which is lack of feeling, is not so much opposed to tem-perance as profligacy, which is excess.

The reasons for this are two. One is the reason derived from the nature of the matter itself: since one extreme is, in fact, nearer and more similar to the mean, we naturally do not oppose it to the mean so strongly as the other; e.g. as foolhardiness

seems more similar to courage and nearer to it, and cowardice more dissimilar, we speak of cowardice as the opposite rather than the other: for that which is further removed from the mean seems to be more opposed to it.

This, then, is one reason, derived from the nature of the thing itself. Another reason lies in ourselves: and it is this—those things to which we happen to be more prone by nature appear to be more opposed to the mean: e.g. our natural inclination is rather towards indulgence in pleasure, and so we more easily fall into profligate than into regular habits: those courses, then, in which we are more apt to run to great lengths are spoken of as more opposed to the mean; and thus profligacy, which is an excess, is more opposed to temperance than the deficiency is.

Perception, not Reasoning

We have sufficiently explained, then, that moral virtue is moderation or observance of the mean, and in what sense, viz. (1) as holding a middle position between two vices, one on the side of excess, and the other on the side of deficiency, and (2) as

aiming at the mean or moderate amount both in feeling and in action.

And on this account it is a hard thing to be good; for finding the middle or the mean in each case is a hard thing, just as finding the middle or centre of a circle is a thing that is not within the power of everybody, but only of him who has the requisite knowledge.

Thus any one can be angry—that is quite easy; any one can give money away or spend it: but to do these things to the right person, to the right extent, at the right time, with the right object, and in the right manner, is not what everybody can do, and is by no means easy; and that is the reason why right doing is rare and praiseworthy and noble.

He that aims at the mean, then, should first of all strive to avoid that extreme which is more opposed to it, as Calypso bids Ulysses—

"Clear of these smoking breakers keep thy ship."

For of the extremes one is more dangerous, the other less. Since then it is hard to hit the mean precisely, we must "row when we cannot sail," as the proverb has it, and choose the least of two evils; and that will be best effected in the way we have described.

❀ 6.5 Determinism ❀

*Selections from The System of Nature
by Baron Henri d'Holbach*

* *

© donatas1205/
Shutterstock.com

Paul-Henri Thiry, the Baron of Holbach (1723–1789), was a French philosopher who lived during the same era as Immanuel Kant. He made a name for himself in the French intelligencia by holding dinner parties or "salons" for famous intellectuals, who would meet and argue with one another. Many of the intellectuals were pursuing social and political reform, and like Holbach, were atheists. Holbach wrote a number of controversial works, including *Christianity Unveiled* and *Common Sense*, which was condemned by parliament and publicly burned.

This selection comes from *The System of Nature*, which was controversial for proposing that the world could be explained as a massive mechanism, consisting only of matter in motion obeying the laws of cause and effect. Holbach denies that there is a soul distinct from the body. Because human beings are part of this material mechanism, human beings could not have any free will.[1]

Holbach's determinism might be called *logical-entailment determinism*. Given prior states of world and the laws of nature, it is not a natural possibility for future events to go any differently than they do. Holbach argues that this follows from the assumption that reality is a system of particles obeying the laws of matter. Free will, says Holbach, is just an illusion.

---

[1]LeBuffe, Michae. "Paul-Henri Thirty (Baron) d'Holbach." *Stanford Encyclopedia of Philosophy*, 2015. E. Zalta, Ed.

Here are some questions to think about when you read:

* Why doesn't a person refusing to drink when thirsty prove that there is free will?

* What is deliberation? Why doesn't the experience of deliberation or "making a choice" prove that there is free will?

* Holbach believed that all human action could be predicted based on an understanding of the brain. Do you think we have more or less evidence of this 250 years later?

* What does Holbach think is the relationship between what causes us to act, and our motives or reasons for acting?

Of the System of Man's free agency

The Soul nothing more than the Body

Those who have pretended that the soul is distinguished from the body, is immaterial, draws its ideas from its own peculiar source, acts by its own energies without the aid of any exterior object; by a consequence of their own system, have enfranchised it from those physical laws, according to which all beings of which we have a knowledge are obliged to act. They have believed that the foul is mistress of its own conduct, is able to regulate its own peculiar operations; has the faculty to determine its will by its own natural energy; in a word, they have pretended man is a free agent.

It has been already sufficiently proved, that the soul is nothing more than the body, considered relatively to some of its functions, more concealed than others: it has been shewn, that this soul, even when it shall be supposed immaterial, is continually modified conjointly with the body; is submitted to all its motion; that without this it would remain inert and dead: that, consequently, it is subjected to the influence of those material, to the operation those physical causes, which give impulse to the body; of which the mode of existence, whether habitual or transitory, depends upon the material elements by which it is surrounded; that form its texture; that constitute its temperament; that enter into it by the means of the aliments; that penetrate it by their subtility; the faculties which are called intellectual, and those qualities which are styled moral, have been explained in a manner purely physical; entirely natural: in the last place, it has been demonstrated, that all the ideas, all the systems, all the affections, all the opinions, whether true or false, which man forms to himself, are to be attributed to his physical powers; are to be ascribed to his material senses. Thus man is a being purely physical; in whatever manner he is considered, he is connected to universal Nature: submitted to the necessary, to the immutable laws that she imposes on all the beings she contains, according to their peculiar essences; conformable to the respective properties with which, without consulting them, she endows each particular species. Man's life is a line that Nature commands him to describe upon the surface of the earth: without his ever being able to swerve from it even for an instant. He is born without his own consent; his organizations does in no wise depend upon himself; his ideas come to him involuntarily; his habits are in the power of those who cause him to contract them; he is unceasingly modified by causes, whether visible or concealed, over which he has no controul; give the hue to his way of thinking, and determine his manner of acting. He is good or bad—happy or miserable—wise or foolish—reasonable or irrational, without his will going for anything in these various states. Nevertheless, in despite of the shackles by which he is bound, it is pretended he is a free agent,

517

or that independent of the causes by which he is moved, he determines his own will; regulates his own condition.

However slender the foundation of this opinion, of which every thing ought to point out to him the error; it is current at this day for an incontestible truth, and believed enlightened; it is the basis or religion, which has been incapable of imagining how man could either merit reward or deserve punishment if he was not a free agent. Society has been believed interested in this system, because an idea has gone abroad, that if all the actions of man were to be contemplated as necessary, the right of punishing those who injure their associates would no longer exist. At length human vanity accommodated itself to an hypothesis which, unquestionable, appears to distinguish man from all other physical beings, by assigning to him the special privilege of a total independence of all other causes; but of which a very little reflection would have shewn him the absurdity or even the impossibility.

The Will a Modification of the Brain

The will, as we have elsewhere said, is a modification of the brain, by which it is disposed to action or prepared to give play to the organs. This will is necessarily determined by the qualities, good or bad, agreeable or painful, of the object or the motive that acts upon his senses; or of which the idea remains with him, and is resuscitated by his memory. In consequence, he acts necessarily; his action is the result of the impulse he receives either from the motive, from the object, or from the idea, which has modified his brain, or disposed his will. When he does not act according to this impulse, it is because there comes some new cause, some new motive, some new idea, which modifies his brain in a different manner, gives him a new impulse, determines his will in another way; by which the action

of the former impulse is suspended: thus, the sight of an agreeable object, or its idea, determines his will to set him in action to procure it; but if a new object or a new idea more powerfully attracts him, it gives a new direction to his will, annihilates the effect of the former, and prevents the action by which it was to be procured. This is the mode in which reflection, experience, reason, necessarily arrests or suspends the action of man's will; without this, he would, of necessity, have followed the anterior impulse which carried him towards a then desirable object. In all this he always acts according to necessary laws, from which he has no means of emancipating himself.

If, when tormented with violent thirst, he figures to himself an idea, or really perceives a fountain, whose limpid streams might cool his feverish habit, is he sufficient master of himself to desire or not to desire the object competent to satisfy so lively a want? It will no doubt be conceded, that it is impossible he should not be desirous to satisfy it; but it will be said,—If at this moment it is announced to him, the water he so ardently desires is poisoned, he will, notwithstanding his vehement thirst, abstain from drinking it; and it has, therefore, been falsely concluded that he is a free agent. The fact, however, is, that the motive in either case is exactly the same: his own conservation. The same necessity that determined him to drink, before he knew the water was deleterious, upon this new discovery, equally determines him not to drink; the desire of conserving himself, either annihilates or suspends the former impulse; the second motive becomes stronger than the preceding; that is, the fear of death, or the desire of preserving himself, necessarily prevails over the painful sensation caused by his eagerness to drink. But, (it will be said) if the thirst is very parching, an inconsiderate man, without regarding the danger, will risque swallowing the water. Nothing is gained by this remark: in this case, the anterior impulse only regains the ascendency; he is persuaded, that life may possibly be longer preserved, or that he shall derive a greater good by drinking the poisoned water, than by enduring the torment, which, to his mind, threatens instant dissolution: thus, the first becomes the strongest, and necessarily urges him on to action. Nevertheless, in either case, whether he partakes of the water, or whether he does not, the two actions will be equally necessary; they will be the effect of that motive which finds itself most puissant; which consequently acts in a most coercive manner upon his will.

This example will serve to explain the whole phaenomena of the human will. This will, or rather the brain, finds itself in the same situation as a bowl, which although it has received an impulse that drives it forward in a straight line, is deranged in its course, whenever a force, superior to the first, obliges it to change its direction. The man who drinks the poisoned water, appears a madman; but the actions of fools are as necessary as those of the most prudent individuals. The motives that determine the voluptuary, that actuate the debauchee to risk their health, are as powerful, their actions are as necessary, as those which decide the wise man to manage his. But, it will be insisted, the debauchee may be prevailed on to change his conduct; this does not imply that he is a free agent; but, that motives may be found sufficiently powerful to annihilate the effect of those that previously acted upon him; then these new motives determine his will to the new mode of conduct he may adopt, as necessarily as the former did to the old mode.

On Deliberation

Man is said to deliberate when the action of the will is suspended; this happens when two opposite motives act alternately upon him. To deliberate, is to hate and to love in succession; it is to be alternately attracted and repelled; it is to be moved sometimes by one motive, sometimes by another. Man only deliberates when he does not distinctly

understand the quality of the objects from which he receives impulse, or when experience has not sufficiently apprised him of the effects, more or less remote, which his actions will produce. He would take the air, but the weather is uncertain; he deliberates in consequence; he weighs the various motives that urge his will to go out or to stay at home; he is at length determined by that motive which is most probable; this removes his indecision, which necessarily settles his will either to remain within or to go abroad: this motive is always either the immediate or ultimate advantage he finds or thinks he finds in the action to which he is persuaded.

Man's will frequently fluctuates between two objects, of which either the presence or the ideas move him alternately: he waits until he has contemplated the objects or the ideas they have left in his brain; which solicit him to different actions; he then compares these objects or ideas: but even in the time of deliberation, during the comparison, pending these alternatives of love and hatred, which succeed each other sometimes with the utmost rapidity, he is not a free agent for a single instant; the good or the evil which he believes he finds successively in the objects, are the necessary motives of these momentary wills; of the rapid motion of desire or fear that he experiences as long as his uncertainty continues. From this it will be obvious, that deliberation is necessary; that uncertainty is necessary; that whatever part he takes, in consequence of this deliberation, it will always necessarily be that which he has judged, whether well or ill, is most probable to turn to his advantage.

When the soul is assailed by two motives that act alternately upon it, or modify it successively, it deliberates; the brain is in a sort of equilibrium, accompanied with perpetual oscillations, sometimes towards one object, sometimes towards the other, until the most forcible carries the point, and thereby extricates it, from this state of suspense, in which consists the indecision of his will. But when the brain is simultaneously assailed by causes

❖ ❖

equally strong, that move it in opposite directions; agreeable to the general law of all bodies, when they are struck equally by contrary powers, it stops, it is in nisu; it is neither capable to will nor to act; it waits until one of the two causes has obtained sufficient force to overpower the other, to determine its will, to attract it in such a manner that it may prevail over the efforts of the other cause.

This mechanism, so simple, so natural, suffices to demonstrate, why uncertainty is painful; why suspense is always a violent state for man. The brain, an organ so delicate, so mobile, experiences such rapid modifications, that it is fatigued; or when it is urged in contrary directions, by causes equally powerful, it suffers a kind of compression, that prevents the activity which is suitable to the preservation of the whole, which is necessary to procure what is advantageous to its existence. This mechanism will also explain the irregularity, the indecision, the inconstancy of man; and account for that conduct, which frequently appears an inexplicable mystery, which indeed it is, under the received systems. In consulting experience, it will be found that the soul is submitted to precisely the same physical laws as the material body. If the will of each individual, during a given time, was only moved by a single cause or passion, nothing would be more easy than to foresee his actions; but his heart is frequently assailed by contrary powers, by adverse motives, which either act on him simultaneously or in succession; then his brain, attracted in opposite directions, is either fatigued, or else tormented by a state of compression, which deprives it of activity. Sometimes it is in a state of incommodious inaction; sometimes it is the sport of the alternate shocks it undergoes. Such, no doubt, is the state in which man finds himself, when a lively passion solicits him to the commission of crime, whilst fear points out to him the danger by which it is attended: such, also, is the condition of him whom remorse, by the continued labour of his distracted soul, prevents from enjoying the objects he has criminally obtained. . . .

Choice no Proof of Free Will

Choice by no means proves the free-agency of man; he only deliberates when he does not yet know which to choose of the many objects that move him, he is then in an embarrassment, which does not terminate, until his will as decided by the greater advantage he believes be shall find in the object he chooses, or the action he undertakes. From whence it may be seen that choice is necessary, because he would not determine for an object, or for an action, if he did not believe that he should find in it some direct advantage. That man should have free-agency, it were needful that he should be able to will or choose without motive; or, that he could prevent motives coercing his will. Action always being the effect of his will once determined, as his will cannot be determined but by a motive, which is not in his own power, it follows that he is never the master of the determination of his own peculiar will; that consequently he never acts as a free agent. It has been believed that man was a free agent, because he had a will with the power of choosing; but attention has not been paid to the fact, that even his will is moved by causes independent of himself, is owing to that which is inherent in his own organization, or which belongs to the nature of the beings acting on him. Indeed, man passes a great portion of his life without even willing. His will attends the motive by which it is determined. If he was to render an exact account of every thing he does in the course of each day, from rising in the morning to lying down at night, he would find, that not one of his actions have been in the least voluntary; that they have been mechanical, habitual, determined by causes he was not able to foresee, to which he was either obliged to, yield, or with which he was allured to acquiesce; he would discover, that all the motives of his labours, of his amusements, of his discourses, of his thoughts, have been necessary; that they have evidently either seduced him or drawn him along. Is he the master of willing, not to withdraw his hand from the fire when he fears it will be burnt? Or has he the power to take away from fire the property which makes him fear it? Is he the master of not choosing a dish of meat which he knows to be agreeable, or analogous to his palate; of not preferring it to that which he knows to be disagreeable or dangerous? It is always according to his sensations, to his own peculiar experience, or to his suppositions, that he judges of things either well or ill; but whatev\ er way be his judgment, it depends necessarily on his mode of feeling, whether habitual or accidental, and the qualities he finds in the causes that move him, which exist in despite of himself . . . .

The Complication of Motion

It is the great complication of motion in man, it is the variety of his action, it is the multiplicity of causes that move him, whether simultaneously or in continual succession, that persuades him he is a free agent: if all his motions were simple, if the causes that move him did not confound themselves with each other, if they were distinct, if his machine was less complicated, he would perceive that all his actions were necessary, because he would be enabled to recur instantly to the cause that made him act. A man who should be always obliged to go towards the west would always go on that side, but he would feel extremely well, that in so going he was not a free agent: if he had another sense, as his actions or his motion augmented by a sixth would be still more varied, much more complicated, he would believe himself still more a free agent than he does with his five senses.

It is, then, for want of recurring to the causes that move him, for want of being able to analyse, from not being competent to decompose the complicated motion of his machine, that man believes himself a free agent; it is only upon his own ignorance that he founds the profound yet deceitful notion he has of his free-agency, that he builds those opinions which he brings forward as a striking proof of his pretended freedom of action. If, for a short time, each man was willing to examine his own peculiar actions, to search out their true motives, to discover their concatenation, he would remain convinced that the sentiment he has of his natural free-agency is a chimera that must speedily be destroyed by experience.

Nevertheless, it must be acknowledged that the multiplicity, the diversity of the causes which continually act upon man, frequently without even his knowledge, render it impossible, or at least extremely difficult, for him to recur to the true principles of his own peculiar actions, much less the actions of others; they frequently depend upon causes so fugitive, so remote from their effects, and which, superficially examined, appear to have so little analogy, so slender a relation with them, that it requires singular sagacity to bring them into light. This is what renders the study of the moral man a task of such difficulty; this is the reason why his heart is an abyss, of which it is frequently impossible for him to fathom the depth. He is, then, obliged to content himself with a knowledge of the general and necessary laws by which the human heart is regulated; for the individuals of his own species these laws are pretty nearly the same, they vary only in consequence of the organization that is peculiar to each, and of the modification it undergoes; this, however, is not, cannot be rigorously the same in any two. It suffices to know that by his essence man tends to conserve himself, to render his existence happy: this granted, whatever may be his actions, if he recurs back to this first principle, to this general, this necessary tendency of his will, he never can be deceived with regard to his motives.

❋ 6.6 Libertarianism ❋

Selections from Metaphysics
by Richard Taylor

✳✳✳

Richard Taylor (1919–2003) was an American philosopher known for his unpretentious style. In this selection from his textbook on Metaphysics, Taylor argues in favor of an agent-causal account of libertarianism, the view that there is free will.

Taylor rejects both determinism and what he calls "simple indeterminism". "Simple indeterminism", which we'll call *non-agent-causal libertarianism*, is the view that an action is free provided that it was a natural possibility for one to do otherwise. This view does not require that we actually are the causes of our own actions; it only requires that whatever physical events do cause our actions, these physical events do not fully determine it – they leave open the possibility that things might have gone differently.

The trouble, says Taylor, is that "simple indeterminism" amounts to saying our "free" actions are matters of random *chance*. But acting randomly or on chance is not freedom. Freedom means that we are in control of our actions: we are at least sometimes the causes of our own actions, *self-d*etermined instead of determined by outside forces or indeterministic chance.

Here are some questions to think about when you read:

* Why can one "hardly affirm the theory of agency . . . without embarassment"?

* What view in the philosophy of mind does Taylor seem to be committed to?

* How is an "agent cause" supposed to be different from ordinary causation by events.

* Taylor denies determinism because he thinks that it requires all causation go back infinitely in time. Why does the think agent causation is more plausible?

Free Agency*

The Refutation of Soft Determinism

My free actions are those unimpeded and unconstrained motions that arise from my own inner desires, choices, and volitions; let us grant this provisionally. But now, whence arise those inner states that determine what my body shall do? Are they within my control or not? Having made my choice or decision and acted upon it, could I have chosen otherwise or not?

But it is not nonsense to ask whether the causes of my actions—my own inner choices, decisions, and desires—are themselves caused. And of course they are, if determinism is true, for on that thesis everything is caused and determined. And if they are, then we cannot avoid concluding that, given the causal conditions of those inner states, I could not have decided, willed, chosen, or desired otherwise than I in fact did, for this is a logical consequence of the very definition of determinism. Of course we can still say that, *if* the causes of those inner states, whatever they were, had been different, then their effects, those inner states themselves, would have been different, and that in this hypothetical sense I could have decided, chosen, willed, or desired differently—but that only pushes our problem back still another step. For we will then want to know whether the causes of those inner states were within my control; and so on, *ad infinitum*. We are, at each step, permitted to say "could have been otherwise" only in a provisional sense—provided, that is, something else had been different—but must then retract it and replace it with "could not have been otherwise" as soon as we discover, as we must at each step, that whatever would have to have been different could not have been different.

Examples

Whether a desire which causes my body to behave in a certain way is inflicted upon me by another person, for instance, or derived from hereditary factors, or indeed from anything at all, matters not the least. In any case, if it is in fact the cause of my bodily behavior, I cannot but act in accordance with it. Wherever it came from, whether from personal or impersonal origins, it was entirely caused or determined, and not within my control. Indeed, if determinism is true, as the theory of soft determinism holds it to be, all those inner states which cause my body to behave in whatever ways it behaves must arise from circumstances that existed before I was born; for the chain of causes and effects is infinite, and none could have been the least different, given those that preceded.

*FONTANA, ANDREA KIM; TAYLOR, RICHARD, METAPHYSICS, 2nd Ed., * 1974. Reprinted by permission of Pearson Education, Inc., New York, New York.

Simple Indeterminism

We might at first now seem warranted in simply denying determinism, and saying that, insofar as they are free, my actions are not caused; or that, if they are caused by my own inner states—my own desires, impulses, choices, volitions, and whatnot—then these, in any case, are not caused. This is a perfectly clear sense in which a man's action, assuming that it was free, could have been otherwise. If it was uncaused, then, even given the conditions under which it occurred and all that preceded, some other act was nonetheless possible, and he did not have to do what he did. Or if his action was the inevitable consequence of his own inner states, and could not have been otherwise given these, we can nevertheless say that these inner states, being uncaused, could have been otherwise, and could thereby have produced different actions.

Only the slightest consideration will show, however, that this simple denial of determinism has not the slightest plausibility. For let us suppose it is true, and that some of my bodily motions—namely, those that I regard as my free acts—are not caused at all or, if caused by my own inner states, that these are not caused. We shall thereby avoid picturing a puppet, to be sure—but only by substituting something even less like a man; for the conception that now emerges is not that of a free man, but of an erratic and jerking phantom, without any rhyme or reason at all.

Suppose that my right arm is free, according to this conception; that is, that its motions are uncaused. It moves this way and that from time to time, but nothing causes these motions. Sometimes it moves forth vigorously, sometimes up, sometimes down, sometimes it just drifts vaguely about—these motions all being wholly free and uncaused. Manifestly I have nothing to do with them at all; they just happen, and neither I nor anyone can ever tell what this arm will be doing next. It might seize a club and lay it on the head of the nearest bystander, no less to my astonishment than his. There will never be any point in asking why these motions occur, or in seeking any explanation of them, for under the conditions assumed there is no explanation. They just happen, from no causes at all.

This is no description of free, voluntary, or responsible behavior. Indeed, so far as the motions of my body or its parts are entirely uncaused, such motions cannot even be ascribed to me as my behavior in the first place, since I have nothing to do with them. The behavior of my arm is just the random motion of a foreign object. Behavior that is mine must be behavior that is within my control, but motions that occur from no causes are without the control of anyone. I can have no more to do with, and no more control over, the uncaused motions of my limbs than a gambler has over the motions of an honest roulette wheel. I can only, like him, idly wait to see what happens.

Nor does it improve things to suppose that my bodily motions are caused by my own inner states, so long as we suppose these to be wholly uncaused. The result will be the same as before. My arm, for example, will move this way and that, sometimes up and sometimes down, sometimes vigorously and sometimes just drifting about, always in response to certain inner states, to be sure. But since these are supposed to be wholly uncaused, it follows that I have no control over them and hence none over their effects. If my hand lays a club forcefully on the nearest bystander, we can indeed say that this motion resulted from an inner club-wielding desire of mine; but we must add that I had nothing to do with that desire, and that it arose; to be followed by its inevitable effect, no less to my astonishment than to his. Things like this do, alas, sometimes happen. We are all sometimes seized by compulsive impulses that arise we know not whence and we do sometimes act upon these. But because they are far from being examples of free, voluntary, and

responsible behavior, we need only to learn that behavior was of this sort to conclude that it was not free, voluntary, or responsible. It was erratic, impulsive, and irresponsible.

Determinism and Simple Indeterminism as Theories

Both determinism and simple indeterminism are loaded with difficulties, and no one who has thought much on them can affirm either of them without some embarrassment. Simple indeterminism has nothing whatever to be said for it, except that it appears to remove the grossest difficulties of determinism, only, however, to imply perfect absurdities of its own. Determinism, on the other hand, is at least initially plausible. Men seem to have a natural inclination to believe in it; it is, indeed, almost required for the very exercise of practical intelligence. And beyond this, our experience appears always to confirm it, so long as we are dealing with everyday facts of common experience, as distinguished from the esoteric researches of theoretical physics. But determinism, as applied to human behavior, has implications which few men can casually accept, and they appear to be implications which no modification of the theory can efface.

Both theories, moreover, appear logically irreconcilable to the two items of data that we set forth at the outset; namely, (1) that my behavior is sometimes the outcome of my deliberation, and (2) that in these and other cases it is sometimes up to me what I do. Because these were our data, it is important to see, as must already be quite clear, that these theories cannot be reconciled to them.

I can deliberate only about my own future actions, and then only if I do not already know what I am going to do. If a certain nasal tickle warns me that I am about to sneeze, for instance, then I cannot deliberate whether to sneeze or not; I can

only prepare for the impending convulsion. But if determinism is true, then there are always conditions existing antecedently to everything I do, sufficient for my doing just that, and such as to render it inevitable. If I can know what those conditions are and what behavior they are sufficient to produce, then I can in every such case know what I am going to do and cannot then deliberate about it.

By itself this only shows, of course, that I can deliberate only in ignorance of the casual conditions of my behavior; it does not show that such conditions cannot exist. It is odd, however, to suppose that deliberation should be a mere substitute for clear knowledge. Ignorance is a condition of speculation, inference, and guesswork, which have nothing whatever to do with deliberation. A prisoner awaiting execution may not know when he is going to die, and he may even entertain the hope of reprieve, but he cannot deliberate about this. He can only speculate, guess—and wait.

Worse yet, however, it now becomes clear that I cannot deliberate about what I am going to do, if it is even possible for me to find out in advance, whether I do in fact find out in advance or not. I can deliberate only with the view to deciding what to do, to making up my mind; and this is impossible if I believe that it could be inferred what I am going to do, from conditions already existing, even though I have not made that inference myself. If I believe that what I am going to do has been rendered inevitable by conditions already existing, and could be inferred by anyone having the requisite sagacity, then. I cannot try to decide whether to do it or not, for there is simply nothing left to decide. I can at best only guess or try to figure it out myself or, all prognostics failing, I can wait and see; but I cannot deliberate. I deliberate in order to *decide* what *to* do, not to *discover* what it is that I am *going* to do. But if determinism is true, then there are always antecedent conditions sufficient for everything that I do, and this can always be inferred by

❀ ❀

anyone having the requisite sagacity; that is, by anyone having a knowledge of what those conditions are and what behavior they are sufficient to produce.

This suggests what in fact seems quite clear, that determinism cannot be reconciled with our second datum either, to the effect that it is sometimes up to me what I am going to do. For if it is ever really up to me whether to do this thing or that, then, as we have seen, each alternative course of action must be such that I can do it; not that I can do it in some abstruse or hypothetical sense of "can"; not that I could do it if only something were true that is not true; but in the sense that it is then and there within my power to do it. But this is never so, if determinism is true, for on the very formulation of that theory whatever happens at any time is the only thing that can then happen, given all that precedes it. It is simply a logical consequence of this that whatever I do at any time is the only thing I can then do, given the conditions that precede my doing it. Nor does it help in the least to interpose, among the causal antecedents of my behavior, my own inner states, such as my desires, choices, acts of will, and so on. For even supposing these to be always involved in voluntary behavior—which is highly doubtful in itself—it is a consequence of determinism that these, whatever they are at any time, can never be other than what they then are. Every chain of causes and effects, if determinism is true, is infinite. This is why it is not now up to me whether I shall a moment hence be male or female. The conditions determining my sex have existed through my whole life, and even prior to my life. But if determinism is true, the same holds of anything that I ever am, ever become, or ever do. It matters not whether we are speaking of the most patent facts of my being, such as my sex; or the most subtle, such as my feelings, thoughts, desires, or choices. Nothing could be other than it is, given what was; and while we may indeed say, quite idly, that something—some inner state of mine, for instance— *could* have been

different, had only something *else* been different, any consolation of this thought evaporates as soon as we add that whatever would have to have been different could not have been different.

It is even more obvious that our data cannot be reconciled to the theory of simple indeterminism. I can deliberate only about my own actions; this is obvious. But the random, uncaused motion of any body whatever, whether it be a part of my body or not, is no action of mine and nothing that is within my power. I might try to guess what these motions will be, just as I might try to guess how a roulette wheel will behave, but I cannot deliberate about them or try to decide what they shall be, simply because these things are not up to me. Whatever is not caused by anything is not caused by me, and nothing could be more plainly inconsistent with saying that it is nevertheless up to me what it shall be.

The Theory of Agency

The only conception of action that accords with our data is one according to which men—and perhaps some other things too—are sometimes, but of course not always, self-determining beings; that is, beings which are sometimes the causes of their own behavior. In the case of an action that is free, it must be such that it is caused by the agent who performs it, but such that no antecedent conditions were sufficient for his performing just that action. In the case of an action that is both free and rational, it must be such that the agent who performed it did so for some reason, but this reason cannot have been the cause of it.

Now this conception fits what men take themselves to be; namely, beings who act, or who are agents, rather than things that are merely acted upon, and whose behavior is simply the causal consequence of conditions which they have not wrought. When I believe that I have done something, I do believe that it was I who caused it to be done, I who made something happen, and not merely something within me, such as one of my own subjective states, which is not identical with myself. If I believe that something not identical with myself was the cause of my behavior—some event wholly external to myself, for instance, or even one internal to myself, such as a nerve impulse, volition, or whatnot—then I cannot regard that behavior as being an act of mine, unless I further believe that I was the cause of that external or internal event. My pulse, for example, is caused and regulated by certain conditions existing within me, and not by myself. I do not, accordingly, regard this activity of my body as my action, and would be no more tempted to do so if I became suddenly conscious within myself of those conditions or impulses that produce it. This is behavior with which I have nothing to do, behavior that is not within my immediate control, behavior that is not only not free activity, but not even the activity of an agent to begin with; it is nothing but a mechanical reflex. Had I never learned that my very life depends on this pulse beat, I would regard it with complete indifference, as something foreign to me, like the oscillations of a clock pendulum that I idly contemplate.

Now this conception of activity, and of an agent who is the cause of it, involves two rather strange metaphysical notions that are never applied elsewhere in nature. \??\ The first is that of a *self* or *person*—for example, a man—who is not merely a collection of things or events, but a substance and a self-moving being. For on this view it is a man himself, and not merely some part of him or something within him, that is the cause of his own activity. Now we certainly do not know that a man is anything more than an assemblage of physical things and processes, which act in accordance with those laws that describe the behavior of all other physical things and processes. Even though a man is a living being, of enormous complexity, there is nothing, apart from the requirements of this theory, to suggest that his behavior is so radically different in its origin from that of other physical objects, or that an understanding of it must be sought in some metaphysical realm wholly different from that appropriate to the understanding of nonliving things.

Second, this conception of activity involves an extraordinary conception of causation, according to which an agent, which is a substance and not an event, can nevertheless be the cause of an event. Indeed, if he is a free agent then he can, on this conception, cause an event to occur—namely, some act of his own—without anything else causing him to do so. This means that an agent is sometimes a cause, without being an antecedent sufficient condition; for if I affirm that I am the cause of some act of mine, then I am plainly not saying that my very existence is sufficient for its occurrence, which would be absurd. If I say that my hand causes my pencil to move, then I am saying that the motion of my hand is, under the other conditions then prevailing, sufficient for the motion of the pencil. But if I then say that I cause my hand to move, I am not saying anything remotely like this, and surely not that the motion of my self is sufficient for the motion of my arm and hand, since these are the only things about me that are moving.

This conception of the causation of events by beings or substances that are not events is, in fact, so different from the usual philosophical conception of a cause that it should not even bear the same name, for "being a cause" ordinarily just means "being an antecedent sufficient condition or set of conditions." Instead, then, of speaking of agents as *causing* their own acts, it would perhaps be better to use another word entirely, and say, for instance, that they *originate* them, \??*initiate* them, or simply that they *perform* them.

Now this is on the face of it a dubious conception of what a man is. Yet it is consistent with our data, reflecting the presuppositions of deliberation, and appears to be the only conception that is consistent with them, as determinism and simple

❖ ❖

indeterminism are not. The theory of agency avoids the absurdities of simple indeterminism by conceding that human behavior is caused, while at the same time avoiding the difficulties of determinism by denying that every chain of causes and effects is infinite. Some such causal chains, on this view, have beginnings, and they begin with agents themselves. Moreover, if we are to suppose that it is sometimes up to me what I do, and understand this in a sense which is not consistent with determinism, we must suppose that I am an agent or a being who initiates his own actions, sometimes under conditions which do not determine what action he shall perform. Deliberation becomes, on this view, something that is not only possible but quite rational, for it does make sense to deliberate about activity that is truly my own and that depends in its outcome upon me as its author, and not merely upon something more or less esoteric that is supposed to be intimately associated with me, such as my thoughts, volitions, choices, or whatnot.

One can hardly affirm such a theory of agency with complete comfort, however, and wholly without embarrassment, for the conception of men and their powers which is involved in it is strange indeed, if not positively mysterious. In fact, one can hardly be blamed here for simply denying our data outright, rather than embracing this theory to which they do most certainly point. Our data—to the effect that men do sometimes deliberate before acting, and that when they do, they presuppose among other things that it is up to them what they are going to do—rest upon nothing more than fairly common consent. These data might simply be illusions. It might in fact be that no man ever deliberates, but only imagines that he does, that from pure conceit he supposes himself to be the master of his behavior

and the author of his acts. Spinoza has suggested that if a stone, having been thrown into the air, were suddenly to become conscious, it would suppose itself to be the source of its own motion, being then conscious of what it was doing but not aware of the real cause of its behavior. Certainly men are *sometimes* mistaken in believing that they are behaving as a result of choice deliberately arrived at. A man might, for example, easily imagine that his embarking upon matrimony is the result of the most careful and rational deliberation, when in fact the causes, perfectly sufficient for that behavior, might be of an entirely physiological, unconscious origin. If it is sometimes false that we deliberate and then act as the result of a decision deliberately arrived at, even when we suppose it to be true, it might always be false. No one seems able, as we have noted, to describe deliberation without metaphors, and the conception of a thing's being "within one's power" or "up to him" seems to defy analysis or definition altogether, if taken in a sense which the theory of agency appears to require.

These are, then, dubitable conceptions, despite their being so well implanted in the common sense of mankind. Indeed, when we turn to the theory of fatalism, we shall find formidable metaphysical considerations which appear to rule them out altogether. Perhaps here, as elsewhere in metaphysics, we should be content with discovering difficulties, with seeing what is and what is not consistent with such convictions as we happen to have, and then drawing such satisfaction as we can from the realization that, no matter where we begin, the world is mysterious and the men who try to understand it are even more so. This realization can, with some justification, make one feel wise, even in the full realization of his ignorance.

✿ 6.7 Selections on Compatibilism ✿

* *

"Compatibilism" is the view that determinism is compatible with free-will. Of course, certain definitions of determinism are not compatible with certain definitions of free-will; but there are also ways to define free will and/or determinism so that the two are compatible.

In the readings quoted here, we'll focus here on a form of compatibilism on which free will is supposed to be compatible with *any* form of determinism, including logical-entailment determinism. According to this type of compatibilism, an agent's action is free provided that the agent did not do the action under external force or compulsion. An act is free when the immediate causes of the act are psychological states of the agent, rather than states of affairs external to the agent.

In the first selection, W. T. Stace (1886–1967) argues that the debate between determinists and libertarians is a verbal dispute. Both sides are mistaken in thinking that "free will" is defined as an undetermined choice. If we paid attention to how "free will" is used in everyday language, we'd see that determinism is consistent with free will.

In the second selection, Samuel Alexander (1859—1938) argues that what makes an action "free" is simply that we *enjoy* the action or *want* to perform it. Enjoyment is a subjective mental state, not a state of particles in motion. While the movements of particles in motion are predictable based on past events, our conscious sense of enjoyment is not predictable.

Here are some questions to think about as you read:

* Why does W. T. Stace think ordinary language will tell us about free will?

* Why is someone "free" when they go without food in protest, but not when they go without food because there is no food?

* Why is someone "not free" when they act because of a threat to their life, even though they could choose to do otherwise?

* What is the use of the notion of free will? Why did we develop a word for it?

Compatibilism

W. T. Stace on Free Will from *Religion and the Modern Mind*, 1952

Stace begins with an example of how "free will" is used in ordinary language:

Jones: I once went without food for a week.
Smith: Did you do that of your own free will?
Jones: No. I did it because I was lost in a desert and could find no food.

Contrast that with:

Gandhi: I once fasted for a week.
Smith: Did you do that of your own free will?
Gandhi: Yes. I did it because I wanted to compel the British Government to give India its independence.

What's the difference? The difference seems to be that Gandhi fasted for his own reasons, but Jones did not. Stace gives another example – suppose he had stolen bread:

Judge: Did you steal the bread of your own free will?
Stace: Yes. I stole it because I was hungry.

Compare this to:

Judge: Did you steal of your own free will?
Stace: No. I stole because my employer threatened to beat me if I did not.

What's the difference? It isn't that one event is less determined by the laws of nature. It's that the first choice involves Stace's personal reasons, and the second choice involves the reasons of Stace's employer. Stace gives another example involving a courtroom:

Judge: Did you sign the confession of your own free will?
Prisoner: No. I signed it because the police beat me up.

Again, consider this:

Jones: Did you go out of your own free will?
Smith: Yes. I went out to get my lunch.

Compared to:

Jones: Did you leave your office of your own free will?
Smith: No. I was forcibly removed by the police.

Stace concludes that the following conversation seems like it would never happen, which is good evidence that philosophy is not talking about the "normal" conception of free will when thinking that free will is incompatible with determinism:

Foreman of the Jury: the prisoner says he signed the confession because he was beaten and not of his own free will.
Philosopher: This is quite irrelevant to the case. There is no such thing as free will.

Foreman: Do you mean to say that it makes no difference whether he signed because his conscience made him want to tell the truth or because he was beaten? Philosopher: None at all.

Obviously, it *does* matter whether a confession was extracted by force or given freely. We do care about the everyday notion of "free will" when we are considering issues of punishment and reward. But the everyday notion of "free will", Stace says, is not in conflict with determinism. Instead, an agent acts freely when the primary, immediate causes of the action are that agent's own psychological states – if the agent acts for his or her own motives, not on the motives of someone else.

Samuel Alexander
From *Space Time and Deity,*
Vol. II 1920

Man is free, and his freedom has been supposed on one ground or another to separate him from the rest of creation. As free, he has been thought either to be exempt from causality, or to possess a causality of a different sort so as to be independent of determination, like the rest of the world, by some antecedent cause. If it were so, causality would no longer claim to be a category as entering into the constitution of every from of finite existence . . .

It remains then to identify the consciousness of freedom that we possess. It will be seen that freedom is nothing but the form which causal action assumes when both cause and effect are enjoyed; so that freedom is determination as enjoyed, or in enjoyment . . .

The novelty alleged to be distinctive of free will . . . turns on the belief that human action is not wholly predictable. . . . Undoubtedly human action is partly predictable. The intercourse of men with one another implies it and is based on it. We resent equally . . . that our action cannot partly be predicted and that it can be wholly predicted . . .

Determinism in mind is therefore not incompatible with unpredictability; and we have seen the reason, that the predictor is a mind, and while he may predict human future regarded as a contemplated object, that is in physiological terms, he cannot predict it wholly in mental terms. . . .

Not only may mental action be determined and yet unpredictable, it may be free and necessary. Necessity conflicts with freedom only if it is taken as equivalent to compulsion which removes the conditions of freedom or makes choices impossible. An external compulsion like a physical force may put the will out of action, or like imminent death it may under certain circumstances unman a person and reduce him to the condition of a brute. But the necessity which the will obeys is the 'necessity' of causation, the determinate sequence of event upon its conditions. . . . it follows that freedom does not mean indetermination.

RELIGION AND THE MODERN MIND*

W. T. Stace

All normal people instinctively believe in free will. Nothing seems more obvious than that I am free to choose whether I will drink tea or coffee. I have no doubt myself that the obvious view is the true view, and that we do have free will. Nevertheless this can be doubted, and has been doubted, by many very clever and learned men. They have used arguments to show that free will, however strongly we may feel that we have it, is in fact a delusion. And the reason why this becomes a part of our story is that these arguments are based upon ideas which have been derived from the scientific revolution. I do not mean to say that science invented the problem of free will, or that the difficulties which are inherent in the conception of it were discovered by modern science. There may be said to have been a problem about free will ever since men began to think. It was discussed in the middle ages by Thomas Aquinas, and in ancient times by Aristotle. What science did was to make the problem acute in the modern period by providing a new argument for disbelieving in free will. And modern disbelief in it—maintained, it should be said, only by a few intellectuals and not by the man in the street, who is usually unaware that there is any problem—is the immediate result of the scientific view of things.

Newtonian science gave rise to the assumption that every event is completely determined by a chain of causes which could, if we knew enough, be traced back indefinitely far into the past. Whatever happens, therefore, has been certain and pre-determined from the beginning of time. This general thesis is called determinism. It was well expressed by Laplace who wrote:

> An intelligence knowing, at a given instant of time, all forces acting in nature, as well as the momentary positions of all things of which the universe consists, would be able to comprehend the motions of the largest bodies of the world and those of the smallest atoms in one single formula, provided it were sufficiently powerful to subject all data to analysis; to it nothing would be uncertain, both future and past would be present before its eyes.[1]

*Excerpts from pp. 135–40, 278–87 from *Religion and the Modern Mind* by W. T. Stace. Copyright © 1952 by W. T. Stace, renewed © 1980 by Blanche Stace. Reprinted by permission of HarperCollins Publishers.

[1] Quoted, *Foundations of Physics*, R. B. Lindsay and H. Margenau (New York: Wiley, 1936), p. 517.

❀ ❀

Recent physics has shown reasons for doubting the complete truth of this view. But it was the view which seemed to follow from Newtonian science, and it was Newtonian science which became influential in the making of the modern mind. Moreover —in spite of the assertions of some physicists —the indeterminism of recent science does nothing to relieve the difficulties of the problem of free will, as will be shown in due course.

The postulate of determinism provided the modern argument against free will. Every event is completely determined by causes. A human action is just as much an event in nature as is a whirlwind or an eclipse of the sun. Therefore a human action is wholly determined by its past causes. Therefore it could not possibly be other than it is. If you know all the causes which produce an event, you can predict the event. The eclipse of the sun which occurred yesterday could have been predicted a million years ago if there had been astronomers alive then who knew all the causes which operate in the solar system. Apply this thought to the actions of human beings, which are, after all, nothing but motions of their physical bodies. Everything which men do could be predicted beforehand by anyone who knew enough about the causes, and the chains of causes stretching back into the past, which produced their actions. This means that whatever you do you were certain to do. You could not have done otherwise. You had no choice. You told a lie yesterday. It was certain thousands of years ago, nay, millions of years ago, that you would tell that lie; and the intelligence imagined by Laplace—the Laplacean calculator, as it is sometimes called—could have foreseen it. But if this is so, what sense is there in saying that, when your life came to the moment of time in which you told that lie, you could have chosen whether you would tell it or not?

The general argument then is simply that all human actions must be wholly determined by causes of some kind, and that this is inconsistent with belief in free will.

Theoretically, if one knew all the relevant meteorological conditions, one could predict every detail of the rainstorm. It will be the same with human actions. And just as the weather is in some degree predictable, so are human actions. The more you know of a human being, and of his psychology, and of the forces, social, environmental, or spiritual, which act on him, the more nearly you can say beforehand what he will do.

Thus there is every reason to think that the law of causal determinism is universal, that it applies in the internal world of mind as well as in the external world of matter. Whether we adopt a materialistic or a dualistic theory of human personality, in either case free will seems to be impossible. However you look at it, Newtonian science implies determinism, and determinism has seemed to most people to imply the denial of free will.

11. THE PROBLEM OF MORALS

Morality is concerned with what men ought and ought not to do. But if a man has no freedom to choose what he will do, if whatever he does is done under compulsion, then it does not make sense to tell him that he ought not to have done what he did and that he ought to do something different. All moral precepts would in such case be meaningless. Also if he acts always under compulsion, how can he be held morally responsible for his actions? How can he, for example, be punished for what he could not help doing?

It is to be observed that those learned professors of philosophy or psychology who deny the existence of free will do so only in their professional moments and in their studies and lecture rooms. For when it comes to doing anything practical, even of the most trivial kind, they invariably behave as if they and others were free. They inquire from you at dinner whether you will choose this dish or that dish. They will ask

❖ ❖

a child why he told a lie, and will punish him for not having chosen the way of truthfulness. All of which is inconsistent with a disbelief in free will. This should cause us to suspect that the problem is not a real one; and this, I believe, is the case. The dispute is merely verbal, and is due to nothing but a confusion about the meanings of words. It is what is now fashionably called a semantic problem.

How does a verbal dispute arise? Let us consider a case which, although it is absurd in the sense that no one would ever make the mistake which is involved in it, yet illustrates the principle which we shall have to use in the solution of the problem. Suppose that someone believed that the word "man" means a certain sort of five-legged animal; in short that "five-legged animal" is the correct *definition* of man. He might then look around the world, and rightly observing that there are no five-legged animals in it, he might proceed to deny the existence of men. This preposterous conclusion would have been reached because he was using an incorrect definition of "man." All you would have to do to show him his mistake would be to give him the correct definition; or at least to show him that his definition was wrong. Both the problem and its solution would, of course, be entirely verbal. The problem of free will, and its solution, I shall maintain, is verbal in exactly the same way. The problem has been created by the fact that learned men, especially philosophers, have assumed an incorrect definition of free will, and then finding that there is nothing in the world which answers to their definition, have denied its existence. As far as logic is concerned, their conclusion is just as absurd as that of the man who denies the existence of men. The only difference is that the mistake in the latter case is obvious and crude, while the mistake which the deniers of free will have made is rather subtle and difficult to detect.

Throughout the modern period, until quite recently, it was assumed, both by the philosophers who denied free will and by those who defended it, that *determinism is inconsistent with free will*. If a man's actions were wholly determined by chains of causes stretching back into the remote past, so that they could be predicted beforehand by a mind which knew all the causes, it was assumed that they could not in that case be free. This implies that a certain definition of actions done from free will was assumed, namely that they are actions *not* wholly determined by causes or predictable beforehand. Let us shorten this by saying that free will was defined as meaning indeterminism. This is the incorrect definition which has led to the denial of free will. As soon as we see what the true definition is we shall find that the question whether the world is deterministic, as Newtonian science implied, or in a measure indeterministic, as current physics teaches, is wholly irrelevant to the problem.

Of course there is a sense in which one can define a word arbitrarily in any way one pleases. But a definition may nevertheless be called correct or incorrect. It is correct if it accords with a *common usage* of the word defined. It is incorrect if it does not. And if you give an incorrect definition, absurd and untrue results are likely to follow. For instance, there is nothing to prevent you from arbitrarily defining a man as a five-legged animal, but this is incorrect in the sense that it does not accord with the ordinary meaning of the word. Also it has the absurd result of leading to a denial of the existence of men. This shows that *common usage is the criterion for deciding whether a definition is correct or not*. And this is the principle which I shall apply to free will. I shall show that indeterminism is not what is meant by the phrase "free will" *as it is commonly used*. And I shall attempt to discover the correct definition by inquiring how the phrase is used in ordinary conversation.

Here are a few samples of how the phrase might be used in ordinary conversation. It will be noticed that they include cases in which the question whether a man acted with free will is asked in order to determine whether he was morally and legally responsible for his acts.

Jones. I once went without food for a week.

Smith. Did you do that of your own free will?

Jones. No. I did it because I was lost in a desert and could find no food.

But suppose that the man who had fasted was Mahatma Gandhi. The conversation might then have gone:

Gandhi. I once fasted for a week.

Smith. Did you do that of your own free will?

Gandhi. Yes. I did it because I wanted to compel the British Government to give India its independence.

Take another case. Suppose that I had stolen some bread, but that I was as truthful as George Washington. Then, if I were charged with the crime in court, some exchange of the following sort might take place:

Judge. Did you steal the bread of your own free will?

Stace. Yes. I stole it because I was hungry.

Or in different circumstances the conversation might run:

Judge. Did you steal of your own free will?

Stace. No. I stole because my employer threatened to beat me if I did not.

At a recent murder trial in Trenton some of the accused had signed confessions, but afterwards asserted that they had done so under police duress. The following exchange might have occurred:

Judge. Did you sign this confession of your own free will?

Prisoner. No. I signed it because the police beat me up.

Now suppose that a philosopher had been a member of the jury. We could imagine this conversation taking place in the jury room.

Foreman of the Jury. The prisoner says he signed the confession because he was beaten, and not of his own free will.

Philosopher. This is quite irrelevant to the case. There is no such thing as free will.

Foreman. Do you mean to say that it makes no difference whether he signed because his conscience made him want to tell the truth or because he was beaten?

Philosopher. None at all. Whether he was caused to sign by a beating or by some desire of his own—the desire to tell the truth, for example— in either case his signing was causally determined, and therefore in neither case did he act of his own free will. Since there is no such thing as free will, the question whether he signed of his own free will ought not to be discussed by us.

The foreman and the rest of the jury would rightly conclude that the philosopher must be making some mistake. What sort of a mistake could it be? There is only one possible answer. The philosopher must be using the phrase "free will" in some peculiar way of his own which is not the way in which men usually use it when they wish to determine a question of moral responsibility. That is, he must be using an incorrect definition of it as implying action not determined by causes.

Suppose a man left his office at noon, and were questioned about it. Then we might hear this:

Jones. Did you go out of your own free will?

Smith. Yes. I went out to get my lunch.

But we might hear:

Jones. Did you leave your office of your own free will?

Smith. No. I was forcibly removed by the police.

We have now collected a number of cases of actions which, in the ordinary usage of the English language, would be called cases in which people have acted of their own free will. We should also say in all these cases that they *chose* to act as they did. We should also say that they could have acted otherwise, if they had chosen. For instance, Mahatma

❖ ❖

Gandhi was not compelled to fast; he chose to do so. He could have eaten if he had wanted to. When Smith went out to get his lunch, he chose to do so. He could have stayed and done some more work, if he had wanted to. We have also collected a number of cases of the opposite kind. They are cases in which men were not able to exercise their free will. They had no choice. They were compelled to do as they did. The man in the desert did not fast of his own free will. He had no choice in the matter. He was compelled to fast because there was nothing for him to eat. And so with the other cases. It ought to be quite easy, by an inspection of these cases, to tell what we ordinarily mean when we say that a man did or did not exercise free will. We ought therefore to be able to extract from them the proper definition of the term. Let us put the cases in a table:

Free Acts	Unfree Acts
Gandhi fasting because he wanted to free India.	The man fasting in the desert because there was no food.
Stealing bread because one is hungry.	Stealing because one's employer threatened to beat one.
Signing a confession because one wanted to tell the truth.	Signing because the police beat one.
Leaving the office because one wanted one's lunch.	Leaving because forcibly removed.

It is obvious that to find the correct definition of free acts we must discover what characteristic is common to all the acts in the left-hand column, and is, at the same time, absent from all the acts in the right-hand column. This characteristic which all free acts have, and which no unfree acts have, will be the defining characteristic of free will.

Is being uncaused, or not being determined by causes, the characteristic of which we are in search?

It cannot be, because although it is true that all the acts in the right-hand column have causes, such as the beating by the police or the absence of food in the desert, so also do the acts in the left-hand column. Mr. Gandhi's fasting was caused by his desire to free India, the man leaving his office by his hunger, and so on. Moreover there is no reason to doubt that these causes of the free acts were in turn caused by prior conditions, and that these were again the results of causes, and so on back indefinitely into the past. Any physiologist can tell us the causes of hunger. What caused Mr. Gandhi's tremendously powerful desire to free India is no doubt more difficult to discover. But it must have had causes. Some of them may have lain in peculiarities of his glands or brain, others in his past experiences, others in his heredity, others in his education. Defenders of free will have usually tended to deny such facts. But to do so is plainly a case of special pleading, which is unsupported by any scrap of evidence. The only reasonable view is that all human actions, both those which are freely done and those which are not, are either wholly determined by causes, or at least as much determined as other events in nature. It may be true, as the physicists tell us, that nature is not as deterministic as was once thought. But whatever degree of determinism prevails in the world, human actions appear to be as much determined as anything else. And if this is so, it cannot be the case that what distinguishes actions freely chosen from those which are not free is that the latter are determined by causes while the former are not. Therefore, being uncaused or being undetermined by causes, must be an incorrect definition of free will.

What, then, is the difference between acts which are freely done and those which are not? What is the characteristic which is present to all the acts in the left-hand column and absent from all those in the right-hand column? Is it not obvious that, although both sets of actions have causes, the causes of those in the left-hand column are

of a different kind from the causes of those in the right-hand column? The free acts are all caused by desires, or motives, or by some sort of internal psychological states of the agent's mind. The unfree acts, on the other hand, are all caused by physical forces or physical conditions, outside the agent. Police arrest means physical force exerted from the outside; the absence of food in the desert is a physical condition of the outside world. We may therefore frame the following rough definitions. *Acts freely done are those whose immediate causes are psychological states in the agent.*

Acts not freely done are those whose immediate causes are states of affairs external to the agent.

It is plain that if we define free will in this way, then free will certainly exists, and the philosopher's denial of its existence is seen to be what it is—nonsense. For it is obvious that all those actions of men which we should ordinarily attribute to the exercise of their free will, or of which we should say that they freely chose to do them, are in fact actions which have been caused by their own desires, wishes, thoughts, emotions, impulses, or other psychological states.

❄ 6.8 The Trolley Problem ❄

Selections
Judith Jarvis Thomson

✳✳

© Scott Richardson/Shutterstock.com

Judith Thomson (1929—Present) is an American philosopher who writes on topics in ethics and metaphysics, including heated topics like abortion and euthanasia. She is on the philosophy faculty at the Massachusets Institute of Technology.

In this selection, Thomson considers a variety of scenarios in which people have to make very difficult moral judgements, which seem to pit the prohibition on letting someone die by failing to act against the prohibition on actively killing. The most famous, which she adapts from Philippa Foot, involves the decision to kill one to save five by switching the direction of a trolley.

Here are some questions to think about when you read:

* How do you think Kant would respond to the trolley problem?

* How do you think Mill would respond to the trolley problem?

* How do you think Aristotle would respond to the trolley problem?

* How would *you* respond to the trolley problem?

Killing and Letting Die: The Trolley Problem

Thomson presents an example originally proposed by Philippa Foot:

> Edward is the driver of a trolley, whose brakes have just failed. On the track ahead of him are five people; the banks are so steep that they will not be able to get off the track in time. The track has a spur leading off to the right, and Edward can turn the trolley onto it. Unfortunately there is one person on the right-hand track. Edward can turn the trolley, killing the one; or he can refrain from turning the trolley, killing the five . . .

Does the wrong of killing the one outweigh the wrong which would result from doing letting the five die? Thomson concludes that:

> The thesis that killing is worse than letting die can not be used in any simple, mechanical way in order to yield conclusions about abortion, euthanasia, and the distribution of scarce medical resources. The cases have to be looked at individually. If nothing else comes out of the preceding discussion, it may anyway serve as a reminder of this: that there are circumstances in which, even if it is true that killing is worse than letting die, one may choose to kill instead of letting die.

You can access the full text through the ASU Library!

http://www.jstor.org.ezproxy1.lib.asu.edu/stable/pdf/27902416.pdf

ASU Login required.

Judith Jarvis Thomson. "Killing and Letting Die: The Trolley Problem." The Monist, Vol. 59, No. 2, Philosophical Problems of Death (APRIL, 1976), pp. 204–217

❉ 6.9 Unit 6 Study Guide ❉

* *

Readings by Ethical Theorists (Kant, Mill, Aristotle)

Kant was a (deontologist/consequentialist/virtue ethicist)?

Aristotle was a (deontologist/consequentialist/virtue ethicist)?

Mill was a (deontologist/consequentialist/virtue ethicist)?

Kant

How did Kant believe we could have knowledge of moral truths?

According to Kant, what can be called "good" without qualification?

What does Kant mean by the "Kingdom of Ends?"

What is the first formulation of the categorical imperative?

What is the second formulation of the categorical imperative?

According to Kant:

> Why shouldn't a person borrow money with no intention to repay the loan?

> Why do I have a duty to tell the truth when testifying in court?

> How should I treat other people I interact with?

> Why do I have a duty to be charitable?

> What duties do I have to myself?

Aristotle

According to Aristotle, a virtue lies in the _____ between ____ _____

According to Aristotle, virtue is acquired by _____ and _____

According to Aristotle, what matters in ethics?

According to Aristotle, what's the supreme good in life?

According to Aristotle, who could be virtuous, and who couldn't?

What is a virtue ethicist concerned with evaluating?

Mill

According to Mill, can a Utilitarian love beauty?

According to Mill, what is the worthiness of self-sacrifice determined by?

According to Mill, what is happiness?

According to Mill, what matters in ethics?

What is a "hedonist" in ethics? In what sense is Mill a "hedonist"?

Does Mill think Utilitarianism is a doctrine worthy of swine? Why or why not?

Mill argues that there are differences in the _____ of pleasure: some pleasures, like poetry, are _____ than others, like eating tasty food.

How would Mill and Kant view the death penalty differently?

How would Mill and Kant disagree over whether it is possible to perform the right action from selfish motives?

How, on Mill's view, could a senseless, random act of murder turn out to be the morally right action?

Meta-Ethics

What does a moral realist believe about morality?

What does a moral anti-realist believe about morality?

Why does central argument for moral anti-realism seem self-contradictory?

What does a moral relativist believe about moral facts?

What is conventionalism (as a form of relativism)?

What is subjectivism (as a form of relativism)?

What does a moral objectivist believe about moral facts?

What does a moral situationalist believe about morality?

What does a moral absolutist believe about morality?

How is objectivism different from absolutism?

How is conventionalism different from subjectivism?

What's the relationship, if any, between:

   Moral relativism and moral realism?

   Moral objectivism and moral situationalism?

   Being a moral realist and being a moral person?

   Moral objectivism and moral absolutism?

Major Ethical Theories

What does a consequentialist believe makes it right or wrong for me to do some action?

What does a deontologist believe about morality and consequences?

For the virtue ethicist, what are the proper subjects of moral evaluation?

A consequentialist holds that an action is right if and only if _____, and an action is wrong if and only if _____.

How did Rawls respond to Utiliarianism?

Applying Ethical Theories to Common Debates

For any given major controversial topic in ethics X, be able to say:

What is an example of a consequentialist reason for the morality of X?

What is an example of a consequentialist reason against the morality of X?

What is an example of a deontological reason against the morality of X?

What is an example of a deontological reason for the morality of X?

Free Will

Fill in the "..." with a definition:

On a <u>compatibilist</u> view of free will like Stace's, an agent's action A at time t is free if and only if . . .

On the view of free will held by <u>agent-causal Libertarians</u>, including Taylor, an agent's action A at time t is free if and only if . . .

On the view of free will held by <u>non-agent-causal Libertarians</u>, an agent's action A at time t is free if and only if . . .

According to the lecture, on the <u>logical-entailment determinism</u> held by d'Holbach, a determinist is committed to the view that . . .

According to the lecture, on <u>causal-exclusive determinism</u> a determinist is committed to the view that . . .

According to the lecture, on <u>emergentist</u> views a determinist is committed to the view that . . .

d'Holbach

If we accept that reality is a system of material particles operating according to fixed laws of motion, then what will we conclude?

Is the experience of having a choice proof of free will?

Taylor

If determinism is true, then there are always _____ _____ sufficient for everything I do.

On the theory of agency, we are sometimes, though not always, _____ _____

Compatibilists/Stace

An act is free when its immediate causes are _____ _____ of the _____, as opposed to _____.

Does the ordinary way people use words every day matter to philosophy?

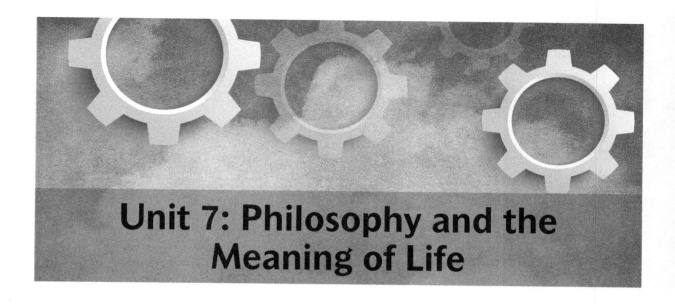

Unit 7: Philosophy and the Meaning of Life

✳ ✳

"Tell them I've had a wonderful life."
Ludwig Wittgenstein

So, what is the meaning of life?

This is probably one of the first questions that your friends and relatives will ask you when you let them know that you've finished a philosophy class. They're joking, of course. But, seriously, how would you answer it?

A. Introduction

Part I: Definitions

    B. Defining Meaning as Representation

    C. Defining Meaning as Narrative

    D. Defining Meaning as Happiness

    E. Defining Meaning as Moral Praiseworthiness

    F. Defining Meaning as Purpose

    G. Defining Life as the Self

Part II: Meditations

    H. Methodology

    I. Three Answers Which I Find Unsatisfying

    J. The Phenomenology of Meaninglessness

Part III: Purposes of the Self

    K. The Accidental Self
    L. The Essential Self
    M. The Agential Self
    N. The Alterior Self

A. Introduction

The first thing that comes to many people's mind when they first hear about philosophy isn't usually logic, or the theory of knowledge, or the nature of consciousness. Typically, they think about the prime example of an *extremely interesting* and *extremely difficult* question: what is the meaning of life?

It's an extremely interesting question, because, as Abraham Maslow held, once one has satisfied all of the more basic needs, like food, shelter, security, friendship, and a sense of self-respect, it seems like a natural next question to begin asking is "now what?" or "what was the point of all of that?" The only goal remaining is living a meaningful life.

However, it's also an extremely difficult question, because even though one thing many people seem to agree upon is that they all want a meaningful life, they don't seem to all share a commonly agreed upon idea of what a meaningful life is. Answering the question "what is the meaning of life?" is perhaps even more difficult than answering "what makes something morally right or wrong?" because the concept of a "meaning of life" is much less clear.

How should I go about answering a question like "what is the meaning of life?"

If you've noticed the pattern from other units by this point, you can probably predict what's next: I have to start by defining my terms.

Part I: Definitions

B. Defining "Meaning" as Representation

So, what does "meaning of life" even mean? What does the word "meaning" mean in this context?

One proposal might be that the word "meaning" in "meaning of life" means the exact same thing as "meaning" means when we talk about the meaning of a word or the meaning of a sentence. The meaning of a word or sentence is its *sense*, the way in which it represents something as being (1.3). So, perhaps the meaning of life is what that life represents.

The meaning of a word is external to what we associate with that word when we think about it. Even if I think of the word "dog" as being about a plant rather than an animal, the word "dog" represents an animal, not a plant. So, even if I conceive of my life as meaning one thing or another, if the "meaning" of life is like the "meaning" of a word, then it would follow that what my life represents is independent of how I conceive of my life.

Someone like Plato (1.5) could hold this view. Plato held that things in this world represented a higher and ideal realm of forms. So, perhaps my life represents some Ideal Form of Life. The meaning of my life would then be the way in which it represents this Ideal Life, and my life can go right or go wrong depending on how correctly or incorrectly it reflects this ideal life.

This could be true. However, it isn't obvious to me that my life is a representation. It isn't obvious to me how precisely my life could represent something else, or how it could be that my life represents another life, or what sort of life the Ideal Life is. It is also not obvious to me that the meaning of my life is independent of how I conceive of my life. So, perhaps I should not assume that the "meaning" of a life is the same sort of "meaning" as the meaning of a word.

C. Meaning as Narrative

Another proposal might be that when people talk of the "meaning" of a life, what they really mean is analogous to when we talk of the "meaning" or "role" of one event in the context of a larger event, such as in a novel or a movie. For example, people might say that the meaning of the assassination attempt on Vito Corleone in the movie *The Godfather* is that it brings his son Michael Corleone out of his "innocence" as a loving college-educated husband proud of his military service, and into his inherited role as murderous Mafia boss, motivated by a desire to defend his father. Or, in the book *To Kill a Mockingbird*, the "meaning" of the death of the innocent man Tom Robinson is that it forces the young girl Scout Finch to "come of age", by exposing her to the evil of racism in her home town. We can speak of historical events in this way also: Pearl Harbor "meant" the entry of the United States into the Second World War; the discovery of penicillin "meant" that infections were far less often fatal.

This might lead me to think of the meaning of events in my life as the role they play in my life as a whole, and the meaning of my life as a whole as the role it plays in some larger mega-story outside of my life. This analogy between a life story and a fictional story can be found in Hume's account of personal identity (4.4). The meaning of someone's life would then be the story they tell about their life. One person might tell a story about a heroic rise from great adversity and pain to amazing success, and another a story about a tragic fall from tremendous privilege and talent to dull mediocrity and failure. When we are telling the story of Abraham Lincoln's life, for instance, we might talk about his growing up in a log cabin on the frontier, his self-educated youth, his many attempts to win political office ending in defeat after defeat, and yet ultimately his election to the presidency and the role his life played in the beginning of the civil war and the end of slavery in the United States. So too, I might think of the meaning of my life as the role of my story in the whole of history.

The novelist Dostoevsky (5.8) often created characters who conceived of themselves as characters in a novel: not the novel he was writing, but some novel that the character had read. Someone who read romances would conceive of his life as the pursuit of unrequited love; someone reading tragedies would conceive of his life as a tragic failure; someone reading revolutionary political literature would conceive of herself as a revolutionary, and so on. Piecing together the story of one's life often involves extensive borrowing from the stories told by others. Yet, for Dostoevsky there seemed to be something deeply inauthentic about living a life of which someone else was the author. Real life was too jumbled and contradictory to make a good story.

After all, "Reality television" only became possible with the invention of digital video editing in the 1990s, when it became practical to edit together short pieces of video to construct a (highly artificial) narrative, and to edit out anything which didn't fit the narrative. The same can be said for journalism: a critical viewer of news coverage always remembers that while the particular events depicted probably happened, the large "event" created by piecing them together probably did not happen at all as it is depicted. So too, the way in which I retell the story of my own past changes to suit my present purposes. The life story one depicts in a job interview will often be very different from the life story one depicts on a first date.

It could be true that the meaning of a life has to do with the way it is narrated or to its role within a larger narrative. It could be that the desire for a meaningful life is the desire to be able to tell a good story before one dies. However, it is not obvious to me that this is the case: This sort of "meaning" seems to be too artificial and arbitrarily constructed to be the thing which I desire to have in desiring a meaningful life. So, I should not assume it to be a definitional truth from the beginning of my investigation.

D. Defining Meaning as Happiness

A third proposal I should consider is that a meaningful life is a "good life", in the sense that it is a life which is *good for* someone; a life which is worth living. For Aristotle (6.4), the good life was identified with a happy life: meaningfulness in life is ultimately happiness. To be clear, "happiness" here doesn't mean a few moments of intense feeling. Rather, the happy life is, as John Stuart Mill (6.3) defines it:

> . . . not a life of rapture; but moments of such, in an existence made up of few and transitory pains, many and various pleasures, with a decided predominance of the active over the passive, and having as the foundation of the whole, not to expect more from life than it is capable of bestowing.

However, while it may be true that having a feeling of happiness or satisfaction about my life is a necessary condition of my having a meaningful life, it is doubtful that my having a happy life is a sufficient condition of my having a meaningful life. Robert Nozick (1938–2002), in his book *Anarchy, State, and Utopia* (1974) proposed the following thought-experiment, which, if one agrees with Nozick, seems to suggest that someone could have a happy life without having a meaningful life:

> Suppose there was an experience machine that would give you any experience you desired. Super-duper neuropsychologists could stimulate your brain so that you would think and feel you were writing a great novel, or making a friend, or reading an interesting book. All the time you would be floating in a tank, with electrodes attached to your brain. Should you plug into this machine for life, preprogramming your life-experiences?
>
> If you are worried about missing out on desirable experiences, we can suppose that business enterprises have researched thoroughly the lives of many others. You can pick and choose from their large library or smorgasbord of such experiences . . . of course, while in the tank you won't know that you're there; you'll think it's all actually happening.

Whatever you want to experience in life, you can experience it within the tank. During your life in the tank, you might experience the greatest sense of accomplishment, experience making the greatest and most popular works of art or music, experience being loved and having many friends and deep relationships, or experience power, prestige, and prominence. Would you plug in?

Nozick concludes that he wouldn't plug in to the machine. While there might be some lives which are so bad that plugging in would be a merciful escape from reality, Nozick would prefer a mediocre but real life on the outside over an extremely happy but illusory inside the machine. Like Nozick, it seems to me that happiness is not enough to feel like one is living a meaningful life. I don't want to just feel like I have friends, I want to actually have friends. I don't just want to feel like I accomplished something, I want to actually do it.

Even if you disagree with Nozick and you think you would plug into the machine, the fact that a wide variety of people share Nozick's judgment mightbe enough to raise doubt for you that happiness is simply the *definition* of "meaningful". So, I don't think I should start out by defining a meaningful life as just a happy life, even if I regard a sense of happiness or satisfaction with my life as closely related to meaningfulness.

E. Defining Meaning as Moral Praiseworthiness

A fourth proposal might be that a meaningful life is not a life which is *good for someone*, but rather a life which we would praise because of its moral value: the sort of life we would congratulate someone on and say of their life, "good for you!" or "that was good of you!" We wouldn't necessarily praise someone simply for living a *happy* life in which they were content and pleased with themselves. "Way to go, you're sure enjoying yourself!" Far from it: we often praise people for doing things which cost them and are unpleasant. We issue awards and medals to those who risk their lives or make large sacrifices for the rest of society.

However, I can see some reasons to think that being morally valuable is neither a necessary condition nor a sufficient condition for being meaningful.

First of all, it seems like not everything which I find meaningful in a life needs to have moral value. Atomic Fission was discovered by Lise Meitner and her colleagues Fritz Strassman and Otto Hahn. Imagine for a moment that I had discovered atomic fission. Wouldn't I think that this contributed to the meaningfulness of my life? It would be quite an accomplishment! However, Meitner did not regard the discovery of Atomic Fission morally valuable; instead, she was distressed by the morally bad consequences of Atomic Fission since it resulted in the creation of atomic weapons.[1] Over 100,000 Japanese civilians, including men and women, the aged and the young, were killed by the two atomic bombs over Hiroshima and Nagasaki, which Meitner regarded as a serious moral evil. The world's terror of nuclear war has never ended since then. Yet, while this might cause someone to question the moral value of the discovery of atomic fission, should it detract from the meaningfulness of the discovery of atomic fission?

Scientific discoveries taken in themselves, when considered independently of their consequences, might be morally neutral. However, this does not mean that they must be neutral when it comes to their meaningfulness as part of someone's life.

On the other side, it seems like not everything which is equally morally valuable is equally meaningful. Suppose that Ralph is a person who is intellectually and physically capable of accomplishing many things, but instead he spends his entire life doing no work, living off of relatives and friends, while indulging his sole passion of watching old episodes of 1980s teen situation comedies. On the other hand, his neighbor Alf improves the lives of hundreds of thousands of homeless children throughout the country through his tireless operation of an innovative charitable organization, while at the same time managing to always be available for his close friends and family. Many people would say that Alf had a more meaningful life than Ralph did. However, it is not so obvious to me that Alf's life has more moral value than Ralph's life, since many people believe that all lives are equally morally valuable; that is, they think that taking Ralph's life would be morally wrong to the same degree, and for the same reasons, that taking Alf's life would be wrong.

Again, it might be true that there is a very close connection between living a meaningful life and living a moral life, but even if that is so, I can't say it is simply true by the definition of "meaningful".

F. Defining Meaning as Purpose

So, I would conclude that the best definition of what we mean by the "meaning" of life is what Aristotle (3.5) called the *final cause* of life, or its *telos*—the ultimate end or *purpose* which the life is for. When we talk of the "meaning" of life, we mean the purpose of one's life. The things which seem to make life more

---

[1] See "This Month in Physics History: Discovery of Nuclear Fission", *American Physical Society News*, Vol 16, No 11 (Dec. 2007).

meaningful are those which make it more purposeful, which relate it to some end goal: Alf's life seems more meaningful because it is directed at a purpose; Ralph's life seems less meaningful because it is fulfills no further purpose at all. The opposite of a meaningful life is a *meaningless* life: a pointless, purposeless life.

Of course, one thing can have many different, even contrary, purposes, depending upon *who* purposes its purposes. Consider a light bulb which burns out. The purpose of the light bulb for the person who flips the switch is to turn on and give light: the light bulb, in burning out, is malfunctioning—it has failed to fulfill its function. However, suppose the light bulb was designed by an unscrupulous factory which wanted to ensure that light bulbs burnt out quickly so that there would always be a market for replacements. The light bulb is well-functioning: it has fulfilled the function for which it was designed. Suppose then that the burnt out light bulb is used in a work of contemporary art. The light bulb has now found a new purpose.

So, some things acquire their purposes from a person willing to have that purpose. However, this does not mean that the purpose of everything *just is* whatever a person wills it to be. It might be true that some purposes exist in part because we make or create those purposes, but that wouldn't automatically mean that all purposes are *whatever* we make them to be. I think someone can be *wrong* about what the purpose of something is. Someone who tries to use a burnt out light bulb as a cigarette lighter, or as a hearing aid, or as a breakfast cereal, has made a mistake.

So, while I think it is true that some of the meaningful aspects of my life have that meaning because I created that meaning, I don't think that this means that all of the meaningful aspects of my life are meaningful just because I believe them to be meaningful. I think someone could simply be objectively wrong about whether some activity was meaningful.

Suppose that Aldo spends his entire life trying to pass legislation to prevent mixed-race couples from having children. This may seem to Aldo, because of his racist beliefs, to be a meaningful cause. He believes that pursuing it gives meaning to his life. However, it seems like Aldo might have a concerned friend who, while knowing his beliefs, still sincerely says to him, "Aldo! Why are you wasting your life on this meaningless, stupid cause? Get a life!" I'd tend to agree with Aldo's friend. So, that someone has a belief about the purpose of someone's life does not tell us all there is to know about the purpose of that person's life.

This principle matters when I consider what relationship there might be between the purpose of life and God. Some philosophers have defended the view that the purpose of human life is assigned by God's will, while other philosophers have argued that no God assigns purposes to life, or that even if God assigns purposes to life, this is irrelevant to the purpose of life. While I will remain neutral on this issue for the moment, it does seem to me that saying that the meaning of life is what God wills it to be doesn't really help me figure out the meaning of life, since it doesn't tell me *what* God wills it to be. I can't claim to know that the purpose of life is X simply because somebody else tells me that God has willed X as life's purpose. How would I know they were right? First, I would need some *a priori* reason to tell me *why* God would assign X as life's purpose and not something else. If I first knew *a priori* that X made life more purposeful, *then* I would have a reason to think that a perfect God would assign X as a purpose to life, and *then* I would have a reason to believe someone who told me that God wills X as life's purpose. Any *a priori* account of why God assigns life purpose X will in the end be an account of why X makes a good purpose for life. So, I should first try to figure out what a good purpose of life is, and *then* I will know what, if God exists, God would will the purpose of life to be.

G. Defining Life as the Self

I've said that I will be defining the "meaning" of life as the purpose or final cause of life. What, though, do we mean by "life" in "meaning of life"?

We might mean "life" in a strictly biological sense. However, it seems like the question, "What is the meaning of *the existence of life among organisms in general*" is not the same question as the one we are asking when we ask, "What is the meaning of *my* life?" Maybe the existence of life within the universe has a meaning: it's an interesting proposal to think about. Is there a meaning to the bacteria ever dividing, the plants spreading seeds and growing and dying every generation?

But even if I learned what the meaning of life in general was, or what this very long process of creatures on earth living and reproducing and dying was all for, I don't see that this would say anything about the meaning of *my* life. I am concerned that *I* should have meaning, not just that my being physiologically alive should have meaning. Instead, when we talk about the meaning of "life" it seems like we are really talking about the meaning of the *self*, the experiences a person has. So, I think I can best define the "meaning of life" as the "purpose of the self".

Part II: Meditations

H. Methodology

So, now that I have a slightly clearer definition to work with, how will I go about determining the purpose of the self?

This isn't an easy question to answer: There's no experiment or empirical test I could perform on the world around me to tell me what the purpose of *me* is. I could try to speculate on my own, or I could try to listen to what other people say, and I could see if any proposed purpose for my life caught my fancy, but even if I heard something that sounded interesting or persuasive, how would I know that it was the purpose of my life?

Perhaps, the best I can do is try to introspect on what I would *want* the purpose of my life to be—what sort of purposes would and would not be genuinely satisfying to me, if they were the purposes of my life.

I would expect a meaning of life to at least be something *satisfying*. If a proposed answer seems unsatisfying as a purpose for life, and I can give some reasons why, then I have a reason to think that it is not really the meaning of life. On the other hand, if some proposed answer does seem satisfying to me, then either I am mistaken in thinking it is meaningful, or else I'm right. If I'm mistaken, then either it is because there is no intrinsic meaning of life, or because there is some other meaning of life. If there is some other meaning of life, then I would expect this to be more satisfying on reflection than something which was not the meaning: So the process of reflecting on what is and is not satisfying as a meaning of life is still the best process to use. If life has no intrinsic purpose, then I suppose whatever I believe the purpose of life to be will be life's purpose for my purposes, which is purpose enough.

So, whether life has the meaning that seems most satisfying to me, or whether I'm mistaken and it has another meaning, or whether there is no intrinsic meaning of life at all, the same method will be useful: I can rule out that something is the meaning of life if it seems unsatisfying to me.

Of course, this process is only so good as my own introspection. The answers I find satisfying may not be satisfying to you, and the answers I find unsatisfying may be satisfying to you. Like everything else in philosophy, nothing in this essay is meant to be accepted on authority, but instead is something that others should consider and come to a conclusion about for themselves.

I. Three Answers Which I Find Unsatisfying

With that said, let me try to explain three answers which seem unsatisfying to me.

1. First, it seems unsatisfying to me to think that the purpose of myself has to do with other contingent events around me—events which could have happened differently. Earlier in this essay I seemed to assume that how things happen independently of me could make my life more meaningful or less meaningful. My life seems more meaningful if I have a positive impact on the world, and seems less meaningful if I have no impact. But now I'm beginning to doubt that.

For instance, suppose that someday humans use nuclear energy to travel to distant galaxies and colonize space. Someone might suggest that the meaning of the life of Lise Meitner and her colleagues was that they invented atomic fission, which led to nuclear energy, which lead to humans colonizing space centuries later. However, this seems unsatisfying to me because it simply moves the question forward: great, but what was the purpose of humans colonizing space?

Or, suppose someone were to say that the purpose of my life is to raise my child well. That sounds good enough, but what is the purpose of raising her well? Does that mean that the purpose of her life is to have children which she raises well? And what are all of these children for? You might say, "maintaining the human race", though I have a feeling the human race will reproduce itself well enough without my help. And even if we take that as an answer, it only pushes the question forward: and what is the purpose of the human race?

When I was a younger, I might have imagined that the purpose of my life was to write The Great Twenty-First Century Novel, a work of incomparable genius which influences people for generations to come. But what is the purpose of influencing people, and what are those influenced people supposed to go on and do, and what if they fail to do it? Or, what if they aren't much influenced at all, or influenced in the opposite of the way I intended? Or what if the novel is lost and forgotten forever?

Perhaps, I find these answers unsatisfying because it seems like so little of the future is under my present control. If the meaningfulness of my life depends upon how other people respond to something I did, or even how my legacy carries on in the years (or centuries) after I die, it seems like whether my life is meaningful or not it largely out of my hands.

Or perhaps my worry is that humans are easily substitutable: if Meitner and her colleagues didn't invent fission, someone would have. If I don't write The Great Twenty-First Century Novel, then someone else will, and it will probably be better anyway. If the purpose of the self is something so far outside of the reach of the self, then it seems like we can do without the self entirely.

2. This brings me to a second purpose for life which people propose, which seems unsatisfying to me. Perhaps, the meaning of my life is to be this small part of our grand cosmos: I'm a drop of water in a vast ocean. Although I have no special meaning, the ocean is meaningful, and I can derive my own purposefulness from it.

Part of what makes me uncomfortable is that this story of the absorption of the individual into the total whole seems like an account on which *my*self doesn't really have any purpose at all as such. Something has a purpose, but it's not me.

Another worry I have is that it seems to lend itself to a kind of totalitarian society. That is, if everyone thinks that their life's purpose is tied up with the advance of something bigger than them, the progress of their Nation or their Race or their Ideology, the result is a very unpleasant social structure to live under. The individuals within the society who are not in charge will actually matter very little, only insofar as they contribute to the whole, while what really matters is the society as a whole and the direction given by its leadership.

3. A third purpose for life that does not seem satisfying to me, although I have great respect for the people who do hold it to be life's purpose, is that the purpose of this life is a kind of cosmic test, that is, life is a test which one must pass in order to obtain a certain outcome in the afterlife. On this view, this life has meaning as a means of achieving a better or worse state in the life after this one on the basis of what one has done in this life, through a principle like *karma* or through a day of judgment. However, there are a couple of reasons that this doesn't seem very satisfying an answer to me.

First, it seems like leaving all of the significance to the afterlife deprives *this* life of most of its meaning and purpose. If one thinks the test is relatively easy to pass, then it sounds like the rest of this life is simply a matter of waiting around for one's own life to end, trying not to do anything too terrible in the mean time, and enjoying what one can. On the other hand, if one thinks the test is relatively difficult to pass, then it sounds like this life is going to be only a means to an end, a source of raw material which one must frantically convert into a higher "test score", without anything in this world having further value. Perhaps, one could think of a better way to think of this life as related to an afterlife than in terms of preparation for a final exam.

Secondly, it seems to me like this only pushes the question forward again: If the purpose of this life is found in the afterlife, then what is the purpose of the afterlife? Suppose the afterlife has some intrinsic purpose. Then, wouldn't that also be the purpose of this life? For instance, if the purpose of the afterlife is to experience a greater degree of enjoyment and pleasure and to avoid the worse degrees of torment, then why wouldn't the purpose of this life also be to experience pleasure and avoid pain? If the purpose of the afterlife is to be united with family and friends, then wouldn't that be the purpose of this life also? If the purpose of the afterlife is to worship God or the gods, then wouldn't that be the purpose of this life also?

Thirdly, if someone believes both in the afterlife and in an omnipotent God, it seems to raise similar questions to those we asked when we were discussing the problem of evil (5.1). If life is a test, then why is the test so very long? If God is capable of bringing it about that I pass the test, then why would God not simply do so for me? If the answer is that passing the test requires an act of my own free will, then why would God not simply register my free decision, for better or worse, and then move me on? If God is omniscient, then God isn't waiting bated breath with to know the outcome.

It seems to me that the purpose of life will not be satisfying if it is reduced to simply passing a test by choosing the right thing and obtaining "moral success". To be satisfying, I would think the purpose of life would have to involve the whole sum what one genuinely encounters in life. My experience of life does include making decisions, but it also includes many other sorts of experiences. It includes experiences of great closeness and intimacy, happiness, immense beauty, the pleasure of learning and creating new things . . . and it also includes many experiences of pain, loneliness, suffering, sadness, and encounters with serious moral failure not only in others, but in myself. The purpose of life must not leave this out, or so it seems to me.

J. The Phenomenology of Meaninglessness

I am beginning to worry that there can simply be no satisfying answer to the question, "what is the meaning of life?" Speaking honestly about the phenomenology (3.1) of being alive, what it is like to be alive is quite often an experience of meaninglessness. There are two experiences which leave me with a strong impression that my life is meaningless: my smallness in the scale of the universe, and the fact that I will die.

The Scale of the Universe

First, there is this feeling or impression of emptiness which I get when I consider the size of the universe and the vastness of space and time. I am only one of billions of people who are alive, not to mention the billions who have lived and died and the billions or trillions who are to come. Yet all of these people taken together live on a planet, earth, which is only a speck of dust relative to the size of the sun, which is over one million times larger. And this sun is only one of hundreds of billions of stars in our galaxy, which is only one of hundreds of billions of galaxies in the universe. If this is not enough to make me feel very small, the duration of my life is nothing compared to the billions of years which have passed before me and which will be after my life has ended. The moment in which I am writing these words is nothing in the big picture. So, why should I expect my life to have a purpose, and why should I think that any purpose my life has would be the least bit meaningful?

However, while it is true that both of these things give me a strong feeling that my life is meaningless, when I look at the arguments that might be constructed from them, I see that I should not consider my life meaningless after all. Looking at the first argument:

1. My life is not very big relative to the universe.
2. Things are important in proportion to their size.
3. The importance of my life is relative to the universe.
C. My life is not very important.

The argument is valid, and the first premise is clearly true. However, the two premises that lead us to the conclusion both seem questionable.

I can question premise two. Are things really important in proportion to their size? Consider a newborn baby. A diamond is very small relative to a mound of dirt. However, does that mean that the mound of dirt is more important than the diamond? Many office buildings in London are massive skyscrapers that are vastly larger than the Prime Minister's office on 10 Downing Street, which is 3,800 square feet. Which is the more important building in London? I don't see any correlation between the size of things and their actual importance. So, why think that the size of the universe makes me any less important, or it any more important?

I can also question premise three. Why think that it is relative to the history of the universe that my life must have meaning? Of course my life does not serve a purpose in causing planets to rotate or stars to explode into supernovae. Why think that the rotations of planets and the explosions of stars are the events within which my life must find meaning?

The moment in which my daughter was born was very short, and she was very small. However, that very short moment seemed to be infused with an intensity of meaning, and in that moment as she began to breathe for the first time and gradually turned from blue-grey to pink it seemed to me that she was the most important thing in the entire world. While it is possible to "zoom out" from my perspective for a moment, and imagine the cosmos as a whole, and feel a sense of emptiness, it is also possible for me to "zoom in" very close within my own perspective, and feel a sense of fullness which seems greater than the feeling of emptiness.

Death

However, there is a second consideration which leaves me with a sense of emptiness: the sense I get when I consider the fact that I will die. I have known other people who died, and I know that my own death will come eventually too, even if I try to avoid awareness of it. Death seems to thwart most attempts at a meaningful life. I have a guarantee that, for anything which I would expend my life toward, the thing will end. Suppose I were to dedicate my life to becoming someone, whether it is a wealthy person, or a powerful person, or a famous one, or a wise one, or a heroic one, or a morally praiseworthy one, or some other image I have of the person who I wish to be. Suppose I achieve it. First, achieving it means the remainder of my life will be meaningless now, because what is left to achieve? However, putting that aside, soon enough I will die and I will no longer be that person I tried to become. I might hope that my legacy will live on, and perhaps it will . . . for a little while. But eventually the people who knew me will die also, and the people they told about me will die also. To expect to be remembered much longer than that will be hard to achieve, and even then the memory of me will eventually be annihilated by time. This brings to mind the poem Ozymandias, by the poet Percy Shelley (1792–1822):

> I met a traveler from an antique land
> Who said: "Two vast and trunkless legs of stone
> Stand in the desert. Near them, on the sand,
> Half sunk, a shattered visage lies, whose frown,
> And wrinkled lip, and sneer of cold command,
> Tell that its sculptor well those passions read
> Which yet survive, stamped on these lifeless things,
> The hand that mocked them and the heart that fed:
> And on the pedestal these words appear:
> 'My name is Ozymandias, king of kings:
> Look on my works, ye Mighty, and despair!'
> Nothing beside remains. Round the decay
> Of that colossal wreck, boundless and bare
> The lone and level sands stretch far away.

All the work I do will be undone. Suppose I dedicate my life to fighting for social reform. Social reform is achieved for a time, but then this society dies and another takes its place which is even worse. Suppose I dedicate my life to academia. I contribute to our body of knowledge, but eventually the knowledge is lost and forgotten in the next dark age. Suppose I dedicate my life to helping my family succeed, whether my immediate or extended family. The generation or two after me do well, but eventually my descendants and relatives will be absorbed into the many other families of the rest of the world and my work will be forgotten.

Death is a problem even for simpler and more modest goals. Suppose that I work very hard, live frugally, and pay off my student loans and pay off the house in which I live. I owe nothing, and I have a reasonable amount in savings. Then, I die. When I die, I am no better off than the person who did not work very hard and spent money freely. Suppose that I work to be respected and thought highly of my co-workers, my neighbors, and the other people I know. Everyone likes me, and no one can say a bad thing about me! Then, I die, and I am no better off than the anti-social jerk who everyone gripes about and can't stand to be around. Suppose that I remodel my house in order to get everything just right, so that everything looks exactly as I would like it to be: shortly after I die, and my house is bulldozed over.

However, let me construct for a moment the argument which seems to be in the background:

1. If my life fulfills a purpose, that purpose will be one of the effects of my life.
2. At some point after my death, my effects will no longer be present.
3. What is no longer present no longer exists.
4. If something does not exist, it does not fulfill a purpose.
C. At some point after my death, my life fulfills no purpose.

Premise 1 is an application of the principle that, if something has a purpose and fulfills it, then the purpose it fulfills must be one of the effects of that thing. For example, when an airplane flight fulfills its purpose, its purpose is that the passengers arrive at their destination, which is an effect of the airplane flight. Premise 2 is what we have just established: that whether it is shortly after my death or a few generations later, there will be a point at which the effects of my actions will no longer be present. Premise 4 is supposed to be uncontroversial: non-existent things, like unicorns and goblins, can't cause anything to happen and can't fulfill a purpose.

However, I think that I can challenge Premise 3. Premise 3 is a statement of a view in the philosophy of time called *presentism*, that only what is in the present moment exists, and that what is in the past and in the future no longer exists. There are many philosophers who have given good arguments for presentism. But there are also many philosophers who have given good arguments for the opposing view, known as *eternalism*. For an eternalist, all moments in time are equally real and equally exist, both the present and the past and the future. And if eternalism is true, the fact that the effects of my life will not always be present is not a reason to say that they didn't have meaning at the time they were present, since that time they were present is just as real 1 billion years from now as it was when it occurred.

Why it's Good Some Things are Meaningless

Perhaps the phenomenology of meaninglessness serves a good purpose in directing me to live a more meaningful life, even if it is mistaken to conclude from the feeling of meaninglessness that in fact my life is meaningless.

Economists have observed that people tend to fall into the fallacy of "sunk costs". We are likely to continue to pursue a course which we have invested in, even when we can clearly see that an alternative would be better for us, out of fear of "losing" our past efforts. A person who has invested heavily in something will naturally be resistant to change, even good change. However, this is a mistake. Change is not a threat to the meaning of my life. If the past is every bit as real as the present, then change in the present does not eliminate the good which happened in the past. It is not necessary for my projects to survive or continue on indefinitely for them to have had weight and meaning.

Likewise, if the importance of something has little to do with how long it lasts or how big it is, then we are mistaken when we regard things as giving meaning to our lives simply because they seem like "big" things, things which will have effects for a little longer, or things which have lasted since the distant past.

If it is a mistake to regard my life as less meaningful simply because I am small compared to the solar system, then it is a mistake to regard small projects in life as less meaningful than big projects in life simply because of their size. If it is a mistake to regard my life as less meaningful simply because its effects will eventually be forgotten, then if it is a mistake to regard the action I take which is quickly forgotten as necessarily less meaningful than the one which everyone remembers for years to come. If it is a mistake to regard my life as unimportant relative to the history of the universe simply because it is shorter, then it is also a mistake to regard today as unimportant relative to the whole of my life simply because it is shorter.

So it is not that the awareness of death or the vastness of the universe should make me doubtful that my life or anything in it could be meaningful. Rather, an awareness of death and the vastness of the universe can be a useful tool to detach myself from things which are not so meaningful as their size and duration might first impress me to think, so that I do not feel compelled or obliged to give them so much weight. In turn, this makes room for me to attach myself to the things which I judge to be genuinely meaningful.

Part III: Purposes of the Self

K. The Accidental Self

So, what is genuinely meaningful?

Earlier I said that by the "meaning of life" I think people mean the "purpose of the self". I have looked at a negative account of some things which it does not seem to me could be purposes for the self, which I ruled out because they were unsatisfying. It have also considered some doubts about whether the self has a purpose at all, but also seen a way around these doubts. Now the task is try to give a positive account of what the purpose of the self is.

Of course, in order to talk about the self, we will have to talk about *personal identity*. I suspect, in light of many of the texts I included in Unit 4, that there is not one unified concept of the self, but several. It seems to me that we can divide these concepts of the self into four distinct categories:

1. Concepts of the Self as the Given, or the **accidental self**. On these, the self is defined in terms of some set of contingent properties, which it has. It is the self *as it has*.

2. Concepts of the Self as the Recipient, or the **essential self**. On these, the self is defined as whatever it essentially is—we know not what—which has or bears the properties of the accidental self. It is the self *as it is*.

3. Concepts of the Self as the Giver, or the **agential self**. On these, the self is defined as the agent behind the actions which are taken by the essential self. It is the self *as it does*.

4. Concepts of the Self as the Received, or the **alterior self**. On these, the self is defined by what some *other* perceives or believes about the agential self. It is the self *as it is known*.

I suspect that sort of self has a distinct purpose which corresponds to it. I will begin in this section by discussing the accidental self.

By "accidental", I mean that the self is defined in terms of properties it just so happens to have but could have failed to have. I've called this the self as it is "given", much like certain premises are given at the start of a proof: it is the self as it appears on the scene and discovers that it exists with no say of its own. I was born, with little or no say of my own, with a certain gender, skin color, physical appearance, and sexual orientation; with certain abilities and disabilities, strengths and weaknesses; part of a certain family, social group, nation and language; at a certain point in history, which may seem "too soon" or "too late"—all of these are part of my accidental self. But all of them are properties I could have failed to have, so none of these properties are part of the essential self. I happen to be 5′11″ and English, but I could have been 4′10″ and spoken Spanish. When I write down a list of properties about myself and include "Born in Tucson, 5′11″, speaks English", I am writing about the accidental self.

Even many of those things in life that I feel I exercise some choice over, appear to me as choices only because of a rich causal background which presented them to me. I chose my job because it was the only offer I had. I chose to buy a car because of advertising. These are also part of the accidental self.

The accidental self matters to me. While parts of my body might not be essential to me—as Locke proposed in Unit 4—they are still very much a part of my accidental self. I would be pretty distressed if I lost a finger, not because I think the finger is conscious, but because it is a part of my body, which is a part of me.

The accidental self might also be called the **social self**, because it is the self insofar as it matters for social purposes. This is the self which others hold *accountable* when I do something wrong, or praise when I do something right. This is the self which matters to others when they are *giving an account*—the person who they tell stories about, and who I tell different stories about. This is also the self which matters for the sake of *keeping accounts*, saying what property belongs to whom and tracking property over time.

Precisely which properties matter for the purposes of being the same social self might differ from context to context. I think that Derek Parfit is probably correct that for most contexts, what matters to the social self is psychological continuity: having the same psychological properties at a later time rather than a previous time. It is possible for two social selves to fuse into one, and possible for one social self to undergo fission into two. However, even when we are dealing with psychological properties, we might in some cases be more concerned with a person's reasoning, and in other cases more concerned with a person's emotions or feelings. In general, Daniels's teleportation cases do not change the social self. However, because the body is also part of the social self, in some cases having the same body will make a difference.

Earlier we considered whether a meaningful life had to do with living a morally good life. Insofar as the accidental self is concerned, the purpose of the self may simply be just that: taking whatever it has been given and whatever situation it has been thrown into, and fulfilling its natural moral duties. The argument is roughly as follows:

1. The accidental self is thrown into the world with a set of properties {P}.
2. If a property includes a purpose, then anything with that property has that purpose.
3. Some properties in {P} include purposes.
C. The accidental self has the purposes which the properties in {P} have.

I have been thrown into the world as a human being. If Aristotle is right, then human beings by nature have a certain function or purpose, which is the life of reason, the life of virtue. The property of being human includes the purpose of living reasonably just like the property of being a can-opener includes the purpose of opening cans; were I born a can-opener, my purpose in life would be to open cans, but I was born a human. So, the purpose of my life is to obtain the intellectual and moral virtues.

Furthermore, I have been thrown into the world as a reasoner. If Kant is right, then the basic principle all rational agents must follow is not to act on self-contradictory principles, and thus to treat others as ends in themselves. This purpose is included in what it is to be a reasoner. So, this is part of my purpose.

I have also been thrown into the world as a being with an aversion to pain and a desire for pleasure, and an ability to empathize and be aware of the minds of others which desire and avoid the same things.

The purpose of seeking to avoid causing pain and to try to maximize pleasure is included in the definition of what it is to be something with these sensations and abilities. So, part of the purpose of my life is to maximize utility.

There may be other duties which I have. I was thrown into a nation, so natural morality may require that I obey the commands of the legitimate authorities in my nation. I was thrown into a network of family and friends who help me, so morality may require that I reciprocate and help them. I was thrown in a system of accountability, so morality may require that I fulfill my responsibilities. I have a certain job and certain social roles, partly by my choice and partly not, and I am in certain social relationships as a friend, a husband, a child, and a father. Part of the definition of each of these roles I have is that these roles exist to fulfill certain purposes, or duties. I may not like all of these duties, and I may not have chosen all of them, but now they are attached me. For me to run away from them is for me to run away from myself. So, for the time being I willingly adopt them.

I might say this: The purpose of the accidental self is *to fully take up all that it is given*. It does not have one intrinsic purpose, but rather dozens and dozens of purposes related to the role it happens to fulfill.

L. The Essential Self

The word "role" for the social self is apt. The Greek word for person, πρόσωπον, originally referred to an actor's mask in a play. The actor put on the mask during the play to represent a character, and fully adopted and dedicated himself to being this character for the duration of the show. However, when the show ended, the mask came off. So, in pre-Socratic Greek thought, we find the notion of the social self as the *person* or "mask" which each of us wears, and which each of us is held responsible for even though the mask was simply handed to us at the start of the show. Yet we also find hidden behind this the notion of another self, the self behind the mask. This is the idea of the essential self.

I could have existed without my particular job and social role: These things are not necessary conditions to being my essential self. And no bundle of accidental properties will ever provide sufficient conditions for being my essential self either, since there will always be the possibility of duplication, as in the teleportation cases.

I've called this the self as "recipient" to get across the idea that which the given self has been given *to*. The essential self is not a bundle of properties, but whatever *bears* or *has* these properties. In this essential sense of "I", I am not my body, and I am also not my mind, because nothing possesses itself. Rather, I am the thing which possesses the body and the mind.

What can I say about the essential self? Almost nothing. My essential self is something which I can know very little about because there is very little to be known. It has very few properties essentially. Perhaps, I am necessarily a thing which thinks and perceives—but I never perceive the thing which perceives, and can't say much about the thing which thinks beyond what it is thinking about. Nothing can be used to distinguish it as myself and not some other self, since anything which could distinguish us would be contingent. The word *haecceity*, or "individual essence", has been used historically to try to say what property it is which makes the essential self distinct from other essential selves—but this is an open admission that there is nothing more which can be said.

I can now see the origins of Hume's skepticism that there even is such a thing as an essential self. For Hume there was a social, "fictional" self, but nothing behind it. But even if I accept that there must be something behind the mask, whatever it is, this self seems as close as one can get to nothing. Kant called it the "Transcendental Unity of the Apperception"—whatever it is that unifies my experiences into a whole and makes them *mine* instead of *yours*.

The social self finds its purpose in moral obligations: that is, the duties of the social role which a person occupies. But the essential self can genuinely wonder why it should be bound by moral norms, or why it should accept them and care about them. "What about self-interest?" someone might ask, since we all wish to obtain rewards and avoid punishment. The social self certainly has a kind of self-interest: that is, the interests of the social role which a person occupies. So, the social self can have prudential motives. However, the essential self has no self-interests, since there is nothing which can change about it. Nothing can make the essential self better off or worse off than it was before.

It is doubtful to me that the essential self has any purpose at all. I can think of two arguments. I will distinguish between a *contingent* purpose, or a purpose which a thing can fulfill or fail to fulfill, and a *necessary* purpose, or a purpose which a thing cannot fail to fulfill.

1. The essential self cannot change.
2. To have a contingent purpose, something must be capable of changing to fulfill that purpose.
C. The essential self does not have any contingent purpose.

1. The essential self is the set {S} of necessary and sufficient conditions of being one's self.
2. There is nothing in {S} which we can speak of without circularity.
3. A necessary purpose for the self will be in {S}.
C. There is no necessary purpose for the self which we can speak of without circularity.

So, if the essential self has any purpose, it is a purpose which it can't fail to fulfill and which we cannot say anything further about. For all practical purposes, the essential self has no purpose. It is meaningless. But, I recall also that the experience of being meaningless is not such a bad thing after all. Meaninglessness provides a kind of freedom, in fact. The essential self can look at the various purposes and duties and roles of the social self, and, taking a step back from them, it can say of them: those aren't really *my* purposes or duties or roles. They belong to the mask. There is nothing to speak of behind the mask, but the "nothing" behind the mask enjoys complete freedom, since it has no purposes at all.

Perhaps, I could put it this way: The purpose of the essential self is *to empty itself*.

M. The Agential Self

But because the essential self has no purposes assigned to it, and complete freedom with respect to what purposes it chooses, the essential self can act freely for its own purposes.

When it acts freely like this, it becomes the agential self, or the self as *agent*. (Recall the example of the bowling ball from Unit 6: the way in which a ball rolls is different from the way an agent rolls a ball). As an agent, I can act for purposes of my own choosing. In choosing a purpose, I make it my purpose. I become defined as an agent by what I do, by my choices.

When I say "I am defined by my choices", I am not thinking about choices like whether I want tea or coffee, or whether I want a Honda or a Toyota. Rather, I am thinking about situations in which there are two options, where I cannot have both, and where even after I think about the decision a very long time there is no way to weigh which option is preferable to me. For example, there have been times when I made a decision after a great deal of reflection and thought to do something—like my choice of college major—not because reasons outside of me weighed more on one side than another, but because internally I desired to be a certain sort of person and not another.

The process of choosing the purposes which I will act upon is a process of self-composition: I am creating a work of art, myself. The agential self is produced by its purposes, and so the purpose of the agential self is whatever purposes it chooses for itself. The meaning of my life is what I mean my life to be. The meaning of life is a creative act. But how is the agential self to go about choosing purposes for life?

One possibility is that the agential self chooses from the list of purposes that the social self has—or the exact opposite of those purposes. I decide to become exactly what life has tossed at me, or exactly what it has not tossed at me. The social self has many purposes on its list, including things which the people it interacts with find purposeful, things which it simply runs into along the way, and things which society has assigned it as a purpose. However, freely choosing whatever purpose was assigned to me does not seem like freedom at all. There is something about exercising my "freedom" by either doing exactly what others want me to do, or reacting in the opposite direction by doing exactly what they do not want me to do, which seems inauthentic. A certain amount of lying to myself is involved.

A second possibility is that the agential self chooses its purposes arbitrarily and randomly. Arbitrary actions are free, since being arbitrary and random can't be turned to serve some social purpose outside of myself. However, choosing randomly does not express anything distinct about myself. It doesn't contribute anything to the process of creating myself out of these choices.

So, I find myself in a bit of a dilemma. I create my purpose by what I freely choose. In a sense, my purpose is to create myself by freely choosing. However, I find that inevitably I either act for purposes which I didn't choose, or I act arbitrarily and purposelessly. If I act for purposes I didn't choose—either by accepting or reacting against the purposes of the social self—then my choice doesn't seem truly free or creative. However, if I act arbitrarily and randomly, then my "free" choice does nothing to create a self.

However, it seems to me like there may be one act which is not arbitrary but manages at the same time to be genuinely free: the act of giving myself over to another. Giving is the only creative act: it takes what is mine by nature and makes it not mine; or what is not mine by nature and makes it mine. By "giving", I do not mean here a social practice of giving money to philanthropic organizations. Giving of that sort is usually simply a part of one's social role. I mean instead something like giving my entire *self* to someone else or something else, whether giving myself to a person in friendship or giving myself to compose a work of music.

Whom or what I give to must be neither arbitrary, nor assigned, but rather chosen. When I choose to befriend someone, for instance, or choose to care especially for someone who will never be my friend, my reason for doing so is not social or moral obligation (who says, "I am your friend because I have to be?"), but it is also not arbitrary (who says, "I pulled your name out of a hat?"). My only reason for engaging in friendship is the person I befriend. And the same can be said for choosing someone to love, or choosing a work of art to create: one loves for the sake of the thing beloved, not for the sake of fulfilling one's given social role, and yet also not randomly. The argument goes like this:

1. Giving oneself to another is for another.

2. What is for another is not for a purpose of the social self.

3. What is for another is not arbitrary.

4. What is neither arbitrary nor for a purpose of the social self is free and creative.

C. Giving oneself to another is a free and creative act.

Thus, while the agential self has whatever purposes it freely chooses in the process of creating itself, the only purpose I can think of which is consistent with choosing freely and creatively is the choice to adopt *another* as one's purpose, and not one's self.

Morality for me as an agent will look very different from the morality I had as a social self. Agential morality tells me not to seek the virtues pertaining to the nature I was given, but to seek the virtues pertaining to the nature I choose to have. Agential morality tells me not to reciprocate what was given to me, but to give to those who I have no obligation to give to. Agential morality does not insist that I obey local authorities, but insists that I obey those who are not in authority and who can make no legitimate claim on me. It does not advise me to try to maximize the sorts of value that are given in the world, but instead advises me to create new types of value. It does not tell me to act on rules which all others can follow, but instead tells me to act on rules which it would be impossible for everyone to follow, which only distinctly *I* could follow. It is not so interested in whether I take responsibility for my own actions as it is whether I take responsibility for the actions of others. It is not concerned with preserving myself, but rather with the adoption of another self as though it were myself.

I questioned earlier whether a meaningful life was necessarily a happy life. I think the best answer now is something like this. It is probably best to try to believe that a meaningful life is not a happy life, because the pursuit of happiness is the surest way not to achieve happiness. Happiness represents that one has reached the goal; it is not the goal itself. However, when I reflect on those moments in life which seemed to me fullest with intense meaningfulness, those moments all involved giving to and receiving from another person, and in those moments I was very happy. And so, while I don't think that meaningfulness is happiness, I do think that the meaningful life is usually a happier life.

I'll call the agential self the "giver" self: the purpose of the agential self is *to give itself to something*.

N. The Alterior Self

In giving to another I am able to extend beyond the natural boundaries of myself, so that I almost become located somewhere else through the process of giving. However, suppose that I give myself to the creation of a beautiful work of art, which is then destroyed; or a piece of music which is never played; or a person who will never understand or appreciate what I'm doing for them? It seems like this is less meaningful than if the work of art is appreciated, the music is heard, and the person understands. It is more meaningful when what I give is also received.

I think of the alterior self as the self as it is *received*. The alterior self is myself as it is known by another. It is me as the other person perceives it. Recall that, when we were trying to give a definition of the self in Unit 4, we ran across a few cases in which we could find necessary and sufficient conditions for defining the self which were not circular:

I_{me} = You$_{you}$
I = *that* guy$_{you\ pointing\ at\ me}$
I = Jeff
I = the actual author of *Introduction to Philosophy: Deducing Answers*

What all of these cases have in common is that reference is fixed by something external to myself: by *you* when you refer to me, or by the proper name that others use to refer to me, or by the actuality of the world. In the first three cases, reference is fixed by how others refer to me. The alterior self is myself as it is referred to by others.

The purpose of the alterior self is simply to be known, to be received. When I first began our investigation, many of the intuitions I had about what sorts of things might make my life more meaningful were intuitions about what would make my life more *memorable* in the minds of other people. What I desired in desiring a meaningful life had something to do with having a legacy or being remembered.

Of course, simply "being remembered" is not very specific. Someone can be remembered negatively; I would rather be remembered in a positive light. Someone can be remembered for something which was passively done to them; I would rather be remembered for something I did actively. But for the alterior self, the meaning of life is to be remembered for the good, creative, and free things one did—for the giving of the agential self.

Becoming famous seems to be appealing at first because it means that I would be known and remembered by many people, possibly for a long time. However, I recall that the duration and size of something does not indicate its meaningfulness. And when I think about it more carefully, it does seem to me like being barely known by many people would not be nearly so satisfying as being known very well by a few people. One can see how loneliness would accompany fame—fame is both being known by many and yet being known by none at all. (Perhaps loneliness is what drives people to seek fame.) Being remembered indirectly, through what other people say about me, could never seem as satisfying as being remembered directly, by people who knew me personally.

So, the purpose of the agential self is to be known. The argument is fairly simple:

1. The purpose of a gift is to be received.
2. The self is a gift given to others.
C. The purpose of the self is to be received.

On Locke's theory of personal identity, I survive my past self because I remember the conscious states of my past self. The way in which other people remember me, from the outside rather than the inside, is not survival. And so, death still seems like a problem for the alterior self. The part of me which others know and remember will be very limited, and it will die when they die. If the past is as real as the present, then as an agent myself and my actions will forever exist in the past, even when I am no longer living. But isn't it a problem for myself as an other, if the *other* in whom I exist will die also?

There are two ways to look at this issue. The first is more cautious. Those who remember me and know me well will not live forever, and I am more afraid of them dying than I am of dying myself. However, even if the audience members forget the play, at the moment of the play, the audience members still exist and are aware of it. And so, even if what I do is forgotten, or those who remember it do not outlive me, what I did was still received. If eternalism is true, the moment at which it was received still exists.

The second is more speculative; I can see both reasons that someone would think it to be true and reasons that someone would not think it to be true (5.1). However, suppose it is true that there exists an omniscient being, God. Then, it follows that there is a way in which I will be remembered that is unlike the way in which anyone else will remember me.

An omniscient being knows all of the facts. According to Jackson's argument in the "Mary's Room" case, there are facts about subjective conscious states—facts about *what it is like* to be me right now. We cannot know these facts about one another. However, an omniscient being would know them, that is, the omniscient being would know firsthand what it is like to experience exactly what I am presently experiencing, and everything I have ever experienced. This means that everything I give is always received, even when it seems to go unnoticed, and everything I give is remembered, even when it seems to be forgotten. If there is an omniscient being, then even after I am dead, this being will remember my conscious states in the same way in which I remember my own past self's conscious states. So, at least on Locke's theory of personal identity, then my whole life would survive death in these memories; nothing is lost.

Furthermore, although it is an even more speculative thought, and perhaps even less clear, if it is true that I form the memories of the omniscient being by my free actions, and yet the cosmological argument is also correct that my existence depends upon the omniscient being, then in giving, being received, and in turn being given again, then someone could say that I become an active participant in my own being: I am no longer the accidental self tossed or thrown into the world. However, I am not sure how clear an idea this is.

I will conclude with one final thought. I noted that there seemed to be four distinct notions of the self, but as I've explored them it seems to me like they are more of a linked chain than four entirely distinct ideas. There is a natural flow from each to the next. So, if I were asked—maybe jokingly on a plane flight after introducing myself as someone who teaches philosophy, "what is the meaning of life?"—then my best answer at the moment would be something like this: *the purpose of myself is to fully take up all that it is given, to empty itself, to give itself to something, and to be received.*

What would your answer be? How would you go about investigating the question?

Appendix A
A.1 Writing a Philosophy Paper

* *

Purpose of An Argument Paper

An argument paper defends your position or thesis on a philosophical issue. A position or thesis is *your* view. An argument paper is not a report on what someone else says on an issue, but instead presents what you have to say about the issue. You aren't writing to inform your reader, but to persuade your reader.

However, it is unlike other persuasive essays you may have written, in the sense that you must appeal only to your readers' best reasoning, not to their emotions or their weakness for powerful rhetoric or beautiful prose. Fallacies are common in part because they are persuasive. You must treat those who disagree with you (your "opponents") charitably, putting their best arguments forward and acknowledging where their arguments are strong. Interpreting someone who disagrees with you in the worst way in order to make them look bad, ultimately backfires and makes you look bad. Exaggerating the evidence to make your own side look better makes you look desperate.

Arguing for a position means that you aren't writing as a neutral third party. You're making a claim at the beginning and trying to argue that you are right. This means that certain words you may have been taught don't belong in academic papers *do* belong in philosophy papers, like the word "I". There is no need to refer to yourself in the third person. You can present your views by saying "I hold that . . . " or "I deny that . . . ", or when you're less certain, "it seems to me that . . . " or "it's not clear to me why . . . ". Present your thesis at the beginning by saying "In this paper, I will argue that . . . "

We know that the paper advocates for your views, so there is no need to apologize for them by saying things like "this is just my opinion" when you write. That said, merely expressing your feelings about something is not an argument. Telling a story or a personal narrative might be engaging, but it isn't a philosophy paper. Do not appeal to anecdotes of personal experiences if few of your readers will share them in common with you. Instead, you have to find premises that your audience is likely to agree with and show how they lead to the view you hold. Think carefully about what a skeptical reader would think about your premises. Imagine what someone who objects to you would say to your argument.

An argument paper includes a discussion of things that other people have written on the topic, but it isn't just an exposition on what others said. Instead, it discusses and interacts with what others have written on the topic. Assume that your reader is interested in what *you think* of Hume's view of personal identity, not just exposition on Hume's view of personal identity.

An argument paper foresees and addresses objections that opponents might offer, but in a way which is charitable and respectful toward those opponent. You will disagree with those who hold a certain view in your paper, but you're not out to demonize them. Ultimately, an argument paper is about your view on the topic and the reasons and arguments you can give for it.

Formatting and Organization

Your paper should be written in clear, easy to understand prose, avoiding confusing or ungrammatical phrasing. Proofread by reading it out loud.

In English classes you may have been encouraged to use a variety of words (with the aid of a Thesaurus) rather than using the same wording over and over. However, in writing Philosophy it is better to use the same exact wording and phrasing when making an argument, so your reader doesn't think you intend to make a distinction between two words. This might make your writing sound "robotic", but being robotic is better than being unclear.

In another point contrary to what you may have been taught in English class, use **bold section headings** in your paper, like this:

Russell's View

This helps break your paper up into easy to manage "chunks".

The structure of your paper should include:

* A short introduction. The final sentence of this paragraph should be a one-sentence statement of your thesis, roughly: "I will argue in this paper that . . . because . . . " Do not include an extensive history of your topic or of humankind in your introduction.

* Following the introduction, a short section which gives context on the issue or an analysis of the situation the prompt, including making connections to readings in the class or outside of class.

* A short section in which you present your argument(s) explicitly as a numbered series of premises leading to a conclusion. You don't need to put this in prose form; number the premises as a list.

* For each premise in your argument, a section explaining what the premise means and why we should believe them. You may need to make sub-arguments for your premises, or you may argue that some of them are things even your opponent is likely to accept, so you don't need to argue for them.

* Then, for each premise in your argument, write out any objections a reasonable person would likely give to each of your premises, and include your reply to these objections.

* A conclusion that wraps up the main line of argument in your paper and what you think we should ultimately conclude. Avoid appealing to emotion in your conclusion and avoid hubris or pride—you have not just proven everyone else wrong, you've only given an argument that suggests they are wrong.

* A work cited in page or bibliography.

You'll need to both cite your sources in the text, using either footnotes or parenthesis like this (Watson 2015), or as well as create a works cited page listing all of the sources you have cited. Remember that a source is any place you got information that you relied on in writing your text, even if the words you use are entirely different than the place you got the information.

❋ A.2 Example Term Paper ❋

✳ ✳

Following is a paper written by a junior-level undergraduate philosophy student, used with permission. It is on a topic in philosophy we haven't covered in this course, so copying the content won't help you write your paper. However, it gives a good illustration of how to *structure* a paper.

Amending Russell on Definite Descriptions

1. Introduction

Definite Descriptions (noun phrases that start with *the*, like "the black cat") have inspired several different philosophical analyses, most notably those of Bertrand Russell and Peter Strawson. In this paper, I will argue that it is better to attempt to amend Russell's view than to adopt Strawson's view.

2. Context: Russell's View

Russell first delved into the question of definite descriptions with a desire to show something seemingly trivial: that non-existent things didn't exist. At the time, the general view was that words and phrases derived their meaning by referring to objects in the real world. But this caused problems: what about sentences of the form "X doesn't exist", such as "The current Shah of Persia doesn't exist"? Or, what about sentences that utilized nonexistent objects, such as "The current Shah of Persia is sloshed"? The sentences were clearly meaningful, but what exactly did "the current Shah of Persia" refer to, if not something in present reality? Was there a separate world full of nonexistent objects floating around and waiting for someone to refer to them? (lecture)

To solve this problem, Russell chose to deny the idea that all definite descriptions derived their meaning by referring to objects in the real world—that they were all necessarily "singular terms". (Lycan, 90) Instead he proposed an analysis in which a singular definite description, of the form "The F is G", was true only if three separate propositions were true:

(a) There is at least one thing that is F.

(b) There is not more than one thing that is F.

(c) If a thing is F, then it is also G. (Russell, 17)

This analysis has the virtue of explaining how "The F is G" can be meaningful and have a value of either true or false, without requiring any direct reference to a particular object F. In other words, if I claim that "The current Shah of Persia is sloshed," then I'm committed to separate claims that there is at least and at most one current Shah of Persia, and that every current Shah of Persia is sloshed. Since it is not the case that there is at least one Shah of Persia, any claims about his relative level of alcoholic intoxication will be necessarily false.

3. Strawson's View

However, there were also problems with Russell's view. For one thing, how many people would intuitively say that "The current Shah of Persia is sloshed" was *false* given that there is no current Shah of Persia? Wouldn't we intuitively say that there was something wrong with the sentence because it failed to refer to something, so it was neither true nor false? It hardly seems that it is false in the same sense that the sentence "The current President of Iran is female" is false.

Strawson developed a very different analysis of definite descriptions. He distinguished between a sentence and a statement (a true/false proposition), and between the meaning of a sentence and the *use* of a sentence. He argued that sentences, on their own, did not make statements that could be true or false or refer to things in the world. Only people, when using a sentence, could make true or false statements or refer to things in the world.

On this analysis, a sentence of the form "The F is G" is true only if it is used by a speaker to make a statement about some intended referent F and G, and the speaker is correct that whatever the speaker intends to refer to with F has the property or identity of G. If F does not refer to something, then the sentence is neither true nor false. "Our nation's current Secretary of War is an idiot" is neither true nor false if spoken today in the United States when there is no such cabinet position as "Secretary of War," but if spoken in a different time or place it could be used to refer to someone specific and make a true statement.

4. My Argument

I will argue that it would be preferable, all things considered, to see whether Russell's view can be amended so that we are not forced to adopt Strawson's view. My argument has this structure:

1. The only available alternatives are Strawson's view and Russell's view.
2. If an alternative to a radical view can be modified to account for the criticisms of the radical view, we have no reason to accept the radical view.
3. Strawson's view is radical.
4. Russell's view can be modified to account for Strawson's criticism.
C. We have no reason to accept Strawson's view.

5. Explanation of Premises

The first premise I'm taking for granted—I haven't learned about any other views in this class. Maybe there is one, but I don't know about it.

The second premise is a principle that says that we should only accept radical views when there is no alternative that can deal with the criticisms they offer. Since radical views go against common sense and conventional wisdom, we need a reason to accept them. But what reason is that?

The third premise says that Strawson is radical. I think Strawson gives a very radical view to take of language. First, he takes meaning out of the sentence and putting it in the hands of the speaker. Sentences don't mean things, but people do. But this seems challenging to reconcile with the human ability to understand combinations of words one has never heard before or to correctly understand translations from other languages. It makes it hard to know how what you mean is the same as what I mean, because meanings are in our heads. Second, I also think it is radical to say that descriptive sentences are neither true nor false. It is a basic rule of logic that sentences are either true or false. Denying this requires us to either change or reject logic. That's a drastic thing to say.

The fourth premise says that Russell's view can be modified to address Strawson's criticisms. I will discuss how I think this can be done in the next section.

6. How to Modify Russell

I think Russell's interpretation of "The blue shirt is wrinkled" need not be taken to mean that "there is at most one thing that is a blue shirt *in the entire universe*". Certainly, the domain of objects under discussion can be implicitly limited by context: "there is at most one blue shirt *in this room*", perhaps. This doesn't require that *the blue shirt* refers to an object determined by the speaker, however; it would be odd if a speaker used that phrase to refer to a red sweater.

Additionally, we can explain why it seems unintuitive to say that it is *false* that "The current Shah of Persia is sloshed," since even in Russell's view this sentence is the conjunction of *three* different statements, of which two are actually *true* (there is at most one Shah of Persia, and the conditional *if something is the Shah of Persia then it is sloshed*). In practice we'd rather explain the one false statement (*There is at least one Shah of Persia*) than declare the entire conjunction false. But this doesn't change how logic works generally.

7. Objections

I am not too worried about objections to the first premise or second premise of my argument. I suppose that Strawson might object that his view is "radical" and instead try to make it to seem intuitive. For example, he could bring up that some sentences, like commands and requests, are neither true nor false. However, "the king of France is bald" is a sentence that someone actually intends to use to describe the world, unlike a command or request. So it must be either true or false.

The main objection to my argument will have to be that my attempt to save Russell from Strawson's criticism doesn't work. Everyone knows that logic says that if any one of the parts of a conjunction is false, the whole conjunction is false. So why is it wrong to say that "The Shah of Persia is Sloshed" is false if it amounts to a conjunction and one conjunct is false? However, suppose it's true that it there is a test tomorrow, and it is true that it is on Kripke, and it is false that we're suppose to bring a blue book. Suppose I know this, and you ask me, "So, there is a test tomorrow AND it is on Kripke AND we are supposed to bring a blue book, right?", and I respond "No, that's false". You'll wrongly conclude that each of the parts of that conjunction are false instead of just one of them.

8. Conclusion

To conclude, Strawson's view seems to give undue weight to the intent of the speaker and ignore the fact that communication is just as dependent on the person hearing and understanding a sentence—a member of the community of competent speakers of a language. While the speaker of "The current Shah of Persia is sloshed" may not be asserting that "There is a current Shah of Persia" and may not be aware that this is implied from what he said, a listener will assume that the speaker believes it to be the case. Likewise, you can use "The current Shah of Persia" to refer to a mutual alcoholic friend of ours, but unless you and I have previously established this as a name for this friend, I will assume that you are talking about a Monarch in Iran. Russell's view, on the other hand, recognizes that there must be a common ground for interpretation between the speaker and the listener.

Appendix B1
❀ Writing a Final Exam ❀

❋❋❋

The key to doing well on a final essay exam in a philosophy course is preparation. You may receive the questions in advance, or you may only know the general topics, but either way doing well means practicing structuring and writing your answer, not simply taking for granted that you feel like you know what you might write. It's easy to forget under pressure if you haven't practiced!

When people grade essay exams in philosophy, they're looking to answer four key questions, starting with the most basic and leading to the less basic.

* When it comes to the **written quality** of the essay, is it readable?

* Does the **relevance** of the essay show that the student has read and studied the source texts for themselves and related them to the question?

* Can this student **explain** what they read to someone else accurately and charitably?

* Can this student **evaluate** what they read critically and either object to or defend it?

Writing Quality

Although handwritten essays in philosophy aren't typically graded on spelling or punctuation or minor grammatical issues, the overall readability and writing quality of the essay does matter. It is hard to give a passing grade on an essay if it is written so poorly that it is not possible to follow the main line of thought in the essay or to understand what it is saying or where it is going.

The best written essays keep the reader in mind at all times. It doesn't simply pour out thoughts from one's head to paper, as they occur in one's head (which may not make so much sense to anyone else). Instead, it makes sure that the writer knows what is going on at each point in the essay. The introduction clearly states what the topic is and what the essay intends to do. Each paragraph of the essay begins with a topic sentence which transitions from the previous paragraph and gives clearly the topic of the new paragraph. Sentences connect to each other within each paragraph and flow one to the other. The later sentences in each paragraph give evidence or argumentation for the claim made in the topic sentence of the paragraph. Arguments are presented formally, as a numbered series of premises leading to a conclusion. All assumptions are made explicit. The conclusion of the essay makes clear how each part of the original essay question has been answered in the essay.

Relevance

Lower-scoring essays are often not very relevant to the question which was asked. The person grading them can see fairly clearly that the student did not pick up much from readings or lectures, but perhaps googled and read a bit of SparkNotes the night before the exam. They may have misinterpreted the question, as a result of missing class, for example. The problem with this strategy is that a philosophy class is always more narrow and specialized than the information one is likely to pull up on the Internet, which is broader and will include many things which were not discussed in class at all. Even if someone manages to find relevant information, learning by this method generally remains at a superficial and basic level.

A better essay is one on which it is clear that the student did the reading in addition to attending class, as answers are deeper and more complete. References are made to actual examples that were used in class or the textbook. It is clear that all of the parts of the question which was asked have been answered in the essay.

Explanation

Quality of explanation is your ability to teach the material to someone else. It requires not just knowing *what* someone said, but *why* they said it and how you would get someone else to understand their argument and view.

Lower scoring essays tend to avoid making many substantive claims about the subject that go beyond simply rephrasing the words in the question itself. When they do make substantive claims they are either completely wrong or deeply misleading.

Middle-range essays will state the various views and positions accurately. However, they don't explain any of the arguments or reasons behind why someone held these views. We're left with the impression that these views were more or less arbitrary, or the result of "crazy" philosophers who lose touch with reality, rather than conclusions derived logically from premises that most of us already accept. We have no idea why someone held these eclectic views.

Better essays don't just state views but actually explain the reasoning and argumentation behind them. Even if they have some mistakes or imprecisions in how they explain the argument, or misstate a few things about the view, we get an impression that these views were the result of careful reasoning. Ideally, if someone who didn't know anything about philosophy read this essay, that person will have learned something. We'd trust the person who wrote the essay to, say, teach a high school class on this topic someday.

The way to do better on the explanation section of an essay is to practice explaining what you've learned without assuming that the person you're speaking to has been in the class. Don't write to your instructor, TA, or even your classmates—write to someone who hasn't learned yet the terminology or references that you are using.

Evaluation

Critical evaluation has to do with your own best judgement on the issues raised in your essay. It is your opinion, but your critical and well-reasoned opinion. Most students, perhaps because they were trained to do so in other disciplines, spend about 90% of a paper on exposition and only 10% on critical evaluation.

Some students don't state anything about their own views at all! However, the proportion should be more like 30–50% critical evaluation in some form or another—whether this is raising objections to someone else's view, presenting and arguing for your own view, or rebutting objections to your own view.

Middle-range essays to give views and reactions that they have, but don't really give a reasoned defense of those views, perhaps only stating *causes* of their view rather than *reasons*. This indicates that the person writing the essay has thought a little bit about what they think, but not enough about how to justify what they think to someone else. They tend to object to the conclusions of arguments but not to the reasoning which lead to those conclusions. They tend to assert positions or views without arguing for them.

The best essays are cases where the student presents a view or argument of their own that they give reasons for, and where the student has genuinely critical thing to say about the writers he or she read. The critical evaluation is insightful, new, and interesting. When objecting to an argument, these essays *attack the premises rather than the conclusion*. Rather than simply saying why the conclusion is wrong, they give reasons to think the premises which got us to the conclusion are unlikely to be true.

To become better at critical evaluation, you can try these exercises.

* When you're explaining arguments for or against a view, make sure to present them in a formal argument structure as a series of premises followed by a conclusion. This makes it easy to evaluate them: you just have to determine whether the argument is valid or not, and then determine how likely each of the premises are.

* Try picking one of the source texts that you've read in this class and trying to find every possible problem with the argument they make. Look for ways they might undermine their own views or break with common sense. Make a list of 10 problems with their view, or ways someone might object, and then narrow this list down to about 3 problems.

* Try to have a dialogue with yourself about these issues, where you switch back and forth between two opposing positions.

* If you aren't sure what you think and can't make up your mind, adopt a position temporarily, *just for the sake of argument*. No one is going to look at your essay years down the road to investigate whether you defended radical skepticism or not. So, take the opportunity to try out a view and see where it will go.

Hopefully this gives you an idea of what someone who grades your essay is looking for. Above all, remember that the person grading your essay is **not** grading it with a checklist of things that you must mention or say in your essay, and they are not giving or taking away points based on whether you get all of the information across in the essay. Rather than rushing to pack in as much information as you can in order to get 'points', focus instead on walking step-by-step through the reasoning of the philosophers you are discussing, and then through your own reasoning. Because grading has to do with quality rather than quantity of information students can get a high grade even if they forget a bit of information here or there, provided that the overall explanation and evaluation is excellent.

❀ B.2 Example Final Exam Essay ❀

"Superior Essay Question" on a PHI 101 Exam
by Shawn S. Student

✳✳

PROMPT: Present, explain, and evaluate three of the arguments given in class regarding the meaning of life associated with the philosophers we read in Units 1,2, and 3, with at least 1 holding that life is meaningless and 1 holding that life is meaningful. Do you think life is meaningful? Present and explain an argument for your own position. How might someone object to your argument? How would you respond?

Answer:

Goldilocks argues that:

1. Pleasure is an end in itself
2. Whatever produces an end in itself is meaningful.
3. A pleasant life is pleasurable
C. A pleasant life is meaningful.

Goldilocks says (1) and (2) are obvious; I can't object. But (1) is controversial. Goldilocks thinks pleasure is the only thing people all agree is valuable, and that makes it an end in itself. But, just because everyone agrees on something doesn't make it true. And couldn't someone pursue pleasure as a means to an end? Sometimes I seek to be happy, not because I want to be happy—I'd rather mope around depressed—but because I know it makes me less of a jerk.

Optimus Prime argues:

1. All struggles are meaningful.
2. Some lives involve a struggle for survival.
3. A life which does not involve a struggle for survival is easy.
4. Anything which is easy is not meaningful
C. A life is meaningful if and only if it involves a struggle for survival.

Optimus holds (1) and (4) because he thinks "meaningfulness" is a feeling of satisfaction, but he's never felt satisfied about any easy task, and great struggles satisfy him. By "struggle", he means something that is risky and difficult. Premises (2) and (3) are supposed to be obvious—some people do struggle to survive, and those of us who don't struggle have it easy. However, I would object, because do not think all struggles are meaningful. Suppose Bob struggles for years to create a perpetual motion machine, which is impossible! This seems meaningless. On the other hand, caring for a beloved pet may be easy, but having a pet can still be a meaningful part of life.

Finally, Necronomicus argues:

1. if x is the purpose of y then x must occur after y
2. if y is the purpose of life, then we must y while alive
3. if y is the purpose of life then y must occur after life (from 1)
4. we do not experience anything after life while alive.
C. nothing is the purpose of life

This is a clever argument, because it says that life's purpose must be both experienced during life (2) and also after life (3), but it can't be both, and clearly we do not experience what's after life while actually alive (premise 4)! To understand (1), consider that the purpose of a sports game is not the game but the victory which follows the game, or the purpose of making money is not the money but what one spends it on. However, why believe (2)? Necronomicus says if the purpose of our lives is something which we can't experience, then "who would care about it?" But I don't understand why he thinks this. I can still anticipate something meaningful in the future, like great-great-grandchildren, even if I'm not around then.

My own view is:

1. If one believes that one is already dead, then one will not be concerned with one's own life or well-being.
2. If one is not concerned with one's own life or well-being, then one can only act for those intrinsically valuable things which are outside oneself.
3. If x seeks to promote something intrinsically valuable outside itself, x is meaningful.
C. If one believes that one is already dead, then one will have a meaningful life.

It's clear enough that no one who is dead can also be alive and have a well-being to be concerned for. So if I believe I'm dead, it would be absurd to try to stay alive (1). Also clear is that what promotes valuable/meaningful things is meaningful (3).

Someone might object by challenging (2). They'll ask: Why would someone have to act for intrinsic value? However, I'd reply with another question: what other ends could my actions seek? Every action seeks some end. My actions can't seek my own ends or something which promotes them on (1). So the only ends left are those which have value independently of me! Although my view is depressing, since it says thinking you're the dude in *The Sixth Sense* is the key to a meaningful life, it's worth a try.

Appendix C
❀ How to Cite your Sources ❀

✳ ✳

My policy is that you must cite everything which you obtain from any source except your own ideas, on every assignment. Citations are required on everything that you don't do during class itself: essay questions on weekly quizzes, discussion board posts, writing assignments, and the final paper. You must cite your sources to prove that you didn't borrow your ideas from elsewhere. Citing sources isn't just a matter of integrity, it's a matter of being a good member of the academy - it shows that you know where an idea came from.

There are two different "Styles" which you may use for citing sources. A **formal style** that you should use for writing a formal argument paper at the end of class, and an **informal style** that you can use for most ordinary assignments.

Formal Citation Style—Required on term paper Only

For the final paper, you need to use one of the three major citation styles: APA, Chicago Style, or MLA. If you're already familiar and comfortable with one of them, use the one you are comfortable with. Your introductory English classes probably used MLA. If you don't already have a style that you're comfortable with, then see if there's an accepted style within your major. For History and Philosophy, Chicago Style tends to be more popular, and footnotes are preferred over endnotes or in-text citations.

Information on MLA, APA, and Chicago Style Citations can be found at the Online Writing Lab at Purdue University: **owl.english.purdue.edu**

Informal Citation Style—for all other Assignments

For all other assignments, you can use the informal citation style which follows. This citation format involves an in-text citation in parentheses with (author's last name or title of work, page number) or, if there is no page number, then (author's last name or title of work and year). Place the citation at the end of a direct quote, the end of a paraphrased statement, or at the end of a paragraph, which relies on that source for any ideas contained in the paragraph. For example:

Direct Quotes

Of course, as Berkeley said, "to be is to be perceived" (Dialogues, 45).
So, "Berkeley was perhaps the most well known proponent of idealism." (Wikipedia, "Berkeley")

End of a Paraphrased Statement
As Berkeley taught, existing is just the same thing as being observed. (Dialogues, 45)
Berkeley was probably the most famous idealist. (Wikipedia, "Berkeley")

End of a paragraph in which you relied on a source for ideas.
. . . so we shouldn't accept idealism. Or, as the rationalists would say, Berkeley and his like are mistaken because they reject *a priori* knowledge. (Stanford Encyclopedia, "Idealism")

Citing my Lectures

For in-class lectures, write (lecture). Nothing further is needed.
For recorded lectures, write (lecture #N) replacing N with the number of the lecture.

Citing Textbooks in the Course

Use this format: (Author/Editor of Textbook, page number). For example: (Huemer, 62). This applies even if the original source is Plato or Kant. Use the original author's name in your text, but cite the editor of the textbook. For instance, if you were reading the excerpt from Hume in this textbook, you'd write:

> Hume argues that we know nothing about causation. (Watson, 54)

Citing Published Books or Articles Outside of the Course

Use this format: (Author's last name or title of work if no last name, page number). For example: (Kripke, 117). Then write a note at the bottom of the page with the last name of the author and the title of the work. For example:

> Kripke, Saul. "Naming and Necessity"

For informal citations, date information and publisher information is not necessary. I can google that stuff for myself if I want.

Citing Internet Resources

If you don't cite an internet resource, even if you forget that you took the information from an internet resource and you manage to put the idea into different words, you will fail. If you do Internet research, keep track of what you read so that you can go back and cite it. Note that I don't care what you cite, as long as you cite it. If you used Wikipedia or "Epistemology for Dummies" or "Gettier's Epistemology Fetish blog" . . . well, much better to tell me that up front than let me uncover it for myself.

In the text, cite the source like this: (name of website). For example, (Stanford Encyclopedia of Philosophy).

Then, at the bottom of the page, note the author (if applicable), the name of the page, the title of the website, and the address of the website. For instance:

> "Immanuel Kant", Wikipedia. http://en.wikipedia.org/wiki/Immanuel_Kant

When you don't Remember the Citation

Sometimes you're in a hurry. You think an idea came from somewhere else and know it isn't your own, but you don't remember where you got it. Here's what you should do.

In the text, note (cf) after every idea, thought, phrase, and so on that you're pretty sure you got from another source

At a note at the bottom of the page, write this:

cf = citation forthcoming and available upon request

If you feel unsure about whether you've relied on a source or not, it's better to cite (cf) than not to. For example, suppose you remember reading through another professor's website at their course notes on Metaphysics, but you're in a hurry, don't remember the site, and don't know whether it's influenced you. Write in (cf), and then look up the information after you submit the exam.

I may ask you when I grade your work to fill in the missing citations before I give you a grade, or I might not, but by noting that you know it came from somewhere, even if you don't remember where, you avoid any accusation of plagiarism.

All exams are open-note. So, even in your own notes for the course, you should cite sources: that way you know where the information came from when it comes time to take the exam.

If you still feel unsure or uneasy about citing sources, contact your university Writing Center, where you may be able to receive writing tutoring to help.

Course _____

LECTURE PARTICIPATION FORM   DATE: _____ / _____ / _____

LAST NAME   **FIRST NAME**

REFERENCE INFO. *Which philosopher was the focus of discussion in this lecture? Which work? What is the reference information?*

EXTRACT AND PRESENT a valid deductive argument from their work
Present it as a numbered series of premises followed by a conclusion, where the truth of the premises would guarantee the truth of the conclusion.

EXPLAIN the premises of the argument
Explain what each premise means, defining specialized terms, and give reasons it might seem plausible.

EVALUATE the argument
Looking at each premise, how likely do you think it is to be true? Can you think of any exceptions to the premises? Can you think of any counterarguments? Can you think of ways to make the argument stronger, or give a better argument for the same conclusion?

What made the least sense in this lecture?